New American World

A Documentary History of North America to 1612

NEW
AMERICAN
WORLD

A Documentary History of
North America to 1612

IN FIVE VOLUMES

VOLUME IV

Newfoundland from Fishery to Colony. Northwest Passage Searches.

Edited, with a Commentary by

DAVID B. QUINN

With the Assistance of

Alison M. Quinn and Susan Hillier

ARNO PRESS
A New York Times Company

and

HECTOR BYE, INC.
New York, 1979

Library of Congress Cataloging in Publication Data
Main entry under title:

Newfoundland from fishery to colony.

   (New American world ; v. 4)
    1. Newfoundland—History—Sources. 2. North-
west Passage—History—Sources. I. Quinn, David
Beers. II. Quinn, Alison M. II. Hillier,
Susan.
E101.N47 vol. 4 [E101.N47]   970.01s
ISBN 0-405-10763-3   [971.8'01] 78-23465

Library of Congress Cataloging in Publication Data
Main entry under title:

New American world.

   Includes bibliographies and indexes.
    1. America—Discovery and exploration—Sources.
2. America—History—To 1810—Sources. I. Quinn,
David Beers. II. Quinn, Alison M. III. Hillier,
Susan.
E101.N47   970.01   77-20483
ISBN 0-405-10759-5

Printed in the United States of America

Contents

PART XVI.   THE NEWFOUNDLAND TRADES: COD-FISHING AND WHALING, 1514–1613   81

Chapter Seventy-two.   Beginnings, 1514–1559   87

Maps
List of Plates

(Notes on the Maps will precede the plate section in each volume.)

VOLUME IV

Preface

NEWFOUNDLAND IN SOME WAYS is the key, or one of several keys of which it is the most significant, to continuing European concern with northeastern North America, since it was there that every year the many ships of all the western European powers—France, Portugal, England, Spain—came to take back cargoes of fish (whose number seemed without end) and oil (from cod, whale, walrus, and seal) to Europe. From there stemmed Basque whaling stations on the Labrador side of the Strait of Belle Isle; from there emerged the first English plans to colonize the island and to dominate the whole fishery and then (briefly) to penetrate the Gulf of St. Lawrence that lay behind. Finally, they were to succeed in establishing the first continuing colony on its island shores, at Cupids.

France tended to regard Newfoundland as so dominated by its fishermen that plans to colonize the island were unnecessary or irrelevant. It looked for settlement farther west only as the fur trade emerged, first as an offshoot of the fishery, then as an end in itself. The Cartier-Roberval dream of a passage through America never quite fades, but it is replaced at a practical level by a determination to command the fur trade of the St. Lawrence River which, after trial and error, brought about the continuing settlement—trading post rather than colony—at Québec. But the fur trade also drew the French to the south. If Acadia had furs, might not its lands and those still farther to the south (in Norumbega, which was still so named in the early seventeenth century) provide for settlers as well? Out of an intensive period of exploration, which has left us some of the best descriptive literature of the period, came in the end only the small *habitacion* at Port Royal, and the relinquishment of the fertile but too fur-scarce coastline down to and beyond Cape Cod.

If we can link French exploration of the later New England, Acadia, and the St. Lawrence River with Newfoundland beginnings, so too can we tie the Northwest Passage searches in with the fishery. One continuing incentive to go north was to see whether whale and cod prevailed in high latitudes. This probably led many more vessels than those of which we have record well up the Labrador coast, while explorers of this barren zone could always rely on replenishing their stores at the island fishery. But theory was still the dominating factor in the Northwest Passage search (the gold fever of 1577 and 1578 an aberration only). There must—argued Portuguese, English, and Dutch—be a way around North America to the Far East. The geographical arguments seemed good. Successive explorers found great expanses of sea, penetrable at least for short seasons, and many supposed passages, as they worked first north and then west. The discovery of just enough westward openings made it feasible for these efforts to continue. Finally Hudson, with the discovery of the strait and bay that bear his name, seemed to have found the entrance to the passage. In 1612 it appeared (although this was to be followed rapidly by further disillusionment) that a way was on the point of being found.

Most North American ventures have more rational short-term economic or social motives than those of the Northwest Passage voyages, but it should be remembered that for none were the potential rewards of success so great. Yet in the northwest (which is, of course, still the northeast on the North American map), land and sea and ice intermingled were to remain for centuries a puzzle and a challenge which, from time to time, men took up. This volume ends with one of the great questions of North American exploration still unanswered.

Introduction

NEWFOUNDLAND IS NOT, at least after its discovery by John Cabot, one of the greatly stressed and admired themes of early American discovery and exploration. The exploitation of the riches of offshore North America by hundreds of European vessels—their number growing steadily throughout the period down to the early seventeenth century—has seemed too prosaic to be particularly interesting or even pertinent to American colonization. Yet it can now be seen as perhaps the main reason why North America continued to retain the interest of the western European powers, even when they were unable to contemplate devoting any large share of their resources toward exploration of other parts, or undertaking a major commitment to establish colonies there. Almost every western European port had its Newfoundlanders, ships and the men in them, which each summer crossed and recrossed what at that time seemed a great waste of water, and returned with fish and fish oil. The Newfoundland trade, as it has been shown in outline in this volume (but which is still largely unknown in detail), had wide ramifications throughout Europe. Religious abstention from meat on Fridays and Holy Days was possible in a Europe with a growing population, if Newfoundland made up its quota of fish. Fish was an essential food. It became, after the Newfoundland fisheries developed, an essential war material—armies marching on their "Poor John" as navies sailed with its aid in victuals. The wet-salted or dried Newfoundland cod became a staple of the European diet. This was at one prosaic end. At another, statesmen wondered how they could keep up the growth in the number of qualified seamen upon which much of their commercial prosperity depended—as, in war, did their navies—without the rigorous training for increasing numbers that the trade brought.

Protestant England brought in Fish Days to keep the merchant seamen flourishing. In between, those who built ships, who arranged their provisioning and manning, who found money in one way or another to charter or purchase them, to pay for their outfitting, to engage men in wages and shares, and to insure their perilous voyages—all were in some way concerned.

Thus, even if conscious thought about developing North America was not a direct offshoot of the practical trade in fish, it had its roots there. It was on account of the fishery that North America itself, and not merely its littoral, seemed to be a matter of interest or concern to men who had a stake in the prosperity of a major industry, as well as those who looked at this industry from a distance. Then, too, whaling was a specialized branch of the fishery that brought mammalian oil into almost every home. Without whale oil few lamps would have burned in Europe. And whale had many more uses. Most whaling was concentrated on one small part of the American shore, the Grand Bay, the Strait of Belle Isle, with some later extension into the Gulf and River of St. Lawrence.

The fur trade was largely a development from the fishery. When Bretons and Basques tracked down walrus for oil and ivory on the Magdalen Islands, and La Roche's released criminals killed walrus and seal on Sable Island, they were making one step in the transition from fish to fur. But it was the fox and marten, the deer and moose, the bear and the lynx, that led on to the prized beaver and to a trade that was not merely casual exchange with growingly sophisticated Amerindians and Eskimo, but a lever to penetrate into the heart of northern North America itself, setting tribes to trade with tribes, who traded with other tribes, and so on, or carried, even, a chain of war and raiding along the line of trade . The St. Lawrence might still represent the best prospect of finding a watershed, if not a passage, by which contact might be made with the Pacific, but very shortly after 1580 it offered also the best chance of tapping the interior trade in furs. The Indians of the St. Lawrence Valley became a people who were exploited by, and exploited in turn, the French traders who came each year in increasing numbers, even if, to the tribes concerned, furs were still often less significant than warfare and traditional ceremonial observance. But the trade goods white men brought, changing a stone-age people into an iron-age people in a matter of two or at most three generations, linked them more and more tightly with the white men's craving for furs. The emphasis on coat beaver, skins used as clothing by Indians and then turned over to the whites in this secondhand state, must, to begin with, have seemed to them to have some arcane ceremonial implication, rather than the practical one of removing the coarse outer hairs, thus making the beaver pelt ready for felting without more ado. It was the fur trade (in the period covered by this volume) that drew the French into attempted settlement on the St. Lawrence River, first at Tadoussac and then, permanently, at Québec, and so created in the end a French Canada. It was the desire to combine a fur-trading and agricultural community that led to the hard and thorough exploration and attempted settlement at Ste Croix and Port Royal, and brought Champlain southward to describe every mile of coast from the head of the Bay of Fundy to Nantucket Sound. Thus, no chance might be missed of a site combining a plenitude of furs with the prospect of a reasonable life for French gentlemen and farmers. In the end, only the outpost of Port Royal was left as the symbol of French claims to Acadia, claims that were by no means firmly acknowledged by the time this collection ends.

Frenchmen were careful and persistent occupiers of unfavorable sites—Cartier had shown this in 1535–1536 and 1541–1542—but they did not consider settlement justified in a harsh, wintry climate unless it produced large profits from some trade, in this case from furs. Ste Croix represented a more careful disposition of forces for settlement than had the earlier attempts of Cartier and Roberval, but more Frenchmen died than survived there. Port Royal proved more beneficial. The closely knit *habitacion*, its gardens, its fields, its watermills, created for the first time an image of New France which, if it did not last, impressed itself firmly in the minds of the Sieur de Poutrincourt and his son Charles Biencourt. It was never wholly lost thereafter. But France was not prepared to pour its sons and daughters into North America unless it offered a better way of life (rather than just richer fur-trade profits) than it appeared capable of doing. The same might be said of the English experience of New England in the years before 1612, although they were to have second thoughts about it not so many years later. The lasting achievement of the French was primarily the *comptoir* (as Marcel Trudel has rightly called the first French presence), down to 1627 at least, in North America. The *coureurs du bois*, the *seigneurs* of the littorine lands of the St. Lawrence, and the missionaries, Jesuit and other, were to appear as later manifestations of the French national genius. Lescarbot's *Histoire de la Nouvelle France*, however, enables us to glimpse a lighter-hued North America, one where poems and playlets were written, where Indians were the source of curious tales, and not merely the objects of serious assessment in their potential role as enemies or trading partners, where for at least odd moments Frenchmen might feel a sense of enjoyment.

There was not much room for enjoyment on the long, icy voyages into the seas that border the broken lands of northern North America. The hardihood learned in the fisheries is shown in the capacity of ships and seamen to survive blows not only of Atlantic winds and waves, but of Arctic ice, in pack or iceberg, as floating islands and as concealers of rocky dangers. The men who served the Muscovy Company on its arduous North Cape to White Sea voyages indeed had a foretaste of the wilder northern waters, on occasion seeking the Northeast Passage. It was not until 1576 and thereafter that Europeans undertook, in seeking a Northwest Passage, to deal with the combination of wind, low temperature, and ice that brought to bear on them the heaviest pressures of sixteenth-century North American navigation. Why should they have risked so much for so little result? The Frobisher voyages of 1576–1578 were luxuriously provisioned by the standards of their day, but the narratives recorded in every case much more hardship to balance the novelties of Eskimo life, the extraordinary characteristics of the larger icebergs now met for the first time in these northern waters (in Newfoundland they might be dangerous too but still a minor peril). And yet the idea of a passage in 1576 was sufficient to give satisfaction to the men who went and returned from the first Frobisher voyage. When to the lure of a passage was added the chance of getting rich through goldmining, in the far from attractive environs of Frobisher Bay, there was competition to go, even in 1578 to stay on over the winter in the harsh north. But it is clear, too, that only the most expert navigators and diplomats could conduct a ship out and home without threats of mutiny and savage recriminations between the men who took part. The Arctic air was bad for human tempers.

Even if lack of gold cooled many Northwest Passage enthusiasts, it created others who were willing to work for the passage alone. In his three voyages from 1585–1587, John Davis showed consummate seamanship in weathering every kind of danger, while he gradually charted that great expanse of water now known by his name. He did much to put western Greenland and Baffin Island on the map, even if he failed to press home his penetration of every inlet until he might find the last one that would bring a ship through, perhaps, to a strait leading to the

Pacific. In the early seventeenth century George Waymouth might well have entered and passed Hudson Strait, if his men had not become too distressed and discontented to allow him to go farther (the same thing happened to Sebastian Cabot as far back as 1508). The grand old slave driver of the Arctic passages was Henry Hudson. Clearly a superb seaman, Hudson thought nothing of driving his men to Novaya Zemlia, then up the coast of East Greenland, across from North Cape to Newfoundland and the Hudson River, and finally through the strait that was to him the Northwest Passage. Next, his *Discovery* was caught in the sack of James Bay, and he emerged to be set on by men who had suffered under him more than they could stand. He was left to sink or swim, almost certainly to sink, with only a handful of sick men and a cross-grained carpenter to keep him company on his last and unknown voyage. The Victorian picture of Hudson as the kindly old man, driven to his icy death by hard-faced villains, is probably far from true. Rather, he was the prototype of the whaling skippers of the nineteenth century, who brought their men to hell and sometimes back, and who had to take the rough of mutiny with the smooth of profits as they came. But the Northwest Passage refused to yield—within a few years not only was Hudson Bay found to be finite, but the exits from it to the northwest were, or appeared to be, blocked. The more persistent tried again farther north, and William Baffin gave his name to still another bay in honor of an English Arctic pioneer, but that was virtually all for more than another century and a half. Samuel Hearne's view of the Arctic Ocean at the Coppermine River was not to be made until 1779.

Note on Presentation of Materials

SOME INDICATIONS of editorial methods must necessarily be given. We have modernized, except in a very few cases (where explanations are given), usages of "u," "v," "i," and "j." We have kept "y^e" although we are well aware that the bastardized thorn it contains annoys linguistic purists. Since we have retained "yt" or "y^t" meaning "it," we have expanded on grounds of possible confusion "y^t" meaning "that."

From 1582 onward continental dating was ten days ahead of English dating. For French and Spanish documents this must be kept in mind and, also, when relating English documents to continental. Where confusion is likely to arise, double dating has been given.

We have not been afraid to expand contracted words, without indication, in either printed or manuscript sources, except where there is a genuine ambiguity. We have capitalized proper names where we have thought fit to do so. We have added full points to complete sentences and occasionally used either the comma or full point for the slash (/) (where ambiguity might arise from its retention).

Sidenotes are frequent in sixteenth-century published works and less frequently in manuscripts. Usually, they simply form a running index to the contents of the document. Where they do so they have been omitted. But from time to time they either convey additional information or express the point of view of the contemporary editor. In such cases they have been added as footnotes.

Square brackets have been used to fill lacunae conjecturally, although usually with a question mark. They also comprise words or phrases in non-English languages that may not be conveyed clearly in the translation or where the exact words of the document appear important. Occasionally, but only occasionally, they are included to explain a word, or a place name, which otherwise might be wholly unintelligible.

Almost all documents have been printed in full, although where omissions have been made they are indicated in the headnotes. In a few cases where the text was not suitable for transcription in full, abstracts have been made.

For each document or closely associated group of documents bibliographical references have been given. In the case of major sources, of which there have been many editions, this has been expanded in the introduction to the appropriate section. The editors have been generous with their own writing. The introductions to each volume attempt to point to the major characteristics of the selection in that volume and to bring out major comparative points of relationship. Longish introductory passages have been given for main sections where it was felt that headnotes alone might not be sufficient. Subsections have been knit together by brief introductory summaries. Finally, individual headnotes have tried to throw light on the nature of the particular document without trying, however, to summarize its contents in detail. Precise consistency in producing introductory matter of these kinds has not been aimed at or achieved. What assistance appeared to be required for each group of documents was given, rather than attempt to follow a completely consistent plan. Over such a wide range of materials it would be surprising if some discrepancies in treatment, which were not intended, will be observed. A broad measure of uniformity has, it is hoped, been maintained. We believe that, within the terms of our brief, this is the best selection on this scale that we could make. We see many ways in which it could have been improved, but we profoundly believe it will be useful, although it cannot within its scale be definitive. Another generation of editors may perhaps put together on film, after spending unlimited time and money, the complete documentary record of earliest European contacts with America. We hope they do so, but we also wish the users of this present set many interesting and productive hours, reading from a well-printed set of books much of what remains on an endlessly stimulating and engrossing topic.

Abbreviations
Used in the Text

A.G.I., Seville. Archivo General de Indias, Seville

A.G. Simancas. Archivo General de Simancas

B.L. British Library, Reference Division (formerly British Museum Library)

Biggar, H.P. *Precursors of Jacques Cartier.* H.P. Biggar, *The Precursors of Jacques Cartier, 1497–1534.* Publications of the Public Archives of Canada, no. 5. Ottawa, 1911.

Calendar of State Papers, Spanish. (a) *Letters, Despatches and State Papers Relating to the Negotiations Between England and Spain, 1485–1558.* 14 vols., London, 1862–1954; (b) *Letters and State Papers Relating to English Affairs, Preserved Principally in the Archives of Simancas, 1558–1603.* 4 vols. London, 1892–1899.

Colección de documentos inéditos de Indias. Colección de documentos inéditos relativos al descubrimiento, conquista y colonización de las posesiones Española en América y Oceanía, edited by Joaquin F. Pacheco, Francisco de Cárdenas, and Luís Torres de Mendoza. 1st series. 42 vols. Madrid, 1864–1889.

Hist. MSS Comm. Historical Manuscripts Commission, *Reports,* London, 1868-.

N.Y.P.L. New York Public Library.

P.R.O. Public Record Office, London.

Quinn, D.B., *Gilbert.* D.B. Quinn, *The Voyages and Colonising Enterprises of Sir Humphrey Gilbert.* 2 vols. London, Hakluyt Society, 1940.

Quinn, D.B., *North American Discovery.* D.B. Quinn, *North American Discovery, c. 1000–1612.* New York, 1971.

Quinn, D.B., *Roanoke Voyages.* D.B. Quinn, *The Roanoke Voyages, 1584–1590.* 2 vols. Cambridge, Eng., Hakluyt Society, 1955.

Taylor, E.G.R., *Hakluyts*. Eva G.R. Taylor, *The Original Writings and Correspondence of the two Richard Hakluyts*. 2 vols. London, Hakluyt Society, 1935.

T.L.S. The Times Literary Supplement. London.

Williamson, J.A., *The Cabot Voyages* (1962). James A. Williamson, *The Cabot Voyages and Bristol Discovery under Henry VII*. Cambridge, Eng., Hakluyt Society, 1962.

Williamson, J.A., *The Voyages of the Cabots* (1929). James A. Williamson, *The Voyages of the Cabots and the English Discovery of North America in the Reigns of Henry VII and Henry VIII*. London, 1929.

VOLUME IV

Newfoundland from Fishery to Colony.
Northwest Passage Searches.

XV

The English at Newfoundland, 1573–1596

I**N THE EARLY** 1570s the English fishery at Newfoundland was at a very low ebb. This may have been due to friction with Spain, 1568–1573, which may well have led to Newfoundlanders from England being in some jeopardy from the Spanish codfishermen and whalers. In 1573 Anthony Parkhurst tells us there were only four vessels taking part, but there was a rapid revival and the figures, in round numbers, went up to 30 in 1575, 40 in 1577, and 50 in 1578. Our informant, Anthony Parkhurst (526), took the trouble to go ashore in Newfoundland between 1574 and 1578 and also collected a substantial amount of information on the codfishery and whale fishery in general which provides an important starting point for reconsideration of these industries as a whole. His particular importance is that he advocated that Englishmen should carry on with their seizure of an increasing share of the trade and, in particular, should seriously contemplate seizing and colonizing posts commanding both the cod and whale fisheries. From this time onward we can date an English interest in the island for its own sake.

Sir Humphrey Gilbert cynically advocated in 1577 that Englishmen should take the lead in aggression there by seizing all the fishing fleets and using them to mount a great force against the Spanish Indies. If this caused too much trouble with France and Portugal, she might limit the attack to Spanish ships alone. Gilbert's colonizing patent (370) and his actions in mounting an expedition in 1578 do not indicate he had a special interest in attacking or colonizing Newfoundland at this time, but he did not forget it; he certainly knew of Parkhurst's schemes. In 1580 Portugal was absorbed by Spain, and Englishmen who complained of failure to get compensation for losses sustained in Spain began to treat both Spanish and Portuguese ships as enemies.

In 1582 Henry Oughtred, in compensation for losses sustained in Spain, took the law into his own hands and raided Newfoundland, taking a Portuguese ship and robbing many others. This outraged English fishermen at Newfoundland as it broke up their peaceful conduct of the trade, and also led to official Spanish protests, but Oughtred was protected by Sir Francis Walsingham, secretary of state (528–533). In 1583 Gilbert turned to Newfoundland on his way to reconnoiter a site for a colony in Norumbega (southern New England). He evidently expected to revictual his ships there and also to take control of St. John's and other harbors so that Englishmen in his pay could issue licenses for shore lots ("rooms") and other fishing rights to nationals of other countries. He accordingly entered St. John's Harbour in August, 1583, and proceeded to declare Newfoundland English territory under his own government (536). He was accepted, superficially, by French and Portuguese fishermen in the harbor, and they acquired from him fishing licenses, one of which, when shown in Spain, created some surprise and alarm (596). Gilbert's companions were divided about Newfoundland. The Hungarian Stephen Parmenius thought it was a mere desert (534); Edward Hayes, one of Gilbert's captains, thought that it had great economic potential as a colony in control of the whole fishery (536). Gilbert sailed away, doing nothing to secure his hold on the island, although his brother, Sir John Gilbert, may have taken some ineffectual steps to try to do so in 1584, and Edward Hayes turned to solicit assistance from Lord Burghley, which he never received, for plans to control and settle Newfoundland (362–364).

In 1585 relations with Spain reached a climax. In May Spain impounded English shipping in Spanish ports. Bernard Drake was diverted from a Virginia voyage to go to Newfoundland. His peaceful mission was to inform all English ships he could contact not to bring fish directly to Spain, as some were accustomed to do, because they would be seized there. His less peaceful mission was to carry through the type of raid Gilbert had advocated in 1577, to seize or destroy all Spanish and Portuguese ships in Newfoundland waters. Drake did not venture into either of the Spanish centers, Placentia Bay for the codfishermen and the Strait of Belle Isle for the whalers, but he scoured the southeastern bays for Portuguese vessels and took some seventeen or eighteen of them prisoner with their crews and their fish. The vessels were retained in England as compensation, many of their men dying there of typhus. (At the prisoners' trial, Drake caught typhus and also died.)

The rest of the political story, if it can be called such, is one of attack and counterattack. In 1584 French Basques took over an English privateer with its Spanish loot. In 1590 some French fishing vessels captured a Spanish prize from an English privateer and kept it themselves. In 1596 French Basque fishermen turned on an English vessel under Richard Clerke at St. John's. These are only a few typical incidents which emerged as cases in the High Court of Admiralty. What does not appear in this type of record is that the Portuguese dropped out altogether, it would seem, from the inshore fishery and confined their attentions to the Banks where they were less obvious. Spanish Basque codfishermen were hampered both by Spanish government demands on their manpower and by attacks on them by English and French privateers, mainly on their homeward voyage; and what was true of them was more true of the whalers, who almost ceased to operate in the 1590s and were reduced to very small numbers. The advantage was taken by the French. French Basques, although harried by the English, were very active; so were other French vessels. Most of all, the English prospered. Special licenses allowed them to build up their fishing fleet even though other trades were hampered by embargoes. At the end of the century, French and English shared the fishery, the French still more numerous, the English growing and very strong.

We have no evidence of English plans to settle Newfoundland in the 1590s, but they may well have still been in minds like those of Edward Hayes and Richard Hakluyt. Much later there is talk of a French failure to colonize the island about 1585 (628), but nothing concrete has emerged about this attempt, if it was made. The Marquis de la Roche, however, in his revived role of governor of New France from 1597 included Newfoundland in his putative dominion. For the time being, however, the English had the initiative there, the French in the St. Lawrence River.

Chapter Sixty-nine
The Beginnings, 1577–1583

REPORTS ON NEWFOUNDLAND, 1577–1578

ANTHONY PARKHURST sent out ships from Bristol to the Newfoundland shore fishery from about 1575 to at least 1578, some of which he accompanied himself. He was one of the first Englishmen to obtain any general conspectus of the European fisheries carried on around its shores, and he appears to have penetrated into the interior from several harbors. He was the first literate person whom we know to have set down his impressions of the island, and the earliest to advocate English colonization there. (It seems likely that he influenced Sir Humphrey Gilbert, to whose project he subscribed.) Of his two letters, the first, the earlier, concentrates on colonization prospects, the second being the more general. (a) [1577] Anthony Parkhurst to [Edward Dyer?], B. L. Lansdowne MS 100, no. 10, printed in E. G. Taylor, *The original writings and correspondence of the two Richard Hakluyts*, I (1935), 123–127 (Document 525); (b) November 13, 1578. Anthony Parkhurst to Richard Hakluyt the elder, printed in Richard Hakluyt, *Principall navigations* (1589), pp. 674–677, reprinted in *Principal navigations*, III (1600), 132–134 (526).

525. 1577. Anthony Parkhurst to [Edward Dyer?].

Right worshipfull, I have byn bold to send yow certain nootes tutchynge the newe founde land, the rather for that I perceved, at my last beynge with yow at the corte, by your rejoysyng hart, what joy yo^{we} conceved to here any thynge that might benefyt your cuntry. And then weying the redynesse of your good nature, so prest to further sutche matter by sygnyfyinge the same to the grave counsellors of this land, which stody contynually nothynge more than gods honor and the proffyt of ther cuntrye, happely yowe beynge ofte tymes amonge them, may in some ower informe them what yowe hard, and what possybylyte there is in tyme to come to be rypte by that land, yf yt wer inhabyted.

Then dowte I not but among many informacions and notes made by me, and other sutche travel-lers that for lacke of power can but wysshe well to the common welthe, and for our partes be redy to put downe matter whereon ther fyne wyttes may some tymes work uppon, and then owt there of to chose some one thynge among many, fyt to take in hand for the commodity of our Land.

1. For first and chefest I holde our trade of fysshynge, which might be made twyse, ye[a] thryse, as good as yet yt ys, which thanked be god ys well amended within v yeres, from iiij sayle of small barkes to fortye, whereof the one halfe ar worthy shippes, so that I dare be bolde to affirme to brynge home as mutche fysshe in some one of these as all the navy did before.

2. Nowe for yf this cuntry wer inhabyted, we might make salt ther mutch more cheper than in Inglond, for that owr wood and the caryage (that makes yt dere) would be saved. And possible not far thense to fynde some apte place to make salt, with the helpe of the sonne as in france and spayne, for the clyme will permyt. And I thyncke that aboute cape bryttayne, beynge fenced from

the cold ayer of the Ise by cape race, to fynde yt very warme, as at rotchell.

3. Our salt beynge saved, which stands us more then the vittels and all that we cary, we might not only sell thynges better chepe, but mighte make grete store of dry fysshe with the bryne y'here is cast away. So might we save halfe the salt we spend, and make twyce as mutch dry fysshe as we do.

4. We shold further more, yf this land wer inhabyted, kepe people fysshynge halfe the yere and busyed in the makynge thereof, where as now not past ii moneths: ffor ther would be saved the tyme we spend in makynge our botes and stages. In grabbynge of botes. In makyng of flakes and other dryinge places.

5. We should also provide in every harborow sutche mete places for dry fysshe that we myght make twyce as mutche as we do, and that with lesse payne, in halfe the tyme, and with halfe the men, which truly ys matter of great importance.

6. Nowe will I showe yowe howe mutche this voyage ys to be preferred before a spanysshe viage or other cuntryes. In primis, they cary forthe nether ware nor mony, nether spend they abrode halfe the vyttels that at home they woulde, and yet brynge they home greate store of fysshe, suffycyent to serve our realme and others from whence with yt we brynge home rytche commodyte.

7. It also increseth the navy, good maryners, good fysshermen, and that which moste strange ys, yt maketh them honest, ritche and good husbonds, against ther onlie custome which seldome they brake unless by constraynt. These men as I saide are honest, for that they fynd not in this country wyne nor women. They wex welthy, for that thier shares ys worthe thre tymes the waiges they have for france, spayne or denmarke. Nether spend they that abrode, or they cum home as in other viages. Thus can their wyves, chyldren, servantes and credytors wytnes with me the swetenes and proffyt of this viage.

8. It also spareth mutche flesshe in this realme and especially in thos partes from whence thes shippes are set forthe. The poverty there greatly refresshed, and mutche by that trade set on worke (over longe to declare). So that the povertye together with the clargy do pray for the prosperus successe of these fysshermen. And I am well assured so doth the gentery, for they all

have some proffyt as yowe shall know more at large when I cum next to London, especyally the power hospytalls and the povertye of thos shiers and portes from whence thes shippes be. For ther is given out of every mans share, and of the shippes parte, and also the vyttellers at the least xiid. uppon every syngell share, which may amounte out of a tall shippe to the valewe of x li., besyde the broken fysshe, which is no small quantity, at the least ii or thre thousand, which may be worthe xx li. or xxx li. yf yt were sale abell, and yet as good to eate as the hole.

9. Farther more yowe shall understand that by this viage a greate number of cuntry people, and of all sortes of occupacyons that cannot lyve, ar by thes meanes made good maryners and fysshermen, and that in one viage.

10. Also mo men set on worke in shippes of equal burden by one halfe then ys to france, spayne and denmarke, for a ship bownde to france requyryng forty men, hathe nede of fower score to the new founde on fysshynge fare. And yf xx^{ti} of thes be good maryners, they shall be abell to conducte the shippe, and make the rest that never wer on see resonable good maryners and fysshermen or they cum home.

11. More over yowe shall understand that thes men that travell thether kepe a longe lent of halfe one yere, and spare mutche drynke and vytteles that at home and in other cuntryes they would wantonly wast. Lyvynge nowe by fysshe, sower bere, bysket, bad syder and that more then halfe myngeled with water.

12. Nowe shal yowe understand what other commodytes may growe by that cuntrye more then hitherto we have had. Chefely above all other the kyllynge of wale, which woulde be one of the rytchest trades in the worlde, as the bascons knowe right well, that use that trade only.

Also there might be had towarde the navy greate aboundance of mastes, yardes, plancke, dele borde, turpentyne, rosin, pytche, tar.

There is also in thes lande grete store of dere, hares, brefylles, beares, foxes, wolfes, lybards, otters, sables and martyns. There groweth roses as common as here bryars. So doth ther of raspes, of hurtes, strawberryes and dewberyes, with many other strange beryes.

13. Also ther might be had greate store of Iron, for there is plenty of the myne, and of alder and berche mete for cole, the chefest charge, so ys

ther trym ryvers for yowr iron mylles and for sawynge mylles for your planckes and bordes.

14. There might also be incresed greate plenty of all kyndes of cattell in a shorte tyme, as by example of the Spanyards in the West Indes, which sence ther cummynge thether have had sutche increase of thos they caryed thether, that I have seen ther one meane man, named lazarus besherano, in the ile of curazao, to have a greter number of beefes then ever I saw or herd any in Inglond to have of shepe. So have they there of horse and excellent Junettes, which for ther skynes they kyll in grete number. What might ther be thoughte the increase of swyne would be in this cuntry, so nere to us in respecte of thos partes of the west Indes. Thes have yonge thryse in the yere and most tymes xiiij, xv or xvi. Thes and conyes would in small tyme multyplye to a number infynyte.

15. There is to this land sutch plenty of fysshe and foule that how many so ever went thether shoulde not nede to kyll any of ther cattell they cary for store. They only nede bred and dryncke for one yere or twayne tyll the grounde may be sowen, which in most places is apte for all kynde of corne, as I have made parte tryall.

Pees growe there naturally on the rockes and beeche, pasture plentyfull and good, for there groweth the clover grasse and hony suckell both whyte and red.

This cuntry is habytable and at all tymes of the yere passable as I wyll prove at large by probabell reasons at my next cummynge. Thus I commyt you to almyghte god, trustynge shortly to make your worship better acquaynted with newland matters.

Yours for ever
[Signed:] Anthony Parkhurst

526. November 13, 1578. Anthony Parkhurst to Richard Hakluyt the elder on Newfoundland.

A letter written to M. Richard Hakluyt of the middle Temple, conteining a report of the true state and commodities of New-foundland, by M. Anthonie Parkhurst Gentleman, 1578.

Master Hakluyt, after most heartie commendations, with like thanks for your manifold kindnesse to me shewed, not for any merits that hitherto have beene mine, but wholly proceeding, I must needs confesse, of your owne good nature, which is so ready prest to benefit your countrey and all such poore men as have any sparke in them of good desires, that you do not onely become their friend, but also humble your selfe as servant in their affaires: for which I would to God I were once in place where I might cause your burning zeale to bee knowen to those that have authoritie, power, and abilitie to recompense your travelling mind and pen, wherewith you cease not day nor night to labour and travell to bring your good and godly desires to some passe, though not possibly to that happy ende that you most thirst for: for such is the malice of wicked men the devils instruments in this our age, that they cannot suffer any thing (or at least few) to proceed and prosper that tendeth to the setting forth of Gods glory, and the amplifying of the Christian faith, wherein hitherto princes have not bene so diligent as their calling required. Alas, the labourers as yet are few, the harvest great, I trust God hath made you an instrument to increase the number, and to moove men of power, to redeeme the people of Newfoundland and those parts from out of the captivitie of that spirituall Pharao, the devill.

Now to answer some part of your letter touching the sundry navies that come to Newfoundland, or Terra nova, for fish: you shal understand that some fish not neere the other by 200. leagues, and therefore the certaintie is not knowen; and some yeres come many more then other some, as I see the like among us: who since my first travell being but 4. yeeres, are increased from 30. sayle to 50. which commeth to passe chiefly by the imagination of the Westerne men, who thinke their neighbours have had greater gaines then in very deed they have, for that they see me to take such paines yeerely to go in proper person: they also suppose that I find some secret commoditie by reason that I doe search the harbors, creekes and havens, and also the land much more then ever any Englishman hath done. Surely I am glad that it so increaseth, whereof soever it springeth. But to let this passe, you shall understand that I am informed that there are above 100. saile of Spaniards that come to take Cod (who make all wet, and do drie it when they come home) besides 20. or 30. more that come from Biskaie to kill Whale for Traine. These be better appoynted for shipping and furniture of munition, then any nation saving the Englishmen, who commonly are lords of the harbors where they fish, and do use all strangers helpe in fishing if need require, according to an old custome of the countrey, which thing they do willingly, so that you take nothing from them more then a boat or twaine of salt, in respect of your protection of them against rovers or other violent intruders, who do often put them from good harbor, &c. As touching their tunnage, I thinke it may be neere five or six thousand tunne. But of Portugals there are not lightly above 50. saile, and they make all wet in like sorte, whose tunnage may amount to three thousand tuns, and not upwarde. Of the French nation and Britons, are about one hundred and fiftie sailes, the most of their shipping is very small, not past fortie tunnes, among which some are great and reasonably well appointed, better then the Portugals, and not so well as the Spaniards, and the burden of them may be some 7000. tunne. Their shipping is from all parts of France and Britaine, and the Spaniards from most parts of Spaine, the Portugals from Aviero and Viana, and from 2. or 3. ports more. The trade that our nation hath to Island maketh, that the English are not there in such numbers as other nations.

Now to certifie you of the fertilitie and goodnesse of the countrey, you shall understand that I have in sundry places sowen Wheate, Barlie, Rie, Oates, Beanes, Pease and seedes of herbes, kernels, Plumstones, nuts, all which have prospered as in England. The countrey yeeldeth many good trees of fruit, as Filberds in some places, but in all places Cherie trees, and a kind of Pearetree meet to graffe on. As for Roses, they are as common as brambles here: Strawberies, Dewberies, and Raspis, as common as grasse. The timber is most Firre, yet plentie of Pineapple trees: fewe of these two kinds meete to maste a ship of threescore and ten: But neere Cape Briton, and to the Southward, big and sufficient for any ship. There be also Okes & thornes, there is in all the countrey plentie of Birch and Alder, which be the meetest wood for cole, and also willow, which will serve

for many other purposes. As touching the kindes of Fish beside Cod, there are Herrings, Salmons, Thornebacke, Plase, or rather wee should call them Flounders, Dog fish, and another most excellent of taste called of us a Cat, Oisters, and Muskles, in which I have found pearles above 40. in one Muskle, and generally all have some, great or small. I heard of a Portugall that found one woorth 300. duckets: There are also other kinds of Shel-fish, as limpets, cockles, wilkes, lobsters, and crabs: also a fish like a Smelt[1] which commeth on shore, and another that hath the like propertie, called a Squid: these be the fishes, which (when I please to bee merie with my old companions) I say, doe come on shore when I commaund them in the name of the 5. ports, and conjure them by such like words: These also bee the fishes which I may sweepe with broomes on a heape, and never wet my foote, onely pronouncing two or three wordes whatsoever they be appoynted by any man, so they heare my voyce: the vertue of the wordes be small, but the nature of the fish great and strange. For the Squid, whose nature is to come by night as well as by day, I tell them, I set him a candle to see his way, with which he is much delighted, or els commeth to wonder at it as doe our fresh water fish, the other commeth also in the night, but chiefly in the day, being forced by the Cod that would devoure him, and therefore for feare comming so neere the shore, is driven drie by the surge of the Sea on the pibble and sands. Of these being as good as a Smelt you may take up with a shove-net as plentifully as you do Wheate in a shovell, sufficient in three or foure houres for a whole Citie. There be also other fishes which I tell those that are desirous of strange newes, that I take as fast as one would gather up stones, and them I take with a long pole and hooke. Yea marrie say they, wee beleeve so, and that you catch all the rest you bring home in that sort, from Portugals and Frenchmen. No surely, but thus I doe: with three hookes stretched foorth in the ende of a pole, I make as it were an Eele speare, with which I pricke those Flounders as fast as you would take up fritters with a sharpe pointed sticke, and with that toole I may take up in lesse then halfe a day Lobsters sufficient to finde three hundred men for a dayes

1. "Called by the Spaniards Anchovas, and by the Portugals Capelinas."

meate. This pastime ended, I shewe them that for my pleasure I take a great Mastive I have, and say no more then thus: Goe fetch me this rebellious fish that obeyeth not this Gentleman that commeth from Kent and Christendome, bringing them to the high water marke, and when hee doubteth that any of those great Cods by reason of shelving ground bee like to tumble into the Sea againe, hee will warily take heede and carrie him up backe to the heape of his fellowes. This doeth cause my friendes to wonder, and at the first hearing to judge them notorious lies, but they laugh and are merrie when they heare the meanes howe each tale is true.

I tolde you once I doe remember how in my travaile into Africa and America, I found trees that bare Oisters, which was strange to you, till I tolde you that their boughes hung in the water, on which both Oisters and Muskles did sticke fast, as their propertie is, to stakes and timber.

Nowe to let these merrie tales passe, and to come to earnest matters againe, you shall understand, that Newfoundland is in a temperate Climate, and not so colde as foolish Mariners doe say, who finde it colde sometimes when plentie of Isles of yce lie neere the shore: but up in the land they shall finde it hotter then in England in many parts of the countrey toward the South. This colde commeth by an accidentall meanes, as by the yce that commeth fleeting from the North partes of the worlde, and not by the situation of the countrey, or nature of the Climate. The countrey is full of little small rivers all the yeere long proceeding from the mountaines, ingendred both of snow and raine: few springs that ever I could finde or heare of, except it bee towards the South: in some places or rather in most places great lakes with plentie of fish, the countrey most covered with woods of firre, yet in many places indifferent good grasse, and plentie of Beares every where, so that you may kill of them as oft as you list: their flesh is as good as yong beefe, and hardly you may know the one from the other if it be poudred but two dayes. Of Otters we may take like store. There are Sea Guls, Murres, Duckes, wild Geese, and many other kind of birdes store, too long to write, especially at one Island named Penguin, where wee may drive them on a planke into our ship as many as shall lade her. These birdes are also called Penguins, and cannot flie, there is more meate in one of these then in a goose: the French-

men that fish neere the grand baie, doe bring small store of flesh with them, but victuall themselves alwayes with these birdes. Nowe againe, for Venison plentie, especially to the North about the grand baie, and in the South neere Cape Race, and Pleasance: there are many other kinds of beasts, as Luzarnes and other mighty beastes like to Camels in greatnesse, and their feete cloven, I did see them farre off not able to discerne them perfectly, but their steps shewed that their feete were cloven, and bigger then the feete of Camels, I suppose them to bee a kind of Buffes which I read to bee in the countreyes adjacent, and very many in the firme land. There bee also to the Northwards, Hares and Foxes in all parts so plentifully, that at noone dayes they take away our flesh before our faces within lesse then halfe a paire of buts length, where foure and twentie persons were turning of drie fish, and two dogs in sight, yet stoode they not in feare till wee gave shot and set the dogs upon them: the Beares also be as bold, which will not spare at midday to take your fish before your face, and I beleeve assuredly would not hurt any bodie unlesse they be forced.

Nowe to shew you my fancie what places I suppose meetest to inhabite in those parts discovered of late by our nation: There is neere about the mouth of the grand Bay, an excellent harbour called of the Frenchmen Chasteaux, and one Island in the very entrie of the streight called Bell Isle, which places if they be peopled and well fortified (as there are stones and things meete for it throughout all Newfound land) wee shall bee lordes of the whole fishing in small time, if it doe so please the Queenes Majestie, and from thence send wood and cole with all necessaries to Labrador lately discovered: but I am of opinion, and doe most stedfastly beleeve that we shall finde as rich Mines in more temperate places and Climates, and more profitable for fishing then any yet we have used, where wee shall have not farre from thence plentie of salt made by fire undoubtedly, and very likely by the heate of the Sunne, by reason I finde salt kerned on the rockes in nine and fortie and better: these places may bee found for salte in three and fortie. I know more touching these two commodities last remembred then any man of our nation doeth; for that I have some knowledge in such matters, and have most desired the finding of them by painefull travaile, and most diligent inquirie. Now to be short, for I have bene over long by Master Butlers means, who cryed on mee to write at large, and of as many things as I call to minde woorthy of remembrance: wherefore this one thing more. I could wish the Island in the mouth of the river of Canada should bee inhabited, and the river searched, for that there are many things which may rise thereof, as I will shew you hereafter. I could find in my heart to make proofe whether it be true or no that I have read and heard of Frenchmen and Portugals to bee in that river, and about Cape Briton. I had almost forgot to speake of the plentie of wolves, and to shew you that there be foxes, blacke, white & gray: other beasts I know none save those before remembred. I found also certain Mines of yron and copper in S. Johns, and in the Island of Yron, which things might turne to our great benefite, if our men had desire to plant thereabout, for proofe whereof I have brought home some of the oare of both sortes. And thus I ende, assuring you on my faith, that if I had not beene deceived by the vile Portugals descending of the Jewes and Judas kinde, I had not failed to have searched this river, and all the coast of Cape Briton, what might have bene found to have benefited our countery: but they breaking their bands, and falsifying their faith and promise, disappointed me of the salte they should have brought me in part of recompense of my good service in defending them two yeeres against French Rovers, that had spoyled them, if I had not defended them.

By meanes whereof they made me lose not onely the searching of the countery, but also forced mee to come home with great losse above 600. li. For recompence whereof I have sent my man into Portugall to demaund justice at the Kings hand, if not, I must put up my supplication to the Queenes Majesty & her honourable councell, to grant me leave to stay here so much of their goods as they have damnified mee, or else that I may take of them in Newfound land, as much fish as shall be woorth 600. li. or as much as the salte might have made. I pray you advertise mee what way I were best to take, and what hope there will bee of a recompence if I follow the suite: many there are that doe comfort me, and doe bid me proceede, for that her Majestie and the councell doe tender poore fisher men, who with me have susteined three hundred pound losse in that

voyage. And to conclude, if you and your friend shall thinke me a man sufficient and of credite, to seeke the Isle of S. John, or the river of Canada, with any part of the firme land of Cape Briton, I shall give my diligence for the true and perfect discoverie, and leave some part of mine owne businesse to further the same: and thus I end, committing you to God. From Bristow the 13. of November, 1578.
Yours to use and command
[Signed:] Anthony Parckhurst.

527. November 6, 1577. Sir Humphrey Gilbert advocates seizure of non-English shipping at Newfoundland.

A cynical plan to seize all non-English shipping at Newfoundland—French, Spanish, and Portuguese—was put forward by Sir Humphrey Gilbert, who was one of the war party that resented the modus vivendi *worked out with Spain in 1573–1574 and that hoped for war. He thought his plan, if put in operation, might provoke reprisals against English trade by Portugal and France, as well as war with Spain, but he believed it would provide ships for an attack on the Spanish Indies which would counterbalance losses. At the time both Portugal and France were allied with England, but he thought, if necessary, their ships could be omitted from the seizure. A similar plan was put forward somewhat later by another hand (P.R.O., SP 12/177, 58), and in 1585 Bernard Drake attempted to carry out something like this against Spanish and Portuguese ships (539–547).*

P.R.O., SP 12/118, 12(i); printed in D. B. Quinn, Gilbert, *I, 170–175, extracts.*

A discourse how hir Majestie may annoy the k: of Spayne.

I am bowld (most excellent Soveraigne) to exercise my pen touching matters of state, because I am a syllie member of this Common Weale of England, and doe not offer myself therein as an Instructor, or a reformer, but as a Welwiller to your Majestie and my Countrie, wherein the meanest or simplest ought not to yeeld them selves second to the best, or wisest. In which respect I hope to be pardoned, if through want of judgement I be mistaken herein. And so to the matter.

The safety of Principates, Monarchies, and Common Weales rest chiefly in making theire enemies weake, and poore, and themselves strong and rich, Both which god hath specially wrought for your majestes safety, if your highness shall not overpas good opportunities for the same, when they are offered. For your neighboures infelicities through civill warres, hath weakened and impoverished them both by sea, and land, And hath strengthened your Majestes Realme both by thone, and thother, which thinge is so manyfest, that it weare more then in vayne, to go about to prove the same. And for that that this your Majestes Realme of England requireth other consideracions then those which are of ther continent, I will omit them, and sypnn a threed propper for our English loomes.

First your highnes owght undoubtedly to seeke the kingdome of heaven, and upon that fowndacion to beleeve that there can never be constant, and firme league of amytie betwene those princes, whose division is planted by the woorme of thier consciences. So that their leagues and fayre wordes, ought to be held but as mermaydes songes, sweet poysons, or macquesites, that abuse with outward plawsabilityie, and gay showes. For in troth as in such leagues there is no assuraunce, so Christian princes ought not for any respect to combyne themselves in amytie, with such as are at open and professed warres with god himselfe. For non est consilium omnino contra deum. So that no state or common weale can florishe, where the first and principall care is not for goddes glorie, and for thadvaunsing of the pollisies of his spirituall kingdom, which donn, your majestie is to thinck that it is more then tyme to pare theire nayles by the stumpes, that are most readie prest to plucke the crowne (as it were in despite of god) from your highnes head, not only by foraine force: also by stirring up of home factions. And therefore the best waie is first to purge, or at least wise to redresse your owne kingdome of theire suspected adherentes, I meane not by banishment, or by fire, and sworde, but by diminishing theire habilities by purse, creditt and force. Then to foresee by all diligente

meanes, that your suspected neighbors may not have opportunity to recover breath whereby to repayre theire decayed losses; which for your safetie is principally to be don, by the farther weakning of theire navies, and by preserving and increasing of your owne.

And the deminishing of their forces by sea is to be done eyther by open hostilytie, or by some colorable meanes; as by geving of lycence under lettres patentes to discover and inhabyte some strange place, with speciall proviso for their safetyes whome pollisy requyreth to have most annoyed by which meanes the doing of the contrarie shalbe imputed to the executors fawlt; your highnes lettres patentes being a manyfest shewe that it was not your Majestes pleasure so to have it. After the publick notyse of which fact, your Majestie is either to avowe the same (if by the event thereof it shall so seme good) or to disavowe both them and the fact, as league breakers, leaving them to pretend yt as done without your pryvitie, either in the service of the Prince of Orange or otherwise. This cloake being had for the raigne, the way to worke the feate is to sett forth under such like colour of discoverie, certayne shippes of warre to the N.L. [New Land] which with your good licence I will undertake without your Majestes charge; in which place they shall certainely once in the yeere meete in effecte all the great shipping of Fraunce, Spayne, and Portyngall, where I would have take and bring awaye with theire fraygthes and ladinges, the best of those shippes and burn the woorst, and those that they take to carrie into Holland or Zeland, or as pirattes to shrowd them selves for a small time uppon your Majestes coastes, under the frendship of some certayne viceadmirall of this Realme; who may be afterwardes committed to prison, as in displeasure for the same, against whose returnes, six monthes provision of bread, and fower of drinck to be layd in some apt place: together with municion to serve for the number of five or six thousand men, which men with certaine other shippes of warr being in a readyness, shall pretend to inhabit St. Lawrence Island, the late discovered Contries in the North, or elswhere, and not to joyne with the others but in some certaine remote place at sea.

The setting forth of shipping for this service will amounte to no great matter, and the retourne shall certainely be with great gayne, For the

N.F. [Newland Fish] is a principall and rich and everie where vendible merchaundise: and by the gayne thereof, shipping, victuall, munition, and the transporting of five or six thousand soldiors may be defrayed.

It may be sayd that a fewe shippes cannot possibilie distres so many: and that although by this service yow take or destroy all the shipping you find of theirs in those places: yet are they but subjectes shippes, theire owne particular navies being nothing lessoned therby, and therefore theire forces shall not so much be diminyshed, as yt is supposed, whereunto I answere.

There is no doubt to performe it without dawnger. For although they may be many in number, and great of burthen, yet are they furnished with men, and munition, but like fishers, and when they come upon the coastes, they do alwaies disperse them selves into sundry portes, and do disbarke the moste of their people into small boates for the taking and drying of theire fish, leaving fewe or none aborde theire shippes, so that there is as little doubt of the easye taking, and carrying of them away: as of the decaying hereby of those princes forces by sea. For theire owne proper shippinges are very fewe, and of small forces in respect of the others, and theire subjectes shipping being once destroyed, yt is likely that they will never be repaired, partly through the decaye of the owners, and partly through the losses of the trades whereby they mainteyned the same / For everie man that is hable to build shippes doth not dispose his wealth that waye, so that their shipping being once spoyled, yt is likely that they will never be recovered to the like number and strength, but if they should yt will requiei [sic] a long time to season timber for that purpose, all which space we shall have good opportunity to proceed in our farther enterprises / And all the meane tyme the forsayd princes shall not only be disapointed of their forces as aforesaid, but also leese great revenues, which by traffick they formerly gayned; and shall therewithall endure great famine for want of such necessarie victualles &c. as they former enjoyed by those voyages.

It may also be objected that although this may be done in act, yet it is not allowable, being against your Majestes league: for although by the reach of reason mens Ies may be obscured, yet unto God nothing is hidden, which I answere thus.

I hold it as lawfull in christen pollicie, to prevent a mischief betime: as to revenge it to late, especiallie seing that god him selfe is a party in the common quarrelles now a foote, and his ennemy malitiouse disposition towardes your highnes, and his Church manifestlie seen, although by godes mercifull providence not yet throughlie felt.

Further it may be saide that if this should be done by Englishmen under what colour soever they should shrowd themselves, yet will that cut us off from all trafficke with those that shalbe annoyed by such meanes; and thereby utterlie undoe the state of merchandise, decaye the mayntenaunce of the shipping of this Realme and also greatly diminishe your Majestes customes to which I replie thus.

To prevent theise daungers (that although your highnes may at the first distres both the French, Spanyshe, and Portingall yet there needeth none to be towched but the Spaniardes, and Portingall, or the Spaniardes alone) by the want of those whose traffick there is no necessity of such decaye and losses as partly appeared by the late restrainte betwene your Majesty and them. And the forces of the Spaniardes and Portingalls, being there so much decayed as aforesaid; The French of necessitie shalbe brought under your highnes eye / assuring your majesty the case being as it is, it were better a thousand folde thus to gayne the start of them, rather then yerely to submitt our selves subject to have all the marchauntes shippes of this Realme stayed in their handes: whereby they shalbe armed at our costes, to beate us with roddes of our owne making, and ourselves thereby spoyled both of our owne wealth and strength.

And touching the contynuaunce of traffick wherewith to increase and maintaine our shipping, and your majestes revenues, and also to provide that the prices of sotherne wares shall not be so inhaunced to the detriment of the Comon weale: there may be good meanes found for the preventing thereof, as hereafter followeth /

It is true if we shold indure the losse of those trades, and not recover those commodities by some other meanes: that then your Majesty might be both hindred in shippinge, and customes, to the great decaie of the comon Weale. But if your highnes will permit me, with my associates eyther overtly or covertly to perfourme the aforesaide enterprise: then with the gayne thereof there may be easely such a competent companie transported to the W[est] I[ndies] as may be hable not only to disposses the S[paniards] thereof, but also to possesse for ever your Majestie and Realme therewith, and thereby not only be countervaile, but by farr to surmounte with gaine, the aforesaid supposed losses: besides the gowld and silver Mynes, the profitt of the soyle, and the inward and outward customs from thence, By which meanes your highnes doubtfull frendes, or rather apparaunte enemyes, shall not be only made weake and poore, but therewith your selfe, and Realme made strong and rich, both by sea, and by lande, as well there, as here. And where both is wrought under one, it bringeth a most happy conclusion. So that if this may be well brought to passe (where of there is no doubt) then have we hitt the mark we shott at, and wonn the goale of our securities to the immortall fame of your Majestie / For when your enemyes shall not have shipping, nor meanes left them whereby to maintayne shipping, to annoye your Majestie nor your subjectes be any longer enforced for want of other trades to submitt them selves to the daunger of theire arrestes, then of force this Realme being an Iland shall be discharged from all forraine perills, if all the Monarchies of the world should joyne against us, so long as Ireland shal be in salf keping, the league of Scotland maintayned, and further amitie concluded with the prince of Orange and the King of Denmark. By which meanes also your majestie shall ingraffe and glewe to your crowne, in effect all the Northerne and Southerne viages of the world, so that none shalbe then well hable to crosse the seas, but subject to your highnes devocion: considering the great increase of shipping that will growe, and be maynetayned by those long vyages, extending themselves so many sundrie wayes. And if I may perceave that your highnes shall like of this enterprise, then will I most willinglie expresse my simple opinion, which waye the W[est] I[ndies] maye without difficultie be more surprised, and defended, without which resolucion it were but labour lost. But if your Majestie like to do it at all, then wold I wish your highnes to consider that delay doth often tymes prevent the perfourmaunce of good thinges: for the Winges of mans life are plumed with the feathers of Death. And so submitting my self to your Majesties favourable judgement I cease to trouble your highnes any further. Novembris: 6. 1577.

Your Majestes most faithfull servaunt and subject.
[Signed:] H. Gylberte

THE OUGHTRED–PERROT PIRACY AGAINST PORTUGUESE SHIPS AT NEWFOUNDLAND, 1582

THE PIRATICAL RAID in the summer of 1582 by a ship belonging to Henry Oughtred and Richard Clerke master and the *Popinjaye* belonging to Sir John Perrot on the ports of Renews and Fermeuse is something of a turning point in Newfoundland's affairs. The ships falsely claimed to have an English commission to take prizes so that they were, in law, pirates. They stripped two Portuguese ships of their fish and oil and loaded into a third which, after taking a lesser toll from other Portuguese vessels, they brought to England. The port admiral at Renews was a French Basque, and there were a number of English ships in the harbors. Although none made any resistance, the masters of the English vessels gave the robbed Portuguese evidence on what happened. In England the Spanish ambassador intervened (529), one of the Portuguese appealed to the Privy Council, and a case against Clerke was brought in the Admiralty Court. There, in the spring of 1583, a number of English seamen testified against Clerke (531–532) and a Portuguese witness was later brought from Portugal (533). The result of the case is not known.

Oughtred apparently received some protection from Sir Francis Walsingham, and Clerke was allowed to sail with Sir Humphrey Gilbert in June. The episode shows the Portuguese being treated by some Englishmen as enemies but also that the old international cooperation of the Newfoundland fishermen still survived.

528. [1582]. Petition to the Privy Council by Francisco Fernandes.

P.R.O., State Papers, Domestic, Elizabeth I, SP 12/151, 36, fol. 97.

State Papers, Foreign, Spain, SP 94/1, fol. 312; in French, translated.

To the Quenes maiestes moste honorable privie councell.

In most humble wise doth showe unto your honours Francisco Farnandus portingale of the towne of Viana as well for my self as the rest of whome I have their procuracions and exhibited before master doctor Lewes highe iudge of the admiraltie touching robberye comitted in newfond land being in Companie of divers englishe shipps that wer a fuishing by an englishe pirat apperteyning to master henrie Whytteredge dwelling besides southampton. The which shipp did robb and spoyle us of our fishe and the other englishe men which wer in our companie would have assissted us, but the capitayne of the same Henrie Witteredge shipp declared unto them that they had comission from the lordes of the Councell of England for ye taking of us as your honours orato I have alredy shewed under the handes of the masters of the other english shippes whiche wer then in our company. And they hering the same durste not succour us and upon the same they tooke away your oratours shipp laden full of fishe and trayne oyles and brought the same to this Realme about Bristowe side....

529. November 9, 1582. Spanish complaints about Richard Clerke's Newfoundland raid.

Bernardino de Mendoza, Spanish ambassador, to Lord Burghley, November 9, 1582. P.R.O.,

Sir,

By my letter written to Master Secretary Walsingham to be laid before the lords of the council I have informed him that a ship or two [ships], which were set out by Master Outred [Oughtred] of Antona [Southampton] had robbed more than twenty ships at Terra Nova [Newfoundland] belonging to subjects of the king my master, who were fishing, ill-treated their men, and took their victuals. Having laden his vessel he [Richard Clerke] took one of them to the "Coast" of Bristol loaded with fish and oil [*poisson et grasses*], where he was stayed by the lieutenant of a gentleman named Herri Bicher [Harry Becher?]. And in conformity with the request made in this letter, orders were given by the said Master Walsingham to the Judge of the Admiralty to see justice done. And so the Judge ordered that the goods be placed in custody until the attorneys of the owners arrived. Now the Judge says that by your order and that of the Lord Admiral the goods and ship have been delivered in the hands of the said Outred, in regard to which I am quite sure that you were not informed of the robbery. Therefore I pray you to order that justice be done, and that the goods be not put in the hands of pirates, but of the person who shall be appointed for this, giving security. I pray that the Creator give you health and a good and long life with compliments and his good and virtuous desires. London, 9 November 1582.

Your wellwisher

[Signed:] Don Bernardino de Mendoza

[Addressed:] The Lord Treasurer of England.
[Endorsed:] 9 November 1582. The Spanish Embassador. A Spanish ship seased by Master Ughtred.

530. April 25, 1583. Examination of Thomas Peers, English fisherman.

P.R.O., High Court of Admiralty, Examinations, HCA 13/25.

25 April 1583. Thomas Peers of Plymowthe maryner aged about xliiiior yeares or thereaboutes sworne and examined before Mr Doctor Lewes Judge of Thadmiraltye upon certen articles geven against him and others on the behaulfe of Fruncis Fernandes and others deposethe thereunto as followethe.

To the first he sayethe that in the monethes of June Julye and August last past he was in Newe founde land in the Harborowghe articulate a fisshinge in the cumpanye of iii Portingall shipps and others as in the article ys deduced.

To the second he sayethe that a shipp of Bayon in Fraunce was Admirall one Domingo Hewes beinge Capitaigne thereof and Master alsoe.

To the third he sayethe that there was iij as before he hathe deposed of one whereof was Master Nicholas Fernandes, of the second Baltaser Mendez was Master Nicholas Fernandes, of the second Baltaser Mendez was Master and of the third was Master tharticulate Frauncys Vernandez. Whoe were owners thereof he knowethe not but he thinckethe the said Masters were parte owners of the said shipps but what partes they had he cannot depose.

To the iiiith he sayethe that a shipp of tharticulate Master Owtredes one Clerck beinge Master thereof came into the Harboroughe articulate aboute the middest of August last past uppon bourd wch shipp this examinant went in the cumpanye of the foresaid Frauncys Fernandes. But what her name ys he cannot declare.

To the fyfte he cannot otherwyse depose then before he hathe to the precedent article.

To the vj he cannot depose. But sayethe that the foresaid Clerck sayed he came not to fishe, notwithstandinge said he fyshe I muste and will have before I goe hence.

To the viith he sayethe that ii of the said Portingall shipps were of the burden of lxxxx tonnes or there aboutes per peece, and the thirde was of lxx tonnes burden, beinge laden for the moaste parte with wett and drye Newe founde land fyshe the ij bigger shipps havinge in them aboute lxx

thousand of fyshe, and the lesser aboute fyftie thousand which this examinant knowethe to be trewe for that as he sayethe he fysshed by them and knewe what they did take.

To the viiith he sayethe, that aboute the beginninge of Auguste last past the said Clerck the Master assaulted and tooke in Newfounde land in the harboroughe of Renowsa the iii Portingale shipps aforesaid and ryfelid and spoyled them of all their ladinges and one of the said shipps he carryed quite awaye with her ladinge in her, havinge in her aboute lxx thousand of fyshe wett and drye, which wett fyshe was worthe viiili per M. and the drye iiiili per thousand, and iij or fower tonn of trayne oyle was in her alsoe. Thother ii shipps after he had ryfelid and spoyled them at his pleasure and laden the fyshe owte of them into his owne he left them soe spoyled in the havon of Firmoosa and so departed and went his way.

Alsoe he sayethe that the said Clerck with his shipp and cumpanye spoyled ii other Portingall shipps in the said havon of Firmoosa. And more to this article he cannot depose.

To the ixth he sayethe. That the foresaid Clerck Master of the said Master Owghtred his shipp did affirme and say in this examinantes heringe that he had aucthoritye and lycence from the Lordes of the Counsell to apprehand and take Portingalls and Spaniardes. But afterwardes beinge called before vi or vii Englishe men Masters of shipps then and there presente he did utterlye deny that he had aucthoritye from the Llordes of the Counsell. But sayed that he had Commission from Don Antonio and soe good aucthoritye there with all that he would make sale thereof at Hampton Key.

To the xth he sayethe that the Admirall of the shipps was not hable to resiste the said Master Owtredes shipp. And otherwyse he cannot depose.

To the xith he cannot otherwyse depose then he hathe to the viiith article before. Savinge he sayethe that the said Frauncys Fernandes shipp taken and spoyled by the said Clerck as before with her tacle and furniture besides her ladinge of fyshe was worthe iiiiC.li at the least.

To the xiith he sayethe that the said Clerck brought one of the said Portingale shipps belonginge to the foresaid Frauncys Fernandes with her ladinge as aforesaid to the quoast of England but to what place he knowethe not.

To the xiiith and xiiiith he sayethe that he sawe suche a Testimoniall in Newfounde land as in tharticle is deduced, which beinge nowe agayne shewed unto him at the tyme of his examination he avouchethe to be the selfe and same that he sawe in Newefounde land aforesaid. And sayethe that the persons which have subscribed the said Testimoniall are men of good creditt, and were presente in the contrey at the tyme of the foresaid spoyles committed and don whoe travelid verye earnestelye unto the said Clerck to make rede-liverye of the said Portingalls shipp and goodes, but he would not doe the same.

To the last he cannot depose.

[Signed:] bye me Thomas Pyres.

531. April 25, 1583. Examination of William Dill.

P.R.O., HCA 13/25.

26 April 1583. William Dill of Plimouthe maryner aged xxviii yeres or thereabowtes sworne and examined before the said Judge of Thadmiraltye uppon the foresaid articles sayethe thereunto as followethe.

To the firste he deposethe bye chardge of his oathe That this examinante beinge masters mate of a shippe of Plimouthe called the John Hawkyns whereof was master Thomas Pierse arryved at Reignosa in Newefounde lande in the monethe of maye laste and in the beginninge of the same where this examinante and the reste of the companye of the said shippe remayned in Fisshinge fare the space of xiiii weekes in companye of thre portingalls shipps and ii biskyns and a Frenche man. Of one of whiche Portingalls shipps Jasper Peres was Captayne and Frauncys Fernandes master, and one Balchys Mendres was Captayne of one of the other portingalls shipps and the other Captayne or master he knowethe not bye name.

To the seconde he sayethe the said Frenche shippe beinge of the portadge of lxx toones was Admirall of the said shippes whereof a Frenche man was Captayne whose name nether the Masters he knowethe not.

To the thirde he sayethe theire was thre por-

tingall shipps in the said harbor a fisshinge whose names he knowethe not nether the masters of Captaynes of more then ys before specified.

To the iiiith and vth he sayethe that of his owne knowledge aboute the ende of Julye or beginninge of Auguste [laste] a greate shippe of Master Henrye Owghtredes of Southampton of cc toones or upwardes arryved at a place in newefounde lande called Fermose abowte a league to the Northwarde from the said harbor of Reignosa together with an other shippe of Sir John Parrattes called the Popiniaye of lx toonnes whereof was master henrye Taylor. And of master henrye Owghtredes shippe Richard Clercke was master but the Captaynes name he knowethe not.

To the vith he sayethe he was never on borde the said shippe of Master Owghtredes, and therefore can not specifye howe the same was appoyncted.

To the viith he sayethe the said Ja[s]per Peres his shippe was to his iudgmente of cx toonnes or thereabowtes, and the other two shippes were the one of an hundrethe tonnes, and the other of forescore toonnes, and were to his iudgmente abowte thre partes laden with newelande fishe severallye. And more he knowethe not.

To the viiith a he sayethe yt ys moste trewe that the said Master Owghtredes shippe and Sir John Perrottes shippe fallinge in consorte togeather, and beinge not able to bringe master Owghtredes shippe into the harbor of Reignosa because of such bignes, and the winde contrarye theye manned the other lesser shippe with abowte xiii of the companye of master Owghtredes shippe whereof the said Richard Clercke the master was one, besides the said Taylers whole companye and soe came uppe into the harbor of Reignosa and in warlicke sorte and forceable maner assaulted and sett uppon the said thre portingalls shippes then ridinge in that harbor, and subdued entered and tooke the same and there detayned them in the harbor the space of viii dayes untill theye had gotten aborde a greate quantitye of fishe and Frayne whiche the companye of the said portingall shippes had taken and was dryeinge on shore, And when theye had gotten the said goodes on borde, the said Clercke, Tayler and theire companye caryed awaye the said thre portingalls shippes furthe of the said harbor of Reignosa, and broughte them to Fermose where master Owghtredes shippe laye. And there they rifled and spoyled the said shippes at theire wills and pleasures both of theire ladinges munition and furniture, and verey wickedlye besides abused, beate, and thretned to kill the companye of the said shippes. Addinge moreover that when the said Clarcke, Tayler and the reste of theire consortes had made spoyle of what they beste liked theye caried one of the said Portingalls shippes with her whole Ladinge whereof the said Jasper Peres was Captayne and Francys Fernandes master, cleane awaye, and lefte the other two shippes spoyled and berefte of theire ladinges munition and furniture in the said harbor. Whiche he knowethe to be trewe for that this examinante was at that presente in the harbor of Reignosa in the John Hawkyns of Plimouthe and sawe the arrivall of the said Sir John Parrattes shipped in that harbor, and the assaulte and spoile whiche theye made uppon the said portingalls shipps in that harbor, and the caryeinge of them awaye in such sorte and order as ys before deposed. Whiche was in the firste daye of Awguste Laste to his nowe remembrance. Ut dicit. And towchinge the valewe of the said goodes spoyled he cannot depose but sayethe the corre fishe was worthe x li the thowsande and the drye fishe iiii^{li}x s. the M. of everye mans moneye.

To the ixth he cannot depose.

To the xth he sayethe that the Admirall of the said shipps then beinge in the said harbor coulde not reskue the said portingalls shippes for that he was a Fissherman and but slenderlye appoyncted for fighte and also the moste parte of his companye were at the tyme of the assaulte made a fisshinge at the sea, as the companye of this examinantes shippe were. And when they had gotten the said shippes in subiection yt was to late to seeke reskue or to recover the same.

To the xith he sayethe that the said Clercke and Tayler and theire companye caried awaye one of the said Portingalls shippes with her ladinge as ys before sayde, and the ladinge of the other ij shippes but the valewe of the shippe and goodes spoyled he cannot otherwise declare then ys before deposed.

To the xiith he sayethe he hathe herde that the said master Owghtredes shippe and the portingall shippes with theire severalle ladinges of the said spoyled goodes were broughte into the Realme bye the said Richard Clercke and his adherentes. And otherwise he cannot depose.

To the xiiith he sayethe he herde John Pocombe Richard Birche Richard Pope, Roberte Cotton and William Stagge all masters of shipps savinge the said Stagge, affirme and saye in the said havon of Reignosa that they woulde geve testimonye unto the portingalls for the recovery of theire said Losses here in Englande and in what sorte and manner theye had byn spoyled and abused bye the said Richard Clercke, Henrye Tayler and theire companye For that theye were all at that presente in the said harbor and sawe the spoile soe committed and don. And more he cannot.

To the xiiiith he sayethe he knowethe all the parties whose names be subscribed to the articulate Testimoniall nowe redde unto him at the tyme of his examination, and that theye are honeste men of good fame and creditt and soe are accowpted and taken and never herde the contrarye. And towchinge the said Testimoniall he sayethe he sawe yt not made nor subscribed by the said parties but sayethe the contentes thereof towchinge the spoyle committed and don uppon the said portingalls shipps and the caryenge awaye of one of them with her ladinge, and the ladinge of the reste of this examinantes sighte and perfecte knowledge are moste trewe as ys before deposed.

To the xvth he cannot depose.

[Attested by his mark]

532. April 27, 1583. Examination of John Heimers.

P.R.O., HCA 13/25.

27 April 1583. John Heimers of Plimouthe Carpenter of the age of xxxvj yeres or thereaboutes sworne and examined uppon the foresaid articles Sayethe thereunto as followethe.

To the firste he confessethe he was in the havon of Reignosa in Newefounde lande on fisshinge fare from the firste of maye laste untill the firste of September followinge in the John Hawkyns of Plimouthe. Durenge whiche tyme there also were in the said harbor on fisshinge thre portingalls shippes whereof Jasper Perez was Captayne of one of them and Balthus mendes was pilott and

Captayne of one other and the thirde Captayne or master he knowethe not.

To the seconde he sayethe there was also in the said roade a Frenche shippe of Bayon of lxx toonnes or thereabowtes whiche was Admirall of the shippes remayninge in that harbor whereof a Frenche man was owner and master whose name this examinante knowethe not.

To the thirde he sayethe there were three Portingalls shipps in the said harbor whose names he knowethe not Jasper Peres as ys before said beinge Captayne of one and Francys Fernandes master of the same, and Balthus Mendes pilott of one other the thirde he knowethe not.

To the forthe he knowethe that a shippe of master Henrye Owghtredes whereof Richard Clercke was Master beinge of cc toonnes burthen togeather with an other smaler shippe of Sir John Parrattes of lx toonnes burthen Henrye Tayler beinge master thereof arryved togeather at Fermose a harbor in Newefounde lande abowte a leage distant from the said Harbor of Reignosa abowte the beginninge of Awguste laste to his nowe remembrance.

To the vth he sayethe Richard Clercke was Master of the said Master Owghtredes shippe the Captaynes name he knowethe not.

To the vith he sayethe the said Master Owghtredes shippe was full of ordenance, and manned with forscore and ten men, and otherwise warlicklye appoyncted.

To the viith he sayethe that ii of the said Portingalls shippes were of an hundrethe toonnes burthen or upwardes and the thirde of abowte forescore toonnes burthen, and were thre partes laden severallye with fishe and salte as he ys well assured. but the quantitye otherwise he cannot specifye.

To the viiith he sayethe that the said Richard Clercke not beinge able throughe contrarye windes to fetche the said harbor of Reignosa with his greate shippe, thereuppon shipped himselfe with twelve of his men into Sir John Parrattes shippe and consorted himselfe with the master and companye thereof, and soe came into the said harbor of Reignosa in Auguste laste where the said thre Portingalls shipps laye, and with force and violence sett uppon, bourded and entered them in warlicke sorte, and there detayned them and theire companye as captyves vj or viij dayes space untill they had broughte on borde suche

fishe and trayne as Portingalls had taken and then was on shore, whiche beinge don the said Clarcke Tayler and theire companye caryed awaye the said thre portingalls shippes in this examinantes sighte (beinge then yn the said harbor on borde the John Hawkyns) and broughte them to Fermose where master Owghtredes shippe rode, and there verey wickedlye they spoyled and robbed two of the said Portingalls shipps of all theire ladinge munition provision apparell and necessarye, and the thirde shippe beinge Jasper Peres his shippe the wholye caryed awaye with her ladinge munition and furniture, and soe departed leavinge the other ii shippes berefte and spoyled as aforesaid. Whiche for trewthe he can instlye verefye for that he was at that presente in the said harbor of Reignosa and sawe the spoyle committed and the shipps caryed awaye as ys before deposed, and also the poore portingalls besides marvelouslye misused, beaten and threatned to be kilde soe as sondry of them for savegarde of theire lyves laye on borde other shippes in the Roade and durste not be sene to the said pirattes leste theye wolde have murdered them as muste wickedlye they threatned them.

To the ixth he sayethe that the said Richarde Clarcke in this examinantes presence and hearinge did openlye affirme and saye that he had aucthoritye and licence from the Quenes majestes of Englande and her privye Counsell to take all Spanierdes and portingalls.

To the xth he sayethe the said Admirall was a shippe of smale force, and was not able to reskue the said portingalls shippes, or to save them from spoyle the said Clarcke and his companye beinge soe stronge as throwghlye appoyncted with men munition and artillerye.

To the xith he sayethe the said Clarcke Tayler and theire adherentes caryed awaye one of the said portingalls shipps and spoyled the other two as ys before deposed but to what valewe the spoyle extended he knowethe not.

To the xiith he hath herde that the said Jasper Peres shippe whiche the said pirattes caryed awaye they broughte into this Realme with her ladinge, and ys here yet remayninge at the Wighte.

To the xiiith he affirmethe that he herde John Pocombe and other Masters of shippes whiche were at the tyme of the said spoyle committed in Newfounde lande affirme and saye that they woulde make a testimoniall and certificatt under theire handes towchinge the said spoile whiche he thinkethe they made accordinglye.

To the xiiiith he knowethe the persons all whose names be subscribed unto the Testimoniall shewed unto him at the tyme of his examination and theye be honeste men of good fame, reporte and credit and verely thinkethe that the said Testimoniall was made and subscribed bye them and towchinge the contentes thereof he sayethe soe muche as concernethe the spoyle and robberye don uppon the said portingalls and theire said shippes he affirmethe of his owne sighte and knowledge to be moste trewe as in the said Testimoniall ys contayned.

To the xvth he cannot depose.

[Attested by a mark]

533. October 16, 1583. Paulo Dies testifies as to Captain Clerke's actions in Newfoundland in 1582.

P.R.O., HCA 13/25, fols. 40v.–42.

Francisco Fernandes and others against Henry Utrighte [Oughtred].

Wednesday, 16 October 1583. Paulus Dies of Avero in Portugal, seaman, aged forty-five years or thereabouts testifies, through the interpretation of Robert Parcke, Citizen of London, in the Portuguese tongue, says he has known the agents of Francisco Fernandes for twenty days and Henry Utrighte not at all.

To the first, second, and third articles he cannot depose.

To the fourth and fifth he swears and affirms and truly says, "That in the monethes of June Julye and Auguste in the yeare 1582 there arryved in the partes of Newefounde Lande a tall Englishe shippe of ij hundrethe tonnes and upwardes whereof one Clarke an Englishe man was Captayne appoyncted and furnished in warlicke sorte with men munition victuall artillery and all other suche nessesaries for the warre. Whereof (as the said Clerke in this examinates presence and hearinge then beinge in Newfounde Lande in

the haven of Fermosa where they said Clerke was) affirmed and said a greate gentleman in Englande was owner and possessor and that he him selfe had aucthoritye from the Quenes Majesty of Englande to take and spoile all Spaniardes and Portingales. Affirminge moreover that at that present there were in the said havon of Fermosa and Reinosa a porte adjoyinge amongste other shipps plyinge fisshinge faire, the shippes of Viena in Portingall called the Saint John Esperaunce and Saint Tiaco whiche remayned there laboringe for and abowt the takinge of fishe as yerelye yt ys accustomed. For this examinate as he sayethe was at that presente master of the Trinitye of Avero in Portugal and in Fishinge in the said partes of Newe founde lande."

To the sixth and seventh he affirms and says "That the said Francys Fernandes of this examinates certayne knowledge was at the tyme aforesaid master and parte owner of the said shippe the Saint John and commonlye soe had in reputation and accompted."

To the eighth he affirms "That the articule Nicholas Fernandes and Belchior Mendes were at the same present masters of the articulate shipps the Esperaunce and Saint Tiago and soe were comonly reputed and taken in the said partes of Newefounde Lande."

To the ninth he deposes "that the said shippe the Sainte John was of the portadge of C toonnes and upwardes and bye this examinates estimation and judgement well worthe with her tacle apparrell munition, victuall and furniture thre thowsand duckettes. For as he sayethe he this examinate was on borde the same shippe and sawe she was a stronge newe shippe verey well apparelled victualed and furnished, and hath had him selfe a shippe of abowte the same burthen whiche standethe him in thre thousandes duckettes and upwardes whereby he ys the rather induced to beleve the premisses to be trewe. What burthen or valowe the other ii shippes mentioned in this article were of this examinate cannot justly saye for that he was not on borde the same but onelye sawe them ride in the said Harbor."

To the tenth he says "that the articulate masters of the shipps named in this article with theire severall companyes bye theire labor and industrye in fisshinge in the monethes articulate did take great store of verey good fishe as this examinate and other masters then did but the quantitye thereof he cannot declare."

To the eleventh he says "That the articulate masters and maryners did also of this examinates certayne knowledge at the same presente make good store of trayne oyle but the quantitye he cannot despose."

To the twelfth he says "he knoweth not what a thowsand of Newe Lande fishe ys worthe sterling moneye. But sayeth that after his comminge into Portingall from Newe founde Lande the said yere 1582 he this examinate solde there of suche fishe as he himselfe tooke by his labor and travell in Newfounde Lande after thirtye Duckettes Portingall money every thowasande wett and drye fishe togeather. And soe muche was yt worthe comonlye to be solde in the Realme of Portingall." As he says, "And every toonn of oyle was well worthye in Portingall the same tyme fifty ducettes. And soe this examinate solde oyle the same yere As he sayethe" And he knows no more.

To the thirteenth he deposes and says it is true "That the said Clerke with his soldiers maryners and companye after theire comminge into Newfounde Lande of this examinates perfecte knowledge did in the monethes articulate invade and enter in warlicke sorte in the havon of Rainosa the said thre Portingall shipps (the companye for the moste parte beinge at that presente at the sea in fishinge) and afterwardes caryed from further of that havon to another havon therebye called Fermosa where the said Clerke and his companye in warlike maner did utterlye spoyle ii of the said shippes of their fishe victuall provision and necessaries, and the thirde beinge the said Francys Fernandes his shippe they also quite caryed away and dispossessed the same Fernandes thereof beinge master and parteowner of the same and commonly reputed and taken, with all her fishe oyle and furniture whatsoever. For this examinate as he sayethe was at the tyme of the said spoile committed and donn in the said Havon for Fermosa and pryvye of the same spoile, and sawe the said Clerke carye the said Fernandes shippe awaye and also the companye of the other two spoyled shipps beinge cleene spoyled of theire victualls fishe and provision and havinge

nothynge lefte to sustayne them selves withall wente abowte a begginge from shippe to shippe for releife to carye them home and amongste other shipps came on borde this examinates shippe and had suche thinges as he coulde spare them. Whiche bye vertue of his oathe he affirmethe to be most trewe."

To the fourteenth he affirms "That the said Clerke in this examinates shippe did affirme that he had aucthority from the Quene of Englande to take all Spaniardes and Portingalls whiche beynge noysed ammongste both English men and Portingalls in Newefoundelande caused them to make noe resistance agaynste the said Clercke, otherwise he ys perswaded there woulde have byn resistance used. As he sayethe."

To the fifteenth he says "That trewe yt ys that the said Clercke caryd awaye the shippe the Saint John belonginge in parte to the said Fernandes and all that was therein togeather also with the severall ladinges of the other two shipps. But whither he caryed them or for whose use he cannot depose."

To the sixteenth, seventeenth and eighteenth he cannot depose.

To the nineteenth he affirms "That the said Clercke with the forsaid shippe the Suzan Fortune did besides the foresaid spoyles committ manye other robberies the said yeare 1582 in the partes of Newefounde Lande of this examinates certayne knowledge For as he sayethe he came with force and violence uppon this examinate and his said shippe in the havon of Bowe in Newefounde Lande and toke from him this examinate ii pipes of wyne, certayne hennes marmelade and other victualls and from other shipps in the same harbor he also tooke xxx thowsande of fishe vii or viii pipes of oyle, with sondry sayles ankers, cables, gonnes munition and other necessaries as the masters and companyes of the said shippes did certifye, and complayne." And more he does not know.

To the twentieth and twenty first he cannot depose. To the last he says that what he has deposed above is true.

For Interpreter Robert Parke

[Signed:] Palles Diz 1583

LETTERS FROM NEWFOUNDLAND, AUGUST 6–8, 1583

WHEN SIR HUMPHREY GILBERT reached Newfoundland early in August, there was an opportunity to send letters home by some of the English fishing vessels in St. John's Harbour. The Hungarian scholar-poet Stephen Parmenius wrote to Lawrence Humphrey at Magdalen College, Oxford. Although the letter has not survived, his Latin letter of August 6 to Richard Hakluyt the younger (534) was printed and translated in Richard Hakluyt, *Principall navigations* (1589), pp. 698–699. It was edited, with both Hakluyt's and a new translation, in D. B. Quinn and N. M. Cheshire, *The New Found Land of Stephen Parmenius* (1972), pp. 167–185. It conveys the romantic poet's harsh reaction to the earthy activities of the fishermen and to the unpromising appearance of Newfoundland. The other optimistic, but laconic, letter was from Sir Humphrey Gilbert to his associate, Sir George Peckham (535). It was printed in Samuel Purchas, *Pilgrimes*, III (1625), 808.

534. August 6, 1583. Stephen Parmenius to Richard Hakluyt the younger from Newfoundland.

To the worshipfull, Master Richard Hakluyt at Oxforde in Christchurche Master of Art, and Philosophie, his friend and brother

I had not purposed to write to you, when the promise of your letters came to my mind: You thought in June last to have followed us your selfe, and therefore I had left order that you should be advertised of my state, by Master Doctor Humfrey: but so you would not be satisfied: I will write therefore to you almost in the same words, because I have no leasure at this time, to meditate new matters, and to vary or multiply words.

The 11. of June we set sayle at length from Englande in good earnest, and departed, leaving the haven and lande behinde us at Plymmouth: our Fleete consisted of five shippes: the greatest, which the Admirals brother had lent us, withdrew her selfe from us the third day, wee knowe not upon what occasion: with the rest wee sayled still together till the three and twentie of July: at which time our view of one another beeing intercepted by the great mistes, some of us sayled one way, and some another: to us alone the first lande appeared, the first of August, about the latitude of fiftye degrees, when as before wee had descended beyond 41. degrees in hope of some Southerly windes, which notwithstanding never blewe to us, at any fitte time.

It is an Ilande which your men call Penguin, because of the multitude of birdes of the same name. Yet wee neither sawe any birdes, nor drewe neere to the lande, the windes serving for our course directed to another place, but wee mett all together at that place a little before the Haven, whereunto by common Counsell wee had determined to come, and that within the space of two houres by the great goodnesse of God, and to our great joy. The place is situated in Newfound lande, between fortie seven and fortie eight degrees, called by the name of Saint Johns: the Admirall him selfe by reason of the multitude of the men, and the smalnesse of his shippe, had his company somewhat sickly, and had all ready lost two of the same company, which died of the Flixe: of the rest wee conceive good hope. Of our company (for I joyned my selfe with Maurice Browne, a very proper Gentleman) two persons by a mischance were drowned, the rest are in safetie, and strong, and for myne owne part I was never more healthy. Wee arrived at this place the third of August: and the fift the Admirall tooke possession of the Country, for himselfe and the kingdome of England: having made and published certaine Lawes, concerning religion, and obedience to the Queene of England: at this time our fare is somewhat better, and daintier, then it was before: for in good sooth, the experience of so long time hath taught us what contrary windes wee have founde, and what great travell we may endure hereafter: and therefore we will take such order, that wee will want nothing, for we founde in this place, about twenty Portingale, and Spanishe shippes, besides the shippes of the Englishe: which being not able to matche us, suffer us not to be hunger starved: the English although they were of them selves stronge ynough, and safe from our force, yet seeing our aucthoritie, by the Queenes letters patentes, they shewed us all manner of dutie and humanitie.

The manner of this Countrey, and people remayne nowe to bee spoken of. But what shall I say, my good Hakluyt, when I see nothing but a very wildernesse? of fishe here is incredible abundance, whereby great gayne growes to them, that travell to these partes: the hooke is no sooner throwne out, but it is eftsoones drawne up with some goodly fishe: the whole lande is full of hilles and woodes. The trees for the most part are Pynes and of them some are very olde, and some yong: a great part of them beeing fallen by reason of their age, doth so hynder the sighte of the Lande, and stoppe the way of those that seeke to travell, that they can goe no whither: all the grasse here is long, and tall, and little differeth from ours. It seemeth also that the nature of this soyle is fitt for corne: for I founde certayne blades and eares in a manner bearded, so that it appeareth that by manuring and sowing, they may easelie bee framed for the use of man: here are in the woodes bushe berries, or rather strawe berries growing up like trees, of great sweetenesse. Beares also appeare about the fishers stages of the Countrie, and are sometimes killed, but they seeme to be white, as I conjectured by their skinnes, and somewhat lesse then ours. Whether there bee any people in this Countrey I know not, neither have I seene any to witnesse it. And to say trueth who can, when as it is not possible to passe any whither: In like sort it is unknowne, whether any mettals lye under the hilles: the cause is all one, although the very colour and hue of the hilles seeme to have some mynes in them, we moved the Admirall to set the woods a fire, that so we might have space, and entrance to take view of the Countrey, which motion did nothing displease him, were it not for feare of great inconvenience that might thereof insue: for it was reported and

confirmed by verie credible persons that when the like happened by chance in another Port, the fish never came to the place about it, for the space of 7. whole yeere after, by reason of the waters made bytter by the turpentyne, and rosen of the trees, which ranne into the ryvers upon the firing of them. The weather is so hot this time of the yeere, that except the very fish, which is layd out to be dryed by the sunne, be every day turned, it cannot possibly be preserved from burning: but how cold it is in the winter, the great heapes, and mountaines of yce, in the middest of the Sea have taught us: some of our company report, that in May, they were sometimes kept in, with such huge yce, for 16. whole dayes together, as that the Islands thereof were threescore fathomes thicke, the sides whereof which were towarde the Sunne, when they were melted, the whole masse or heape was so inverted and turned in manner of balancing, that that part which was before downeward rose uppwarde, to the great perill of those that are neere them, as by reason we may gather. The ayre upon land is indifferent cleare, but at Sea towardes the East there is nothing els but perpetual mistes and in the Sea it selfe, about the Banke (for so they call the place where they find ground at fourty leagues distant from the shoare, and where they began to fishe) there is no day without rayne, when we have served, and supplyed our necessitie in this place, we purpose by the helpe of God to passe towards the south, with so much the more hope every day, by how much greater the thinges are, that are reported of those Countries, which we go to discover. Thus much touching our estate.

Now I desire to know somewhat concerning you, but I feare in vaine, but specially I desire out of measure to know how my Patrone Master Henry Umpton doth take my absence: my obedience, and dutie shall alwaies be readie towardes him as long as I live: but indeede I hope, that this journey of ours shalbe profitable to his intentions. It remayneth that you thinke me to be still yours, and so yours as no mans more. The sonne of God blesse all our labors, so farre, as that you your selfe may be partaker of our blessing. Adewe, my most friendly, most sweete, most vertuous Hakluyt: In Newfound lande, at Saint Johns Port, the sixt of August, 1583.

[Signed:] Steven Parmenius of Buda, yours.

535. August 8, 1583. Sir Humphrey Gilbert to Sir George Peckham from Newfoundland.

Sir George, I departed from Plymouth on the eleventh of June with five sailes, and on the thirteenth the Barke Rawley ran from me in faire and cleere weather, having a large winde. I pray you solicite my brother Rawley to make them an example of all Knaves. On the third of August wee arrived at a Port called Saint Johns, and will put to the Seas from thence (God willing) so soone as our ships will be ready. Of the New-found Land I will say nothing, untill my next Letters. Be of good cheare, for if there were no better expectation, it were a very rich demaynes, the Country being very good and full of all sorts of victuall, as fish both of the fresh water and Sea-fish, Deere, Pheasants, Partridges, Swannes, and divers Fowles else. I am in haste, you shall by every Messenger heare more at large. On the fifth of August, I entred here in the right of the Crowne of England; and have engraven the Armes of Englande, divers Spaniardes, Portugals, and other strangers, witnessing the same. I can stay no longer; fare you well with my good Lady: and be of good cheare, for I have comforted my selfe, answerable to all my hopes. From Saint Johns in the New-found Land, the 8. of August, 1583. Yours wholly to command, no man more,

[Signed:] Hum. Gilbart

536. 1583. Edward Hayes's narrative of Sir Humphrey Gilbert's voyage.

This celebrated narrative was first published by Richard Hakluyt in Principall navigations *(1589), pp. 679–697. It gives a full account of Sir Humphrey Gilbert's preparations and objectives and deals with the voyage to Newfoundland, its formal annexation to the English crown by Gilbert, and of the later tragic stages of the voyage when the* Delight *sank off Sable Island, and Gilbert, in the* Squirrel, *disappeared in mid-Atlantic. It also gives an important description of Newfoundland. Hayes returned to safety in his* Golden Hind *and proceeded to attempt, unsuccessfully, to obtain support to develop Gilbert's plans for Newfoundland (362–364).*

A report of the voyage and successe thereof, attempted in the yeere of our Lord 1583 by sir Humfrey Gilbert knight, with other gentlemen assisting him in that action, intended to discover and to plant Christian inhabitants in place convenient, upon those large and ample countreys extended Northward from the cape of Florida, lying under very temperate Climes, esteemed fertile and rich in Minerals, yet not in the actuall possession of any Christian prince, written by M. Edward Haie gentleman, and principall actour in the same voyage, who alone continued unto the end, and by Gods speciall assistance returned home with his retinue safe and entire.

Many voyages have bene pretended, yet hitherto never any thorowly accomplished by our nation of exact discovery into the bowels of those maine, ample and vast countreys, extended infinitely into the North from 30 degrees, or rather from 25 degrees of Septentrionall latitude, neither hath a right way bene taken of planting a Christian habitation and regiment upon the same, as well may appeare both by the little we yet do actually possesse therein, & by our ignorance of the riches and secrets within those lands, which unto this day we know chiefly by the travell and report of other nations, and most of the French, who albeit they can not challenge such right and interest unto the sayd countreys as we, neither these many yeeres have had opportunity nor meanes so great to discover and to plant (being vexed with the calamities of intestine warres) as we have had by the inestimable benefit of our long and happy peace: yet have they both waies performed more, and had long since attained a sure possession and setled government of many provinces in those Northerly parts of America, if their many attempts into those forren and remote lands had not bene impeached by their garboils at home.

The first discovery of these coasts (never heard of before) was well begun by John Cabot the father, and Sebastian his sonne, an Englishman borne, who were the first finders out of all that great tract of land stretching from the cape of Florida unto those Islands which we now call the Newfoundland: all which they brought and annexed unto the crowne of England. Since when, if with like diligence the search of inland countreys had bene followed, as the discovery upon the coast, and outparts therof was performed by those two men: no doubt her Majesties territories and revenue had bene mightily inlarged and advanced by this day. And which is more; the seed of Christian religion had bene sowed amongst those pagans, which by this time might have brought foorth a most plentifull harvest and copious congregation of Christians; which must be the chiefe intent of such as shall make any attempt that way: or els whatsoever is builded upon other foundation shall never obtaine happy successe nor continuance.

And although we can not precisely judge (which onely belongeth to God) what have bene the humours of man stirred up to great attempts of discovering and planting in those remote countreys, yet the events do shew that either Gods cause hath not bene chiefly preferred by them, or els God hath not permitted so abundant grace as the light of his word and knowledge of him to be yet revealed unto those infidels before the appointed time.

But most assuredly, the only cause of religion hitherto hath kept backe, and will also bring forward at the time assigned by God, an effectuall and compleat discovery & possession by Christians both of those ample countreys and the riches within them hitherto concealed: whereof notwithstanding God in his wisdome hath permitted to be revealed from time to time a certaine obscure and misty knowledge, by little and little to allure the mindes of men that way (which els will be dull enough in the zeale of his cause) and thereby to prepare us unto a readinesse for the execution of his will against the due time ordeined, of calling those pagans unto Christianity.

In the meane while, it behooveth every man of great calling, in whom is any instinct of inclination unto this attempt, to examine his owne motions: which if the same proceed of ambition or avarice, he may assure himselfe it commeth not of God, and therefore can not have confidence of Gods protection and assistance against the violence (els irresistable) both of sea, and infinite perils upon the land; whom God yet may use an instrument to

further his cause and glory some way, but not to build upon so bad a foundation.

Otherwise, if his motives be derived from a vertuous & heroycall minde, preferring chiefly the honour of God, compassion of poore infidels captived by the devill, tyrannizing in most woonderfull and dreadfull maner over their bodies and soules; advancement of his honest and well disposed countreymen, willing to accompany him in such honourable actions; reliefe of sundry people within this realme distressed: all these be honorable purposes, imitating the nature of the munificent God, wherwith he is well pleased, who will assist such an actour beyond expectation of man. And the same, who feeleth this inclination in himselfe, by all likelihood may hope, or rather confidently repose in the preordinance of God, that in this last age of the world (or likely never) the time is compleat of receiving also these Gentiles into his mercy, and that God will raise him an instrument to effect the same: it seeming probable by event of precedent attempts made by the Spanyards and French sundry times, that the countreys lying North of Florida, God hath reserved the same to be reduced unto Christian civility by the English nation.[1] For not long after that Christopher Columbus had discovered the Islands and continent of the West Indies for Spaine, John and Sebastian Cabot made discovery also of the rest from Florida Northwards to the behoofe of England.

And whensoever afterwards the Spanyards (very prosperous in all their Southerne discoveries) did attempt any thing into Florida and those regions inclining towards the North, they proved most unhappy, and were at length discouraged utterly by the hard and lamentable successe of many both religious and valiant in armes, endevouring to bring those Northerly regions also under the Spanish jurisdiction; as if God had prescribed limits unto the Spanish Nation which they might not exceed: as by their owne gests recorded may be aptly gathered.

The French, as they can pretend lesse title unto these Northerne parts then the Spanyard, by how much the Spanyard made the first discovery of the same continent so far Northward as unto Florida, and the French did but review that be-

---

1. Sidenote: "Probably conjectures y'these lands North of Florida, are reserved for the English nation to possesse."

fore discovered by the English nation, usurping upon our right, and imposing names upon countreys, rivers, bayes, capes, or headlands, as if they had bene the first finders of those coasts; which injury we offered not unto the Spanyards, but left off to discover when we approched the Spanish limits: even so God hath not hitherto permitted them to establish a possession permanent upon anothers right, notwithstanding their manifolde attempts, in which the issue hath bene no lesse tragicall then that of the Spanyards, as by their owne reports is extant.[2]

Then seeing the English nation onely hath right unto these countreys of America from the cape of Florida Northward by the privilege of first discovery, unto which Cabot was authorised by regall authority, and set forth by the expense of our late famous king Henry the seventh: which right also seemeth strongly defended on our behalfe by the powerfull hand of almighty God,[3] withstanding the enterprises of other nations: it may greatly incourage us upon so just ground, as is our right, and upon so sacred an intent, as to plant religion (our right and intent being meet foundations for the same) to prosecute effectually the full possession of those so ample and pleasant countreys appertaining unto the crowne of England: the same (as is to be conjectured by infallible arguments of the worlds end approching) being now arrived unto the time by God prescribed of their vocation, if ever their calling unto the knowledge of God may be expected. Which also is very probable by the revolution and course of Gods word and religion, which from the beginning hath moved from the East, towards, & at last unto the West, where it is like to end, unlesse the same begin againe where it did in the East, which were to expect a like world againe.[4] But we are assured of the contrary by the prophesie of Christ, whereby we gather, that after his word preached thorowout the world shalbe the end. And as the Gospel when it descended Westward began in the South, and afterward spread into the North of Europe: even so, as the same hath begunne in the South countreys of America, no

lesse hope may be gathered that it will also spread into the North.

These considerations may helpe to suppresse all dreads rising of hard events in attempts made this way by other nations, as also of the heavy success and issue in the late enterprise made by a worthy gentleman our countryman sir Humfrey Gilbert knight, who was the first of our nation that caried people to erect an habitation and government in those Northerly countreys of America. About which, albeit he had consumed much substance, and lost his life at last, his people also perishing for the most part: yet the mystery thereof we must leave unto God, and judge charitably both of the cause (which was just in all pretence) and of the person, who was very zealous in prosecuting the same, deserving honourable remembrance for his good minde, and expense of life in so vertuous an enterprise. Whereby neverthelesse, least any man should be dismayd by example of other folks calamity, and misdeeme that God doth resist all attempts intended that way: I thought good, so farre as my selfe was an eye witnesse, to deliver the circumstance and maner of our proceedings in that action: in which the gentleman was so infortunately incumbred with wants, and woorse matched with many ill disposed people, that his rare judgement and regiment premeditated for those affaires, was subjected to telerate abuses, & in sundry extremities to holde on a course, more to upholde credit, then likely in his owne conceit happily to succeed.

The issue of such actions, being alwayes miserable, not guided by God, who abhorreth confusion and disorder, hath left this for admonition (being the first attempt by our nation to plant) unto such as shall take the same cause in hand hereafter not to be discouraged from it: but to make men well advised how they handle his so high and excellent matters, as the cariage is of his word into those very mighty and vast countreys.[5] An action doubtlesse not to be intermedled with base purposes; as many have made the same but a colour to shadow actions otherwise scarse justifiable: which doth excite Gods heavy judgements in the end, to the terrifying of weake mindes from the cause, without pondering his just proceedings:

2. Sidenote: "The French are but usurpers, upon our right. The French also infortunate in these North parts of America."

3. Sidenote: "A good incouragement for the English nation, to proceed in the conquests of the North of America."

4. Sidenote: "The due time approcheth by all likelihood of calling these heathens unto Christianity. The word of God moveth circularly."

5. Sidenote: "The planting of Gods word must be handled with reverence. Ill actions coloured by pretence of planting upon remote lands."

and doth also incense forren princes against our attempts how just soever, who can not but deeme the sequele very dangerous unto their state (if in those parts we should grow to strength) seeing the very beginnings are entred with spoile.

And with this admonition denounced upon zeale towards Gods cause, also towards those in whom appeareth disposition honourable unto this action of planting Christian people and religion in those remote and barbarous nations of America (unto whom I wish all happinesse) I will now proceed to make relation briefly, yet particularly, of our voyage undertaken with sir Humfrey Gilbert, begun, continued, and ended adversly.

When first Sir Humfrey Gilbert undertooke the Westerne discovery of America, and had procured from her Majesty a very large commission to inhabit & possesse at his choice all remote and heathen lands not in the actuall possession of any Christian prince, the same commission exemplified with many privileges, such as in his discretion he might demand, very many gentlemen of good estimation drew unto him, to associate him in so commendable an enterprise, so that the preparation was expected to grow unto a puissant fleet, able to encounter a kings power by sea: neverthelesse, amongst a multitude of voluntary men, their dispositions were divers, which bred a jarre, and made a division in the end, to the confusion of that attempt even before the same was begun. And when the shipping was in a maner prepared, & men ready upon the coast to go aboord: at that time some brake consort, and followed courses degenerating from the voyage before pretended: Others failed of their promises contracted, and the greater number were dispersed, leaving the Generall with few of his assured friends, with whom he adventured to sea: where having tasted of no lesse misfortune, he was shortly driven to retire home with the losse of a tall ship, and (more to his griefe) of a valiant gentleman Miles Morgan.

Having buried onely in a preparation a great masse of substance, wherby his estate was impaired, his minde yet not dismaid, he continued his former designment & purpose to revive this enterprise, good occasion serving. Upon which determination standing long, without meanes to satisfy his desire; at last he granted certaine assignments out of his commission to sundry persons of meane ability, desiring the privilege of his grant, to plant & fortifie in the North parts of America about the river of Canada, to whom if God gave good successe in the North parts (where then no matter of moment was expected) the same (he thought) would greatly advance the hope of the South, & be a furtherance unto his determination that way. And the worst that might happen in that course might be excused without prejudice unto him by the former supposition, that those North regions were of no regard: but chiefly a possession taken in any parcell of those heathen countreys, by vertue of his grant, did invest him of territories extending every way two hundred leagues: which induced sir Humfrey Gilbert to make those assignments, desiring greatly their expedition, because his commission did expire after six yeres, if in that space he had not gotten actual possession.

Time went away without any thing done by his assignes: insomuch that at last he must resolve himselfe to take a voyage in person, for more assurance to keepe his patent in force, which then almost was expired, or within two yeres.

In furtherance of his determination, amongst others, sir George Peckham knight shewed himselfe very zealous to the action, greatly aiding him both by his advice & in the charge. Other gentlemen to their ability joyned unto him, resolving to adventure their substance & lives in the same cause. Who beginning their preparation from that time, both of shipping, munition, victual, men, and things requisit, some of them continued the charge two yeres compleat without intermission. Such were the difficulties and crosse accidents opposing these proceedings, which tooke not end in lesse then two yeres: many of which circumstances I will omit.

The last place of our assembly, before we left the coast of England, was in Causet bay neere unto Plimmouth: then resolved to put unto the sea with shipping and provision, such as we had, before our store yet remaining, but chiefly the time and season of the yeere, were too farre spent. Neverthelesse it seemed first very doubtfull by what way to shape our course, and to begin our intended discovery, either from the South Northward, or from the North Southward. The first, that is, beginning South, without all controversie was the likeliest, wherein we were assured to have commodity of the current, which from the cape of Florida setteth Northward, and would have furthered greatly our navigation, discovering from the foresayd cape along towards cape Briton, and all those lands lying to the North.

Also the yere being farre spent, and arrived to the moneth of June, we were not to spend time in Northerly courses, where we should be surprised with timely Winter, but to covet the south,[6] which we had space enough then to have attained; and there might with lesse detriment have wintred that season, being more milde and short in the South then in the North where winter is both long and rigorous.

These and other like reasons alleged in favour of the Southerne course first to be taken, to the contrary was inferred: that forasmuch as both our victuals, and many other needfull provisions were diminished and left insufficient for so long a voyage, and for the wintering of so many men, we ought to shape a course most likely to minister supply: and that was to take the Newfoundland in our way, which was but seven hundred leagues from our English coast. Where being usually at that time of the yere, and untill the fine of August, a multitude of ships repairing thither for fish, we should be relieved abundantly with many necessaries, which after the fishing ended, they might well spare, and freely impart unto us.

Not staying long upon that Newland coast, we might proceed Southward, and follow still the Sunne, untill we arrived at places more temperate to our content.

By which reasons we were the rather induced to follow this Northerly course, obeying unto necessity, which must be supplied. Otherwise, we doubted that sudden approch of Winter, bringing with it continuall fogge, and thicke mists, tempest and rage of weather; also contrariety of currents descending from the cape of Florida unto cape Briton and cape Rase, would fall out to be great and irresistable impediments unto our further proceeding for that yeere and compell us to Winter in those North and colde regions.[7]

Wherefore suppressing all objections to the contrary, we resolved to begin our course Northward, and to follow directly as we might, the trade way unto Newfoundland: from whence after

our refreshing and reparation of wants, we intended without delay (by Gods permission) to proceed into the South, not omitting any river or bay which in all that large tract of land appeared to our view worthy of search. Immediately we agreed upon the maner of our course and orders to be observed in our voyage; which were delivered in writing unto the captaines and masters of every ship a copy in maner following.

Every shippe had delivered two bullets or scrowles, the one sealed up in waxe, the other left open: in both which were included severall watch-words. That open, serving upon our owne coast or the coast of Ireland: the other sealed, was promised on all hands not to be broken up untill we should be cleere of the Irish coast; which from thencefoorth did serve untill we arrived and met altogether in such harbors of the Newfoundland as were agreed for our Rendez vouz. The sayd watch words, being requisite to know our consorts whensoever by night, either by fortune of weather, our fleet dispersed should come together againe; or one should hale another; or if by ill watch and steerage one ship should chance to fall aboord of another in the darke.

The reason of the bullet sealed was to keepe secret that watch-word while we were upon our owne coast, lest any of the company stealing from the fleet might bewray the same: which knowen to an enemy, he might boord us by night without mistrust, having our owne watch-word.

Orders agreed upon by the Captaines and Masters to be observed by the fleet of Sir Humfrey Gilbert.

First the Admirall to cary his flag by day, and his light by night.

2. Item, if the Admirall shall shorten his saile by night, then to shew two lights untill he be answered againe by every ship shewing one light for a short time.

3. Item, if the Admirall after his shortening of saile, as aforesayd, shall make more saile againe: then he to shew three lights one above another.

4. Item, if the Admirall shall happen to hull in the night, then to make a wavering light over his other light, wavering the light upon a pole.

5. Item, if the fleet should happen to be scattered by weather, or other mishap, then so soone as one shall descry another, to hoise both toppe sailes twise, if the weather will serve, and to strike them twise againe; but if the weather serve

---

6. Sidenote: "Commodities in discovering from South Northward."
7. Sidenote: "Cause why we began our discovery from the North. Incommodities in beginning North."

not, then to hoise the maine top saile twise, and forthwith to strike it twise againe.

6. Item, if it shall happen a great fogge to fall, then presently every shippe to beare up with the admirall, if there be winde: but if it be a calme, then every ship to hull, and so to lie at hull till it be cleere. And if the fogge do continue long, then the Admirall to shoot off two pieces every evening, and every ship to answere it with one shot: and every man bearing to the ship, that is to leeward so neere as he may.

7. Item, every master to give charge unto the watch to looke out well, for laying aboord one of another in the night, and in fogges.

8. Item, every evening every ship to haile the admirall, and so to fall asterne him, sailing thorow the Ocean: and being on the coast, every ship to haile him both morning and evening.

9. Item, if any ship be in danger any way, by leake or otherwise, then she to shoot off a piece, and presently to hang out one light, whereupon every man to beare towards her, answering her with one light for a short time, and so to put it out againe; thereby to give knowledge that they have seene her token.

10. Item, whensoever the Admirall shall hang out her ensigne in the maine shrowds, then every man to come aboord her, as a token of counsell.

11. Item, if there happen any storme or contrary winde to the fleet after the discovery, whereby they are separated: then every ship to repaire unto their last good port, there to meet againe.

Our course agreed upon.

The course first to be taken for the discovery is to beare directly to cape Rase, the most Southerly cape of Newfound land; and there to harbour our selves either in Rogneux or Fermous, being the first places appointed for our Rendez vous, and the next harbours unto the Northward of cape Rase: and therefore every ship separated from the fleet to repaire to that place so fast as God shall permit, whether you shall fall to the Southward or to the Northward of it, and there to stay for the meeting of the whole fleet the space of ten dayes: and when you shall depart, to leave marks.

A direction of our course unto the Newfound land.

Beginning our course from Silley, the neerest is by West-southwest (if the winde serve) untill such time as we have brought our selves in the latitude of 43 or 44 degrees, because the Ocean is subject much to Southerly windes in June and July. Then to take traverse from 45 to 47 degrees of latitude, if we be inforced by contrary windes: and not to go to the Northward of the height of 47 degrees of Septentrionall latitude by no meanes: if god shall not inforce the contrary; but to do your indevour to keepe in the height of 46 degrees, so nere as you can possibly, because cape Rase lieth about that height.

Notes.

If by contrary windes we be driven backe upon the coast of England, then to repaire unto Silley for a place of our assembly or meeting.

If we be driven backe by contrary winds that we can not passe the coast of Ireland, then the place of our assembly to be at Beare haven or Baltimore haven.

If we shall not happen to meete at cape Rase, then the place of Rendez vous to be at cape Briton, or the neerest harbour unto the Westward of cape Briton.

If by meanes of other shipping we may not safely stay there, then to rest at the very next safe port to the Westward; every ship leaving their marks behinde them for the more certainty of the after commers to know where to finde them.

The marks that every man ought to leave in such a case, were of the Generals private device written by himselfe, sealed also in close waxe, and delivered unto every shippe one scroule, which was not to be opened untill occasion required, whereby every man was certified what to leave for instruction of after commers: that every of us comming into any harbour or river might know who had bene there, or whether any were still there up higher into the river, or departed, and which way.

Orders thus determined, and promises mutually given to be observed, every man withdrew himselfe unto his charge, the ankers being already weyed, and our shippes under saile, having a soft gale of winde, we began our voyage upon Tuesday the eleventh day of June, in the yere of our Lord 1583, having in our fleet (at our departure from Causet bay) these shippes, whose names and burthens, with the names of the captaines and masters of them, I have also inserted, as followeth:

1. The Delight aliâs The George, of burthen 120 tunnes, was Admirall: in which went the Generall, and William Winter captaine in her and part owner, and Richard Clearke master.

2. The Barke Raleigh set forth by M. Walter Raleigh, of the burthen of 200 tunnes, was then Vice admirall: in which went M. Butler captaine, and Robert Davis, of Bristoll master.

3. The Golden hinde, of burthen 40 tunnes, was then Reare admirall: in which went Edward Hayes captaine and owner, and William Cox of Limehouse master.

4. The Swallow, of burthen 40 tunnes: in her was captaine Maurice Browne.

5. The Squirrill, of burthen 10 tunnes: in which went captaine William Andrewes, and one Cade master.

We were in number in all about 260 men: among whom we had of every faculty good choice, as Shipwrights, Masons, Carpenters, Smithes, and such like, requisite to such an action: also Minerall men and Refiners. Besides for solace of our people, and allurement of the Savages, we were provided of Musike in good variety: not omitting the least toyes, as Morris dancers, Hobby horsse, and Maylike conceits to delight the Savage people, whom we intended to winne by all faire meanes possible. And to that end we were indifferently furnished of all petty haberdasherie wares to barter with those simple people.

In this maner we set forward, departing (as hath bene said) out of Causon bay the eleventh day of June being Tuesday, the weather and winde faire and good all day, but a great storme of thunder and winde fell the same night.

Thursday following, when we hailed one another in the evening (according to the order before specified) they signified unto us out of the Vizadmirall, that both the Captaine, and very many of the men were fallen sicke. And about midnight the Vizeadmirall forsooke us, notwithstanding we had the winde East, faire and good. But it was after credibly reported, that they were infected with a contagious sicknesse, and arrived greatly distressed at Plimmouth: the reason I could never understand. Sure I am, no cost was spared by their owner Master Raleigh in

setting them forth: Therefore I leave it unto God.

By this time we were in 48 degrees of latitude, not a little grieved with the losse of the most puissant ship in our fleete: after whose departure, the Golden Hind succeeded in the place of Vizadmirall, and remooved her flagge from the mizon unto the foretop.

From Saturday the 15 of June untill the 28, which was upon a Friday, we never had faire day without fogge or raine, and windes bad, much to the West northwest, whereby we were driven Southward unto 41 degrees scarse.

About this time of the yere the winds are commonly West towards the Newfound land, keeping ordinarily within two points of West to the South or to the North, whereby the course thither falleth out to be long and tedious after June, which in March, Apriell & May, hath bene performed out of England in 22 dayes and lesse. We had winde alwayes so scant from West northwest, and from West southwest againe, that our traverse was great, running South unto 41 degrees almost, and afterward North into 51 degrees.

Also we were incombred with much fogge and mists in maner palpable,[8] in which we could not keepe so well together, but were disseuered, losing the companie of the Swallow and the Squirrill upon the 20. day of July, whom we met againe at severall places upon the Newfound land coast the third of August, as shalbe declared in place convenient.

Saturday the 27 of July, we might descry not farre from us, as it were mountaines of yce driven upon the sea, being then in 50 degrees, which were caried Southward to the weather of us: whereby may be conjectured that some current doth set that way from the North.

Before we come to Newfound land about 50 leagues on this side, we passe the banke, which are high grounds rising within the sea and under water, yet deepe enough and without danger, being commonly not lesse then 25 and 30 fadome water upon them: the same (as it were some vaine of mountaines within the sea) doe runne along, and from the Newfound land, beginning Northward about 52 or 53 degrees of latitude, & do extend into the South infinitly. The bredth of this

8. Sidenote: "Great fogges upon the Ocean sea Northward."

banke is somewhere more and somewhere lesse: but we found the same about 10 leagues over, having sounded both on this side thereof, and the other toward Newfound land, but found no ground with almost 200 fadome of line, both before & after we had passed the banke. The Portugals, and French chiefly, have a notable trade of fishing upon this banke, where are sometimes an hundred or more sailes of ships: who commonly beginne the fishing in Apriell, and have ended by July. That fish is large, alwayes wet, having no land neere to drie, and is called Corre fish.[9]

During the time of fishing, a man shall know without sounding when he is upon the banke, by the incredible multitude of sea foule hovering over the same, to pray upon the offalles & garbish of fish throwen out by fishermen, and floting upon the sea.

Upon Tuesday the 11 of June, we forsooke the coast of England. So againe Tuesday the 30 of July (seven weekes after) we got sight of land, being immediately embayed in the Grand bay, or some other great bay: the certainty whereof we could not judge, so great hase and fogge did hang upon the coast, as neither we might discerne the land well, nor take the sunnes height. But by our best computation we were then in the 51 degrees of latitude.

Forsaking this bay and uncomfortable coast (nothing appearing unto us but hideous rockes and mountaines, bare of trees, and voide of any greene herbe) we followed the coast to the South, with weather faire and cleare.

We had sight of an Iland named Penguin, of a foule there breeding in abundance, almost incredible,[10] which cannot flie, their wings not able to carry their body, being very large (not much lesse then a goose) and exceeding fat: which the French men use to take without difficulty upon that Iland, and to barrell them up with salt. But for lingering of time we had made us there the like provision.

Trending this coast, we came to the Iland called Baccalaos, being not past two leagues from the maine: to the South therof lieth Cape S. Francis, 5. leagues distant from Baccalaos, between which goeth in a great bay, by the vulgar sort called the

9. Sidenotes: "The banke in length unknowen, stretcheth from North into South, in bredth 10. leagues, in depth of water upon it 30. fadome. A great fishing upon ye banke."
10. Sidenote: "Iland and a foule named Penguin."

bay of Conception. Here we met with the Swallow againe, whom we had lost in the fogge, and all her men altered into other apparell: wherof it seemed their store was so amended, that for joy and congratulation of our meeting, they spared not to cast up into the aire and overboard, their caps & hats in good plenty. The Captaine albeit himselfe was very honest and religious, yet was he not appointed of men to his humor and desert: who for the most were such as had bene by us surprised upon the narrow seas of England, being pirats and had taken at that instant certaine Frenchmen laden, one barke with wines, and another with salt. Both which we rescued, & tooke the man of warre with all her men, which was the same ship now called the Swallow, following still their kind so oft, as (being separated from the Generall) they found opportunitie to robbe and spoile. And because Gods justice did follow the same company, even to destruction, and to the overthrow also of the Captaine (though not consenting to their misdemeanor) I will not conceale any thing that maketh to the manifestation and approbation of his judgements, for examples of others, perswaded that God more sharpely tooke revenge upon them, and hath tolerated longer as great outrage in others: by how much these went under protection of his cause and religion, which was then pretended.

Therefore upon further enquiry it was knowen, how this company met with a barke returning home after the fishing with his fraight: and because the men in the Swallow were very neere scanted of victuall, and chiefly of apparell, doubtful withall where or when to find and meete with their Admiral, they besought the captaine they might go aboord this Newlander, only to borrow what might be spared, the rather because the same was bound homeward. Leave given, not without charge to deale favorably, they came aboord the fisherman, whom they rifled of tackle, sailes, cables, victuals, & the men of their apparell: not sparing by torture (winding cords about their heads) to draw out else what they thought good. This done with expedition (like men skilfull in such mischiefe) as they tooke their cocke boate to go aboord their own ship, it was overwhelmed in the sea, and certaine of these men there drowned: the rest were preserved even by those silly soules whom they had before spoyled, who saved and delivered them aboord the Swallow. What became afterward of the poore Newlander, perhaps destitute of sayles and furniture sufficient to carry them home (whither they had not lesse to runne then 700 leagues) God alone knoweth, who tooke vengeance not long after of the rest that escaped at this instant: to reveale the fact, and justifie to the world Gods judgements inflicted upon them, as shalbe declared in place convenient.

Thus after we had met with the Swallow, we held on our course Southward, untill we came against the harbor called S. John, about 5 leagues from the former Cape of S. Francis: where before the entrance into the harbor, we found also the Frigate or Squirrill lying at anker. Whom the English marchants (that were & alwaies be Admirals by turnes interchangeably over the fleetes of fishermen within the same harbor)[11] would not permit to enter into the harbor. Glad of so happy meeting both of the Swallow and Frigate in one day (being Saturday the 3. of August) we made readie our fights, & prepared to enter the harbor, any resistance to the contrarie notwithstanding, there being within of all nations, to the number of 36 sailes. But first the Generall dispatched a boat to give them knowledge of his comming for no ill intent, having Commission from her Majestie for his voiage he had in hand. And immediatly we followed with a slacke gale, and in the very entrance (which is but narrow, not above 2 buts length) the Admirall fell upon a rocke on the larboord side by great oversight, in that the weather was faire, the rocke muche above water fast by the shore, where neither went any sea gate. But we found such readinesse in the English Marchants to helpe us in that danger, that without delay there were brought a number of boates, which towed off the ship, and cleared her of danger.

Having taken place convenient in the road, we let fall ankers, the Captaines and Masters repairing aboord our Admirall: whither also came immediatly the Masters and owners of the fishing fleete of Englishmen, to understand the Generals intent and cause of our arrivall there. They were all satisfied when the General had shewed his commission, and purpose to take possession of those lands to the behalfe of the crowne of En-

gland, and the advancement of Christian religion in those Paganish regions, requiring but their lawfull ayde for repayring of his fleete, and supply of some necessaries, so farre as conveniently might be afforded him, both out of that and other harbors adjoyning. In lieu whereof, he made offer to gratifie them, with any favour and priviledge, which upon their better advise they should demand, the like being not to bee obteyned hereafter for greater price. So craving expedition of his demand, minding to proceede further South without long detention in those partes, he dismissed them, after promise given of their best indevour to satisfie speedily his so reasonable request. The marchants with their Masters departed, they caused foorthwith to be discharged all the great Ordinance of their fleete in token of our welcome.

It was further determined that every ship of our fleete should deliver unto the marchants and Masters of that harbour a note of all their wants: which done, the ships aswell English as strangers, were taxed at an easie rate to make supply. And besides, Commissioners were appointed, part of our owne companie and part of theirs, to go into other harbours adjoyning (for our English marchants command all there) to leavie our provision: whereunto the Portugals (above other nations) did most willingly and liberally contribute. Insomuch as we were presented (above our allowance) with wines, marmalads, most fine ruske or bisket, sweet oyles and sundry delicacies. Also we wanted not of fresh salmons, trouts, lobsters and other fresh fish brought daily unto us. Moreover as the maner is in their fishing, every weeke to choose their Admirall a new, or rather they succeede in orderly course, and have weekely their Admirals feast solemnized: even so the General, Captaines and masters of our fleete were continually invited and feasted. To grow short, in our abundance at home, the intertainment had bene delightfull, but after our wants and tedious passage through the Ocean, it seemed more acceptable and of greater contentation, by how much the same was unexpected in that desolate corner of the world:[12] where at other times of the yeare, wilde beasts and birds have only the fruition of all those countries, which now seemed a place very populous and much frequented.

11. Sidenote: "English ships are the strongest and Admirals of other fleetes, fishing upon the South parts of Newfoundland."

12. Sidenote: "No Savages in the South part of Newfoundland."

The next morning being Sunday and the 4 of August, the Generall and his company were brought on land by English marchants, who shewed unto us their accustomed walks unto a place they call the Garden. But nothing appeared more then Nature it selfe without art: who confusedly hath brought foorth roses abundantly, wilde, but odoriferous, and to sense very comfortable. Also the like plentie of raspis berries, which doe grow in every place.

Munday following, the General had his tent set up, who being accompanied with his own followers, sommoned the marchants and masters, both English and strangers to be present at his taking possession of those Countries. Before whom openly was read & interpreted unto the strangers his Commission: by vertue whereof he tooke possession in the same harbour of S. John, and 200 leagues every way, invested the Queenes Majestie with the title and dignitie thereof, had delivered unto him (after the custome of England) a rod & turffe of the same soile, entring possession also for him, his heires and assignes for ever: And signified unto al men, that from that time forward, they should take the same land as a territorie appertaining to the Queene of England, and himselfe authorised under her Majestie to possesse and enjoy it. And to ordaine lawes for the governement thereof, agreeable (so neere as conveniently might be) unto the lawes of England: under which all people comming thither hereafter, either to inhabite, or by way of traffique, should be subjected and governed. And especially at the same time for a beginning, he proposed & delivered three lawes to be in force immediatly. That is to say: the first for Religion, which in publique exercise should be according to the Church of England. The 2. for maintenance of her Majesties right and possession of those territories, against which if any thing were attempted prejudiciall, the partie or parties offending should be adjudged and executed as in case of high treason, according to the lawes of England. The 3. if any person should utter words sounding to the dishonour of her Majestie, he should loose his eares, and have his ship and goods confiscate.

These contents published, obedience was promised by generall voyce and consent of the multitude aswell of Englishmen as strangers, praying for continuance of this possession and governement begun. After this, the assembly was dismissed. And afterward were erected not farre from that place the Armes of England ingraven in lead, and infixed upon a pillar of wood. Yet further and actually to establish this possession taken in the right of her Majestie, and to the behoofe of Sir Humfrey Gilbert knight, his heires and assignes for ever: the Generall granted in fee farme divers parcells of land lying by the water side, both in this harbor of S. John, and elsewhere, which was to the owners a great commoditie, being thereby assured (by their proper inheritance) of grounds convenient to dresse and to drie their fish, wherof many times before they did faile, being prevented by them that came first into the harbor. For which grounds they did covenant to pay a certaine rent and service unto sir Humfrey Gilbert, his heires or assignes for ever, and yeerely to maintaine possession of the same, by themselves or their assignes.

Now remained only to take in provision granted, according as every shippe was taxed, which did fish upon the coast adjoyning. In the meane while, the Generall appointed men unto their charge: some to repaire and trim the ships, others to attend in gathering togither our supply and provisions: others to search the commodities and singularities of the countrey, to be found by sea or land, and to make relation unto the Generall what eyther themselves could knowe by their owne travaile and experience, or by good intelligence of English men or strangers, who had longest frequented the same coast. Also some observed the elevation of the pole, and drewe plats of the countrey exactly graded. And by that I could gather by each mans severall relation, I have drawen a briefe description of the Newfound land, with the commodities by sea or lande alreadie made, and such also as are in possibilitie and great likelihood to be made: Neverthelesse the Cardes and plats that were drawing, with the due gradation of the harbors, bayes, and capes, did perish with the Admirall: wherefore in the description following, I must omit the particulars of such things.

A brief relation of the New found lande, and the commodities thereof.

That which we doe call the Newfound land, and the Frenchmen Bacalaos, is an Iland, or rather (after the opinion of some) it consisteth of sundry Ilands and broken lands, situate in the North regions of America, upon the gulfe and entrance of the great river called S. Laurence in Canada. Into the which, navigation may be made both on the South and North side of this Iland. The land lyeth South and North, containing in length betweene three & 400 miles, accounting from cape Race (which is in 46 degrees 25 minuts) unto the Grand bay in 52 degrees of Septentrionall latitude. The Iland round about hath very many goodly bayes and harbors, safe roads for ships, the like not to be found in any part of the knowen world.

The common opinion that is had of intemperature & extreme cold that should be in this countrey, as of some part it may be verified, namely the North, where I grant it is more colde then in countries of Europe, which are under the same elevation: even so it cannot stand with reason and nature of the clime, that the South parts should be so intemperate as the brute hath gone.[13] For as the same doe lie under the climate of Briton, Amjou, Poictou in France, betweene 46 and 49 degrees, so can they not so much differ from the temperature of those countries: unlesse upon the outcoast lying open unto the Ocean and sharpe windes, it must in deede be subject to more colde, then further within the land, where the mountaines are interposed, as walles and bulwarkes, to defend and to resist the asperitie and rigor of the sea and weather. Some hold opinion, that the Newfound land might be the more subject to cold, by how much it lyeth high and neere unto the middle region. I grant that not in Newfound land alone, but in Germany, Italy and Afrike, even under the Equinoctiall line, the mountaines are extreme cold, and seeldome uncovered of snow, in their culme and highest tops, which commeth to passe by the same reason that they are extended towards the middle region: yet in the countries lying beneth them, it is found quite contrary. Even so all hils having their discents, the valleis also and low grounds must be likewise hot or temperate, as the clime doeth give in Newfound land: though I am of opinion that the Sunnes reflection is much cooled, and cannot be so forcible in the Newfound land, nor generally throughout America, as in Europe or Afrike: by how much the Sunne in his diurnall course from East to West, passeth over (for the most part) dry

land and sandy countries, before he arriveth at the West of Europe or Afrike, whereby his motion increaseth heate, with little or no qualification by moyst vapours. Where, on the contrarie he passeth from Europe and Afrike unto America over the Ocean, from whence it draweth and carieth with him abundance of moyst vapours, which doe qualifie and infeeble greatly the Sunnes reverberation upon this countery chiefly of Newfound land, being so much to the Northward. Neverthelesse (as I sayd before) the cold cannot be so intollerable under the latitude of 46 47 and 48 (especiall within land) that it should be unhabitable, as some doe suppose, seeing also there are very many people more to the North by a great deale. And in these South parts there be certaine beastes, Ounces or Leopards, and birdes in like maner which in the Sommer we have seene, not heard of in countries of extreme and vehement coldnesse. Besides, as in the monethes of June, July, August and September, the heate is somewhat more then in England at those seasons: so men remaining upon the South parts neere unto Cape Rece, untill after Hollandtide, have not found the cold so extreme, nor much differing from the temperature of England. Those which have arrived there after November and December, have found the snow exceeding deepe, whereat no marvaile, considering the ground upon the coast, is rough and uneven, and the snow is driven into the places most declyning as the like is to be seene with us. The like depth of snow happily shall not be found within land upon the playner countries, which also are defended by the mountaines, breaking off the violence of winds and weather. But admitting extraordinary cold in those South parts, above that with us here: it can not be so great as in Swedland, much lesse in Moscovia or Russia: yet are the same countries very populous, and the rigor of cold is dispensed with by the commoditie of Stoves, warme clothing, meats and drinkes: all which neede not to be wanting in the Newfound land, if we had intent there to inhabite.

In the South parts we found no inhabitants, which by all likelihood have abandoned those coastes, the same being so much frequented by Christians: But in the North are savages altogether harmelesse. Touching the commodities of this countrie, serving either for sustentation of inhabitants, or for maintenance of traffique, there

13. Sidenote: "New found land is habitable."

are & may be made divers: so y^t it seemeth Nature hath recompenced that only defect and incommoditie of some sharpe cold, by many benefits: viz. With incredible quantitie, and no lesse varietie of kindes of fish in the sea and fresh waters, as Trouts, Salmons and other fish to us unknowen: Also Cod, which alone draweth many nations thither, and is become the most famous fishing of the world. Abundance of Whales, for which also is a very great trade in the bayes of Placentia & the Grand bay, where is made Traine oiles of the Whale: Herring the largest that have bene heard of, and exceeding the Malstrond herring of Norway: but hitherto was never benefit taken of the herring fishing. There are sundry other fish very delicate, namely the Bonito, Lobsters, Turbut, with others infinite not sought after: Oysters having pearle but not orient in colour: I tooke it by reason they were not gathered in season.

Concerning the inland commodities, aswel to be drawen from this land, as from the exceeding large countries adjoyning: there is nothing which our East and Northerly countries of Europe doe yeelde, but the like also may be made in them as plentifully by time and industrie: Namely, rosen, pitch, tarre, sopeashes, dealboord, mastes for ships, hides, furres, flaxe, hempe, corne, cables, cordage, linnen-cloth, mettals and many more. All which the countries will aford, and soyle is apt to yeelde.

The trees for the most in those South parts, are Firre-trees, pine and Cypresse, all yeelding Gumme and Turpentine.

Cherrie trees bearing fruit no bigger than a small pease. Also peare trees, but fruitlesse. Other trees of some sorts to us unknowen.

The soyle along the coast is not deepe of earth, bringing foorth abundantly peason small, yet good feeding for cattel. Roses passing sweet, like unto our muske roses in forme, raspases, a berry which we call Hurts, good and holesome to eat. The grasse and herbe doth fat sheepe in very short space, proved by English merchants which have caried sheepe thither for fresh victuall and had them raised exceeding fat in lesse then three weekes. Peason which our countreymen have sowen in the time of May have come up faire, and bene gathered in the beginning of August, of which our Generall had a present acceptable for the rarenesse, being the first fruits comming up

by art and industrie in that desolate and dishabited land.

Lakes or pooles of fresh water, both on the tops of mountaines and in the vallies. In which are said to be muskles not unlike to have pearle, which I had put in triall, if by mischance falling unto me, I had bene letted from that and other good experiments I was minded to make.

Foule both of water and land in great plentie and diversitie. All kind of greene foule: Others as bigge as Bustards, yet not the same. A great white foule called of some a Gaunt.

Upon the land divers sorts of haukes, as faulcons, and others by report: Partridges most plentifull larger then ours, gray and white of colour, and rough footed like doves, which our men after one flight did kill with cudgels, they were so fat and unable to flie. Birds some like blackbirds, linnets, canary birds, and other very small. Beasts of sundry kindes, red deare, buffles or a beast, as it seemeth by the tract & foote very large in maner of an oxe. Beares, ounces or leopards, some greater & some lesser, wolves, foxes, which to the Northward a little further are black, whose furre is esteemed in some Countries of Europe very rich. Otters, bevers, marternes: And in the opinion of most men that saw it, the Generall had brought unto him a Sable alive, which he sent unto his brother sir John Gilbert knight of Devonshire: but it was never delivered, as after I understood. We could not observe the hundreth part of creatures in those unhabited lands: but these mentioned may induce us to glorifie the magnificent God, who hath superabundantly replenished the earth with creatures serving for the use of man, though man hath not used a fift part of the same, which the more doth aggravate the fault and foolish slouth in many of our nation, chusing rather to live indirectly, and very miserably to live & die within this realme pestered with inhabitants, then to adventure as becommeth men, to obtaine an habitation in those remote lands, in which Nature very prodigally doth minister unto mens endevours, and for art to worke upon.

For besides these alreadie recounted and infinite moe, the mountaines generally make shew of mineral substance[14]: Iron very common, lead, and

---

14. Sidenote: "Newfoundland doth minister commodities abundantly for art & industrie."

somewhere copper. I will not averre of richer mettals: albeit by the circumstances following, more then hope may be conceived thereof.

For amongst other charges given to inquire out the singularities of this countrey, the Generall was most curious in the search of mettals, commanding the minerall man and refiner, especially to be diligent. The same was a Saxon borne, honest and religious, named Daniel. Who after search brought at first some sort of Ore, seeming rather to be yron then other mettall. The next time he found Ore, which with no small shew of contentment he delivered unto the General, using protestation, that if silver were the thing which might satisfie the Generall & his followers, there it was, advising him to seeke no further: the perill whereof he undertooke upon his life (as deare unto him as the Crowne of England unto her Majestie, that I may use his owne words) if it fell not out accordingly.

My selfe at this instant liker to die then to live, by a mischance, could not follow this confident opinion of our refiner to my owne satisfaction: but afterward demanding our Generals opinion therein, and to have some part of the Ore, he replied: Content your selfe, I have seene ynough, and were it but to satisfie my private humor, I would proceede no further. The promise unto my friends, and necessitie to bring also the South countries within compass of my Patent neere expired, as we have alreadie done these North parts, do only perswade me further. And touching the Ore, I have sent it aboord, whereof I would have no speech to be made so long as we remaine within harbor: here being both Portugals, Biscains and Frenchmen not farre off, from whom must be kept any bruit or muttering of such matter.[15] When we are at sea proofe shalbe made: if it be to our desire, we may returne the sooner hither againe. Whose answere I judged reasonable, and contenting me well: wherewith I will conclude this narration and description of the Newfound land, and proceede to the rest of our voyage, which ended tragically.

While the better sort of us were seriously occupied in repairing our wants, and contriving of matters for the commoditie of our voyage: others of another sort & disposition were plotting of mischiefe. Some casting to steale away our shipping by night, watching oportunitie by the Generals and Captaines lying on the shore: whose conspiracies discovered, they were prevented. Others drew togither in company, and caried away out of the harbors adjoyning, a ship laden with fish, setting the poore men on shore. A great many more of our people stole into the woods to hide themselves, attending time and meanes to returne home by such shipping as daily departed from the coast. Some were sicke of fluxes, and many dead: and in briefe, by one meanes or other our company was diminished, and many by the Generall licensed to returne home. Insomuch as after we had reviewed our people, resolved to see an end of our voyage, we grewe scant of men to furnish all our shipping: it seemed good therefore unto the Generall to leave the Swallowe with such provision as might be spared for transporting home the sicke people.

The Captaine of the Delight or Admirall returned into England, in whose stead was appointed Captaine Maurice Browne, before Captaine of the Swallow: who also brought with him into the Delight all his men of the Swallow, which before have bene noted of outrage perpetrated and committed upon fishermen there met at sea.[16]

The Generall made choise to goe in his frigate the Squirrel (whereof the Captaine also was amongst them that returned into England) the same Frigate being most convenient to discover upon the coast, and to search into every harbor or creeke, which a great ship could not doe. Therefore the Frigate was prepared with her nettings & fights, and overcharged with bases and such small Ordinance, more to give a shew, then with judgement to foresee unto the safetie of her and the men, which afterward was an occasion also of their overthrow.

Now having made readie our shipping, that is to say, the Delight, the golden Hinde, and the Squirrell, and put aboord our provision, which was wines, broad or ruske, fish wette and drie, sweete oiles: besides many other, as marmalades, figs, lymmons barrelled, and such like: Also we had other necessary provisions for trimming our ships, nets and lines to fish withall, boates or

---

15. Sidenote: "Reasons why no further search was made for the silver mine."

16. Sidenote: "God brought togither these men into the ship ordained to perish, who before had committed such outrage."

pinnesses fit for discovery. In briefe, we were supplied of our wants commodiously, as if we had bene in a Countrey or some Citie populous and plentifull of all things.

We departed from this harbour of S. Johns upon Tuesday the twentieth of August, which we found by exact observation to be in 47 degrees 40 minutes. And the next day by night we were at Cape Race, 25 leagues from the same harborough.

This Cape lyeth South Southwest from S. Johns: it is a low land, being off from the Cape about halfe a league: within the sea riseth up a rocke against the point of the Cape, which thereby is easily knowen: It is in latitude 46 degrees 25 minutes.

Under this Cape we were becalmed a small time, during which we layd out hookes and lines to take Codde, and drew in lesse than two houres, fish so large and in such abundance, that many dayes after we fed upon no other provision.

From hence we shaped our course unto the Island of Sablon, if conveniently it sould so fall out, also directly to Cape Briton.

Sablon lieth to the sea-ward of Cape Briton about 25 leagues, whither we were determined to goe upon intelligence we had of a Portugal, (during our abode in S. Johns) who was himselfe present, when the Portugals (above thirty yeares past) did put into the same Island both Neat and Swine to breede, which were since exceedingly multiplied. This seemed unto us very happy tidings, to have in an Island lying so neere unto the maine, which we intended to plant upon, such store of cattell, whereby we might at all times conveniently be relieved of victuall, and served of store for breed.

In this course we trended along the coast, which from Cape Race stretcheth into the Northwest, making a bay which some called Trespassa. Then it goeth out againe toward the West, and maketh a point, which with Cape Race lieth in maner East and West. But this point inclineth to the North: to the West of which goeth in the bay of Placentia. We sent men on land to take view of the soyle along this coast, whereof they made good report, and some of them had wil to be planted there. They saw Pease growing in great abundance every where.

The distance betweene Cape Race and Cape Briton is 87 leagues. In which Navigation we

spent 8 dayes, having many times the wind indifferent good: yet could we never attaine sight of any land all that time, seeing we were hindred by the current. At last we fell into such flats and dangers, that hardly any of us escaped: where neverthelesse we lost our Admiral with al the men and provision, not knowing certainly the place. Yet for inducing men of skill to make conjecture, by our course and way we held from Cape Race thither (that thereby the flats and dangers may be inserted in sea Cards, for warning to others that may follow the same course hereafter) I have set downe the best reckonings that were kept by expert men, William Cox Master of the Hind, and John Paul his mate, both of Limehouse.

Reckonings kept in our course from Cape Race towards Cape Briton, and the Island of Sablon, to the time and place where we lost our Admirall.

August 22. West,	14. leagues.
West and by South,	25.
Westnorthwest,	25.
Westnorthwest,	9.
Southsouthwest,	10.
Southwest,	12.
Southsouthwest,	10.
August 29. Westnorthwest.	12. Here we lost our Admiral.

Summe of these leagues, 117.

The reckoning of John Paul Masters mate from Cape Race.

August 22. West,	14. leagues.
23 Northwest and by West,	9.
24 Southwest and by South,	5.
25 West and by South,	40.
26 West and by North,	7.
27 Southwest,	3.
28 Southwest,	9.
Southwest,	7.
Westsouthwest,	7.
29 Northwest and by West,	20. Here we lost our Admirall.

Summe of all these leagues, 121.

Our course we held in clearing us of these flats was Eastsoutheast, and Southeast, and South 14 leagues with a marvellous scant winde.

The maner how our Admirall was lost.

Upon Tewsday the 27 of August, toward the evening, our Generall caused them in his frigat to sound, who found white sande at 35 fadome, being then in latitude about 44 degrees.

Wednesday toward night the wind came South, and wee bare with the land all that night, Westnorthwest, contrary to the mind of master Cox: nevertheless wee followed the Admirall, deprived of power to prevent a mischiefe, which by no contradiction could be brought to hold other course, alleaging they could not make the ship to worke better, nor to lie otherwaies.

The evening was faire and pleasant, yet not without token of storme to ensue, and most part of this Wednesday night, like the Swanne that singeth before her death, they in the Admiral, or Delight, continued in sounding of Trumpets, with Drummes, and Fifes: also winding the Cornets, Haughtboyes: and in the end of their jolitie, left with the battell and ringing of dolefull knels.[17]

Towards the evening also we caught in the Golden Hinde a very mighty Porpose, with a harping yron, having first stricken divers of them, and brought away part of their flesh, sticking upon the yron, but could recover onely that one. These also passing through the Ocean, in heardes, did portend storme. I omit to recite frivolous reportes by them in the Frigat, of strange voyces, the same night, which scarred some from the helme.

Thursday the 29 of August, the wind rose, and blew vehemently at South and by East, bringing withal raine, and thicke mist, so that we could not see a cable length before us. And betimes in the morning we were altogether runne and folded in amongst flats and sands, amongst which we found shoale and deepe in every three or foure shippes length, after wee began to sound: but first we were upon them unawares, untill master Cox looking out, discerned (in his judgement) white cliffes, crying (land) withall, though we could not afterward descrie any land, it being very likely the breaking of the sea white, which seemed to be white cliffes, through the haze and thicke weather.

Immediatly tokens were given unto the Delight, to cast about to seaward, which, being the greater ship, and of burden 120 tunnes, was yet formost upon the breach, keeping so ill watch, that they knew not the danger, before they felt the same, too late to recover it: for presently the Admirall strooke a ground, and had soone after her sterne and hinder partes beaten in pieces:

whereupon the rest (that is to say, the Frigat, in which was the Generall and the Golden Hinde) cast about Eastsoutheast, bearing to the South, even for our lives into the windes eye, because that way caried us to the seaward. Making out from this danger, wee sounded one while seven fadome, then five fadome, then foure fadome and lesse, againe deeper, immediatly foure fadome, then but three fadome, the sea going mightily and high. At last we recovered (God be thanked) in some despaire, to sea roome enough.

In this distresse, wee had vigilant eye unto the Admirall, whom we sawe cast away, without power to give the men succour, neither could we espie any of the men that leaped overboord to save themselves, either in the same Pinnesse or Cocke, or upon rafters, and such like meanes, presenting themselves to men in those extremities: for we desired to save the men by every possible meanes. But all in vaine, sith God had determined their ruine: yet all that day, and part of the next, we beat up and downe as neere unto the wracke as was possible for us, looking out, if by good hap we might espie any of them.

This was a heavy and grievous event, to lose at one blow our chiefe shippe fraighted with great provision, gathered together with much travell, care, long time, and difficultie. But more was the losse of our men, which perished to the number almost of a hundreth soules. Amongst whom was drowned a learned man, an Hungarian, borne in the citie of Buda,[18] called thereof Budaeus, who of pietie and zeale to good attempts, adventured in this action, minding to record in the Latine tongue, the gests and things worthy of remembrance, happening in this discoverie, to the honour of our nation, the same being adorned with the eloquent stile of this Orator, and rare Poet of our time.

Here also perished our Saxon Refiner and Discoverer of inestimable riches, as it was left amongst some of us in undoubted hope.[19]

No lesse heavy was the losse of the Captaine Maurice Browne, a vertuous, honest, and discreete Gentleman, overseene onely in liberty given late before to men, that ought to have bene restrained, who shewed himselfe a man resolved, and never unprepared for death, as by his last act

17. Sidenote: "Predictions before the wracke."

18. Sidenote: "Stephanus Parmenius a learned Hungarian."
19. Sidenote: "Daniel a refiner of mettals."

of this tragedie appeared, by report of them that escaped this wracke miraculously, as shall bee hereafter declared. For when all hope was past of recovering the ship, and that men began to give over, and to save themselves, the Captaine was advised before to shift also for his life, by the Pinnesse at the sterne of the ship: but refusing that counsell, he would not give example with the first to leave the shippe, but used all meanes to exhort his people not to despaire, nor so to leave off their labour, choosing rather to die, then to incurre infamie, by forsaking his charge, which then might be thought to have perished through his default, shewing an ill president unto his men, by leaving the ship first himselfe. With this mind hee mounted upon the highest decke, where hee attended imminent death, and unavoidable: how long, I leave it to God, who withdraweth not his comfort from his servants at such times.

In the meane season, certaine, to the number of foureteene persons, leaped into a small Pinnesse (the bignes of a Thames barge, which was made in the New found land) cut off the rope wherewith it was towed, and committed themselves to Gods mercy, amiddest the storme, and rage of sea and windes, destitute of foode, not so much as a droppe of fresh water. The boate seeming overcharged in foule weather with company, Edward Headly a valiant souldier, and well reputed of his companie, preferring the greater to the lesser, thought better that some of them perished then all, made this motion to cast lots, and them to bee throwan overboord upon whom the lots fell, thereby to lighten the boate, which otherwayes seemed impossible to live, offred himselfe with the first, content to take his adventure gladly:[20] which nevertheles Richard Clarke, that was Master of the Admirall, and one of this number, refused, advising to abide Gods pleasure, who was able to save all, as well as a few.

The boate was caried before the wind, continuing six dayes and nights in the Ocean, and arrived at last with the men (alive, but weake) upon the New found land, saving that the foresayd Headly, (who had bene late sicke) and another called of us Brasile, of his travell into those Countreys, died by the way, famished, and lesse able to holde out, then those of better health. For such was these poore mens extremitie, in cold and wet,

to have no better sustenance then their owne urine, for six dayes together.

Thus whom God delivered from drowning, hee appointed to bee famished, who doth give limits to mans times, and ordaineth the manner and circumstance of dying: whom againe he will preserve, neither Sea, nor famine can confound. For those that arrived upon the Newe found land, were brought into France by certaine French men, then being upon that coast.

After this heavie chance, wee continued in beating the sea up and downe, expecting when the weather would cleere up, that we might yet beare in with the land, which we judged not farre off, either the continent or some Island. For we many times, and in sundry places found ground at 50, 45, 40 fadomes, and lesse. The ground comming upon our lead, being sometimes oazie sand, and otherwhile a broad shell, with a little sand about it.

Our people lost courage dayly after this ill successe, the weather continuing thicke and blustering, with increase of cold, Winter drawing on, which tooke from them all hope of amendement,[21] seting an assurance of worse weather to growe upon us every day. The Leeside of us lay full of flats and dangers inevitable, if the wind blew hard at South. Some againe doubted we were ingulfed in the Bay of S. Laurence, the coast full of dangers, and unto us unknowen. But above all, provision waxed scant, and hope of supply was gone, with losse of our Admirall.

Those in the Frigat were already pinched with spare allowance, and want of clothes chiefly: Whereupon they besought the Generall to returne for England, before they all perished. And to them of the Golden Hinde, they made signes of their distresse, pointing to their mouthes, and to their clothes thinne and ragged: then immediately they also of the Golden Hinde, grew to be of the same opinion and desire to returne home.

The former reasons having also moved the Generall to have compassion of his poore men, in whom he saw no want of good will, but of meanes fit to performe the action they came for, resolved upon retire: and calling the Captaine and Master of the Hinde, he yeelded them many reasons, inforcing this unexpected returne, withall protesting himselfe, greatly satisfied with that hee had seene, and knew already.

---

20. Sidenotes: "A wonderfull scape and deliverance. A great distresse. A desperate resolution."

21. Sidenote: "Causes in forcing us to returne home againe."

Reiterating these words, Be content, we have seene enough and take no care of expence past: I will set you foorth royally the next Spring, if God send us safe home. Therefore I pray you let us no longer strive here, where we fight against the elements.

Omitting circumstance, how unwillingly the Captaine & Master of the Hinde condescended to this motion, his owne company can testifie: yet comforted with the Generals promises of a speedie returne at Spring, and induced by other apparent reasons, proving an impossibilitie, to accomplish the action at that time, it was concluded on all hands to retire.

So upon Saturday in the afternoone the 31 of August, we changed our course, and returned backe for England, at which very instant, even in winding about, there passed along betweene us and towards the land which we now forsooke a very lion to our seeming, in shape, hair and colour, not swimming after the maner of a beast by mooving of his feete, but rather sliding upon the water with his whole body (excepting the legs) in sight, neither yet diving under, and againe rising above the water, as the maner is, of Whales, Dolphins, Tunise, Porposes, and all other fish: but confidently shewing himselfe above water without hiding: Norwithstanding, we presented our selves in open view and gesture to amase him, as all creatures will be commonly at a sudden gaze and sight of men. Thus he passed along turning his head to and fro, yawning and gaping wide, with ougly demonstration of long teeth, and glaring eies, and to bidde us a farewell (comming right against the Hinde) he sent forth a horrible voyce, roaring or bellowing as doeth a lion, which spectacle wee all behelde so farre as we were able to discerne the same, as men prone to wonder at every strange thing, as this doubtlesse was, to see a lion in the Ocean sea, or fish in shape of a lion. What opinion others had thereof, and chiefly the Generall himselfe, I forbeare to deliver: But he tooke it for Bonum Omen, rejoycing that he was to warre against such an enemie, if it were the devill.

The wind was large for England at our returne, but very high, and the sea rough, insomuch as the Frigat wherein the Generall went was almost swalowed up.

Munday in the afternoone we passed in the sight of Cape Race, having made as much way in little more then two dayes and nights backe againe, as before wee had done in eight dayes from Cape Race, unto the place where our ship perished. Which hindrance thitherward, and speed back againe, is to be imputed unto the swift current, as well as to the winds, which we had more large in our returne.

This munday the Generall came aboord the Hind to have the Surgeon of the Hind to dresse his foote, which he hurt by treading upon a naile: At what time we comforted ech other with hope of hard successe to be all past, and of the good to come. So agreeing to cary out lights alwayes by night, that we might keepe together, he departed into his Frigat, being by no meanes to be intreated to tarie in the Hind, which had bene more for his security. Immediatly after followed a sharpe storme, which we overpassed for that time. Praysed be God.

The weather faire, the Generall came aboord the Hind againe, to make merrie together with the Captaine, Master, and company, which was the last meeting, and continued there from morning untill night.[22] During which time there passed sundry discourses, touching affaires past, and to come, lamenting greatly the losse of his great ship, more of the men, but most of all of his bookes and notes, and what els I know not, for which hee was out of measure grieved, the same doubtles being some matter of more importance then his bookes, which I could not draw from him: yet by circumstance[23] I gathered, the same to be ye Ore which Daniel the Saxon had brought unto him in the New found land. Whatsoever it was, the remembrance touched him so deepe, as not able to containe himselfe, he beat his boy in great rage, even at the same time, so long after the miscarying of the great ship, because upon a faire day, when wee were becalmed upon the coast of the New found land, neere unto Cape Race, he sent his boy aboord the Admirall, to fetch certaine things: amongst which, this being chiefe, was yet forgotten and left behind. After which time he could never conveniently send againe aboord the great ship, much lesse hee doubted her ruine so neere at hand.

Herein my opinion was better confirmed diversly, and by sundry conjectures, which maketh me have the greater hope of this rich Mine. For

22. Sidenote: "Our last conference with our Generall."
23. Sidenote: "Circumstances to be well observed in our Generall, importing the Ore to be of a silver mine."

where as the Generall had never before good conceit of these North parts of the world: now his mind was wholly fixed upon the New found land. And as before he refused not to grant assignements liberally to them that required the same into these North parts, now he became contrarily affected, refusing to make any so large grants, especially of S. Johns, which certaine English merchants made suite for, offering to imploy their money and travell upon the same: yet neither by their owne suite, nor of others of his owne company, whom he seemed willing to pleasure, it could be obtained.

Also laying downe his determination in the Spring following, for disposing of his voyage then to be reattempted: he assigned the Captaine & Master of the Golden Hind, unto the South discovery, and reserved unto himselfe the North, affirming that this voyage had wonne his heart from the South, and that he was now become a Northerne man altogether.

Last, being demanded what means he had at his arrivall in England, to compasse the charges of so great preparation as he intended to make the next Spring: having determined upon two fleetes, one for the South, another for the North: Leave that to mee (hee replied) I will aske a pennie of no man. I will bring good tidings unto her Majesty, who wil be so gracious, to lend me 10000 pounds, willing us therefore to be of good cheere: for he did thanke God (he sayd) with all his heart, for that he had seene, the same being enough for us all, and that we needed not to seeke any further. And these last words he would often repeate, with demonstration of great fervencie of mind, being himselfe very confident, and setled in beliefe of inestimable good by this voyage: which the greater number of his followers nevertheles mistrusted altogether, not being made partakers of those secrets, which the Generall kept unto himselfe. Yet all of them that are living, may be witnesses of his words and protestations, which sparingly I have delivered.

Leaving the issue of this good hope unto God, who knoweth the trueth only, & can at his good pleasure bring the same to light: I will hasten to the end of this tragedie, which must be knit up in the person of our Generall.[24] And as it was Gods ordinance upon him, even so the vehement perswasion and intreatie of his friends could nothing availe, to divert him from a wilful resolution of going through in his Frigat, which was overcharged upon their deckes, with fights, nettings, and small artillerie, too cumbersome for so small a boate, that was to passe through the Ocean sea at that season of the yere, when by course we might expect much storme of foule weather, whereof indeed we had enough.

But when he was intreated by the Captaine, Master, and other his well willers of the Hinde, not to venture in the Frigat, this was his answere: I will not forsake my little company going homeward, with whom I have passed so many stormes and perils. And in very trueth, hee was urged to be so over hard, by hard reports given of him, that he was afraid of the sea, albeit this was rather rashnes, then advised resolution, to preferre the wind of a vaine report to the weight of his owne life.

Seeing he would not bend to reason, he had provision out of the Hinde, such as was wanting aboord his Frigat. And so we committed him to Gods protection, & set him aboord his Pinnesse, we being more then 300 leagues onward of our way home.

By that time we had brought the Islands of Açores South of us, yet wee then keeping much to the North, until we had got into the height and elevation of England: we met with very foule weather, and terrible seas, breaking short and high Pyramid wise. The reason whereof seemed to proceede either of hilly grounds high and low within the sea, (as we see hilles and dales upon the land) upon which the seas doe mount and fall: or else the cause proceedeth of diversitie of winds, shifting often in sundry points: al which having power to move the great Ocean, which againe is not presently setled, so many seas do encounter together, as there had bene diversitie of windes. Howsoever it commeth to passe, men which all their life time had occupied the Sea, never saw more outragious Seas. We had also upon our maine yard, an apparition of a little fire by night, which seamen doe call Castor and Pollux. But we had onely one, which they take an evill signe of more tempest: the same is usuall in stormes.

Munday the ninth of September, in the afternoone, the Frigat was neere cast away, oppressed by waves, yet at that time recovered: and giving foorth signes of joy, the Generall sitting abaft

24. Sidenote: "Wilfulnes in the Generall."

with a booke in his hand, cried out unto us in the Hind (so oft as we did approch within hearing) We are as neere to heaven by sea as by land. Reiterating the same speech, well beseeming a souldier, resolute in Jesus Christ, as I can testifie he was.[25]

The same Monday night, about twelve of the clocke, or not long after, the Frigat being ahead of us in the Golden Hinde, suddenly her lights were out, whereof as it were in a moment, we lost the sight, and withall our watch cryed, the Generall was cast away, which was too true. For in that moment, the Frigat was devoured and swallowed up of the Sea. Yet still we looked out all that night, and ever after, until wee arrived upon the coast of England: Omitting no small saile at sea, unto which we gave not the tokens betweene us, agreed upon, to have perfect knowledge of each other, if we should at any time be separated.

In great torment of weather, and perill of drowning, it pleased God to send safe home the Golden Hinde, which arrived in Falmouth, the 22 day of September, being Sonday, not without as great danger escaped in a flaw, comming from the Southeast, with such thicke mist, that we could not discerne land, to put in right with the Haven.

From Falmouth we went to Dartmouth, & lay there at anker before the Range, while the captaine went aland, to enquire if there had bene any newes of the Frigat, which sayling well, might happily have bene before us. Also to certifie Sir John Gilbert, brother unto the Generall of our hard successe, whom the Captaine desired (while his men were yet aboord him, and were witnesses of all occurrents in that voyage,) It might please him to take the examination of every person particularly, in discharge of his and their faithfull endevour.[26] Sir John Gilbert refused so to doe, holding himselfe satisfied with report made by the Captaine: and not altogether dispairing of his brothers safetie, offered friendship and curtesie to the Captaine and his company, requiring to have his Barke brought into the harbour: in furtherance whereof, a boate was sent to helpe to tow her in.

Neverthelesse, when the Captaine returned aboord his ship, he found his men bent to depart, every man to his home: and then the winde serving to proceede higher upon the coast: they de-

manded money to carie them home, some to London, others to Harwich, and elsewhere, (if the barke should be caried into Dartmouth, and they discharged, so farre from home) or else to take benefite of the winde, then serving to draw nearer home, which should be a lesse charge unto the Captaine, and great ease unto the men, having els farre to goe.

Reason accompanied with necessitie perswaded the Captaine, who sent his lawfull excuse and cause of his sudden departure unto sir John Gilbert, by the boate of Dartmouth, and from thence the Golden Hind departed, and tooke harbour at Waimouth. Al the men tired with the tediousnes of so unprofitable a voiage to their seeming: in which their long expence of time, much toyle and labour, hard diet and continuall hazard of life was unrecompensed[27]: their Captaine nevertheless by his great charges, impaired greatly thereby, yet comforted in the goodnes of God, and his undoubted providence following him in all that voyage, as it doth alwaies those at other times, whosoever have confidence in him alone. Yet have we more neere feeling and perseverance of his powerfull hand and protection, when God doth bring us together with others into one same peril, in which he leaveth them, and delivereth us, making us thereby the beholders, but not partakers of their ruine.

Even so, amongst very many difficulties, discontentments, mutinies, conspiracies, sicknesses, mortalitie, spoylings, and wracks by sea, which were afflictions, more then in so small a Fleete, or so short a time may be supposed, albeit true in every particularitie, as partly by the former relation may be collected, and some I suppressed with silence for their sakes living. it pleased God to support this company, (of which onely one man died of a maladie inveterate, and long infested): the rest kept together in reasonable contentment and concord, beginning continuing, and ending the voyage, which none els did accomplish, either not pleased with the action, or impatient of wants, or prevented by death.

Thus have I delivered the contents of the enterprise and last action of sir Humfrey Gilbert knight, faithfully, for so much as I thought meete to be published: wherein may alwaies appeare, (though he be extinguished) some sparkes of his

25. Sidenote: "A resolute and Christianlike saying in a distresse."
26. Sidenote: "A fit motion of the Captain unto sir Humfrey Gilbert."

27. Sidenote: "An ill recompense."

vertues, he remaining firme and resolute[28] in a purpose by all pretence honest and godly, as was this, to discover, possesse, and to reduce unto the service of God, and Christian pietie, those remote and heathen Countreys of America, not actually possessed by Christians, and most rightly appertaining unto the Crowne of England: unto the which, as his zeale deserveth high commendation: even so, he may justly be taxed of temeritie and presumption (rather) in two respects.

First, when yet there was onely probabilitie, not a certaine & determinate place of habitation selected, neither any demonstration of commoditie there in esse, to induce his followers: nevertheles, he both was too prodigall of his owne patrimony, and too careles of other mens expences, to imploy both his and their substance upon a ground imagined good.[29] The which falling, very like his associates were promised, and made it their best reckoning to bee salved some other way, which pleased not God to prosper in his first and great preparation.

Secondly, when by his former preparation he was enfeebled of abilitie and credit, to performe his designements, as it were impatient to abide in expectation better opportunitie and meanes, which God might raise, he thrust himselfe againe into the action, for which he was not fit, presuming the cause pretended in Gods behalfe, would carie him to the desired ende. Into which, having thus made reentrie, he could not yeeld againe to withdraw, though hee sawe no encouragement to proceed, lest his credite foyled in his first attempt, in a second should utterly be disgraced. Betweene extremities, hee made a right adventure, putting all to God and good fortune, and which was worst, refused not to entertaine every person and meanes whatsoever, to furnish out this expedition, the successe whereof hath bene declared.

But such is the infinite bountie of God, who from every evill deriveth good. For besides that fruite may growe in time of our travelling into those Northwest lands, the crosses, turmoiles, and afflictions[30], both in the preparation and execution of this voyage, did correct the intemperate humors, which before we noted to bee in this

28. Sidenote: "Constancie in sir Humfrey Gilbert."
29. Sidenote: "His temeritie and presumption."
30. Sidenote: "Afflictions needfull in the children of God."

Gentleman, and made unsavorie, and lesse delightfull his other manifold vertues.

Then as he was refined, and made neerer drawing unto the image of God: so it pleased the divine will to resume him unto himselfe, whither both his, and every other high and noble minde, have alwayes aspired.

537. 1584. Richard Clerke's account of the wreck of the *Delight* and of his return to England by way of Newfoundland.

Richard Clerke (or Clarke), who had been master of Henry Oughtred's ship in her piratical attack on Portuguese vessels at Newfoundland in 1582 (528–533), was master of Sir Humphrey Gilbert's ship Delight *when she struck and broke up on Sable Island. His narrative is a vivid account of how he and fifteen others escaped in the ship's boat and after great hardships reached the south coast of Newfoundland from which they were brought to France by a French Basque ship. It was printed by Richard Hakluyt,* Principall navigations *(1589), pp. 700–701.*

A relation of Richard Clarke of Weymouth, master of the ship called the Delight, going for the discovery of Norembega, with Sir Humfrey Gilbert 1583. Written in excuse of that fault of casting away the ship and men, imputed to his oversight.

Departing out of Saint Johns Harborough in the Newfound land the 20. of August unto Cape Raz, from thence we directed our course unto the Ile of Sablon or the Isle of Sand, which the Generall Sir Humfrey Gilbert would willingly have seene. But when we came within twentie leagues of the Isle of Sablon, we fell to controversie of our course. The Generall came up in his Frigot and demanded of mee Richard Clarke master of the Admirall what course was best to keepe: I said that Westsouthwest was best: because the wind was at South and night at hand and unknowen sands lay off a great way from the land. The Generall commanded me to go Westnorthwest. I told him againe that the Isle of Sablon was Westnorthwest and but 15. leagues off, and that he should be upon the Island before day, if hee went that course. The Generall sayd, my reckoning was untrue, and charged me in her Majesties name, and as I would shewe my selfe in her Countrey, to follow him that night. I fearing his threatnings, because he presented her Majesties person, did follow his commaundement, and about seven of the clocke in the morning the ship stroke on ground, where shee was cast away. Then the Generall went off to Sea, the course that I would have had them gone before, and saw the ship cast away men and all, and was not able to save a man, for there was not water upon the sand for either of them much lesse for the Admirall, that drew fourteene foote. Now as God would the day before it was very calme, and a Souldier of the ship had killed some foule with his piece, and some of the company desired me that they might hoyse out the boat to recover the foule, which I granted them: and when they came aboord they did not hoyse it in againe that night. And when the ship was cast away the boate was a sterne being in burthen one tunne and an halfe: there was left in the boate one oare and nothing els. Some of the company could swimme, and recovered the boate and did hale in out of the water as many men as they coulde: among the rest they had a care to watch for the Captaine or the Master: They happened on my selfe being the master, but could never see the Captaine: Then they halled into the boate as many men as they could in number 16. whose names hereafter I will rehearse. And when the 16. were in the boate, some had small remembrance, and some had none: for they did not make account to live, but to prolong their lives as long as it pleased God, and looked every moment of an houre when the Sea would eate them up, the boate being so little and so many men in her, and so foule weather, that it was not possible for a shippe to brooke halfe a coarse of sayle. Thus while wee remayned two dayes and two nights, and that wee saw it pleased God our boate lived in the Sea (although we had nothing to helpe us withall but one oare, which we kept up the boate withall upon the Sea, and so went even as the Sea would drive us) there was in our company one master Hedly that put foorth this question to me the Master. I doe see that it doth please God, that our boate lyveth in the Sea, and it may please God that some of us may come to the land if our boate were not overladen. Let us make sixteene lots, and those foure that have the

foure shortest lots, we will cast overboord preserving the Master among us all. I replied unto him, saying, no, we will live and die together. Master Hedly asked me if my remembrance were good: I answered I gave God prayse it was good, and knewe how farre I was off the land, and was in hope to come to the lande within two or three dayes, and sayde they were but threescore leagues from the lande, (when they were seventie) all to put them in comfort. Thus we continued the third and fourth day without any sustenance, save onely the weedes that swamme in the Sea, and salt water to drinke. The fifth day Hedly dyed and another moreover: then wee desired all to die: for in all these five dayes and five nights we saw the Sunne but once and the Starre but one night, it was so foule weather. Thus we did remaine the sixt day: then we were very weake and wished all to die saving onely my selfe which did comfort them and promised they should come soone to land, by the helpe of God: but the company were very importunate, and were in doubt they should never come to land, but that I promised them the seventh day they should come to shore, or els they should cast me over boord: which did happen true the seventh day, for at eleven of the clocke wee had sight of the land, and at 3. of the clocke at afternoone we came on land. All these seven dayes and seven nights, the wind kept continually South. If the wind had in the meane time shifted upon any other point, wee had never come to land: we were no sooner come to the land, but the wind came cleane contrary at North within halfe an houre after our arrivall. But we were so weake that one could scarcely helpe another of us out of the boate, yet with much adoe being come all on shore we kneeled downe upon our knees and gave God praise that he had dealt so mercifully with us. Afterwards those which were strongest holpe their fellowes unto a fresh brooke, where we satisfied our selves with water and berries very well. There were of al sorts of berries plentie, & as goodly a Countrey as ever I saw[1]: we found a very faire plaine Champion ground that a man might see very farre every way: by the Sea side was here and there a little wood with goodly trees as good as ever I saw any in Norway, able to mast any shippe, of pyne trees, spruse trees, firre, and very great birch trees. Where we came on land we

---

1. Sidenote: "The fruitfulnesse of the south part of Newfound land."

made a little house with boughes, where we rested all that night. In the morning I devided the company three and three to goe every way to see what foode they could find to sustaine themselves, and appointed them to meete there all againe at noone with such foode as they could get. As we went aboord we found great store of peason as good as any wee have in England: a man would thinke they had bene sowed there. We rested there three dayes and three nights and lived very well with pease and berries, wee named the place Saint Laurence, because it was a very goodly river like the river of S. Laurence in Canada, and we found it very full of Salmons. When wee had well rested our selves wee rowed our boate along the shore, thinking to have gone to the Grande Bay to have come home with some Spanyards which are yeerely there to kill the Whale: And when we were hungry or a thirst we put our boate on land and gathered pease and berries. Thus wee rowed our boate along the shore five dayes: about which time we came to a very goodly river that ranne farre up into the Countrey and saw very goodly growen trees of all sortes. There we happened upon a ship of Saint John de Luz, which ship brought us into Biskay to an Harborough called The Passage.[2] The Master of the shippe was our great friend, or else we had bene put to death if he had not kept our counsayle. For when the visitors came aboord, as it is the order in Spaine, they demaunding what we were, he sayd we were poore fishermen that had cast away our ship in Newfound land, and so the visitors inquired no more of the matter at that time. Assoone as night was come he put us on land and bad us shift for our selves. Then had wee but tenne or twelve miles into France, which we went that night, and then cared not for the Spanyard. And so shortly after we came into England toward the end of the year 1583.

2. Sidenote: "Foureteen of our men brought out of Newfound land in a ship of St. John de Luz."

538. 1580–1583. Richard Whitbourne's recollections of Newfoundland.

In A discourse and discovery of New-found-land *(London, 1620), sig. C5, Richard Whitbourne recalled his earliest contacts with the island.*

My first Voyage thither was about 40 yeeres since, in a worthy Ship of the burthen of 300. Tunne, set foorth by one Master Cotton of South-hampton; wee were bound to the grand Bay (which lyeth on the North-side of that Land,) purposing there to trade then with the Savage people, (for whom we carried sundry commodities) and to kill whales, and to make Trayne oyle, as the Biscaines doe there yeerely in great abundance. But This our intended Voyage was overthrowne, by the indiscretion of our Captaine, and faint-heartednesse of some Gentlemen of our Company.

Whereupon we set saile from thence, and bare with Trinity Harbor in New-found-land: where we killed great store of Fish Deere, Beares, Beavers, Seales, Otters, and such like, with abundance of Sea-fowle: and so returning for England, we arrived safe at South-hampton.

In a Voyage to that Countrey about 36. yeeres since, I had then the command of a worthy Ship of 220. Tun, set forth by one Master Crooke of South-hampton: At that time Sir Humfrey Gilbert, a Devonshire Knight, came thither with two good Ships and a Pinnace, and brought with him a large Patent, from the late most renowned Queene Elizabeth, and in her name tooke possession of that Countrey, in the Harbour of S. Johns, whereof I was an eye-witnesse. He sailed from thence towards Virginia, and by reason of some unhappy direction in his course, the greatest Ship he had, strucke upon Shelves, on the Coast of Canadie, and was there lost, with most part of the company in her: And hee himselfe being then in a small Pinnace of 20. Tun, in the company of his Vice-Admirall, (one Captaine Hayes) returning towards England, in a great storme, was overwhelmed with the Seas and so perished.

Chapter Seventy
Privateering and Piracy Become Endemic,
1584–1596

539. 1584. French Basques take advantage of an English privateer at Newfoundland.

Apparently, in 1584 Hugh Jones, in the privateer Jacquet, made profitable seizures from Spanish ships in the Caribbean. On his way home his men developed some fatal disease and all, except the master Edward Spicer, died. The ship reached Plancentia Bay, Newfoundland, and when Jones appealed to some French Basque vessels for aid, they attacked him, and his ship was plundered and broken up. Jones and Spicer survived and were brought to France thanks to the humane treatment of a French captain, Martin Sance de Zerea of Ciboure. In May, 1586, Jones claimed redress from the French for the damages he had suffered.

British Library, Additional MS 11405, fols. 304–305, courtesy of Dr. K. R. Andrews.

Hugh Jones captaine of a shipp of 90 tonnes called the Jaquet of Falmouth with his company abowt ii yeares past undertoke a vyage to the West Indias and after they had bene a yeare and upwardes upon the said vyage and gotten soundry Jewells spices and other thinges of valewe, in there vyage homewardes they put in with a bay in Newefound land called Playsaunce, where all his company died excepte Edward Spicer the master of the said shippe, And on the 18. of May, 1586 there aryved xv^th sailes of French ships of St John de Luce, Beirrie Soubiboroughe and places there-abowtes, who the next daie entred there said shippe the Jaquet, and toke the same, with her whole furniture munition and such thinges as were in her, And there came aland, where they toke from the said Captaine his chest with all the Juelles and other thinges therein, Although the said Jones mad humble request, that they wold save his life and his goodes and bringe him to Fraunce, And he wold in consideracion thereof give them 300. Crownes, which at the first they promised they would doe notwithstanding when they had him, and his said master on bourd theire ships, and put them asunder, they toke all to them selves, And brake up the said captaines ship to seke for gold. And saith that after they were on bourd the said Frenchemen, they had determined to have murdered the said captaine Jones and his said master, And so had done, but that one Martine Sance de Zerea of Soubeborough captaine of one of the said ships, beinge made acquainted with the practice of the rest wold not only not agre to such murder, but also toke the said captaine Jones and his said master into his shippe and kept them against the will of the rest, insomuch that he and the rest of the Captaines fell out and became Enemyes abowte the same and so he cawsed them to be brought into Spaine and preserved them from the fury of the rest. Afterwardes the said Captaine Jones and his said master at theire comminge into Fraunce bothe at St. John de Luce and Bayon mad suite to the Justice for restitucion of the said goodes and tould them where the same were remayninge notwithstandinge they could not obtaine any thinge but stoode in great daunger of theire lives, And were often harased and pursued in St John de Luce so that they hardlie escaped.

The thinges taken from the said Jones were theise as followeth.

His shipp lying In a bay litell perished the said Frenchemen brack up and cutt the same and so used it to theire uses and behoofes wourth	CL^li
of peeces of cast Iron and wrought Iron to the weight of 14100 which at St. John de Luce wold have yelded 26s.8d. the C amountinge	CLxxxviij^li
One Copper Fawlconett	xx^li
Thirtie Muskets with theire furniture	xL^tie li
fiftie Callivers with theire furniture	xxxiij^li vj^s viij^d
Tenne Case of Pistolls	xx^li

vj fier lock peces	x^{li}
Tenne targettes and tenne Armors of proofe	Lxx^{li}
Twenty Corsleetes	xxiij^{li} vj^s viij^d
Twenty Jackes and cotes of plate	xx^{li}
Swordes daggers and targattes of wood covered with lether	xL^{tie li}
Longe bowes shefes of arrowes & Pikes	x^{li}
Crosse bowes Slurre bowes with their arrowes & furniture	x^{li}
Shackleshotte diceshotte, Crosse barres & rownd shotte	xxx^{li}
halfe a tonne of Leade	v^{li}
Thre Cables whereof one never occupied	xxviij^{li}
Item other ropidge abowt his ship wourth	x^{li}
Twoe anckers weyinge abowt 800 di.	x^{li}
Silke clokes garded with vellet, silk stockes Bever hattes Cappes of velvet, and in other apparell, Naprie, of sheetes and souchlike provision which was carried for theire uses to the value of	CC^{li}
Thre Ensignes of silke on dromme, one trompett and one trompett penon	xxiiij^{li}
five sea plottes or cardes astrolobies and other instrumentes for the sea	x^{li}
They had in plate as in saltes, spones, whistles and buttons of silver to the value of	xxx^{li}
They had of black fox, the rarest furres that are knowen xv^{ten} skinnes estimated to be wourth C^{li} a skinne	xv^{c li}
They had a glasse of the Right and pure Balsomomey which is supposed to be worth	v^{c li}
They had of pearle to the value of	v^{c li}
They had of Sinamon pepper Gallingall and other spices to the value of	CC^{li}
They had a bracelet of pearle & Corrall and one stone Cutt in squares verilie supposed to be a Diamond, as broad as a mans naile of the midle finger, laide about with a round hoope of gold verie finelie wrought, iudged to be wourth	CC^{li}
a pece of Russett Taffata	x^{li}
Summa Totalis	3961^{li}

540. 1584 or 1585. A plan to seize Spanish ships at Newfoundland.

This document appears to be rough notes in the hand of Sir Francis Walsingham, secretary of

state. If it is, it may well be a summary, with a few added comments, of Sir Humphrey Gilbert's plan of 1577 (527), which it might be possible to revive since relations with Spain were worsening. That it existed in such a hand may indicate how the Bernard Drake enterprise was conceived and executed so rapidly.

P.R.O., State Papers, Domestic, Elizabeth I, SP 12/177, 58, fols., 153–153 v.

A plotte for the annoyeng of the K. of Spayn
The entrepryce is to surprise Spanyshe shippes as voyage yerely to the fishing of the newe fownde Lande and the Grande Baye.
For the execution whereof yt shall be necessarye to have thre shyppes well fournished of 200 tonnes at the least.
The charges of the sayd shyppes will amount unto being thoroughly manned and fornished the somme of [blank].
The tyme of proceeding to the execution of the enterpryse wyll be abowt the ende of Aprill.

The benefytes that wyll follow of the enterpryce
The greatest shipps belonging to the K. of Spayne sobjectes shall be dystressed.
The nomber of his maryners which can not in many yeares be supplyed shall be distressed.
They shall be put to great extremitye in Spayne for lacke of the sustentation of victull that they receive yerely by the seid waye.
The benefit that may be made of the shyppes tacles ordynaunce trayne oyle and fishe wyll be worth at the least 4000^{li}.

Necessary consyderations
Yt is fyrst to be considered at whos charges thes shyppes shall be sett forth.
Yf by her majestie then may the shyppes with the forniture be borne and the K. of Spayne weakened as is before expressed. Yf by her subjectes, then must they take the shyppes and ther ladyng and bringe hether either into this realme or into the Lowe Countreys.
To converte the benefit herof to the defraying of her charges yf they shoold be brought into this realme then would the K. of Spayne regard yt an open act of hostylytye matter wourthye of consyderatyon. To carry them into the Lowe Countreys yt is dowbtfull that they wyll not be receyved for that yt woold cut of the presente good traffycke the States have into Spayne.

The inconvenience be moste [?] expected of this ploot

The trafficke into Spayn wyll be cutt of.

The K. wylle seeke to take revenge by sendyng [?] under arrest of the Low Contreys and Scotlande. He wyll omytt no other revenge that he may take by producing [?] trobles in her majesties owne realme.

To answer with these inconveniences

1. The K. of S. Fraunce ether[?] to be tried [?] towchinge as assocyacon for the annoying of the K. of Spayne and the destroyinge of his greatness.

2. Scotlande is to be assured.

BERNARD DRAKE IS AUTHORIZED TO WARN THE ENGLISH TO TAKE PRIZES AND SHIPS IN NEWFOUNDLAND, JUNE, 1585

IN THE MONTHS after the Virginia voyage of 1585 got under way (434–435), Amyas Preston and Bernard Drake were preparing a second small fleet to reinforce the Virginia colonists. The *Golden Royal* of Exmouth (110 tons), Bernard Drake captain, and the pinnace *Good Companion*, Hugh Drake captain, were almost ready to sail when Sir Walter Ralegh was instructed to divert them and other ships to go to Newfoundland instead. His own ship *Job* (70 tons), Andrew Fulford captain, was among them. They were to warn English ships not to take their catch to Spanish ports and also to seize Spanish or Portuguese fishing vessels in reprisal for the embargoing of English ships in Spanish ports. We do not know how many ships Drake had with him at his departure. When they reached Newfoundland, they made contact with the *Golden Lion* of Chichester, George Raymond captain, which had delivered some colonists to Roanoke Island and then sailed to Newfoundland. Together they took either sixteen or seventeen Portuguese Newfoundlanders. One of them and the *Job* they lost to the French (547) and some others went astray, but eleven or twelve were brought to England. This was a major blow to the Portuguese inshore fishery from which, apparently, it did not fully recover.

The draft commission (541) is from P.R.O., State Papers, Domestic, Elizabeth I, SP 12/179, 21–22.

541. June 20, 1585. Commission to Bernard Drake.

Elizabeth by the grace of god Quene of England Fraunce and Irland defendor of the faythe &c. To all and singuler our subiectes tradinge to the new found land for fishe and to all other owr subiectes whatsoever on the seas or land unto whom in this case it shall apertayne and to everie of them gretinge. Wheras wee have bene given to understand that divers shipps perteynynge to our subiectes within this our Realme with their persons and goodes have latelie bene arested in Spayne by expres order from the kinge there. And beinge also further enformed that others of our subiectes that doe employ them selves in the fishinge at the new fownd land ar determined after they have finyshed their said fishinge to repaire into Spayne with entent to make a sale of their fish there. Wee have therfore thought meete tenderinge the saftie and weale of our subiectes to send our trustie and welbeloved servaunt Barnard Drake Esquire the berer herof not onlie to advertise our said subiectes of the said entent and determinacion to thend they maye avoide perill and danger that might otherwise ensue theirbie. But also our expres will and comandement is, that as many of our subjectes as shall come to have the sight and knowlege of this our presente comission shall joine with the said Barnard Drake, in doinge your best endevours accordinge to such direction as you shall receave from him, to cease and take into your possession all such shipps as you shall knowe and find to aperteyne unto the said kinge of Spayne or unto any of his subiectes which said s[h]ipps by you so seased our pleasure is, that you and the said Barnard Drake shal by vertue of this our comission bringe into some of the westerne portes of this our Realme, and there to remayne without dispersinge any part of their ladinge untill our further pleasure shalbe knowen in that behalfe And as for the shipps perteyninge to other princes our neighbours, our pleasure is you shall in no case deale with them, but use them in suche courteouse and frindlie sort as heretofore hathe bene accustomed. / Fayle you not herin as you will answer to the contrarie at your uttermost perills: And this our Lettars shalbe your sufficient warrant and discharge in that behalfe given under our Signett at our mannour of Grenewich the xxth days of June in the xxvijthe of our Reigne:/

[Endorsed:] The coppie of her majesties commission, given to Sir Barnard Drake at his going to new found lande.

542. October 10, 1585. The allowances to the Spanish [-Portuguese] seamen taken by Bernard Drake are cut down.

The Privy Council was concerned that the prisoners taken at Newfoundland were being too generously treated so their allowance was to be cut from three shillings and four pence a week to one shilling and nine pence a week. This was to be paid from a third of the fish sales credited to the victuallers of the ships. The venture is described as Sir Walter Ralegh's since Bernard Drake was in his service and was preparing to go to Virginia at the time he was commissioned for Newfoundland.

P.R.O., SP 12/173,13, draft.

After our harty commendacions wheras uppon knowledge receivid here of a generall arrest made in Spayne of dyvers of her maiesties subiectes shippes and goodes, yt was of late thought meete by her maiesty to direct Sir Walter Rawlegh knight to set fourth certen shipps to the seas out of the west partes of this realm for the intercepting of such of the king of Spaynes subiectes as should repeire to the fishing at new found land, which the said shippes have accordingly executed with so good successe as to bring into this realm a good number of Spanish vessells taken by them at the said fishing, wherein there are by estimacion above sixe hundreth maryners, and forasmuch as we are credibly advertisid that her maiesties subiectes yet stayed in Spayne, by vertue of the said generall arrest, are nowe of late used there in verie hard and unsufferable sorte, we do therfore thincke meete that, where the said Spanishe maryners are nowe as we understand dyetid at three shillings and fower pence a man by the weeke, their said dyet should hereafter be rated but at three pence a man by the day, the chardges wherof are to be allowid out of the third part of the fish to be by you allottid unto the vittallers of the said shippes of warre, with thother two third partes one to the owners and the other to the maryners of the same all which fish we thincke meete should be sould ether within the realm or in forren Countryes that are in league or good amity with her maiesty, where yt may be utterid to most proffit. In the doing wherof we pray you to caule three of the Commissioners of the Admiralty there to your assistaunce, by whos advice and travell theis thinges may accordingly be put the better in execucion and so we bid you hartely fare well. At Richmond the xth of October 1585 Your very loving frendes

[Signatures of privy councellors would have been attached to the original.]

543. 1586. An outbreak of typhus as a result of the Newfoundland raid.

Many of the Portuguese seamen were kept in prison after Sir Bernard Drake's raid (for which he was knighted). It is not clear with what offenses they could have been or were charged, but they were eventually brought to trial at the Exeter assizes with tragic results for their prosecutors as well as themselves.

Raphael Holinshed, Chronicles, *2nd edition, 3 vols. (London, 1587), 1547–1548.*

Some do impute it to certeine poore Portingales, then prisoners in the said gaole [Exeter]. For not long before, one Barnard Drake esquier (afterwards dubbed knight) had beene at the seas, and meeting with certeine Portingals, come from New found land, and laden with fish, he tooke them as a good prise, and brought them into Dartmouth haven in England; and from thense they were sent, being in number about eight and thirtie persons, unto the gaole of the castell of Exon, and there were cast into the deepe pit and stinking dungeon.

These men had beene before a long time at the seas, and had no change of apparell, nor laine in bed, and now lieng upon the ground without succor or reliefe, were soone infected; and all for the most part were sicke, and some of them died, and some of them was distracted: and this sickenesse verie soone after dispersed it selfe among all the residue of the prisoners in the gaole; of which disease manie of them died, but all brought to great extremities, and verie hardlie escaped. These men, when they were to be brought before the foresaid justices for their triall, manie of them were so weake and sicke, that they were not able to go or stand; but were caried from the gaole to the place of judgment, some upon handbarrowes, and some betweene men leading them, and so brought to the place of justice.

[This caused the justices to arrange for assizes to be held at quarterly sessions so that prisoners were not incarcerated for so long in such conditions and for the state of the prison to be improved. The prisoners were brought into the judgement hall and placed, as was the custom, near to the judge's seat.]

And howsoever the matter fell out, and by what occasion it happened, an infection followed upon manie and a great number of such as were there in the court, and especiallie upon such as were neerest to them were soonest infected. . . . And besides the prisoners, manie were there of good account, and of all other degrees which died thereof: as by name sargeant Floredaie who then was the judge of those trials upon the prisoners, Sir John Chichester, Sir Arthur Basset, and Sir Barnard Drake knights; Thomas Carew of Haccombe, Robert Carie of Clovelleigh, John Fortescue of Wood, John Waldron of Bradfield, and Thomas Risdone esquires, and justices of the peace.

REPERCUSSIONS OF BERNARD DRAKE'S NEWFOUNDLAND EXPEDITION, 1585

IN 1588 AMIAS PRESTON complained that in the venture of 1585 he had been in partnership with Bernard Drake and that he had not obtained his share of £2000 of the £20,000 prizes taken. As the defendant was dead, the case was carried on against his heir John Drake. Witnesses give a few details of the exploits at Newfoundland and in the Atlantic of Drake's ship, the *Golden Royal*, in company with George Raymond's *Red Lion* of Chichester.

Extracts are from P.R.O., High Court of Admiralty, Examinations, HCA 13/27; November 8, 1588, deposition of John Marshall (544), and November 30, 1588, deposition of Henry Browne (545). Further details of the case are in D. B. Quinn, *Roanoke voyages*, I, 234–242.

544. John Marshall.

That the said shipp the Golden Riall beinge so victualed and sent to sea did with the healpe of the Red Lion of Chichester surprise and take foure shippes laden with sugers some gould & silver and other commodities, and also svi sayle of Portingalles laden with fishe in the Newe founde lande whereof the first foure and xi or xii of the Newe founde lande men were brought into this Realme beinge all lawfull prize excepte for some smale quantity of sugers and one of the shippes which was claymed by Englishemen.

545. Henry Browne.

Master Drake and Amias Preston with this examinate and company beinge victualled and furnished as aforesaid did proceede with the said shipp the Golden Riall in the viadge aforesaid and first they apprehended a Brasil man laden with sugers wherewith Master Preston was sente for Englande, and then the said Drake with the said shipp and company proceeded to the New found land where they took xvii Portingall shipps laden with fishe which they sente home and then meeting with Captine Riman [Raymond] in the bay of Bulls they consorted together and sayled to the Isles of Surreys. Where they took thre Brasil men and an India men laden with sugers wynes oliphantes teeth and some goulde which were brought into Portesmouth or Chichester and Exmouth of this examinates knowledge beinge presente at the taking of all the said prizes.... He knoweth that master Bernard Drake and Captaine Riman had the disposinge of the goodes in the thre Brasill men and one Indian man of this examinates knowledge and of parte of the fish also.

546. October 18-27, 1586. Newfoundland fish brought to Weymouth.

In 1585 Captain George Raymond (Ryman) and Captain Amias Preston had taken part in Bernard Drake's capture of Portuguese ships at Newfoundland. In 1586 they were at sea on their own and took some further Newfoundlanders, although it is not known whether the seizures occured at Newfoundland or at sea on their way home or, indeed, whether the captured ships were Portuguese or Spanish. The cod, wet and dry,

were unloaded at the twin town of Weymouth and Melcombe Regis in Dorset under the eyes of the agent of the Lord High Admiral, Lord Charles Howard, who was entitled to one-tenth of all prize goods brought in by licensed privateers. The remainder of the catch went in equal share to the owners, victuallers, and crew of the vessels. The total number of fish, 129,360, would suggest the two privateers took from one to three Newfoundlanders. Of the cod 18,600 are described as wet fish and 12,000 as dried fish, the remaining 98,460 being more likely to be dry than wet fish. Raymond's ship thus got 64,680 gross, and Preston's the same, subject to the Lord High Admiral's deduction of 12,936 between the two. Each crew got 21,560. The total value lay between £ 500 and £ 600.

The document is in Weymouth, Dorset, Municipal Records, Miscellaneous no. 145.

For the cost of fish, etc., G. M. Cell, The English Fishery at Newfoundland 1577–1600 (Toronto, 1969), pp. 3–4, 15–16, 130, 133, 150. The Roman figures may be confusing: M = 1,000, C = 100, d = one-half of a hundred (50).

+86 [–1586]

Tewsday morninge fest St Luce [October 18, 1586]

In prymis brought to shoare one Waymouth syde to thuse of capitayne Ramon	xix^M
Item one thother syd for Captayne Preston devide into iii vix. thowners vittaylers and compart [= company] amountinge to vi^M 3^C 40 coupell [e]che part	xix^M
Item brought to shoare the said daye on Melcomb syde for wett fysh not devided	ii^M vi^C

Wensday the xixth of October 86

Item brought to shoare one Weymouth syd to thuse of Capten Rayman	vi^M iiii^C
Item one thother syd for Capten Preston devided into iii viz. thowners vitteylers company amounting to ii^M one C & x coupell ech part	vi^M iiii^C
Item brought to shore the said day at Weymouth syde to thuse of Capten Ryman of wett fyshe	ii^M vii^C

Item onn thother syd for Capten Preston devided into iii viz. thowners vittaylers & company amounting to ix^C & x coupell ech part — ii^M vii^C

Thursday the xxth of October
Item brought to shoar one Weymouth syde — 4^M 7^C d

Item one thother syd for Capten Preston devided into iii viz. thowners vittayliers & company amountinge to one^M C1 coupell [e]che part — 4^M 7^C d

Friday the xxith of October
Item brought to shoare one Thyrsday night & this morninge to thuse of Capten Riman one Waymoth syde — vi^M

+ 86 Octobre
Thursday
Item brought to shore one Weymouth syd to thuse of Capten Ryman — ii^M

Item one thother syde to Capten Preston devided into iii partes viz. to thowners victayllers and company amountynge to vi^C & xl coupells eache parte — ii^M

Item brought one shore the same day one Waymouth side and to the use of Capten Ryman — v^M iiii^C

Item to Capten Preston devided into three partes viz. to thowners victellers and company amountinge to i^M viii^C eche parte — v^M iiii^C

Fridaye
Item brought one shore one Waymouth side to Capten Ryman use — ii^M ii^C 30

Item to Capten Preston devided into thre viz. to thowners & to victellers & companye amountynge to vii^C l cuppelles each parte The whole beinge 5000 where of my Lords part was taken out viz. v^C — ii^M ii^C 30

Item brought to shoar the said daye on Weymouth syd to the use of Capten Ryman — ii^M

Item one thother syde to capten Preston devided into iii viz. to thowners & victelers & company amountynge to [blank, though figure would be "vi^C & xl coupells eache part"] — ii^M

Item one thother syde for Capten Preston devided into iii viz. thowners vittaylers & cumpany amountynge to ii^M eche part — vi^M

Item brought to shoar the said day of drye fysh with my Lords part — vi^M

Satterday the xxiith of October
Item brought to shoar one Waymouthsyde of wett fishe to Capten Ryman of — ii^M v^C

Item one thother syde for Capten Preston devided into iii viz. thowners vittlers & company amountynge to viii^C xx coupell eache part — ii^M v^C

The Monday the xxiiith of October
Item brought one shoar one Waymouth syde to thuse of Capten Ryman — ii^M v^C

Item on thother syd for capten Preston devided into iii viz. thowners vittelers & company amountyne to viii^C eche parte — ii^M v^C

Twesday
Item brought to shoare one Waymouth syd to thuse of Capten Ryman of wett fyshe — ii^M vii^C

Item one thother syd for Capten Preston devided into iii parts viz. thowners vittlers & company amountynge to viii^C & xl coupell eche part the whole beinge 6000 whereof my lordes part was taken out viz. 600. / — ii^M vii^C

Wensday
Item brought to shore one Waymouth syd to the use of Capten Ryman — ii^M ii^C

Item one thother syd to Capten Preston devided into iii partes viz. to thowners & vittlers & company amountynge to vii^C & xx couppelles each parte the — ii^M ii^C

whole beinge 5000 wherof my
Lordes parte was taken out viz
v^c

547. 1586. Petition of Andrew Fulford and Thomas Raynfford on losses sustained from the French when coming from Newfoundland.

Fulford, captain of Sir Walter Ralegh's small ship, the Job, *and Thomas Raynfford, captain of the Portuguese prize, the* Lion of Viana, *were returning from Bernard Drake's raid on Newfoundland when they were obliged to put into Breton ports. Their ships and their contents were seized there, and they and their men were imprisoned (perhaps because they tried to sell Portuguese fish and were taken, not unnaturally, for ordinary pirates). Eventually they were released and made their way to England. They petitioned the Privy Council for aid in recovering some part of their goods, if not their ships, from the French. They are not likely to have been successful. The petition (not previously printed in full) is P.R.O., State Papers, Domestic, Elizabeth I, SP 12/185, fol. 133.*

To the right honorable the Lordes & others of her majestes moste honorable Privie Councell./

Moste humbly complayninge showe unto your honours your humble Suppliants Androwe Fulforde gentleman Capten of the Shippe called the Jobe belonginge to Sir Walter Raleighe Knighte and Thomas Raynfforde gentleman Captayne of a Shippe called the Lyon of Viana which was taken as prize by Sir Bernard Drakes Knighte and Thomas Raynfforde your honours said Suppliants were appoynted for her Majestes service with others by the Direccion of the said Sir Walter Raleigh Knighte with comissione accordinglye/ And in there returne home wards were urged by foule weather, and other neadfull wantes to putte into certen Harbours on the Coste of Bryttayne, As the said Fulford into the Towne of Dariana [Douarnanez?] one Cremenicke Governoure there And the saide Raynfford into Morebeane in

the Ile of Ruze [Morbihan in Presquile de Rhuis] monsier Dillinge Ruler therof / Nowe so yt ys good Lords yf yt maye please your honours that your Suppliants cominge on shore with certen of theire Companyes for theire better provision were all sodenly apprehended, stript of all the had, caste into Prison, theire ships & goods taken, & all confiscated they knowe not howe withoute eny cause gyven. And so remayned Prisoners a longe time expectinge nothinge more Sure then deathe. Yet by the providence of the Almightie they departed thence with lyffe althoughe in great penurye & injurye to their great sorrow in herte & griefe of mynde Aswell for theire wone distressed estate as for theire miserable Companye./ And were urged for the reliefe of theymselves and the reste of theire Companyes to borrowe money of Englishe merchauntes enteringe into bands to repaye the same which as yet they are altogeather unhable to doe, and so rest in great feare of the daunger that maye ensue./ In tender consideracion whereof maye yt please your honours of youre accustomed clemencye, and to whome yt chiefelye belongethe to see reformacion had for the relyffe of the oppressed, to cause by some good measures (as your honours shall like beste) that restitucion may be had, If not of the Shipps yet of the goodes & value of theyme. Whereby your said Suppliants with manye others shall not onely be encouraged (so farre as lyffe to attempte any worthie exploite for the service of her Majestie your honours, & theire Countrey. But will as moste bounden daylye praye for the longe preservacion of your honours in all health & perfecte felicitie.

The Jobe whereof the said Fulforde was capten.
The shipps Burthen 70 tonnes
Of Cedar wodde xvj tonnes
Of caste pieces xiiii
Of Calevers xx^{tie} with there furniture
Powder & shotte
With all the shipps provision & furniture whiche furniture of the Companyes by estimacion worth M^{li}.
The Lyon wherof the said Raynfford was Capteyn
The shipps burthen 180 tonnes of thereaboutes full fraighted with Fyshe & oyles from the Newe founde Lande.
The Shipps Companyes furniture estimated to the value of 2000^{li}.

Andrewe Fulforde, Thomas Raynfford

548. 1587. A further English plan to strike at Spain through her Newfoundlanders.

On February 5, 1587, the Spanish ambassador in Paris, Bernardino de Mendoza, forwarded to Philip II a document which he said was a plan drawn up by Sir Francis Drake and Sir John Hawkins to attack Spain through her Newfoundland shipping, largely by privateers returning from their Caribbean raids on Spanish shipping. This was a return to earlier projects (540).

Abstracted in Calendar of State Papers, Spanish, 1587–1603 *(London, 1899), pp. 20–21, extract.*

You may leave the Indies from June to the middle of August, and go to Newfoundland, where you may get victuals, and capture a great number of Spaniards, Biscayners and others.

From there go to the Great Bay [Strait of Belle Isle], where you may take very many Biscayners who fish there. By calculating the times and places set forth above, you may capture so many ships and Spaniards that they will not recover the loss for years, if you take care to deprive them of their sails.

549. 1590. A Norman Newfoundlander seizes a Spanish prize from English privateers.

William Irish as captain of the English privateer, the Bark Young, *had a profitable cruise in the Caribbean in 1590, taking in May, among other vessels, a Spanish vessel of 40 tons on which he put a prize crew. On August 6 the two vessels had reached the roadstead of Notre Dame Bay, well up the east coast of Newfoundland, when they were attacked by seven Newfoundlanders from Le Havre and Honfleur, who took the prize, sank her, and brought her cargo to Le Havre. The* Bark Young *escaped and on her return proceedings were begun in the High Court of Admiralty with a view to bringing charges against the Frenchmen concerned.*

P.R.O., HCA 13/28, January 22 [William Irish], and March 27 (John Cade) 1591, printed in Kenneth R. Andrews, English Privateering Voyages to the West Indies 1588–95 *(Cambridge, Eng., Hakluyt Society, 1959), pp. 91–94).*

[a] William Irish of Westham gentleman of the age of xxx yeares or thereaboutes sworn & examined before the righte worshipfull master Doctor Cesar Judge of her majestes high Courte of the Admiralty. . . .

To the thirde he affirmeth most true yt ys that this examinate and his company with the said shipp followinge the contentes of theire said commission did aborde and take of the S\ᵗDomingo in the West Indies aboute the vᵗʰday of May laste paste a Spanishe shippe of aboute forty tonnes laden with suger & hides comminge from Sᵗ Domingo bounde for the Avana. . . .

To the iiiiᵗʰ and vᵗʰhe sayth truth yt ys that this examinate and company beinge possessed as aforesaid of the said Spanishe shippe and her ladinge did bringe the same as farre as New founde lande in theire viadge towardes Englande, and comminge out of the Roade of Noterdam [Notre Dame] with the same seven greate shipps of Newhavon and Humfleur in Fraunce belonginge to the Leage [Catholic League], and being there on fisshinge did violently assaulte and sett uppon the said prize and foughte with her and his examinate in his shipp of warre a whole daye and at laste this examinate beinge soe fiersly assaulted by the said vii shippes & xv pinnaces which they had manned out was inforced to take his men out of the prize to defend his man of warre from them, and soe they tooke the said prize from this examinate, and he hardly escaped with his man of warre from them, beinge chased by them soe longe as the day lasted which he affirmeth to be most true.

To the viᵗʰ he saythe the said Spanishe shippe was full laden with suger & hides, and he verely thinketh the same was very well worth xvCˡⁱ sterling when they were taken from this examinate by the said Frenche men.

To the viiᵗʰ he was tould by one Denise de Parcke of Garnsey who was in Newe found lande that the said vii shippes and pinnaces were of Newhavon & Humfleur in Fraunce. And one

Cade of Barstable who was lately... at New havon in Fraunce & sawe the suger and hides landed there out of the said Spanishe shippe thither broughte by the said vii shipps comminge from Newfound lande with fishe.

[b] John Cade of Barnestable in the Countye of Devon merchante aged xlviii yeares or thereaboutes....

To the first second, third, iiii th & v th vi & vii th articles he deposeth by chardge of his oathe that aboute the monethe of October last this examinate beinge at Newhavon in Fraunce sawe there seven shippes arrived there from before from the Newefound lande laden for the most parte with dry fishe and he knoweth that there were landed in New havon furth of the said shippes fyve hundreth & odde hides & eightene greate chestes of S t Domingo suger whiche the Captaines and companye reported & commonly boasted of all aboute the towne that they had taken in a Spanishe Carvell from an Englishe man of warre which this examinate knewe to be the Barcke Yonge whom they foughte withall all one whole day in the Newfound lande, and forced the Englishemen to forsake her. And sayth the Admirall of the said vii shipps was called John Blondell dwellinge in Newhavon [Le Havre] to which place the shipp belonged, The Captaine of the viceadmirall was called Captaine Bountainace of Roane, the Captaine of the second Admirall ys called Peter Mabbile of Feckam [Fécamp], and the shipp belonged to Feckamb also. The Captaine of the second viceadmirall was called Nicholas Mabbile of Feckam and the Captaines of the other thre shipps were named Peter de Mounte, Nicholas Gaffey, and the third John Rokerall all of Fecambe and the shipps belonged to the same place which he knoweth to be true for that beinge at Newhavon and hearinge bragges made by the Frencheman of the takinge of the said prize from the Englishe man of warre at Noterdam in Newe found lande this examinate harkened thereunto and tooke note of theire Captaines names which were as ys before declared, Addinge also that the Frenche men confessed that after they had taken out of the prize the suger & hides aforesaid and such other thinges as were in her, they soncke the Spanishe vessell in the bay of Noterdam or thereaboutes.

550. 1596. French Basque fishermen turn on the English at St. John's Harbour, Newfoundland.

As has been indicated, the French Basques suffered because they were in the middle between the English and the Spanish, but they also could be aggressive. The owner and the master of the ship Pilgrim *of Newport in the Isle of Wight reported such an incident when they tried to buy salt from three French Basque ships in St. John's Harbour in 1596.*

P.R.O., HCA 24/66, no. 51, extracts and abstract. (There is also a statement in P.R.O., State Papers, Colonial, CO 1/1,8.)

Richard James, owner of the *Pilgrim* of Newport, Isle of Wight, complains against Michael De Sance, Martin de Sance and Nicholas de Biscay.

He is the owner of the *Pilgrime* of Newport (100 tons), which went on a voyage to Newfoundland within the months March to September 1596. She fished on "the Bancke *prope* Newefoundland" and had almost a complete lading but lacked salt to finish it ("some was wasted through stormy and foule weather"). They understood that certain ships of "St Mallowes" had left salt behind at the harbor of "St Joanes" and slaied there in hopes of making up their voyage.

They arrived at St. John's on September 24 and found there three ships of "St Johns" [St Jean de Luz] in France. Casting anchor, they sent a boat to board the Admiral "according to the order used in that Countrey to acknowledge themselves fishermen" and to report that they lacked salt to complete their voyage.

On Saturday, September 25 some one or more of the company of the *Pilgrim* were invited aboard the Admiral where they found the masters of the ships at breakfast. There was "very loving and frendly talke" and the Frenchmen asked what they wanted of the voyage. They said "about ten thousand fishes".

The Frenchmen, pretending friendship and meaning spoil, offered to help to fish for them, Michael De Sance, master of the Admiral, and Nicholas [de Biscay], master of the Rear-admiral, each promising a boat and men to help them.

In "requital" the master and company of the *Pilgrim* the next day, Sunday, invited the masters and some of their company to dine on board the *Pilgrim*, but each framed his excuses, the Admiral saying he had an ague and would send his chiefest men, and sent one of his mates and the master gunner. The other masters "said they would not come because of necessity they muste send theire boats to sea."

In the afternoon on Sunday the captain and master [Richard Clarke] sent twelve men on shore "to untwist a cable to makes roades for the boates to stay them as they fished." Immediately after, the Captain of the Admiral [Michael de Sance] "sent for the master or governor of the Pilgrime to entrete him to visit him in his sicknes". He did so.

After he [Richard Clarke] came on board the said captain or some other "did by a false token as from the Maister of the *Pilgrime* sende some other of his chiefest men to come aboarde." When they did so "on the sudden upon a watchworde of the Captaine diverse of the Company of the French in the sayd ship ran upon the Englishmen therein being unarmed with naked rapiers halbards, pikes and javelins crying out '*rende vous rende vous*' viz. *Anglice*, yeeld your selves, yeeld your selves and surprised them and kept them in hold nyne dayes or thereaboutes." And with the company of the other ships "they boarded the sayd ship the Pilgrime and tooke and robbed the English of all the fish formerly taken all their ordinance shot and other munition." After about ten day's imprisonment, "the French Company delivered to the English the bare hull only of theire ship the Pilgrim with fewe sayles and very small quantity of victualls."

Chapter Seventy-one
English, French, and Basques in the Gulf of St. Lawrence, 1580–1597

MATERIALS ARE NOT yet available to illustrate all the aspects of French and Spanish Basques, Breton and English activity in the Gulf of St. Lawrence in the later sixteenth century. By 1580 Spanish Basques were installed in a number of whaling bases on the north side of the Strait of Belle Isle, occupying themselves with catching whales from boats and processing their oil and other products at shore bases. They appear to have begun to penetrate farther into the Gulf shortly after 1580. French Basque vessels, operating from Cape Breton Island and, probably, from western Newfoundland, carried on a codfishery at the Cabot Strait and in the southern part of the Gulf, while they also hunted whale (probably mainly the *beluga* or white whale), walrus and seal, as well as doing some trading in furs with the Indians. Sir Humphrey Gilbert, acting on suggestions from Anthony Parkhurst (525–526), leased rights to exploit the territories in and around the Gulf to a Southampton syndicate headed by Edward Cotton and probably including Henry Oughtred. Oughtred got special permission to send vessels to fish and trade in this year (528–533), and Cotton, as Richard Whitbourne noted much later in his *Discourse and discovery of New-found-land* (1620) (538), set out to catch whale and trade, though with no success.

After 1580, French ships, mainly Bretons at first, were regularly crossing the Gulf on their way into the St. Lawrence River where they went each summer to trade in furs with the Indians, while Basques, fishing for *beluga*, were also active there. In 1590 a straggler from the Breton fur trading fleet picked up information on a Basque walrus fishery on the island of Ramea, that is, the Magdalen Islands, in the Gulf. The ship *Bonaventure*, returning from a profitable experimental walrus-hunting season the following year (1591) was captured by the English and aroused their interest (553), while in the same year a rich French Basque fur-trading vessel, the *Catherine*, was also captured and released (557). These events led to an expedition from Bristol in 1593 under George Drake, which had only limited success in obtaining a cargo of walrus at the Magdalen Islands (559), while a further expedition under Sylvester Wyet cruised the Gulf in 1594, with a Basque pilot, searching for whale, although again with very limited success (560). Clearly, by this time, some Englishmen also wished to establish a more permanent base on the Magdalens.

Brownists, who refused to conform to the Church of England, had been in prison since 1592 under threat, at the least, of banishment (562). In 1597 it was agreed they might prospect the Magdalens as a possible site for a colony. Four of them sailed with Captain Charles Leigh in 1597, although only one ship reached the islands. She found there Basques, Bretons, and Micmac Indians, who chased her and the would-be Pilgrim Fathers away, the four Brownists forgetting their colonizing task in the heat of theological argument at sea (567). Leigh, later in 1597, put in a further plan for a settlement in which he still hoped to house some nonconforming

Protestants (569), but he received no more support and English interest in the area faded. The documents, however, illuminate a part of North America almost unmentioned since Cartier's voyage in 1534.

551. February 22, 1580. Henry Oughtred obtains permission to send his ships fishing, possibly one going to the Strait of Belle Isle.

Decision of the Privy Council, February 22, 1580, Acts of the Privy Council, 1580 (1901), pp. 395–396.

This day, at the humble request of Mr. Henry Outrede, esquier, of the county of Southampton, who made suit unto ther Lordships that notwithstanding a General Restraint given by them for the staying of all the shippes and mariners within the Realme from going to the seas, ether by way of traffique or otherwise, untill further direction should bee given to the contrary, he might have liberty to putt certain of his shippes to the seas for the trade of fishing, it was ordered by ther Lordships that in respect of the great charges which he had sustened in building vj shippes for the service of her Majestie and the Realme, he should have licence (so as he did leave his greatest ship and ij others, such as the Lord Admirall should appoint for that purpose, to serve her Majestie when occasion should bee offred) to send the rest of his shippes to the seas to

pass into any part that is in good league and amity with her Majesty by way of trade and not otherwise....

552. 1580. Edward Cotton's expedition to the Grand Bay (Strait of Belle Isle).

The recollections of Richard Whitbourne, Discourse and discovery of New-found-land (1620), sig. C5, form our only record.

My first voyage thither was about 40 yeares since, in a worthy Ship of the burthen of 300. Tunne, set foorth by one Master Cotton of South-hamptom; wee were bound to the grand Bay (which lyeth on the Northside of that Land,) purposing there to trade with the Savage people, (for whom we carried sundry commodities) and to kill whales, and to make Trayne oyle, as the Biscaines doe there yeerely in great abundance. But This our intended Voyage was overthrowne, by the indiscretion of our Captaine, and faint-heartednesse of some Gentlemen of our Company.

WALRUS-TAKING AT RAMEA (MAGDALEN ISLANDS), GULF OF ST. LAWRENCE, 1591, AND ENGLISH REACTIONS TO IT

THE FIRST document (553) is the narrative of a Breton ship's voyage to the Magdalen Islands in 1591; the second (554) is a letter recording the ship's capture by the English and noting the information it provided; the third (555) a note by Richard Hakluyt the younger on the potential uses of walrus products. First printed in Richard Hakluyt, *Principal navigations* (3 vols., 1598–1600), III, 189–191; reprinted (12 vols. 1903–1905), VIII, 150–157.

553. "A relation of the first voyage and discoverie of the Isle Ramea" with the ship called the *Bonaventure*.

For the performance of our said voyage, we departed from S. Malo with the fleete that went for Canada, and kept companie with the ships called The Soudil and the Charles halfe the way, and then lost them; a violent wind arising at Northwest, which separated us. After which we had faire wether, and came to the coast of Cape Rase, & had no further knowledge thereof, because the winde was at the Southwest but a scarce gale: and we came to the sounding Southwest of the Isles of S. Peter about 10. leagues, where we found 20. fathoms of water, and we sayled Northwest one quarter of the North, and came within 12. leagues of Cape de Rey.

The next day being the 6. of May 1591, we were come to Cape de Rey, & saw a ship Southwest off us, and stayed there that night.

The next day being the seventh of the sayd moneth, we came to the Isles of Aponas, where we put foorth our boat, because we had not past 8. leagues to our haven, which we kenned very clearly, although the coasts lay very low: and because the night approached, and the wind grew very high, we sought not to seeke our port, because it is very hard to find it when the wind is lofty, because of the shoalds that are about it. And we thought to keepe our course untill the next morning between the Isle of Brion & the Isle of Aponas. But there arose so great a tempest at the Southwest, that without the helpe of God we had bene in great danger among these Isles. And we traversed up and downe eleven dayes, making our prayers unto God to ende the tempest and to send us faire weather, that we might obteine our haven: which of his goodnesse he gave us. The last of May we ranged the Isle Ramea on the Northnorthwest side, unto the contrary part of the land, where it trendeth to the Southsoutheast: and seeing no land on the West side, wee ranged the sayd land to the East one quarter to the North at the least 15. leagues, and being from the shore some eight leagues, we found 15 fathoms water, and passed betweene the Isle of Duoron and the Isle of Ramea, where goeth a chanell of 3. leagues bredth; in the midst whereof you shall have 7. 8.

and 9. fathoms water. And the lowe poynt of the Isle Ramea, and the Isle Duoron lie Northnortheast, and Southsouthwest. And take heede you come not neere the low point of the Isle Ramea by a great league, for I have sounded it at 3. fathoms water. The Isle is marked. And the harbour of the Isle Ramea lyeth Northeast and Southwest, one quarter to the East and West. And if you would enter the sayd harbour, keepe you a league off the shoare: for often times there is great danger.

And that you may know the sayd haven, to the Eastnortheast of the sayde Isle there are high lands appearing to them that are without on all sides like a number of Islands, but in very deede they are all firme land: and if you come on the South and Southwest side, you shall see a hill divided into 3. parts, which I called the three hillockes, which is right within the haven. And for another better marke of the sayd harbour, you shall see an Isle like unto a Floure de lice, distant from the sayd haven 6. leagues at the least: and this Isle and the sayd haven lie Northeast and Southwest, a quarter to the North and South. And on the sayd Isle there is good pebble stone to drie fish upon: But to the west thereof there is a very faire countrey: and there is a banke of sand, which runneth the length of a cable, having not past one fathom water upon it. From the sayd Isle along the firme land the coast lyeth East and West, and you shall see as it were a great forrest running eastward: and the Easterne Cape is called Cape du Chapt, and is great and red toward the Sea. And betweene the sayd lands you shall see as it were a small Island, but it joyneth to the firme land on the Southwest part: and there is good shingle to drie fish on. And you must coast the shore with boates and not with ships, by reason of the shallowes of the sayd coast. For I have seene without Cape du Chapt in faire weather the ground in two fathoms water, neere a league and a halfe from shore, and I judged by reason of the highnesse of the land, that there had bene above thirtie fathoms water, which was nothing so: and I have sounded comming neere the shore, in more or lesse depth. The coast stretcheth three leagues to the West from Lisle Blanch, or the white Isle, unto the entrance of a river, where we slewe and killed to the number of fifteene hundred Morses or Sea oxen, accounting small and great, where at full sea you may come on shoare with boates, and within are two or three fathoms water. From thence the coast trendeth four leagues to the West one quarter to the Northwest unto the Isle Hupp, which is twentie leagues in circuit, and is like the edge of a knife: upon it there is neither wood nor grasse: there are Morses upon it, but they bee hard to be taken. From thence the coast trendeth to the Northwest and Northnorthwest; which is all that I have seene, to wit, the two sides and one ende of the Isle. And if I had had a good lucke as my Masters, when I was on the Northwest side with my shippe, I would have adventured to have sayled South-southeast, to have discovered the Easterne shoare of the sayd Isle.

In your returne to the East, as you come from the haven of Cape du Chapt unto the sayde haven, are sandes and sholds. And three good leagues from Cape du Chapt there is a small Island conteining about a league of ground: where there is an haven toward the Southeast: and as you enter into the sayd haven on the starreboord side, a dented Cape all of redde land. And you cannot enter into the said haven but with the flood, because of a barre which lieth halfe a league without the poynts of the sayd haven. The tydes are there at Southeast and Northwest; but when the wind is very great, it bloweth much into the haven at halfe flood. But ordinarily it floweth five foote and an halfe. The markes to enter into the sayd haven are to leave the Isle Blanche or White Island at your coming in on the starreboord; and the poynt of the haven towarde the West hath a thick Island, which you shall see on the other side, and it hath a little round Buttresse, which lyeth on the East side of the Island. There are also two other buttresses more easie to bee seene then hidden: these are not to the East but to the West, and they have markes on them. Here you shall not have above two fathom and an halfe at a full sea upon this barre. And the sounding is stone and rough ground. At your entring in, when you shall finde white sand which lyeth next the Southeast of the Cape, then you are upon the barre: and bee not afrayd to passe up the chanell. And for markes towarde the West athwart the barre, when you have brought an Island even, which lyeth to the westward without, with the thicke part of the high land which lyeth most to the West, you shall bee past the barre: and the chanell runneth due North. And for your anchoring in the sayd haven, see that you carefully seeke the middest of the

sayd Thicke land, which lyeth in the bottome of the sayd haven: for you must anchor betweene two bankes of sand, where the passage is but narrow. And you must anker surely: for there goeth a great tyde: for the Sea runneth there as swiftly and more than in [   ]. There is good ground and ankorage here: and you shall ride in three fathom water. And within the sayde haven there is nothing to hurt you, for you are free from all winds. And if by chance you should be driven Westward of the sayd haven, you may seeke an entrance, which is right over against the small Island named before, which is called The Isle of Cormorants; and you may enter in there as at the other haven at a full sea: And you must passe upon the West side, and you shall finde on the Barre at a full sea fourteene foote water, and great depth when you are entred in: for the Sea runneth very swiftly in that place: and the entrie thereof lyeth Southeast and Northwest.

Right over against you on the other side, you may passe with boates at a full sea. And all these entrances make all but one haven, which is good within. I say this, because I have passed into the maine Sea by the one and the other passage. And the said Isle is not past two leagues over in the middest. It is but two bankes of sande, whereof one is like that of S. Malo, which let the Sea from passing through the middest of all the Isle: But the two endes are high mountaines with Islands altogether cut and separated with streames and rivers.

To anker in the sayd harbour, you must not ride farther than five or sixe cables length from the sayd haven.

554. September 14, 1591. Letter from Thomas James of Bristol to Lord Burghley.

Right Honourable, my humble duetie to your good Lordship done, I thought good humbly to advertise your honour of the discovery of an Island made by two smal shippes of Saint Malo; the one 8 daies being prised neare Silley, by a ship of which I am part owner, called the Pleasure, sent by this citie to my Lord Thomas Howard, for her Majesties service. Which prise is sent backe to this Port of those of the sayd shippes, with upwards of fortie tunnes of Traine. The Island lyeth in 47. degrees, some fiftie leagues from the grand Bay, neere Newfoundland: and is about twentie leagues about, and some part of the Island is flat Sands and shoulde: and the fish commeth on banke (to do their kinde) in April May & June, by numbers of thousands, which fish is very big: and hath two great teeth: and the skinne of them is like Buffes leather: and they will not away from their yong ones. The yong ones are as good meat as Veale. And with the bellies of five of the saide fishes they make a hogshead of Traine, which Traine is very sweet, which if it will make sope, the king of Spaine may burne some of his Olive trees. Humbly praying your Lordship to pardon herein my boldnes, betaking your Honour to the keeping of the Almightie. From Bristoll, this 14 of September. 1591.

Your Honours most humbly at commandement.
Thomas James.

two Oxe or Buls hides in England. The Leatherdressers take them to be excellent good to make light targets against the arrowes of the Savages; and I hold them farre better then the light leather targets which the Moores use in Barbarie against arrowes and lances, whereof I have seene divers in her Majesties stately Armorie in the towre of London. The teeth of the sayd fishes, whereof I have seene a dryfat full at once, are a foote and some times more in length: & have been sold in England to the combe & knife-makers, at 8 groats and 3 shillings the pound weight, whereas the best Ivory is sold for halfe the money: the graine of the bone is somewhat more yellow then the Ivorie. One M. Alexander Woodson of Bristoll my old friend, an excellent Mathematician and skilful Phisition, shewed me one of these beasts teeth which were brought from the Isle of Ramea in the first prize, which was half a yard long or very little lesse; and assured mee that he had made tryall of it in ministring medicine to his patients, and had found it as soveraigne against poyson as any Unicornes horne.

555. 1600. "A briefe note of the Morsse and the use thereof."

In the first voyage of Jacques Cartier, wherein he discovered the Gulfe of S. Laurence and the said Isle of Ramea, in the yeere 1534, as you may reade in pag. 205 of this present volume, he met with these beasts, as he witnesseth in these words. About the said Island are very gret beasts as great as oxen, which have two great teeth in their mouthes like unto Elephants teeth, and live also in the sea. Wee sawe one of them sleeping upon the banke of the water, and thinking to take it, we went to it with our boates, but so soone as he heard us, he cast himselfe into the sea. Touching these beasts which Jacques Cartier saith to be as bix as Oxen and to have teeth in their mouthes like Elephants teeth: True it is that they are called in Latin Boves Marini, or Vaccæ Mariæ, & in the Russian tongue Morsses, the hides whereof I have seene as big as any Oxe hide, and being dressed I have yet a piece of one thicker then any

556. 1591. Notices of the capture of the *Bonaventure*.

[a] *Note of prizes in which her majestie is interested, 1591. B.L., Lansdowne MS 67, fol. 190.*

Item at Bristol, by Thomas Jeames a prize with fishe and Oyle.

[b] *Dr. Julius Caesar's notes of prizes. B.L., Harleian MS 598, fol. 15v.*

1591 October ye first Bristoll
Brought into Bristoll by the Pleasure of yᵉ same porte wherof honors and vyctalers Thomas James and Thomas Jeninges captaine wherof master William Trenche is and brought home on Leager pryse Laden with trayne oyell feshydes and teethe the tenthes wherof weare sol. (= paid) for 79ˡⁱ3ˢ which standeth yppon 79ˡⁱ3ˢ [cargo valued at £791. 10s] Dewe to me yppon my patten at 5ˡⁱ

per centum [blank] The tenths of y^e pryshe ship delivered master Souche

[c] *Lord Burghley's notes. Prizes brought in by way of reprisal 15th October 1591. B.L., Lansdowne MS 67, fol. 146.*

Item A Bristoll prize of Thomas Jeames with oyll and Fish. Thomas Jamis. from a New foundlandman by Frenchmen of St. Mallows.

557. 1591. Report of a further fur-trading ship taken coming from the St. Lawrence.

October 29, to November 8, 1591. P.R.O., State Papers Foreign, Spain, SP 94/4, fol. 65v.

In the extract below Edmund Palmer alerted Lord Burghley from St. Jean-de-Luz as to the landing of the recently captured French Basque ship. Other sources show that she was the

Catherine de St. Vincent *of Ciboure, in which the Princesse de Bourbon, sister of Henry IV, had an interest.*

The ship was released by Privy Council Order (Acts of the Privy Council, 1591–1592 [1901], p. 35) after representations by the Princesse de Bourbon and M. de Chasteaumartin to Lord Burghley (P.R.O., State Papers Foreign, France, SP 78/26, fols. 62–63, 95).

Yt maye plese yore Honor a Shippe of this tonne comynge home from the canada is taken by a Inglishe Shippe of Waymouthe & thither caryd the Setter owte of her was one Page of the Sayd plase / the Shippe hathe in her trayne oylle Salmon & newland feshe And greate Store of Riche Fures as bevers martrenes otters & manye other Sortes./ Some tymes the do Bringe Blacke foxe Skynes - no soche thinge to Ease a man of the payne of the gowte as thes blacke Foxe Skynes & for that cawse I do wryte yore honnor hereof the owner of theme is bownd over in this Shippe to Recober his Shyppe & goodes...

ENGLISH EXPEDITIONS TO THE GULF OF ST. LAWRENCE, 1593 AND 1594

DOCUMENT (558) was first printed in R. Hakluyt, *Principal navigations*, III (1600), 191–193; reprinted, VIII (1904), 1157–1161; and document (559) in *ibid.*, III (1600), 194–195; VIII (1904), 162–165.

558. 1593. The voyage of the *Marigold.*

The ship called the Marigold of 70 tunnes in burthen furnished with 20 men, wherof 10 were Mariners, the Masters name being Richard Strong of Apsham, the Masters mate Peter Langworth of Apsham, with 3 coopers, 2 butchers to flea the Morsses or sea Oxen (whereof divers have teeth above a cubit long & skinnes farre thicker then any buls hide) with other necessary people, departed out of Falmouth the 1 of June

1593 in consort of another ship of M. Drakes of Apsham, which upon some occasion was not ready so soone as shee should have bene by two moneths. The place for which these two ships were bound was an Island within the streightes of Saint Peter on the backe side of Newfoundland to the Southwest in the latitude of fortie seven degrees, called by the Britons of Saint Malo the Isle of Ramea, but by the Savages and naturals of the Continent next adjoyning, Menquit: On which Isle are so great abundance of the huge and mightie Sea Oxen with great teeth in the moneths of April, May and June, that there have bene fifteene hundreth killed there by one small barke, in the yeere 1591. The two English shipps aforesayde, lost companie before they came to Newfoundland: and never came after together in all their voyage.

The ship of M. George Drake fell first with Newfoundland, and afterward very directly came to the Isle Ramea, though too late in the yeere to make her voyage: where shee found a shippe of Saint Malo three parts fraighted with these fishes: the men whereof enquiring whence our shippe was and who was the Master thereof, being answered that shee was belonging to Master George Drake of Apsham, fearing to bee taken as good prize being of a Leaguer towne, and at that time out of league with England, fled so hastily that present night that they left three and twentie men and three Shallops behind them, all which our men seazed upon and brought away as good prises home.

Here our men tooke certaine Sea-oxen, but nothing such numbers as they might have had, if they had come in due season, which they had neglected. The shippe called the Marigolde fell with Cape Saint Francis in Newfoundland the eleventh of Julie, and from thence wee went into the Bay Rogneuse, and afterward doubled Cape Razo, and sayling toward the straight of Saint Peter (which is the entrance betweene Newfoundland and Cape Briton,) being unacquainted with the place. beate up and downe a very long time, and yet missed it, and at length over shot it, and fell with Cape Briton.

Here diverse of our men went on land upon the very Cape, where, at their arrivall they found the spittes of Oke of the Savages which had roasted meate a litle before. And as they viewed the countrey they sawe divers beastes and foules, as blacke Foxes, Deere, Otters, great Foules with redde legges, Pengwyns, and certaine others. But having found no people here at this our first landing wee went againe on shipboorde, and sayled farther foure leagues to the West of Cape Briton, where wee sawe many Seales. And here having neede of fresh water we went againe on shore. And passing somewhat more into the land, wee founde certaine round pondes artificially made by the Savages to keepe fish in, with certaine weares in them made to take fish. To these pondes wee repayred to fill our caske with water. Wee had not bene long here, but there came one Savage with blacke long hayre hanging about his shoulders who called unto us, weaving his handes downwarde towardes his bellie, using these wordes, Calitogh Calitogh: as wee drewe towardes him one of our mend musket unawares shot off: whereupon hee fell downe, and rising up suddenly againe hee cryed thrise with a loude voyce, Chiogh, Chiogh, Chiogh. Thereupon nine or tenne of his fellowes running right up over the bushes with great agilitie and swiftnesse came towardes us with white staves in their handes like halfe pikes, and their dogges of colour blacke not so bigge as a greyhounde followed them at the heeles; but wee retired unto our boate without any hurt at all received. Howbeit one of them brake an hoghead which wee had filled with fresh water, with a great branche of a tree which lay on the ground. Upon which occasion we bestowed halfe a dousen muskets shotte upon them, which they aboyded by falling flatte to the earth, and afterwarde retired themselves to the woodes. One of the Savages, which seemed to bee their Captaine, ware a long mantle of beastes skinnes hanging on one of his shoulders. The rest were all naked except their privities, which were covered with a skinne tyed behinde. After they had escaped our shotte they made a great fire on the shore, belike to give their fellowes warning of us.

The kindes of trees that wee noted to bee here, were goodly Okes, Firre trees of a great height, a kinde of tree called of us Quickbeame, and Cherie trees, and diverse other kindes to us unknowne, because wee stayed not long with diligence to observe them: and there is great shewe of rosen, pitch and tarre. Wee found in both the places where wee went on land abundance of Raspeses, Strawberies, Hurtes, and herbes of good smell, and divers good for the skurvie, and grasse very ranke and of great length. Wee sawe five or size boates sayling to the Southwestwardes of Cape Briton, which wee judged to bee Christians, which had some trade that way. Wee sawe also, while wee were on shore, the manner of their handing up of their fish and flesh with withes to dry in the ayre: they also lay them upon raftes and hurdles and make a smoake under them, or a softe fire, and so drie them as the Savages use to doe in Virginia.

While wee lay foure leagues South of Cape Briton wee sounded and had sixtie fathomes nlack ozie ground. And sayling thence Westwarde nine or ten leagues off the shore, we had twenty foure fathomes redde sande, and small whitish stones.

Wee continued our course so farre to the Southwest, that wee brought our selves into the latitude of fourtie foure degrees and an half, having sayled fiftie or sixtie leagues to the Southwest of Cape Briton. We found the current betwene this Cape Briton and Cape Rey to set out toward the Eastsoutheast. In our course to the West of Cape Briton we saw exceeding great store of seales, and abundance of Porposes, whereof we killed eleven. We sawe Whales also of all sortes aswell small as great: and here our men tooke many berded Coddes with one teate underneath, which are like to the Northeast Cods, and better than those of Newfoundland.

From our arrivall at the haven of Saint Francis in Newfoundland (which was as is aforesayde the eleventh of July) we continued beating up and downe on the coast of Arambec to the West and Southwest of Cape Briton until the twentie eight of September, fully by the space of eleven weekes: and then by the perswasion of our Master and certaine others wee shaped our course homeward by the Isles of the Açores. and came first to Corvo and Flores, where beating up and downe, and missing of expected pray, we sayled by Tercera, and from thence to Saint Michael, where we sought to boorde a Portugall shippe, which we found too well appointed for us to bring along with us, and so being forced to leave them behinde and having wasted all our victuals, wee were constrained against our willes to hasten home unto our narrowe Seas; but it was the two and twentieth of December before wee could get into the Downes: where for lacke of winde wee kept our Christmas with dry breade onely for dropping of our clothes. One thing very strange hapened in this voyage: to witte, that a mightie great Whale followed our shippe by the space of many dayes as we passed by Cape Razo, which by no meanes wee coulde chase from our ship, untill one of our men fell overboord and was drowned, after which time shee immediately forsooke us, and never afterward appeared unto us.

559. 1593. A note of the voyage of George Drake of Apsham to Ramea.

In the beginning of the former relation written by Richard Fisher servant to the worshipfull Naster Hill of Redriffe is, as you reade, a briefe reporte of their loosing of their consort shippe of Master George Drake of Apsham: which though shee came directly to the Isle of Ramea, yet because shee was not ready so soone by two moneths as she ought to have bene, she was not onely the hinderance of her consort the Marigolde, & lost the season of the yere for the making of her voyage of killing the Morses or Sea Oxen, which are to be taken in Aprill, May and June: but also suffered the fit places and harboroughs in the Isle which are but two, as farre as I can lerne, to be forestalled and taken up by the Britons of Saint Malo and the Baskes of Saint John de Luz, by comming a day after the Fayre, as wee say. Which lingering improvidence of our men hath bene the overthrowe of many a worthy enterprize and of the undertakers of the same.

The relation of this voyage at large I was promised by the Authour himselfe: but the same not comming to my handes in tyme I am constrained to leave it out. The want whereof, for the better understanding of the state of the sayde Island, the frequenting of that gainefull trade by the aforesayd nations of the Britons and Baskes, may in part be supplyed by the voyage of Master Charles Leigh to the sayde Island of Ramea: which also comming much too late thither, as Master George Drake had done, was wholly prevented and shutte out to his and his friendes no small detriment and mischiefe, and to the discouraging of others hereafter in the sayd gainefull and profitable trade.

Neverthelesse albeit hitherto the successe hath not answered our expectation through our owne default, as is abovesaid, yet I was very willing to set downe in briefe and homely stile some mention of these three voyages of our owne men. The first of M. George Drake, the second of M. Silvester Wyet, the third of M. Charles Leigh, because they are the first, for ought that hitherto is come to my knowledge, of our own Nation, that have conducted English ships so farre within this gulfe of S. Laurence, and have brought us true relation of the manifold gaine which the French, Britaynes, Baskes, and Biskaines do yerely returne from the sayd partes; while wee this long time have stood still and have bene idle lookers on, making courtisie who should give the first adventure, or once being given, who should continue or prosecute the same.

560. 1594. The voyage of the *Grace* of Bristol.

We departed with the aforesaid Barke manned with twelve men for the place aforesaid from Bristoll the 4 of Aprill 1594. and fell with Cape D'Espere on the coast of Newefoundland the nineteenth of May in the height of 47. We went thence for Cape Raz, being distant from thence 18 or 19 leagues, the very same day.

The 20. day we were thwart of Cape Raz.

Then we set our course Northwest for Cape S. Marie, which is distant from Cape Raz 19 leagues, and is on the Eastside of the great Bay of Placentia almost at the exntrie thereof.

From thence we shaped our course for the Islands of S. Pedro passing by the broken Islands of the Martyers: and when we were thwart of the said Isles of the Martyers our course to the Isles of S. Pedro was West by North. In these Isles of S. Pedro there is a faire harbour, which we went into with our barke, and found there 2 ships of Sibiburo fishing for Cod: where we stayed 2 dayes, and tooke in balest for our ship. There are as faire and tall firre trees growing therein, as in any other part of Newfoundland. Then wee departed thence, and as we came out of the harbours mouth we laid the ship upon the lee, and in 2 houres space we tooke with our hookes 3 or 4 hundred great Cods for our provision of our ship. Then we departed from the Isle of S. Pedro to enter into the gulffe of S. Laurence betwene Cape Briton and the said Isle, and set our course West North West, and fel with Cape de Rey which wee found to be distant from the Isles of S. Pedro 42 leagues. From Cape de Rey to Cape de Angullie we set our course Northnorthwest being distant thence 12 or 13 leagues. From the Cape de Angullie into the Bay of S. George we ran Northeast and by East some 18 or 19 leagues.

In this bay of Saint George, we found the wrackes of 2 great Biskaine ships, which had bene cast away three yeeres before: where we had some seven or eight hundred Whale finnes, and some yron bolts and chaines of their mayne shrouds & fore shroudes: al their traine was beaten out with the weather but the caske remained still. Some part of the commodities were spoiled by tumbling downe of the clifts of the hils, which covered part of the caske, and the greater part of those Whale finnes, which we understood to be there by foure Spaniards which escaped, & were brought to S. John de Luz. Here we found the houses of the Savages, made of firre trees bound together in the top and set round like a Dovehouse, and covered with the barkes of firre trees, wee found also some part of their victuals, which were Deeres flesh roasted upon wooden spits at the fire, & a dish made of a ryne of a tree, sowed together with the sinowes of the Deere, wherein was oile of the Deere. There were also foules called Cormorants, which they had pluckt and made ready to have dressed, and there we found a wooden spoone of their making. And we discerned the tracks of the feete of some fortie or fiftie men, women and children.

When we had dispatched our businesse in this bay of S. George and stayed there ten dayes, wee departed for the Northren point of the said bay, which is nine or ten leagues broade. Then being enformed, that the Whales which are deadly wounded in the grand Bay, and yet escape the fisher for a time, are woont to shoot themselves on shore on the Isle of Assumption, or Natiscotec, which lieth in the very mouth of the great river that runneth up to Canada, we shaped our course over to that lond Isle of Natiscotec, and wee found the distance of the way to the Estermost ende thereof to be about forty fourse leagues: and it standeth in the latitude of 49. Here we arrived about the middest of June at the East end, and rode in eighteen fadome water in faire white sand and very good ankerage, and for tryall heaved a lyne overboorde and found wonderfull faire and great Cod fish: we went also seven of us on shore and found there exceeding fayre great woods of tall firre trees, and heard and sawe store of land and sea foules, and sawe the footing of divers beastes in the sand when we were on shore. From the Easter end we went to the Norther side of the Island, which we perceived to be but narrow in respect of the length thereof. And after wee had searched two dayes and a night for the Whales which were wounded which we hoped to have found there, and missed of our purpose, we returned backe to the Southwarde, and were within one league of the Island of Penguin, which lyeth South from the Eastermost part of Natiscotec some twelve leagues. From the Isle of Penguin wee shaped our course for Cape de Rey and had sight of the Island of Cape Briton: then returned wee by the Isles of Saint Pedro, and so came into the Bay of Placentia, and arrived in the Easterside thereof some ten leagues up within the Bay among the fishermen of Saint John de Luz and of Sibiburo and of Biskay, which were to the number of threescore and odde sayles, whereof eight shippes onely were Spaniares, of whom we were very well used and they wished heartily for peace betweene them and us. There the men of Saint John and Sibiburo men bestowed two pinnesses on us to make up our voyage with fish. Then wee departed over to the other side of the Bay, where we arrived in an harbour which is called Pesmarck, and there made our stage and fished so long, that in the ende the Savages came, and in the night, when our men were at rest, cut both our pinnesse and our shippes boate away to our great hinderance of our voyage, yet it was our good fortune to finde out our pinnesses and get them againe. Then for feare of a shrewder turne of the Savages, we departed for Cape Saint Marie, and having passed Cape Raz, we passed Northwarde fourteene leagues and arrived in Farrillon, and finding there two and twentie sayles of Englishmen, wee made up our fishing voyage to the full in that harborough the twentieth foure of August to our good content: and departing thence we arrived first in Combe and staied there a seven night, and afterward in Hungrod in the river of Bristoll by the grace of God the 24 of September 1594.

561. 1595. A Basque pilot for the Englishmen.

The Basque pilot, Stevan Bocall, evidently a Huguenot, supplied by Edmund Palmer for the 1594 whaling voyage, was dissatisfied with his Bristol associates. Edward Palmer reported to Lord Burghley, on 6/16 March 1595 (P.R.O., State Papers, Foreign, Spain, SP94/6, fols. 9–10), that Bocall wished to make a further expedition to cut off a Spanish Basque ship which had wintered in Newfoundland (or more probably on the northern shore of the Strait of Belle Isle). We do not know whether this expedition was made.

This yere there is wyntered in newfoundland in the grande Baye a newe Shippe of St. Sebastaynes one of 4 hondred tones whoo went thither to kill the whale & the Shippe cannot be but Ryche with trayne oylle another Small Shippe is preparynge to get to her with vyttlles and other 2 Shippes bownd to the killynge of the Sea cowse owte of home the do geste greatte Store of balyne which is a Ryche comodyttye.

Seynge thes thinges I have hade conferrences with one of this towne the onlyeste fellow to pilott in this Land (who hathe geven me his worde to go over to Ioyne with Some onieste mane in England for a Shippe & men and to go and brynge home thes spanishes he Shall Repayre fyrste to yore honner / his name is Stevan de Bocall callyd here prince of conde he knowes wher the coper bynes be in newfoundland / wherof I have showe but I never Sawe better in all my Lyffe / this mane hathe hade greatte trafycke in the contrye with the Salvages / & will warrant any mane to pase that waye over a poynte of a land to the Sowthe Sea / for that contrye & thes passages I thinke [he has] not his fellow in the worlde / I have knowen hime brynge owte of the canada in a paltrye barke 3 thowsand pownd worthe in feres [furs] / besides other thinges of Ryche vallew / whos fortune So never yt to be Sette hime forth wilbe a Ryche mane all the beste men of this countrye as pilottes ar agaynste hime & have wrotte all the menes the cane to kepe him at home / thes ij yers he hathe Saylled frome brystow. but he cowlde not have that as he woolde have for the vytlinge & when he came thither his men woold do nothinge / & in a barke of 35 tones, he hathe yeven me his feythe & trothe to prosed & all theme in the worlde Shall not stope his goynge to yore honner fyrste of all for he hath Soche a mynd to theis Spanyses that he cannot be in quyet till he hathe the new Shippe with her Ladynge / By the party I will wrytte tore lord Shippe who wilbe redye to departe henes of a 3 dayes and thus god preserve yore honner /

THE PLAN TO PERMIT ENGLISH BROWNISTS TO SETTLE IN AMERICA, 1593–1597

SOME FIFTY-SIX Brownists, forming a nonconforming London congregation, were imprisoned early in 1593, including their pastor, Francis Johnson and his brother George. Repeated attempts were made to obtain their release, for example (a) a petition by John Johnson to Sir Robert Cecil on behalf of his sons, Hatfield House, Cecil Papers, Petitions 1055 (*Calendar of Cecil MSS*, XIV (1923), 281 (562); (b) Sir Walter Ralegh's plea for the Brownists in debate in the House of Commons, 1593, on a bill to banish nonconforming Protestants. Simonds D'Ewes, *The Journals of all the Parliaments during the Reign of Queen Elizabeth* (1682), p. 517 (563); (c) petition by the imprisoned Brownists early in 1597 to be permitted to go to the Province of Canada (Ramea, now the Magdalen Islands), P.R.O., State Papers, Domestic, Elizabeth I, SP 12/246, 46 (564). Permission was finally granted in 1597 (565).

562. Petition by John Johnson to Sir Robert Cecil, on behalf of his Brownist sons, Francis and George.

To the right honorable Sir Robert Cissell Knight and one of hir Majestes most Honorable priue counsell.

Most humble saeth to your Honour your poore Orator John Johnson to take notice and compassion of the distressed estate of his Two sonnes Franncis Johnson and George Johnson who have ben close prisoners theone in the Clynke a yeare and an halfe thother in the Fleete xvj monethes onlie for that uppon Conscience they refuse to have spirituall communion with the present Ministrey of the Land. Both of them have ben schollers and masters of Artes in the universitie of Cambridge and their brought up in lerning at the greate charges of your said Orator their Father whoe with all the suite he can make to hir Majestes high Commissioners, fynding not release for his sonnes is inforced to make his humble suite to your Honnor Beseeching your Honnorable and Christian favor That his sonnes maie either be discharged alltogether or have the benefit which the Preachers had Two yeres since whoe being prisoners were suffered to be at some honest men howses in the Cittie uppon sufficient assurannce there to be forthcoming uppon warning duelie geven. And that (till this enlargement be graunted) they maie for their health and lessening of their charge have the libertie of the prisons where they are. And the yonger (called George) be removed from the Fleete where he

hath ben most unchristianlie and unnaturally intreated so as he hath ben kept sometymes Two dayes and Two nightes togeather without anye manner of sustenance sometymes xx^{ty} nightes together without anie bedding and as longe withoute annie change of lynnen and all this xvj monethes in the most dankish and unholsom roomes of the Prison they could put him into not suffering anie of his freindes to come unto him, and now of late not permitting your Orator his Father so much as to see him. In all which respectes your poore suppliant is forced even in the bowels of his nature and of the Lord Jesus Christ to sue to your Honnor to be a meanes for reliefe of the moste unhealthfull chargeable and lonnge continewed ymprisonment of his Twoe sonnes aforesaid. And thus both he and they shalbe bound dailie to pray unto God for your Honnors health and happiness in this lyfe and for ever.

(Endorsed) The humble petition of John Johnson, in behalf of his Two sonnes Franncis and George Johnson having ben close prisoners thone in the Clink above a yere and a half, and the other in the Fleete above .16. Moneths onely for their conscience in religion.

563. 1593. Sir Walter Ralegh's plea for the Brownists in the House of Commons.

Sir Walter Ralegh:

If two thousand or three thousand Brownists

meet at the Sea ... at whose charge shall they be transported, or whither will you send them? I am sorry for it. I am afraid there be ten thousand or twelve thousand of them in England. When they be gone, who shall maintain their wives and children?

564. The imprisoned Brownists petition the Privy Council.

To the Right Honorable the Lords of her Majestes most honorable privie Councell:

Thereas wee her Majestes naturall borne Subjectes true and Loyall now lyving many of us in other Countries as Men exiled her highnes Domynions, and the rest which remaine within her Graces land greatlie distressed thorough imprisonment and other great troubles sustained onlie for some matters of conscience in which our most lamentable estate, wee cannot in that measure performe the dutie of Subjectes, as wee desier. And also Whereas meanes is now offered for our beeing in a forraigne and farre Countrie which lieth in the West from hence in the Province of Canada where by the providence of the Almightie, and her Majestes most gratious favour, wee may not onlie worshippe god as wee are in conscience perswaded by his Word, but also doe unto her Majestie and our Country great good service, and in tyme also greatlie annoy that bloodie and persecuting Spaniard about the Baye of Mexico. Our most humble suite is that it may please Your Honors to bee a meanes unto her excellent Majestie that with her most gracious favour and protection wee may peaceablie Depart thither, and there remayning to bee accounted her Majestes faithfull and loving Subjectes, to whom wee owe all dutie and obedience in the Lord. Promising heerebie, and takeing god to record who searcheth the hartes of all people. That wheresoever we become we will by the grace of god live and die faithfull to her highnes and this Land of our Nativitie: /

565. March 25, 1597. Instructions by the

Privy Council to permit Brownists to leave for Ramea.

P.R.O., *Privy Council Registers, PC 2/22, p. 167* (Acts of the Privy Council, 1597 [*1903*], pp. 5–6).

25° Martii 1597. A Lettre to the Customer & Serchers of London. Whereas Abraham Van Harwick and Stephan Van Harwick merchaunt strangers and Charles Leigh merchaunt of London have undertaken to adventure a voyage of fishinge and discovery into ye Bay of Canyda, and to plant them selves in an Island called Ramea or there aboutes whence they hope and Intend to bringe divers very necessarie comodyties of speciall use for this Realme and to establish a Trade of Fishinge there, And this present yere they have prepared to make ready two shippes to be sent thether. called the Hopewell, and the Chauncewell, the one being appointed to wynter there and thother to Retorne hether; For as moche as they have made humble suite unto her majeste to Transport out of this Realme divers Artificers, and other persons that are noted to be Sectaryes whose names are contained in a scedule hereunto anexed wherof fower shalbe at this present sent thether in those shippes that goe this present voyage; Yo^w shall therefore understand that her majestie ys pleased they shall carry with them the foresaid persons this present voyage So as note be taken of theire Names by yow, and good Bondes to her Majestes use of ye said merchauntes of anie one of them, that they shall not repaire againe hether unto this her majestes Realme unles they shalbe contended to reforme themselves, & to Lyve in obedyence to her Lawes established for matters of Religion. And that they nor any of them shall serve her Majestes forreine Enemyes. / And before theire departure they are to tender also there othe to beare trewe faith & obedyence to her majestie as becommeth dutyfull.

These are therefore to Requier yo^w to cause such Bondes to be taken of the said Merchauntes, or of any one of them, and thereuppon to permytt those fower persons to be Imbarqued in ye foresaid shippes. And because they do meane to take with them soch howshold stuff and other Implementes as may serve them for there necessary use, yo^we shall see what those Thinges are which shall carry with them, and to permytt them to take those thinges with them that may be fytt for theire necessary use there, They haveinge Intencion to Reside and Inhabit those partes. So

Requyring yo^w to take order herein accordingly, & to certyfy us ye same, wee &c.

THE EXPEDITION OF CAPTAIN CHARLES LEIGH TO THE MAGDALEN ISLANDS, 1597

THE EXPEDITION combined an attempt by the English to take over the walrus fishery on Ramea (the Magdalen Islands) from the Basques and Bretons with the provision of a colony of refuge for the Brownist congregation, four of whose members were released to reconnoiter the proposed site for a settlement. The main document is the account (a) by Charles Leigh of his voyage, first printed by Richard Hakluyt, *Principal navigations*, III (1600), 195–201 (reprinted VIII [1904], 166–180), without reference to the Brownists (566); (b), an extract from George Johnson, *A discourse of some trouble and excommunications in the banished English church at Amsterdam* (Amsterdam, 1603), pp. 111–113 (567); and (c) a deposition by a Basque seaman, Francisco de Cazanova, on Leigh's attempt to take a Basque prize off Newfoundland, P.R.O., High Court of Admiralty, Instance and Prize, Examinations, HCA 13/91, November 7, 1597 (568).

566. 1597. The voyage of Charles Leigh to Cape Breton and the Magdalen Islands.

The Hopewell of London of the burthen of 120 tunnes, whereof was M. William Crafton, and the Chancewel of London of the burthen of 70 tunnes, whereof was M. Steven Bennet, bound unto the river of Canada, set to sea at the sole and proper charge of Charles Leigh and Abraham Van Herwick of London merchants (the saide Charles Leigh himselfe, and Steven Van Herwick brother to the sayd Abraham, going themselves in the said ships as chiefe commanders of the voyage) departed from Graves-end on Fryday morning the 8 of April 1597. And after some hindrances, arriving at Falmouth in Cornewal the 28 of the said moneth put to sea againe. And with prosperous windes the 18 of May we were upon the banke of Newfoundland. The 19 we lost the Chancewel. The 20 we had sight of land and entred within the bay of Assumption, where our men contrary to my knowledge fought with a French ship: and after ward in the same bay wee met with our

consort. Whereupon we presently put to sea againe: and the next day we arrived at Caplen bay, where we remained by extremitie of foule weather, and to mend a pinnes of 7 or 8 tunnes (which was given us at Farrillon by M. Wil. Sayer of Dartmouth the Admiral of that place) untill the last of May. On which day departing from thence in the afternoone we put in to Rognause to seeke Shallops but could find none. The first of June we set saile from Rogneuse, and the second we put roone to a bay under the Northside of Cape Raz being inforced in by an extreme storme. The 4 we set saile, and this day we saw a great Island of yce. The 5 at night we lost the Chancewell in a fog at the mouth of the bay of Placentia. The 11 at Sunne setting we had sight of Cape Briton. And the 12 by reason of contrary windes we cast anker under the Northweat ende of the Isle of Menego to the North of Cape Briton in 16 fathome reasonable ground. In that place we caught great store of Cods, which were larger and better fish than any in Newfoundland. The 13 wee weyed anker againe, and being becalmed about a league from the shore we fell to fishing where the Cods did bite at least 20 fathomes above ground, and almost as fast as we could hale them into the ship. The 14 we came to the 2 Islands of Birds some 23 leagues from Menego: where there were such abundance of Birds, as is almost incredible to report. And upon the lesse of these Islands of Birds, we saw great store of Morsses or Sea Oxen, which were a sleepe upon the rockes; but when we approched nere unto them with our boate they cast themselves into the sea and pursued us with such furie as that we were glad to flee from them. The 16 we arrived at Brians Island, which lyeth 5 leagues West from the Island of Birds. About this Island ther is as great aboundance of cods as in any place can be found. In litle more than an houre we caught with 4 hookes 250 of them. Here we caught also a great Turbut which was an elle long and a yard broad: which was so great that the hooke could not hold her into the ship: but when she was above water she bent the hooke & escaped. In this Island we found exceeding good ground both for corne and meadow, & great store of wood, but of smal groweth. Springes of fresh water we found none in all the Island, but some standing pooles of raine water. The same day at night we weyed anker againe. The 17 we had stormy weather. The 18 we came to the Isle of Ramea, where we appointed to meet with our consort. And approching neere unto the harborough of Halabolina we cast anker in 3 fadomes water and sent out great boate into the harborough, with the masters mate and some dozen more of the company: who when they came in, found 4 ships. Namely 2 of Saint Malo in Britaigne, and two of Sibiburo adjoyning to Saint John de luz being the French Kings subjects, whom they supposed to have bene of Spaine, and so affirmed unto us. Whereupon wee went presently into harborough, finding but eleven foote and an halfe of water upon the barre and a mightie great current in, when wee had cast anker we sent presently to speake with the masters of all the ships: but those onely of Saint Malo came aboord, whom wee entertained very friendly, and demaunded of whence the other two shippes were. They sayde as they thought of Saint John de Luz or Sibiburo. Then we presently sent our boate for the Masters of both the sayd shippes, to request them to come aboord, and to bring with them their Charters parties and other evidence, to the ende we might knowe of whence they were. At which message one of the sayde Masters came

aboord, with the Pilote and Masters mate of the other shippe: whom when we had examined, they sayd that they were of Sibiburo, and the French King subjectes. We requested them for our better securitie in the harborough peaceably to deliver up their powder and munition: promising them that if we found them to be the French Kings subjectes it should be kept in safetie for them without diminishing. But they woulde not consent thereunto: whereunto we replyed, that unlesse they would consent thereunto we could hold them to be our enemies. They not consenting, we sent the boate well manned to fetch their powder and munition from aboorde their ship: but straightly commanded our men not to touch any thing else in the ship upon their further perill: which they promised to performe. When they came aboorde the saide ships which were mored together, they were resisted by force of armes, but quickly they got the victorie: which done, they fell presently to pillaging of the Baskes, contrary to their promise: whereupon we sent another to forbidde them; but when he came to them, none was more ready of pillage than he. Whereupon I went my selfe, and tooke away from our men whatsoever they had pillaged, and gave it againe to the owners; onely I sent aboord our owne ship their powder and munition to be kept in safetie until we knew farther what they were. When I had done, I gave the Baskes possession of their shippe againe and I tolde them they should not loose the valewe of one penny if they were the French Kings subjects. Then I caryed away all our men, and also tooke with me two or three of the chiefest of them, and when I came aboord went to examining of them, and by circumstances found one of the ships to belong to France: whereupon I tolde the master of the said ship, that I was thoroughly satisfied that he was of France and so dismissed him in peace. Of the other ship we had great presumption that she was of Spaine, but had no certaine proofe thereof, wherefore wee dismissed them likewise in peace. After I had thus dismissed them, our ships company fell into a mutiny, and more than half of them resolved to cary one of those ships away. But they were prevented of their evill purpose by ayde which the saide ships received from their counteymen in the other harborough: For the next morning, which was the twentieth of June, we earely there were gathered together out of all the ships in both harboroughs, at the least

200 Frenchmen and Britons, who had planted upon the shore three pieces of Ordinance against us, and had prepared them selves in al readinesse to fight with us, which so soone as we had discried them gave the onset upon us with at least an hundred small shot out of the woods. There were also in readines to assault us about three hundred Savages. But after we had skirmished a while with them, we procured a parley by one of the men of Saint Malo, whose ship rowed hard by us: In which parley they required some of our men to come on shore unto them: whereupon wee requested M. Ralph Hill and the Boatswaines mate to go on shore to them: whom when they had they detained as prisoners; and then required the powder and munition, which we had of the Baskes in possession; which we surrendred unto them in safetie as our intent alwayes was, which done, there came aboord unto us one Captaine Charles, who was captaine of the great ship of Saint Malo, which rode in the other harborough: who challenged our great boate which we had at Farrillon to be his. And while we were in talke with him about the two Baskes which at first we thought to be Spaniards, we had almost bene betraied. For the said Captaine Charles with halfe a dozen more of his company kept themselves aboord of our ship and held us in a talke, while thirtie or fortie others should have entred our ship unawares from one of the ships of S. Malo, which professed to be our friend, & unto whom we shewed all courtesie. But we perceiving their trecherous intent, threatned to set fire on the said ship, which was then thwart our hawse, from which they would have entred. By which resolution of ours God did discourage them from effecting their mischievous purposes. Now the said captaine Charles when he saw himself prevented of his wicked intents, took his boate presently to go on shore, and promised that all things should be ended in peace betweene us, and that he would send us our two men againe. But when he was on shore he presently sent for our great boat which he claimed to be his, & withall commanded us out of the harborough; but he sent not our men as he promised, we being now the weaker side did not only deliver his boat but also determined to be gon and then requested them to help us with our anker which was on shore; but they would not. Then we desired them to cut the bent of the cable upon the anker on shore (for we durst not send our boat lest they

should have kept from us both our boat and men) which they promised to do for us, as also to send our men; but when they were on shore, they would do neither. We therefore seeing their falshood in every thing, durst no longer tary for feare of farther treachery; wherefore we concluded to cut our cable in the hawse; which we did, & so departed from the harborow about 9 of the clock, leaving two of our men with our cable and anker, and 20 fadoms of a new hawser behind us. And as we were going away, they made great shewes of friendship, and dranke unto us from the shore; but more for feare then love, and requested us to come on shore for our men, whom then they delivered. The same morning in passing over the barre before the harborowes mouth, and by that time that we had all our men aboord, our ship came on ground upon the sands; where we lay some 8 houres: during which time, at low water we trimmed our ship without boord, and by the great providence of God found our leake which then we stopped. About six of the clocke at night we got our ship on float againe, and that night ankered within part of the barre, which then because of the wind we could not passe. But it pleased God to send us faire weather all that night, and the next day by noone we had gotten our ship cleane over the bar. The 21 day after we got over the barre the wind arose at east & eastsoutheast, we blew right into the bay: which if it had come before we were cleere of the bar, we had both ship and men perished in the sands. The same day, because the wind kept us within the bay, we went to the Isle Blanch, where the ships of the other harborow had their stages: but it was at least two leagues from their ships: where we hoped by friendship to procure a shallope & assurance of our cable and anker againe. But when we had approached nere the shore with our ship, & weaved them with a white flag, they in sted of comming unto us, sent their message by a buttel out of a piece of great ordinance, which they had placed on shore of purpose against us; so that they would neither speake with us, nor permit us to come nere them. Thus we departed, and would have put to sea that night: but there was much wind at East, which kept us within the bay, & inforced us to come to an anker under Isle Blanch. The next morning being the 22, we put to sea, and about 12 of the clocke the same day, the wind being at Northeast and foule weather, the master sayd he could not ply up to Grande Coste, because of the leeshore, & the wind against us, and therefore asked what we should do. I asked then how farre we had to the river of cape Briton: he sayd a little way. Then sayd I, If it be not farre, we were best to go thither to trade with the Savages while the wind is contrary, and to take in water & balist, which we wanted. To which the master sayd, that if I would he would cary us thither. I thinking it to be the best course, sayd I was content, so farre forth as that from thence we tooke the first faire wind for Grande Coste. Hereupon the master willed him at the helme to keepe his course southeast and southeast by south. Presently after I asked him how many leagues we had to the sayd river and from the sayd river to Grande Coste. He then sayd that we had 40 leagues to the river, and from the river to Grande Coste 120 leagues. Hereupon I said I would not consent to go so far out of our way, but willed him to keep his directest course for Grande Coste; which he did. Within one halfe houre afterwards the 23 day the gunner and company of the ship presented me & the master with a request in writing to returne for England or to goe for the Islands of Açores for a man of war, for they would not proceed on their voyage to Grande Coste; and therefore do what I could they turned the helme homewards. The 14 of June we sent our boat on shore in a great bay upon the Isle of Cape Briton for water. The 25 we arrived on the West side of the Isle of Menego, where we left some caske on shore in a sandy bay, but could not tary for foule weather. The 26 we cast anker in another bay upon the maine of Cape Briton. The 27 about tenne of the clocke in the morning we met with eight men of the Chancewell our consort in a shallope; who told us that their ship was cast away upon the maine of Cape Briton, within a great bay eighteene leagues within the Cape, and upon a rocke within a mile of the shore, upon the 23 of this moneth about one of the clocke in the afternoone: and that they had cleered their ship from the rocke: but being bilged and full of water, they presently did run her up into a sandy bay, where she was no sooner come on ground, but presently after there came aboord many shallops with store of French men, who robbed and spoiled all they could lay hands on, pillaging the poore men even to their very shirts, and using them in savage manner: whereas they should rather as Christians have aided them in

that distresse. Which newes when we heard, we blessed God, who by his divine providence and unspeakable mercy had not onely preserved all the men, but brought us thither so miraculously to ayd and comfort them. So presently we put into the road where the Chancewell lay; where was also one ship of Sibiburo, whose men that holpe to pillage the Chancewell were runne away into the woods. But the master thereof which had dealt very honestly with our men stayed in his ship, and came aboord of us: whom we used well, not taking any thing from him that was his, but onely such things as we could finde of our owne. And when we had dispatched our businesse, we gave him one good cable, one olde cable and an aker, one shallop with mast, sailes, and other furniture, and other things which belonged to the ship. In recompense whereof he gave us two hogsheads of sider, one barrell of peaze, and 25 score of fish. The 29 betimes in the morning we departed from that road toward a great Biskaine some 7 leagues off of 300 tun, whose men dealt most doggedly with the Chancewels company. The same night we ankered at the mouth of the harborow, where the Biskain was. The 30 betimes in the morning we put into the harborow; and approaching nere their stage, we sawe it uncovered, and so suspected the ship to be gone; whereupon we sent out pinnesse on shore with a dozen men, who when they came, found great store of fish on shore, but all the men were fled: neither could they perceive whether the ship should be gone, but as they thought to sea. This day about twelve of the clocke we tooke a Savages boat which our men pursued: but all the Savages ran away into the woods, and our men brought their boat on boord. The same day in the afternoone, we brought our ship to anker in the harborow: and the same day we tooke three hogsheads and an halfe of traine, and some 300 of greene fish. Also in the evening three of the Savages, whose boat we had, came unto us for their boat; to whom we gave coats and knives, and restored them their boate againe. The next day being the first of July, the rest of the Savages came unto us, among whom was their king, whose name was Itarey, and their queene, to whom also we gave coats and knives, and other trifles. These savages called the harborow Cibo. In this place are the greatest multitude of lobsters that ever we heard of: for we caught at one hawle with a little draw net above 140. The fourth of

July in the morning we departed from Cibo. And the fift we cast anker in a reasonable good harborow called New Port under an Island some eight leagues from Cibo, and within three leagues from the English port. At this place in pursuing certaine shallops of a ship of Rochel, one of them came aboord, who told us that the Biskainer whom we sought, was in the English port with two Biskainers more, and two ships of Rochel. Thereupon wee sent one of our men in the Rochellers shallop to parle with the admiral & others our friends in the English port, requesting them ayd for the recovery of our things, which the other ship called the Saint Maria of S. Vincent (whereof the Master Johannes de Harte, and Pilot Adame de Lauandote) had robbed from the Chancewell. To which they answered, that if we would come in unto them in peace, they would assist us what they might. This answere we had the sixt day: and the seventh in the fornoone we arrived in the English port, and cast anker aloofe from the other ships: which done, I went aboord the Admirall, to desire the performance of his promise: who sent for Johannes de Harte, who was contended to restore most of our things againe: whereupon I went aboord his ship to have them restored. This day and the eighth I spend in procuring such things as they had robbed; but yet in the end we wanted a great part thereof. Then we were briefe with them, and willed them either to restore us the rest of our things which they had, or els we would both inforce them to doe it, and also have satisfaction for our victuals and merchandises which by their meanes we lost in the Chancewell. The ninth in the morning wee prepared our ship to goe neere unto them. Whereupon their Admirall sent his boat aboord, and desired to speake with mee: then I went aboord unto him, and desired to have our things with peace and quietnesse, proffering to make him and the Masters of the two ships of Rochel our umpires, and what they should advise I would stand unto. Heereupon he went aboord the other ship to make peace; but they would heare no reason, neither yet condescend to restore any thing else which they had of ours. Then I desired that as I came in peace unto them, they would so set me aboord by ship againe: which they denied to doe, but most unjustly detained me and Stephen van Herwicke who was with me. A while after our shallop came with foure men to know how I did, and to fetch me aboord: but so soone as she came to the Admirals ships side, his men entred, and tooke her away, detaining our men also as prisoners with us. Then presently all the three Biskainers made toward our ship, which was not carelesse to get the winde of them all: and having by the mercy of God obtained the same; shee then stayed for them: but when they saw they had lost their advantage, they presently turned their course, making as great haste in againe as they did out before. Afterwards I attempted twise to goe aboord, but was still enforced backe by the two other Biskainers, who sought our lives: so that in the end the Master of the Admirall was inforced to main his great boat to waft us: and yet notwithstanding they bent a piece of great ordinance at us: for we were to passe by them unto our ship: but we rescued our shallop under our Masters great boat; and by that meanes passed in safety. The next morning being the tenth of the moneth, we purposed if the winde had served our turne, to have made them to repent their evill dealing, and to restore us our owne againe, or else to have suncke their ships if we could. But the winde served not our turne for that purpose; but carried us to sea; to that the same morning wee tooke our course toward the bay of S. Laurence in Newfoundland: where wee hoped to finde a Spanish ship which as we had intelligence, did fish at that place. The thirteenth day we had sight of S. Peters Islands. And the fourteenth day being foggy and misty weather, while we made towards the land, we sent our shallop before the shippe to discover dangers: but in the fogge, through the mens negligence which were in her, she lost us: yet we kept on our course, thinking that although we could not see them, yet they might see our ship: and coming into sixteene fathoms water we cast anker, supposing our selves to be neere the shore: and in the evening it pleased God to give us for the space of one quarter of an houre clere weather, by which we found our selves to be imbayed, and also had sight of our shallop, which was at the point of a land about one league from us. The same night we went further into the same bay, where we had very good riding. The fifteenth we went on shore, and in that place found footing of deere, and before we returned we killed one. The eighteenth we departed toward S. Laurence: the same evening we had sight of S. Laurence, and sent off our boat in the night with our Master and sixteene men to surprise the Spanyard, which lay in Litle S. Laurence; who presently upon the entrance of our men surrendred up their ships and goods. The nineteenth in the morning before day, the Master of our ship with two more, and three Spanyards, tooke a boat and came foorth to meet our shippe, but being foggy, he cast anker by the mouth of the harborow (thinking in faire weather to put out to our ship, which through the current and foggy weather was put five or sixe leagues to leeward: & while they were at anker in the boat they were surprised again by certaine Basks of S. John de Luz who were in Great S. Laurence hard by. These Basks with their forces (having received intelligence by one of the Spanyards, who sleeping on shore, escaped unto them overland) on the sudden surprised the sayd boat with our Master and others: and then presently made unto the ship; but our men aboord defended them off. In the end they threatned that unlesse they would yeeld, they would kill M. Crafton and other men before their eyes. So at last upon M. Craftons intreaty and our mens, to save their lives, they yeelded up the ship againe, upon condition, that they should not injury any of our men, but should let them all with their weapons peaceably depart: yet when our men had yeelded, they brake their covenant, profering them great violence, threatning to kill them, disarming them, stripping their clothes from their backs, and using them like dogs then man. After they had thus robbed our men of their prize and weapons, they presently towed the shippe with their boats out of that harborow into Great S. Laurence, where their owne shippes did ride, and within lesse than an houre after they had carried our prize away, our shippe arrived in the bay: where after we had bene a while at anker, our shallop came aboord unto us, with most part of our sixteene men, who tolde us the whole story before recited, as also that captaine Laurence had caried away our Master, and Stephen van Herwicke prisoners, and turned the rest of our men on shore in the woods, without either meat, drinke, or almost any apparell. The 20 all our men came aboord, except the two prisoners: and the same day we tooke with our boats three of the Spanyards shallops, with five hogsheads of traine oile in ech of them, & in one boat foure Spanyards; but the men of the other two shallops fled on shore. The same day also we tooke the Master of one of the ships which was in the harborow with

three other of his men, whom we detained prisoners to ransome M. Crafton & Stephen van Herwick. The 22 captaine Laurence sent them abooord, and we also released all our prisoners, except one Spanyard, who was boatswaine of the Spanish ship, whom we kept with us: and the same day we set saile from thence. The 24 we had advice of our Spanyard of certain Leagers which were in the harborow of cape S. Mary. Whereupon the same night, being within five or six leagues of the harborow, I sent off our two shallops with thirty men to discover the harborow, and to surprise the enemy. The 25 in the morning we approached the harborow with our ship, and in the mouth thereof we espied three shallops, two whereof were ours, and the third of a ship of Rochel, which they had surprised with foure men in her: who told them that there were but two ships in the harborow, whereof one was of Rochel, and the other of Bell isle. And as we were discoursing with the Rochellers, we had sight of the ships whereupon we sent our boat aboord the Rocheller to certifie him that we were his friends, and to request him not to hinder our fight with the enemy. This message being sent, we made all the haste we could unto the ship of Bell isle, which first began with us with three great shot, one whereof hit our maintopsaile, but both the others missed us. And we also sent one unto them: then being approched nere unto them ten or twelve of us went in a shallop to enter them, and we caried also a warpe with us to make fast unto their ship, whereby our ship might the better come up to ayd us. And when we boorded them in our boat, they betooke themselves to their close fights, playing chiefly upon us with shot and pikes out at two ports, between which we entred very dangerously, escaping neere dangers both by shot & pike. Some of our men were wounded, but no great harme was done. And mine owne piece in entring, was shot out of my hand into the sea; which shot also burst one side of the ladder, by which I entred. We had not long bene aboord, but through the helpe of God we caused them to yeeld unto our mercy. There were of them in the ship above forty men, most whereof we sent aboord of our shippe, there to be kept in holde, with order to our chyrurgion to dresse the wounded men, one of which was wounded unto death. That done, we had then time to view our prize, which we found of great defence, and a notable strong ship, almost two hundred tun in burden, very well appointed, and in all things fitted for a man of warre. They had also foureteene men more, which were then absent from the ship; otherwise we should have had the hoter fight. The same day we got our sailes to the yard, and our top masts on end, and rigged the shippe what we could. The 26 day we got some oile aboord, and there we taried untill the second of August, fitting our selves for the sea, and getting fish aboord as weather served us. During our abode there we divided our men, and appointed to ech ship their company, my selfe and my friends being resolved to take our passage in the prize; wherein when we were shipped, and the company, there arose great enmity against us by the other shippe, which afterward was quieted. The second day of August, having taken in water and wood, we put to sea from that harborow in company of the Hopewell, with purpose to go directly to Parlican, which is an harborow in the North part of Newfoundland, where we expected another prize. But when we came to sea we found our sailes so olde, our ropes so rotten, and our provision of bread and drinke so short, as that we were constrained to make our resolution directly for England: whereupon we drew out our reasons the fourth day of August, and sent them aboord the Hopewell, to certifie them the cause of our resolution for England: wherat they were generally offended, thinking and saying, that we in the prize went about to cousin and deceive them. To conclude, they sent us word that they would keepe us company for England. But I had given William Crafton commission before to go for the Islands of the Açores, and there to spend his victuals for a man of warre. The next day being the fift of August, having a faire winde, we put off from the coast of Newfoundland, and kept our course directly for England, the Hopewell keeping us company untill midday, whenas having lost us in a fogge, she shot off two pieces of ordinance, and we answered her with three: afterwards we spake not with her, supposing that she went for the Islands. The 27 of August, drawing neere the coast of England, we sounded and found ground at seventy fadoms. Some of the mariners thinking we were in Bristow channell, and other in Silly channell: so that through variety of judgements, and evill marinership we were faine to dance the hay foure dayes together, sometimes running to the Northeast, sometimes to the Southeast, then

againe to the Easte, and Eastnortheast. Thus did we spend faire winds, and lose our time untill the last of August. And then it pleased God that we fell with the Island of Lundy within the channell of Bristoll; from whence we shaped our course: and after divers dangers, the third of September we met with the Tramontane of the Queene of Dartmouth; to the captaine whereof we gave certaine things that he had need of. The fift of September I landed on the outside of the Isle of Wight, and within few dayes after it pleased God to bring the ship in safety to London, where she was made prize as belonging to the enemies of this land.

Certaine observations touching the countreys and places where we travelled.

The Newfoundland we found very subject to fogs and mists. The ground of it is very rocky: and upon it there is great store of firre trees, and in some places red; and about the shore it hath great abundance of codfish. We were on land in it in foure severall places: 1 At Caplin bay and Farrillon: 2 At Cape Rase: 3 At the harborow of Lano, which lieth foure leagues to the West beyond Cape Laurence: 4 At S. Marie port.

The Island of Menego for the soile is much like Newfoundland, but the fish about it, as also throwout the Grande Bay within Cape Briton, is much larger and better then that of the Newfoundland. This Island is scant two leagues long, and very narrow. In the midst of it, a great way within the wood is a great poole. Here we were thrise on shore: once at the East side, and twise at the West.

The three Islands of birds are sandy red, but with the multitude of birds upon them they looke white. The birds sit there as thicke as stones lie in the paved street. The greatest of the Islands is about a mile in compasse. The second is a little lesse. The third is a very little one, like a small rocke. At the second of these three lay on the shore in the Sunshine about thirty or forty seaoxen or morses: which when our boat came nere them, presently made into the sea, and swam after the boat.

Brions Island wee found to be very good, and sandy ground. It hath in it store of firre trees. It is somewhat more than a league long, and about three leagues in compasse. Here we were on land once, and went from the one side of it to the other.

The Island of Ramea we tooke to be like ground as Brions Island, having also abundance of firre trees. It seemeth to be in length about twelve or thirteene leagues at least. We were there in harborow, but not on shore, which we much desired, and hoped to have bene; but the conflict which we had there with the Basks and Britons, mentioned before, prevented us.

The Isle Blanche likewise seemeth in quality of the ground and bignesse of it to be much like Brions Island aforesayd, but somewhat lesse. We were not on shore upon it, but rode before it at anker.

The land of Cape Briton we found to be somewhat like the Newfoundland but rather better. Here towards the West end of it we saw the clouds lie lower then the hils: as we did also at Cape Laurence in Newfoundland. The Easterly end of the land of Cape Briton is nothing so high land, as in the West. We went on shore upon it in five places: 1 At the bay where the Chancewell was cast away: 2 At Cibo: 3 At a little Island betweene Cibo and the New port: 4 At the New port: And 5 at Port Ingles, or the English port.

Concerning the nature and fruitfulnesse of Brions Island, Isle Blanche, and of Ramea, they do by nature yeeld exceeding plenty of wood, great store of wild corne like barley, strawberries, gooseberries, mulberies, white roses, and store of wilde peason. Also about the sayd Islands the sea yeeldeth great abundance of fish of divers sorts. And the sayd Islands also seeme to proffer, through the labour of man, plenty of all kinde of our graine, of roots, of hempe, and other necessary commodities.

Charles Leigh.

567. 1603. George Johnson, *A discourse of some troubles... in the banished English church at Amsterdam.*

Hereupon all things were ended, peace and agreement againe made, the seal of the covenant the next Lordes day (so far as I remember) administered : much joy was there among the brethren, and at the Pastors house was there a meeting of many, as at a love feast : in which (as afterward appeared) Master Studly was a spott and blot, keeping writing in secret against George Johnson and laying waite to catch him : Yet the Brothers continued frendship : things seamed to be not onely forgiven, but presently forgotten : so as (being banished, sent to America, and staied by contrary windes at Famouth) the Pastor stoode very fast and faithfull to his brother being likely (thorow the envy of a Master of one of the Ships, and some of the Meriners) to come into trouble about our printed confession of faith, which he there had, and lent to one of them : also when they came into newfound Land, one of the Captaines reviling George Johnson behinde his back about the same matter, the Pastor defended him, and openly rebuked the Captaine, as was to George Johnson afterward signified : yea George Johnson suffering Shipwrack, the ship being thorow the headines of the Master in a faire sunne shine day run upon the Rocks, whereby the Captaine and all the rest had great losse (the Frenchmen thereby making a pray of all their goods, which they could wel have saved, having gott the Ship from among the Rocks, and with much labour and paines running her a shore) by which losse they came to be in great distresse, specially the two banished, John Clarke, and George Johnson to whom the Captaine propounded that they must either leave them their, and so they should be subject to be devoured by the wilde : deliver them to the French men to be brought for France, and by them their, and so they should be subject to be masse : or they must adventure with them in shallops, wherein they would go, and seeke purchase, if they could finde a leager, or Spanyard : three hard choices: none whereof John Clarke and George Johnson would chuse, telling the Captaine they would not have theire owne hands in choosing, but which he would lay upon them, that by Gods help they would undergoe, hoping he would worke al for good : at which answer the Captaine was trobled, being unwilling to lay any one upon us. At length continuing in that wilde place three or foure daies while they prepared their shallops, and made redy so wel as they could to take purchase, Gods providence, who never faileth, no not in the mountaine or wildernes, shewed it selfe : for the Captaine walking with George Johnson and conferring of these things, suddenly (being quick sighted) he saw a ship far of in the sea, and said I see a shipp, to whom George Johnson said, it may be the Lord wil send us help thereby, and requested the Captaine to man out a shallop to them, to signify our shipwrack and distresse unto them, and no doubt the Lord would move their hearts to pitie: which presently the Captaine commaunded to be done : and we stil walking under hope, at length one who was very quick eied, discerned it to be an English ship, and put us in hope that it was our fellow, which was bound to make the same jorney with us, which made the marriners to hasten the more with their shallop, who coming to them, finding them to be the ship which was bound with us (wherein were the Pastor and Master Studly the other two banished) and relating to them the distresse wherein we were, Oh what heavines was there among them, specially in the Pastor for his brother, and in that loving man Master Charles Leigh the Captaine thereof, who was not so heavy for the losse (thogh a principal of the ship was his) and he was joyful, that all the men were safe : and presently (by reporte) commanded the Maister to make to the bay, where our distresse was : at whose meeting what teares there were (not for the losse, but) for joy that we so met, specially betwene the brothers, I cannot expresse, yea I cannot now write without teares, remembering such a wonderous providence of God even in a strange land : Which as it is my duetie alwaies to recorde to Gods praise : so here also I recorde it, to shew that not onely natural, but godly love appeared in the Pastor to his brother : he and the Captaine not onely comforting him in respects of the losse, but shewing tokens and fruites of love, helping him with things necessary, the Frenchmen having taking his provision from him : but in all these I observed that Master Studly shewed not so much affection, as many of the mariners did, who had no religion : whereas in a true Christian and brother there ought, and wil be a fellowfeeling.

The said Master Leigh taking al the distressed into the ship, and George Johnson being now in the same ship with the Pastor and Master Studly, there was familiaritie and much frendship betwene the Captaine and the brothers : but Master Studleys countenance was cast downe, yet he would use good wordes to George Johnson complaining of some things hee saw amisse in Master Leigh, who was a brother in the faith with us, and stirred up George Johnson to exhort and ad-

monish him : which he did, being to simple and sleight to marke Master Studlys crafty practise, who hereby wroght occasion of mislike betwene us, and at length set the one against the other, who before had lone bene deare frends : for if Master Studly had dealt uprightly, he ought not to have opened the infirmities of Master Leigh a brother unto an other, but have himself admonished him : yet this he did not, and so was the cause of contention : and here let brethren be exhorted to take heede of such crafty pates, who under a shew of godlines exhort others to performe the duety of godly admonition, and wil not do it themselves. At length this Master Studly shewed himselfe in his colours : for having sowen sundry occasions, and wroght some dislike (one day there being some wordes betwene Master Leigh and George Johnson) he propounded the matter about Jeremiah 3. 3. drawing the Pastor and Master Leigh to deal with George Johnson about it : the pastor was not very willing to deal thereabout, ye Master Studly so dealt as George Johnson must shew his judgment thereabout, which he did, namely, that seeing the offenders offended in like nature, to wit, not to confes offence, but on the contrary boasted righteousnes : the same scripture might be alledged against the one as against the other. Which also the scriptures shew. Master Studly fel to his olde maner of cavilling about apparel, and now and then would stir up the Paster now and then Master Leigh to shew their judgment : George Johnson shewed them that if it were in a strange land as in newfoundland land etc. the apparel should not troble him, neither put he religion in apparel : but there being offences given by apparel, Christians though no certeine rule or fashions could be directly prescribed, yet ought to observe modestie according to the places wherein they live : that so the least occasion of offence might not be given by them to any within, or without : the Pastor for this time brake of the matter, seeming not very willing to talke thereof : and in my conscience I think the brothers had continued goode frens, if Master Studly had not alwaies raised contentions betweene them. Shortly after he stirred up the coles againe, and laid more wood on, so as very hoate wordes passed betwene the brothers, and he lying in his cabbing would now and then put forth his head, the minister questions and matter to the Pastor, which he urged his brother withal : Which George Johnson marking, and calling to minde Master Studlys seeking occasions to deal hereabout, tolde him, that he dealt very evilly, and should rather seeke to hold, then breake the peace : then begun he to call George Johnson contentious etc : who seeing him so to lie in his cabbing, sometimes putting out his head, and speaking bitterly, straight waies pulling it in againe, he tolde him he dealt like barking dogs who thogh they can not bite as they would, yet barke running in and out of the house, and stirr up other to vex the pore travelling man which would passe on his way in peace : with this reproof his mouth was stopped, so as for that time he plucked in his head, and saide no more, and his mouth being stopped the Pastor presently ceased contending. The Apostle exhorteth us to take hede of dogs : that is (as I take it) men of doggish nature, who barke against, bite and would devour the godly, if they could : Which dogs God will judg. Though for this time his mouth was stopped, yet his envious nature not changing, and that which was bread in the bone shewing itself in the flesh, when we drew nere to England, he pretending that George Johnson would be bolde in going abrode stirred up Master Leigh to make George Johnson promise, that when he came to London, he should tary in the house, and no go to any place without consent of the Pastor and Master Studly or else to keepe him on ship boorde. George Johnson answered them, that they had no such authority to make him so to promise : that he ought not to abridge himselfe of his owne liberty and for his part he would by Gods helpe be so carefull of his liberty as they, but would make no such promise to go but where they pleased : Master Studly begun to persuade Captaine Leigh, then to keepe him per force on ship borde : to whom George Johnson said : the Captaine hath no such authority over me, neither can he do it, yea (quoth George Johnson) Master Leigh you know that thogh they had promised to go with you, so they might have liberty, yet I never promised you, neither would receive liberty upon such a condition : and yet when you had got my liberty, and I was free to go, or stay, as I saw good, then I promised that I would go with you, and so I have : yea you confessed in Newfound Land that I had performed my promise, and you there freed me : all which the Captaine confessed to be true : yet said Master Studly if I had your authority, I would keepe him in the ship : George Johnson answered I would then write ashore, and it may be you would wish that you had not dealt so violently with me : wel said Master Studly I would lock you up in the holde, where you would have no light : so (quoth George Johnson) might the Captaine beshrew himselfe by oppressing of me : and I see if you Master Studly you had power you would be as tirannical (if not worse) as the Prelates, but I hope God wil give courage against your malice, and the Captaine wil be wiser, then to follow your counsel, as in deede he was : for he used George Johnson kindely, suffering him, and dealing frindly for him a shore, as he did for them : the Lord recompense it into his bosome.

The Pastor herein spake litel, and when he did, it seamed to be by Master Studlys motion. Riding together to London from Southampton, Master Studly visited his friends who dwelt neere the way, but they would not be content that George Johnson should speak to his frends, though they rode thorow the townes, and by the doores, where some of them dwelt : which he put up at their hands, yet sory and greeved to see such partiall dealing. Being come to London, and every one in several lodgings for the more safety, that if one came in troble, yet the other might escape : after a day or two, they sent Master Bishop to George Johnson to certify him that it was knowen they were in the citie, and that he must provide to go forth to Gravesends tilt boate : where Master Studly would mete him, and go with him : George Johnson trusting the messenger (who was his sisters husband) tolde him he would make redy, and desired him to lend him some money, for he had but 6. pence with some few halpentes left he promised, that mony should be sent to him to Gravesend : so they parted, and he made redy to go to the boate, where (when he came) he found not Master Studly yet he went on his journey, not doubting, but Master Studly would be there also with the next boate : being come to Graves end, he waited one day, they came not : the send day, they came not : then George Johnson begun to suspect that they dealt craftely with him. by such a devise to gett him to go out of the city, and was much greeved, that his sisters husband should so use him, he having told him how litel mony he had, and not to keepe promise with him, so as even there he had beene driven to some exigent, had not the Lord by his providence in the way given him to meete with a kinsman, of whom he borroed 10.s. The third or fourth day they came, and divers frends with them : George Johnson asking Master Studly why he met him not, and asking them how they thoght he lived, they knowing that 6. pence was to be paied for his passage they put it of, and said they knew George Johnson might have gone to a brothers house (who dwelled within 3. or 4. miles) and there needed not to spend, he asking them how he should have knowne when they came, they said they would have sent for him he tolde them, that though they disappointed him, yet God provided for him having borowed some mony, and so thinking of there dealing more then he spake, perceived there practice to be as before he suspected, but passed it over, they taking ship together the next day to come for Amsterdam.

568. November 7, 1597. Deposition of Francisco de Cazanova.

P.R.O., HCA 13/91.

Franceso de Casaneava of St Sebastians in Biscaia mariner and late boateswaine of a shipp called the Catalina of Orio nere St Sebastians in Bisky and xxxvj yeares or thereaboutes sworne and examined in her maiestes high Courte of the Admiralty by interpretation of Frances Marquino speakinge the spanishe language sworne truly to interpret towchinge the takinge & property of the said shippe & her ladinge Sayth by charge of his oathe that the said ship the Catalina is of the porte of Orio in Spaine nere St Sebastians and of the portadge and burthen of Cxx tonnes or thereaboutes and belongeth to Petro de Chavis and Joseph de Chavys two brothers dwelling in Orio beinge Spaniardes, and was sett to sea in Aprill last manned with xxxiiij men all Spaniardes savinge the pilott & one other to make a viage to the Neue found lande on fisshinge [fare], and accordinge to theire direction the said ship sayled to the Bay of St Lawrence in Neue found lande, and there made one hundreth and twenty thowsand of fishe & xxxvj hosheades of trayne, whereof twenty thousand of the said fish was

broughte on borde the said shippe the Catalina and after the ladinge of the same, all the reste beinge ashore, there arived an english shippe in the said harbor called the hope whereof Charles Leighe was Captaine and William Craston Master, who in the nighte tyme layde the said spanishe shipp on borde & tooke her, and were in quiett possession of the same aboute fyve howers space, and then foure French shippes whereof one was of Rochell of CCC tonnes, manned with men of St John de Luze & the other thre being of St John de Luze, and fisshinge in the said bay after they harde that Englishemen had taken the said Spanishe shipp they manned out there boattes & thereaboutes tooke Captaine Craston as he was goinge to his shipp with six or viij of the company of the said spanish shippe, and caried them backe to the said spanishe shipp the Catalina, and comminge thither the Englishe men whom the Captaine had lefte on borde would not suffer them to come into the shippe and thereuppon the french men threatned to kill the said Craston if he caused not his men to yelde upp the shipp to them, and by reason of those threates the Captaine commaunded them to redeliver the shipp & soe by that meanes the shipp was reskued by the said Frenche men from the Englishe men & restored to the Spaniardes : And this he knoweth to be true for that he was boatswaine of the said Spanish shippe and presente in her when she was taken by the said englishe men & afterwardes reskued from them by the said frenche men of St John de Luze as is before said, and the nexte day after, this examinate was with others taken againe by the said Englishe men as he came from the shore in a boate with brame and was broughte into Englande. And sayeth that the said shipp the Catalina was wholy victualed & sett out for the said viadge by the said owners, & one of them victualed the one haulf & Martyn de Gomez of St Sebastians beinge Captaine of the said shipp victualed the other haulf of his certaine knowledge. Affirminge that the said shipp was made thre yeares past at Oreo, and there accompted worth two thousand duckettes without her tacle furniture and ordinaunce, and at the tyme of the takinge of the said shipp by the said Englishe men the said shipp with her tacle furniture ordinaunce fishe & traine on borde & on shore ready to be laden was worth vj thowsand viij^c Duckettes & soe esteemed by the Captaine master & company.

And sayth that if the french men had not reskued the said shipp from the Englishe men, the same englishe men might have laden all the fishe on shore beinge one C thowsand and xxxvj hogsheades of traine / for that yt was all made, & ready to be laden at that instante /

And sayth he knoweth not eany of the names of the Frenche men whoe reskued the said shipp from the Englishe Savinge that the Captaine of the said shippe of Rochell was called Mattelyne and is of Rochell and the reason why the frenche men ayded the Spaniardes in the said reskue is as he thinketh because they of Sᵗ John de Luze are neighbors of them of Sᵗ Sebastians & trade one with the other and, at the comminge of the Catalina into the said Bay to fishe the Captaine thereof wente on borde the said frenche shippes & intreated theire ayde against Englishe men if eany offered him & his company wronge duringe there fishinge, & the French men promised him all favor, & that they would stand by him & his company come life or death /

Beinge asked whether he knoweth Martin de Baro, S John de Vyce and Rodrigo de Fernandes sayeth he knoweth them well / & that they are Spaniardes & were of the company of the said shipp the Catalina and were taken by the said Englishe men in the boate togeather with this examinate, and after they were broughte into the englishe shipps they were examined by master Charles Leighe and did depose in such maner as ys conteyned in theire examinations under these handes shewed to him at the tyme of his examination For this examinate harde them examined & sawe them firme to the same / Which he affirmeth to be most true

> [Signed:] Francisco Marquino [interpreter].
> The marcke of Francisco de Cazanova [a triangle inside a triangle, making a regular hexagon.]

569. October 4, 1597. Charles Leigh's final plan for the English occupation of the Magdalen Islands.

Leigh's original is British Library, Additional MS 12505, fols. 447–478v. It was first printed in John D. Rogers, The Historical Geography of Newfoundland *(Oxford, 1911), pp. 249–250; and again in Robert Le Blant and René Baudry, etc.,* Nouveaux documents sur Champlain et son époque, *I (Ottawa, 1967), 22–23.*

A Briefe platforme For A voyadge with three shipes vnto the Iland of Ramea in Canada where I purpose god willinge to leave Inhabitauntes (accordinge to my intente the laste yeare) which shall keepe the Ilande to hir maiesties vse, as allso Forbid the Frenchmen from the trade of Fisshinge in that place, who this laste yeare by force (as havinge firste possession of this harboroughes) did expell my selfe & others her highnes subiectes From the said Iland./

The Iland of Ramea is About 16. leagues in length scituated within the Bay of Cannada & lyeth From the south lyne but 47. degrees or lesse yeat is yt much colder then in England. The soyle is sandy & seemeth exceedinge good for tylladge, yt yealdeath naturally wild corne lyke barly, allso peasse, strawberries, goosberies, Mulberies, & wild roses./ of wood there is overmuch plenty the moste parte wherof ar Firr trees & Birche, within the land there runneth which I did not see on [one] faire ryver of Freshe water, replenyshed as I was informed with severall sortes of Freshwater fisshe, About this said Iland there is Abonndaunte plenty of Codd, And for the refudge of shipes two good harbours, on[e] wherof may be Strongly Fortefied with few men, by meanes of A very smale Iland which lyeth in the mouth therof, vpon which 20. men beinge entrenched they may without daunger defend them selves from .500. And lykewyse with ordinaunce And muskettes from their Forte maye easily Command the whole harborough./ In the other harbour about .3. leagues in distaunce from the Former, I know not what meanes of Fortification there is, And therefore purposse (for the more securytie yf god permytt with the helpe of my Friendes who have promysed the furtheraunce hereof) to send thither three good shipes well Furnyshed, to be there yf possible .30. daies before any Frenchmen use to come, & to fortefie this other harborough allso both by sea and land as we shall see most meete, whiche don such as ar apoynted to remayne in the contrie shall presently betake them selves to tilledge plantinge, & buyldinge, And the rest to be imployed in fisshinge, For the speedy ladinge & retorne of the shipes./

Now wheras the fishinge in this Iland is allwayes sooner ended by 40. or 50. dayes then in other places, by which meanes the shipes in re-torninge may with smale preiudice, and lyttle losse of tyme view all the harboroughes Alonge the coaste of cape Brytton And so from thence in the south part of Newfoundland, where yf so yt stand withe her highnes pleasure, And the good lykinge all so of the lordes of the Counsell, very sufficiente service (thorough god his providence) may be performed, against such shipes of Bayon, St Jn⁰ [John] de Lus, And Ciborrow in Fraunce (which are aparanntly knowne every yeare from those partes to serve the Kinge of Spaigne with Fishe,) to the great prejudice of the Kinge of Spaigne who were not able to maynteine his shipes at sea yf he were not supported by theise fishermen./

Further as towchinge the inhabytinge in the said Iland and the countries thereaboutes in few yeares yt may be effected to the peaceable con-tinuaunce of the inhabitanntes, only by the keepinge the Commaund of the Chieffeste har-bours in those countries, by which meanes all other nations wilbe discoraged in shorte tyme & wholly worne out of that trade, then shall the Inhabitauntes without resistaunce enioy all the fishinge in the Bay which is as yeat An unknowne benefitt, as allso have the whole trade of all the inland Countries only in their owne handes./ by this meanes her maiesties revenues & dominions may in shorte tyme be greatly enlarged to her endles honor in all posteryties which the lord of heaven graunte yf yt be his will./
London. this 4th of October / 1597

[Signed:] by me Charles Leigh

[*Endorsed:*] 4 Octobris 1597
A platforme of one Charles Leigh of a Voyage intended with 3 shippes to the Island of Ramea within the baye of Canada, for fishing & inhabita-tion,
Against the French./

570.   1597–1598. Proceedings regarding an-other Brownist.

It might appear from the following documents that the sending of Brownists to the Magdalen Islands or some other part of North America was still being considered late in 1597 and early in 1598. Thomas Elmes, Elme, Nelme, or Nelmes was a prominent nonconforming Brownist. The entries are from Acts of the Privy Council 1597–1598 *(1904), pp. 153, 256.*

[a] 25 November 1597. A lettre to the Lord Anderson, Requiring his Lordship that whereas about Marche last order was taken for the banishment of Certaine Brownistes out of the Realme intendinge a voyage to the bay of Canyda, and amongst others one Thomas Nelme being a principal; of that sect was then at see by that meanes omitted: He would takes bondes of him to her Maiestes use to depart the Realme & not to retorne agayne, and thereupon to sett him at liberty Remayning in Newgate.

[b] 22 January 1598. A lettre to the Recorder & Sherifes of London. Whereas wee understand that one Thomas Nelmes a condempned prisoner in Newgate for publishing sedicious bookes, is like shortlie to be put to execution according to the sentence of iustice giuen against him (the said Nelmes being of the profession of the Brownistes:) These are to let yoʷ understand that wee have thought meete for somme speciall consideracions that the said Nelmes shalbe reprived untill the next Sessions for Newgate. And do therefore pray and require yoʷ to take order that he may be so reprived as is aforesaid and forborne from execucion: to th'end that his offence being farther considered of, it may be by humble suite pre-sented unto her Majestie either to have pardon by her mercie, or to receave Justice. And so &c /.

[c] 24 January 1598. A Lettre to yᵉ Lord chiefe Justice of the Common Pleas. Requiring him to cause stay of Execution to be made of one Thomas Nelmes a condempned prisoner in Newgate (for publishing a lewd & seditious booke) & to take order for the repriving of him untyll farther order & direction shold be given from their Lordship-pes.

XVI

The Newfoundland Trades: Cod-fishing and Whaling, 1514–1613

Mᴜᴄʜ ʀᴇᴍᴀɪɴꜱ to be written about the growth and development of the Newfoundland codfishery and the Labrador whaling industry which will pull together the business practices and experiences of western Europeans in this important sphere of European activity in the sixteenth century. Harold A. Innis, *The Cod Fisheries* (New Haven, 1940), memorably sketched it in fifty pages. Charles de la Morandière, *Histoire de la pêche française de la morue dans l'Amérique*, 3 vols. (Paris, 1962–1967), told all about how codfishing was done, but his specific references to the sixteenth century alone cannot cover more than a twentieth of his vast book. Jacques Bernard's chapter, "Les premiers armements pour Terre-Neuve," in his *Navires et gens de mer a Bordeaux*, 3 vols. (Paris, 1968), II, 805–826, indicates precisely what can be done with the records for a single port when they both survive and are analyzed effectively, but his chapter ends with 1550. Gillian T. Cell, *English Enterprise in Newfoundland, 1577–1660* (Toronto, 1969), is the type of monograph needed for so many other periods and areas, but her concern with the sixteenth century begins late and does not cover more than fifty pages of the volume. Selma Barkham's calendars in the Public Archives of Canada and her own pioneer work on the Basque whaling and codfishery indicate the vast store of business information and local history which is locked up in Spanish notarial archives and which Spaniards themselves have been slow to publish. Nor have the Portuguese done anything to reveal how their fishing industry worked.

A general documentary selection must therefore be both limited and eclectic. It can attempt to give some idea of the types of organizations as well as the documentary ramifications that the industries produced, but it can only whet an appetite which might too easily be sated by a diet of charter parties and insurance policies in bulk. Materials including charters, voyages, and the political implications of the fisheries have appeared, or will appear, elsewhere and also something of the connections between fishing and fur trading, though the latter is not as easy to document from the business aspect.

There was little that was really novel about the business framework into which the fisheries fitted. The western European economy may have been far from integrated, but the methods of its seamen and merchants were reasonably homogeneous, and there was a high degree of cooperation between the various specialists in particular ports and areas, and a measure of international cooperation and association in the fitting-out stages and at the marketing end as well. Shipbuilders, seamen (from captain or master down to ship's boy), victualers, repairers, shipowners, ship investors, victualing investors, money investors, insurers, wholesale fish merchants, secondary fish merchants, retailers of fish, and ultimately consumers made up the same hierarchy in the codfishing and whaling industries as in a number of others. But fishing was a universal occupation for the littoral peoples of western Europe and was engaged in more widely than any other single occupation except growing grain. It therefore ranged in its alignments from the supremely local to the most broadly international. It often had political connotations and therefore was affected by state policy, rivalries, and wars, as well as the endemic piracy and the more or less licensed privateering which affected all European waters and, by the mid-sixteenth century, American littoral waters as well.

Transatlantic fisheries were to some extent specialized in their nature. It remained possible throughout the period for a shipmaster to own his own ship, victual her, and reward her crew without dependence on others, but it must always have been exceptional for him to have done so, and even if a single man could do this, he would have to get others to complete the marketing and distribution for him as he would not be there to do it himself. A ship might have a single owner and a number of Newfoundlanders did so. On the other hand a shipowner might have sole ownership of a large number of Newfoundlanders—the Ango family is believed to have given the Normans a fast start in the Newfoundland trade because they owned the ships with which to do it. But more generally a ship was held in shares (as many as sixty-four in England was not unusual), the master owning some, perhaps a few members of crew others, but most were held by merchants, shipowners, other shipmasters (spreading their risks), professional men such as doctors and lawyers, and even corporate owners like monasteries. The *armateur* in France often owned a substantial share in at least one ship, but he very often spread the risks by getting the victualing done on shares with others (again with the shipmaster sometimes having a stake in the victualing). Generally, in Spain the *armador* seems to have involved himself in either total or shared victualing rather than shipowning. In England it seems that the shipmaster often arranged money for the victualing with London or Bristol merchants or wherever he might be sailing from (usually some small West Country port), and would pay them some 35 percent for what they lent him (the payment often to be made in fish); the "money men," in turn, borrowed from others at 10 percent to enable them to make up their investment. How far this was general or exceptional is not known.

What about the proceeds in general? The usual old procedure over much of western Europe was for operation in shares in thirds, one-third of the proceeds going to the ship (and her owners), one-third to the victualers, and one-third to the master and crew in regularly contracted shares of this one-third. Wages were paid only in exceptional circumstances, although there were probably many cases where advances in the form of wages were paid before the ship sailed and were then recouped from shares at the end of the voyages. Gradually over the century, insurers developed their own tariffs for the rather high-risk Newfoundland and Labrador runs. Often the preparation of a fishing or whaling expedition was done within a very tiny locality, but just as often it was not. Because they had extensive hinterland trades, the Bay of Biscay, Bayonne, and Bordeaux attracted vessels from ports ranging from Brittany to the Spanish Basque country which came there for their victuals and other stores. Later La Rochelle gained a virtual monopoly of the victualing trade in this area though she lost it later. Usually seamen came from a small local area, but ports like London, Le Hâvre, and La Rochelle had very mixed populations of seamen and there was a good deal of regional and even national intermixture among the men. Most of the seamen who emerge in late-sixteenth-century English Newfoundlanders tend to be Thames-siders by residence, even if they were born in the West Country. Portuguese and Bretons made the best pilots; Spanish Basques, uniquely, made the best harpooners, and there were probably other regional specialists also. But how far the seamen who sailed across the Atlantic needed to be specialists is questionable for many if not most of them. Line fishing both on the banks and inshore was tedious and active work, but it did not involve much in the way of specialized training, only experience of local conditions on foggy seas (as on the banks) and rocky bays (as in the inshore fishing) when cod was being caught. Skillful boat work and the techniques of handling sails and rigging were an integral part of the training of seamen at that time. It is difficult to determine how firmly the majority stuck to the fishing trade or moved from one branch of the shipping industry to another. On the whaling side the harpooners were specialists of a very high order, but the boat work in whaling (since whales were caught from shallops and "galions" not from ships) was also highly specialized and demanded an exceptional degree of experience.

The distinguishing characteristics of the employment offered by these American branches of the European fishing industry were mainly in the shore work involved. Splitting, gutting, and heading fish, laying them in the hold if they were salt fish, with just enough salt and a certain amount of water, demanded teamwork rather than seamanship; in the dry fishery there was a good deal of construction work on shore of stages, "flakes," and cookhouses, demanding carpentering skills. The business of salting, turning, and stacking the drying fish was simply laborer's work requiring no skill (later the men brought out to do this were known as "green men"). Others were employed in rendering cod livers for oil ("train oil" was any kind of fish or marine mammal oil, though most usually from cod).

In the whaling industry there was still more shore work. The whales were towed to shore bases in suitable harbors, flensed, and all the usable parts removed, hard bone, whalebone, spermaceti, blubber—the last being the main objective of the industry. On land the blubber had to be rendered down in great brick-based furnaces, which carried heavy metal cauldrons (the Spanish Basques called these constructions "hornos," which is usually translated "ovens" and which is hardly correctly descriptive of their function). Thereafter the oil was purified by allowing it to remain in barrels until it settled. After settling it was poured into other barrels, and this chain process was maintained until the oil was relatively clear (or at least this process was done later when we have fuller descriptions of the process). Because much of their work was done on shore, whalers needed camps and there is some information on the substantial sheds used by them on Northeast Greenland in the 1620s and 1630s. Whalers were the aristocrats of the fisheries and the Spanish Basques rigorously defended their bays and camps along the north shore of the Strait of Belle Isle against intruders.

The inshore codfishers liked to come to the same bay each year, at least to start the season, because they could then take over and repair their installations. However, they could not be sure they would find their places unused when they arrived. What they had to leave behind, in particular, were boats. Newfoundlanders—the term normally used of codfishing vessels as distinct from whalers—were usually too small to carry enough boats to employ their men fully, therefore the codfishers tended to leave boats behind, carefully marked and secured, for the next season. If Indians stole or damaged them, little could be done about it, but if other fishermen touched the boats, quarrels resulted. Indeed, inshore, when fishermen of up to four nationalities came to a single port (as they did to St. John's Harbour), the possibilities for strife, sometimes taken to the full, were endless. The institution of the port admiral, a senior shipmaster, either the first to arrive or one who took the post by some local custom, was developed so that he acted as arbitrator in as many quarrels as he could and, in a large port, he appears to have been assisted by a group of other shipmasters, who acted as assessors. In the great centers such as St. John's and Placentia, much intertrading was done between the ships, the English especially trading their salt from Portuguese or whoever else brought a surplus. And before the end of the sixteenth century "sack ships" were making an appearance, sent out to buy cargoes of fish and not to catch them, so that the trading element in the harbors was steadily growing.

When ships turned homeward with a cargo of fish or oil, or both, they usually came back to their home port, but they might not do so, and might well be instructed to go to another port in their own country (as Spanish Basque ships went down to Cadiz to supply the ships of the Indies fleets), or to a port in another country whose merchants had arranged for a cargo to go to them, or merely to go on chance to a foreign port because trade information stated that markets were good there. English ships began, it is not known when precisely, engaging in a triangular trade, to Cadiz with their fish, then lading Spanish produce and bringing it back to England; when war stopped this they might bring it to the Mediterranean (when they were said to be bound for the Straits), to Toulon, Marseilles, or to an Italian port like Leghorn, and carry from there a local cargo back to England. Or else ships from several countries might arrive at a port known to have a good Newfoundland fleet, like Plymouth at the end of the century, and await the return of the ships so as to buy their cargoes. Once fish, or whale oil, had been sold in bulk it found its way into the normal internal distribution channels of the particular country.

Lawyers and courts are also important in the study of the fishing trades. Notaries made and recorded the thousands of documents which are gradually emerging and which throw light on almost all aspects of the business side of these industries. Other legal specialists were involved in varied aspects of the contracting and insuring side. Many cases of disputes about money and ships found their way into the civil courts and might be found almost anywhere in the multifarious legal records of most western countries. After the middle of the century at least, most civil cases in England involving the industry were adjudicated by the High Court of Admiralty in London or perhaps by local admiralty courts. In England most of the evidence (where there are no notarial records for this period) comes from this source. But, with the help of several people, Mr. John Roberts and Professor Gillian T. Cell among them, it has proved possible to assemble from local and other sources a reasonable sample of English business documents, mainly for the later part of the period. The provincial admiralty courts in France had also cognizance of this type of case though much of this evidence has been destroyed or scattered. Legal records are in themselves often dull and do not make for lively reading, even though examinations in the High Court of Admiralty provide some racy narrative passages. In Spain, if there was a political angle or if an incident impinged on the working of the trade or navigation of the Indies, there might be lengthy inquiries and interminable depositions in which detail was accumulated in tiresome but often illuminating ways. But straightforward descriptive accounts of exactly how things were done are hard to uncover.

The material in this section is inevitably somewhat eclectic and uneven in its coverage, but it will illustrate a number of the points which have been mentioned. The rest must depend rather on the quantitative research, still largely in the future, of the economic historians. Yet cod and whale in themselves provided the main justification for western European interest in North American waters for over a century. Selma Barkham and the Public Archives of Canada have made it possible to provide some important samples of the manuscript riches of the Basque country archives, especially those in the Archivo Histórico de Protocolos de Guipúzcoa at Oñate. Although a few French examples are in print and have been used, the great mass of material in the notarial registers for the ports for which they survive remains in manuscript. Almost nothing appears to be in print from Portuguese sources for this period.

Chapter Seventy-two
Beginnings, 1514–1559

571. December 14, 1514. Attempt to levy tithes on Breton fishermen operating at Newfoundland.

The monks of the Abbey of Beauport attempted to oblige the fishermen of the Île de Bréhat (Brittany) to pay a tithe on every fish caught in Newfoundland and elsewhere. This case was adjudicated in the courts and the men of Bréhat agreed to pay an annual sum instead of the levy.

Archives départmentales, Côtes-du-Nord, fonds de l'abbaye de Beauport, série H, printed by H. P. Biggar, Precursors of Jacques Cartier (1911), pp. 119–123, extract, translated.

On the action... between the reverend father in God, Jehan, abbot of the Abbey of Our Lady of Beauport and the convent of the same on the one part, and the parishioners, dwellers and inhabitants in the Île de Bréhat on the other part, that the said abbot and convent and each of them had said and proposed or intended to say and propose to the aforesaid inhabitants of the said Île de Bréhat that all and each of the men of the said isle who are above the age of eighteen years and who fish in the sea with rod, nets or other engines to take fish, of whatever sort of fish it is, as well conger eels, cod, hake or other fish, in any part where they may be in Brittany, Newfoundland [*La Terre-Neuffve*], Iceland, as elsewhere, ought to be and are subject to pay and let the said abbey and convent of Beauport their receivers, commissioners and deputies have as a duty the tenth of their fish and fishery....

572. February 18, 1520. Bayonne ship preparing to go to Newfoundland.

The initiative in early voyages to Newfoundland from France appears to have been taken and held by vessels from Normandy and Brittany. The earliest record of a Newfoundlander leaving Bordeaux is 1517 (cited in J. Bernard, Navires et gens de mer à Bordeaux, 3 vols. [Paris, 1908], II, 806), while this document from Bayonne, providing that a ship preparing for Newfoundland should complete her lading at Cape Breton, a port a little farther south, is the earliest document so far known of the activities of French Basques in the fishery.

It was published by H. P. Biggar, Precursors of Jacques Cartier (Ottawa, 1911), pp. 124–125, from Archives Municipales de Bayonne, Délibérations en Gascon du Corps de Ville, série BB. 6, fols. 95–96.

To you, most Honourable Lords, Messrs. the Lieutenant of the Mayor, Sheriffs and Council of Bayonne:

Pes de Le Lande makes humble petition, setting forth that it is his intention, at God's pleasure, to send to Newfoundland [Terre Nave] his ship called the *Senct Pe* [*St. Peter*], which is already partly loaded in the said city, and he would be willing to load the remainder, if the said vessel could easily pass the channels, but this will not be possible, for the reason that the said vessel draws much water. In consideration of this, the said petitioner begs that of your goodness you will be pleased to grant him permission and licence to be allowed to complete the cargo of the said vessel below Capbreton, without prejudice to the regulations of the said city; and you will do well.

The present request having been read, permission has been granted to the said petitioner to be allowed to complete his cargo below Capbreton, and this by special favour, without prejudice to the regulations and edict of the king, our lord. Given in council, 18 February, 1519 [=1520].

573. March, 1521. Provisioning a Bayonne ship for Newfoundland.

Some details of procedures in equipping a vessel for a voyage from Bayonne to Newfoundland in 1521 emerge.

Documents of March 6 and March 31 printed by H. P. Biggar, Precursors of Jacques Cartier (1911), pp. 125–126, 132–133, from Archives Municipales de Bayonne, série BB.6, fols. 189, 191–192.

[a] To My Lord the Lieutenant of My Lord the Mayor, Sheriffs and Notable Council of Bayonne:

Messrs. Michael de Segure and Matthew de Biran make humble petition, setting forth that they have decided, at God's pleasure, to send their vessel as far as Newfoundland to fish, and they need a large quantity of provisions, and among other things the number and quantity of forty butts of cider, of the best that can be found. And this being so, that the said de Segure has an orchard on his farm at St. Stephen, which is worked at his expense and from this he has a certain amount of cider; and also the said de Biran has certain debts at Seinhanx, for which he is willing to take payment in cider. In consideration of this, the said petitioners beg, supplicate and ask that you will be pleased to grant them permission, by special favour and without prejudice to the regulations of the said city, to load on board the said vessel forty butts of outside cider, part from the farm of the said de Segure and the surplus from Seinhanx, for the provision and victualling of the said vessel; and you will be doing well.

[Signed:] M. de Biran.

The present request having been read and considered here in council, it has been ordered that the said petitioners, after they have taken oath before My Lord the Lieutenant, shall be allowed and permitted to load cider in their said vessel for the provisioning of the same, half the amount necessary thereto being grown in the city, and the other half being that belonging to the said petitioners. And this by special favour, in consideration of the voyage the said vessel is to make, and without prejudice to the regulations of the

city making mention of wines and ciders, and to other restrictions and edict of the king, our lord, relating to the ports, loading and unloading. And should they be found doing the contrary, they will incur a fine of one hundred livres tournois, to be applied to the affairs of the city. Given in council, 6 March, 1520[=1521].

[Signed:] Daymar.

[b] To You, Most Honourable Lords, Messrs. the Lieutenant, Sheriffs and Council of the city of Bayonne:

Messrs. Pes de Le Lande and Matthew de Biran, merchants of the said city, humbly set forth, how at present their vessel, called *Le Marie*, has arrived within the Bocau, loaded with red lead, and on account of the great currents, it is not possible to bring her up to unload her in the said city; and as they have now decided to send the said vessel to Newfoundland [*Terre Nave*], since the weather is favourable for making the said voyage; and if they do not do so at once, the said voyage will be lost for this year: likewise the sailors boast they will leave them, if the said voyage is not promptly begun, to which end they have made several Shallops [*galions*] and other supplies; wherefore they beg and humbly petition you, my Lords aforesaid, that, taking the above into consideration, you will be pleased of your kind favour to grant them permission and licence to unload at the said Bocau or higher up, where it shall be quickly done, and to bring the said red lead in barges here to this said city, in order to set off on the said voyage; for otherwise if the said permission be not given them, they will miss the said voyage, which will be a very great loss to them; and this you will be pleased to prevent. And in so doing you will put the said petitioners under obligation to serve the said city wherever possible.

The present request having been read, and here in council considered, permission and licence have been given to the said petitioners to unload the said red lead at the said Bocau or higher up, in order to bring it in barges here to this city, according to their request; and this by special favour, on payment of the accustomed dues, without prejudice to the regulations of the said city and edict of the king, our lord. Given in council, the last day of March 1520. [=1521].

574. August 21, 1523. Claim regarding the victualing of a Le Croisic Newfoundlander at La Rochelle.

Archives départmentales de la Charente-Inférieure, La Rochelle, registre, Jacques Hémon, fol. 48, in H. P. Biggar, Precursors of Jacques Cartier, p. 159, now translated.

Jehan le Moyne, in person, makes out a case (the same having nominated as his proctors Jacques Hemé and Thomas Mannoury of Marennes, and each of them for all) in form of a pleading and special procuration to proceed against and receive from Yvon Le Fleuchier, called Piedecerf, master of the ship named *La Marie* of Croisic, the right to the victuals with which the said Le Moyne has provided him, as appears by an obligation passed by Jehan Mosnier this 17th of June last past of all as settled etc. And besides to receive his proportion of cod, oils, gains and profits of the ships which he has assisted to victual to go to the New Land [*Terre Neufve*], and to supply acquittances for it. Made in the presence of Pierre Le Génet, Jehan Quynault and Loys Avrault, clerks, the day and year as below [August 21, 1523].

575. September to October, 1523. French Newfoundlanders from Binic and Pornic, victualed at La Rochelle.

Archives départmentales de Charente-Inférieur, registre Hémon, fols. 68–69, 105v., 118v.; printed in H. P. Biggar, Precursors of Jacques Cartier, pp. 160–162, now translated.

Pierre Jourdain, the younger, merchant and citizen of La Rochelle makes out a case in person (as well in his own behalf as making and carrying equal strength for André Morisson, his *parsonnier* [associate]) and has appointed their procurators general, men honorable, wise etc.... And the said Denibault [the leading procurator] in form of a plea and especially for the said Jourdain for himself and the said Morisson, his said associate, has given authority and power, aid and

agreement to take and receive their right, part and portion of the fish, oils, gains and profits which Michiel Tredieu, master by Gods will of the *La Catherine* of Benic in Brittany and his company, made in the voyages to the New Land [*Terre Neufve*]. With whom the said Jourdain and Morisson were associated, according to the charter-party passed between them by the same notary, which are these presents, the 14th day of April last past. And also to receive from Guillaume Le Gludic, master of *La Marguerite* de Pornix and of all other masters of ships and their companies, then before freighted by the said Jourdain and Morisson to go to the fishing of the New Land, their right and quota of fish, oils, gains and profits, which they have made in their voyages to the New Land, according as they were associated with the said shipmasters according to the charter-parties beforehand made and passed. And also to receive from the said shipmasters and their companies all and each of the cod which they had sold to them before their departure. And also to receive from the said shipmasters all and each of the pieces of artillery, and munitions of war, which the said Jourdain and Morisson lent to the said shipmasters and their companies to defend themselves in their said voyage.

And the said fish, oils, gains and profits, cod and fish sold by the said masters, Jourdain and Morisson, together with the artillery and munitions of war, giving and conceding by the said Thebault, procurator as below, to the said shipmaster and others to whom they pertain good and effective acquittances. And to give effect to this at all times and places Jourdain and Morisson will do, as they can and ought to do, at all times as well when present in their own persons as before jury, judge, etc. Made in La Rochelle in the presence of Jehan Joubert, the said son of the master, and Bastien Roy, clerk, the 15th day of September, the year 1523.

576. October 15, 1523. Division of cod between victualers and seamen where a ship of Blavet was victualed at La Rochelle for Newfoundland.

Archives départmentales, Charente-Inférieure,

registre Hémon, fols. 68v.–69, printed in H. P. Biggar, Precursors of Jacques Cartier, pp. 161–162, now translated.

Jehan Boisseau, merchant and citizen of La Rochelle, appearing personally, the which has constituted as his procurators [blank], Françoys Pingault, his factor, or one of them for all, in form of a pleading and by special authority and power to the said Pingault, to demand, take and receive from Allain Feullagat, master by God's will of the ship called *La Margaritte* of Blavet and his shipmates and seamen and others to whom it appertains, all the right which belongs to the said Boeceau consisting of fish, cod, oils, gain and profit which the said Feullagat and his company have made this present year in their voyage from the New Land [*Terre Neufve*], which the said Boeceau and Jehan Le Moyne, also merchant and citizen of La Rochelle, have freighted out to go to fish at the New Land [*Terre Neufve*] and all according to the partnership in which the aforesaid Feullagat associated the said Boesseau and Le Moyne by their charter-parties passed between them, by the same notary (which are these presents) the 26th day of March last past. Furthermore the said grantor has given authority and power to the said Pingault, his said factor, to receive of the said Feullagat his half of two and three quarter thousands [=2750] of cod of which mention is made in the said charter-party. And also his half of half a thousand [=250] which the said Feullagat promised to sell, as appears by letters passed by the said notary (which are these presents), the last day of March also last past. And further had given power to the said Pingault to cite, assign and appoint with the said Feullagat, Yvon Crever, boatswain of the said ship, and pleaders or one of them according to good and effective form etc. Done in presence of Nycolas Pocheau and Bastien Roy, the 15th day of October in the year 1523.

577. October 22, 1523. Agreement about shares for a Newfoundland voyage.

Archives départmentales, Charente-Inférieure,

La Rochelle, registre Hémon, fol. 118, printed in H. P. Biggar, Precursors of Jacques Cartier, p. 162, now translated.

John Tredian, master by God's will of the *La Marguerite* of Saint Brieux, appears in person, the same having promised Yvon Bonsoul, Estienne Lauret and Gilles Calvan, his shipmates and seamen of the said ship, stipulating and accepting for them and their absent shipmates to keep for them and render their third part of the fish, oils, gains and profits which they have made in their voyage to the New Land [*Terre Neufve*], according to the custom of the sea, to protect for them their rights and profits as if they were there in their proper persons. And to do and accomplish this to the utmost the said party has pledged his goods to do so, etc. Made in La Rochelle, in the presence of Lambert Bardet, Mathurin Marteau and Bastien Roy, the 22nd day of October 1523.

578. February 6, 1527. Victualing a Bayonne ship for Newfoundland.

Translated by H. P. Biggar, Precursors of Jacques Cartier (1911), pp. 162–164, from Archives Municipales de Bayonne, série BB. 6, fols. 641–642.

To You Most Honourable Sirs, Messrs. the Lieutenant, Sheriffs and Council of the city of Bayonne:

Bartholemew de Montauser, citizen of the present city, makes very humble petition, setting forth how he has loaded his ship to go, at God's pleasure, to Newfoundland for fish, and this being so, in order to undertake the said voyage several things are wanting. Among others it is necessary to have twenty-four butts of cider, which the said petitioner possesses at Seinhanxs [Cénac?], and he would like to have them put on board his said vessel if you, Sirs aforesaid, are willing; or even twenty butts, and to take four butts from the present city; and it is not possible for him to take more for the reason that the said petitioner has no money; or if you should wish to force him to do otherwise, the said petitioner would have to procure money on change, which would be to his prejudice and harm. In consideration of which the said supplicant begs, petitions and asks you, Sirs aforesaid, to grant him licence and permission to be allowed to take the said twenty-four butts of cider in the manner aforesaid; and in doing this you will be doing well, and the said petitioner will be under obligation to pray God for your noble estates.

The present request having been read, it has been ordered that the said petitioner [take] two-thirds of his cider from that free from duty, before the ship leaves port, and this done, he shall come before My Lord the Lieutenant who will examine or cause the said cider to be examined: and afterwards the said petitioner will be allowed to load the rest. Done in council the sixth of February one thousand five hundred and twenty-six [=1527].

[Signed:] Daymar, clerk.

579. Between September 23 and December 31, 1533. Obligation of the master of the *Christophe* of Ploumanac'h, going to Newfoundland, to a merchant of La Rochelle.

*Registre Gaschet, fol. 371*v. *(then in private hands), printed in H. P. Biggar,* Precursors of Jacques Cartier, *pp. 181–182, now translated.*

To all those to whom these presents will be known, know that Yvon Raymond, merchant and master of the ship called the *Xpristofle [Christophe]* of Plusmanac has been present and personally makes out a case. Who, of his own good intent and will, has admitted and confessed etc. to owe and to be bound well, justly and loyally to the honorable man, Julien Giraud, merchant and citizen of La Rochelle, at this present, stipulating and accepting the sum of thirty livres tournois. The which sum the said Raymond has confessed to have had and received of the said Giraud before the passing of these presents, and is held and holds to content it, also that he has cognizance and confesses in the presence of the notary as written below this. The said Raymond renounces this in the event of the said money not

having been had, received, nor counted, and with all other manner and exception and deletions whatsoever. And the same said sum of 30 livres tournois the said Giraud has relinquished and relinquishes to them and to the said Raymond toward the bottomry of the first voyage which he is preparing and hopes to make from this town of La Rochelle to the New Lands [*Terres Neufves*] or other place to which he will go, and going and coming in safety into the said Rochelle or other place in its vicinity. And for, after this return made, by the said Raymond to render, release and deliver to the said Giraud at the port and harbor of the said Rochelle or elsewhere for the payment of the said sum of 30 livres tournois, two thousand dressed [dried?] cod, so that he will bring them, provided they are good and saleable. On the condition that all obligations, schedules, and charter-parties which have been made and passed formerly between themselves and by notaries or otherwise remaining will be and remain broken and annulled. Also the said Giraud will be able to give aid against the said Raymond by the original obligation, only as far as to overrule (?) [*rizer*] and to dismiss other creditors. For the said payment, etc.

580. January 29, 1541. Spanish Basque ship chartered to French Basque merchant for the Newfoundland codfishery.

Joanes de Mendiçabal of St. Jean de Luz charters the ship Salvador *from Martin de Artalecu of Fuenterrabia for the Newfoundland codfishery, the former to act as captain, the latter as master, and defining their respective obligations in detail. We owe this document to Selma Barkham.*

Archivo Histórico de Protocolos de Guipúzcoa, Oñate, Partido de San Sebastian (Fuenterrabia), no. 327, fols. 6–7 (of 1541), translated.

Let it be known by this charter party that I, Joanes de Mendiçabal, burgess of San Joan de Lus, declare and recognise in this present letter that I am chartering from you, Master Martin de Artalecu, burgess of Fuentarrabia and inhabitant in the place of the Passage [Pasajes], your caravel called *Salvador* which at present is moored in the port of the Passage and which is of the burden of 100 tons, more or less, for the Terranova fishing; and in order to proceed on the said voyage you, the said Master, have to have your said ship ready and equipped with her sails, anchors and rigging, necessary for the said ship on such a voyage, and with the ship's boat, by the end of the month of February of this present year, and you, the said Master, have to take in the said ship, in your company, the boatswain and the carpenter and two other mariners and a grummet and two boys; and I, the said Joanes de Mendiçabal, the charterer, must take in the said ship, apart from myself, ten mariners, one of whom I shall appoint as steward for the said ship, and another of the mariners that I am to take shall be the pilot, who has to be competent, and to help towards his wages, you, the said Master, shall pay out eight *escudos del sol* from your ship's part, and all the rest that he should have for his wages as pilot the ship's company shall pay, and likewise I, the charterer and Captain, have to give for the said voyage three fishing boats [*galiones*] in good and fit condition with their sails and equipment as is usual and customary.... [Then come several lines that have been half torn, but that clearly refer to the share of the profits the Captain is to receive and to his responsibility towards the outfitting of the ship.]

Moreover, if that should occur which God does not want, and before departing on our voyage a war should break out between the Princes of Spain and of France, in such a case I, the said Captain, shall be obliged to contribute to and pay the cost of the provisioning and supplies that are the quota belonging to the crew and company that I am to provide, and you, the Master, shall pay the quota belonging to the boatswain and carpenter and sailors and grummet and boys, and the costs will be shared by each of us in respect of the number of crew we are each taking; and as to the costs that would arise in such a case over the outfitting, the fourth part, you, the said Master, shall be obliged to pay, and all the rest I, the said Captain, shall be obliged to pay for me and all the companions that are to go in the said ship, and it is understood that the ship does not have to contribute to the furnishing of the victuals but only to the rest of the outfitting; moreover, if peradventure

the fishing should be insufficient to pay the said costs of the outfitting and victuals of the said ship and company, in that case I, the said Captain, shall be obliged to pay all outstanding costs and to keep you and your ship free from indebtedness.... [Then come several more torn lines which go into further detail about the part the crew would have to contribute, and the fact that the Captain has to send the cider and part of the provisions to be put on board the ship.]

And if there is some impediment to the embarkation of the cider on the part of the people from San Sebastian, in that case if I let you know two or three days before that I am sending you the cider as I wish to send it, and you receive notice of this, then in that case you, the said Master, are obliged to unload the cider at your cost and charge; moreover, I, the said Captain, shall be obliged to give you, the said Master, all other provisions that are needed for going from the port of the Passage to La Rochelle, and thus having been given the said provisions by me, the said Captain, for the voyage to La Rochelle, you, the said Master, shall be obliged to leave here for La Rochelle by the end of next February, there being good weather, and after arriving in La Rochelle, I the said Captain, must give and supply for the said voyage all the salt and all the other provisions necessary for the voyage to Tierranova as soon as possible, and thus having taken aboard all the necessary supplies and salt, with the first good weather that God shall give, you, the said Master, shall raise sail and set forth on the said voyage; and of all the catch of fish that God shall give, after counting up the costs, the fourth part shall be for you, the said Master, and after your said ship with the fishing completed returns to the said La Rochelle, or Bordeaux or wherever seems best to us, within 20 days, I, the said Captain must discharge and unload the said ship.... [There are more torn lines here which stipulate that the penalty for any breach of this contract shall be 200 *escudos*, while on the fourth page of the contract there is the usual repetition of the legal formulas which make the contract binding for both parties.]

[...] as surety for which we are executing this charter-party in the presence of Fernand Gomez de Çuloaga, scrivener and notary public of His Majesty and one of the number of this town, who we have asked to draw up this document and authorise it, and those present have been asked to witness it; done and executed in the said town of Fuenterrabia on the 29th day of the month of January, the year of the birth of our Saviour Jesus Christ one thousand five hundred and forty one. . . .

[The torn lines make identification of the witnesses a little difficult; one is Joanes de Azcue, one appears to be Joanicot de Yriarte, and the other's surname is "de Orosco" but his christian name has been torn off. Likewise, only "Min de Artalequ" and the notary's signature remain intact although Joanes de Mendiçabal also signed the document.]

[Signed:] Min de Artalequ Fernand Gomez de Çuloaga

581. December 1, 1547. Contract for the supply of barrels for the Spanish Basque whale fishery in Labrador.

The background to the Spanish Basque whale fishery involved an elaborate business organization in Spain itself. What follows is one of a large number of supply contracts to be found in the notarial archives. We owe this document to Selma Barkham.

Archivo Histórico de Protocolos de Guipúzcoa, Oñate, Partido de Vergara, no. 2574, part i, fols. 18v.–19, translated.

In the town of Motrico, on the first day of December of 1547, in the presence of me, Domingo Ybañes de Laranga, notary of their Majesties and of the number of the said town, and of the undersigned witnesses, appeared present Joan de Aguirre and his brother-in-law, Joan de Andonegui, coopers and burgesses of the said town, and bound themselves with their persons and goods and agreed to make and give to Andres de Armendia, burgess of the said town, 300 new half-pipes fashioned and finished; it should be known: the said Joan de Aguirre, 200, and Joan de Andonegui, 100, the said Andres giving them the necessary staves within the next following ten days, and that the barrels are to be well enough

made to have what oil put into them and are to be watertight and of good workmanship and sufficient hooped with good hoops and osier binding and well covered withal, and that there should be no lack of hoops or anything else, and they should be finished and handed over to the said Andres by the end of the coming month of February under pain of the double with costs and interests and damages payable to the said Andres.

And for the price of the fabrication and the hoops and osiers, let it be known: 80 maravedis of good money, paid as the work progresses, and as part of the down payment the said Joan de Aguirre has received 4 ducats and the said Joan de Andonegui 3 ducats for which they declared themselves content inasmuch as they received them in the presence of me and witnesses in ready cash. The aforesaid barrels are to be for taking to the New Land and for putting whale oil in; and thus agreed, they bound themselves to do good work and sufficiently water tight and newly and well constructed, under the said penalty. Moreover they contracted, both and each of them, to go in person with the said Andres on the said voyage to serve as mariners and in their own trade in the ship with the said Andres without fail, taking in the ship the necessary tools, and for this each of them bind themselves, their persons, goods, furniture and real estate, acquired and to be acquired; and the said Andres agreed to the above and contracted to give to the said workmen the necessary wood on the quay of this town within the said ten days, and to pay them whatever the work amounted to over and above the said ducats that they have already received, thus as the work progressed so he would continue paying them; moreover, he would pay and give to the said Joan de Aguirre and Andonegui individually for the voyage to the New Land and the time spent there and the voyage back, one share each for their persons as is customary plus, on account their trade, for each one of them all that is normally paid to similar coopers on similar ships that have gone from Orio, or San Sebastian, or Guetaria, or Zarauz (which is the place that has taken the most and will take the most this coming summer) in consideration of their trade in which they have to serve, and he will pay them all of this according to the charter-party, not only the shares for their persons but also the extra wages for their trade, and for this he binds himself and his goods, acquired and to be acquired wherever and in whatever place he has them; moreover, the said coopers agreed with the said Andres under the said obligation to go on the said ship and voyage... [here begins part of the common formula for ending such contracts where all the penalties for failure to comply with the stated conditions are reiterated]

... and the said Andres and the said Joan de Aguirre signed this with their names, and the said Joan de Andonegui said that he did not know how to write and asked Lope de Jansoro to sign for him and he signed it; witnesses, the said Lope de Jansoro and Pedro de Ampuero and Joan de Mezta and Joan de Çabala, burgesses of Motrico/ Item that the said Joan de Andonegui shall take his *Ballesta* with him on the said voyage; witnesses, the aforesaid.

[Signed:] Jn de Aguirre Andres de Armendia

By request of the above for witness: Lope de Jansoro

Passed before me: Domingo Ybañes

582. April 22, 1552. Charter party for a ship of La Rochelle victualed at Bordeaux for a voyage to Newfoundland.

Archives départmentales de Gironde, Registre Bigot, 22ᵉ Avril 1552; printed by E. Ducéré, Les corsaires sous l'ancien régime (Bayonne, 1895), pp. 25–26, translated.

The *Saint-Esprit* of Saint-Jean-de-Luz, commanded by the master Augerot Damisquet, and of which the sieurs du Halde and de Chebery were co-owners, negotiate with Simon de Béhère for the victualing of a ship which will be laden for codfishing at Terre-Neuve. Of the proceeds of the voyage the ship will have a quarter, for the rest the victualing will have forty parts and the ship's company thirty-four parts.

The 16th of April Gaucem du Halde borrowed on the ship, in bottomry, divers sums between the gentlemen Mathieu de Belin, J. Delesplan, Marsault Bordes, Jacques de Martin, Ramon de Soubies, and on the 23rd François de Pontcastel. He received the cash in *pistoles, angelots, ducats,* rose nobles, double ducats and current money. The 22nd was the place of account for victualing.

It is laid down that the said du Halde, in order to fit out the ship *Saint-Esprit,* of the burden of 140 tons, for cod fishing at Terre-Neufve, ought to place on her 40 men, each equipped with an arquebus or cross-bow, together with 20 pieces of artillery, furnished with bullets and powder, 2 dozen great pikes, 2½ dozen half-pikes, besides, 6 shallops and 1 boat. The said Béhère, victualer, has furnished 1 ton of powder, 20 tons of wine, 120 quintals of biscuit, 10 quintals of lard, 2½ quintals of olive oil, 22 barrels of vinegar, 120 pounds of candles, 1 hogshead of beans, 2 barrels of peas, and other small victuals, in order to make the voyage. It is agreed between the parties that all the return merchandise will be brought (saving the fortune of the sea) to the port of Bordeaux to be discharged there; and that of all the return merchandise the shipowner [*bourgeois*] will take for the ship's hull a quarter, the ship's company a third and all the rest the said sieur de Béhère for the victualing. The said ship's company will divide between them 34½ parts [the detailed division is not given by Ducéré]. The said Béhère has paid half the living expenses the ship's company sustained in coming from Saint-Jean-de-Luz to Bordeaux. And as for *mortes-payes* of the galleon [*galion*], the sieur de Béhère will be held responsible for their payment, according to the custom of the ships of Saint-Jean-de-Luz. All the victuals which remain in the ship on her return from her Newfoundland voyage, remain the property of Béhère, who will be held liable for the costs of the ship's company of the said ship until the discharge of the return merchandise which will take place at the port of Bordeaux.

And if, in making the said voyage, the said ship or crew make prize on any of the enemies of the king of France, the said ship's company will take half; the said Béhère, for his victuals, a complete third, and the shipowner, for the ship's hull, the remainder.

THE IMPACT ON THE NEWFOUNDLAND FISHERIES OF THE HABSBURG-VALOIS STRUGGLE, 1553–1559

ALTHOUGH THE CARRYING of the Franco-Spanish war into the waters of the Strait of Belle Isle and to the Avalon Peninsula, as well as leading to the seizure of large numbers of whaling and codfishing vessels on their way back from American waters, is scarcely directly concerned with the business aspect of the fisheries, it had some effect on the way they were conducted later on. Governments were inclined to intervene and to order the vessels to proceed in close squadrons so that they were less likely to be attacked by privateers, or even provided them with escorts from the royal navies. Governments also might have insisted that the ships of their nationality carry passports to help identify them against privateers from their own country. The times of sailing might be prescribed, or sailings even be prohibited for the season. The outbreaks of violence in the years 1554–1555, although continued until 1559, did not reach the intensity of this year until the 1580s, and indeed the impression is conveyed that the fishermen themselves determined, seeing the damage that was done during the war, to cooperate in future so far as possible in a peaceful manner in carrying on the fisheries, and especially in settling local disputes through the agency of the port admirals.

The attack in 1554 of French Basque whalers on Spanish Basques at Puerto de los Hornos in the Strait of Belle Isle is discussed by Selma Barkham in "The Spanish province of Terra Nova," *Canadian Archivist* (November, 1974), and, briefly, in D. B. Quinn, *North America from Earliest Discovery to First Settlements* (1977), p. 518. The major attack by the Spanish Basques on the French codfishery on the Avalon Peninsula is treated in Charles de la Roncière, *Histoire de la marine Française*, 2nd ed., III (Paris, 1923), 592, and elsewhere. E. Ducéré, *Les corsaires sous l'ancien régime* (Bayonne, 1895), pp. 333–343, prints a Spanish account of the Newfoundland attack and other depredations on French Newfoundlanders from *Colección Vargas Ponce*, Vol. L, 1, 18, Real Academia de Historia, Madrid, from which extracts (translated) are given (583).

583. 1555. The great fight at Newfoundland and the destruction of the French Newfoundland fleet.

The document from which extracts are given was the report of an inquiry held at San Sebastian in October, 1555, before Baltazar de Egurza, lieutenant, and Miguel de Idiacaiz, the royal scrivener who recorded the inquiries. As usual, interrogatories were drawn up and these were administered to a number of the leading sailors who were involved in the fray. Questions 6 and 7 of the interrogatories are given, followed by extracts from seven of the depositions (the remaining seven being largely repetitive).

[a] Interrogatories

6. Item: if they can attest that these captains and shipowners, natives and inhabitants of this province of Guipúzcoa, during the time of this current war, apart from the warlike opposition they have brought against the French enemy, both by land and sea, and on the high seas, have fitted out many large ships of over three hundred tons each and gone with them to the New Land, a voyage of over a thousand leagues; they have gone into the ports of the New Land, both by sea and disembarked on land, and have fought a number of battles and skirmishes, in which many of the enemy have died, more than five hundred, not counting the wounded; they have captured

from them more than two hundred large ships laden with cod, of high price and value; and even this very year the inhabitants of the town of San Sebastián and of Pasajes have taken forty-two large ships which they have stripped and destroyed; this meant that more than three hundred French ships that went off to the New Land fishing for these cod did no fishing, or if they did it was very little, and returned back to France without any, fleeing from these armed ships of this town and of Pasajes; in this way the subjects of the French King, just in this year of 1555, have suffered to the extent of over 400,000 ducats, as is common knowledge.

7. Item: if they can attest that, for the reasons explained in the previous question, the French enemy are in great terror and fear; they admit themselves that during this war there has to stop any sailing to the fishing grounds off the New Land, which is their main trade, as well as all other sailing from these parts of Western France; and this too is common knowledge.

[b]   Depositions

1st witness: Martin Cardel... recounts what he has heard of what has happened in the New Land, where have gone armed Guipúzcoan ships of three and of four hundred tons, and taken ships captive that he has seen. The French who live in those provinces cannot put up with this nor make a living, and have made emphatic representations to their Council, as a result of which, at the orders of the King of France, six large ships set out in an armed force, and were defeated. He calculates the dead in the province during the war at over a thousand men; ships captured from the enemy, large and small, at over a thousand, including more than four hundred of two hundred tons and upwards, with more than five thousand artillery pieces of iron and bronze, and 12 to 15 thousand prisoners, not counting the dead; he can be sure of all this, for he has been involved in the war since it started.

2nd witness. Domingo de Albistur, Captain, inhabitant of San Sebastián. He quoted the actions of other captains and then said that a little over a year before he set out with a large warship he had fitted out and armed, and on the high sea he met with two large French armed galleons that were going towards the coast of Galicia; they had a fierce fight, he sunk one with all the crew, the other fled from him and got away. On the same voyage he captured with his ship eleven other large French ones on their way back from the New Land laden with cod, well armed and in good order, among them being two powerful armed warships as guards, one called the *Bravosa de San Pau de Leon* and the other the *Bravosa de isla de Ré;* he fought with all these eleven ships for a day and two nights; and after many of his men had died, but he had killed many more of the enemy, he made them all surrender, including the two armed ships, and brought them all to the town of San Sebastián and to Galicia; there were over 600 men in these ships, many of them dead or wounded; and in addition to this, with Captain Francisco de Illareta and Captain Pablo de Aramburu he went on to capture the great galleon from Bayonne called *Bretona*, which was one of the strongest and best fitted warships in France. He was present at the rescue of the transport ship that the French were taking from Motrico to St Jean de Luz; there was no such piece in France nor is there in the navy. The witness, with his one ship, and Captains Francisco de Illareta, Pablo de Aramburu, Juan de Erauso, Juan de Lizarza, Miguel de Egurquiza, Martín Ruiz de Echave, Domingo de Mendaro and Miguel de Iturain, with theirs, have captured and taken this year forty-two large French ships laden with cod, with a lot of artillery of bronze and iron, not counting many others that other captains have destroyed in the New Land itself, which meant that over three hundred ships that went out for the fishing came back to France without doing it, at a loss of over 400,000 ducats. All this is common knowledge, as also that the French are in great fear and terror; for about a month ago the Captain General of Bayonne, at the express orders of the King, ordered there to sail out six large armed ships from St Jean de Luz, with all the best men from the frontier, to recover the fishing ships that had been captured by the Captains from San Sebastián, and these six French ships met those from San Sebastián on the high sea, and the battle lasted for a whole day, with many dead and wounded on each side, but still the ships from San Sebastián defended their captives and destroyed the enemy, and came with their captives to San Sebastián; this witness was involved in this with his ship; he calculated at one thousand two hundred the ships captured from the enemy.

Third witness: Francisco de Illareta, Captain, inhabitant of San Sebastián, said: that during the war over three hundred and fifty sailing ships have been fitted out in Guipúzcoa, so well supplied that they could hardly be better, even at the orders of His Majesty. About two months ago the witness captured a French ship called the *Cuba de Bayona*, one of the most powerful in France; he was involved in the recovery of the transport ship which six French ships were taking from Motrico to St Jean de Luz; in the battle with those that were trying to recover the ships from the New Land, when the French ones were destroyed, and he has captured on his own account several ships laden with cod with his own ship, or together with those of the other captains mentioned, and others that were going to Portugal with wheat, linen and other goods, and to Scotland, Ireland and England, in which he has done very great damage....

Fifth witness. Martín Pérez de Hoa, pilot, inhabitant of San Sebastián, said that he recalled that Captain Miguel de Ituráin, last Whit Sunday night, took by force of arms the great galley of St Jean de Luz, which was fitted for war: Captain Martín de Echave captured another large ship, similarly armed: Captain Xuárez captured a galley and a big *zabra*, also armed: other captains have captured other ships, and he has been present as pilot at many of the occasions being inquired about. This Year he went with Captain Juan de Erauso to the New Land, with three hundred men in a ship of four hundred tons, and there they joined the ships of Captains Juan de Ligarza and Miguel de Ituráin; all three fought at a port of the New Land and, with great damage and death, they captured twelve large French ships laden with cod, among them the one called *Gran Fatasia de San Brin*, with a lot of artillery of iron and bronze; these French ships were in order, tied one to the other, hoping to defend themselves from all the might of the Spanish ships. Afterwards they shared out the captured ships among the three; with the share that fell to Captain Juan de Erauso they fitted out the ship called the *Gran Fatasia*, putting some of their men on board, and went to another port in the northern part of the New Land, and found eight large French ships laden with cod, very much in war formation, with a large well armed ship as guard and escort, called the *Gran Francesa de San Maló*. They had forts and bastions at the entrance to the port, with a lot of artillery fixed and placed there, which they began to fire, and effectively prevented the Captain Juan de Erauso from coming in to the port. When he realized this, he withdrew with his ships to another point and set most of his men on land, and, with their flag, in squadron formation, they went by night very close to where the enemy's forts and bastions were, attacked and overpowered them; and with the same artillery that they found there, after the Spanish ships were brought close, they attacked the eight enemy ships that were tied one to another and made them surrender. In this battle there died of the men of Juan de Erauzo, nine, and of the enemy, seventy-two, not counting the many wounded. On the way back he captured some other ships laden with cod, eighteen in all, with over two hundred pieces of artillery of bronze and iron; he separated some of the ships so that the men could go back home to France in them, after taking the artillery and ammunition away first, and he came back safely to the town of San Sebastián. Including these ships and those captured by the other captains, it comes to 48 that have been captured this year in the New Land, worth at least 100,000 ducats. This same Captain Juan de Erauso, with a ship of three hundred and sixty tons, went to the New Land in former years also, and captured many French ships; choosing the eight best, he set loose the others for the French to go off in and came back to San Sebastián; and he did the same on another voyage, and this witness has been on all three voyages as pilot and was present at what happened; also when six large armed ships set out from St Jean to take back the ships that Captain Erauso had captured, he defended them and repelled the enemy, setting them to flight and almost captured two of these French ships, but because the weather went calm they escaped rowing; and they came with their native ships into San Sebastián.

6th witness. Juan del Puerto, Chief pilot, inhabitant of the town of Orlo, said: that he had gone to the New Land with Captain Juan de Erauso, and confirmed everything said in the previous testimony. Since the French ships brought back to Guipúzcoa were so many, their value has gone down, but in French hands they were worth over a million in gold; and the French, upset at the damage, estimate their worth at much higher;

there have been over fifteen thousand prisoners, not counting the dead; so that there can hardly be a man on the French coast who has not been captured once, and the ships they have at the moment have very little artillery, because it has been captured and taken off in the captured ships.

7th witness. Juan de Erauso, Captain and ship-owner, repeated the declarations of his pilots and added that in the New Land he took more than five hundred prisoners, and in the first encounter gave them ships and provisions to go back to France; in the second encounter, at the forts, which happened on the day of Our Lady in August, he killed 72 of the enemy, wounded 100 and took 500 prisoners, and gave these ships too to go home in; he took the captured ships to San Sebastián, armed with 130 pieces of artillery, repelled the ships that sailed from St Jean de Luz to rescue them, and almost captured two of them, but they escaped rowing; and that Captain Xuárez, of Fuenterrabia, captured this year a galley and a large *zabra* that was going on its way....

10th witness. Miguel de Ituráin, Captain, ship-owner, inhabitant of Pasajes, said: that since the start of the war he set out armed in a galleon of two hundred tons, met another larger ship from Bayonne whose captain was Martin de Vina, who was on his way from the whalefishing of the New Land, fought with it for a long while and defeated it, and brought it captive to the port of Pasajes; that on Whit Sunday night he took by force of arms the *Grande Gatera* of St Jean de Luz, which

was journeying armed; that sometimes alone, other times in the company of other captains, he has gone along the coast of France and made landings with his men, and has surrounded and taken by assault some castles, burnt and sacked villages and done considerable harm; that this year he went to the New Land with Captains Juan de Erauso and Juan de Lizarza; they went to a port where they found twelve large very well armed ships, fought them, and captured them, with dead and wounded on each side; they turned out to be laden with cod, with over 600 men and a lot of artillery, worth over 5,000 ducats; the captive ships were shared among the three captains, and each set off on their own to see what they could find; this witness took the high sea on the way back to the fishing-banks of the New Land, and fought with five ships he found on the codfisheries; after a very fierce battle he overcame them and made them surrender, and with the eight captive ships he came back to the port of Pasajes; that Captain Juan de Erauso, after leaving his company, had fierce and great battles in other ports of the New Land and took up to fourteen ships captive, one of them a warship that was there as guard; that the Captain Lizarza took up to eight ships captive, and took them to sell them at Lisbon; with the result that more than three hundred French ships that went to the New Land came back without having fished; and this has meant a loss of over 400,000 ducats, as is common knowledge.

Chapter Seventy-three
Growth of Sophistication in Business Dealings, 1562–1580

584. April 13, 1562. Charter party for an English voyage to the Newfoundland fishery.

The charter party was universal in western Europe as an instrument which tied together the interests of the shipowners, victualers, investing merchants (if they were not precisely described as either of the previous two), the captain or master of the ship, and the crew, while it also sometimes included arrangements about marketing fish. This charter party is the earliest found for an English voyage to Newfoundland (I owe it to John Roberts), and it is clear that the ship was to be ready to expect violent attack and was equipped to deal with it. Lawlessness, piracy or privateering, and such were already the lot of the fishermen. Its terms should be compared with the French charter party of 1552 (582) and the Spanish charter party of 1571 (580).

The ship made a good voyage, but it was claimed that on her return voyage, which was undertaken around the north of Great Britain, she was robbed by pirates in the Orkneys.

P.R.O., HCA 24/34, no. 289, April 13, 1562, spelling modernized (other documents in the case in the same bundle nos. 90–93, 234–235, 272, 290, also HCA 24/35, no. 208).

It is agreed by charter party indented between James Barret of Tenby in Pembroke gentleman, John Philkyn, John Pallmer, and John Kilberye of the same town, merchants and owners of the good ship the *Jesus* of Tenby, master and governor John Garrett of Plymouth on the one part, and William Philpott of Tenby merchant and half "vitler" [victualler] of the said ship and the said James Barret and William Lougher, two other half victualers, of the other part, that the said

ship shall take in all things necessary, salt victuals and other things for her voyage and shall sail from Tenby Quay to the Newfound land with the first wind and weather and sail and remain until fully laden with fish according to the quantity of the lading of salt and victuals and discharge her lading with twenty days after her arrival there and her lading shall be equally divided into three parts between the owners, victuallers and master and company by equal division of her lading, each party to stand by their division, the owners to make the ship "styff and staunch," well-apparelled with shot and powder, 1 dozen bows, 14 sheaves of arrows, 6 dozen strings with pikes, munitions and all furnishings, the owners to put in the ship with the master forty mariners and four boys, and it is agreed that if the ship be robbed and spoiled, any lading or artillery taken away shall be put in a general average, paying pound for pound, and the goods in the ship shall be equally divided in three parts, pound for pound, as above, towage, dunnage and petty loadmanship to be at the costs of the merchants and loaders, the owners and victualers to find a pilot or to agree with the master. In witness the parties have put their seals April 13,4 Elizabeth (1562).

[Signed, and two seals:] Jamys Barett, Rafe Barett, John Filkyn, John Kilbery.

585. September 5, 1567. Trade in Newfoundland fish among French Basques from Ciboure and Bilbao.

This document records the costs to a French Basque Newfoundland fisherman from Ciboure in disposing of his fish in Spain at Bilbao. The record of taxation and transport costs throws light on problems of distribution and indicates the considerable burden they placed on the primary producers, the fishermen. We owe the document to Selma Barkham.

Archivo Histórico de Protocolos de Guipúzcoa, Oñate, Partido de San Sebastian (Fuenterrabia), no. 373, fols. 86–86v., translated.

I, Anton de Trucios, Public Notary of His Majesty and of the number of the noble town of Bilbao, witness and testify to whomsoever it may concern, that on September 5, 1567, this present year, before the magnificent gentleman, Sanistian de Ysasi, mayor of the said town, representing His Majesty, and in my presence, and before witnesses, Adame de Arrape, Frenchman, burgess of Çubiburu [Ciboure], which is in the kingdom of France, publicly declared in the name of Juanes de Ybayeta, Frenchman, burgess of the same place, that from the Province of Tierranova to the port of Castro de Urdiales the said Juanes de Ybayeta had brought about 230 quintals of codfish, cured in the said Tierranova, in the ship *Maria Madalena de San Vicens*, master the said Juanes, and transported it from the port of the said town of Castro de Urdiales to this town of Bilbao in two pinnaces and to ensure that he would give a detailed account of the sale of the cod. [Mateo de Salinas, burgess of Bilbao, had come with him as guarantor and had put up sufficient surety, and today, 20 December 1567, he had given an account of the sale.] And the 230 quintals of codfish were worth 3741 *reales*, from which said *reales* he declared that he had paid out:

To Ochoa de Terreros, burgess of Eslares [Islares] and to Martin de Quartas, burgess of Castro de Urdiales, for the hire of their pinnaces to bring the said codfish from the said port of Castro to the said town of Bilbao... 230 *reales* plus 82 *reales* paid in this way:

To the girls for carrying the said fish from the riverbank where the pinnaces were to the storehouse where it was to be put... 8 *reales*.

Paid out in wages to 5 men brought to fold and pile the said fish which took them 4 days because it was raining and so had to be done little by little... 48 *reales*.

For straw to put under the said fish and on the sides and on top to cover it... 12 *reales*.

To the girls who took the fish in batches to the public scales of the said town to weigh it each time fish was sold to the mulateers... 7 *reales*.

Paid in dues at the scales for weighing the said fish to the man in charge of the scales... 7 *reales*.

Paid to his host, Mateo de Salinas, for the storehouse where he put the fish in order to sell it... 34 *reales*.

Paid to Juan de Urteaga in duty on the said codfish imposed on the bar of Portugalete... 34 *reales*.

Paid to Simon de Plaça, the servant of Juan Martinez de Recalde who is charged with collecting the dues for the Provostry in His Majesty's name... 85 *reales*.

For buying pieces of coloured cloth for himself and some of his companions for their clothes, and for the making of the same... 260 *reales*.

Costs for himself and one companion in eating and drinking from the 5th of September to the 20th of December of this present year while they were in this said town, selling the said codfish, in the house of Mateo de Salinas amounting to 107 days at 4 *reales* a day which they paid for bed and board... 430 *reales*; plus the cost of the journey on horseback from this town to San Juan de Luz... 66 *reales*; which last two items together come to 496 *reales*, and thus the costs and dues paid for the said codfish, and the clothes made for himself and his companions sum up and amount to 1221 *reales*, and the rest, which are 2520 *reales*, the said Adame de Arrape declared that he wished to take and was taking with him from this said town of Bilbao to the Province of Guipuzcoa to use them for buying iron goods and other merchandise allowed and permitted by the royal decrees of His Majesty's kingdoms, and these same goods were to be loaded, taken and sent to the said kingdom of France....

[The final part of the manifest explains that the declarant and his guarantor must ensure that a deposition showing that the 2520 reales which had been spent in the Province of Guipuzcoa would be sent back to Bilbao, and that no one should be allowed to cause any further difficulty for the declarant or his guarantor.]

INSURANCES FOR SPANISH SHIPS GOING TO THE COD AND WHALE FISHING IN NEWFOUNDLAND AND LABRADOR, 1569–1572

AN ELABORATE insurance system was developed during the sixteenth century to protect the interests of the merchants, shipowners, and seamen. In the Archives of the Consulado at Burgos, Spain, many hundreds of such documents still survive. Below are translated (586) a contract for insurance for a codfishing voyage from San Sebastian to Newfoundland and back, made in May, 1563 (Archivo del Consulado, Burgos, Legajo 99), and (587) a contract for insurance of a whale fishing voyage from Motrico to San Sebastian (or Pasaje) to the Grand Bay of Newfoundland (Strait of Belle Isle), made on May 23, 1572 (Archivo del Consulado, Burgos, Legajo 43, fol. 514v). We owe these to Selma Barkham; see Manuel Basas Fernández, *El seguro marítimo en España del siglo XVI* (Bilbao, 1963).

586. Fair of May, 1563. Jhoan de Quintañadueñas.

In the city of Burgos on the 4th day of April, 1563, Jhoan de Quintañadueñas, burgess and councillor of Burgos, through commission of Martinon de Sociondo and in the name of Miquelon de Agorreta, agreed to insure from San Sebastian to Terranova, the voyage out, the time there and the voyage back to the said San Sebastian or to Bilbao, on the outfitting and victuals and equipment for codfishing belonging to the said Miquelon de Agorreta, or to whomsoever it may or should belong, at 10 per cent, payable at the fair of May, 1569, in the ship called *La Catalina* of San Juan de lus, master Martinon de Sociondo, or another, and the undersigned insured the following sum:

Francisco de La Presa for 450 ducats at nine per cent [for ten?]... 450.
Checked by Alonso de Madrid

through commission of Andres de Arriçavalaga, burgess of Eibar, and in the name of Juan de Ayardia, burgess of Ondarroa, from the bay of Motrico to San Sebastian or the Pasaje or between them and either of them, and the time there, and from there to the Grand Bay of Terranova to any port or ports of that coast, and from one to the other, and from another to another, and for the time spent there in any of them while fishing for whales, and for the voyage back from the said port to San Sebastian or the Pasaje, on the hull, artillery and munition of the galleon, which God save, called the *San Miguel*, master Felipe de Ynurriça, burgess of Zarauz, or any another, insured according to the recent pronouncement of His Majesty on the insuring of the hulls of ships, at 15 per cent the next October, and the following insurers signed:

Juan de Aguero in the said ship, that God save, for 500 ducats at 15% in October [signed] the same day [and twelve other underwriters for a total of 2000 ducats].

587. Fair of October, 1570. Juan Lopez de Soto.

In the city of Burgos on the 23rd day of the month of May, 1572, Juan Lopez de Soto insured

588. April 7, 1571. Charter party for a Spanish Basque whaling voyage to Labrador.

The whaling industry was a large and highly capitalized one, and the agreements that preceded a voyage were correspondingly complex.

Throughout Europe the charter party was the agreement that was made for a fishing or trading voyage. The following example gives a very full indication of what was involved in a whaling voyage from the Spanish Basque country to Labrador and back. We owe this document to Selma Barkham.

The document is from the Archivo Histórico de Protocolos de Guipúzcoa, Oñate, Partido de Azpeitia, no. 1913 (Deva), fols. 79–80; translated.

In the town of Deva, on the seventh day of April, 1571, in the presence of me, Antonio de Arezti, public notary of His Majesty and of the number of the said town, and the undersigned witnesses, appeared present on the one hand Domingo de Sorasu, burgess of the said town, owner and master of the ship named *Nuestra Senora de Yçiar* of about 500 tons burden which at this date has been made and built in the shipyards of the said town, ready to launch into the sea, and on the other hand Martin Garcia de Lasao, burgess of the same town, to whom the said Domingo de Sorasu has chartered his ship for the fishing voyage for whale oil in the New Land this present year, about which, aforehand, both the said parties had come to an agreement, and are now agreed, to sign this charter party with the following conditions and in the following manner:

Firstly, they established that the said Domingo de Sorasu shall give and is giving his said ship for the said voyage, launched and masted, watertight in keel and sides and decks, within the following 20 days, ready to receive the necessary food and equipment, and well and sufficiently rigged with mooring cables, hawsers, sails and all other necessary tackle, in accordance with the ships tonnage and with the voyage to be undertaken, with the ship's boat and skiff for the service of the said ship, and with the artillery and armament of lances and pikes and gunpowder.

Item, that the said Domingo de Sorasu for the said voyage shall appoint the master and boatswain, carpenter and caulker, boatswain's mate and man in charge of the lombards [cannon], and shall pay their extra shares and gratuities at his own cost, without Martin Garcia being charged with providing more than one single share person taken from the crew's portion; and that the total number of crew that are to go in this ship, includ-

ing the above mentioned officers, shall be 85 persons; and that Martin Garcia shall be responsible for seeing that there are a sufficient number of shallops; and for the said 85 persons Martin Garcia shall provide all the victuals: bread, biscuit, cider, wine, bacon, oil, vegetables, and other things needed for 8 months as from the time the ship leaves the port and bay of Motrico, where the food and equipment shall be put aboard along with all the harpoons, javelins, knives, whaling lines, harpoon handles, barrel heads, cauldrons, barrels, equipment and armament and all other necessary things . . . [Martin Garcia shall undertake to put everything aboard] in the port and channel of Deva, and in the bay of Motrico, within the following 20 days, so that from thence with the said crew, the said ship may leave and go on her good voyage.

Item, that the said ship after the said food and outfitting has been received should go straight to the Province of Terranova, to the Grand Bay, to fish for whales and there reside and remain until the fishing has been totally finished and the whale oil has been stowed aboard, in any port or ports, and for as long as there are sufficient victuals, and the fishing having been done and the said ship having been loaded, the cargo shall be brought to the port of El Pasaje where God willing the cargo is to be unloaded and, after it has arrived at this port there can be a period of thirty days for unloading, and Laredo and Castro can be used as ports of call.

Item, they established that of all the cargo of whale oil barrels that the said ship shall bring back and whatever other profit or prize that should result from the said voyage, the fourth part shall be for the said Domingo de Sorasu net without him having to contribute to any costs save only that he should contribute the fourth part of the cost of outfitting of the said ship and of the equipment, except for the supplies of food and drink, as is customary, and for the fourth part of the shares and gratuities of the shallops and harpooners and coopers and the whale cutters and the gunners, and moreover he has to give and shall give in all to the said Martin Garcia, the voyage once finished, four shares of those which each mariner shall individually earn in the said ship in the said voyage.

Item, that in case any grave damage occurs during the said voyage, that the outfitters and crew and the said Domingo de Sorasu have to contribute and shall contribute in the damages according to the amount of shares that they receive in the profits and therefore in accordance with the custom of the said town to which in similar events they are bound.

Item, they declare that the said Martin Garcia has to return at his own cost the said ship in ballast after she has been unloaded, to Domingo de Sorasu in the same way as she is given at present.

Item, the said parties establish that on the said voyage and journey Martin Garcia de Lasao shall go and act as captain in the said ship and as principal commander and administrator of the said outfitting and voyage, or whatever person the said Martin Garcia shall appoint in his place.

Item, they put as a condition that if through fault of the said Martin Garcia, he does not put into the said ship and voyage all the victuals and equipment and barrels and shallops and crew and all other necessities as stipulated above for the said voyage, so that the ship is unable to bring back a full cargo, the said Martin Garcia has to pay to Domingo de Sorasu the part that is lacking.

And with each and every one of these conditions, both the said parties have made and executed this contract and charter party, and each one of them for the part for which they are responsible and pertains to them and in which they are obliged to comply and pay, bind themselves, their persons, and all their goods, furniture and real estate, acquired and to be acquired, etc. . . .

[They agree to abide faithfully by all the aforesaid points in the document, with other customary legal formulae.]

    [Signed:] Martin Garcia de Lassao, Domingo de Sorasu
    [And the notary:] Antonio de Arezti

589. September 7, 1572. Agreement about the sale of boats made at a Spanish Basque whale fishing base on the Strait of Belle Isle.

Business arrangements for the conduct of whale and codfishing continued to be made after the vessels had arrived in Labrador or Newfoundland waters. Whalers used the same base for months on end, sending out their boats to attack and overpower the whales coming through the Strait of Belle Isle. One of these bases was Chateo, as it was known to the Spanish Basques (to the French it was Baie de Chasteaux, in English Bay of Castles, now Chateau Bay), situated on the Labrador side just to the north of the entrance to the Strait. It may be the earliest business document made in modern Canada to survive. We owe this document to Selma Barkham.

Archivo Histórico de Protocolos de Guipúzcoa, Oñate, Partido de San Sebastian, no. 335 (Fuenterrabia, 1574), fol. 11; printed in Selma Barkham, "Two documents written in Labrador, 1572 and 1577"; Canadian Historical Rev., LVII [1976], 236, translated.

I Joanes de Leço, inhabitant of the place of Leço in the jurisdiction of the town of Fuenterrabia, declare that I owe you, Joanes de Langorrieta [Landagorrieta], inhabitant of the said town of Fuenterrabia, twenty ducats which are for four shallops that I have bought from you, the said Juanes de Landagorrieta, for the price of the said twenty ducats for all four, the which aforesaid twenty ducats I am bound to give and pay to you, the said Joanes de Landagorrieta, or to any other person that in your name shows proof that they were asked [to collect it], without lawsuit or dispute of any sort under pain of double costs, and for this I bind myself and very good, acquired and to be acquired, under obligation, and give my power of attorney, complete and in form, to all judges and justice of His Majesty, and this I sign with my name, which is done in the port called Chateo on the seventh of September 1572.

    [Signed:] Joanes de Leço

590. 1574. Times of sailing and return of Spanish Basque vessels.

A note by Cristóbal de Barros, 1574, in M. Fernández de Navarrete, Obras, II (1964), 117, translated.

The ships which go to the cod fishing at Newfoundland set out from that coast at the end of March and the beginning of April and return to it in the middle of September and in October. Those which go to the whale fishery set out from this coast about the middle of June and return to it in December and at the beginning of January.

591. February 12, 1577. Charter to the Muscovy Company for an English monopoly of whale fishing.

English seamen are not known to have attempted to involve themselves at an early stage in the whale fishery in North American waters. Information on the nature and profitability of the Basque whaling industry based in the Gulf of St. Lawrence no doubt reached them, perhaps from Anthony Parkhurst (525). It may be, also, that whale sightings during Martin Frobisher's expedition in 1576 to Baffin Island helped to lead the company to obtain on February 12, 1577, a twenty-year monopoly of whatever whale fishery Englishmen might create. No direct initiatives by the company in this respect are known.

The charter is printed from P.R.O., Patent Roll, 19 Elizabeth I, pt. 12, C 66/1162, in C. T. Carr, ed., Select Charters of Trading Companies A.D. 1530–1707 *(London, Selden Society, 1913), pp. 28–30.*

Elizabeth by the Grace of God etc., To all manner our officers true liege men ministers and subjects, and to all other our people as well within this our Realm as elsewhere under our obeisance jurisdiction and rule or otherwise, to whom these our Letters Patents shall be seen read or shewed, Greeting:

We being given to understand by our faithful and loving subjects Sir Rowland Heyward and Sir Lionel Duckett, Knights, Governors of the Fellowship of English Merchants for Discovery of New Trades, that the said Fellowship do mind shortly to attempt the killing of whales in the ocean and other seas, for to make train oil to the great commodity and benefit of this our Realm of England, And for that purpose have already to their great costs and charges procured certain Biscayans men expert and skilful to instruct our subjects therein,

We, well liking and allowing of this their attempt and enterprise as a thing likely to be very beneficial both for the increase of our Navy and mariners and also for furnishing of this our said Realm and Dominions with so necessary a commodity, of our certain knowledge free will mere motion special grace and of our regal authority for Us our heirs and successors by these presents do grant to the Governor or Governors Consuls Assistants and Fellowship aforesaid and their successors for ever, That they the said Governors and their successors by their factors servants ministers deputies and assigns and none other shall and may from henceforth for the space of twenty years next ensuing the date hereof use and exercise the killing of whales within any seas whatsoever, and thereof to make train oil to their most commodity and profit:

And further for Us or heirs and successors We do expressly enjoin prohibit forbid and command all and singular person and persons whatsoever as well denizens as strangers and all other persons being in any wise subjects to the Crown of England, being not of the said Society or Fellowship, that they nor any of them shall kill any whale to make train oil thereof, or shall hire or set on work or cause or procure to be hired or set on work directly or indirectly any person or persons to kill any whale or make any oil thereof, Upon pain that all and every person or persons whatsoever doing the contrary shall suffer imprisonment during the will and pleasure of Us or heirs or successors, and not to be discharged thereof without special warrant from Us our heirs our successors, And also to forfeit and pay to Us our heirs and successors the sum of five pounds of lawful money of England for every ton of oil sc made, the one half to be to the use of Us our heirs and successors, the other half to the use of the said Fellowship and their successors:

And to the intent this present grant may the better effect to the encouragement of the said Fellowship in this their enterprise and attempt, our further will and pleasure is, and We straitly charge and command all our Customs Officers Comptrollers and other our ministers of our ports that they nor any of them in any wise during the said term of twenty years do take any entry or make any composition of or for any oil commonly called train oil which shall be made of any whale that shall be killed or caused to be killed by any Englishman or other person inhabiting within this our Realm and brought into this our Realm of others than the said Fellowship of English Merchants for Discovery of New Trades or their successors factors or assigns, upon pain of our high displeasure:

Provided always that if the said Fellowship [etc.] by the space of four years in time of peace shall discontinue or surcease the killing of whales and making of train oil as is aforesaid, that then it shall be lawful to and for every other of our subjects whatsoever to enterprise and attempt the killing of whales and making of train oil where they might lawfully have done it afore this our special grant or licence, Anything in this our special grant to the said Fellowship made to the contrary notwithstanding:

In witness whereof etc. witness our self at Westminster the xii day of February [1577].

per breue de priuato sigillo.

592. *Circa* 1580. Conditions under which French and English Newfoundland ventures were said to operate.

Robert Hitchcock was a propagandist for the development of the English fishing industry, who made some incidental reference to the Newfoundland trade although his main concern was with fishing in local waters. He makes the following remarks about the French Newfoundland industry in his A politique platt, for the honour of the Prince (London, 1580), *Sig. Fir.–Fiv., D3r.*

[a] There goeth out of Fraunce commonly five hundreth saile of shippes yearely in March to Newfoundlande, to fishe for Newland fishe, and comes home againe in August. Amongst many of theim this is the order, tenne or twelve Marryners doeth conferre with a Money man, who furnisheth them with money to buy Shippes, Victualls, Salte, Lines and Hookes to be paied his money at the shippes returned, either in fishe or in money, with five and thirty pounde upon the hundrethe pounde in money lent. Likewise here in Englande, in West countrye the like order is used, the fisherman conferres with the money man, who furnishethe them with money to provide victualls, salte and all other needfull thinges to be paied twentie five pounde at the shippes returne, upon the hundreth pound in money lent.

And some of the same money men dothe borrowe money upon ten pounde in the hundreth pounde and puts it in this order to the Fishermen. And for to be assured of the money ventured, they will have it assured, gevyng six pounde for the assuring of every hundreth pound to hym that abides the venture of the Shippes returne.

[b] For every Shippe, beeyng but of the burden of lxx tunne, if God blesse it with safe retourne from Newfounde lande, will bryng home to his Port (in August), twentie thousande of the beste and middle sort of wette fishe (at the leaste) called blanckfishe, and tenne thousand drie fish, whiche beyng solde uppon the Shippes retourne, as it maie be at Newhaven in Fraunce, but for fourtie shillynges the hundreth of wette fishe, which is not fower pence the fishe, and xx shillynges the hundreth of drie fishe, which is not twoo pence the fishe, amounteth to five hundreth pound at the least.

593. 1579. A rutter for a Basque whaling voyage.

Martin de Hoyarsabal, of Cibiburu (Ciboure), published Les voyages avantureux du Capitaine Martin de Hoyarsabal *(Bordeaux, 1579), setting out the routes (hence the name rutter) to be followed from point to point along a considerable part of the northeast coast of North America once a landfall had been made. The extract (translated by Selma Barkham) specifies the route taken by Basque whalers in* La Grande Baie *(the Strait of Belle Isle). This is taken from the 1633 edition, pp. 108–111, which is virtually unaltered from that of 1579.*

Here follow the routes from Cap de Grat to "Toutes Isles" of the Grand Bay, all the Bay lies East-West.

Know that from the Cap de Grat to Beaulsanim there are 30 leagues and when you wish to go from Cap de Grat to Beaulsanim go West, quarter Northwest, and when you wish to go out come West quarter Northeast, on account of the tides and currents which are within [the Bay] on that course for 30 leagues.

Cap de Grat and Chasteau lie Northwest and Southeast, quarter North and South; there are 10 leagues.

Cap de Grat and Baye de Sacure lie East-West, quarter Northeast and Southwest; there are 4 leages.

Cap de Grat and Pointe Basse lie East-West; there are 7 leagues.

Cap de Grat and Boytus lie Northwest and Southeast, quarter East-West; there are 16 leagues.

Chateau and Berille lie Northwest and Southeast, quarter East-West; there are 5 leagues.

Cap de Grat and Borille, which is in the middle of the Bay, lie North and South taking Northeast-Southeast; there are 7 leagues.

Pointe Basse and Boytus lie Northwest and Southeast; there are 10 leagues.

Pointe Basse and Chasteau lie North Northeast and South Southwest; there are 8 leagues, and there is a covered shoal at the entrance to Chasteau on the port side; come close to the small island.

Chasteau and Boytus lie East-West, quarter Northeast and Southwest; there are 12 leagues, and between Chasteau and Boytus there is no place for ships to shelter except at a point in the middle of the way which is not good for ships, as it is a bad spot, and know that you will find no ports until Boytus and you will find at Boytus a covered Shoal which is very bad and dangerous and lies Northwest and Southeast, quarter East-West of the large island of Boytus, and to the seaward side of Flower Island [or the Isle of Flowers], within a bombard shot length; you can pass very well to the landward side if you follow along the land westwards from Chasteau.

Item from Boytus to Port de Ballene there is a league, and at Boytus on the West point there is a Shoal covered at times and you can pass to the landward side, and watch out for the shoal.

Item from Port de Ballene to Furx there are 3 leagues and know there are two large islands going out from Furx across from the island which is to the west.

Item from Furx to Samadeg there are 2 short leagues, and from Samadeg to Eaue Forte where the ships lie there are [also] 2 short leagues.

Item from Eaue Forte to Beaulsablom there are 3 leagues and know that there is a bay between the two and a very bad place as the sea

breaks just outside when the wind is Southwest. From Beaulsanim to the bay there is one small league.

Item close by Beaulsanim to East Northeast opposite some little islands are the covered shoals which are dangerous and for safety when you come to Beaulsanim, when you are opposite the sand, first send [a shallop] on ahead to the West then you will be in no danger.

Beaulsanim and Isle Danser lie East Northeast and West Southwest; there is 1 league.

Isle Danser and Brest lie Northwest and Southeast quarter East-West; there are 6 leagues.

Item you should know that Beaulsanim to The Islands is 2 leagues and if you wish to go from Beaulsanim to The Islands with the ship, watch out for the Pointe Prime for over it the sea breaks on land for a league, and do not approach at all until you have passed well beyond it towards the West and you will find good shelter at Isle Danser and be not afraid of Pointe Prime; and near Isle Danser, near the Islands, there is a shoal amongst them in the middle of the bay and it is covered, and if you do not go aground there is no danger.

Item from The Islands to Droget is 2 leagues and there are shoals well covered and dangerous over the Droget and when you go to Droget with the ship beware of the shoals.

Item from Droget to Cradon is a league, and there are shoals over the Droget half a league to sea which are covered, and watch for them when you go with the ship.

Item you should know that from Gradon to Sachobodege is a small league, to the entrance to Sachobodege, and there are considerable shoals seawards and watch out for them; men take great care there.

Item from Sachobodege to Brest is 2 leagues and there are shoals between the two and watch out for them.

594. 1581. Instructions how to navigate east and west across the Atlantic.

Michiel Coignet, in his Instruction nouvelle des poincts plus excellent & necessaire touchant l'art de naviguer *(Antwerp, 1581), claimed to be able to instruct ships to cross the ocean safely. They should sail down the appropriate latitude, use his "nautical hemisphere" or "astronomical ring," a device which allowed time and variation to be estimated, and by also using a 24-hour sand clock (or sand glass) they could find their longitude. The difficulties were that (a) this scheme presumed a constant change of variation, increasing from 0° to 45°W and decreasing from 45° to 90°W, and (b) it relied on the accuracy of the clock to an extent that was wholly unrealistic. The extracts (pp. 96–97, translated), however, give examples such as a few sailors on voyages to and from North America may have tried to use. His league was presumably the Portuguese league of 4 miles, commonly used by experts on navigation. See David W. Waters, The Art of Navigation in England in Elizabethan and Early Stuart Times (London, 1958), pp. 154, 215, 316.*

[1]   A ship being at Cape S. Vincent in Spain, wishes to navigate exactly to the West. For this the pilot regulates the sand clock so that it begins its run precisely at noon. Then he navigates eight or nine days until he arrives at one of the islands of the Azores called S. Maria. Now he wishes to know how many leagues he has sailed. For this he turns to his glass (which he has turned each day) which had recorded his course exactly, because it is known that it is noon at Cape S. Vincent, but in the island of S. Maria he finds by the astronomical ring that it is precisely 11 hours, 10 minutes, which is 50 minutes less than noon or 12 o'clock and shows the difference between these two meridians or the difference of longitude. He enters in the foregoing table the number of the height of the Pole [latitude], that is 37° (because these two places are on the same parallel) and finds on the righthand side 209 ¾ leagues, for each hour of this parallel. Therefore he multiplies 209 ¾ leagues by 50 minutes below and the product is 10487 ½, the which divided by 60 the quotient is 174 $^{19}/_{24}$ leagues, which is the entire course navigated.

[2]   A ship sails from Terra-nova [Newfoundland] precisely eastward under the exact parallel of 50°, having previously set his sand clock, so that it began to run exactly at noon, turning it as instructed once a day, until the fifteenth day of sailing. Now one wishes to know how many leagues have been sailed. Therefore he sees that the sand glass has made its run precisely and takes it from the astronomical ring, which is (because he is sailing eastward) 2 hours 12 minutes after noon. Entering this in the foregoing table he finds on the parallel of 50° 168 ½ leagues for the hour, so that 2 hours give 337 leagues and the 12 minutes give approximately 33 ¼ leagues, the which added to the 337 leagues aforesaid give in all 370 ¼ leagues sailed.

Chapter Seventy-four
Effects of War on Business Activity, 1583–1603

AN ENGLISH PASSPORT FOR A PORTUGUESE FISHERMAN AT NEWFOUNDLAND, AUGUST 7 TO OCTOBER 27, 1583

AFTER FORMALLY annexing Newfoundland to the English Crown in August, 1583, Sir Humphrey Gilbert went on to issue English passports to masters of the non-English ships present in St. John's Harbour (596). Such a passport, dated August 7, 1583 (August 17, new style, as used in Spain), was given to Tomas Andre, for what consideration we do not know, and came to the attention of the municipal judge of Aveiro after his return to Portugal. The judge forwarded it to Philip II with a Spanish translation and with information that the English leader was proposing to continue his expedition to Cape Breton and "Florida" (in Spanish and Portuguese usage any part of the coast northward to Cape Breton). The documents are in A.G.I., Seville, Patronato 2-5-1/20, no. 40, and were first published in translation in D. B. Quinn and N. M. Chesire, *The New Found Land of Stephen Parmenius* (1972), pp. 209–210. No reaction of the Spanish government to this information is known.

595. October 27, 1583. Gonzalo Estevez to Philip II.

SIRE

From persons who have come this year from the Newfoundland [*Terra Nova*] fisheries it has been learnt that there went to that coast certain English ships which had for commander one Huiz, a great lord of England, who took possession of certain ports, saying that they were to be settled, and that those who went to fish in those parts were to pay him duty. And it is also said that they were going to winter at Cape Breton [*cabo de bertāo*] and from thence go to Florida. It seemed necessary to give an account of this to your highness as these lands are held to be of your conquest. And for greater certainty I acquired a public instrument which I am sending with this,

together with a passport in English which they were giving to each ship. Our Lord preserve the Catholic and royal person of your majesty and enlarge his realms and states. From Aveiro, 27 October 1583.

[Signed:] Gonçallo Estevez

[Addressed:] To our lord the king. From the municipal judge of the town of Aveiro.

Note added that the letter has been translated into Spanish (from Portuguese) by Tomas Gracián Dantisca, notary public and servant to the king.

Covering paper to say that these papers were in Portuguese and have been translated into Castilian. To this is added an endorsement in a contemporary or nearly contemporary hand: "1583. Advices how the English have discovered a strait in Newfoundland at the cod [*Bacallaos*] fishery, from whence they pass into the South Sea and take possession of those ports."

596. August 7, 1583. Passport issued by Sir Humphrey Gilbert to Tomas Andre.

To whomsoever it may concern, know that I, Humfrey Gilbert, knight [*Humberto Guilberto cauallero de armas*], in the name and under the authority of her majesty, the queen of England, give and concede to Tomas Andre of Avero in the kingdom of Portugal that he may have free access to and liberty in the fishing and trade of the New-foundland. Requiring all those who may be asso-ciated with me in any way that they should not harm or annoy him, but rather that they should help and protect him and his ships and goods as much as they are able. Give in St John's [*Sot Rones*] after my taking possession of Newfound-land, 7 August 1583.

[Signed:] H. Guilberto

597. 1584. A legal dispute arising out of a Southampton voyage to Newfoundland in 1583.

While most cases posing legal problems arising in the Newfoundland trade in England tended to be adjudicated in the High Court of Admiralty, they might also emerge in another court. A. K. R. Kiralfy, A Source Book of English Law (London, 1957), pp. 252–254, provides one case that was heard during February, 1584, arising out of the terms under which the master of the Archangel, *Peter Bewieio, was hired to make a voyage to Newfoundland in 1583. The case is in P.R.O., Queen's Bench, roll for Hilary term, 27 Elizabeth I, KB 27/1292, m. 445. I am indebted to John Roberts for the reference.*

SOUTHAMPTON RECORD

City and County of City of Southampton:

Pleas at the court of our lady the Queen of

Piepowders held in the vill of Southampton on Tuesday, 18 February in the 26th year of her reign [1584] at 9 a.m. in the Guildhall of South-ampton before the Mayor and Bailiffs according to the custom of that vill from time immemorial observed and used in that vill.

At this court there appeared before the aforesaid Mayor and Bailiffs in the Guildhall John Hopton and Thomas Dumareske in person and offered themselves against Peter Bewieio in this suit. And thereupon John Ridge, Serjeant of the Mace of this court, was ordered to attach Peter Bewieio by a good attachment, to wit by John Hart and Richard Smart, to be before the said Mayor and Bailiffs to answer John Hopton and Thomas Dumareske in that suit, as he was or-dered. And thereupon Peter Bewieio then and there appears in court in person to answer John Hopton and Thomas Dumareske in this suit as he was attached.

DECLARATION

John Hopton and Thomas Dumareske, by Robert Harrison their attorney, complain against Peter Bewieio in a plea of trespass on the case. They complain that whereas on 12 November in the 25th year of the Queen's reign, at the vill of Southampton within the jurisdiction of this court, the plaintiffs retained the defendant to serve them in the office of master of a certain ship called "The Archangel" of Hampton, to make a voyage from the vill of Southampton to Newfoundland in parts abroad, to fish and to remain there until the said ship was fully laden, and thereupon to return to the port of the vill of Southampton, the defen-dant, in consideration thereof and for 6/– paid to him in hand by the plaintiffs; and of the plaintiffs finding food and drink for him during the voyage and for £14 to be later paid to the defendant by the plaintiffs, to wit, after the arrival of that ship from Newfoundland before the vill of South-ampton, then and there undertook and faithfully promised the plaintiffs to serve them well and truly in that office throughout the voyage, yet the defendant, disregarding his promise and design-ing and deceitfully intending to deceive and de-fraud the plaintiffs, although often requested, has altogether refused to serve and still so refuses, to the grave deceit and no mean damage of the plain-tiffs, so that they say that they have suffered damage amounting to £200 &c.

John Hopton and Thomas Dumareske put

Robert Harrison in their place against Peter Bewieio in a plea of trespass on the case.

Peter Bewieio appears in person and denies force and wrong and craves leave to imparl until the court of Piepowders to be held in the Guildhall of Southampton before the Mayor and Bailiffs on Friday 21 February next following, at 9 a.m. &c. The plaintiff has the same day.

PLEA

Pleas at the court of Piepowders &c. on 21 February of 26th year at 9 a.m. To this court came John Hopton and Thomas Dumareske on the one part and Peter Bewieio on the other. Peter Bewieio denies force and wrong and says the plaintiffs ought not to have their action against him, for, protesting that their statement of claim is insufficient in law and that the plaintiffs had no interest in the ship "The Archangel" of Hampton on the day they began this action, he says for his plea that he did not undertake or faithfully promise the plaintiffs to serve them in that ship to Newfoundland and then to return to Southampton with a full cargo, as they allege.

And of this he puts himself on his country, and the plaintiffs likewise. Therefore, in accordance with the custom of this vill, John Ridge, Serjeant of the Mace and officer of this court, is ordered to summon to the Queen's Court of Piepowders in the said Guildhall before the Mayor and Bailiffs of the vill at 3 p.m. on Friday 21 February in the said 26th year jurors, to wit 12 honest and lawful men of the said vill, by whom the truth of the matter may best be known, who neither &c &c. And the same hour is given the parties. (Jury process continues.)

Court of Piepowders held on 25 February of the 26th year at 3 p.m.: (The parties appear &c. 12 jurors appear, being named.)

VERDICT

The jurors, now appearing, being picked, tried and sworn to tell the truth in the premises say on their oaths that Peter Bewieio did undertake and faithfully promise John Hopton and Thomas Dumareske to serve them faithfully and well in the office of master during the said voyage, as the plaintiffs claim. They assess the damages suffered by the plaintiffs at £20 and their costs at 6d. John Hopton and Thomas Dumareske ask judgment on the premises.

JUDGMENT

Therefore it is adjudged by the court that John Hopton and Thomas Dumareske recover from Peter Bewieio his damages assessed by the jury as above and a further 22 shillings and 8 pence costs awarded the plaintiffs by the court as increment, to the total amount of £21.3.2. Peter Bewieio is to be amerced.

EXECUTION

Thereupon John Hopton and Thomas Dumareske by their attorney ask for execution on the premises against Peter Bewieio according to the custom of the vill. Therefore, in accordance with the custom of the vill, John Ridge, Serjeant of the Mace and officer of the court is ordered to arrest Peter Bewieio if &c and to keep him safely, so that he have him before the Mayor and Bailiffs of the said vill on Monday the last day of February at 9 a.m., to be held to satisfy John Hopton and Thomas Dumareske in the said sum of £21.3.2 for the damages sustained by them by reason of the premises, of which the same Peter has been convicted. And to have this precept here then.

WRIT OF ERROR

(On 9 March in the 26th year at 9 a.m. Peter Bewieio presents a royal Writ of Error, tested at Westminster on 29 February in the 26th year, returnable in the Queen's Bench one month after Easter. The Mayor's court does not comply by sending up the record and further Writs of Error are filed on 2 June, 7 July.)

PROCEEDINGS IN ERROR IN THE QUEEN'S BENCH

Later, to wit, on Saturday after the Octaves of Saint Hilary there appeared in the Queen's Bench at Westminster Peter Bewieio in person. And straightway he said that there were obvious errors in the record, the process and the passing of judgment.

ASSIGNMENT OF ERRORS

(1) Where by the record it appears that the title of the said court is "Pleas at the Queen's court of Piepowder held at the vill of Southampton on Monday 17 February in the 26th year &c at 9 a.m. of that day in the Guildhall of the said vill before the Mayor and Bailiffs of the said vill, according to the immemorial custom used and approved in the same vill" the title of the court ought to have taken this form:

"Pleas at the Queen's court of Piepowders by reason of a market held each day in that vill of Southampton, on 17 February in the 26th year &c at 9 a.m. of that day &c &c."

(2) The said John Hopton and Thomas

Damareske have not declared in their statement of claim that the aforesaid ship legally belonged to them as proprietors or possessors at the time they retained the master or at the time of his arrest.

(3) The plaintiffs also failed to declare at what time Peter Bewieio was to carry out the said voyage with that ship.

(*Scire Facias* to the plaintiffs to appear in Easter Term in 15 days to show cause for the judgment. The plaintiffs deny the errors and the judgment of the Queen's Bench is postponed to Michaelmas Term.)

JUDGMENT

Having carefully examined the record and process and the judgment given thereon in this cause and the matters alleged and the errors assigned by Peter Bewieio it appears to the Queen's court that the record is in no wise defective and that there are no errors therein, and it is adjudged that the said judgment be affirmed in all points and be in full force and effect, notwithstanding the matters assigned as errors by Peter Bewieio. It is ordered that John Hopton and Thomas Dumareske recover £2.13.4 adjudicated by this court against Peter Bewieio for expenses caused by the stay of execution of their judgment by reason of the prosecution of the Queen's writ of Error. And that John Hopton and Thomas Dumareske have execution thereon.

598. April 11, 1584. The question of the ownership of the *Swallow*.

The Swallow *was one of Sir Humphrey Gilbert's ships in the voyage to Newfoundland (536); many of its men were former pirates, who caused much trouble on the way out. At Newfoundland a number of men on other ships were too ill to go further. Gilbert decided to send home the ship and get rid of the sick and the troublemakers at the same time. He seems to have offered to give the ship to any of his men who could put up enough money to buy stores to bring it home. Apparently, Robert Boyce did so, and the* Swallow *eventually (after some considerable delay and further expenditure by Sir Humphrey's heir, his brother Sir John Gilbert) reached England where it was impounded by the courts. It had in fact belonged to*

the recently executed pirate John Chalice, who had apprently taken it from a Scottish merchant. Boyce, however, although he was shipwrecked off Sable Island, survived and returned to England in 1584 and claimed that Gilbert's gift of the ship held good. Walter Ralegh complicated matters by saying that the ship had already been sent by Gilbert to recoup his losses (599). The High Court of Admiralty ruled that Boyce should have the ship, but that he must put in bond to hand it back within a year if anyone established better title to it. The case, although not directly involved with the fishery, indicates how complex the question of ship ownership could become.

P.R.O., High Court of Admiralty, Exemplifications, 1583–1585, HCA 14/22, 98–100. printed in D. B. Quinn, Gilbert, II, 429–431.

Tenetur in cxl li. xxvi° Regine Eliz.

The condicion of this Recognisaunce is souch That whereas a sh[ip] called the Goulden Chalis otherwyse the Swallowe whereof Jo[hn] Chalis was late owner is forfieyted and belonging to the Quenes Majesty for that the said John Chalys whilest he was owner therof did felonyousley commytt piracy in the same upon the Sea and flede for the same which ship with her tackling afterwardes came to the possessyon of Sir Humfrey Gilbert knight who taking him selfe to be owner to the same gave yt to the above bounden Richard Boyse upon consyderacion that he at his owne charges should bring or send home into this Relm[e] of England certayne English marynours which were syke in newfound Land, and therefore lefte there by the sayd Sir Humfrey Gilbert as he went foreward on of his voyage towardes [   ] the said R[ichard Boyse afore]s[aid] who thereupon hath made humble suyt to this Court that he may enjoy the sayd shippe and her tackling without lett or molestacion of the Quenes Officers or any other untill the truth shalbe knowne whither the same shall belong to her Majesty by reason of the said Piracy or for any other cause or to him selfe by the sayd gifte or to any other by any other tytle and that yf yt shall [be] founde to belong to the Quenes highnes that then he may enjoy yt without paying any thing payd to her majesties use for yt in consyderacion that he sent the sicke maryn[ers] into England at his owne charges and goeing forward with the sayd Sir Humfrey Gilbert systeyned great losses upon the sea and was in great daunger to be drowned with xv others by the space of eyght dayes being in a lyttell Shippe boate dryving upon the Seas without meate drinke Clothes or any other reliefe to mayntayne there lyfes and without oares or other meanes to bringe the boate to any Land untill yt pleased god that yt was dryven one shore on an unknowne place in Newfound Land In consyderacion whereof And for the avoyding of the great Charges that the keping of the sayd shipp will requier to preserve yt frome decay It is thought meate and so ordered that the same shippe and fornytuer abovesayd to be delyvered to the above bounden Richard Boyse yelding and paying to the Quenes Majesties use so much as they shalbe valued to be worth by the auctoritie of the Court of Exchequer or as by the same Court shalbe lymytted to [be] payd for the same being not duely proved in the Court or [sic] admiraltie to belong to the sayd Boyse or some other person or persons Yf therefore the sayd shipp and furnytuer shall not within one yere and a day now next ensuing after the date herof by claymed & proved in the sayd Court of Admiraltie by due Course of Lawe to belong to the sayd Richard Boyse or to some to [sic] other person or persones other then the Quenes majesty then yf [the] sayde Richard Boyse his executours administratours or assignes doe before the end of the terme of St. Hillary the next ensuing pay or cause to be payd to the use of our sayd Soveraigne Lady of the Queen her heyres & successores at one entier payment the value of the sayd premisses to be sett or lymytted as afore sayd without [any] delay And yf yt shall h[appe]n the sayd s[hip] with the furnytuer to be claymed and recovered out of her Majesties handes within the sayd tyme by the true owner or owners thereof other then then [sic] the sayd Richard Boyse the[n] yf the said Richard Boyse his executours or administratours shall & doe stand to performe and fulfill souche order as the Judge of the sayd Court of Admyraltie shall take mkae & ordeyne touching the sayd shippe and furnytuer and the restytucion of the same or the value thereof to the sayd recoverers according to the discrecion of the sayd Judg. That then &c. Or els &c.

[Endorsed:] Uppon the saide shippe ys hys uppon prisse made in lawe to hawe for allowance of his necessary chardges bestowed upon the said shippe. And there with I humbly take my leave of you[r] honor. From tharches the xith of Aprill 1584

Mr [H]arward [make] a tes[tymonyall] under the lytle seall that Paule Wilson hathe and the [shipp] deliver after to hym

[Signed:] D. Lewes

599. [April, 1584]. Walter Ralegh to Dr. D. Lewes.

Mr Lewis ther is a matter between my brother Sir John Gilberd and a Skottisman about a shipp which he now possesseth / first she was taken by a piratt delivered to the Queens use praysed and sold befor Sir John had her / aftre ward she was leaft att newfoundland from whence he was att great charge to bringe her home, then she arivd in cornwall wher she spent her mastes besids he hath new built her / so that I thinke he should be very extremely dealt withall to have the ship taken from hyme without recumpence having furst bought her by good ordre and hawinge lost a great ship going to newfoundland he hath sent her thither with another small barkes to save sum part of his charges / Sir I pray lett hym have your lawfull favor and yow shall ric'mand mee in anye otre matter.

Your very asured freinde
[Signed:] W. Ralegh

[Addressed:] To the righte wor: my very good frend Mr Doctor Lewes.

600. April 11, 1584. Sir Francis Walsingham to Dr. Lewes.

After my hartie comendations Wheras Sir Humfrey Gilbert redeemed a certaine shippe

from pirates at the sea which shippe is in the possession of Sir John Gilbert and clamed by a Scottishman: for that heretofore an other heth clamed propertie to this shippe and the clame of this Scottishman may be greatly doubted to be just: and moreover Sir Humfrey and Sir John Gilbert have been at great charges as well in the redemption of this shippe as the reparyng of hir, I would be glad to knowe your opinion what were fitt to be done in this case and what the lawe is towching the same. this bearer is able to informe you more at large of this cawse to whome I referre you desyring your answere hereunto. And so commend you hartely to God. From the Court the xith of Aprill 1584 /
Your loving frend

[Signed:] Fra Walsyngham

[*Addressed:*] To my verie loving frend Mr doctour Lewes Judge of the Admiraltie: or to his deputie Judge of the same Court.

601. July 20, 1584. Sir John Hawkins to the Earl of Shrewsbury.

English aristocrats and highly placed officials were not above taking part in the Newfoundland fishery and expecting good returns.
Shrewsbury and Talbot MSS, College of Arms, London.

Right honorable myne especyall good lord I do send unto your lordship a trew coppy of the charge dysborsyd by my servaunt Humfre Jones [or Fones?] for the settyng forthe of the barke Talbut to the newfound lond firmyd with my hand, of which your Lordship dysborsyd by the hondes of your servaunt Ananias Baylye. one hundrethe pownde, There remayneth more to be payd by your Lordship lxxij^{li} xvij^{s} v^{d} which I have answeryd & payd.

I humbly pray your lordship to gyve order the same 72^{li} 17^{s} 5^{d} may be payd here in london by your lordshipes appoyntment

I hope by the xxth day of Awgust next your Lordship shall here of the aryvall of the ship well loden. to acquyt our charg & bring some proffytt.

and so I humbly take my leve from Deptford the xxth of July 1584
Your Honorable Lordships most bownden
    John Hawkyns

[*Addressed:*] To the Right Honorable my synguler good lord therle of Shresbery gyve this

[*Endorsed:*] Master hawkins bill for the charges of the barke Talbott 20 July 1584

602. 1584. English Newfoundlander goes to Spain to sell her fish.

A triangular voyage was often profitable to the men of Newfoundland—for example, from England to Newfoundland, then from Newfoundland to Spain with fish, and finally back to England with wine, oil, and other Spanish produce. This case, arising in 1585, relates to such a voyage and is concerned also with the lack of discipline on board. Two of the men criticized the master for negligence, and he and his witnesses in turn criticized them for insubordination. Spain eventually put a stop to these voyages by the embargo of May, 1585. Bernard Drake was sent in 1585 (541) to see that, in view of the embargo, no further ships went directly to Spain.
P.R.O., HCA 13/25, January 26, 1585, extracts.

26 January 1585. Examination of John Hayes of Paynton, Devon, mariner, before Dr. Cesar, judge of the Admiralty, upon certain articles given against him on the behalf of William Shotton, master of the *White Hinde* of London.

To the seconde he affirmeth that the said wente maryner in the articulate shippe the White Hinde to Newfoundelande on fishing fare, and from thence to Cales [Cadiz] in Spayne, and soe to this porte of London the said William Shotten beinge master that viadge.

To the seconde he affirmeth that the said William Shotton duringe the saide viage did his beste endevor for the merchantes beste profitt and comoditye, and offered not eany abuse eyther towardes the merchauntes or the companye to this examinates knowledge.

To the thirde he deposethe that the said Shotton used all spede and diligence that winde and weather would permitt both for the takinge of his fishe and complyenge his viadge, and performed the same to the merchantes beste avantadge soe farre further as this examinate ever perceaved.

To the fourth he sayethe that the articulate Henry Weste and Anthonye Boyne duringe theire fishinge tyme did not theire labor as they ought to have don, where of the said Master blamed them, and one tyme this examinate herde the said Weste say to the Master in Newefounde lande that he knewe his tymes for labor as well as he did, and woulde [fishe] sea when pleased him, By which occasion and other such like misdemeanour and stubbornes agaynst the master, he and the said Weste and Boyne often tymes fell at variance, and to gevinge same, and the said Boynce in this examinates presence two severall tymes smote the Master at sea when he offered him bloes for theire ill speeches and disobedience used agaynste him.

To the fifth he affirmeth the said Weste and Boyne did not there dewties as appertayned unto them duringe the said viadge, of this examinates sighte and perfecte knowledge and woulde not be commaunded by the Master in the fisshinge tyme but when pleased them, and the said Weste in this examinates hearinge beinge commanded by the Master to goe a Fishinge sayde he knewe his tyme better then he, and woulde goe when he listed.

To the sixth he sayeth he hathe herde the said Weste and Boyne call the said William West in the partes of Spayne and at sea a Rascall knave and boye and woulde make him a boye, and to his greate discreaditt he was not a sufficient Master, nor able to take chardge, and often tymes they have threatened to heate [hit?] him in this examinates presence and hearinge with manye other unsemely speeches that this examinate hath herde passed betwene them duringe the viadge.

To the seventh he affirmethe that he hath herde the said Weste call the Master dronkerde both at Sea and before the owners how be it this examinate never sawe the said master droncke duringe the said viadge.

To the eighth he denieth that he ever knewe that the said Master wente abowte to confiscate shippe or goodes in Spayne, or to doe the merchauntes eanye damadge, but did his beste endeavor for theire benefitt to his knowledge.

To the ninth he affirmeth the shippe boote was loste duringe the said viadge by extreamitye of verye foulde weather and not by eany necligence of the Master and companye of this examinates perfecte knowledge for this examinate was present on borde when the same boate was loste and knowethe theire coulde noe more more diligence be used for savinge thereof then was shewed, yet coulde not prevaile the extreamitye of the weather was suche at that presente."

603. 1584. Samples of metallic ores from Newfoundland come to Ireland.

Sir Henry Wallop wrote to Sir Francis Walsingham that a Dublin ship had brought to Ireland from Newfoundland samples of metallic ore that appeared promising.

P.R.O., State Papers, Ireland, Elizabeth I, SP 63/118, 73, extract.

May it please your honour here came lately unto my handes a sample of Certen Oare brought over (as I am enformed) from Newfound Lande by a merchant shipp of this towne [Dublin] which of late came from thence: both by owtwarde shewe and also by a kynde of hott brymestone sente which (in stryckinge or rubbinge one piece against an other) it yealdethe, it seameth to have some metall in it: wherefore knowinge your honours disposicion and desier to trye and prove such experymentes, I thought it not amiss to acquainte yow therwith havinge here with sent your honour certen peeces of the said Oare. And of it shalbe judged by men of skill there that it is lyke to yealde any good comoditie, the merchant (as he saythe) knoweth where the lyke is to be hadd, rysinge in great aboundance.

604. March 22, 1587. Philip II warns of the perils to the fisheries in time of war.

After 1580 the fishery was increasingly troubled by piracy, privateering, and the effects of war.

English and French privateers began to take their toll of Spanish Basque ships in both the whale and the cod fisheries; demands of the Spanish navy on both the ships and seamen of the Basque country interfered with the normal routine of the fleets. Warnings to ships leaving Spain or returning from the fishery to protect themselves against attacks were given by Philip II as ships were preparing in March, 1587, to leave for the fishing grounds. We are indebted to Selma Barkham for this document.

Archivo General de la Provincia de Guipúzcoa, Tolosa, Sec. II, no. 12, legajo no. 16, translated.

The King

Representatives of the Assembly, honourable gentlemen of the very noble and very loyal Province of Guipuscoa, from information that I have received it is known that corsairs (English, and from La Rochelle and other parts) are fitting out in haste a number of ships with the sole object of going to Terranova and doing in those posts any damage they can to those who go there from this land, and other parts of the seacoast of these my realms, to the cod and whale fisheries, and because it is well to prevent that which could occur, and provide in time a possible remedy, that which at this moment is seen set to put forth is that the ships which this year have to leave this Province for the said whale and cod fisheries are to go in the best order and as well armed as possible; I require that you, in communication with Garcia de Arce and the Governor of this Province unto whom I have also ordered to be written, give orders that the ships which this said year have to leave from this land and go to the said Terranova, whether for cod or whale fishing, are to go with much caution and with good provision of crew, artillery, arms, ammunition and other equipment suitable for defence and capable of offence when necessary, and so that this can be done with greater security it would be well that they should go together, as many as possible in convoy, and not separately as they normally go, so that in case there are those who wish to lie in wait for them on the way out or back, they have more force with which to defend themselves and even to offend the enemies. Warning should be given to the masters and crews of such ships that because it

might be that when they arrive in the ports of the said Terranova they might find the said Englishmen or corsairs, or some of them, or that the latter might arrive after our ships, and to protect themselves and to make themselves more safe from the damage that could be wished upon them it should be understood that they too go to the fishing to take the enemy with this stratagem without any risk to themselves, who should in this case be thoroughly forewarned, in order that they should receive no damage whatsoever. You must procure that this is complied with and that they are warned in such a way that they cannot pretend to ignorance. Inform me as to what is done in this matter, and what ships go and of what burden, and that they go in good order, so that I can be sure of what is happening.

From Sant Lorenço on the 23rd of March, 1587.
[Signed:] I THE KING

By order of the King our Lord Andres de Alva

605. January 25, 1588. Passport for an English vessel going to Newfoundland.

P.R.O., HCA 14/24, 31, January 25, 1588, draft.

Charles Lord Howard &c

To all and singular Viceadmiralls Justices of Peace &c. Whereas Nicholas Newman, Thomas Morris and William Payne of Dittisham in the County of Devon owners of the ship called the Hope of Dittesham having noe other trade nor being otherwise broughte uppe but in Fysshinge fare at the Newfound lands are authorised and licensed to furnish and sett furhter the said shipp under the conduction and guidinge of Nicholas Bennett Master, Andrewe Cutt Masters mate and twenty mariners more being fishermen to passe unto the Newfound lande on fisshinge fare and to make return for Dittesham with such fish and trayne as by theire industry and travell shalbe there taken and made. And fearinge leste the said shippe beinge furnished and victualed at the great coste and chardges of the said owners should be hereafter stayed and hindered in eany of her majestes partes or at sea from proceedinge and finishinge the said viadge to their utter spoile and undoinge have therfore requested theise our Lettres of pasporte licence and safeconducte for the same which we have graunted unto them.

Theise are therefore on her Majestes behaulfe straightly to charge and commaund you and every of you her Majestes lovinge subjectes to whom in this case by sea or land yt shall or may appertayn to permitt and suffer the said Nicholas Bennett with the said shipp and company quietly and freely to use theire navigation and to departe furth sayle passe and goe by you and every of you to the Newfound lande on Fishinge fare and to returne with such fishe and trayne as shalbe there provided without eany your lett stay ympeachement molestation trowble greife or arreste to be made or done by the way by you or eany of you as you and every of you will answere for doing the contrary at your uttermmost perills. We also most hartely desire &c. Dated the .xxv[th] of January 1587 stilo Anglie and in the xxx[th] yeare [of Queen Elizabeth].

606. 1589. Spain stops French Basque Newfoundlanders from leaving port.

Spain virtually controlled the French Basque Newfoundlanders since the roadstead at El Pasaje (meaning the passage, in the English of the time) was the only place they could assemble for their departure. This might be done to embarrass France, but it was more often done in an attempt to take over the ships' stores for use by the Spanish navy or to prevent Spanish Basque seamen, needed for the Spanish fleet, from going to Newfoundland on French-owned ships. Examples are given in Calendar of State Papers, Foreign, January–July 1589 *(London, 1950), pp. 151, 231–232.*

[a] March 14, 1589. Edmund Palmer to Sir Francis Walsingham from St-Jean de Luz.

The General of Fuenterabya, by the King's orders, eight days ago embargoed seventy ships of this town riding in the Passage ready to go to the Newfoundland fishing. All are ships of a hundred to two hundred and fifty tons, the French victualled for eight months. The Spaniard may get the ships and victuals, but he will not get men. If they do not go to the fishing this country is wholly destroyed.

[b] May 7, 1589. John Welles to Sir Francis Walsingham from Rouen.

A shipmaster come from Bayon says that sixty Bayon and St John the Luyse ships, bound for the Newfoundland fishing, have been stayed at the Passage.

607. 1588. Passport for an English Newfoundlander.

Passports were issued to English ships going to Newfoundland after war had broken out with Spain, because they might offer some slight safeguard in case a vessel was intercepted by an English privateer. In 1588 there was an embargo on vessels leaving without a safe conduct.

P.R.O., High Court of Admiralty, Instance and Prize, Libels, HCA 14/24, 11, brief abstract.

Safe conduct by the Lord High Admiral to Walter Berryman and others, owners of the *Marye* of Northam, her tackle and furniture, under the conduction and guiding of Richard Braddon, master of the same, and seventeen other men and mariners, "on fishinge farre to Newfounde Lande," furnished with victuals and necessaries for such a voyage at their own proper costs and charges.

608. *Circa* 1592. English Newfoundlander in a triangular trade with Toulon.

When Spain closed her doors in 1585 some English fish dealers attempted a triangular trade with French Mediterranean ports. Henry Glanham was cruising in the Mediterranean, ostensibly as a privateer, in practice as a pirate. He had recently caught and released a French vessel from Toulon.

Henry Roberts, News out of the Levane seas (London, 1594), sig. B3v.

Three days after theyr departure earely in the morning wee descried a great sayle, and gave her chace, and about two a clocke came up with her. Thys sayle was the *Salomon* of London which came from New-found Lande laden with fishe, whose Master and Company came aborde of us. Theyr Maister was of the Generall [Glenham] well entertayned. Of them our Generall bought six hundred of theyr fish gyving them ready money for the same. So they departed for Tellone [Toulon] which was their port....

609. January to February, 1594. War interferes with the sailing of English Newfoundlanders.

Letters to prevent ships going on long voyages from sailing were frequently issued by the English government during the war with Spain. At times the Newfoundland trade was exempt, as fish was needed for ships' stores. In 1594 there was doubt about the letters, and local officials queried official orders.

Cecil Papers, Hatfield House, abstracted in Historical Manuscripts Commission, Calendar of Cecil Manuscripts, IV (London, 1892), 479.

[a] Sir John Gilbert forwards an order from Lord Howard of Effingham to the Customers of Dartmouth.

Charles, Lord Howard to Sir John Gilbert, vice-admiral of Devon, signifying her Majesty's pleasure for the stay of all ships, as well merchants as men of war ... and in the meantime to take the sails from the yards, and to carry them ashore for more security. From Hampton Court, 7 January 1593–[1594].

[b] Customers of Dartmouth to John Dawse and other surveyors of customs causes for the outports.

Have received copy of a restraint directed to the Vice-Admiral, and a letter from him, prohibiting them to take any entries of goods or ships which may not return within the time limited in his letter [end of April]. Being unwilling to attempt anything without authority, have sent to pray them to move the Lord Treasurer or Sir John Fortescue, or both, whether Sir John Gilbert's letter stands with their good liking or not, and to receive their direction thereupon. The Newfoundland men whom he toucheth have all made their provision to their great charge, yet they mind to perform that part of his letter until they receive their answers; but in the mean time wish all their honours were remembered that in these hard times of trade it is the only voyage that maketh both owner and mariner to flourish; and that if this restraint be but for her Majesty to be served with men, there will no doubt be had, out of the ships of this harbour bound for Newfoundland, 100 men for her Highness' service, and yet the voyage of the Newfoundland (if they may have leave to depart by the 10th or 20th of March) to proceed with good contentment of the adventurers and owners. Dartmouth, 18 February, 1593=[1594].

610. 1591. Suspicion of an Englishman trading Newfoundland fish to Spain in time of war.

An Englishman was alleged to have sent his lading of Newfoundland fish to Spain. He denied that the ship was his or that he had an interest in the voyage.

Admiralty Proceedings before Dr. Julius Caesar, Judge of the Admiralty, at Weymouth. P.R.O., HCA 13/96, August 20, 1591.

Whereas Richard Pitt ys presented that he sente a barck to Newfound lande on Fishinge which went from thence to Spayne with such fishe as was taken there. It is ordered (for that Richard Pitt deposed that the same Barcke was a French Barcke and furnished with Frenche men and that he had noe adventure at all in the said viadge) that he should be discharged from further trouble for that cause.

611. 1593. Report that the Dutch were intervening in the Newfoundland trade.

In the House of Commons in 1593 Sir Walter Ralegh claimed that the Dutch were already intervening in the Newfoundland trade, although this is rather earlier than other indications that exist.

Sir Simonds D'Ewes, The journals of all the parliaments during the reign of Queen Elizabeth (London, 1682), p. 509.

The Dutchman by his Policy hath gotten Trading with all the World into his hands, yea he is now entring into the Trade of *Scarborough* Fishing, and the Fishing of the *New-found-lands*, which is the stay of the *West-Countries*. They are the people that maintain the King of Spain in his Greatness.

612. 1595. French Basque ships sail to Newfoundland with English passports.

Such was the position of the French Basque ships, many of them attacked and taken on the pretext that they were Spanish, that after repeated complaints in England it was arranged that they could obtain passports to cover them on their way to and from Newfoundland from the Lord High Admiral in England. Martizan (or Martin) Sance de Aristega, in spite of receiving such a passport for the Ste Marie de St-Vincent *of Ciboure, which in turn was reinforced by a pass from the English port admiral at St. John's Harbour, was attacked and had his ship taken by an English privateer (or pirate) Henry Carpenter. The lengthy proceedings in the High Court of Admiralty in London indicate some of the issues.*

P.R.O., High Court of Admiralty, Instance and Prize, Examinations, HCA 13/32, January 17, 1596, brief extracts.

[a] Stephen de Harembellet, said the St. Mary of St Vincent was built in 1592, was of 280 tons, and was worth 5000 crowns: "she sett oute ... to make a viadge to the Newfoundeland on fishinge," in 1595.

"William Parfey hath tould [him] in this city of London that he had perceived the said ship in the Newefoundelandes and fished in her company, and that he had given him a pasporte for his more free passage for St. John de Luze."

[b] Martizan de Aristega. The *St. Mary* went to Newfoundland under his charge as master "who had a pasporte from the L. Admirall of Englande; which was procured for him in England before the undertakinge of the said viadge."

"William Parfrey being an Englisheman and commander of the said River of St. John in Newfoundlande [where he laded fish and oil] gave them a pasporte for there shippe companye and ladinge to departe them for their native contrye."

[c] John de Sabirea. The *St. Mary* left for St. John's "with pasporte which was provided by master Jackson of this city of London of the L. Admirall for the said owners as they toulde this examinate at Subiboroughe [Ciboure] as master Jackson hath tould this examinate in London."

They took 16,000 fish and made 18 tons of oil, "fished and laded."

[d] Peter de Chevenne. He "sawe a pasporte that was granted to them from the L. Admirall of Englande for the said viadge." They made 16,000 wet and dry fish.

"William Parfey an Englisheman beinge commander of the River of St. John in Newfoundlande where the said fish was taken uppon sight of the pasporte which was granted by the L. Admirall to the said shipp and company, gave them his pasporte likewise for there more securrity."

613. 1594–1595. English boats left at Newfoundland said to have been misappropriated.

Inshore fishing at Newfoundland required a large number of boats to be profitable. The fishermen preferred to bring out only a small number each year, as it was difficult to stow any appreciable number. Consequently, they were marked and left at the "room" that had been used during the season on shore at Newfoundland. Sometimes the Boethuk Indians damaged them. In this case one English master accused another of misappropriating his stock of boats and so ruining his voyage.

Francis Cherie, John Stoakes, deceased (by his executrix, Magdalene Stoakes), John de Clerke and William Parfay, owner of the David *of London, against William Baker.*

P.R.O., HCA 24/63, 23, abstract and extracts from deposition of William Parfay.

The ship *David* of London, William Parfay master, was at Newfoundland fishing in 1593 and 1594, and had there their "Boates and shalloppes" necessary for fishing.

William Parfay prepared in 1594 twelve shallops for fishing and and at the end stowed them in the accustomed places namely "five in one place and two in the other hard by or not farre."

Of the five boats left in one place "They were marked somme on the keele and somme on the kelse with a no [an "o"] and an auger hole wherein a muskett shott was putt and with two compasse notches or scratches like half moones with the pointes downeward on their sternes, and the two other boates of the said seavon were marked with an Auger hole in the inside of ther starnes, and with a small auger hole in the insides of the keles in the waterway."

In the months of April, May, June, July, August, September and October 1595 William Parfay came to use the boats in "St Johns Harborough *apud* Newe founded Land" with the *David* but they were missing.

William Parfay learnt that they were in the hands of and were used by William Baker. "They were used by him or by some of the companie of hys ship wherin he was *tempore predicto* and the same were seene tied or clemed to his said shippe, and were all some or one of them by him or hys order appointment or consent deteined and kept away from the said William Parfay, [as] the said William could not have the use thereof in the saide fishinge time."

He said "The said complainentes had and might have had their said fishinge viadge yf it had not bin hindered by the meanes of the saide [Baker] their said shippes beinge at Newfoundlande in Anno 1595, and by reason of the want of these

boates and lacke of takinge in due time in [longe] stayinge charges and other damages they had and have to such value *viz.* to the value of CCCC^li.

"Item that before the said shippe called the David went forth in the viadge aforesaid, the said William Parfay told the owners and setters forth of the saide shippe that he had boates sufficient to fishe or take fishe for the ladinge of the said shippe and in deed the yeare before there were left of his at Newfound Land twelve boates which he hoped to finde and have there again at the saide fishinge time in *anno domini* 1595 that he should have had." (No explanation is offered of what became of the remaining five boats Baker was not charged with misappropriating.)

614. September 23, 1595. Newfoundland fish being distributed from England to France and the Netherlands.

The European war created an unprecedented demand for Newfoundland fish. There was now competition for the catch brought by the West Country fishing fleet.

W. Stalling, mayor of Plymouth, to Sir Robert Cecil, September 23, 1595. Historical Manuscripts Commission, Calendar of Cecil Manuscripts, V (London, 1894), 387, extract.

There is arrived in these parts within these fourteen days past, to the number of fifty sail, the country shipping, all laden with Newland fish which, as it is thought, will be laden away again by Flemings and Frenchmen that have their ships here ready for the same. If hereafter there should be cause to use any for her Majesty's service, no doubt there would be money saved in taking the same as the price now goeth.

615. 1597. Fishing at Newfoundland combined by French Basques with fur trading.

Martizan Sance de Aristega (or Martin Arrit-

saga) lost an additional ship to the English in 1597: He claimed she had been trading with the Indians for furs as well as fishing. See also (612).
    P.R.O., HCA 13/32, December 30, 1597, abstract from his deposition.

Martin Arritsaga. His ship, the *Bonaventure* of Subiborowe [Ciboure] was sent from St Jean de Luz to Newfoundland in April 1597 and got there fish and train oil "and besides they gott of the Savadges in trucke for tobacco fifty buckskynnes, forty bever skinnes, twenty martins" and two barrels of fish roes.

    Off Cape Finisterre the ship was taken by Captain Hubbarde of Southampton. The fish was to be taken to St Jean de Luz and to no part of Spain or Portugal.

Chapter Seventy-five
Business in Peacetime, 1602–1613

616. 1602. A Newfoundland seaman's inventory.

The will of Maurice Cozens of Dartmouth, dated November 21, 1599, shows what a seaman engaged in the Newfoundland fishery might accumulate, and that a share in a voyage was reckoned by him to be worth £2 13s 4d. It is cited in his inventory, taken July 6, 1602. Abstracts of English Records *(privately printed, Boston, 1929), p. 245 (reference from John Roberts).*

A cheste in the norther chamber of his mothers house, astrolabe with 2 seabooks, 2 crosses, 2 payre of compasses and a tinder box, his seachest. Lease of a house in Hardnes for 70 years £40; 2 old trammell nets; ¾ of a share from the Newfoundland £2, a pare of spectakels 1s. Total £74 12s. 4d.

remain to the other and if both die, the money to remain to my wife.

To my said sons all my apparel to be equally divided between them. His wife to be executrix, paying to the Mawdling House of Totnes 2s.

Witnesses. John Germaine, John Barens, William Cowse, William Cleyfe, William Germaine, Robert Yeabsly, John Barens and William Germaine [*sic*].

Proved 12 October 1602 and administration committed to Rabbidgie his relict. Inventory sum £7 12s. 8d.

Inventory praised by Henry Furneaux and William Eastley 24 September 1602.

Household goods. For his Newfoundland voyage the year £5, etc.

Total £7 12s. 8d.

Exhibited 12 October 1602 by Rabidgia the executrix.

617. 1602. A share in Robert Hill's Newfoundland voyage is left by a will made in Newfoundland.

Will formerly in Exeter Consistory Court, abstract in Exeter Public Library. (From John Roberts.)

Will of Robert Hill of Paington, sayler, dated 23 August at Newfoundland, 44 Elizbeth [1602]

To my sons £4 apiece, to be laid out for their maintenance for space of 4 years, but if my wife do marry before, then the said money to be paid immediately upon her marriage, unto my children. If either die without issue, the money to

618. 1605–1606. The Spanish Company tries to organize the trade in Newfoundland fish.

An argument developed in 1606 on whether the Company of Merchants trading to Spain should try to organize the trade in Newfoundland fish. This was contested as an infringement of freedom of trade and defended as a means of developing commerce and preventing overcompetition. Pauline Croft, The Spanish Company *(London, 1973), p. 224, extracts and summary.*

It is alleged that charters to companies of merchants are an impediment to free trade and "that where as mariners do now increase by fishing at Newfoundland, if they should be restrained to sell their fish in Spain they should be discouraged to go fishing and so navigation decay."

It is replied that the Company of Merchants trading to Spain would but £40,000 of fish from them and take the risks of selling it in Spain, whereas now "the fishers now thrusting into every port of Spain without order do but glut the market."

619. 1606. Alleged Spanish maltreatment of an English ship from Newfoundland.

After the Treaty of London, English Newfoundlanders felt free to revive the triangular trade in fish to Portugal and Spain, but the *Spanish authorities do not appear to have been willing to admit this. The Spanish Company was established in 1605 to look after the interests of English merchants in the Iberian lands, but it could do little and was soon dissolved. Pauline Croft, ed., The Spanish Company (London, London Record Society, 1973), p. 121, extract.*

1606. Petition of the Spanish Company to the Privy Council

A western bark going directly from Newfoundland (where she took fish) and arriving at Lisbon, they did confiscate both ship and goods, and committed the mariners to the galleys without any offence by them given, where they still remain for anything we hear to the contrary.

EARLY SEVENTEENTH-CENTURY ENGLISH BUSINESS DOCUMENTS RELATING TO NEWFOUNDLAND

SERGEANT HELE'S "Precedent Book" in the Plymouth City Archives provides examples of a number of forms of document used in the business arrangements that preceded a Newfoundland fishing voyage. The names of the parties often are not given in full, and it is not always clear whether these were copies of documents actually employed or simply formulas for possible arrangements.

In the first (620) the Plymouth merchant agrees with the master of a Newfoundland-bound ship to accept such bills of exchange as are sealed by another master of the same ship and his purser at Newfoundland, who were to take the ship on with its cargo to the Mediterranean ("the Straightes"). The merchant would pay the bills after forty days to the master first mentioned. The second (621) is described as a condition for an adventure to Newfoundland, but appears to cover a voyage (with Newfoundland fish?) from Saltash to San Lúcar and back, when a certain sum was to be paid by one party to another, if the voyage were a success; if not, a smaller sum was to be paid. Without the bond that would go with it, the document is not fully intelligible, but it may be concerned with the insurance of the vessel. The third (622) is a bond and obligation by a Salcombe merchant to deliver certain Newfoundland fish to another merchant on the return of a ship from Newfoundland with a penalty to be paid if the ship does not bring the fish. The fourth (623) is an obligation by a merchant to pay a certain sum within forty days after the return of a Newfoundlander to England. I am indebted for the transcripts to Professor Gillian T. Cell.

The ramifications of the business documents relating to the fishery are by this time considerable in extent.

620. Agreement of a Plymouth merchant to accept bills of exchange.

Be it knowen unto all men by these presentes that I T. R[   ] of Plymouth in the Countye of Devon merchant doe herby Covenaunte & promyse for me my executors admynystrators to & with John D[   ] of Marreldon in the said Countye maryner (master of a shippe called the Provydence of London in the nowe pretended vyage at the Newfoundland) not onlye to accept of suche billes of Exchaunge as shalbe sealed unto me from & out of the parties of the Newfoundland in the nowe pretended viage from & under the handes of Thomas Duffeild of Ratcliff (who goeth master of the seid shippe from the Newfoundland into the Straightes) and Richard Newman of London Fishemonger purser of the seid shippe But also within Fortye dayes nexte after sighte had of the seid billes by me the seid T. R[   ] to satisfye & paye or cause to be payde unto the seid John D[   ] or his laufull assynes suche sommes of moneyes as shalbe therin mentyoned In wytnes &c /

621. Condition for an adventure to Newfoundland.

The Condycion of this oblygacion is suche that wheras the good shippe called the Margarett of Saltashe nowe beinge within the Roade of Salt[ash] aforseid wherein is master (under god) R. Beile is intended by gods helpe with the first good wind etc. to go to St. Lucas in Sp[ain] & then return to Saltash if R. B[eile] or other master shall sail speadily & directly to St. Lucars & return again & if the abovebounden Henry P[errye] his executors etc. pay unto the above-bounden Jo. Y[   ] in 1 payment the sum of £24 within 30 days after the return of the ship from St. Lucars If weather or any stay, restraint etc keep the ship in an English port & if then Henry Perrye his executors etc pay to J. Y[   ] at his dwelling in Hatherlye the sum of £20 within

20 days after such a stay or arrest or any other accident then &c.

622. Bond by a Salcombe merchant to deliver Newfoundland fish.

Noverit &c me Gilbert Bryce de Salcombe &c Teneri &c in Triginta libris Dat. &c /

The Sweet Rose of Salcombe, 40 tons, Robert Asherman master, is bound on voyage from Salcombe to Newfoundland on fishing voyage at direction of said master & then to return directly to Salcombe. If Gilbert Bryce causes to be delivered to William Putt, his executors etc. at or in the cellar of B. A[   ] in Salcombe or any whay or quay etc. there 4400 good dry fish of Newfoundland as they shall come out of the hold without choice, 120 to every 100, within 40 days of the return of the Sweet Rose to Salcombe—if any accident cause Sweet Rose to return without reaching Newfoundland then if Gilbert Bryce pay William Putt £15 within 30 days after her return then this obligation is to be void.

623. Obligation by a merchant to pay money after the return of a Newfoundlander to England.

The condycion of this obligacion is suche that where the good Shippe called the Judithe of Stonehouse nowe beinge within the harboroughe of Stonehouse wherof is master under god Tho: Webber intendethe by gods helpe with the firste good wynde & weather that god shall sende next after that the seid Shippe shalbe readye to sayle in a voyage to the Newfoundland for Fyshe and after hir Fisherye there ended to retorne directlye to Stonehouse aforseid. Yf the abovebounden George Moiles his executors administrators or assignes or anye of them doe within the tyme & space of fortye dayes nexte after that the seid shippe shall make her first retorne & arryvall from the seid Newfoundland in to anye Porte Haven Harbor or Creeke within the realme of England will & trewlye content satisfye & paye or cause to be satisfied & payde the somme of Treskore twoe poundes & tenn shillinges of lawfull monye of England without Coven or fraude, And also yf the seid belonge unto me for & at the rate of one halfe share. In wytnes &c

624. 1583–1612. Examples of business arrangements made at Southampton for Newfoundland voyages: abstracts.

There are a number of the actual agreements made by merchants and seamen regarding Newfoundland voyages entered in the Book of Instruments, 1575–1587 (a) and the Book of Instruments, 1597–1689 (b–g) in the Southampton City Record Office. Abstracts of them have been provided for me by Professor Gillian T. Cell.

(a) lacks the name of the ship and its burden but is otherwise a simple obligation by a merchant to pay a certain sum to another man (evidently adventured in the voyage) after the return of a ship from Newfoundland and to be liable to a penalty if he does not do so. In (b) the two seamen who own half shares in a Newfoundlander are to pay each of two merchants, who have ventured £20 each in the voyage, £25 on its arrival at a French port or in England, under penalty if they do not do so. (c) provides that the master of a Newfoundlander is to bring a surgeon (evidently an apprentice) to Newfoundland and to the Mediterranean and to pay his passage back from there, but not more than £12 besides. (d) is an outline of a complex transaction by which the master of a Newfoundlander undertakes with the owner of the ship to go to France for salt, then to Newfoundland and back, or else pay a penalty (not all the details are included). (e) is a charter party for the lease of a French ship to Southampton men, for £23, for a voyage to Newfoundland, Malaga, and Southampton. (f) is a letter of "Health" by the mayor of Southampton for a Newfoundlander that intended to proceed from Newfoundland to Marseilles (presumably to establish that the ship was in good standing in her port of origin, and not a privateer). (g) is a charter party by which a master mariner undertakes to sail a new ship to Newfoundland and is to pay a sum of money to be so appointed. (625) is part of a Star Chamber case, where there was a charter party of the usual sort for a Newfoundland voyage, but the return and price of the catch are given. The master is alleged to have cheated the mariners and the shipowner.

[a]   April 1583. Thomas Dumareske of Southampton merchant is bound to Luke Griston of Michen in Sussex for £40 with the condition that if he pay Griston £23 6s. 8d. at the next return of the [   ] of the burden of [   ] tons, from a pretended voyage to Newfoundland on fishing, to the port of Southampton & also if the ship go no further than Newfoundland.

[b]   February 1600–1601. A pair of Indentures of Covennantes between George Lyde & George Balin of Swanage, mariners & owners of half of the bark the *George* of Southampton, 40 tons, of the one part & John Jeffrey of Southampton merchant of the other. Jeffrey paid Lyde and Balin £20 each which he adventures in the said ship in its voyage to Newfoundland in consideration of which they promise to pay him £25 within 14 days of the arrival of the ship from Newfoundland either at Bordeaux or Rochelle or, if she does not go there, within one month of her arrival in England.

It is agreed that the port of discharge shall be either Bordeaux, Rochelle, Poole or Southampton. It is agreed that the ship shall leave by 1 May. if through anye restrainte or some other reason the ship does not sail then they are to pay Jeffrey £20 13s. 4d. on or before 30 June. Lyde & Balin bind themselves jointly to the performance of this & their half of the bark is to be enjoyed by Jeffrey as his own proper goods. A bond of £50 from them both for performance of these covenants.

[c]   31 March 1600. A bill of debt of £12 from Robert Cleere of Fowey, Cornwall, master of the *Swan* of Southampton bound for a fishing voyage

to Newfoundland & then to the Straights to discharge her cargo; the bill unto Thomas Lyte surgeon & servant to Richard Hewes of Poole, surgeon, in that Lyde goes surgeon in the said voyage & is to have only £12 for payment of all his shares due to him in the voyage which is to be paid immediately on discharge of the ship at the Straights. Cleere is to ship Lyde in another ship from the Straights for England & is to pay for his good as well as for his transport home.

[d] 10 January 1602/1603. A pair of indentures of covenants between Richard Cornellis, of Southampton merchant, owner of the *Lyon* of Southampton, & Edward Taulbott of Sandwich, Dorset, mariner & master of the ship & the company (Tawlbott & company the second party). The ship to go under his conduct to the Isle of May for salt, & to Newfoundland "for fish" & then back to Southampton or whichever other port Cornéllis shall direct—with other covenants to be performed on either side as in the indenture now at large doth appear. Bond between James Corbett of [ ] merchant & Richard Cornellis for £[ ]. Corbett is factor in the *Lyon* on the said voyage—if he behave properly on the said voyage (etc.)

[e] 8 June 1603. Charter party Clement Bason of Cherbourg, mariner, master & part owner of the *Clemence* of Cherbourg, 76 tons, lets his ship to fraight to Richard Cornellis merchant of Southampton, for the whole voyage to be made from Southampton to Newfoundland to St. Johns or "Polican" or "Soano" there to do what is laid down in the charter party & then to go to Malaga & back to Southampton. The fraight to be paid 18 crowns for every ton's lading & the advantage £6. Stephen Herrell & Sherbrooke, mariner, Richard Cornellis, and Gaspard Fridlocke, gentlemen of Southampton to be bound to pay £23 within the space of 8 days after the arrival of the *Clemence* from the voyage aforesaid into any English port, and to be bound in double if she doesn't arrive.

[f] 28 March 1604. A letter of "Health" under the mayor's seal & my masters hand for the ship the *Lyon* of Southampton, 240 tons, bound for Newfoundland & then to Marseilles—owner & merchant Richard Cornellis

[17–19 September 1604: other "letters of health" for ships bound to Venice & France.]

[g] 2 January 1606/1607: Charter party between Richard Strowe of Poole mariner master of the [ ] of Southampton of 55 tons now built & lying in the stocks in Southampton, And Peter Pryaulx & John Pryaulx of Southampton merchants. The ship as soon as she is ready is to go with the next wind to Newfoundland on a fishing voyage & to stay till has full lading of fish & train, then to return to Southampton. The master in consideration of £18 is to cause the Ship to be manned with 20 sober men &c.

625. 1612. Case in the Star Chamber, 1616–1617, *Thomas Eliot* v. *Thomas Bedford.*

Southampton City Record Office, Star Chamber Miscellanea, Box 1. From Gillian T. Cell.

Full details of the case are not abstracted but include the following data:

1. 16 March, 1611–1612. Charter party made between Thomas Eliot [shipowner and victualer] and Thomas Bedford [seaman?] for a voyage to Newfoundland.

There was to be a crew of 32 and the fish and oil were to be divided into three equal parts, whereof Eliot was to have for his ship, victuals, salt, nets, etc., two-thirds and the master and company one-third, while the master was also to allow Eliot 200 dry fish out of each man's share.

2. The letter of lading on the return of the ship shows 103,000 dry fish, 4,200 wet fish, and 23 tons of oil.

3. William Wilkins was master of the ship and, to deceive the mariners, he made 35 shares, although there was a crew of only 30, but he deducted 200 fish for Eliot out of only 30 shares.

4. All the fish and oil were sold to Eliot at a rate of 7s. the 100 for dry fish, 14s. the 100 for wet fish, and train oil at £8 a ton, so that, after deductions made, Eliot owed the master and company £124. 6s. [The action is to the effect that Bedford and Wilkins conspired to defraud Eliot.]

626. February 14, 1612. William Lewis sells his shares in the Newfoundland Company.

A colonizing company such as the Newfoundland Company of 1610 was a joint stock venture in which a member could dispose of his shares. Nottingham University Library, Middleton MS Mi x 1⁄4.

To all people to whom this present writinge shall come, I William Lewis of the Citie of Bristoll gentlemen sende greetinge in our Lord God Everlastinge, Whereas the kinges moste Excellent Majestie by his highenes Lettres Patents under the greate seals of England bearinge date the seconde daie of Maio in the eight yeare of his highnes Raigne of England France and Ireland, And of Scotland the three and Fortieth hath Graunted unto me the saide William Lewis John Slanye and divers others free Libertie power and authoritie for the Colonye or Plantacion in Newfoundland with other rights as in and by the same Lettres Pattentes more at large doth Appeare Towardes which charge and Plantacion aforesaide I the said William Lewis have putt in Adventure and stocke with the said Adventurers and planters the sume of Threscoare Poundes of lawfull money of England. Now knowe yee that I the saide William Lewis for and in consideracion of the sume of threescore poundes of lawfull money of England to in hand at and before then sealinge hereof by the saide John Slanye Treasurrer for and in behalfe of himselfe and companye of Adventurers and planters of the Citye of London and Bristoll for the Colonye and plantacion in Newfoundland aforesaide Have graunted Bargained and sould assigned transported remised relessed and sett over And by this my present writeinge doe clearelie fullie and absolutelie graunt bargaine sell assigne transferre remise release and sett over unto the said John Slanye and companie of Adventurers and planters of the Citie of London and Bristoll for the Colonye or plantacion in Newfoundland aforesaide and theire successors and assignes aswell all my saide Adventure of threescore Poundes and all that my share and halfe which I the saide William Lewis my Executors administrators or assignes and everie or anie of us have may might shoulde or of

right ought to have of in and to the Cuntrie of newfoundland aforesaide and all benefitt and profytt that hath or shall or may arrise or growe by reason of the saide Plantacion as amply fullye and effectuallie as I the saide William Lewis my executors administrators or assignes may might shoulde or ought to have holde or injoye the same by force virtue or meanes of the saide recited Lettres Pattentes or otherwise howsoever./ And I the saide William Lewis for me my executors administrators and assignes and for everie of us do Covenaunt promise and graunte by theis presentes to and with the said John Slany and company theire successors and assignes That I the saide William Lewis my executors or administrators shall and will hereafter upon reasonable request and at the cost and charges of the saide John Slany and company make passe seale and deliver to the saide John Slanie and company theire successours and assignes such further conveyaunce and assurance of my said Adventure of threescore Poundes and share and a halfe aforesaide and of all other the saide bargayned premisses, As by the saide John Slany and Companye theire successors or assignes shall be reasonably advised devised or required. In witnes whereof I the saide William Lewis have here unto putt my hand and seale, yeoven the Fourteenth day of Februarye, anno: 1611. And in the nineth yeare of the raigne of our soueraigne Lord king James:

[Signed:] William Lewis

[Endorsed:] Sealed and delivered in the presence of me William Alexander: servant to Thomas Hill Richard Holworthy And of me Francis Pensar: servant to the said [Richard Holworthy?].

627. April 3, 1613. Provisioning of a ship for Newfoundland.

Nottingham University, Middleton MS Mi x 1⁄1, fols. 16v.–17.

Plimoth accompt of provision receaved of Nyce Opie Humphry Randele of Salcom for provision for my selfe and twelfe fishermen for a voiage to the Newfoundland.

March 1612 Receved of Master Slanye in London upon my one bond & master Luckames to be paid in fish the some of

49^l 00^s 00^d

Receved and borowed upon my bond and my brothers to be paid in fish which money for the adventure

303^l 00^s 00^d

Receved for our fishing voiage one Seane 6 neates 7 dosen of lynes one great drifat to packe them in 3 dosen of leades qth 52½ [one quarter 52½ pounds] with 10 dosen of hookes won dosen of squidhookes with Irones 3 boate buckettes 4 boles 1 trayne buckett 8 fisher knives one dosen of small maunes to small compase for the boates on C wight of wick qth [1 quarter] 46 pece 4 hatchettes 3 bread boxes 3 wooden flaggens v^{li} wighte of twine one yeard of cloth for spilting gloves 3 great wooden Cans 4 small cans 4 kypnettes of Irone 5^{li} weight of candels one old kettell wight 7^{li}½ [7½ pounds] 6 wooden platters to small coyle of ropes weighte 1 C 3 qth and 10^{li} for boates hallers and roades one latten fuell one wooden fenell one lyne 18^d for bolings 3 bread baskettes 2 trayes and cans 3 bundells of small squidlynes 3 great drifattes 1 dry hogged wher in is 12^l of bread one hogged full of beefe on small barrell of porcke one barrell full of pease 3 tounes of beere 6 hundred of dry fish 3 gallentes of butter more for vittells paid in Plymoth for their dyett

3^l 8^s 10^d

All which provitions I the said [Hu]mphrie Randell do acknowledg to have receaved of the said Nicholas Opie in good condiscion according for the other accomptes at large which I have put

my hand unto the 3th of Aprill 1613 and do promise] to be a carefull steward in spending the victualls for the g[ood] of master Slany and company wytnes my hand the 3th of Aprill 1613/

A noate for the provition of 20 men for the Newfoundland for fishing which may make some 112 thousand of fish 6 quarters of salt accompting 3 quarters for eache man at 18 gallanes to the bushell and 14^d a bushell which may bee the some of

28 00 00
30 00 00
30 00 00

50 hoggheds of beere at 48^s per tonn

50 C of besq[uit] at 12^s per C is

2 hoggheds of beefe 120 peces in each hogghed and everie pece some 3^{li} or 3½ [3½ pounds] which serveth 4 men and 6 sides of bacone is [   ]

6 bushells of pease at 7^s per bushell

50 or 60^{li} of butter

some ½ pecke of musterseed

a littell barrel of viniger for 6 neattes at 24^s per nett

for one Seane at 3^{li} for 10 dozen of lynes at 10^s per dossen

4 or 5 dozen of leades some 60 weight

15 dozen of hookes at 10^d per dosen

1 dozen and a ½ of squid hookes

Provition for landmen for one yeare for Newfoundland

For eache man as followeth

3 hoggheds and a ½ of beere at 12^s

3 C ½ of bread at 12^s per C

For beefe 2 per weeke for each man at 2 per 1

For fishe

For oyle and viniger

XVII

The First English Settlement in Newfoundland, 1610

THE GROWING SHARE that the English codfishing vessels had in the Newfoundland industry at the end of the sixteenth century is well attested and this advantage continued in the early years of the new century, reaching a level very soon of some 200 ships a year—still much less than the French but an enormous increase on their earlier share. John Guy, a Bristol merchant and adventurer, went to Newfoundland with one of his ships in 1608 and, like Anthony Parkhurst thirty years before, returned enthusiastic about the prospects of a colony there. His pamphlet, which he wrote and circulated (but did not apparently publish), must have attracted much attention in London as well as Bristol. In particular, the important London firm of John and Humphrey Slaney took up the promotion of a venture for which Guy was busily assembling support in Bristol. The precise course of events is not certain, but early in 1610 a strong petition was put together (with support from officials and courtiers as well as London and Bristol merchants and speculating gentlemen like Sir Percival Willoughby). After scrutiny of the possible effects of a colony on the fishery, a charter was granted to the Newfoundland Company in May, 1610, authorizing it to settle in a very extensive area in eastern Newfoundland and to carry on trade with the island provided that it did not interfere with the freedom of the fishery as it was traditionally carried on.

The foundation of the tiny settlement was smoothly carried through. Guy brought thirty-nine settlers in August, 1610 to Cupids or "Kippers," now Cupers Cove, in Conception Bay, well away from the main centers of the fishery at St. John and Placentia. He settled them on a site that was excavated in the early 1970s by Dr. R. A. Barakat of the Department of Anthropology,

Memorial University of Newfoundland. His men were skilled artisans and engaged busily in making rough homes for themselves and preparing a cargo of dressed timber for export the following season. They searched for possible naval stores and other exportable products as well as for traces of minerals. Guy was soon very hopeful of iron being extracted cheaply and profitably. As to the fishery, the colonists would have the first choice of "rooms" on the nearby harbors, which might well lead to hostility by the traditionalist fishermen, but was, potentially, good business for the company. A barracklike residence, a store, and a workshop were completed before late winter. They were kept at work building boats throughout the winter season. In late spring they received supplies from the company and set to work to send back in late May cargo the colonists had ready and also to help with the inshore fishing carried on by the company's ships. Guy planned to try to regulate the practices of the regular fishermen, but it was quite impractical, if not wholly unwise, for him and his men to attempt anything of the sort.

Guy came home in the fall of 1611, leaving Philip Guy and William Colston to run the colony. He came back in 1612 confident that the colony could root itself, for he had brought sixteen women with him so that family life could develop. A second group of settlers arrived a little later, some of them, along with the cattle they brought, intended for a second tiny settlement at Renews, where some materials were collected to build and enclose a settlement. The depredations of the pirate Peter Easton on the fishermen in the summer of 1612 interfered with the settlement, led to the abandonment of the plans for Renews, and took up the men's time building a fort, but they were not otherwise disturbed by the pirate. Ships were sent home with good cargoes, after which, in October, Guy took two boats northward to explore part of Trinity Bay and made some aboriginal contacts—and acquired a few furs—when a party of Beothuk Indians was encountered. After some adventures they arrived back on November 25.

There were 62 people in the settlement during the winter of 1612–1613 (in rather more generous quarters than those of the first winter) setting out from the colony to trap and hunt as continuously as the weather made possible. There was more severe weather than in previous winters and some scurvy (8 people died), but a company vessel reached them by the end of March before they ran out of supplies (many of their livestock died in the harsh winter weather). By 1613 it had been clearly demonstrated that English men and women could live in Newfoundland and keep themselves usefully occupied. The years following, however, demonstrated also that to keep the company afloat and also to subsidize a colony were very difficult, and that many problems, some of them insuperable, still lay ahead.

The only good study of the early settlement (an excellent one) is that in Gillian T. Cell, *English Enterprise in Newfoundland* (1969), pp. 53–70. She has lent us the transcripts of the Middleton Manuscripts in Nottingham University Library which are included below.

Chapter Seventy-six
The Establishment
of the Newfoundland Company, 1610

628. February 9, 1610. Petition of merchants of London and Bristol to the Privy Council for a Newfoundland charter referred to the master and wardens of Trinity House.

We do not have the original petition, with names attached, that was made to the Privy Council for a Newfoundland colony charter (the Privy Council Register is not extant for this year), but it would have included the London group, headed by John Slany, and the Bristol group, headed by John Guy, who were named in the charter when it was granted on May 2.

Trinity House, London, was a body primarily concerned with pilotage on the Thames, but it had much prestige and influence in maritime affairs generally. The reference of the petition to this body was to test the opinions of the mercantile community on a measure that might affect the great Newfoundland fishery that was largely financed from London.

Trinity House, London, Transactions, 1609–1625, fol. 1–1v.

Certaine Articles and Reasons towching a Plantation to be made in Newfoundland, Exhibited by Certeyne marchantes of London and Bristoll unto the Lordes of his majestes privie Counsell, and by them referred to the Consideracion & reporte of the master wardens & Assistantes of the Trinity House. February 9. 1609 [–1610].

Certaine Marchantes of London and Bristoll having used the Fishing trade of Newfoundland, being Confident that the same is habitable in winter, lying in 47 degrees being more to the Southward then any parte of England, and in the height of Burdeux, and being full of woodes, faire Rivers, storde with good Fishe, with Fowle and birdes also, and many stagges, or beastes of that nature, which our Fishermen have tasted of, and as neare to England as it is to Spaine, being but 3. weekes sayle from England & Ireland, with reasonable windes.

Theis Marchauntes desire to have leave with a fewe men fitting for Plantation to make tryall thereof; the rather because it is presumed they may be there free of molestation by any salvages, none having bene seene in any parte of the Countrie where our usuall fishinges are, therefore for the good of the fishinge trade they woulde make plantation, and the Reasons followinge may be Considered of.

1. First, whereas at this presente there is greate resort of our nation thither for Fishing, by which there are ymployed yearely to the number of 200 shippes, with 6000 mareners or thereaboutes whereby great benefite accreweth not only to manie private persons, but also to the whole Comon welthe, by the increase of Navigation & trade in Marchandize, which shippes going thither to Fishe and in manner empty, are fitt to Carry all matter for plantation.

2. Nowe if by anie forraine Prince or State it should happen the saide land within the Circuite aforesaid to be possessed & fortefied, whereby our nation shoulde be debarred from the quiet enjoying of the saide harbours & fishing, the losse, and prejudice thereby, woulde be of more Consequence then nowe Can be imagined, the which purpose hath bene heretofore thought upon by the Frenche, for about the yeare .1580. they enterprized to winter there, but by want of foresight they all perished for want of necessaries for plantation.

3. And if it so fall out that this plantation succeed, the places for fishing may forever become secure for our nation, whereby not only the presente benefitt may be Continued, but much

more Commoditie may growe to this our state thereby, aswell by the increasing of the number of shippes, and marreners in their yearely resort thither, which must ensue in all probability, for that manie places which nowe Cannot be used for fishing within the same Circuite, for whant [*sic*] of harbours may be frequented by the planters in boates.

4. As also the inhabiters there being industrious, will accomodate such as shall repaire to the Coaste, with manie necessaries for their ymployment, and otherwise stand them in greate stead in Case of visitation of sicknes, and preservinge their boates saufe to the right Owners &c.

5. And moreover if it so fall out that the planters may there inhabite, the grounde by man-nuran[ce] may be fitt for tillage and pasture of Cattell (wherewith it may be easily stored) & the woodes Converted to greate Comoditie.

6. And whereas the skill & practise of whales hath afforded greate Commoditie to ye Biskaines upon the Coaste neare adioyninge, yt is not to be doubted but our nation inhabiting there, will soone attaine to the skill thereof, and so become partakers of the like benefitte.

7. It is also hoped that the Country will affoarde Furres, heath, pitche, turpentyne, boardes, made of pyne trees, mastes, and yardes for small shippinge, soapeashes, stagges, skyns & hawkes of all sortes, together with Seale, skynnes, & trane made of seales, and very like to affoard eyther Copper or Iron mynes, which in regard of the quantity of woodes and faire Rivers might easily raise greate proffitt.

8. And which is not the least of ymportance in the intended Course of Virginia, the Plantation, or any fortefication upon the saide Coaste, may serve for important uses for that the scituation thereof is about the middle of the direct Course to virginia, and therefore howe serviceable the havinge of the Randevous [there] may be, it may be easily Conjectured &c.

Nowe the premisses Considered, and found fittinge to be attempted as aforesaid, theise marchantes desire to have letters patentes for a small parte of the saide Countrie yet never inhabited by any Christian people, with reservation for all the Fishinge & use of the said land as ever hath bene used heretofore by any trading thither eyther of our owne nation or of other Countries, which heretofore have used fishing upon the said Coaste &c.

629. February 24, 1610. Observations by the master, wardens, and assistants of the Trinity House on the petition for a Newfoundland charter.

The comments of the master, warden, and assistants of the Trinity House were favorable to the plantation, provided only that it did not interfere with the fishery.

Trinity House, London, Transactions 1609–1625, fol. 1v.

The Answer or Reports of the master, wardens, and Assistantes of the Trinity house to the lordes of the Counsell towchinge to foresaid Articles.

Whereas there hath bene brought unto us by master John Slanye of London Marchant, & master John Guye of Bristoll marchaunt, & other marchauntes of both the saide Cityes, a particuler in writinge, towching a plantation to be made & undertaken by them upon their owne Costes, & Charges in the Newfoundland./ In which writing is sett downe the latitude of the place where they intend to make their aboade, with diverse Reasons laid downe in particuler, & severall articles, of benefitt that may redowne to our Countrie thereby, yf please god to blesse them & the effectes thereof.

So it is Right Honorables that this 24th of February .1609. at our meeting about our busines of our Trinity house in Ratcliffe, we have Reade all theise articles towchinge the foresaide busines of Plantation, and have hadd it debated respectively & Considered of amongest us And for the said intended plantation we are of opynion that people may very well lyve there, and that it may redowne to the greate Comodity of our Country, aswell in respecte of the greate fishinge used there yerely by our nation, as otherwayes.

Provided alwaies that thereby the freedome of Fishing which nowe we enioy may not be altered.

Hugh Merritt, master, William Jones, William Bygate, Robert Rickman, William Jordan,

William Hare, William Sims, Nicholas Diggens, John Goodland, William Goodladd, Robert Kitchen.

630. May 2, 1610. Charter by King James I to the Newfoundland Company.

The royal charter was issued to a group of prominent courtiers, most of whom were merely subscribers in, rather than initiators of, the venture, Many London merchants, notably John Slany, who remained treasurer for eighteen years, country gentlemen (among whom the most prominent was Sir Percival Willoughby of Wollaston Hall, Nottingham), and a number of Bristol merchants, of whom the brothers John and Philip Guy were to be the most active. The form of the charter was closely linked with those already granted to the Virginia Company, very close indeed to the form of the 1609 charter (801). The powers to settle in Newfoundland were wide, but it was firmly provided that the activities of the colonists and company members should not interfere with the general freedom of fishing, long practiced there. A full account of the charter and the persons named in it is given in Gillian T. Cell, English Enterprise in Newfoundland (1969), pp. 53–61.

P.R.O., Patent Roll, 8 James I, part viii, C66/1826; printed in Cecil T. Carr, ed., Select Charters of Trading Companies (London, 1913), pp. 51–62, from which it is reprinted.

James by the Grace of God of Great Britain France and Ireland King, Defender of the Faith etc., To all people to whom these presents shall come, Greeting:

Know ye whereas divers our loving and well-disposed subjects are desirous to make plantation to inhabit and establish a colony or colonies in the southern and eastern parts of the country and isle or islands commonly called Newfound Land, unto the coast and harbours whereof the subjects of this our Realm of England have for the space of fifty years and upwards yearly used to resort in no small numbers to fish, intending by such plantation and inhabiting both to secure and make safe the said trade of fishing to our subjects for ever, and also to make some commendable benefit for the use of mankind by the lands and profits thereof which hitherto from the beginning (as it seemeth manifest) hath remained unprofitable, and for better performance of such their purpose and intentions have humbly besought our regal authority and assistance.

We being well assured that the same land or country adjoining to the foresaid coasts where our subjects use to fish remaineth so destitute and so desolate of inhabitants that scarce any one savage person hath in many years been seen in the most part thereof, And well knowing that the same lying and being so vacant is as well for the reasons aforesaid as for many other reasons very commodicus for Us and our Dominions, And that by the law of nature and nations We may of our royal authority possess our selves and make grant thereof without doing wrong to any other prince or state, considering they cannot justly pretend any sovereignty or right thereunto in respect that the same remaineth so vacant and not actually possessed and inhabited by any Christian or any other whomsoever.

And therefore thinking it a matter and action well beseeming a Christian King to make true use of that which God from the beginning created for mankind, and thereby intending not only to work and procure the benefit and good of many of our subjects but principally to increase the knowledge of the Omnipotent God and the propagation of our Christian faith.

Have graciously accepted of the said intention and suit, And therefore do of our special grace certain knowledge and mere motion for Us our heirs and successors give grant and confirm by these presents unto our right dear and right wellbeloved Cousin and Counsellor Henrie Earle of Northampton, Keeper of our Privy Seal, and to our trusty and right wellbeloved Sir Lawrence Tanfeild Knt, Chief Baron of our Exchequer, Sir John Doddridge Knt, one of our Sergeants at law, Sir Frauncis Bacon Knt, our Solicitor General, Sir Daniell Dun, Sir Walter Cope, Sir Percival Willoughby and Sir John Constable, Knts, John Weld Esquire, William Freeman, Raphe Freeman, John Slany, Humfrey Slanye, William Turner, Robert Kirkam gent., John Weld gent.,

Richard Fishborne, John Browne, Humfrey Spencer, Thomas Juxon, John Stokeley, Ellis Crispe, Thos Alporte, Frauncis Needham, Willyam Jones, Thomas Langton, Phillipp Gifford, John Whittington, Edward Allen, Richard Bowdler, Thomas Jones, Symon Stone, John Short, John Vigar, John Juxon, Richard Hobby, Robert Alder, Mathewe Haveland, Thomas Aldworth, Willyam Lewis, John Guy, Willyam Merridith, Abram Jenings, and John Dowghtye, their heirs and assigns, and to such and so many as they do or shall hereafter admit to be joined with them in form hereafter in these presents expressed, whether they go in their persons to be planted in the said plantation or whether they go not but do adventure their monies goods and chattels, That they shall be one body or communalty perpetual, and shall have perpetual succession, and one common seal to serve for the said body or communalty and they and their successors shall be known called and incorporated by the name of The Treasurer and the Company of Adventurers and Planters of the City of London and Bristol for the Colony of Plantation in Newfound Land:

And that they and their successors shall be likewise enabled by the name aforesaid to plead and be impleaded before any our Judges or Justices in any of our Courts and in any actions or suits whatsoever:

And We do also of our said special grace certain knowledge and mere motion for Us our heirs and successors give grant and confirm unto the said Treasurer and Company and their successors under the reservations limitations and declarations hereafter expressed, All that part and portion of the said country commonly called Newfound Land which is situate lying and being to the southward of the parallel line to be conceived to pass by the cape or headland commonly called or known by the name of Boniviste inclusive, which cape or headland is to the northward of the bay commonly called Trinitye Baye, and also which is situate lying or being to the eastward of the meridian line to be conceived to pass by the cape or headland commonly called or known by the name of Cape Sancta Maria or Cape Saint Maries inclusive, which cape or headland is to the eastward of the bay commonly called the Bay of Placentia, together with the seas and islands lying within ten leagues of any part of the sea

coast of the country aforesaid, and also all those countries lands and islands commonly called Newfound Land which are situate between forty and six degrees of northerly latitude and two and fifty degrees of the like latitude, And also all the lands soil grounds havens ports rivers mines, as well royal mines of gold and silver as other mines, minerals perals and precious stones woods quarries marshes waters fishings huntings hawkings fowlings commodities and hereditaments whatsoever, together with all prerogatives jurisdictions royaltie privileges franchises and preeminences within any the said territories and the precincts thereof whatsoever and thereto or thereabouts both by sea and land being or in any sort belonging or appertaining and which We by our Letters Patents may or can grant, and in as ample manner and sort as We or any of our noble Progenitors have heretofore granted to any company body politic or corporate or to any adventurer or adventurers undertaker or undertakers of any discovery plantation or traffic of in or unto any foreign parts whatsoever, and in as large and ample manner as if the same were herein particularly mentioned and expressed:

Nevertheless our will and pleasure is and We do by these presents express and declare that there will be saved and reserved unto all manner of persons of what nation soever and also to all and every our loving subjects which do at this present or hereafter shall trade or voyage to the parts aforesaid for fishing, all and singular liberties powers easements and all other benefits whatsoever as well concerning their said fishing as all circumstances and incidents thereunto in as large and ample manner as they have heretofore used and enjoyed the same, without any impeachment disturbance or execution, anything in these presents to the contrary notwithstanding:

To have hold possess and enjoy all and singular the said lands countries and territories with all and singular other the premises heretofore by these presents granted or mentioned to be granted to them the said Treasurer and Company their successors or assigns for ever, to the sole and proper use of them the said Treasurer [etc.] to be holden of Us our heirs and successors as of our manor of East Greenwich in the county of Kent in free and common socage and not in capite, Yielding and paying unto Us our heirs and successors the fifth part of all the ore of gold and silver that from time to time and at all times hereafter shall be there gotten had and obtained for all services duties and demands:

And forasmuch as the good and prosperous success of the said plantation cannot but chiefly depend, next under the Blessing of God and the support of our royal authority, upon the provident and good direction of the whole enterprise by a careful and understanding Council, And that it is not convenient that all the Adventurers shall be so often drawn to meet and assemble as shall be requisite for them to have meetings and conferences about their affairs.

Therefore We do ordain establish and confirm that there shall be perpetually one Council consisting of twelve persons here resident in London which shall govern and order all matters and causes which shall arise grow or happen by reason of the said plantation or which shall or may concern the government of any colony or colonies to be established in any the said territories or countries of Newfound Land before limited or any the precincts thereof, Which Council shall have a seal for the better government and administration of the said plantation besides the legal seal of the Company or Corporation, Each of which seals shall have our arms engraven on the one side thereof and our portraiture on the other side, And that the legal seal of the said Treasurer and Company shall have engraven round about on both sides thereof these words, Sigillum Thesaurarii et Communitatis Terre Noue, and that the seal of the Council shall have engraven round about on the one side these words, Sigillum Regis Magne Britannie Franc. et Hibernie, and on the other side this inscription round about, Pro Consilio Terre Noue:

And further We establish and ordain that Sir Percivall Willoughby Knt, John Welde Esquire, Raphe Freeman, Richard Fishburne, John Stokeley, Willyam Turnor, Willyam Jones, John Slany, Humfrey Slany, John Weld, Thomas Juxon and Thomas Jones shall be the Council for the said Company of Adventurers and Planters in the said territories and countries before limited, And the said John Slanye We ordain to be Treasurer of the said Company, which Treasurer shall have authority to give order for the warning of the Council and summoning the Company to their Courts and meetings, And the said Council and Treasurer or any of them shall be from thence-forth nominated chosen continued displaced changed altered and supplied, as death or other several occasions shall require, out of the Company of the said Adventurers by the voice of the greater part of the said Council and Adventurers in their assembly for that purpose:

And We do also by these presents of our special grace certain knowledge and mere motion ordain establish and agree for Us our heirs and successors, That the said Treasurer and Company shall or lawfully may establish and cause to be made a coin to pass current in the said territories of or in Newfound Land before limited between the people inhabiting in any the said territories or in any the precincts thereof for the more ease of traffic and bargaining between and amongst them of such nature and of such metal and in such manner and form as the said Council here shall limit and appoint:

And We do by these presents of our special grace certain knowledge and mere motion for Us our heirs and successors that if it happen at any time or times the Treasurer for the time being to be sick or to have any such cause of absence from the City of London as shall be allowed by the said Council or the greater part of them assembled, so as he cannot attend the affairs of that Company, in every such case it may and shall be lawful for such Treasurer for the time being to assign constitute and appoint one of the Council for that Company to be likewise allowed [as aforesaid] to be the Deputy Treasurer for the said Company, Which Deputy shall have power to do and execute all things which belong to the said Treasurer during such time as such Treasurer shall be either sick or otherwise absent upon cause allowed of [as aforesaid] so fully and wholly and in as large and ample manner and form to all intents and purposes as the said Treasurer if he were present himself may or might do and execute the same:

And further [etc. We etc.] grant full power and authority to the said Council here resident as well at this present time as hereafter from time to time to nominate make constitute ordain and confirm by such name or names style or styles as to them shall seem good, and likewise to revoke discharge change and alter, all and singular governors officers and ministers which hereafter by them shall be thought fit and needful to be made or used for the government of any colony or plantation to be had or made of or in any of the said territories of

Newfound Land before limited and by these presents granted or meant to be granted, And also to make ordain and establish all maner of orders laws directions instructions forms and ceremonies of government and magistracy fit and necessary for and concerning the government of the said colony or colonies and plantation or plantations, and the same at all times hereafter to abrogate, revoke or change, not only within the precincts of the said colony or colonies as they in their good discretions shall think to be fit for the good of the adventurers and inhabiters there:

And We do hereby ordain that immediately from and after such time as any such governor or principal officer so to be nominated and appointed by the said Council for the government of any colony or colonies aforesaid shall arrive in Newfound Land or in any the territories aforesaid and give notice of his commission in that behalf, all officers governors and ministers formerly constituted or appointed shall be discharged, Straitly charging them and commanding them and every of them and every other person resident or which hereafter shall reside in the said colony or colonies upon their allegiance that they forthwith be obedient to such governor or governors as by the said Council here resident shall be named and appointed as aforesaid and to all directions orders and commandments which they shall receive from them as well in their present resigning and giving up their authorities offices charges and places as in all other attendance as shall be by them from time to time required:

And we do further by these presents ordain and establish that the said Treasurer and Council here resident in London and their successors or any five of them being assembled (the Treasurer being one) shall from time to time have full power and authority to admit and receive any other person into their Company Corporation or freedom, And further in a general assembly of the Adventurers with the consent of the greater part upon good cause to disfranchise and put out any person or persons out of the said freedom and Company:

And We do also grant and confirm for Us our heirs and successors that it shall be lawful for the said Treasurer and Company and their successors by direction of the Governors there to dig and to search for all manner of mines of gold silver copper iron lead tin and other minerals as well within the precincts aforesaid as within any part of the main land not formerly granted to any other, and to have and enjoy the gold silver [etc.] and all other minerals to be gotten thereby to the use and behoof of the said Company of planters and adventurers, Yielding therefore and paying yearly unto Us our heirs and successors as aforesaid without any other manner of profit or account to be given or yielded to Us our heirs or successors for or in respect of the same:

And we do further of our special grace certain knowledge and mere motion for Us our heirs and successors grant by these presents to and with the said Treasurer and Company and their successors, That it shall be lawful and free for them and their assigns at all and every time and times hereafter out of our Realm of England and out of all other our Dominions to take and lead into the said voyage and for and towards the said plantations all such and so many of our loving subjects and live under our allegiance, as shall willingly accompany them in the said voyage and plantation, with sufficient shipping armour weapons ordnances munitions powder shot victual and such merchandises or wares as may be fitting to transport and carry into those parts, and clothing implements furniture cattle horses and mares and all other things necessary for the said plantation and for the use and defence and trade with the people there if any be inhabiting in the said country or shall come out of other parts there to trade with the said planters and in passing and returning to and fro all such commodities or merchandises as shall be from thence brought, without yielding or paying subsidy customs or imposition or any other tax or duty to Us our heirs or successors for the space of seven years from the date of these presents Provided that none of the said persons so taken and carried for the plantation be such as shall be hereafter by special name restrained by Us our heirs or successors:

And that for their further encouragement of our special grace and favour we do by these presents for Us our heirs and successors yield and grant to and with the said Treasurer and Company and their successors and every of them their factors and assigns, that they and every of them shall be free and quit of all subsidies and customs in Newfound Land or any the territories or precincts aforesaid for the space of one and twenty years and from all taxes and impositions forever upon any goods or merchandises at any time hereafter either upon importation thither or exportation from thence into our Realm of England or into any other of our Dominions by the said Treasurer and Company and their successors their deputies factors and assigns or any of them except only the five pounds per centum due for customs upon all such goods and merchandise as shall be brought or imported into our Realm of England or any other of these our Dominions according to the ancient trade of merchants, which five pounds per centum only being paid it shall be thenceforth lawful and free for the said Adventurers the same goods and merchandise to export and carry out of our said Dominions into foreign parts without any customs tax or other duty to be paid to Us our heirs or successors or to any other our officers or deputies, Provided that the said goods and merchandises be shipped out within thirteen months after the first landing within any part of those Dominions:

And We do also confirm to the said Treasurer and Company and their successors as also grant to all and every such governors or other officers or ministers as by the said Council shall be appointed to have power and authority of government and command in or over any colony or plantation in any the limits or precincts aforesaid, that they and every of them shall and lawfully may from time to time and at all times for ever hereafter for their several defence and safety encounter expulse repel and resist by force and arm as well by sea as by land and by all ways and means whatsoever all and every such person and persons whatsoever as without the special licence of the said Treasurer and Company and their successors shall attempt to inhabit within the said several precincts and limits of the said colony or plantation and also all and every such person and persons whatsoever as shall enterprise or attempt at any time hereafter destruction invasion hurt detriment or annoyance to the said colony or plantation:

And it shall be lawful for the said Treasurer [etc. as aforesaid] from time to time and at all times hereafter, and they shall have full power and authority, to take and surprise by all ways and means whatsoever all and every person and person whatsoever with their ships goods and other furniture trafficking in any harbour creek or place within the limits and precincts of any colony or plantation to be made in any the limits or precincts aforesaid, and, being allowed by the said Company to be adventurers and planters of the said colony, until such time as they, being of any Realms or Dominions under our obedience, shall pay or agree to pay, to the hands of the Treasurer or of some other officer deputed by the governor in any the said territories or precincts aforesaid, over and above such subsidy and custom as the said Company is or hereafter shall be to pay, five pounds per centum upon all such goods and merchandises so brought in thither other than such as shall be brought in for the necessary use of fishing as hath been heretofore accustomed, and also five pounds per centum upon all goods by them shipped out from thence other than fish and other necessaries requisite to fishing, And, being strangers and not under our obedience, until they have paid, over and above such subsidy and custom as the same Treasurer and Company and their successors is or hereafter shall be to pay, ten pounds per centum upon all such goods likewise carried in and out, And the same sums of money and benefits as aforesaid for and during the space of one and twenty years shall be wholly employed to the benefit and behoof of the said Company or plantation, and, the said one and twenty years ended, the same shall be taken to the use of Us our heirs and successors by such officer and minister as by Us our heirs and successors shall be thereunto assigned and appointed:

Also We do for Us our heirs and successors grant and declare by these presents that all and every the persons being our subjects which shall go and inhabit within any colony or plantation within any the precincts aforesaid, and every of their children and posterity which shall happen to be born within the limits thereof, shall have and enjoy all liberties franchises and immunities of free denizens and natural subjects within any of our other Dominions to all intents and purposes as if they had been abiding and born within this our Realm of England or any other of our Dominions:

And forasmuch as it shall be necessary for all such our loving subjects as shall inhabit within the said territories or precincts of Newfound Land aforesaid to determine to live together in the fear and true worship of Almighty God Christian peace and civil quietness each with other, whereby every one may with more safety pleasure and profit enjoy that whereunto they shall attain with great pain and peril, We for Us our heirs and successors are likewise pleased and contented and by these presents do give and grant to the said Treasurer and Company and their successors and to such governors officers and ministers as shall be by the said Council constituted and appointed according to the natures and limits of their offices and places respectively, that they shall and may from time to time for ever hereafter within the said territories or precincts of Newfound Land or in the way by the seas thither and from thence have full and absolute power and authority to correct punish pardon govern and rule all subjects of Us our heirs and successors as shall from time to time adventure themselves in any voyage thither or that shall at any time hereafter inhabit in the precincts and territories of the said land called Newfound Land aforesaid according to such orders ordinances constitutions directions and instructions as by the said Council as aforesaid shall be established, and in defect thereof in cause of necessity according to the good discretions of the said governors and officers respectively as well in cases capital and criminal as civil, So always as the said statutes ordinances and proceedings as near as conveniently may be shall be agreeable to the laws statutes government and policy of this our Realm of England:

And We do further of our special grace certain knowledge and mere motion grant declare and ordain that such principal Governor or Governors as from time to time shall duly and lawfully be authorised and appointed in manner and form in these presents heretofore expressed, shall have full power and authority to use and exercise martial law in cases of rebellion or mutiny in as large and ample manner as our Lieutenants in our counties within our Realm of England have or ought to have by force of their commission of Lieutenancy:

And furthermore if any person or persons adventurers or planters of the said colony or any other at any time or times hereafter shall transport any monies goods or merchandises out of any our Kingdoms with a pretense or purpose to land sell or otherwise dispose the same within the limits and bounds of any the said territories or precincts of or in Newfound Land, and yet nevertheless, being at sea or after he hath landed within any part of the said territories and precincts, shall carry the same into any foreign country with a purpose there to sell and dispose thereof, that then all the said goods and chattels of the said person or persons so offending and transporting, together with the ship or vessel wherein such transportation was made, shall be forfeited to Us our heirs and successors:

And further our will and pleasure is that in all questions and doubts that shall arise upon any difficulty of construction or interpretation of any thing contained in these our Letters Patents, the same shall be taken and interpreted in most ample and beneficial manner for the said Treasurer and Company and their successors and every member thereof:

And finally our will and pleasure is, and We do further hereby for Us our heirs and successors grant and agree to and with the said Treasurer and Company and their successors that all and singular person and persons which shall at any time or times hereafter adventure any sum or sums of money in or towards the said plantation of any colony or colonies in Newfound Land or any the territories or precincts thereof, and shall be admitted by the said Council and Company as adventurers of the said Company in form aforesaid and shall be inrolled in the Book or Record of the adventurers of the said Company, shall and may be accounted accepted taken held and reputed adventurers of the said colony and shall and may enjoy all and singular grants privileges liberties benefits profits commodities advantages and emoluments whatsoever as fully largely amply and absolutely as if they and every of them had been precisely plainly singularly and distinctly named and inserted into these our Letters Patents:

And lastly because the principal effect which We can desire or expect of this action is the conversion and reduction of the people in those parts (if any be there inhabiting) unto the true worship of God and Christian religion, in which respect We would be loth that any person should be permitted to pass that We suspected to affect the superstitions of the Church of Rome, We do hereby declare that it is our will and pleasure that none be permitted to pass in any voyage from time to time to be made into the said country but such as first shall have taken the Oath of Supremacy, for which purpose We do by these presents give full power and authority to the Treasurer for the time being and any three of the Council and to every three such person or persons as shall be by the said Treasurer and any three of the said Council thereunto authorised (whereof the Treasurer for the time being to be one), and to any our Mayors Bailiffs or any other our chief officer or officers in any our ports havens or towns where any such person or persons shall take shipping to tender and exhibit the said oath to all such persons as shall at any time be sent and employed in the said voyage to remain or plant there:

Provided always and our will and pleasure is, and We do hereby declare to all Christian Kings Princes and Estates, that if any person or persons which shall hereafter be of any colony or plantation in any the territories or precincts of Newfound Land before limited or any other by this their or any of their licence or appointment shall at any time or times hereafter rob or spoil by sea or land or do any act of unjust or unlawful hostility to any the subjects of Us our heirs or successors or any the subjects of any King Prince Ruler Governor or Estate being in league and amity with Us our heirs or successors, or that upon such injury or upon just complaint of such Prince Ruler Governor or State or their subjects We our heirs or successors shall make open proclamation within any the parts of our Realm of England commodious for that purpose, that the said person or persons having committed any such robbery or spoil shall within the time to be limited by such proclamation make full restitution or satisfaction of all such injuries done, so as the said Princes and others so complaining may hold themselves fully satisfied and contented, And that if the said person or persons having committed such robbery or spoil shall not make nor cause to be made satisfaction accordingly within such time so to be limited, that then it shall be lawful to Us our heir and successors to put the said person or persons having committed such robbery or spoil out of our allegiance and protection, and that it shall be lawful and free for all Princes and others to pursue with hostility all the said offenders and every of them:

Witnes our self at Westminster the second day of May

per breve de privato sigillo.

631. May, 1610. Councilors and adventurers in the intended plantation in Newfoundland.

The Middleton Manuscripts in Nottingham University Library contain much material on the early history of the colony assembled by Sir Percival Willoughby, one of the most active participants (with John Slany and John Guy) in the colony in its early years. Middleton MS Mi x 1/1 contains a copy of the charter, a list of the councilors and adventurers (631), the instructions issued by the Council to John Guy for the establishment of the settlement (632), and the commission to Guy as governor (633).

Here Followeth the names of the [counsellors] and adventurers in the inten[ded plantation in] the newfowndlande Anno 1610

Imprimis
Henery Earell of Northampton ⎫
The lord of the privie Seale ⎪
Sir John Dodrige knight ⎪
Sir Frances Bacon knight ⎬
Sir Danyell Dun knight ⎪
Sir Walter Coape knight ⎪
Sir John Constable knight ⎭
Sir Lawrence Tanfeild lord Cheeff barron
Sir Percivall Willughby
Thomas Cuttpepper
John Well gentelman
Robert Kertam gentelman
Phillipp Gifford gentilman
John Slany merchaund tayler
William Freeman clothwoster
Raphe Freeman clothwo[ster]
Humfry Slany haberdasher
Thomas Juxon ⎬ merchaund taylers
John Stockelye
William Turners ⎬ Salters
Ellis Chrispe
Richard Fishborne mercer
Symon Stone ⎬ All these be adventurers for London
Thomas Allen ⎬ gentleman
John Browne merchand Tayler
Thomas Alport Nediham ⎬ haberdashers
Ritchard Hobby
John Short Iremonger
William Jones ⎬ mariners
William Diggens

Edward Allen ⎰ Fishmongers
Thomas Knighton ⎱
Ritchard Bowdler ⎱
Thomas Jones   ⎰ merchaunttaylers
John Vigers   ⎰
John Juxon
John Whittington grocer

632. May 26, 1610. Instructions from the Council to John Guy.

Nottingham University Library, Middleton MS Mi x 1/1.

Instructions directed by the counsaile For the Plantation in newfoundland to John Guy to be observed in the charge recommend[ed] to him.

First you shall use all possible diligence after the pattent and these instructions become in to your hands to depart from Bristoll to proceede one your voidge to newfoundland Furnished at the least with twelfe months victualls and necessaries for all such persons which shall go with youe and bee of our colonie together with monition nettes hoockes For fishing and all manner of tooles and instrumentes necessarie For the skill and manuall artes of all such as ar to goe with you and whatsoever else you shall thincke Important For the Service//

Secondly you shall take with you one or two smale boates for your present use in fishinge untill such as you shall ther provide moare except you be sure to find boates at your coming to serve your turne untill you provide other wayes.

Thirdly you shall take with you according to your discretion having respect to the conveyence of transportation a small nomber of domesticall creatures as goates hogges Connyes hens and pigeons of eache kind of them male and female with meat walter [for water] and other thinges needfull for the transportation which wee would have safely bestowed and carfully preserved and not anye to bee killed without greate and urgent cause.

Forthly you shall make a trewe inventorie of all the cattell munnition and nescessaries which you shall take with you and there of shall cause a trewe accoumpt to be keepte.

Fifftlye and to the end that almightie god withoute whose remembrance no beginning hath a good foundation may blesse your jornye and plantation with happy and prosporous successe you shall take order that devine servis be pubblickely read and attentively harkened unto especially one the Sabeth daye both Fornoone and afternoone as well duringe the tyme of your aboade upon the seas as after your arivall upon the land.

Sixtly when god shall send you with your company to arive in Newfoundland at the place youe desire to plant if you shall in anye wise perceive the fishermen there present entertayne anye Jelouzies or Suspicions as though your plantation tended one there prejudice in anye such cause onely and not other wise yt ys it [*sic*] thought Fitt and wee do ordayne that you do publishe your pattent and comission by causinge the same to be reade in presence of Some fewe of the cheife of them to the end that by the tenner thereof the maye be satisfied that there former right and custome of fishing is in everie cercumstance reserved unto them.

Seventhly havinge maid Choise of a stronge Fortile place and some Seate of habitation in which regard you shall bee carefull to avoid Lowe and moiste places as unhelthfull and place over burdned with woodes which besides the tedious and difficultie of clensinge maye serve as a covert For enemyes and noysom beastes you shall consider and fore See prudently that there be nowe wastinge of victualls no tymes lost or mispent in Idelnes or vaine imploymentes but that all industrious Courses to be pracktised to sett foreward the enterprise you goe aboute as namely buildinge to bee ereckted for habitations store houses for victualls and merchandise So[me] Fortification and defence against forrayne Irruptions or invasions a [sawe] mill to be ereckted the opertunitie for fishinge For Codd Salmon [and] Seales not lett shipp [= slip] at Ward Howse [= Vardö] in winter the greate fishe Co[me] to the shoare which is pulled upp with hookes of Iron one the ende of a poole and ys dryed with wind and frost and maketh Stockfishe and with all diligence to searche after mynes of all sorts of especially after Iron lead or tynne proofe to be made Concerning the naturall making of Salt by the heat of the sune in those parttes or that fa[i]llinge by the heate of fier as is used in manye places of Ingland of which wee purpose hearafter to informe your [for You] exerience to be maid how our Seedes graine corne pulse will growe and prosper in those parttes to which purpose you shall carrye with you theather of eache kind of grayne Some reasonable quantitie and by hunting shewtinge trapps and gins you shall tacke and kill stagges beavers beards [for bears] catters Foxes and have care to sarve and preserve the Furres.

Eightlye what fishe and trayne you shall have mayde and shall nott need for your owne use you shall uppon returne of the next shipp that shall be sent you cause to be transported to London by whome the one may send some quantetie of the myne you shall have gotten that triall here may bee made thereof as allsoe of the Sarcaparille to be had as reported in Bell Ile and Porrican a smale Iland in the side of Trinitie Bay as allso in such other small Ilands growing a[lo]ng in the mossiye ground hid in the gracsse [= grass] and mosse Spreading licke a vine baring a flower somthing licke a thistele youe must gather yt in somer and lay it upp to be dried with the wind since and so roled upp in bondels.

Nynthly you shall send whome [= home] some of your ferne ashes to be considered of For makinge of glasse as allso such ashes as you shall there make that the sope makers maye have triall therof.

Tenthly you shall lickwise remember kept ashes good for divers [uses] and used at glasse howses as allso turpintyne and hearth pitches you shall also trie the nature of the countrie For hopps the pine boards there will serve to make or mend fishing boastes [= boats] weare the sawe mill once sett and wee herd that pipps [= pipes] have been made of pine tymber and for hoopes yong birches will serve and Fur for caske in Mu[s]kovia ys used anth [= and] that the memorie of accurrantes perrishe not you shall keepe a Journall of all accidentes and what wynds and wether everie day especially betweene September and March.

Elaventhly yt ys thought fittinge that if anye Savige shall come voluntarie to you that you use him kindly and by no meanes not to detayne [him] against his will nor to let him see your house and provissions but if you can uppon ackquaintance made with them and with there good lickinge and consent send over one or to of experience in those Count[r]eys to be kept untill we could Learne

ther langwage or thei oures for there farther discoverie of [the] Countrie wee wish you herin to Followe our advise and otherwise not to meddle with them.

Twelfely For the relading backe of this shipp which is now to transporte you you [sic] & your Companye wee refer that [to] your consideration to considder when you come theare what is Fittest to be done that maye turne to proffitt yf you would by [= buy] store of trayne oyle at 8^li or under the toune yt would yeeld good proffitt or dry fish 7^s or 7^s 4^d must needs yeeld proffitt Corrfishe beinge good and resonable bought will bee heer vented For both dry and Corrfishe begines heere to be in use but the large fish though it be much dearer then the small will be better to send heather.

And for want of fish and trayne one may send such wood as the time will permitt to Cutt downe beinge such as you thincke best will Sell here of all the best sortes serve with some Iron stone and other mineralles if anye may bee so readely found before the Comminge away of ye shipp.

Lastely and finallye wee require you to have a regard of the good reservation & accomplishment of this our instructions so far as the shall not at any way or by anye accident prooffe in convenyent and For all other thinges that are heer omitted which may anye way tend to the furtherence of this enterprise wee committ and leave to your good discretion Committinge and commendinge you and all your companye with the good enterprise now in hand for the plantacion of the gospell and name of our lord and Savior Jesus Christ in that contrie wheare we hope by the eternall providence of the allmightie maker therof it shall remayne untill his cominge at the Last daye to Judgement
Dated in London this 26th day off maye Anno 1610

633. May 26, 1610. Instructions to John Guy as governor of the Newfoundland colony.

Nottingham University Library, Middleton MS Mi x 1/1.

The comission direckted by the Counsaill to John Guy For his government there in Newfoundland

Unto all Chiristian people to whome this writinge shall come greetinge know you that wheare as our Soveraigne lord king Jeames by the grace of god king of Ingland Scotland Fraunce and Iirland defender of the faith etc, hath by pattentes under his great Seale baring date the 2th daye of may in the eight yeare of his majesties raigne of Ingland Fraunce and Iirland & of Scotland the thre and Fortith appoynted us whose names ar under writing with some others to bee of the counsaile for Newfoundland gifving unto us full authoritie & power to nominate and appoynt such governers whom wee shall thinke fitt to sett over the Collonye intended by gods grace to be planted there and to give and to give [sic] direction to him or them for his or there better goverment there in wee havinge such due respect as is requisite to a service of Such impportuance being assembbled to gether for the choise of such governer and for the better orderinge and direckting of the said Service doe by this our writings syngned with our one hands ordayne constitute and appoynt John Guy of Bristow merchant to be our soll governer and commander of the colonye to be planted in the Newfoundland consistinge of the number of fortie persons wee doe ordayne and appoynt the Said John Guy to have the soll commaunde & Conduction as well upon the Seas as after there arived uppon the land and the same to hold and continue untill we shall otherwise dispose thereof to gether with the charge and over sight of all munytion victuall and other provissions goods and merchandize as ar and shall be shipped at the publicke charge of the adventurers for Newfoundland and in anye shipp whatsoever as well upon the Seas or after the landinge and in cause anye of the Said persons of the Colonye shall be found Seditious mutious [= mutinous] and may not without apparent danger bee detayned there untill the next shippinge ther hence or yf anie Such persons shall committ any thefft murder or other offence For which hee ought to die withoute allowance of Cleairgie by the law of Ingland then doe we ordayne and appoynt that the said John Guy Called unto him twelfe other persons of the Said Colonye the person be convickted by there voice and consent upon dew exammination had of the offence committed shall cause execution of Justice to be maid accordinge to the forme nowgh used in Ingland and as for other offences of a lower nature not extendinge unto the losse of life or member wee ordayne that the same shall be punished by soll discretion of the said John Guy where in never the lesse hee may if hee shall please crave ye assistance and advice of fowre others of the said colony and leasste question and strife may grow in poynt of Succession in cause it should please god to tacke away the said governer John Guy ether in the way or after his arivall to newfoundland yt is determyned and ordaynad by us the said counsell that such person shall succeede him in the goverment of the said Colonye as the said John Guy shall nominate under his hand writinge untill such tyme as wee shall tacke further order in that behalffe and in cause the said John Guy shall not nominate any person as affore said or that the person so nominated shall dye then doe wee ordayne Phillipp Guy to succeed him in the government who shall undertake and continue his chardg following the instructions herunto annexed untill such tyme as wee shall otherwise dispose therof and in cause the said Phillipp Guy so succeding shall likewise dye then doe we ordayne such person to Succeed him as the [said] Phillipp shall nominate us as affore said and in default [of] such nomination or in cause the person so nominate shall dye do wee ordayne William Chatchmayde to succeed in the said goverment Followinge the instructions aforesaid and in cause the said William Chatchmaide shall likewise dye then do wee ordayne such person such [= so?] to succeed him as hee the said William Chatchmaid shall nominate as aforesaid and in default of such nomination wee do ordayne that that [sic] the successor shall bee therunto eleckted by the most voices of such persons that shall servaye [survive?] and if equall voices choose too persons then lett [it] be cast whether of them shall be preferred and wee the said counsell do furthermore will and requier as such persons as shall be resident in the collonye to be subjeckt and obedient unto the said Governer John Guy and his successors in all his and ther just and lawfull commaunds whearin if any person be found reb[e]llious or refrectable then do wee give full power and authoritie unto the said g[overner] John Guy and his successors to inflict such punishment [uppon] everie person so offendinge by his or there direction as the quallitie and nature of the offence shall worthely deserve in witnes wherof we the said counsell have signed this our commission and warrant with our hands and dated in London this 26th of maye anno domini 1610.

[Unsigned.]

and so wee committ you to the lord his mercifull protecktion. London the 9th August. 1610

Your loving Frends

[Signed:] John Slanye, William Jones, Raphe Freeman, Ritchard Fishborne, John Wilde, Humfrey Slany

634. August 9, 1610. The Council of the Newfoundland Company to negligent Bristol subscribers.

Nottingham University Library, Middleton MS Mi x 1/2.

[a] The coppye of a letter sent to Bristoll and dereckted unto the woorshipful aldermen William Merideth and and [sic] Humfry Hooke.

Wheare as you agreede and give in your names to be adventurers with Master John Guy of bristoll and us of London For the plantation of Newfoundland and your names with other of Bristoll being by him sent upp weare put into the pattent as the rest weare now by the accoumpte brought wee find you have not brought in your moneye which is 25^{li} for everie mans first adventure thes ar therfore to request you uppon Sight herof that you pay unto Ritchard Hallworthie or John Langton by us deputed for those receictes the said somes of 25^{li} a piece which if you refuse to do then wee must take in others in your places which wee ar loth to doe and dismis you from the benefitt of our pattent beinge in our power so to doe

[b] At an assemblye at the house of John Slany in London the 19th of August 1610 weare these persons Following

John Slany treasurer
William Jones
William Didggins
Ellis Crispe
John Short
Edward Allen
Humfry Spencer
John Wigars
Ritchard Hobbye
John Juxon

At this assembly Ritchard Hollworthy presented the account of the charges laid out at Bristow For the voiage of Newfoundlande and signified to the company that some of the adventurers of Bristoll did adventure but 12^{li} 10^{s} [a] piece and yet would have ther names sett downe in in [sic] the booke heare kept as free as wee of London which this comp[any] thought not fitting to be done consideringe ther many voices might heare prevaile against the goverment of the busynes as it is nowgh established and some of them of Bristoll which had given in the[r] names to be adventurers and weare putt in to the patent had not put in theare money therfor it was ordered that a letter sho[uld] be sent them to this purpose the coppie whereof is above mentioned.

Chapter Seventy-seven
The Progress of the Colony at Cupids, 1610–1612

635. October 6, 1610. John Guy to Sir Percival Willoughby.

Nottingham University Library, Middleton MS Mi x 1/2.

Right worshipfull, yt may please y[ou] to understand, that havinge sett sayle from Kingroade the port of Bristoll The fifte day of July laste, wee were forced with Contrary windes with losse of an ancker, to putt into Myniott from whence departinge the eleventh day of the sayd moneth, we were glad to putt into Milforde, where wee remained untill the tow and twentieth day of the said moneth: and then proceedinge, the [   ] day of [A]ugust, we arrived (God be praised) all in safetie in the bay of Conception, in Newfoundland, [in the] harbour here called Cuperres Cove; which is a branch of Sammon Cove, and is in the latitude of fortie and seaven degrees, and thirtie and seaven minuites, as I founde by observacion taken on the land. For on the 24th day of September, beinge a hott and most fayre cleare sunshininge day the sunne was elevated above the horizon at noone beinge in the meridian, thirtie and eight degrees the declinacion then was in the meridian of London to the southwardes four degrees and twentie minuites but noone beinge here about three houres after, therefore the declinacion was three minuites more so that the Equinoctiall is elevated above the horizon here 42 degrees and 23 minuites which deducted out of 90: there resteth 47 degrees 37 minuits in the elevation of the pole. The windes we had over bound were most southerlie sometimes northerlie and now and then easterly, but very little at west, contrary to the generall opinion of all men, in which manner we have found it ever since our comminge hereunto. All our company was well savinge one which had the smale poxe taken in Bristoll, who is

well recovered, without that any other was infected with it: for which we are all to give greate thankes to God. This harbour is three leagues distant from Colliers Bay to the Northeastward and is preferred by me to beginne our plantacion before the said Colliers Bay, for the goodnes of the harbour the fruitfullnes of the soyle the largenes of the trees, and many other reasons wee landed here tenne goates, havinge lost one at Minniott, and one which was killed aboard with the romadginge of the boate: the residue are all well, stronnge, and lustie, and like well of the Countrie, except one which was ill aboard, and could not recover, so that now there are remayninge nine; moreover a boare, and tow sow-piggs, poultrie, cunnies, and pigeons, all which came hether very well. At our first cominge we saw a Beare now and then, that haunted this place, makinge accompt the fishermen were gone, but beinge shott at, we have not seene nor hard of any these three weeks. If we had never so many goates here, the[y] would live as well as in Fraunce, and be as profitable, and in as little danger of wilde beastes, for the pasturinge of which sorte of cattle, the land would serve without riddinge, as also for the Swine//

Att our arrivall here we found the fishinge shippes not departed, havinge ended there fishinge and expectinge a faire wind, kept in by easterlie windes, very little Fish hath beene here since our comminge, some mackerell, and Cods and a greater quantitie of dogfish at Cape St Fraunces and Bacaleau, after the ship is departed we purpose to send to fishinge for ou[r] p[ro]vision.

We have spent the time since our arrivall much in landinge of our victualls, and provision, and makinge safe places for it and our selves to shroude us in untill our house could [be] builte, but moste of all in ladinge the shipp backe againe with trees and sparrs, th[e] quantit[ie w]hereof appeareth in the bill of ladinge inclosed. We have

144

found the weather ever since our comminge, soe temperate as in England and rather better, otherwise we should not have attended almost alltogeather the ladinge of the shipp, we have digged a saw-pitt hard by the sea side, and put a timber house over it [co]vered with pine bordes; there are tow paire of Sawyers workinge in it, the pyne trees make good and large bordes and is gentle to saw, they be better then the deale bordes of Norway, there is now a pine tree at the saw-pitt, that is above tenne feete about at the butt, and thirtie feete longe is eight feete about; our companie is much confirmed in a good conceipt of this Climate, seeing the weather prove contrary to the fame, and especially for that a fisherman lefte with us by one Master Alexander Sanford of Lime that was bound to the Ilands, that had the disease of the scurvy confirmed in him, to be sent home in the Flemminge, is by our Surgeon very well amended, the scurvy grasse groweth here hard by us, I have seene it and tasted of it since my comminge hether there is also hearbe yarrow, or nose bleed that is good for it, likewise the peason of the Country and many other hearbs here are good for it; the sixte of September the said Master Sanford gave me wheate which he found growinge by his stage that was ripe, and sprang up of graines of wheate that fell out of the mats used under the salte which I send you to have a sight of, He tolde me likewise of a brooke towardes the south of Reanose, with in tow leauges, that hath a kind of shelfish, in it which he calleth Clammes in which were found the last yeare faire and orient pearles, and that some were solde for 20 crownes, and that this yeare if the fishinge had not proved good there abouts they woulde have sought there for more, the same kind of shelfish tow yeres agoe I saw in Colliers Bay which, as also that to the Southwardes of Renose, I purpose (God willinge, after our house is built to make search for such manner of pearls, as the muskles that growe in this harbour yeelde, I send you to have the sighte of, they may happen prove better when we dragg for them in deepe water. The turpentine that commeth from the firr and pine and frankincense of the spruce is likewise sent, I doubt not but that it will prove that shippinge may come hether at all times of the yeare, and that the worst time is when the fishermen come to fishinge, because the drifte Ice from the northen Countries, at that time only

troubleth them, I have heard credibly since my comminge heather, That one Master Hutchins of Salteash was in St Jones harbour on Christmas day laste. The fish of the sea, the fo[wlls] of th[e] aire, the hills full of woodes, the varietie of herbes and berries growinge there of there owne accord, the Climate, the trade of fishinge and many other circumstances are most a[va]ylable to drawe Inhabitantes to it. The soyle likewise is good, not rockie, in most place[s] but very good mould, and deepe in some places without stones, and in other pla[ces] with loose stones amonge, there want[et]h nothinge to make a flourishinge Country but cattle and the industry of men, without which our Count[ry] would be as bad as this. And seinge God hath ordeyned that the earth of it selfe should bot be fruitfull without the sweate of mans browes; it is more to be marveiled at; that there is here that which it yeeldeth naturally, then that there is want of what wee have. Adam havinge the whole earth to make choise of, could not find any place fruitfull without his labour and travell. Seinge all thinges cannot be done at one time, having considered what is most fitt to be set forward this nexte succeddinge yeare, what is my opinion I think good to propound, leaving the resolucion thereof to your good discretions, which is husbandrie, fishinge, and trade by husbandrie and fishinge, the Colonie wilbe soone able to supporte it selfe and by the fruits of the earth, and cattle undertakers and tennents to take land of the Company wilbe in aboundance drawne hether; when they shall heare of our health, whereof by the grace of God I make no doubt, no more then if we were in England. For fishinge I thinke fitt that a ship of an hundred and fiftie tunns were sent hether, with only thirtie fishermen and foure Spilters, there are here already eight that are fishermen, and one spilter, and the rest here will serve for land men; boats shalbe made ready by us now in the winter God willinge, here is a good beach and the fishinge neare, to be assured of a good place to fish and a beach, boates and stage may be worth more then one or tow hundreth poundes yearely for a shipp of that burthen, which the company may be assured of by the plantacion because they shalbe sure to be first here every yeare to take what stage they shall have need of for there owne use. There must be greate care had that the fishermen be good, for that is the ground of the voyage for trade, greate shippinge may be imployed betweene Rochall and this place, To bring salte and to returne laden with maste sparrs, and deales. Three voyages may easily be made in an yeare, which salte maye be solde to the fishinge shipps before they come out of England, when there is any here in store; who to be assured of it, will gladly give either fish or trayne for it at the end of the voyage. Traine also may be bought of such shipps as goe to the straights or Spaine, but agreement must be made with them for it in England before they beginne there voyage, for then they doe dispose of it. If lead be sent hether in the sacke, for a smale matter is [it?] maybe sent hence to any parte of Spaine, or Italy, servinge so fitt for ballaste under the fishe. If an expert ma[n] to make pitch and tarr were sent hether a double[e] commoditie would arise because by that meanes the woodes would be ridd the sooner. When a saw-mill is erected here we maye serve the fishinge fl[ee]te w[ith] boords to make fishinge boats whereof they bringe good store yearely from England. I sawe so[me] of them in Italie, and tooke such particular notic[e the]reof, as I am in good hope with the workman I have here to sett up one. The accoumpt of a glasse-house, I send you by which you maye perceave, that there is nothinge wantinge here to make it but worke men. At the end of the fishinge the next yeare, the number of such if [= of] the [c]ompanie as now are here, that will returne home will be easily, and at better rates [s]upplied by spare men that are to be had out of the fishinge shipps; / A learned and godlie minister would be a greate comforte to us all and a credit to the plantation./

One Master Peter Coxe of Poole hath beene here coasting this summer, who when he heard that I was to come and that a patent was obtained, was desirous to have spoken with me. He hath taken hom with him som mine which he found at an Iland called Belile, which, he is in greate hope will prove good; I doubt not but you may informe your selfe of the qualitie thereof. Hereafter at more leasure, I will make diligent search concerninge the mines. How the blommer man came away from the shipp at minyott, I wrote Master Holworthy of, and doe expect one by the next shipp that cometh hether, if the yron mine here should not prove of good quantitie or qualitie yet the matter of yron is not to be despaired of; for by means of greate shipps going with a fewe men, good may be done by yron mine brought out of England hether as I suppose consideringe that for the extraordinary chardge of the fraighte of the mine wood and all necessaries are to be had for nothinge, and that yron is now above fortie shillinges a tonne deerer then it was wont to be custome and imposte free, and for little or no fraighte, because it will serve for good ballaste under the fish, 800 tonne of mine will make 200 tonnes of barr yron which will not stand in above 400^{li} the fraighte after the rate of 10^s per tonne outwards and for the lading to be had here hence of trees, sparrs, and deales, I doubt not but that will make up the rest if the fraighte be after the rate of the Flemminge fraighte this voyage.

A note of such thinges I thinke fitt should be sent hether the next yeare I send inclosed./- because all fishermen were upon departure at our arrivall, and no house built not any settled habitacion effected. I thought good to forbeare this yeare, and to reserve it for the next yeare, to give solemne notice in an assemblie, of this our purpose of plantacion and the warrant and auctoritie, whereupon it is grownded, but privately so much was done as no man here was ignorant thereof, and that there is no intent to prejudice any fishermen./

When experience of the winter season is made, what is wantinge now in this my letter to give your worshippes further satisfaction, I hope shalbe in some sort then supplied; and in the meane time doe take my leave, prayinge God to give his blessinge to this our enterprise and to preserve your worshipps in safetie./

In Cupers Cove the sixte of October 1610

Your worshipps to command

[Signed:] John Guy

636. May 11, 1611. John Guy reports on the first winter and spring in the Newfoundland colony.

S. Purchas, Pilgrimes, *IV (1625), 1877–1879 (XIX [1907], 110–116).*

Master John Guy his Letter to Master Slany Treasurer, and to the Counsell of the New-foundland Plantation.

Right worshipfull, it may please you to understand, that it was the tenth day of this moneth of May before the Barke of Northam, called the Consent, arrived here in New-found-land; notwithstanding that a Ship of Bristoll, called the Lionesse, came to this Countrey the second of May in a moneths space: and the Trial of Dartmouth arrived here before in sixteene dayes: By reason of which stay of the aforesaid Barke, nothing could be done to take any of the places desired: all being possessed before. So that the Ship that commeth, whereof as yet there is no newes, is to trust to the place here, which is reserved for her; which I hope will prove a good place. Some yeeres as great a Voyage hath bin made here, as in any place in this Land: God send her hither in safetie. I have not yet seene any of the Countrey to the Southward, or Northward of this Bay of Conception since this spring, because I expected daily the arrivall of the Barke, and thought it not fit to be absent herehence untill she were arrived, and dispatched: but presently upon her departure, no time, God willing shall be lost. The care that was taken to require generally the Fishermen to assist us, and to supply our wants, if any should be, was most joyfull and comfortable to us, which was most willingly accomplished by the most part of those which I have yet seene: yet, God be praised, such was the state of all things with us, as we were in no want of victuals, but had a great remainder, as you shall after understand.

The state of the Autumne and Winter was in these parts of New-found-land after this manner.[1] In both the moneths of October and November, there were scarce six dayes wherin it either freezed or snowed: and that so little, that presently it was thawed and melted with the strength of the Sunne: All the residue of the aforesaid two moneths being both warmer and drier then in England. In December we had sometimes faire weather, some times frost and snow, and sometime open weather and raine: for in the latter end it was rainie, and was open weather. All these three moneths the winde was so variable, as it would every fortnight visite all the points of the Compasse.

The most part of January and February unto the middle of March the frost continued: the winde being for the most part Westerly, and now and then Northerly; notwithstanding three or foure times, when the winde was at South, it began to thaw and did raine. That which fell in this season was for the most part Snow, which with the heate of the Sunne would be consumed in the open places within a few dayes. That which abode longest was in February. During this time many dayes the Sun shone warme and bright from morning to night: notwithstanding the length of this frosty weather, small brookes that did run almost in levell with a slow course, were not the whole winter three nights over frozen so thicke, as that the Ice could beare a Dogge to goe over it, which I found by good proofe: for every morning I went to the brooke which runneth by our house to wash. The Snow was never above eighteene inches thicke generally out of the drift; so that the feare of wanting wood or water never tooke hold of us: for albeit we made no provision for them, yet at a minute of an houres warning we were furnished where there were Lakes of fresh water that stood still and did not run, there it remained frozen able to beare a man almost three moneths, and was not dissolved untill the middle of Aprill. But where the ayre had entrance and issue out of them, there was no frost. When the winde in the winter time in England is at the North-east one moneth together, the frost is greater, and the cold more sharpe, then it is here at all. There was no moneth in all the winter that some of our company did not travell in, either by land or by water, and lie abroad and drinke water, in places distant two, three, foure and five leagues from our habitation, and sometimes lay in the woods without fire, and received no harme. When Aprill came our Spring began, and the first that did bud was the small Resen or the Corinth tree. Our Company was not letted in working abroad, & in the woods and open ayre fifteene dayes the whole winter. We never wanted the company of Ravens and small Birds: So that the doubts that have bin made of the extremity of the winter season in these parts of New-found-land are found by our experience causelesse; and that not onely men may safely inhabit here without any neede of Stove, but Navigation may be made to and fro from England to these parts at any time of the yeare.

Concerning the healthfulnesse of these Countries, we having bin now more then ten moneths upon this Voyage, of nine and thirty persons, which was all our number which wintered here,

1. Purchas notes in the margin; "I have by me a written journall, declaring the winde and weather of every day from 24. November 1610. till the last of Aprill 1611. but thought it would seeme tedious, the substance thereof being here contained." This has not survived.

there are wanting onely foure; whereof one Thomas Percy Sawyer died the eleventh of December of thought, having slaine a man in Rochester; which was the cause, being unknowne unto mee untill a day before he died, that he came this Voyage. And one other, called John Morris Tyler, miscarried the first of February by reason of a bruse. The third, called Marmaduke Whittington, was never perfectly well after he had the small Poxe, which he brought out of Bristoll with him, who died the fifteenth of February. And the fourth, called William Stone, having at the first onely a stiffenesse in one of his knees, kept his bed ten weekes, and would never stirre his body, which lasinesses brought him to his end, who died the thirteenth of Aprill. Of the rest foure or five have bin sicke, some three moneths, and some foure moneths; who now are better then they were, except one. All of them, if they had had as good will to worke, as they had good stomackes to their victuals, would long since have bin recovered. One Richard Fletcher, that is Master Pilot here and a director of the Fishing, reported unto me, that he was one of the company consisting of forty persons, that went in a drumbler of Ipswich, called the Amitie, to the North part of Ireland about eleven yeeres agoe from London in the late Queenes service, under the charge of one Captaine Fleming, and continued there the space of two yeares: In which time two and thirty died of the Scurvie, and that onely eight of them returned home, whereof the said Richard Fletcher was one. So that the accident of death or sicknesse of any persons in these our parts of New-foundland is not to argue any unhealthfulnesse of this Country, no more then Ireland is to be discredited by the losse of those two and thirty men: notwithstanding that there were to be had fresh victuals and many other helpes, which this Country as yet hath not, but in good time may have.

From the sixt of October untill the sixteenth of May our Company had bin imployed in making of a Storehouse to hold our provisions, and a dwelling house for our habitation, which was finished about the first of December; with a square inclosure of one hundred and twenty foot long and nintie foot broad, compassing these two houses, and a worke house to worke dry in to make Boates or any other worke out of the raine: and three peeces of Ordnance are planted there to command the Harboroughs upon a platforme made of great posts, and railes, and great Poles sixteene foot long set upright round about, with two Flankers to scoure the quarters. A Boat about twelve tuns big with a decke is almost finished to saile and row about the headlands: six fishing Boates and Pinnesses: a second saw-pit at the fresh Lake of two miles in length and the sixt part of a mile broad, standing within twelve score of our habitation, to saw the timber to be had out of the fresh Lake, in keeping two paire of Sawyers to saw plankers for the said buildings, in ridding of some grounds to sow Corne and garden seedes: in cutting of wood for the Collier, in coling of it: in working at the Smiths Forge Iron workes for all needfull uses: in costing both by Land and Sea to many places within this Bay of Conception: in making the frame of timber of a farre greater and fairer house, then that which as yet we dwell in, which is almost finished, and divers other things. We have sowed all sorts of graine this Spring, which prosper well hitherto. Our Goates have lived here all this winter; and there is one lustie Kidde, which was yeaned in the dead of winter. Our Swine prosper. Pidgens and Conies will endure exceeding well. Our Poultrie have not onely laied Egges plentifully, but there are eighteene yong Chickins, that are a weeke old, besides others that are a hatching.

The feare of wilde Beasts we have found to be almost needelesse. Our great Ram-Goate was missing fifteene dayes in October, and came home well againe, and is yet well with us. If the industry of men and presence of domesticall Cattle were applied to the good of this Countrey of New-found-land, there would shortly arise just cause of contentment to the inhabitants thereof. Many of our Masters and Sea-faring men seeing our safetie, and hearing what a milde winter we had, and that no Ice had bin seene fleeting in any of the Bayes of this Countrey all this yeare (notwithstanding that then met one hundred and fifty leagues off in the Sea great store of Ilands of Ice) doe begin to be in love with the Countrey, and doe talke of comming to take land here to inhabit: falling in the reckoning aswell of the commoditie that they may make by the banke fishing, as by the husbandry of the Land, besides the ordinary fishing. At the Greene Bay, where some of our Company were a fishing in November, they report there is great store of good grounds without woods, and there is a thousand acres together which they say may be mowed this yere. There is great store of Deere, whereof they saw some divers times, and twice they came within shot of them; and the Greyhound, who is lustie, had a course, but could not get upon them. But neerer unto Cape Razo, Revonse, and Trepasse there is great quantitie of open ground and Stagges. It is most likely that all the Sackes will be departed out of England before the returne of this our Barke, which shall not make any matter; because I am now of opinion that nothing should be sent hither before the returne of the Ships from fishing. For as concerning sending of Cattle, it will be best that it be deferred untill the next Spring. And concerning Victuals, in regard of the quantity, we have of it remaining of old, together with that that is come now, as with the dry fish that here we may be stored with, I am in good hope there will not want any to last till this time twelve moneths. And according to the victuals which shall be found at the end of the fishing, the number of persons that shall remaine here all the next winter shall be fitted, that there shall not want: notwithstanding about Alhollantide, or the beginning of December, a Ship may be sent, such a one as our Fleming was with Salt from Rochel; for at any time of the winter Ships may as well goe and come hither, as when they doe, especially before January. This Summer I purpose to see most places betweene Cape Rase, Placentia, and Bona vista, and at the returne of the fishing Ships to entertaine a fit number of men to maintaine here the winter; and to set over them, and to take the care of all things here, with your patience, one Master William Colton, a discreete yong man, and my brother Philip Guy, who have wintered with me, and have promised me to undertake this charge untill my returne the next Spring, or till it shall be otherwise disposed of by you, and then together with such of the company as are willing to goe home, and such others as are not fit longer to be entertained here, I intend to take passage in the fishing Ships, and so returne home: And then betweene that and the Spring to be present, to give you more ample satisfaction in all things, and to take such further resolution, as the importance of the enterprise shall require: wherein you shall finde me alwayes as ready as ever I have bin to proceede and goe forward, God willing. And because at my comming home it will be time enough for mee to lay before you mine opinion touching

what is to be undertaken the next yeare, I will forbeare now to write of it; because you should be the sooner advertised of our welfare: and because such of the Company as are sent home both for their owne good, and that the unprofitable expence of victuals and wages might cease: I have laden little or nothing backe, that the said Company might the better be at ease in the hold. Onely there is sent three hogsheads of Charcoles: where Numero 1°. is, they are of Burch: n°. 2°. is, of Pine and Spruce, n°. 3°. is of Firre, being the lightest wood, yet it maketh good Coles, and is used by our Smith. I send them because you shall see the goodnesse of each kinde of Cole. Also I send you an Hogshead of the Skinnes and Furres of such Beasts as have bin taken here, the particulers whereof appeare in the Bill of lading.

While I was writing I had newes of the Vineyard, the Ship which you send to fishing, to have bin in company with another Ship that is arrived on this side of the Banke, and that the Master intended to goe to Farillon or Fer-land: God send her in safety. So praying God for the prosperity of your Worships, and the whole Company, with hope that his divine Majestie which hath given us so good a beginning, will alwayes blesse our proceedings: my dutie most humbly remembred, I take my leave. Dated in Cupers Cove the sixteenth of May, 1611.[2]

637. June 17, 1612. John Guy to Sir Percival Willoughby.

Nottingham University Library. Middleton MS Mi x 1/7

[Ri]ghte worshipfull I have received your moste kind, & curteous lettres [y]our love, & good opin-

---

2. Purchas notes: "I have also a Journall of the winde and weather from the latter end of August 1611. till June 1612. written by Master William Colston; and delivered to Master John Guy, Governour of the English Colony in Newfoundland, at his returne from England thither, June the seventh 1612. By which it appeareth that the weather was somewhat more intemperate then it had beene the yeare before, but not intolerable, nor perhaps so bad as we have it sometimes in England. Their Dogges killed a Wolfe, Otters, Sables, &c. Captaine Easton a Pirat was troublesome to the English, and terrible to the French there: of whom I have added this Letter; for the Diarie of the weather and occurrents each day would be very tedious." This has not survived.

ion expressed thearein I will endeavour to be thankefull for what I may. The enterprise of plantacion I hope every day you shall have juste cause to like better, & better, Master Olney, & Edward Poulton are heere with me: the gentleman your sonne, [Thomas Middleton] & Master Croute are well at Renoose, whom I hope to see shortelie. Theare shalbe nothing omitted of my parte to give them satisfaction in all thinges. The young man Edward Tottle misliked to be heere in the nature which he came in as one apprentice & became earneste to returne againe, which for diverse reasons I yeelded unto. All those which came by your direction are very willing, & towardlie how the state of all matters is heere, you shall understand by the generall lettres, to which I make bold to referre you. The matter of the pirates I pray you to thinke ove[r] seriouslie, & to advise ane effectual course to be sodaineleε imbraced to stoppe yt now at the firste breaking out principiis obsta fero medicina paratur. And soe praying god for your contynewall happiness, I humblie take my leave.

Your worships to commaund
    [Signed:] John Guy

From Cupers cove the 17th day of June 1612
[Endorsed:] To the righte worshipfull his especiall good Friend Sir Percevall Willughby Knighte give thease.

638.   July 29, 1612. John Guy to John Slany.

The arrival of the pirate Peter Easton to plunder the fishing fleet for stores diverted the colonists toward building a fort at Cupids to protect the colony against further attacks. It also led to the abandonment of the plans (well advanced) to leave a second colony to winter at Renews. S. Purchas, Pilgrimes, IV (1625), 1879–1880 XIX [1907], 417–418.

To Master John Slany Treasurer, and others of the Councell, and Company of the New-foundland Plantation, the twenty nine of July 1612.

Right Worshipfull, by my last of the seventeenth of June, I wrote you of the estate then, of all matters here, by the Holland Ship, which (I hope) is long since safely arrived, together with Master Colston, who hath (I doubt not) made by word of mouth, full relation of all matters. Because the proceedings of one Captaine Peter Easton a Pirate, and his company since, are most fit to be knowne, before I touch our Plantation businesse, you shall understand, what they have bin unto this time: untill the seventeenth of this present, the said Captaine Easton remained in Harbor de Grace, there trimming, and repairing his Shipping, and commanding not onely the Carpenters of each Ship to doe his businesse, but hath taken victuals, munition, and necessaries from every Ship, together with about one hundred men out of the Bay, to man his Ships, being now in number six. He purposed to have before he goeth, as is said, out of the land five hundred men; while he remained there, two severall Companies to the number of about one hundred and eightie persons to each Company, being discontented, stole away from him in a Shallop, and tooke two Ships that were fishing in Trinitie Bay, one belonging to Barnstable, and one other to Plimmouth, and so intend, to begin to be new heads, of that damnable course of life. As I sailed from hence towards Renoose, in a small Barke, I fell into one of their hands: and one of my company was hurt with a Musket. There was one of their crew that wintered with me here the first yeare, by whose meanes, and because I was in the Barke, they made shew, that they were sorry that they had medled with us: And so they departed from us, without comming aboord. That which they sought after was men, to increase their number. Before the said Captaine Eastons departure, he sent three Ships into Trinitie Bay, to store himselfe with victuals, munition, and men, who are said to be worse used, then the Ships here, he taketh much ordnance from them. The said Easton was lately at Saint Jones, and is now, as farre as I can learne, at Feriland, where he taketh his pleasure, and thereabouts the rest are to meete him. It is given out, that we will send one Captaine Harvy in a Ship to Ireland, to understand newes about his pardon, which if he can obtaine in that large and ample manner as he expecteth, then he giveth out, that he will come in: otherwise, it is thought, that he will get Protection of the Duke of Florence, and that in his course herehence, he will hover about Westwards of the Ilands of the

Azores, to see whether he can light upon any of the Plate fleete, or any good rich bootie, before his comming in. Albeit, he hath so prevailed here to the strengthening of himselfe, and incouraging of others to attempt the like hereafter: yet, were there that course taken, as I hope shall be, it is a most easie matter to represse them.

639. August 18, 1612. Richard Holworthy to John Slany.

Nottingham University Library, Middleton MS Mi x 1/12.

In Bristol the 18th August 1612. Worshipfull Sir the last weeck cam a barke from Newfoundland, but noe letters from master Guye, such newes as came I spedyly wrot up to London, & by this tyme I count you are uppon going thither, yet for that the bearer telleth me you staye a weeck longer in the contry, I proceed to writ you thes feyowe lines, the bark com brings newes that Easton was with master Guye some 14 dayes with near 100 men, in & out, offring noe wrong to other, & parted frindly, while he was in that baye he landed & ayred all his cloth, & the 18th last month he was com to Saint Joanes, wher wear about 30 Englishe ships he taking victuall & men from them all, sending som of his ships all along the coaste to doe the like from other shipes, and a tyme apointed when they shold all meet at Ferryland, wher it is thought they wilbe about 1000 men. In thear drinck they gave out they wold therhence for the Ilands to attend the West India fleet, he used much Crueltey to the Portingals & French wherby near all thear fishing voyages wear overthrowen, & maney of them left thear ships & fled into the woodes, in soe much as master Guye doubting they might in thear extremytey goe for Renose, it is thought will withdraw the Colonell therhence to be together at Kippers Cove, & himself going by sea in the action about Cape Sannct Francis, som of the pirotes hayled the bote he was in because he cam not presently to them, they shot & wounded on of master Guy companey, which they wear sorry for when they hard they wear master Guye & his

companey, but heruppon he crossed the land going to Bellile & went back to Koppers Cove, sending Master Spence & other for Renose. The kine & goates that went herhence, cam thether in salftey & in good liking, this being the newes now here going which I thought good to writ you of accompting now shortly we shall here from master Guye at larg of all thinges, & soe doubting of your departure for London I rest and am the briefar, taking leave. Comitting you to the protection of Almighty God

Yours alwayes to Comand
    [Signed:] Richard Holworthy

I pray comend me to your good brother & his wief. I Received lettars from thear son in Civill dated 24th last month, thear being much hope of a good vintage

[Endorsed:] To the worshipfull my verry good frind Master John Slaney merchant at the Hem near Brignorth delivered per a friend

640. August 23, 1612. Thomas Cowper, Edward Carton, and John Harrington to Sir Percival Willoughby.

Nottingham University Library, Middleton MS Mi x 1/14.

Sir may it please you after your humble dutie remembred we have thought good to be bowld to wryte unto you woorship Conserninge our servis and our partes of land which we are to have heere which is to everie on of us 50 acers at the 5 yeares end or else yf we dislike of the land your promise was to give us 30¹ a peece so it is now that we beinge sumwhat aquainted with the Cuntrie findings our usage far woorse then we expected our labour verie much and harde and with all beinge dubtfull of the goodnes of our land we do ernestlie beseech you to fulfill your promis unto us that we may have the better Corage to serve owt our time or else that it may please you to favou[r] us so much that we may cum home againe th[en on our] returne we are willinge to do your woorship anie serv[i]se that it shall please you to imploy us in but to the Cumpanie we will not serve as prentises for thise much land we are Contente to Continue owt this yeare untill we here further of your woorships pleaser thus praying the Almightie god to bles you with everlastinge happines we moste humblie take our leave

Your poore servants in all dutie
[Signed in one hand:] Thomas Cowper, Edward Garton, John Harrington
This xxiij^th of August

[Endorsed:] To the right woorshipfull Sir Persifall Willoughbie Knight at Wollerton give this I pray you

[Written on the Back of this letter are the following notes:]
store of sassaparilla in ye Ile of Backalas
New-Foundland ye Faukner & Ollney Quarell
who should bring ye beare & Haukes to P. W.
From Crowt T. Will [oughby] wanting clothes
Store of Beavers P. W. lot next ye Savages
their Barley spoiled by Goats
newfoundland Master Guy Bart. Person T. Will sent thither
Complaints of Pirates there.

641. October 7 to November 25, 1612. Expedition made by John Guy in the *Indeavour*.

The autumn journal is important for its ethnography, and the original manuscript (well preserved, except in one or two places) has a unique sketch of a Beothuk Indian canoe. Lambeth Palace Library, Lambeth MS 250, fols. 406-412. The only published edition appeared in The New World. A Catalogue of an Exhibition... *at Lambeth Palace Library between 1 May and 1 December 1957 (London, 1957), pp. 52-64, 90-92, which includes useful identifications of places, although they can be traced more adequately in E. R. Seary,* Place Names of the Avalon Peninsula of the Island of Newfoundland *(St. John's and Toronto, 1971).*

Discoverie made by John Guy in Newfoundland in anno 1612 in and about 48: degrees of Latitude towards the pole Articke:

A Journall of the voiadge of discoverie made in a barke builte in Newfoundland called the *Indeavour*, begunne the 7 of October 1612, & ended the 25th of November following: By John Guy of Bristow:

The Jornall of our voiadge in the Indeavour begunne the 7 of October 1612.

October 7.
This night by sayling & rowing we came to Harbor de Grace, as farre in as the Pirates forte, wheare the banke shippe roade, wheare we remayned untill the 17th day of the sayde moneth, & in the meane time did bring the banke shippe a shoare, land the salte upon the higheste parte of the grownd thereaboutes, putting yt up in a round heape, & burning of yt to preserve yt. Two anchors, & two old Junkes we lefte upon the beache. The quantetie of salte was about fifteene tonnes.

[October] 17.
We departed from Harbor de Grace, & that nighte came to Greene bay, bothe the barke & the shalloppe. Theare weare in the barke fowerteene. viz. 1. John Guy. 2. Mr. Teage. 3. Mr. Groote. 4. George Whittington. 5. Fraunces Tipton. 6. Edwarde Perrie. 7. James Holworthy. 8. John Crowder. 9. James Babacucke. 10. Georg Davies. 11. Thomas Rowlie. 12. George Lane. 13. George Vaughen. 14. Thomas Tayler.
And in the shallope five: viz. 1. George Wichalle. 2. Wm. Hadden. 3. Bartlemew Percevall. 4. George Frewin. 5. Samuell Butler.

[October] 18.
At two a clocke in the morning we put out of Greene bay, the wind North, we spent all that day in the barke to double the Grates to goe into Trinitie bay, but could not, & soe late at nighte come backe to Greene Bay againe. The shalloppe proceeded, & that nighte attayned unto a harbour of the South side of Trinitie bay called Hartes content.

[October] 19 [-25].
We put out againe, the wind N.W., a stiffe gale. We crossed Trinitie bay, & came to a roade under the land good for a [ship to lie?] [We had?] westerlie, & Northerlie windes, theare was harde by u[s an] Iland, wheareby we tooke yt to be that which is called S. Catalinaes, yt lyeth from Baccalean N.N.W. Heere we roade without being able to goe ashoare for want of a boate, untill the 21th

day, when at 4 of the clocke in the afternoone the wind came Northerlie, & soe we put to sea to get up into Trinitie bay, & sayled all that nighte untill midnighte with our mainsaile out, but after taken in untill day. Our course was SW & SWBS moste commonlie, & sometimes S. & SBE to fetch the Souther side of the bay. When it was daylighte, we found our selves neerer the south side, then to the Northside, about two leagues farther up in the bay then Hartes Content. By twelve of the clocke the same day, we came to the Harbour that the way overland from Avon in the bay of Conception is marked unto wheare we fownde good stoare of scurvie grasse. Heere we stayed until the 24th day, & then both the barke & shalloppe proceeded partelie by sayling, & partelie by rowing unto a harbour in the South bottome of Trinitie bay, which now is called by us Savage Harbour. Heere we fownd some savage housen a holberte a wooden target, & small coffins made of the barke of trees & a broad way leading from the seaside throughe the woodes.

[October] 26.

The 26th day being about to departe heerehence, & under sayle, contrarie windes put us in againe & then I sent some to follow the said way to see how farre yt went, & wheather they could see any savages. Who within one houre returning, declared that they saw a great freshe water lake, wheather the said way did lead them, & two fires, one upon ane Iland in the said lake & ane other upon the side of the lake. Wheareupon John Guy, with fourteene more, went to the said lake, whare they had sight of the said fires, & of a canoa with two rowing in her in the said lake, and soe goeing through the woodes with what silence was possible, alongste the lake side at twilighte, they came within halfe a mile of the place of the said fires, wheare remayning two houres within nighte after they proceeded, & came to the said place, wheare they fownde noe savages, but three of theire housen, wheareof two had bin latelie used, in one of the which the hearth was hot. The savages weare gone to the said Iland, wheather we could not goe for want of a boate. We fownd theare a copper kettle kepte very brighte, a furre gowne, some seale skinnes, ane old sayle, & a fishing reele. Order was taken that nothing should be diminished, & because the savages should know that some had bin theare, everything was re-

moved out of his place, & broughte into one of the cabins, and laid orderlie one upon the other, & the kettle hanged over them, whearin thear was put some bisket, & three or fower amber beades. This was done to beginne to winne them by fayre meanes. This time of the yeare they live by hunting, for we fownd twelve stags hoofes that weare latelie killed. A little peece of fleshe was broughte away, which was fownde to be a a beaver cod which is foorthcoming to be seene. Theire housen theare weare nothing but poules set in a rownde forme, meeting all togeather alofte, which they cover with deere skinnes. They are about tenne foote broade, and in the middle they make theire fire. One of them was covered with a sayle, which they had gotten from some Christian. Soe all things in this manner lefte, everyone returned by the moonelighte, goeing by the brinke of the lake unto the entraunce of the made way, & a little before they came theather they passed by a new savadge house almoste finished, which was made in a square forme with a small roofe & soe came to the barke.

[October] 27.

The nexte day we put foorth a flag of truce being a white flag. The lake is about a mile from any parte of the harborough. Theare issueth out of yt a very great brooke enough to drive three fordges with the currant. Theare was seene at theire cabanes showes made of deere, and seale skinnes very artificiallie. They have two kind of oares, one is about fower foote long, of one peece of firre, the other is about 10 foote long made of two peeces, one being as long, big & rownd as a halfe pike made of beeche wood, which by likelihood they made of a Biskaine oare, th'other is the blade of the oare, which is let into th'end of the long one slit, & whipped very stronglie. The shorte one they use as a paddle, & thother as ane oare.

[October] 30.

The 30th without any further business with the savadges, we departed thence to the northerne side of Trinitie bay, and anchored all that nighte under ane Iland.

[October] 31.

The 31th we rowed unto ane harboure which now is called Alhallowes, which hath adioyning unto yt very high land from whence was seene a great bay which ranne into the land North. Yt was to the neereste place about 3 leagues over land S.W. & some parte of yt did lie N.W. This muste needes be the bay of Placentia.

November 1.

The barke & shalloppe put out of the said harborough to discoover the bay within the headland which now is called the Elbow, & being foorth, the shalloppe was sent before to see wheare theare was any harborough theare, & the barke returned to Alhallowes. Word was brought that theare was noe harborough, but a sandie banke for a league, of a gray colour, & that a brooke came foorthe apparantlie in one place, but that theare went soe greate a sea as they could not get a shoare. They gave a good reporte of the likelihood of the place to yeeld good land. When they weare a league of theare was not fower fadome water.

[November] 3.

The 3 day we departed from Alhallowes, & went Northwards towards a sound, which we weare in good hope woulde bring them to Placentia & theare in a harborough one the wester side of the sound we anchored. This lieth 7 leagues from Alhallowes North within a league of this harbour. In the waye from Alhallowes lieth ane other harbour, that hath before the entraunce a good space of two rockes. Theare our boate saw nine savage housen, used by them in their coasting: the sound heere is about two miles broad.

[November] 4.

The 4th we put forward in the sound. The firste reach lieth N.B.W. westerlie one league, from thence N.N.W. halfe a league & from thence W.N.W. one league, wheare the sound did end. In that place was fownd eighte or nine savage housen in severall places, and a way cut into the woods, which being prosequuted, yt was fownd to lead directlie to a harborough in the bay of Placentia distant onlie two miles W., which harbour in Placentia bay is now called "Passage harbour". A river came unto yt from the N.N.E.; they which went, fownd theare fishe hookes, a small copper kettle, a fishing line, & a lead, a target, a staffe & a French basket, but noe shew of housen. In two houres & a halfe twelve of the companie which went returned. Here was fownd a new canoa ashoare, which now remayneth in the woods at Pernecam; by reason of stormie weather yt could not be broughte any further.

[November] 5.

The fifte day John Guy & tenne with him went from the barke by land to the top of a very high hill, to take a full view of the bay of Placentia, and all the contrey about. In their way they waded over the river that runneth into Passage harborough, yt is five times greater then any other river or brooke yet seane to the Southwards. Because the foggienes of the weather hindred the prospecte they remayned theare all nighte. About sunset yt cleered up from the SSW to the Northwards by the weste, & then the wester side of the bay of Placentia was seene to lie W. WSW. & SWBW & SW. About 10 leagues of theare was ane open(ing) into the maine sea, noe land appearing, in which sound weare small Ilands in a righte line; SWBS theare was land by which I thinke that all that lyeth betweene the said open[ing], & Cape St. Lawrence, which is the Cape one the wester side of the bay of Placentia are Ilands, & that Passage harbour before spoaken of is in the bottome of the bay of Placentia:

[November] 6.

The 6 day they returned to the barke from the high hill, & about two of the clocke in the afternoone, about two houres after the returne, theare was perceived a fire in the sownd a mile of whereupon all the companie repayred aboorde, because yt could be noe other then the doeing of savages. Presentlie two canoaes appeared, & one man alone comming towards us with a flag in his hand of a wolfskinne, shaking yt, & making a lowde noice, which we tooke to be for a parlie, whereupon a white flag was put out & the barke & shallope rowed towards them: which the savages did not like of, & soe tooke them to theire canoaes againe, & weare goeing away. Wheareupon the barke wheared onto them & flourished the flag of truce, & came to anker, which pleased them, & then they stayed. Presentlie after, the shalloppe landed Mr. Whittington with the flag of truce, who went towards them. Then they rowed into the shoare with one canoa, th'other standing aloofe of, & landed two men, one of them having the white skinne in his hand, & comming towards Mr. Whittington, the savage made a loude speeche & shaked the skinne, which was awnsweared by Mr. Whittington in like manner & as the savage drew neere he threw downe the white skinne into the grownde. The like was done by Mr. Whittington. Wheareupon both the savages passed over a little water streame towards Mr. Whittington daunsing leaping, & singing, & coming togeather, the foremoste of them, presented unto him a chaine of leather full of small perwincle shelles, a spilting knife, & a feather that stucke in his heare. The other gave him ane arrow without a head, & the former was requited with a linnen cap, & a hand towell, who put presentlie the linnen cap upon his head, and to the other he gave a knife. And after hand in hand they all three did sing, & daunce. Upon this one of our companie called Fraunces Tipton went a shoare, unto whom one of the savages came running: & gave him a chaine such as is before spoaken of, who was gratefied by Fraunces Tipton with a knife, & a small peece of brasse. Then all fower togeather daunced, laughing, & makeing signes of joy, & gladnes, sometimes strikeing the breastes of our companie & sometymes theyre owne. When signes was made unto them that they should be willing to suffer two of our companie more to come one shoare, for two of theires more to be landed, & that bread, & drinke should be brought ashoare, they made likewise signes that they had in their canoaes meate also to eate. Upon this the shalloppe rowed aboorde and broughte John Guy, & Mr. Teage a shoare, who presented them with a shirte, two table napkins & a hand towell, giving them bread, butter & reasons of the sun to eate, & beere, & aquavitae to drinke. And one of them blowing in the aquavitae bottle yt made a sound, which they fell all into a laughture at. After Mr. Croote, & John Crouder came ashoare, whom they went to salute giveing them shell chaines, who bestowed gloves upon them. One of the savages that came laste ashoare came walking with his oare in his hand, & seemed to have some command over the reste, & behaved him selfe civillie. For when meate was offred him, he drew of his mitten from his hand, before he would receive yt, & gave ane arrow for a present, without a head, who was requited with a dozen of pointes. After they had all eaten, & drunk, one of them went to theire canoa, & broughte us deeres fleshe dryed in the smoake, or wind, and drawing his knife from out of his necke he cut every man a peece, & yt savoured very well. At the firste meeting, when signes weare made of meate to eate one of the savadges presentlie came to the banke side, &

pulled up a roote, & gave yt to Mr Whittington. Which t'other savage perceiving to be durtie, tooke yt out of his hand, & went to the water to washe yt, & after devided yt among the fower. Yt tasted very well. He that came ashoare with the oare in his hand went, & tooke the white skinne, that they hayled us with, & gave yt to Master Whittington, & presentlie after they did take our white flag with them in the Canoa, and made signes unto us that we should repaire to our barke, & soe they put off for yt was almoste nighte.

In the two canoaes theare weare eighte men, yf none weare women (for commonlie in every canoa theare is one woman). They are of a reasonable stature, of ane ordinarie middle sise; they goe bareheaded, wearing theire haire somewhat long, but rounded, they have noe beards. Behind they have a great locke of haire plattered with feathers, like a hawke's lure with a feather in yt standing uprighte by the crowne of the head, & a small locke platted before. A shorte gowne or cassocke made of stag skinnes, the furre innermost, that came downe to the middle of theire leg, with sleves to the middle of their arme, & a beaver skinne about their necke, was all their apparell, save that one of them had showes & mittens, soe that all went bare legged, & moste barefoote. They are full dyde of a blacke colour, the colour of their haire was diverse, some blacke, some browne, & some yellow, their faces something flat & broad, red with okir, as all theire apparell is, & the reste of their bodie. They are broad breasted, & bould, & stand very uprighte.

Theire canoaes are about 20 foote long, & 4 foote & a halfe broad in the middle alofte, & for their keele, & timbers they have thinne lighte peeces of dry firre rended, as yt weare lathes and in steede of boorde they use the utter birche barke which is thinne & hath many foldes, sowed togeather with a thread made of a small roote quartered, they will carrie fower persons well, & way not one hundred weight. They are made in forme of a new moone, stemme, & sterne alike & equallie distant from the greateste breadth. From the stemme & sterne theare riseth a yarde highe a lighte thinne staffe whyped about with small rootes, which they take hold by to bring the canoa ashoare. That serveth in steede of ropes, and a harbour, for every place is to them a harboorugh, wheare they can goe ashoare themselves they take a land with them theire canoa, & will neaver put to sea but in a calme, or very fayre weather. In the middle the canoa is hygher a great deale then in the bow & quarter. They be all bearing from the keele to the porteles, not with any circular line but with a righte line. They had made a tilte with a sayle, that they got from some Christian, & pitched a dozen poules in the grownd neere, one which weare hanged divers furres, & chaines made of shells, which at that instant we fell not in the reckoning to what intent yt was done, but after yt came to our mindes as heereafter you shall perceive.

[November] 7.

The 7th day we spent in washing, & in beginning a house to shelter us when we should come theather heereafter, upon a small Iland of about five acres of grownd which is Joyned to the maine with a small beache; for any bartering with the savages theare can not be a fitter place.

[November 8].

Yt beganne to freeze, & theare was thinne Ice over the sound & because we heard nothing more of the savages we beganne to returne out of the sound, & coming to the place which the savages had made two dayes before the fire in, we fownd all things remayning theare, as yt was when we parted, viz. ane old boate sayle, three, or fower, shell chaines, about twelve furres (of beavers moste), a foxe skinne, a saple skinne, a bird skinne, & ane old mitten set everye one upon a severall poule, wheareby we remayned satisffied fullie that they weare broughte theather of purpose to barter with us, & that they would stand to our curtesie to leave for yt what we should thinke good. Because we weare not furnished with fit things for to trucke, we tooke onlie, a beaver skinne, a saple skinne, & a bird skinne, leaving for them, a hatchet, a knife & fower needles threaded. Mr. Whittington had a paire of sezers which he lefte theare for a small beaver skinne, all the reste we theare untouched and came that nighte to the harbour that we weare in at our entring, which we call Flagstaffe Harbour, because we fownd theare the flagstaffe throwen by the savages away. Thease savages by all likelihood weare animated to come unto us, by reason that we tooke nothing from them at Savage bay, & some of them may be of those which dwell theare. For in noe other place wheare we weare,

could we perceive any tokens of any aboade of them at this point.

[November] 10.

We departed from Flagstaffe harbour, & came that nighte to a harbour called Hartes content.

[November] 11.

The wind being NE, & the snow contynewing all day kepte us in Hartes content.

[November] 13.

The barke, & shalloppe departed from Hartes content. Before nighte the barke doubled the Grates, & sayled betweene Baccalean, & the maine into the Bay of Conception, and as they sayled they saw above a dozen stags upon the bare hills neere Greene Bay. After seaven houres turning in the bay, we boare roome with Greene bay to stay for the shalloppe, and at II of the clocke at nighte we anchored in the Eastermoste roade of Greene Bay.

[November] 14.

We fownd by waying of one anchor, that the rocks had worne a sunder our hawser that we roade by, for the anchor, & twentie fadome of the hawser was lefte behind, for that & by reason of a sea which came into the roade out of the South, we soughte to recover th'other roade of Greene bay: which as we weare about to doe, the shalloppe came sayling out of Trinitie bay without the canoa, which they had towed from Truce sound unto Old Pernecam, wheare foule weather forced them to land yt: & the sea was so wroughte as they could not come aboord us. We in the barke because we could not double the head of Greene Bay, stoode to the offing, and standing backe againe, perceiving that by reason of sagging in with the smalnes of the winde we went to leewarde, we stoode out againe, & being foorth in the offing, Yt blew soe much wind at South as we weare forced to hull the moste part of that nighte.

[November] 15.

This day when yt cleered up, we saw land to the N.W. of us, which because we imagined that we had gone to the Northward by hulling, we made accompte that yt had bin parte of the land one the Northside of Trinitie bay: this nighte also we weare forced to hull by reason of the fiercenes of the wind.

[November] 16.

This day we saw the land againe, & still accompting yt to be betweene Bonaviste, & the Horselips we wroughte theareafter, sometimes goeing S. & SSW & SBE as the wind would permit us, & sometimes NW to get neere the land.

[November] 17.

Yt was a fog & we could not see above a mile from us, untill noone we went S.S.W. & then, being desirous to get neare the land to make yt, to be sure wheare we weare, we went N.W. & weare within hearing of the rut of the shoare before we could see yt, and presentlie yt pleased God to send us a cleere, the wind WNW & then we fownd our selves something to the Southward of Renoose. Then knowing that yt was the currant that carried us the firste nighte that we hulled, to the Southwarde and that the land which we saw alwayes was to the South of Cape St. Fraunces, yt was Gods doeing that we went not to the South of Cape Razo.

[November] 18.

Being in the offing from Cape Broile, a SE wind came & broughte us to Torrebay, wheare we ancored at nighte.

[November] 19.

We remayned heere expecting a fayre wind, & having noe boate with us we made meanes by oares, & a hogshead to get some of our companie ashoare.

[November] 20.

About 2 of the clocke in the morning the wind came to S.E. wheareupon we departed from Torrebay, but before day, the wind came to S.W., & soe weare faire to recover Greene Bay againe in the roade which we lefte. This nighte was one exceeding great storme, the wind WNW.

[November] 21.

We put foorth of Greene Bay, choosing rather to continew turning in the bay, then to ride in such a roade, to the hazard of the losse of all our anchors.

[November] 22.

We got into the roade of great Belile, yt blowing a fierce gale of wind at W.N.W.

[November] 24.

About Midnighte the 24th day the wind being S.B.E., we departed from Belile, but before we had proceeded as farre as the end of the said

Iland, the wind came to the S.W. & W.S.W., & blew soe much as we could beare noe sayle, but lay a hull untill day, in doubte to be put out of the bay, & makeing accompte that we had great good hap, yf we could recover the roade from whence we came. And while we weare thus perplexed, the wind came to the North and broughte us in safelie, God be praysed to Cupers Cove by tenne of the clocke in the forenoone the 25th day of this month of November, wheare we understoode that the shalloppe which we lefte in Greene bay eleaven dayes agoe was caste away the morrow after, but all the men saved, who put the sayle, & theire apparell in safetie ashoare, & came homeward by land to Carbonera in 8 days, having nothing to eate, but what they could find by the way, & from thence came in safetie home one sunday the 22th. of this month. Presentlie after the barke was arrived the wind was westerlie.

642. September 1, 1612 to April 1, 1613. "Occurrents in Newfoundland."

Weather diaries were a feature of the colony's record-keeping from the beginning, but those for 1610–1611 and 1611–1612 were in Samuel Purchas's possession, but he printed only brief notes of them and the full versions are lost. Purchas preserved for us something more in the way of a summary of the winter diary of the 1612–1613 journal (Purchas, Pilgrimes, IV [1625], 1880–1882 [XIX (1907) 418–424]), but there is a full version surviving in Nottingham University Library, Middleton MS, Mi x 1/66, fols. 2–18. The diary is unique as a record of early modern North American weather and is of considerable climatological interest.

Journall from the first of September u[ntill] the last of Aprill 1613 in Cupe[rs Co]ve Ne[wfo]und land wher the Colonie is kept 1612. September first the winde at weste al the daie verie faire the sune shi[ning]e all the daie untill night: this morning 8 of us wen[t forward] for Trinitie Bay markinge the way: we founde verie faire burch trees passing thorowe the woodes and 4 places of open grounde and passed 3 Fresh watter lakes with divers beavers nesses in them: this [= thus] we went some Six milles the first daie / this night we had the winde at southeast with raine untill daie:

2th. The winde at southeast verie Fowlle weather and much raine all the day the winde beinge cold: the sune not showinge hir selffe all that d[aie] wher we wear forced to staie under a tree all this day and night conteinuinge rayninge untill the morninge: which by no mayner we coud not kept our bread drie but was all waitte

3th. in the morninge we proceedid: being the winde at north west: abowte an houre after sune rissinge: we had some showers of small Raine passing thorow much open ground: with a fresh watter lake in it after passing a wood and thickett came againe into open ground wher was a verie faire river ca[me] thorowe and a path which made showe of much deer had passed that way from thence thorowe other faire woodes some 3 milles: and so came into a great Campion countrie and much open ground which was some 3 or 4 mylles from Trinitie bay: this night we lay in a wood by a freshe watter lake wher we killed some 5 or 6 ducks for our supper in that lake was some 4 beavers nesses // this night proved verie faire the wind at west all night

4th. in the morninge we proceedid Farther thorowe verie faire woodes passing faire lakes and freshe rivers: beinge abowte 10 of the clock in the middest of a wood at the top of a great hill and could not see any part of the bay: and dowtting to find it before such time as our bread was spentt: being all weett resolved amongest our selves to retorne againe: so that night we came unto that fresh watter lake wher we departed from the morninge: the wind all the daie at west north and small raine // but the night faire

5th. in the morninge the winde at northeast verie faire weather all the daie untill night with fair sune shininge: that night we logged by a freshe river the night being verie faire in a wood // at the head of a Fresh lake which did prove after ward that we wear not above 6 mylls from Trynitie Baye but beinge our bread was spent we durst not hazard [or] venture any fur[ther] but returned back again all the [way which we had travelled] forth

[September 1]612

6th. in th[e] morninge the winde at east verie faire sune shininge all the day untill night // at night we retorned againe at Cupers Cove the night beinge verie faire weather: all our Bread spent the day before we came home: this eveninge master robartes shipp came from Reenoose

7th. in the morninge the wind all at east untill night with verie faire sune shininge all the day untill night the weather verie warme the night in like mannor gorg wichalls and elles norton killed 2 musk rattes at Cammon Cove

8th. in the morninge the wind at weste very much winde all the day untill night the night allso much winde this day master robertes departed with his shipp: to go for London:

9th. in the morninge the winde at weste with some Raine in the after noone untill it was night this morning departed 8 of our people againe for Trinitie Bay to find it by land the night proved verie faire weather all night

10th. the wind at weste verie faire and cleare weather untill night the night allso the winde verie faire weather

11th. the wind all easterly verie faire sune shininge weather all the daie untill night the night verie faire allso the wind beinge still at east

12th. the winde westerlie with much raine all the daie untill it was night also it rayned some parte of the night the wind still at weste

13th. the winde at weste untill noone after noone at easte verie faire weather untill night the night allso proved verie faire

14th. the winde in the morning at north with some raine but towardes night reasonable faire weather and likewise the night allso

15th. in the morninge the wind at Southweste verie faire sune shininge weather all the daie untill night

16th. in the morninge the wind at west south west windie and verie Close weather all the daie untill night the n[igh]t verie clear and faire

17th. in the morninge the winde at Southweste verie f[aire] sune shininge weather all the daie untill night th[e] ni[ght] allso verie faire and Cleare

18th. in the morninge the wind at weste south-west ve[ry] Faire sune shining weather all the daie unt[ill] night The night allso verie faire and Clear

19th. in the morninge the wind at west south-west verie Faire sune shininge weather and clear untill nigh[t] The night allso verie clear

September 1612

20th. in the morninge the wind at east south east [veri]e Close weather all daie with small raine untill night The night allso small raine untill after midnight

21th. in the morninge the winde at east north east faire sune shyninge all the daie untill night the night allso verie Faire untill day

22th. in the morninge the winde at weaste verie faire sune shininge wether all the daye untill night the night allso verie Clear and faire

23th. in the morning the winde at south weste verie hard but very faire Sune shininge weather all the daie untill night the night allso verie faire

24th. in the morninge the winde at south weste with some small Rayne // but all the reste of the daie verie faire sun[e] Shyninge untill night the night allso verie faire

25th. in the morninge the winde at Northweste a whitt froost: but all the after[noon] verie faire sune shyninge weather untill night. The night allso faire

26th. in the morninge the winde at south east: a whitte froost but all the daie after a verie faire sune shyninge weather untill // night the night allso verie faire

27th. in the morninge The winde at northweast a Froost but all the daie a verie faire sune shyninge // untill night The night allso verie faire

28th. in the morninge The winde at south weste verie much winde but very Faire sunne shininge all the daie untill night: the night very faire

29th. in the morninge the winde at Southweste reasonabell Faire weather all the daie the night some raine untill Morninge:

30th. in the morninge the wind at south weste with some raine all the daie and most parte of the night//

October 1612

1th. in the morninge the wind at South weste with Some small raine and much wind in the night very much raine

2th. in the morninge the wind at weast verie hard all the daie dry and verie faire sune shyninge some 4 howres before sune settinge

3th. in the morninge the winde at south weste with some Raine and some tymes the sune shyninge: in the night some 3 or 4 howres before day raine

4th. in the morninge the wind at Southweste with litell Raine but all the night verie much raine

5th. in the morninge the winde at southweste somthinge cold: with some rayne in the after noone sune shininge untill night the night verie Faire

6th. in the morninge the wind at southweste very mylde weather untill noone verie close weather/ in the after noone verie faire sune shyninge all the after noone untill night

7th. in the morninge The wind at weste some raine untill noone the after noone abowte 2 of the clocke we departed from Cupers Cove with our panice the governer and 18 more of us bound For the Baye of Trinitie a coasting this night we put in at Harbroo de Grace: abowte ii of the clocke in The night the wind at west faire weather

8th. in the morninge the winde at weste south-weste all the daie raine untill night: the night allso much raine//

9th. in the morninge the winde at weste verie faire weather and the sune shininge all the daie the wind somthing hard the night allso much wind

10th. in the morninge the wind at weste verie faire weather the sune shininge all daie untill night but the wind somthing hard and so it was all night

11th. the wind in the morning at weste verie faire weather with sune shyninge: but the wind somthing hard: Litell all night but some 2 howres before daie much wind and raine with thunder and lightning

October 1612

12th. in the morninge the wind at weste northweste all the fore noone verie close weather and much winde in the after noone verie faire sune shininge but verie much wind untill night the night verie calme but very colde we landed out of the French shipp left ther by captaine Eastone some 15 tonns of Salts upon the beache allso lefte 2 cabells and a anker which we lefte ther allso the some 60 Fadome the shipp 120 tonne

13th. in the morninge the winde at Northweste with faire sune Shyninge all the daie and the night allso verie faire weather the wind all night at northweste

14th. in the morninge the winde at nerly weste verie faire weather but a litell Froost this morn-ing but all the daie verie faire sune shyninge untill night // in the night some raine but small as drivinge Fogge

15th. in the morninge the winde at weste with a

storme and Raine all the daie untill night the night allso verie much raine and much winde all night

16th. in the morning the winde at weste north weste verie much winde all daie but sune shyninge all the daie The night verie faire and litell wind

17th. in the morninge the wind at north weste this morninge we departed from Harbour de Grace abowte 7 of the clocke all this daie verie faire sune shyninge untill night and at night abowte the setting of the sune we ankered in Green Bay of the wester side the wind at northwest in the night we had some showers of snowe this night after midnight we wayed anker to go abowte Backaloo // but ther finding the wind contrarie bonding too and froo

18th. in the morninge the winde at northeaste some parte of the day Sune shyninge and some tymes showers of snowe but the wind being Contrary this night we put backe againe and ankered againe in Green [Bay] this night we had much snowe most parte of the night

19th. in the morning the winde at northwest much wind but faire sun shininge this morning we departed againe from green Baye For to gett the Baye of Trinitie but the wind comyng more at weste in the afternoone cold recover under a land neer unto an Island called Sainct Cattlins in this place wher we ankered under the hie land was a great heape of stonnes made up like unto a chappell we had this night a Reasonable galle of winde the night proving reasonable Faire

October 1612

20th. in the morninge the wind at west very much winde all the daie but the sune shyninge verie Faire all the daie untill night the night verie much wind untill it was towardes day

21th. in the morninge the winde at weste verie much wind and raine // in the after noone we putt from thence abowte 3 of the clocke the wind Comyng in a shower of raine at north and north and be [= by] east all this night we crossed the Baye of Trinitie with the wind at north east

22th. in the morning the wind at north east we wear neer by Harts Content of the souther side with very faire weather and sune shyninge all the after noone the wind at south west this after noone betwine 1 or 2 of the clocke went into Mounte Eagle Baye and ther ankered this night verie much wind and rayne all the night

23th. in the morninge the wind at southwest faire sune shining all the daie untill night the night the wind at weste verie faire weather this daye in the morninge we went at the mouth of Mountte Eagell Baie and landed upon a fine litle Iland which was excellent good ground and grasse upon it and ther we gathered store of scurvy grasse allso this litell we found that ther had ben great store of birdes had haunted

24th. in the morninge the wind at south east verie faire sune shininge weather // untill night and calme this morninge we departed out of Mountte Eagell Baye coastinge towardes the bottom of Trinitie Baye passed by Iland of the south side rowing all the day with our pennice and Tawing hir with our shallopp abowte 3 or 4 of the Clocke we entered with our Barke in a sound some 4 mylles and Right of the north side before the harbours mouth 3 fine Ilandes which will make that place a good harbour this night we ankered in this sound this night verie faire weather the wind at west untill morninge a litell raine

25th. in the morninge the wind at south and at south west but faire sune shininge most parte of the daie some small showers at tymes the weather verie mylde this daie our people did find divers things of the solvages bouckellers, long staffes or pikes one arowe and litell boolles and sundry housses wher they had bin in allso they had made a great path thorowe the woodes this night the wind at weste very much winde

October 1612

26th. in the morninge the wind at weste very Faire sune shininge weather all the daie but very much wind this morning we wayed our ankers and rowed forth at the mouth of the harbour finding the wind contrarie we retorned backe againe and did anker in the same place from whence we parted after our comynge in some of our people sought out the path of the solvages which brought them unto a Fresh watter lake wher they had sight of 2 or 3 of ther Fiers they retorned againe advertissed our governer of it so in the eveninge wentt him Selfe with 14 more thinking to have in trapped them in ther housses but beffore they came the solvages wear departed and gone into an litell Iland in the mydest of the Freesh watter lake our people had sight of a canno and 2 men which wear Rowinge unto the Iland but our man had never a bootte to go unto them: the governer entered into ther housses ashoore / but gave charg nothing should be touched by any of his Companie Finding and felling in the night divers good Foures // and the Feett of 3 deer which they had newly killed // so the governer lefte all ther thinges but leaving in a litell brassen kettell which they had in there house lefte in it some biskitt pointtes and Brassletes Takeng some 2 or 3 Childrin showes: and brought away and so departed this night the wind at north east verie faire weather

27th. in the morninge the wind at east north east verie close weather all daie the night somthing faire but some 2 or 3 howers befffore daie some rayne //

28th. in the morninge the wind at east south east with small Raine and much wind all the day the night allso very much Raine the wind still at east south east all night//

29th. in the morninge the wind at south east verie thicke Fogg untill noone / in the after noone much raine the wind still southerlye / the night reasonable faire untill towardes the morning then it Rayned

30th. in the morninge the winde at south easte but verie litle but verie full of Fogg this morning we departed from Solvage Baye for so we have named it because we found them ther so coasting towardes the bottome we sent our shallope thinking to find a sound some leag from this our bootte went no Farther being thick Fogg our bootte being at a pointe of another bay one of our people was ashoore upon a fine parselles of gound of some 12 ackars of very good land and excellent good grasse // in the other side William Hatton being in the bootte had the sight of some Irone stone: in the point of a rock: but by no maynes could go ashoore the sea so loftie: over leffe but came away Fearinge to louse the sight of our penice the governor makinge to retorne backe that way againe homewardes // in the after noone very clear and faire weather rowinge over for the north sid of Trinitie at night we ankered under a pointte of an Ilande which is to be named by the governor and the other places which we have bin at // this night the wind at north east but verie full of Fogg all night

31th. in the morninge the winde at sowth weste very faire weather all the daie: this morning we removed anker from this Iland and coasting the

baye abowte 10 of the clocke rowing along came into a Fine sound which did ly west & west north west from this Iland some 2 leages betwine the Iland and this place: in the after noone the governer and some 5 more went up unto the topp of very hie hills: thinking to discover some passagg thorowe some soundes into the Bay of Pleasaunce but we could [not] perceav any but a deep sound which went in: thorowe // this night very faire weather some of our people lying ashore and some abord

November 1612

1th. in the morninge the wind at southeaste very much wind and mayne after 8 of the clocke this morninge we removed anker thinking to have gone into a sound called Sanndy Baye which is within the elbowe so being Fowll weather and rayne // we returned back againe unto the place we removed anker this morning but the governer sent our boott to see if ther wear any harbour but they could finde noone // but an excellent beache and verie fine sannde and earth: a verie likely place and by Jugment not farr by land from thence to Pleasaunce this night proved verie Faire the wind at southwest

2th. in the morninge the wind at north & be west verie Close weather with some showers of rayne this morninge we went with our bootte: and found 2 fine harbors more not abowe ech a mille of anuder [= another] from the plac we ankered be all in one baye in thes places we see divers solvages housses: but not that they had bin ther in long tyme // the winde this night was at west and west south west verie much raine and much fogge after mydnight and the wind very hard allsoe

November 1612

3th. in the morninge the wind at west south weste very much wind but Clear and sune shininge weather this morning we did remove anker from this harbour: and torned into the next sound which went up north or north and be east thinking to find a passage thorowe for Pleasaunce but goeinge up this sound we found another sound and sent our bootte ashoore in one litell Creeke wher they did find 9 solvagges housses: so the bootte came unto the next sound wher we ankered and stayed all night supping ashoore / ther we found allso 3 solvagges housses more this sound went in north west this night very myld weather

4th. in the morninge the wind at north west very faire sune shininge weather some parte of the daie this morninge we removed anker and went up farther in to the other sound which went up north and north be west we went unto the verie bottome thinking sure to have found a passag thorowe: so that after noone we found a canno verie artifically made which was halled upon the shoore // after dinner we wentt some 9 of us and followed a path which the solvagges had made which brought us unto a very faire river which goeth in Pleasaunce which was but 2 mylles overland from the place wher our Barke was: of the other wher we found the path to go into Pleasance we found divers places wher the solvagges had bin and they do cary cannose over land to Imbark them selves at the other side ther we found a baskett full of Fishermens hookes, flentt stones and a goate skynne and a lame skine and a little brassen kettell which we brought with us and a bouckeller // ther we see 2 very great wollves // also we found ther a calking yerone for a shipp: in our cannoe we found a fishing lynne one of our men a Fisher mans caepe / in this place we found wher our Barke is we found in all some 8 or 9 solvages housses // and wher they had tanned a beares skine ther path over land is a great beatten path into Pleasaunce Baye this night verie faire weather

5th. in the morninge the wind at northweste verie faire myld weather but no sun shyninge but close weather a litell froost in the morninge this morning our governer wentt a coasting at the tope of a hill with some ii more of our people to di[s]cover Pleasaunce Bay but it was verie thick and close untill towardes night which he doth Imagine ther may be a passage near a bowte Hartes Ease which we had no time to trye this after noone a litell raine but the night proved very faire but ther was a litell froost this night our gover[ner] stayed Forth all the night

6th. in the morninge the wind at north north west with some Fogge abowte dinner tyme our governer and his Companie retorned agayne so some howre after dinner we did espie a solvagges fier being some mylle from the place wher we made our fier being we discovered ther fier did go all abord and advertised our governer of it howe they made a Fier for a signe for us to come unto them: so we removed anker and made towardes them with our penice and shallope // Comyng neer

them both with our penice and shallop they began to be fearfull: retorned againe unto ther concouse [canoes?] being 2 of them and 8 personnes // seeing them to be Rowinge away we made signes with our flagg of truce: which made them retorne but first they showed a Flage of truce unto us with a wolffes skine and they made showes we should come ashoore unto them but seeing both bark and boott come made them to fear and gett into ther cannouse // then the governor sent but the boote to go ashoore and ther landid one man called Master Whittington: with our flagg of truce then ther landid one of thers out of the cannow and so came to parlea by signes one to the other with handing and dauncing togeather // they laughinge much with verie great voyces // then ther came another of ther men ashoore presently ther landid another of ours // then afterward the governer landid and some 4 more of us: the governer maid them a banquet with reassons bread and butter and beare and aquavitae which they liked well // but first they gave us at our comyng ashoore chaines of sheelles and putt abowte our neckes for great presentes // the governer bestowed one them a shirte napkinge hankerchers and pointes and our flagg of truce // they gave us some of ther drie venicon they wear very Joifull of our flagg of truc allso they Brought ashoore at ther first comyng certaine Fours some 14 in all more they had in ther cannouse / and did haunge them upon stages by the beach we thinking they did drie them but we perceived after ward it was to trock with us being towardes night they hasted to be gone // making showe they would go into ther cannouse and they made showe unto us to go abord our Bark which we departed instantlie as they did // but they lefte all ther skins behind except a wolffe skine which they bestowed one master Whittington which was ther flage of truce so we removed with our bark and boott up to the bottome of the sound againe we call this sound Truce Sound because we made truce with them ther // ([margin]: the wind at northeast but some froost this night) this night very mild//

November 1612

7th. in the morninge the winde at northeaste verie faire sune shininge in the after noone Some snow blanckes this daie we began to build a house upon a litell Iland which is in the verie bottome of Truce Sound and in the verie trad waye of the solvages as they go unto Pleasaunce this bay lieth in neerest north north east and out south south weste: this night very faire starr light but a Froost in all the bottome of this harbour which we dowtted to be kept in if we should have stayed longer which made us to forsake to Furnish the buildinge of our house

8th. in the morninge the wind at south some thing close weather but verie myld: this morninge we removed anker from this sound of truce and in goinge Forthe we wennt ashoore at the place wher we had parley with the Solvages comyng ashoore we founde all ther skines still standing upon the poolles // so the governer taking veiwe of them all did take 2 beavers skines one sabell skynne and a skine of a kind of straunge Fowell leavinge For the same thinges // one hachett one kniffe 3 neells [= needles] threedid for the rest we lefte one the poolles as we founde them being verie sorowe we could not staie any longer for to have spoken with them ther wear lefte in all some 14 skines lefte of Beavers the most parte this day in the after noone we ankered in a sounde comynge into Truce Sound when we came first in // which we ankered in the 4th ditto: the wind still at south this daie we had some raine and snowe blanckes: this night we had in this harbour verie Fowlle weather the wind at north west verie much winde and good store of snowe // we Feared much to be put From our anker

9th. in the morninge the wind at north west verie much wind and close weather untill noone: then sune shininge and verie faire weather untill night the night allso proved verie faire but somthing cold

10th. in the morninge the wind at North weste verie faire weather the sune shininge at tymes and some tymes snow blanckes this morning we removed anker caring [= carrying] the canno with us // being crossing all this day the Bay of Trinitie and at night we came unto Hartes Content this night verie faire and litell wind mending hear our canno//

11th. in the morninge the winde at North east much wind showinge verie thicke all the daie this place is some 8 leages from Mountt Eagell Bay this morninge we removed anker and goinge forth the harbour mouth found the winde contrarie so retorned in to the harbour agayne all this night it did snowe very thicke and very much wind at northeast

12th. in the morninge the wind at northeast much winde but verie faire sune shininge weather all the day in the night Froost but verie clear and litell wind

13th. in the morninge the wind at west sune shininge some parte of the daie // this morninge we departed from Hartes Content coastinge along before we came unto Backalo and Green Baye // passinge the pointe we see at the tope of hill in one companie 12 or 13 deer marching along one after another so at the verie pointe this night we ankered in a litell cove to the easter side of Green Baye: the night being very Faire and litell wind the wind at south west all the night our bootte staying behind us and the canno at the Old Perlican // being much sea could not bring her aboute the Graates

14th. in the morninge the wind at south and south & be easte with small raine // in the after noone we removed anker but in waying our cabell was cutt with rocke // so wear Forced to leave him behind us when it was towardes night we espied our bootte being adreefe with our Bark // and speaking unto our bootte being much wind willid them to fish for our anker but the weather being so Fowlle they could not find it they going ashoore into Green Bay shipping a sea filled ther bootte and all they in daunger to be drownned but gott ashoore upon oores and other thinges and so did save them selves being 5 of them lost all ther apparrell and vittelles from saterday untill monday they wear coasting too and froo at green [= Green Bay] not knowing the way for wante of a compase diall // so after wardes considered with them selves did kept by the Sea coaste: but at Green Bay they had sight of some 4 companies of deer 6 - 5 - 4 and 3 in ech companie comyng verie neer unto them so long as they kept going but standing still they would come no neer them easily to be shoote but they wannted a pece // making the beste shifte they could eatting some routes [= roots] and Beeres [= berries] which they found being in great extreemitie untill they came unto Carbonnire wher they Found in a stadge // a salt codd head and 2 Fishes // and ther lanched a bootte the 22th ditto and came to Cupers Cove the 23th abowte 9 of the clock at night being all most famished comyng thorowe the woodes they did see verie faire berche trees as possible might be and somthing near Carbonire for abowt Green Bay very much open ground and good grasse and ther great store of partridge at Green Bay by reasson of the open grownd for ther is ther hantt most / all thes partes they came therowe was in Sir Percivall Willaghby lotte: they lefte the canno at the Old Perlioan in the bootte was Bartholemew Prison and William Hatton

15th. in the morninge the wind at south and be east with Fogg until 10 of the clocke then the sune shininge but afterward with very much wind until night allso all the night a verie great storme of wind and Raine the wind at west and could bear no saille but hulled all night the Sea being verie wraught: this night by force of the Corrantt we wear put to the southwardes of Cape Sannct Frauncis wher we made accompt that we had bin betwin Backalo and Trinitie so we wear deceived

16th. in the morninge the wind at northeast verie faire sune shininge but the weather cold the night verie faire the wind at southeast being to the southward of the cape at Frauncis // but being mistaken we thought still to be in the Bay of Trinitie: which we have come backe againe verie well if we had not bin mistaken this night reasonable faire weather

17th. in the morninge the wind at north much Fogg untill noone: then abowtte one of the clocke it cleared up and we made the land which was betwine Rennouse and Fermouse that we wear in the stead of Trinitie Baye: a hard galle of wind in the after noone we could not recover into any harbour the wind blowing hard at west but cast abowt to the northwardes agayne // this night proved verie faire but cold: in the morning we wear right against the Ile of Speares//

18th. in the morning the wind at southeast verie faire sune shininge but a verie Freesh galle of winde abowt 3 of the clocke the wind came at south and raine and like of Fowell weather which made us to put into Torbay that night with very much wind at weast all this night

19th. in the morninge the wind at west with some snowe blanckes at times and some times sune shininge most parte of the daie about 3 of the clocke we made a raffte and wentt ashoore and suped and allso lanssed a bootte // and came abord that night the night being verie faire untill after midnight: then we removed anker from thence being forth of the harbour we had the wind at east: but after we wear forth of Torbay we had verie Fowell weather verie much wind and rayne

being abowte day we weare neer Cape St Fraun-cis

20th. in the morninge the wind having dubbed [= doubled?] Cape St frauncis the wind at south and south west with verie much Rayne and much wind not being abell to recover any harbour in the Bay of Consumption // but wear Forced this evenynge to put back for Green Baye and ankered in the same place at the easter parte wher we loste before our anker. Riding ther all night with a great storme of wind in great fear our cables or anker would have Failled

21th. in the morninge we removed anker and the wind at south weast torninge up the bay to gett to Cupers Cove but the wind and Rayne so exstreame could recover noe place all this daie // this night somthing Faire untill day

22th. in the morninge the wind at south weste some tymes the sune Shininge and some tymes snowe in the after noone much wind at weste but towardes night the wind at west north weste which made us to gett to the souther side of Great Bellill against the stadges wher the shipes fish and ther ankered all night with verie much winde all night at west north west this night a great froost against the morninge

23th. in the morning the wind at weste north weste verie much wind and exstreame cold weather: but faire sune shininge all the day Freessing hard // the night somthing milder with the wind still at west north west

24th. in the morninge the wind at west north west the sune shininge verie faire but somthinge a cold Froost and some snowe in the after noone / at night the wind at south: and abowt 12 of the clock at night we removed anker from Bell Ille to go For Cupers Cove // but abowte 4 of the clock we had verie Fowle weather not abell to beare any Saille at all but hulled in the baye making first 2 or 3 bordes // with snowe and raine at tymes: we wear lik to be put out of the bay this night the wind and sea being so exstreame

25th. in the morning the winde at north with snowe showers which Came abowte 8 of the clock continued untill none which brought us into Cup-ers Cove so abowte ii of the clock we arived hear but the after noone allso divers showers of Snowe untill it was night the night Froost and good store of Snowe

26th. in the morninge the wind at weste and

some showers of snowe and some parte of the daie Faire sune shininge at night some store of Snowe and froost the wind at west all the night

27th. in the morninge the winde at west and be north verie faire sune shininge all the daie but cold all the days freessinge somthing untill night: reasonable faire weather untill midnight but after midnight the winde at south west varie much wind with a great storme and much raine all that parte of the night which did consume the greater parte of the snowe and Ice which did fall before//

28th. in the morninge the winde at south west somthing myld weather but verie close all the daye / the night allso somthing mild The wind at south west with some small raine but after mydnight ther was a litell frooste//

29th. in the morninge the winde at south: verie myld weather but some showers of snowe most parte of the daye verie close weather // at night the wind at north weste with much snowe and some Froost

30th. in the morninge the wind at North west much winde and cold and froost Freessing hard all day but sun shininge most part of the day at night the wind at west north west with very much snowe

1th December 1612 in the morninge the wind at south east untill noone in the after noone at east but all the day very much snowe untill night at night the wind at east with showers of snowe and some froost

2th. in the morninge the wind at north west verie much winde all the day but faire sune shyninge all the day Freessinge all the day The night the wind at west & be north with froost and much snowe

3th. in the morning the winde at west north west verie cold freessinge hard all the daye with clear sune shininge all the daye // the night more mylder the wind at west south west all night

4th. in the morninge the wind at west south west verie mild wether the sune shininge all the day: at night myld weather the wind at north east and very much snowe

5th. in the morninge the wind at north all the daie verie close weather Freessing hard and allso snowe some parte of the Daie: the night very cold the wind at South weste with snowe after midnight untill day

6th. in the morninge the winde at weste north weste snowinge very thick all the daie untill it was 4 of the clock in the after noone it did break up to verie faire weather but very much winde all The night: after midnight it Freese verie hard untill the morninge the winde at weste

7th. in the morninge the winde at west north west verie faire sune shininge all the daie butt Freessinge verie hard untill night in the night allso the wind at weste north weste verie clear night litle winde but Freessing exstreeme hard all the night

8th. in the morning the winde at west north west very faire sune Shininge and clear weather Freessing verie hard all the daie untill night: at night verie much winde at west north west Freessing but litell

9th. in the morninge the winde at west north west verie Close weather all the daie not Freessing much // at the night the winde at south west thawing all the night being somthing mild

10th. in the morninge the wind all southerly but somthing Calme all the daie with Fogg thawing much all the daie but verie mild weather in the after noone the sun shinned towardes night the wind at west north west at night the wind at south west very mild weather all night: thawing still // but a litel beffore daye was a litell Froost

11th. in the morninge the winde at southwest and be south verie myld weather all the daye thawinge verie much it thawed and uncovered the housses from snowe which had bin Froossen 8 dayes beffore: the sune showing hir selffe abowte 12 of the clock and so contenued allmost untill night this morning was verie close weather with Fogg // the skie in the morning verie reed // at the rissing of the sune and verie litell winde mylder day could not be in England in the night after 9 of the clock verie much winde at Southweste with verie much raine all the night: which did consume near all the Froost and snowe which was upon the ground before litell lefte except in some certaine places//

12th. in the morninge the winde at west with much wind and shower of Raine untill it was 9 of the clock then it Cleared up and some sune shininge after dinner verie faire weather sune shining untill night Freessing hard towardes night with much winde at west north weste: all the night Freessinge verie hard and exstreeme which our Freshe watter lak by the Fortt was frossen over and the litell pond by the brue [=brew] house

13th. in the morninge the wind at west north west litell winde the sune shininge most parte of the daie but Freessinge verie hard all the daie untill night at night the wind somthing a freesh gall west north west // after midnight Freessing very hard untill morninge

14th. in the morninge the winde at west north west litle wind but Faire sune shininge all the daie: Freessinge // verie hard all the daie untill night: this day after dinner our boote departed for Green Baye to Coast for some deer and to bring home our Canno which was lefte at Perlican there are gone some 6 of our men this night verie litell wind butt a verie hard Froost Frossen so Farr out in the harbour as the Spettacles

15th. in the morninge the wind at north and be west litell wind but close weather Freessinge verie hard untill 10 of the clock then verie faire sune shininge all day untill night thawing verie much after dinner untill it was night and very warme and pleasante weather as thought it had bin at midsummer calme in the after noone no wind but a litell at south // this morning the governer and my selffe tok a sabell in the trape a litell from the house // towardes night setting of the sune began to Freese verie hard // and so likewise all the night it did Freese verie hard but verie litell wind

16th. in the morninge the wind at west north west somthing calme but abowte tenn of the clock the wind somthing freesh the sune shining verie faire all the daie untill night but freesing all the day untill it was night but the weather very temperat in the evenynge the wind at south south west the weather verie myld and all the night verie warme and mylde the morning towardes daye a litell cold // but nothing to any purpose

17th. in the morninge the wind at southwest wind and reasonable myld weather sune shyninge // aboute 12 of the clock the wind at North weste verie faire sune shininge untill night more temperatte I have not seen in England for this time of the year but abowte 9 of the clock at night it did begine to Snowe the wind all night at verie calme at north easte but verie milde weather and warme all night

18th. in the morninge the wind at south verie litell winde untill tenn of the Clock then the wind Fresshed up at the north east with some snowe untill it was 12 of the clock ther was in the morninge a litell Fogge in the after noone Close weather untill night against night it begane to freese The winde at north west but all night it Freessed very hard but litle winde//

19th. in the morninge the winde at south west verie litle winde but a verie cold Freesinge verie hard and Close weather untill noone then the sune showinge herselfe and the after noone somthing milder weather with litle winde at weste a bowte 4 of the Clock it began to snowe verie faste and so it Continued untill it was midnight with a freesh gall of winde and some 2 howers before daie it did begine to thaw verie Fast this eveninge master Teage killed a gray Fox which he found had killed 2 of our goates being then Feedinge one them this night the winde at southwest and south south west

20th. in the morninge the winde at South weste litle winde but close weather untill 9 of the clock: then afterward verie faire sune Shininge all the daie untill night which disolved all the snowe from the houses beinge some 2 ynches thicke which had fallen the night before mylder weather cold not be desired / towardes night the aire was a litle cold and freessinge: but all the night litle winde but verie close skie and verie mylde all night

21th. in the morninge the wind at South litle winde but verie Close weather and reasonable mild: after 12 of the clock it did begine to Snowe and so contin[u]ed untill night but litell winde but the snowe did fall verie thicke it continued Snowinge untill it was midnight some 4 ynches thick agaynst the morninge all the night the wind at southeaste the weather somthing mild

22th. in the morninge the wind at South west with some snowe but abowte 12 of the clock it snowed verie thicke for the space of too howres then the sune showing hir selfe somthing pleasaunt at tymes // and some small snowe now and then amonge // the after noone did prove to be reasonable faire // but the aire some Cold // Freesing a litle all night beinge verie faire starr light

23th. in the morning the wind at west north weste untill it was noone very fresh winde and cold untill 12 of the clock after ward the sune shining verie faire untill night abowte 8 of the Clock at night close weather but calme untill midnight then afterward the wind began to blowe very hard with Small Rayne untill it was daie//

24th. in the morninge the wind verie hard at south west with verie much Rayne and so it Continued untill night which did consume very neer all the snowe which was upon the ground verie much wind all the daie untill night // the night verie mild untill it was 2 houres before daie: then it was somthinge cold freessinge very hard

25th. in the morninge the winde at north north east freessing verie hard and exstreeme all the daie untill night but the sune Shining verie faire and clear untill night the wind still at north east verie cold at night the winde verie calme untill day but freessing hard all night

26th. in the morninge the wind at North east freesh galle of winde this morninge snowinge very thicke but verie much wind all the daie no appearinge of the sune all daie untill night at night the wind calme and very myld weather all night

27th. in the morninge the winde at North but verie litle winde untill 9 of the clocke then at south west allso litle winde all the day but verie milde weather and close all the daie untill night: at night abowte 8 of the clocke yet did begine to snowe but after midnight abowte 2 of the clocke very much winde with some haille and Snowe untill it was day

28th. in the morninge the winde at west verie freshe with some showres of snowe and haille but verie much winde the sune at tymes did showe hir selfe betwine certaine showres of snowe untill night but at night verie much winde with a greate storme which I have not sene many the like and very exstreeme cold all the night the winde beinge still at west the floud being so hie it wentt all over our stadge before the brue house

29th. in the morninge the winde at weste and be north with verie much winde and verie cold the sune showing hir selffe at tymes in the forenoone and many showres of snowe before noone and so likewise in the after noone untill it was night abowt 8 of the clocke it did continue with verie much winde untill it was tenn of the clock after ward reasonable myld weather all The night untill day the wind still at weste south weste somthing cold Freessing a litle all the night

30th. in the morninge the winde at west south weste much wind with certaine showres of snowe untill it was noone the sune showing hir selfe 2 or 3 tymes the tide was so hie this morninge it hath caried away the bridg from the staddge the tide was never seen so hie before hear somthing cold

also and freessing untill noone // in the after noone snowinge very thicke untill night and so continued untill tenn of the clocke with verie much winde at south weste a litell frooste towardes the morninge

31th. in the morninge the wind at north and north north weste freessing untill noone and some snowe: the after noone verie faire sune shininge untill it was night Froessinge a litle all the night but verie litle winde

Januarie 1th 1613. in the morninge the winde at weste clear weather but somthing cold in the morninge the sune shininge verie pleasaunt all the daie untill it was night verie mylde weather but a litle snowe in the beginninge of the night

2th. in the morninge the winde at south weste litle winde with varie faire sune shininge all the daie and so pleasaunte and warme as thought [= though] it had bin at mid sommer the aire a litle cold in the morninge abowte one of the clock after dinner master Whittington and the rest of his company cam from coasting from Green Bay of whom we made great dowt being they had bin wantting 20 daies thought they had bin starved with the cold and wannt of food they killed in ther vaige at Green Bay and other places 3 foxes 2 dozen of ducks and some dozen of partridges in Green Bay they see them by great Companies they could not bring out canno but lefte hir in the woodes betwine Green Baye and New Perlican and at Harbour de Grace they lost ther boote but gote another comynge in ther upon Christmas even // this night verie mylde but after mid night it did blowe much wind with many haille showres before day

3th. in the morninge the wind at weste much wind and so continued all the daie // but verie faire sune shininge untill it was night which did disolve the snowe verie much a litell froost was this morninge all the night verie myld and litle winde untill morninge

4th. in the morning the winde at south west litle winde all the daye very myld weather and pleasaunte the sune shininge very faire in the after noone untill night in the fore noone verie close weather: in England not mylder for the time and seasone the night allso verie milde no froost at all but a little cold//

5th. in the morninge the winde at south weste close weather and very mylde and temperate as might be desired abowte noone the sune did showe hir selfe 3 or 4 tymes but afterward close weather untill it was night // abowte 9 of the clocke in the night it began with small raine which did continue some parte of the night with the wind at southeast but verie warme all the night

6th. in the morninge the winde at south weste verie close weather with small raine in manner of a Fogge thawinge verie much all the daye: but for mylder weather can not be in England but after dinner very thick raine which did disove [= dissolve] the snowe verie much untill it was night being verie warme // at night the wind very freesh at west most part of the night in the morning somthing cold

7th. in the morninge the winde at west north west // verie Sharp cold weather fressing hard untill noone // but the sune shininge very pleasaunte all the daie untill night being very clear weather at night litle winde at weste freessing a litle but not much

8th. in the morninge the wind at west south weste close weather with some litell snowe blanckes from 7 of the clock it contived snowinge untill it was 3 in the after noone with verie much wind the sune in the after noon abowte 3 of the clock did showe hir selfe divers tymes the weather reasonable myld this morning departed 10 of our company to go by land for to find out the solvages in Solvage Bay: for to see ther manner of life in the winter with provition for 15 or 20 days this night verie myld weather and calme the wind at southweste // untill daye

9th. in the morninge the winde at east north easte not much winde but abowte 7 or 8 of the clocke it did begine to snowe verie faste and so it continued all the daie: but at the settinge of the sune yt cleared up: but this night verie clear weather with litell winde but Freessinge hard all the night

10th. in the morninge the winde at weste verie cold freessing hard untill it was noone the sune shininge verie pleasaunte in the after noone varie close snowinge verie faste untill night the weather reasonable mylde and litle winde // the night proved exceeding warme as possible might be: this evenynge thos that went towardes the Salvages returned againe by reasone they found the snowe so deep that they could not travell: and went but 2 mylls in all // from Sammon Cove

11th. in the Morninge the winde at south weste verie close weather untill noone and then the sune opened and showing hir selfe divers times in the after noone but from morninge untill night verie warme weather // thawinge very faste all the day abowte settinge of the sune it did begin to Snowe but not much all the night verie warme untill 4 of the clocke in the Morning the winde did begine to freesh at west and be north

12th. in the morninge the winde at north weste much winde and close weather untill it was 8 of the Clocke then afterward very faire sune shininge untill night abowt 2 of the clock was a little snowe did Fall // abowte 4 of the clock it did begine To Freese hard and so it continued all the night untill day the wind still at North west

13th. in the morninge the wind at north west all the day untill night with verie Faire sune shininge all the day Freessing very hard untill night the night litell wind but verie clear weather Freessinge verie hard all night

14th. in the morninge the wind at weste north weste verie cold Freessing very hard all the day untill night the sune shininge very pleasante untill night: / the night allso freessing very hard untill it was day the wind still at west north weste

15th. in the morninge the winde at weste and be north a Freshe gall of winde the sune shininge all the daie verie pleasante: reasonable myld weather at 4th of the clock close weather makinge show of some rayne so at 8 of the clocke at night it did begine to raine with much winde at weste and continued most parte of the night but verie mylde weather

16th. in the morninge the wind at weste verie faire weather all the day the sun shininge most parte of the daie and all the daie verie warme weather untill night: which gave great content unto our workemen in the woods / at night verie clear starr light Freessinge all the night the wind still at west

17th. in the morninge the winde at west: all the day the sune shininge verie faire and pleasante untill night very cold Freessinge hard all the night and exstreeme untill morninge: but verie litle winde

18th. in the morninge the wind at weste south west: litle winde freessinge till it was noone the sun shininge verie faire and pleasante till noone the wind at weste very close weather making show of some Snowe but the weather verie myld: what it was in the forenoone the wind at south west untill night the litell ponnd by the brue house was this morninge froossen over // at night abowte 8 of the clock at night it did begine to snowe and continued most part of the night was against the morninge some inche and halfe thicke the wind very hard all night at southwest

19th. in the morninge the wind at Northweste much wind and so continued all the daye untill it was night the sune shyninge verie warme and pleasaunt all the daie but somthing cold and Freessinge but in The night verie cold freessing verie hard untill daie but litle wind

20th. in the morning the wind at west and be north verie faire sune shyninge weather all the daie and warme the sune // but yt did from the sune freese verie hard untill night the skie verie clear // till it was towardes night then all overcast with cloudes in the night the wind at southwest somthing myld all the night

21th. in the morninge the wind at Southwest untill noone with some snowe which it did continue untill it was one of the clocke then it cleared up and after verie faire sune shyninge untill it was night: the wind at weste south west // but all the night Freessing exstreem hard untill morninge this night Barthellmew Presson killed a verie fair Black fox and 3 daies sethince a verie faire gray fox which wear delivered unto the governer//

22th. in the morning the wind at west north west the wind verie sharp and cold freesing verie hard and exstreeme all the daie untill night but the sune shininge verie faire and pleasant untill night // the night allso exstreeme and cold Freessing verie hard the wind still at west northwest//

January 1613

23th. in the morninge the wind at west and be north litle wind but an exstreeme sharpe cold the sune shyning verie pleasant all the daye Freessing verie hard untill night the weather being very clear // this morning delivered unto the governer the black Fox skine and the grey skine of the Fox which weare very faire and excellent good and all the night Freessing verie hard the wind still at west and be north the freesh watter lak betwine the Fort and the house all Frosen over

24th. in the morning the wind at west verie cold and close weather in the morning a little snowe in the after noone verie fair sune shining weather untill night freessing very hard untill night with some litle showers of snowe amonge untill night litle winde // at night the wind at west with some snowe the night reasonable myld//

25th. in the morning the wind at west north west a Faire gall of winde the sune shining all the daie untill night very faire this daie was our lak by the brue house all Froossen over and the harbour so farr as the Spectakells as allso all the harbour from Samon Cove unto the Spettacles was froosen // this daye we began to drink beverage in one quarter can three cans of watter & one of beere this night proved to be Reasonable myld

26th. in the morning the wind at west and be north with some litell snowe being very close weather but very cold untill noone the sune shining hir selffe at tymes // in the after noone the wind at west South very myld but close weather but abowte 3 or 4 of the clock towardes night yt did begin to snowe // for the space of some hower then after ward it did begin to rayne verie much all the night with the wind at south very warme weather all night but the rayne which consumed part of the snowe that was on the ground

27th. in the morning the wind at south verie myld weather but very close // the sune opening some certayne tymes // thawing very much all the daie allso at night the wind at south verie myld weather and warme with small Rayne all the night but abowt 4 of the clock in the morning much wind at west and be south

28th. in the morning the wind at North west much wind freessing very hard and exstreeme cold but the sune shining hir selfe often in the forenoone // and likewise in the after noone but the wind still at north west this day a great storme of wind, this day was buried one of our companie called Gorg Davies a cooper who died the last night // freesing very hard all this night untill it was daye//

29th. in the morning the wind at South west verie litell wind Freessing a litell but the sun shininge verie pleasaunte untill ten of the clock and then it began to be close weather with some showers of snowe the winde then blowing verie Freesh and so yt continued untill it was night but at tymes the sune showed hir [self] in the after noone this after noone master Teage killed a reed Fox this night litle winde but snowinge some parte of the night but reasonable warm weather

30th. in the morninge the wind verie Freesh gall at Northwest and very cold all the daie untill night but verie Faire sune shininge all daie and the sune verie warme but only the exstreemity of the wind made it verie cold that day master Thomas Willughby and my selfe was at Breegas // this night allso verie cold the Ice all gone that was in this harbour but a litell remayned in our litell ponnd by the brue house

31th. in the morninge the wind at weste but the weather verie mylde and verie faire sune shininge and warme untill it was night and yt thawed verie much all this daie with the sune // at night the wind at south west verie little wind but the night very myld weather untill morning as any man might desire

February 1613

1th. in the morninge the wind at south weste litle wind verie close weather with a litle hoare Froost in the morninge but it was soone desolved with the sune showinge hir selffe at tymes // but in the after noone betwine 2 and 3 of the clock yt did begin to snowe // very thick the wind at east or east and be south but the weather very myld and warme as any might desire this night allso did continue verie myld and warme // this night Edwarde Garton died

2th. February in the morning the wind at east litle wind but so it did untill night verie mild weather but close untill 3 or 4 of the Clock in the afternoone then the sune shining untill night no man could desire mylder weather abowt 4 or 5 of the clock this after noone was Edward Gartoun buried abowt 9 of the clock at night yt did begine to snowe continuinge all night being Fallen against the morning some 3 ynches all this night the wind at southeast but the night verie myld not aching cold

3th. in the morninge the wind at north east not much wind but close weather all the daie myld weather thawing verie much from the morninge untill night but yt continued snowing most part of the daie: but abowte 4 of the clock in the after noone then the wind at north west verie much wind and so continued all night Freessing hard but yt did cease from snowinge//

4th. Februarie 1613. in the morning the wind at north west not much wind litell cold Fressing a litell but the sune shininge very faire all the daie which did thawe verie much wher they had hir

powre // a very pleasaunte day to the contentment of all our people // which in England it could not be mylder the wind at abowte 3 of the clock in the after noone at west and so yt did continue all the night but not much wind Freessing somthing hard untill the morninge//

5th. in the morninge the wind at east litell wind untill noone the weather close Freessing a litell which our litle pond and the harbour was craymed over with Ice: in the after noone a Fressh gall of wind at east with verie faire sune shininge untill night and the sune verie warme // but from the sune yet did freese all the day the skie being verie clear: the night very cold Freessing very hard all the night the wind at north east in the morning ther was a crayme of Ice all this Bay over within the Burnte Head

6th. in the morning the wind at south west little wind: but abowte 11 of the clock a reasonable freesh gall of wind the sune shining verie warme untill yt was 3 of the clock in the after noone then yt was verie close weather making showe of Rayne or snowe // so about a 11 or 12 of the clock in the night ther did arise a great storme with the wind at south west with much snowe and rayne amonge // which continued untill morninge the night being somthing myld thought [= though] fowll weather//

7th. in the morning the wind at west south west a freesh gall of wind with small driving snowe and rayne // but yt did desolve so fast as yt did fall // and so did the snowe which did fall the last night before // verie close weather untill 12 of the clocke then yt cleared up but very Faire sune shininge untill night but a great storme of wind at west south west untill night the night the wind somthing calme: with a litle catching froost against the morning

8th. in the morning the wind at South west litle wind with some snowe for the space of halfe an howre but a verie close morninge untill it was noone the weather verie myld: 4 dayes sethince Fredrick the Duchman killed at Samman Cove a musk ratt and one outter the after noone allso very close but yt did thaw very much abowt 3 of the clock it did begin to rayne: and abowt 7 of the clock at night yt did rayne very Fast but the weather very myld and warme the wind at south

9th. in the morning the wind at west south west rayning small rayne very thick untill ten of the clock then the wind at west with some small snowe abowt a ii of the clock the sune began to appear shyning at tymes in the after noone the wind blowing cold the sky verie clear freesing hard the wind blowing hard which did drive all the Ice out of the harbour the night very cold Freessing verie hard all the night

10th. in the morning the wind at west not much wind the sune shininge all the daie verie pleasaunte and warme // thought [= though] a litell cold but all our men did work in the woodes with great Content but in the after noone abowt 4 of the clock the skie verie cleare begyninge agayne to Freesse very hard // after dynner died one of our Companie called Edward Hartland a tailler and prentice for the companie // this morning the litle pound betwine the house and the Brue house and allso the harbour was all taken over with a crayme of Ice this night the wind at west north west litle wind but Freessing hard all the night

11th. in the morning the wind at west south west abowte 9 of the clock the wind was somthing hard Freessing verie hard untill noone but the sune shininge verie pleasaunte at certayne tymes // Falling some snowe now and then all the harbour Froossen over with a crayme of Ice // in the after noone abowte 4 of the clock verie close weather and like of snow // the wind at southwest something cold: at 4 of the clock Edward Hartland was buried at 9 of the clock at night it did begine to snowe verie thick and so it continued untill mydnight blowing a great storme of wind at southwest after midnight began to Raine verie Fast and so continued untill day the night very warme

12th. in the morning the wind at south west much wind and close weather Snowing verie thick which continued untill noone thawing very Fast the weather warm which consumed all the snowe allmost in the after noone yt snowed allso untill 3 of the clock then yt did clear up beginning to Freese verie hard this morning all the Ice in this harbour was consumed away // this 2 dayes hath fallen a great Quantetie of snowe not all this wintter the lik this night the wind at west north west verie verie hard all the night

13th. in the morning the wind at west north west somthing cold and Freessing somthing hard all the daie / the harbour all over Froossen with a crayme of Ice the sune shininge verie pleasaunt and warme untill 12 of the clocke after wardes for the space of an hower verie Close weather and

after ward verie close weather untill night but Freesing hard from the sune the night very myld with the wind at south west

14th. in the morning the wind at south west snowing verie thick but litle wind close weather continuing snowing untill noone then yt began to rayne verie fast which consumed all the snowe allmost and the Ice // in the harbour Rayninge still very fast untill night this night verie myld the wind at south west thawing very Fast all the night

15th. in the morning litell wind at southwest verie myld weather the sun shining unt[ill] ii of the clocke then the weather somthing close thawing very fast consuming the greater parte of the snowe on the ground at this Instant wear some 20 or 22 of our people sick in this countrie disease the scurvy // at 3 of the clock it did begine to rayne and so continued untill night but after 8 of the clock at night began to rayne verie fast untill it was midnight and at 4 of the clock in the morning began to snowe very thick till it was day against the morning abowte one ynch thick one the ground this night our goat house did fell downe and killid 2 goates//

16th. in the morninge the wind at south west litle wind untill 9 of the clocke then a reasonable gall of wind more fressher the sune shininge verie warme untill noone // which desolved the snowe and ice verie much very moderate weather as hart cold wishe which putteth every one in hope that winter is now paste for this year this night verie myld untill it was midnight then the wind round at east northeast verie cold and freessing hard untill it was daie

17th. in the morninge the wind at east and continued all the daie verie close weather untill night snowing a litle this morninge untill 8 of the clocke Freessing a litle all the daie untill night the wind somthing cold the sune abowt 3 or 4 of the clock in the after noone began to shine verie pleasaunt untill night this night somthing cold Freessing all The night but not verie exstreeme//

18th. in the morning the wind at south west somthing sharp and cold untill it was noone but the sune shininge verie pleasaunte and warme that in the after noone the sune thawed verie much in the open places // the wind blowing somthing hard: this after noone some of our people with a boott went for Harbour de Grace to seke for scurthe grasse for our companie which are sicke this night the wind at south west very myld weather

19th. in the morning the wind at southwest litle wind the sune showing hir selfe at tymes untill noone in the morning a litle hoare frooste upon the ground // in the after noone the sune showinge hir selfe at certayne times the skie somthing overcast with cloudes and lik of Raine yt thawed this after noone verie much at 3 of the clock yt did begine to raine verie fast untill night the wind at south the weather verie warme // which disolved the snowe and ice in great abundaunce // all the night yt did raine with a great storme of wind untill daie

20th. in the morninge the wind at west Blowing verie hard all the daie untill night somthing cold freessing verie litle the sune showing hir selfe at times both in the fore noone and after noone but most parte of the daie close weather this morning died one of our men called Jnᵒ [John] Toncks a mazone a hired man for wagges in the after noone buried abowt 4 of the clock at 7 of the clock at night yt did begine to snowe // but scarse covered the ground // all this night yt hath Freesin[g] verie hard the wind at north west which hath made a crayme of ice in the litle pound and the harbour over by the gallowes//

21th. in the morning the wind at North west verie cold freessing verie hard but the sune shininge verie pleasaunt all the daie untill night and warme thawing wher the sune had some power after it was night yet did begin to be myld the wind at west south west abowt 4 of the clock in the night yt did begine to snowe // verie thick and so continued untill 7 or 8 of the clock in the morning which was abowe one ynch thick

22th. in the morning the wind at west south west much wind and so continued all daie // thawing verie litle // untill noone / then after noone the sun shininge some time verie pleasaunte this day came 4 or 5 of our men at Sammon Cove which had bin sick ther came unto our surgent hear this night yet did freesse somthing but not much

23th. in the morninge the wind at North west litell wind untill 8 of the clock then somthing freeshe the sune shininge very pleasaunt and warme all the daie untill night thawing very much wher the sune had power but from the sune yt did freese all the night yt did freese but not much

24th. in the morninge the wind at south west Blowinge verie hard with some haill showers untill yt was 8 of the clocke then yt did begine to

raine verie fast untill yt was noone in the after noone a great storme of wind at south not the like this year with very much Raine // which continued untill night // the wind so fyrce that yt did blowe of the one quarter part of the bordes from our upper house this Raine hath consumed very much the snowe and ice in most places // the Rayne ceassed abowt 5 of the clock at night and so yt cleared up this night was a litle frose but to no purpose

25th. in the morning the wind at east abowte 6 of the clock yt did begine to snowe and raine // and some times haille but abowt 9 of the clock yt did begine to snowe verie thick and so continued untill night which did fall at lest 2 ynches and halfe thick of snowe upon the ground close weather all the daie // in the after noone some showers of raine with the wind at east south east untill night all the night the wind at west north west verie cold and freesing verie hard // untill it was daye

26th. in the morning the wind at north west verie cold and freessing very hard untill noone // but the sune shininge verie pleasaunte & warme thawing wher the sune had power from the sune freesed hard the after noone somthing close weather and so continued all the night after myd-night began to Raine verie fast untill the morning the wind all night at south and the weather very warme

27th. in the morninge the wind at south west and so continued untill night in the morning small raine untill 9 of the clocke the weather very myld and warme // towardes noone the sune shininge very pleasaunte untill night which disolved the most parte of all the snowe which was upon the open ground yt was verie warme all the day yesterday Frederick the Duchman toke a Fox in the trapp at Sammon Cove the night allso very warme and myld thawing very very much all night which consumed very neer all the ice / this night died one of our company called Willes who hath bin sicke sethince Christmas

28th. in the morning the wind at and last of February [sic] the wind at south south west verie myld and warme weather as hart could wish the sune rissing in the morning very pleasaunte and so yt continued untill night this day making showe of noe more wintter being so pleasaunt and warme // the birds Singing very pleasaunt in the woodes this after noone Willes was Buried all this day the wind somthing hard this night abowte tenn of the clocke it began to raine very Fast and yt continued untill 4 or 5 of the clocke in the morninge // and then ceassed and afterwardes yt did begin to Freesse very hard//

1th March 1613. in the morning the wind at west freessing verie hard untill noone the sune shininge very pleasaunt and warme thawing verie much in the sune which hath consumed all the snowe uppon the open ground and most part in the woodes. this day our governer went oft Avon Hill to seeke for Reed beeres for our sick men but could find noone this night the wind at west south west and yt freessed after midnight a litle froste against the morning but not much

2th. in the morninge the wind at south west the sune showing hir selff at the rissing but afterward cloudy and over cast untill noone freesing a litle but in the after noone allso verie close weather and abowt 3 of the clock yt did begin to snowe but yt was but litle this morning died one of our companie called Tobias an Irishe man who was an apprentice and was buried this after noone this after noone our boote came home which hath bin at Harbour de Grace for scurvy grase but found noone which hath bin wanntting this 12 daies this night hath bin mild Falling a litle snowe which covered all the ground over whittel litle wind all night at southeast they brought from Harbour de Grace 4 geese with them//

3th. in the morning the wind at east litell wind all the daie untill night the sune showing at some times in the forenoone but the weather verie myld and warme // which did disolve all the snowe which did fall the last night: all the daie verie warme untill night this night after midnight yt did begin to freese a litell continued untill daie but not much

4th. in the morning the wind at east litle wind close weather all the day abowte 8 of the clock yt did begin to snowe and continued untill noone but in the after noone it did snowe verie faste and so yt continued untill night // no showe of the sune all this day this night allso the wind at east snowing verie thick all the night

5th. in the morning the wind at east north east with a verie great storme the lik not seen in a long tyme snowing very fast untill 4 of the clock in the after noone // this night allso a great storme of wind which continued all the night

6th. in the morning the wind at east all day untill night very much wind abowt a ii of the clock it did begin to snowe verie fast and so yt continued

untill night this morning died one of our company called Mathew Greeges a torner and was buried in the after noone // a hired man for wagges // this night snowing and haill showers all the night and freessing allso // very fowell weather

7th. in the morning the wind at east very much wind with very much Rayne and snowe and some times haill showers very fowell weather untill night snowing continually this day Fredrick killed a sabell at Sammon Cove this night proved somthing myld thawing very much all the night verie litle wind

8th. in the morning the wind at east north east litle wind but a Fogge all the Fore noone // thawing verie much: but after dinner the sune opened and shyned very warme for some 4 howers and then close weather untill night the wind all night at east thawing very much

9th. in the morning the wind at east full of Fogg close weather all day Thawing verie much after dinner the wind at east north east untill night // at night the wind at east south east the night very warme & myld rayning most part of the night which did disolve the snowe verie much

10th. in the morning litle wind at east south east thawing very much: most part of the day close weather but very warme the sune showing hir selffe at times at 2 of the clock in the after noone the wind at south and south and be west at 4 of the clock yt began small Rayne and so yt continued all that night which it did consume the snowe verie much

11th. in the morning the wind at east north east a freash gall of wind all the day untill night but this morning small snowe falling thick very close weather all the daie the weather somthing cold all the daie but the snowe in the open ground consumed much: this morning died William Wattes one of our Cheeffes carpenters // a hirrid man for wagges and buried abowte 4 of the clock in the after noone: this night verie much wind at east northeaste snowing a litle in the beginninge of the night and a litle frooste ther was this night

12th. in the morninge the wind at east much wind untill night this morning was a litle snowe all this day very cold untill night very close weather all the daie abowte 4 of the clock in the after noone some small raine the night the wind somthing hard with some litle snow which did fall which did not scarse cover the ground with some froost allso against the morning

13th. in the morning the wind at northeast much wind verie thick weather all the day untill night and small rayne this morning was a litle froost ther came in this morning into this harbour a verie hudg great Iland of ice this daie proved verie cold untill it was night with much wind and abowte 4 of the clock yt did blowe a verie great storme at east snowing verie thick untill night and continued so all the night snowing Continually and Freessing

14th. in the morning the wind at north east with small snowe untill noone after 12 of the clock the wind chaunged at west and west north west snowing verie thick with much wind untill night the weather verie close all the daie: this night litle wind Freessing somthing

15th. in the morning the wind at north west not much wind but somthing cold untill noone in the after noone the sun shininge somthinge pleasaunt thawing a litle wher the sune had power towardes night the wind at west litle wind but this night a hard froost which made a crayme of ice all over our litle ponnd by the brue house

16th. in the morning the wind at west litle wind somthing cold but the sune shining verie pleasaunt the after noone somthing warme which did desolve the snowe very much and a very pleasaunt daye this after noone William Glissen did tak some 4 or 5 troutes in our brook hard by the house // this night yt did freese somthing hard the wind at west southwest litle wind all the night

17th. in the morning the wind at west south west litle wind and abowt 9 of the clock the wind at west north west much wind the sune from the Rissing untill noone shyning verie pleasaunt and warme all the daye which did disolve the snowe verie much and verie comfortable unto all our sick people // at one of the clock after noone the wind at east north east litle wind and so continued untill night this day our people took more troutes: this night the wind came at west freessing very hard all the night

18th. in the morning the wind at west north west all the day untill night much wind the sune shyning from morning untill night but in the after noone very warme / desolving the snowe very much very pleasaunt and comfortable weather the turnnopes which have bin under the snowe all the winter hath done them great good for the scurvie this night the wind at west with some froost against the morning

19th. in the morning the wind at west south west a fressh gall of wind all the daie untill night but the weather very myld the sune shyning very warme and pleasaunt all the daie untill night in the after noone extreeme warme as thought [= though] yt had bin at myd sommer which did disolve the snowe very much which left litle or noone upon the open ground this night the wind at west Freessing very hard with the litle ponnd by the brue house all craymed over and the harbour also with ice this night master Fredrick tok a Fox in the trapp

20th. in the morning the wind the wind [sic] at east litle wind: the sune shininge very pleassunt all the forenoone and warme // in the after noone exstreeme warme // which yt did revy[ve] all our sick people very much desolving the snowe verie much the sune being of such force this night came master Teag and master Willughby from Breegas watching ther all the night which had there killed a Fox and 3 partridges this night very cold freesing very hard after mydnight the wind at east south east

21th. in the morning the wind at east litle wind but at 8 of the clock the wind at south west and so yt continued untill night the sune shyning very warme all the fore noone // but the after noone somthing close weather but the weather very myld which did disolve the snowe very much the night a litle froost but to no porpose//

22th. in the morning the wind at south south east begyning to snowe very Thick for the space of 2 howers and afterwards yt did begine to Raine very fast untill yt was noone // which consumed all the snowe which did fall this morning // abowt 4 of the clock in the after noone the wind blowing hard at south untill night and at 5 of the clock began to snowe which yt did not continue long this night the wind at west freessing very hard all the night and snowing somthing thick against the morning

23th. in the morning the wind at west north west much wind and very sharp and cold all the day Freessing hard all this morning: the sune shyning very pleasaunt most part of the day. but thawing very litle abowt 4 of the clock yt did begin to snowe the wind blowing very hard untill night and some like of snowe but abowt 2 of the clock in the after noone yt did snowe very thick untill morninge the night myld and not cold

24th. in the morning the wind at west south west snowing all this morning vary thick was at lest 3 ynches thick after 12 of the clock yt did clear up and the sun shined very pleasaunt which consumed the snowe very much after noone the wind at west much wind and so continued untill night this night yt freesed very hard all night against the morning but all night litle wind

25th. in the morning the wind at west northwest some fresh gall the sune showing hir selfe at times in the after noone yt thawed very much but yt snowed allso at times the aire somthing cold all the day untill night: this night yt freessed very hard and many haill showers this night did fall//

26th. in the morning the wind at west somthing cold a crayme of ice all over The litle ponnd by the brue house: the sune shyning from the morning untill night very pleasaunt and warme which did consume the froost very much in the after noone thawed very much but toward night somthing cold this night allso a Froost: this morning I went at Burnt Head//

27th. in the morning the wind at south west and sune showing hir selfe abowt 7 of the clocke but abowt 9 of the clock yt did begine to snowe very thick untill 12 of the clock but yt did consume awaye so fast as yt did fall thawing very much all the day. in the after noone the sune showed hir selfe at times but something cold: this night was Guy wiffe [Guy's wife] brought a bede with a young sonne // some halfe hower in travell // this night a litle froost but to no porpose//

28th. in the morning the wind at east litell wind untill ytt was 9 of the clocke the sune rissinge very Faire and shyning very pleasaunt and warme all the day the wind after 12 of the clock came at southwest and continued untill night mylder weather ther could not be if ytt had bin at mydsommer desolving the snowe very much this morning Fredrick killed a sable at Samon Cove in the trap this night allso very faire and myld the wind at southwest

29th. in the morning the wind at south west with Fogg but very myld weather but the weather very close untill noone then the sune shyned very pleasaunt and warme // untill night this morning master Bowlling arived hear in the Hoope which came from London departing from thence 24th November last 1612 allso this day our fresh watter lake by the Forte did breake up

30th. in the morning the wind at Southwest litell wind the weather very myld the sune shininge very warme all the daie as thought ytt had bin at mydsommer the night allso very warme & faire weather

31th. in the morning the wind at east untill 9 of the clock then yet [it?] chaunged at south west litle wind untill night from morning untill night very close weather but after 12 of the clock yet did begine to raigne // untill yet was night the night the wind at south west very myld weather [A space was left for April 1, but no entry was made.]

April 1613

2th. in morning the wind at east very much Fogg and small Rayne untill it was noone in the after noone much rayne untill yet was night all the night allso very much Rayne untill yet was day, the wind at east north east

3th. in the morning the wind at north east very thick Fogg and much Rayne and very much wind continuing untill noone in the after noone small Rayne untill night and very thick weather somthing cold all the day at night the wind at east north east snowing very much with a great storme of wind and Fowle weather

4th. Aprill. the wind at east a great storme snowing verie thick all the daye untill night verie cold freessing hard all day untill night at night verie much wind snowing thick and some tyme snowe and some showers of haill all the night

5th. in the morning the wind at south east with a greate storme snowing all the daie small snowe and some thing cold: freessing in the morning and continued untill night allso the night very much wind all night the wind at east with small snowe freessing hard all night

6th. in the morning the wind at east with a very great storme of wind snowing verie thick which continued untill noone // then ytt ceassed the wind all the day very cold and freezing something this night the wind at east north east freessing after mydnight a litle

7th. in th'morning the wind at northeast much wind and verie close weather but yt thawing very fast which disolved most part of the snowe which did fall the daie before in the after noone the sune showing hir selfe at times this somthing cold the wind at east north east ther arived shipp at Pherrilland [Ferryland] and St Joanes the 23th March 1613

8th. in the morning the wind at noreast litle wind with some Fogg in the morninge but after 12 of the clock some tyme showers of small snowe but at 5 of the clock at night began to snowe and so yt did continve all the night but very litle wind

9th. in the morning the wind at north west litle

wind snowing thick untill yt was noone the weather reasonable myld the snowe hath Fallen verie thick any time this 3 dayes // yt hath bin such fowle weather that hear hath bin 3 or 4 boottes From Harbro de Grace which could not gett away Bound for St. Joanes // this after noone yt snowed very thick untill night the night very myld the wind at west

10th. in the morning the wind at west litle wind the sune rissing verie pleasaunt and faire the day verie warme and pleasaunt thawing the snowe verie fast this day abowte 12 of the clock our governer master Guy departed for England in the Hoop Master Bowling master undergod Bound for Bristoll this night proved verie myld weather some small raine

11th. in the morning the wind at west not much wind the sune shining very warme untill noone after noone somthing close weather for an howre but after the sun shininge very pleasaunt desolving the snowe very much this night a litle froost but not much

12th. in the morning the wind at south untill after 12 of the clock the sune shyning verie warme which disolved the snowe verie much after noone much wind at west and close weather untill night lik of raine this night verie myld and warme abowt 4 of the clock after mydnight rayned verie Fast untill the morning//

13th. in the morninge the wind at south west with verie much raine all the day which consumed the snowe very much the sune showing hir selff at times but the weather very warme all the daye this night allso very warme with some showers of rayne

14th. in the morning the wind at southwest the sune rissing and shining very pleasaunt untill 12 of the clock at 9 of the clock the wind came at northeast and continued untill 2 of the clock in the after noone after ward at southwest with some store of rayne untill night most part of all the snowe consumed upon the ground the weather very thick with much wind at west

15th Aprill 1613. in the morning the wind at west north west much wind and very cold in the morning a litle snowe in the after noone thawing very fast which consumed most part of the snowe which did fall the last night the sune shyning at times this night yt Freessed very hard the night verie cold

16th. in the morning the wind at east and east south east untill night the sune shining very pleasaunt and warme all the day this morning the litle ponnd betwine the house and the brue house all craymed over Ice and all the harbour over hear wher the shipps anker about 4 of the clock the wind came at west this night some froost

17th. in the morning the wind at south the sune shyning very warme all the daie which disolved the froost last night this day our people sowed divers sortes of seedes in our gardins this night very myld the wind at south west with sondrie showers of Rayne//

18th. in the morning the wind at southwest verie close weather all the daie the sune showing hir self not all the daie but the weather very myld lik of rayne // the night allso very warme with many showers of small rayne // the wind at south all the night

19th. in the morning the wind at south west untill 9 of the clock litle wind after 9 of the clock at east south east all the daie untill night the sune shyning all the daie verie warme // the night allso very myld with small raine all the night

20th. in the morning the wind at south litle wind rayning untill 12 of the clock but verie warme weather this morning our bark departed for Harbour de Grace to fatch our cables and ankers from the French shipp that was taken by captaine Eastone // after noone continued Rayning untill night the night very myld Rayning all night

21th. in the morning the wind at east full of fogg and rayne untill 12 of the clocke in the after noone at south east with much Rayne untill 4 of the clock then clear weather the sune shyning the day somthing cold all the day but the night very myld and warme

22th. in the morning the wind at west faire sune shining and very warme all the daie // the after noone the wind very calme // untill night the night allso very myld and warme // this evenyng master Whittington from Harbour de Grace with the Biskiners in their shallopp

23th. in the morning the wind at east and so continued untill night but a verie thick Fogg untill 8 of the clock the weather very warme the sune shining at times this after noone a very thick fogg the night very myld and warme the wind still at east

24th. in the morning the wind at east all the daie untill night the wind something cold but the sune shyning verie warme: in the after noon about 3 of the clock a verie thick Fogg which did continue untill night this night the wind still at east full of fogg and somthing cold

25th. in the morning the wind at east verie full of fogg all the day untill night // the wind and fogg somthing cold in the night some small rayne being somthing cold

26th. in the morning the wind at east north east full of rayne and some snowe // verie close weather untill noone // and cold the after noone very faire sune shyning and warme // untill night somthing cold

27th. in the morning the wind at east north east all the daye clear weather untill noone // the sune shining at times in the after noone very close weather with a thick Fogg untill night being somthing cold the night allso proved verie cold

28th. in the morninge the wind at east north east close weather all the day and something clowd all the day untill night the night somthing cold with Rayne some part of the night

29th. in the morning the wind at east north east clear weather untill noone in the after noone full of small rayne the weather somthing thick and cold all this night very much rayne // and snowe with much wind continued untill yt was daye

30th. in the morning the wind at east north east very thick weather snowing so Fast as any time this year untill noone the wind somthing cold but the snowe consumed so fast as yt did fall // forthwith the night the wind at northeast very cold

1th Maye 1613. in the morning the wind at north-east much wind untill untill [sic] yt was noone the sune shyning at times // but in the after noone very faire sune shyning: but the wind somthing cold: at 2 of the clock our bark came from Harbour de Grace: but lost the shipp boott of the French-man by the way which sunck // this night very clear but yt freesed very hard // that the litle ponnd all craymed over with ice against the morn-ing//

2th maye. in the morninge the wind at south west the sune rissinge very faire and shined verie warme all the daie which had soone disolved the froost the night allso very myld and very calme all the night

3th. in the morninge the winde at southwest much untill it was noone // the sune rissinge verie faire and shined very warme all the day which had

disolved soone a litle hoare froost which was this morninge the night allso verie warme and myld

4th. in the morninge the wind at south west not much wind with some Small raine untill yt was noone: after noone very much rayne and thundar and lightninge for the space of an howre but continuing rayning untill yt was night with very close weather all the daie this night proved very myld

5th. in the morninge the wind at west south west somthing cold but verie faire sune shininge all the day a litle froost this morninge the night proved very myld

6th. in the morning the wind at south litle wind the sune shininge all the daie very pleasauntt this morninge came from Harbour de [Grace?] 2 Bes-kinners with one master Lukhame master of the Great Portion of Plymouth who would have put the French men out of ther places but we went by the Frenchmens requeste at Harbour de Grace and sett all matters in good order this after noone the wind at northwest with some showers of Rayne this night somthing cold with a litle froost

7th. in the morning the wind at west litle wind: the sune rissing very faire and shininge very warme all the day this night a litle cold the wind at east

8th. in the morninge the wind at south east close weather with some small raine in the after-noone the wind at west untill night the sune shining very warme all the after noone but all the night the wind at north very fair weather

9th May 1613. in the morninge the wind at west and so continued untill night very faire weather the sune shininge verie faire all the day this day came one Master Rice of Bristoll who fisheth at Bellill he brought us a hogghed of beer which he bestowed one us // this night very myld and litle wind at southwest

10th. in the morninge the wind at southeast close weather and litle wind but abowte 9 of the clocke yt did begine to snowe very thicke untill yt was 4 of the clock in the after noone // but con-tinued Rayninge untill night yt covered the ground some ynch and more thicke but all con-sumed this night against the morninge all the night the wind at east without raine or snowe

11th. in the morninge the wind at east much wind all the day and somthing cold and very close weather all the day the night very much wind at east north east all the night

12th. in the morninge the wind at north east much wind all the day and close weather untill night but abowt 6 of the clock before night yt did begine to snowe which continued not long the night very myld

13th. in the morninge the wind at north east litle wind which continued untill noone // in the after noone the wind at [ends in mid-entry]

XVIII

The Northwest Passage

THE NORTHWEST PASSAGE QUESTION IN THE LATE SIXTEENTH CENTURY

THROUGHOUT THE GREATER PART of the sixteenth century and into the following century, the lure of the supposed northerly passages to Asia provided one of the more significant topics for discussion in Europe, especially in England. They sprang from the northwest concepts of Sebastian Cabot and the Portuguese early in the century and from the polar theories of Robert Thorne. They led to practical experiments in the 1550s, which produced not a passage to Cathay but a trading route to north Russia. In the second half of the century discussion continued. In the 1560s Humphrey Gilbert and Anthony Jenkinson argued the relative theoretical merits of Northwest and Northeast Passages, and this argument led to the eventual publication in 1576 of Sir Humphrey Gilbert's tract on the topic. Throughout, the emphasis at discussion level was on geographical theories of landmasses and ocean currents and is of considerable importance in geographical thought.

At a more material level the main incentive was to reach Asia and tap the very rich Asiatic trade without sailing through the zones to the East and the West monopolized by Portugal and Spain. A great additional advantage was a much shorter route to China and the Spice Islands, which ought to have been available if a passage existed. This was held to counterbalance the known dangers from cold and ice that would, almost inevitably, be encountered. But a third incentive also existed; this was exploration for exploration's sake. It is impossible not to feel that some of the men who went to search for a Northwest Passage, and so contributed substantially to the discovery of the northern parts of North America, were not themselves attracted, even fascinated, as later generations of Arctic explorers were to be, by the sheer excitement of discovery among harsh, unfamiliar, but challenging lands and seas. John Davis is the great explorer here in the earliest phase, and he is recognized as such in the extensive literature of the Arctic North. His discoveries did little to reveal a passage, but they did a great deal to bring home the nature of the waters making up the strait that bears his name and the lands, Greenland, Baffin Island, and Labrador, that bounded it.

The Portuguese were more active in the northwest than there is clear evidence to support. It seems difficult to differentiate the continuing activities of the Barcelos family (which was at least partly concerned with colonization) from those of the Corte Real family, which were concentrated to some extent on the discovery of a passage through the St. Lawrence (perhaps) and certainly by way of Labrador. Both families are likely to have exercised some significant position in the fishing industry also. It seems best here to keep them together, if only to make it clear that the English were not the only Europeans concerned, in the middle and later sixteenth century, with the problem of getting around or through North America to Asia.

A phase of discussion starts in England about 1565 and merges into the period of practical experiment that began in 1576. It may be said to have reached some sort of terminus about 1590, since little of theoretical importance emerged after that date. The return of Drake in 1580 showed that the longer passages through the Iberian zones were practicable. Only the war with Spain prevented major English attempts to exploit them, and it was as part of their own war effort against Spain that the United Provinces threw so much of their strength into breaching the monopolies in the 1590s. But the Northwest Passage idea retained its hold and was regarded as a valuable secondary outlet for enterprise and capital.

From 1576 to 1578 it seemed as if northeastern North America could become a major area of English involvement. Michael Lok organized London merchants and a few courtiers to back the first experimental voyage in 1576 under Martin Frobisher, purely to discover a sea route to the Far East. The expedition had some qualified success. Baffin Island was discovered; a deep inlet (Frobisher Bay) was found, the terminus of which could not be reached because it was still icebound, but it was optimistically believed to be a strait leading to Asia. The omens were good enough to lead to further investment in another expedition in 1577. This was not merely an exploration voyage, but also a commercial one. Some mineral samples brought from Baffin Island (or more precisely from islands near the mouth of Frobisher Bay) were found by self-interested, credulous, or criminal "mineral men" to contain significant amounts of gold. So the second voyage turned into what was primarily a mining speculation. Frobisher did little further discovery (not even to determine finally whether Frobisher Bay was genuinely a passage or only an inlet). All his energies were needed to extract significant quantities of mineral matter to bring to England. The return of his fleet led to interesting publications, notably by Dionyse Settle, on the newly discovered terrain and its inhabitants, but practical attention was concentrated on the minerals. Elaborate arrangements for testing were put into effect, and the "experts" (or most of them since there were a few skeptics) continued to produce optimistic results. A sort of gold fever now overcame merchants, courtiers, government officials, and even the queen. Before any definitive results from the smelting of the minerals were available, eleven ships were equipped in 1578 to bring back a substantial quantity of mineral matter, and also to leave a permanent mining camp on Baffin Island (given the noncommittal name, Meta Incognita), so as to lay foundations for a permanent exploitation of the supposed riches of the area. Frobisher's men duly dug out, under harsh conditions, several thousand tons of rock and loaded it for return (most of it duly arrived). Fortunately perhaps, much of the equipment to establish the mining colony was lost in a shipwreck, so no English community was left behind to endure an Arctic winter. As an offshoot of the venture a genuine discovery was made. Frobisher's own ship was carried off course and into what he could only call "the Mistaken Straits," which was almost certainly Hudson Strait and so a genuine channel going farther to the West.

Before the ships returned, exhaustive tests at Bristol and Deptford had established that, whatever minerals might be contained in the rocks brought from Baffin Island, neither gold nor silver was among them, nor indeed anything else of value that could be extracted. When Frobisher returned, his lading had proved to be useless, the Company of Cathay, optimistically chartered in 1577, was discredited and bankrupt, and the boom exploded. The residue of the experiment was a mass of business records, invaluable of their kind, but not very digestible for a collection such as this. Many documents reflected the personal rivalries and jealousies that emerged during the ventures, and a kernel of knowledge was to provide not only a public for the narratives of the expeditions, but also narratives and maps of an informative nature that could help future explorers. The Frobisher voyages were the first extensive English investment in North America, and many investors who had their fingers burned there would never touch any future project connected with North America. The interest of the published narratives kept the idea of a Northwest Passage alive. The enthusiasms of a smaller group of merchants and explorers, in spite of the general attitude of skepticism about further northwest ventures, enabled exploration to keep going and to continue to build slowly a picture of northeastern North America in its higher latitudes.

The Davis voyages that followed, from 1585 to 1587, were small-scale exploring expeditions. They were mainly the private venture of the London merchant, William Sanderson, with a small group of his London friends, and of Exeter merchants who gave some support, although in the end very grudgingly, largely because John Davis, a Devon man, remained the prime mover in the conduct of the expeditions. Davis, in the course of three comparatively inexpensive ventures, charted and defined the west coast of Greenland, reaching well up into the seventies of north latitude, where the open-sea North Water enabled hope of an eventual route over the Pole still to be entertained. He followed the long eastern coast of Baffin Island and he made a significant contribution to linking Labrador with the other northern coastlines. He also identified the Middle Pack, a vast ice island between Greenland and Baffin Island. Unfortunately, the charts which he brought back no longer exist—and he was an outstanding chartmaker—but the narratives of his three voyages, laconic, clear, precise, occasionally illuminating, leave us with a scientifically drawn picture of the first of the great water and land groupings in the high northeast of North America. What Davis did not do, almost inexplicably, was to locate, identify, and penetrate Frobisher's "Mistaken Straits" and so discover Hudson Strait and Hudson Bay more than twenty years before Hudson. In this sense he did little to help forward the search for the Northwest Passage. He did bring back reports not only of Eskimo, but also of whale and cod, of furbearing seal and of walrus. However, these were not to be exploited extensively until a later generation.

The Spanish War had allowed Davis just enough time to complete three voyages. It did not permit others to be made for the remainder of the century. The new phase of activity from 1602 to 1613 was, however, to be based on the experiences of 1576 to 1587, especially since Richard Hakluyt had made them accessible to the reading public, first in 1589 and again in 1600. The Northwest Passage voyages must be regarded, however, as of considerable significance in the first stages of defining long stretches of North America's coasts and islands, and establishing especially the character of its northern seas.

The literature of the Frobisher voyages is substantial. Dionyse Settle, *A true report of Capteine Frobisher his last voyage into the West and Northwest regions this present yere 1577* (London, 1577) (659), led to translations into French, German, and Italian over the next three years. Thomas Ellis, *A true report of the third voyage* (London, 1578) (662), had only a single separate edition. The narrative by George Best, *A true discourse of the late voyages of discoverie for the finding of a passage to Cathaya* (London, 1578), is the fullest account of all three voyages (too long to print in this collection). Richard Hakluyt in *Principall navigations* (1589) gave from manuscript Christopher Hall on the first voyage (658), reprinted Settle and Ellis, and supplemented Ellis with a note by Thomas Wiars. In *Principal navigations* (1598–1600) he included Best (with some omissions). The Hakluyt Society republished the Hakluyt versions of the texts in 1867, *The Three Voyages of Martin Frobisher*, ed. Richard Collinson, adding materials from the Public Record Office on finance, as well as a third voyage narrative by Edward Sellman. V. Stefansson and E. MacCaskill, *The Three Voyages of Martin Frobisher*, 2 vols. (London, 1938), reprinted Settle, Ellis, Best, Wiars and Sellman, together with a reprint of Collinson's P.R.O. material, ignored other similar unpublished material in the same repository, but drew attention to a manuscript on the third voyage (discovered by G. B. Parks) in the Huntington Library.

For John Davis, the three voyage narratives published by Hakluyt in 1589 and in 1600 can only be supplemented from Davis's summary in *The worlds hydrographicall discription* (London, 1595), which Hakluyt added in 1600. *The Voyages and Works of John Davis*, ed. A. H. Markham (London, Hakluyt Society, 1880), also includes Davis's navigational works.

Chapter Seventy-eight
The Portuguese in Northeastern
North America, 1562–1574

THERE IS very little concrete evidence of Portuguese activity in northeastern North America between the early 1520s and the 1560s. During the 1560s and early 1570s both the Barcelos and Corte Real families were active in this area—the former, it would appear, in the vicinity of Cape Breton (including Sable Island), the latter farther north, on the Labrador coast and in the Strait of Belle Isle. Whether the rumored Portuguese colonies of 1566–1567, directed to the Strait of Belle Isle or farther north, had any concrete existence or not cannot so far be ascertained. The principal body of evidence relates to the activities of the Barcelos family in Sable Island and elsewhere (presumably in the later Maritimes) (643–646). There is also some specific information about the Corte Real ventures (648, 650–651) and vague allegations of Portuguese activity in the northeast from French and Spanish sources, respectively (641, 649). In our present state of knowledge, this could apply either to Barcelos or Corte Real initiatives, although perhaps more probably to the latter.

BARCELOS FAMILY INITIATIVES IN SABLE ISLAND AND ELSEWHERE, 1562–1568

IN THE PRAIA da Vitoria papers in the Arquivo Publico de Angra, Terceira, Azores, are a petition and depositions on behalf of Manoel de Barcelos relating to expeditions sent to the Island of Barcellona de Sam Bardão, which has been identified with Sable Island (although there seems a possibility that there may have been Barcelos expeditions to Cape Breton Island as well). They were found by Manuel C. Baptista de Lima and published by him in "A ilha Terceira e a colonização do Nordeste do Continente Americano no século XVI," *Boletim do Instituto Histórico da Ilha Terceira*, XVIII (1963), 5–37, app. i–xiii. His paper, "Uma tentativa açoriana de colonização da ilha denominada 'Barcellona' no século XVI," Congresso Internacional de História des Descobrimentos, *Actas* (6 vols., Lisbon, 1960–1961), V, part I, 161–177, is also valuable. The materials have been summarized and partly translated into English by L. A. Vigneras, "The voyages of Diego and Manoel de Barcelos to Canada in the sixteenth century," *Terrae Incognitae*, V (1973), 61–64, from which they have been extracted.

They report that Manoel and his first cousin Marcos made several voyages to Terra Nova after the death of Manoel Barcelos the elder (643–646). One voyage was made "five or six years" before 1568, that is, in 1562 or 1563, another "two years ago" (1566 or possibly 1565). In 1568 the current Manoel Barcelos, with his cousin Marcos de Barcelos Machado, acquired an interest in the ship *A Vera Cruz*, João Cordeiro, master and part owner, and proposed to lead a further expedition to America, under himself or his second son. Manoel de Barcelos Machado petitioned the King's Purveyor in Angra, on January 8, 1568, against an embargo on his ship imposed by the Portuguese authorities in Terceira. Four extracts are given.

643. Testimony by Manoel de Barcelos Machado.

"Manoel de Barcelos Machado, who resides in this city of Angra in Terceira Island, says that he bought a new ship, whose master is João Cordeiro, to go and settle the Island Barcellona de Sam Bardão, in which discovery his late father and he spent more than 5000 cruzados, and in which they have been breeding herds of cows, sheep, goats and swine; and because the petitioner did not acquire that ship to go trading, but only to colonize the said island, and because he plans to leave in March or April with people to settle the said island; he asks Your Grace that you let him draw up certain testimonies proving what he says, and that orders be given so that his ship, which was embargoed to transport the King's wheat, will not go beyond Lisbon and will return home in time to go to the said isle. [He also asks] that for the years to come his ship will not be requisitioned, since he bought it to colonize and for no other reason; and through the disembargo of his vessel, he will receive justice and favour, and His Highness will benefit and be greatly served thereby."

644. Testimony by Diego de Vieira, uncle of Manoel de Barcelos's wife.

He stated that Manoel de Barcelos "about five or six years ago on his part . . . sent two ships as he knows for the first time was six years more or less and left there cattle, and two years ago he also sent cattle there which were cows, sheep and goats, which he set down in the said land and where they have fattened, flourished and multiplied."

645. Testimony of Gaspar Rodriguez, inhabitant of Santa Barbara, Terceira.

He says that Manoel de Barcelos had discovered the island Barcellona and about six years ago, more or less, had sent a ship there and within the two years last past had brought animals "who testifies he [Manoel de Barcelos] is going to the said land and he testifies that he [Barcelos] sent to the same much cattle which have there flourished and multiplied and brought other wise cattle which are established in that land."

646. Testimony of Marcos de Barcelos, first cousin of Manoel de Barcelos.

He says that the ship (*A Vera Cruz*) was bought at the island of S. Jorge with the object of "going to that new isle of São Bardão [Sam Bardam] where Marcos de Barcelos and Manoel have set down much cattle."

647. March 2, 1567. A report of a proposed Portuguese plan for an expedition to Canada.

The indications of Portuguese activity with regard to northeastern North America include this suggestion that a fleet was ready to go to Canada by way of the Azores to find a land route to the Pacific if Pierre de Monluc had not recently raided Madeira and so diverted their attention. It is suggested that they were anxious to find a new short route to the Pacific to strengthen their claim to the Moluccas in view of the recent Spanish annexation of the Philippines.

M. de Fourquevaux to Queen Catherine de Médicis, Dépêches de M. de Fourquevaux au roi Charles IX, edited by Célestin Douais, I (1896), 187, extract translated.

I am assured, Madame, that they will not be in the aforesaid country [Portugal] so enthusiastic nor so ardent as to set out with their army against the said [Algerian] pirates, as they were recently against the late Captain Monluc [Pierre de Monluc who had attacked Madeira in revenge for Portuguese help to Spain in Florida]; and I am informed that if it had not been for the Madeira alarm a little while ago throughout all the islands subject to the king of Portugal, a fleet which set out for the Azores would have gone on to Terre Neuve (of your ancient conquest), to take possession of the land and people in the Grand Bay of Canada [the Strait of Belle Isle], and they would not have been mistaken. For Spain and Portugal want the whole of the New World to be theirs and to exclude the French from sailing there, even to the north, which the Bretons discovered more than a century ago. And your Majesty should know that the said Portuguese had hopes of finding a much shorter route to the South Sea and the Moluccas from the said Canada by crossing the country by land, and not by the ordinary route they use. For from the said Azores to the said Canada is not more than four hundred leagues and if they can find the said route they will advance their cause against the Spaniards about the difference between them which they have over the said Moluccas [the contest over the half-way line], which each of the parties wishes to have in the event of a repartition.

It would, Madame, be very much better if this discovery could be made for your crown and to send your subjects to inhabit and people the said country than to put up with such a usurpation.

648. May 4, 1567. Appointment of a legal official to take part in the government of a proposed Corte Real colony in Terra Nova.

The somewhat theoretical Portuguese settlement somewhere in northeastern North America—on the Strait of Belle Isle or Labrador, rather than in Newfoundland itself—takes some legal shape in the royal permission received by Manoel Corte Real from King Sebastian on May 4, 1567, to appoint a governor with legal qualifications to administer the proposed (or actual?) Portuguese settlement. The permission was to last until March 4, 1570.

Lisbon, Archivo da Torre do Tombo, Privilegios de D. Sebastian, VI, no. 237, printed in Henry Harrisse, Les Corte-Reals (Paris, 1883), pp. 235–236, translated.

I, the King, make known to you, Gaspar Ferar, *corregidor* of the Azores, that Manoel Corte Real, governor of Angra in the island of Terceira told me that he, his father and uncles had sent out the people who discovered the land now called Terra Nova. Now he was sending there two ships and a caravel with people and provisions to begin to colonize it. He was sending with them a person who would act in his name as governor [*Capitana*] of the said Terra Nova. which had been granted to him. This person must perforce perform the duties of a governor, judge and administrator of justice. Thus he would need to find a person who, being a public scrivener, could draw up deeds of ownership and record whatever related to the administration of justice. Since people will come from the said island of Terceira and he does not yet know who is going to go, he has asked me for this time only to give him written authority for the same. This is in order that the *corregidor* of the said island may place one of those persons who are going in this position and grant him authority. Therefore I require you to choose out of these persons who are going to Terra Nova the person who is most suitable and proper to draw up all documents and record whatever happens in the said land. He must swear upon the Bible to write and tell the truth. You should put it on record in the book of the registers of the chancery [*Livro dos Registos da Chancellaria*], where this person will record his usual public signature. This grant is valid for three years only.

The said land can begin to be colonized and then we shall know what is necessary for this purpose, so that I can then grant the offices necessary for the rule and government of the said land. This my permission will not confer upon the said Manoel Corte Real, nor on his heirs, rights and donations in the said land additional to those I have given him. You should give that person who is appointed a letter, signed by you, conveying the authority given by this deed, with instructions that he should observe the rules of the writers and scriveners of this Kingdom which are written in the first book of ordinances [*primeiro livro das ordenaçãos*]. This will be valid as a charter, since it will have validity for more than a single year, notwithstanding the ordinance of the second book, chapter 20 [*ordenação 2° Livro titulo xx*] to the contrary.

João Gallvão made it in Lisbon the 4th of May 1567. João de Castilho ordered it to be written.

649. March 28, 1568. Pedro Menéndez de Avilés considers the Portuguese to have colonized Terra Nova two to three years before.

The evidence of Pedro Menéndez de Avilés was taken before the inquisitor, Juan de Ovando, during the course of inquiries being made at Fuenterrabia. It must be remembered that he considered that his authority to colonize Florida for Spain extended also to Terra Nova, but he was extremely vague about the location of the latter (putting it, on one occasion, at the northern limit of his own explorations in 1561 as extending from the head of Chesapeake Bay). His geographical location of the Portuguese settlement is therefore worthless.

B.L., Additional MS 33983, fol. 328v., extract, translated.

27. The Portuguese fortified in Terra Nova and Florida. Item he says that on the coasts of Florida and Terra Nova which are in his charge, and the discovery of which has been made [i.e. the exploration of which has been completed] two years ago [1566?], the Portuguese settled it after he had taken possession of that land in the name of his majesty and fought the Huguenots [*luteranos*]. And it is said they have fortified more than two hundred leagues inland from the conquest of that

discovery [from the part he has explored?]. This, certain persons, inhabitants of Fuenterrabia, who were with them, told him in the presence of Don Juan de Acuña, captain general of that kingdom, and the licentiate Arcila, one of his majesty's servants, inhabitant of San Sebastian, accountant of the garrison [*gente de guerra*] of that town of Fuenterrabia. He wrote that the French had told him there in San Sebastian that they had seen colonies of Portuguese in Florida, each village of very big Indians, and in their company they have entered by way of Tierra Nova which he understands to be a branch of the sea between the land of Florida. And this he had given to the royal Council of the Indies.

It appears that unless they are beaten out of there, on account of the design which the Portuguese have of reaching China and the Moluccas, they are certain to fortify themselves there, to go later from there, especially in view of the ease with which they can be supplied from the Azores (which are the King of Portugal's) and from which the sailing time in good weather is twelve to fifteen days.

650. 1574. Report of a voyage to northeastern North America by Vasques Eanes Corte Real.

When Richard Hakluyt the younger was completing the compilation of his Divers voyages touching the discoverie of America *(London, 1582; published in facsimile with an introductory volume entitled* Richard Hakluyt Editor, *by D. B. Quinn [Amsterdam, 1967]), he picked up from Don António de Castillo, the Spaniard who was representing Portugal at the English Court, some rather vague information about a voyage up the Labrador coast by Vasques Eanes Corte Real in 1574 that was said to have reached a latitude of some 58°N.*

[Sig.* 2v.]

A verie late and great probabilitie of a passage, by the Northwest part of America in 58. degrees of Northerly latitude.

An excellent learned man of portingale, of singuler gravety, authoritie and experience tolde mee very lately, that one *Anus Cortereal*, captayne of the yle of Tercera about the year 1574. which is not above eight yeres past, sent a Shippe to discover the Northwest passage of America, & that the same shippe arriving on the coast of the saide America, in fiftie eyghte degrees of latitude, founde a great entrance exceeding deepe and broade, without all impediment of ice, into whiche they passed above twentie leagues, and found it alwaies to trende towardes the South, the lande lying lowe and plaine on eyther side: And that they perswaded them selves verely, that there was a way open into the south sea. But their victailes fayling them, and being but one shippe, they returned backe agayne with joy. This place seemeth to lie in equal degrees of latitude, with the first entrance of the sounds of Denmark betweeen Norway and the head land called in Latin *Cimbrorum promontorium*, and therefore like to bee open and navigable a great parte of the yeere. And this report may bee well annexed unto the other eight reasons mentioned in my epistle dedicatorie, for proofe of the likelihood of this passage by the Northwest.

651. Between 1578 and 1580. Confirmation for Vasques Corte Real of charter granted to Manoel Corte Real (July 12, 1574).

Manoel Corte Real apparently died before 1578, after having received a confirmation of his Newfoundland charter, dated July 14, 1574, from King Sebastian. His son, Vasques Eanes Corte Real, who had been on a Labrador voyage in 1574, asked for and obtained from Cardinal King Henry (1578–1580) a reissue of the confirmation of 1574, granted to his father. No information appears so far to have emerged to indicate that he or other members of his family continued to make exploratory voyages up the North American coast, although it is probable that they continued to be involved with the Newfoundland fishery. Lisbon, Archivo da Torre do Tombo, Confirmações Geraes, III, no. 149, printed in Henry Harrisse, Les Corte-Reals (1883), pp. 236–237, translated.

I, Henry [*Amrique*] make known to those who shall see this charter that on behalf of Vasqueanes Corte Real, eldest son of Manoel Corte Real— may his soul rest in peace—there was presented to me a charter of the late king my nephew [Sebastian *d.* 1578], signed by him and given by the chancellor, which says the following:

Dom Sebastião etc. to those who shall see this my charter of ratification I make known that on behalf of Manoel Corte Real, a member of my Council, this charter was presented to me, a charter of my late lord and grandfather [João III], signed by him and given by his chancellor of which the content is the following: [it repeats the charters of 1500, 1506, 1522 and 1538 already recorded.]

The said Manoel Corte Real asked me as a favor to ratify this charter. After seeing his petition and wishing to grant this to him, I confirm and ratify it. I wish it to be carried out and maintained in its entirety and in the manner described. Antonio Carvalho made it in Lisbon on July 12, 1574.

I, Duarte Dias ordered it to be written.

Chapter Seventy-nine
Northwest Passage Theories:
The English Discussions, 1565–1580

Dıscussıon IN ENGLAND, having been silent since the speculations of Sebastian Cabot (1547–1553) on the possibilities of a passage to the northwest, started again in 1565. Humphrey Gilbert's *Discourse for a discoverie for a new passage to Cataia,* although written in 1566, did not appear until a decade later. But Doctor John Dee, Richard Willys, William Bourne, and, above all, Michael Lok, were prepared to put down some of their speculative ideas on paper between 1565 and 1580.

652. December, 1566. Humphrey Gilbert petitions the queen for privileges to promote the discovery of a Northwest Passage, with William Cecil's comments.

P.R.O., State Papers, Domestic, Elizabeth I, SP 12/42, 23 (ii), printed in D. B. Quinn, ed., Voyages and Colonising Enterprises of Sir Humphrey Gilbert, *I (1940), 108–110.*

To the Quenes moste excelente Majesti.

Forasmuche as yt hathe pleasid your Majesti to Establishe by parliament the Corporacion for discooverye of new trades I your highneis Humble servant & Subject Humfrey gilberte beyng on of the same Companye am therby encoorraged and mynd with your Majesties licence & favor to enterpryse & geve the attempt with all possible spede for the discooverye of A passage to Cataya and all other the ryche partes of the worlde as yet unfounde which takynge good success shalbe greate honor & strengthe to your majeste with ymmortall fame thoroughte all the world besides the great enrichinge of your highnes & your Countrye with increace & mayntenaunce of your navye, yt maye therfore please your Majesti to grante me thes previleges followinge, aswell in Consideracion of the premisses as also of the greate Chargys that I shall sustayne by the set-

tynge forwarde the same, besides the apparent mysserable trawayll hassarde & perell of my lyffe, wherin I submyte my selffe to the good wyll & pleassure of god.

1. Firste that yt maye plese your honour for the fowre furste voyages to graunte frelye to me, the use & occupacion of suche two of your majestis shippes with ther fornytures as by your honours Lord admyrall shalbe thought moste fyttest to be employed yn that service, with your Majestis Commission yf nede shalbe for the apprestinge and hiring of maryners & other parsons necessarye for that voyage; & also for the vittailynge of suche number of shippes as shalbe used yn that fowre firste voyages at your Majestis pryce.

2. Also that your honour wyll please to graunte to your sayd servante his heyres Executores & assighnes that he or they maye & shall at his or theyr will & Election yerely during the space of xl. yeres, trafficq with anye kynde of merchandise to anye the plases hereafter to be discovered by the said Corporacion for discoverye of new trades with one or two shipes at the moste with oute payeng any maner of custome, imposicion subsedes or other dutyes which may growe to your Majesti for any merchandise to be laden in any of them eyther in their voyage thether or yn ther returne hether except only xii d. for everye toonne according to the burden of the said shippe or shippes.

3. Also that I maye have to me & my ayers yn fee the tenthe parte of all suche landes & Countres as shall so happen to be Diskovered with all manour of proffites thereunto appertayninge. havinge lyberty to take to that quantyty to any our usses yn any parte of thes diskoveryd Counterys where as to us shall seme good, holdinge yt of your Majesti as of ye Crown of Englond at the yerely rente & valew of A knightes fee withoute any impossityon subside oyssing oute. or any other charge or servis for the same.

4. Also to graunte to me duringe my lyfe the Capitaneshipe chefe rule & government too your Majestis use of all suche Contres & terytoryez as shalbe by me or by my meanes or advice discoveryd, with convenyent fee & alowancez for suche a charge as to your Majesti shall seme good, & the same to be occupyd & exercyside by me or my sufficient deputye or deputyez.

5. Also the moyete of her Majestis parte of suche goodes as shall hereafter happen to be forgyted by infrenginge the prevlgis of the said corporacion to be to the use of me & my ayers in fee for every answeryng 12d. by the yere for the same.

6. Also that all suche shippes as shall from tyme to tyme be imployed aboute the traffike into suche discoveryd countres owtewardes or homewardes with there gingez may be fre for ever of all arestes impreste or ympechementes for any common service of the realme unleas yt be by vertu of her majestis speciall commyssion under her byll assind.

[Notes by Sir William Cecil at the end of the petition.]

1. in what tyme the foure voyadges shall be / if any of ye first shuld perish

ye Queens own shippes to be vyctelled by [contractors?] for redy mony

2. He hymself his heyres of his body or the heyres of his fathers body for yeirs half custom for thynges contained. without colloryng of strangers into ye partes towardes ye north and west that shall be discovered. /

3. To hym and his heyres of his body, or the heyres of his fathers body.

4. ye Deputy to be alloued by ye Queens Majesty.

5. to hym and his heyres males of his body or of his fathers ut supra

for infrynging of ye priviledges of ye Corporation for any thyng doon or Commetted in ye voyadg north west ward /

[Endorsed:] Humfery Gilberte. Mr Gilbertes sute.

653. January 24, 1567. The Muscovy Company comments on Gilbert's petition.

P.R.O., State Papers, Domestic, Elizabeth I, SP 12/42, 5 (ii), printed in D. B. Quinn, Gilbert, *I (1940), 111–115.*

1. Firste that ytt maye please your highenes for the iiii[or] firste voyages, so, as the same be performed within the space of tenne yeres nexte followinge Marche come twelve monthes: vz. beynge in anno 1569 to graunte to me the use and occupacion at your majestes adventure, of suche twoe of youre majestes shippes with theire furnytures mete For suche a voyage, as by your highenes Lorde Admyral shalbe thought fytt for suche a servyce with your majestes Commyssion, yff nede shalbe for the apprestinge off maryners and other personnes mete for the same

2. And also that I and the heires males of my boddy and for defaulte of suche Isshewe then the heires males of the bodye of Otes Gylberte deceassed may and shall paye but halfe custome and subsedye payable by Englishe men borne, for suche goodes and merchandyse, as we shall by the space of [blank] yeres by oure selves, deputes or assigneis, beynge Englyshe borne, transporte or cause to be transported in one or twoe shippes or vesselles into any place or places; hereafter to be by me, my ayde or advise dyscoveredde towardes the northweste, or takinge any parte of the weste and also shall paye but xiid. for everye tonne of merchandyse broughte frome suche places duringe the sayde tyme in two suche shipps aforsaid, ande no more whatsoever myghte otherwyse have growin to your highnes your heires or successours for anye suche merchandise, soe broughte or transported, as ys aforsaid

Annswers to the firste and second Artycles

Touchinge the ayde of shippinge and releacemente of custome yt is not prejudytiall to the

Companye yf yt please her majeste to graunte them, notwithstandynge, sythence the Company have frome the begynnynge of the fyrste attempte mynded the discovery of Cathay and have made dyvers attemptes therof and arre determyned so to doe againe aither by the northeaste or by the northweste, They desyer to have the rule and orderinge of all discoveries towardes the said parties, agreynge to their pryveledges etc. wherin they will not refuse: but desyer the good advise, helpe and conference of Mr Gilbarte yf yt please hyme, with reasonable condytions to enterpryse yt or to assyste theme therin

3. Also that I and my heires maye have and enjoye of your majestes gyfte, the tenthe parte of all suche landes terrytories and Contries, as shalbe dyscovered as ys aforsayde towardes anye parte of the northe and weste, as shalbe by us chosen with the proffyttes thereto apperteynynge with Free passage, egresse and regresse to the same, holdinge the same of your majeste your heires and successours by the yerlye rente of a knyghte Fee, for all manner of servyce and other paymentes to be sett or taxedde.

Annswere to the iiide Artycle

Item the sayde fellishippe dothe mislyke wholy the iiide requeste, as derogatorye to the pryveledges. / for yt is graunted to them, that they shall and maye subdue possesse and occupy all manner townes Isles and maynlandes of Infydelytie lying northwardes, northeastwardes or northwestwardes which shalbe founde: as vassalles and subjectes of this Realme / And to acquire the domynion, tytle and Jurisdiction of those places to be founde, unto the Quenes Majestie and her successours for ever /moreover ytt is graunted to the said fellyshippe that none shall traffike vysytt or saille to any suche contry lyinge as is aforsaid undiscoverede withoute the order and agreemente of the sayde fellyshippe

4. Also that ytt maye please your majeste to graunt to me durynge my lyffe the Captenshippe rule and governement to your majestes use, of all suche Contries and territories as shalbe by me or my advise discovered as is aforsaid / with convenyente Fee and allowaunce for suche a chardge / and the same to be occupied and exercysed by me, or my deputie or deputies soe, as your majeste shall allowe of hyme or theme by me to be nomynatedde
[Answer]

Touchinge the iiiith requeste the sayde fellyship can very well lyke Mr Gylbarte acceptinge the freedome of the said socyetye mayebe appoincted in persone and not by substytute, to be Captane and governour of the Contries by hys travell to be founde / So as the Lybertye off traffyke and the Pryveledges aforsaid be entierly reserved to the sayd felliship/.

5. Also that ytt maye please your majeste to graunte me and to the heires males of my boddy: and for defaulte of suche Ishewe, to the heires males of Otes Gylberte deceassed, the one halffe of your majestes parte of suche goodes, fynes, forfeytures or penaltyes: as shall hereafter fortune to be forfaycted by ynfrynginge the pryveledges of the said Corporacion for any offence commytted towardes the northweste or takynge anye parte of the weste

6. Also that all suche shipps as shall from tyme to tyme be ymployed aboute the traffyke into anye the dyscovered Contries of any Corporacion for dyscoverye of newe trades, bothe owtwardes and homewardes with theyre gynge may be Free for ever of all arestes, ymprestes and ympecchementes for anye comon servyse of the Realme, unleste yt be att the settinge forthe of a generall Armye and Navye, and by vertue of your majestes spetyall Commyssyon for the same, under your Bill sygnedde.
[Answer]

To the fyvethe and syxte: the sayde Socyetye submytte them selves to the Quenes majesties pleasure

654. 1576. The inception of the Frobisher voyages to the Northwest.

Michael Lok, during the course of the Frobisher ventures, sat down in 1577 to write an account of the inception of the northwest project, probably on the basis of diaries or notes compiled at the time. It is not always easy to judge how reliable he is and his manuscript is, in any case, damaged by fire. Yet it has some appreciable authority.

B. L., Cotton MS, Otho E. VIII; first printed (with modernized spelling) in E. G. R. Taylor, Tudor Geography (London, 1930), pp. 269–270.

[The] learned man Master John Dee hearing

the common [report] of this new enterprise, and understanding of the prepa[ration] for furniture of the Ships, being thereby persua[ded] that it would now proceed, and having not been acquainted with our purpose in any part before, about the 20th. day of May, A° 1576 of his own good nature favouring the enterprise in respect of the service and commodity of his natural country, came unto me desiring to know of me the reasons of my foundation and purpose in this enterprise, and offering his furtherance therof, with such instructions and advice as by his learning he could give thereon. Whereupon I conceived a great good opinion of him, and therefore appointed a time of meeting at my house, whereat were present Martin Frobysher, Steven Burrough, Christopher Hall, with other. Where freely and plainly I laid open to him at large my whole purpose in the traffic of merchandise by that new part of the world, for the benefit of the Realm by many means, as well in the countries of East India if this way the sea be open, as also otherwise, though that this New land should chance to bar us from the sea of India. And also declared such conjectures and probabilities as I had conceived of a passage by sea unto the same sea of East India by that way of the north-west from England. And for the proof of these two matters, I laid before him my books, authors, my cards and instruments, and my notes thereof made in writing as I had made them of many years study before. Upon which matters when he had thus heard and seen, he answered that he was right glad to know of me this much of this matter, and that he was greatly satisfied in his desire above his expectation, and that I was so well grounded in this [here the MS. is burnt, and conjectural words are added in brackets]... [Like]wise he shewed me all his [books, authors, and certain writings of] his own: and also showed me his [cards? instruments?] which I did very well like. And afterw[ards so long as] the ship remained here, he took pains [to demonstrate] the Rules of Geometry and Cosmography for [the better instruct]ion of the Masters and Mariners in the use of Instruments for Navigation in their voyage, and for [Cas]ualities happening at sea, which did them service, whereby he deserves much commendation.

655. October 28, 1577. Michael Lok on the

ideas behind Frobisher's second voyage.

B. L., Cotton MS, Otho E VIII; first printed by E. G. R. Taylor, Tudor Geography *(1930), p. 271.*

Neither nede I [say any]thing touching the naturall Riches and infinite T[reas]or, and the great Traffic of rich Merchandise that is in those countries of Cathay, China India and o[ther] countries thereabouts, for that every boke of history and cosmography of those parts of the world, which are to be had of every Prynters shop, does declare the same at large.... But of the matters that chiefly moved me to enterprise my money therein so largely, I will say briefly that three things chiefly moved me thereto. First the great hope to fynd our English seas open unto the Seas of the East India, by that way, which I conceved by the great likelyhood thereof which I found by reading the histories of many men's travailes toward that parte of the Worlde. Whereby we might take passage by sea to those rich Cuntries for traffik of merchandize, which was the thynge I chiefly desired.

Secondly I was assured by manifold good proofs of divers Travailers and histories, that the countries of Baccaliaw [sic] Can[a]da, and the new found Landes thereto adjoining, were full of people: and full of such commodities and Merchandize as are in the countries of Lappia, Russia, Moscovia, Permia, Pechora, Samoietza, and the Cuntries thereto adjoining: Which are furres, hydes, wax, tallow, oyle and other. Whereby if it should happen those new Landes to stretch to the North Pole, so that we could not have passage by Sea that way which we sought to the Northwestward, to pass into East India, yet in those same new lands to the northwestward might be established the like Trade of Merchandize as is now, in the other said countries of the....

656. 1580. William Bourne on the Northwest Passage.

William Bourne was one of the most influential of the practical Elizabethan writers on navigation. His advice in his (a) preface to and (b) his text of A regiment for the sea *(1580) is therefore of value. The latter was a section headed "A Hydrographicall discourse to show the passage unto Cattay five manner of waies, two of them knowen and the other three supposed." The known ways were by the Cape of Good Hope and the Strait of Magellan, and the "supposed" by way of passages to the northeast, north and northwest.*

Passage (a), preface to his second edition of A regiment for the sea *(London, 1580), is taken from E. G. R. Taylor,* Tudor Geography *(London, 1930), p. 237, spelling modernized; passage (b) is from William Bourne,* A Regiment for the Sea, *ed. E. G. R. Taylor (Cambridge, Eng., Hakluyt Society, 1963), pp. 307–308.*

[a]   It is also very necessary for them that would attempt any voyages of discovery to find out the passage to come to Catay and China and the Islands of the Moluccas, into the northwards, or into the east by Nova Zemla, or to the west by that way that Captain Frobisher hath begun to the northwards of Baculayas and Labrador, for it is to be supposed that amongst the broken lands and islands, that there may be found passage upon the north part of America, but the great quantity of ice may somewhat hinder the prosperity of that discovery. And yet, notwithstanding, my opinion is, that it is not frozen there so much to have such huge quantities of ice, but that it may be frozen more farther unto the north parts, and so by some current or stream brought thither, and so is stayed upon the coast of Labrador and Baculayas, by the means of this great current that cometh out of the bay of Mexico all alongst the north side of Florida, unto Baculayas or Newfoundland.

[b]   And now furthermore, for to discourse the third way that is not knowen, but supposed that it may be passageable, that is by the Northwest, as now of late Captaine *Forbisher* hath begun, and hath discovered as farre as a place nowe called *Meta Incognita*, which he himselfe did call *Forbishers Straights*, but yet notwithstanding it is doubtfull, whether that be a Straightes to give passage to come into the East Occean Sea, or south sea, for any thing that is knowen yet, it maye bee as well a Baye as otherwise, but notwithstanding whether that bee a Straight or not, it is possible that there maye be passage there about, between the Norther parte of America, as betweene *Labradorre* and *Groynland*, and such landes as lyeth unto the North Polewardes.

Wherefore now for to depart from *England* to go unto *Cattay* by the Norwest, first this for to make their direction from the West part of *England*, unto the place called *Meta Incognita*, the course is West Norwest about *650.* leagues, and the latitude thereof *63.* Degrees, and on the Starboord is first *Ireland* and *Iseland*, and *Freeseland*, and on the Larboord side, is the Occean Sea. And now beeing at *Meta Incognita*, they must discover there abouts, where that they may finde Sea for to give them passage, & yet if they do finde sea, they must hold on their course West untill y^t they have passed *1000* or *1100* leagues. For if that they should hold on any Southerly course, then they should imbaye themselves in the maine land of *America*, for the extention of the backe Side, or North side of *America*, is not much lesse than 1000. leagues, before that they shal open ye way into the East Ocean Sea, and in this West course on the Starboord side is the North Pole, and such lands as lyeth that way if there be any, and on the Larboord side, is the maine of *America*.

And after that they have sailed West *1000.* leagues on the North part of *America*, they may then direct a more southerly course, for that then they may be open of the East Ocean sea, for that the most parte of the best Cosmographers laye the opening of that sea opposite unto us in our Meridian, & then holding on a southerly course, then they may have unto the great bay of *Quinsay* about 400. or *500.* leagues. And the latitude of ye North part of ye Bay of *Quinsay* in *Cattay* is about 46. degrees, and on the Starboord side is the coast of *Asia*, as *Mangie* and *Cattay*, and on the Larboord side *America*. And thus much have I saide as touching the third way to goe to *Cattay*, &c.

Chapter Eighty
The Frobisher Voyages, 1576–1578

BEGINNING IN a small way in 1576 the expeditions emerged as a great speculation in 1577 and continued to expand in 1578, only to explode, as its gold reef was exposed as false, before the end of the year. Yet the voyages did gain experience for Englishmen in northern waters, in numbers that might otherwise never have reached there, and so provided knowledgeable personnel for later voyages. For the first time the series also produced an impression in Europe of English exploring activity in North America.

657. 1576. Accounts for the purchase and fitting out of the *Gabriel* and *Michael*.

Michael Lok left an unequalled series of accounts and correspondence for the Frobisher expeditions. Those in State Papers, Domestic, Elizabeth (SP 12) were given at length as an appendix to R. Collinson, ed., The Three Voyages of Martin Frobisher (London, Hakluyt Society, 1867), and these were reprinted in V. Stefansson and E. MacCaskill, eds., The Three Voyages of Martin Frobisher, 2 vols. (London, 1938). No systematic attempt has been made to present the material in the PRO E164 series, or to print in full the accounts for the third voyage in the Huntington Library (see G. B. Parks, "New material on the third voyage," Huntington Library Quarterly, II, 59–65). What follows is, for the first voyage, a representative sample of what the unpublished PRO series contains and indicates its value for obtaining a full picture of the equipment of a vessel for a transatlantic voyage. In this case it is one more generous than representative, since it was hoped the ships would sail as far as China or Japan.
P.R.O., E 164/35, fols., 9–26.

The paymenttes of monye paid by me Michaell Lok for the Furniture of the fyrste voyage made by Martyne Frobiser gentelman for the discovery of Cathay by the Northwestwardes Anno 1576.

	li	s	d
Paid to Mathewe Baker shipwrit, for release of a bargane made with him for buyldinge of a shippe anno 1575 which tooke none effecte for lake of the venturars mony paid him	5	0	0
paid to John Cockes maryner, who was highred for master of the voyage in that yere of anno 1575 and was releassed for the consideracone for said	5	0	0
paid to Mathew Baker & John Addye shippe wrightes, for buildinge a newe shipp called Gabriell of Burden 30 tons & a pynace of 7 ton & carpenters worke to furnishe the same, & plankes tymber mastes and ther stuffe therto anno 1576	105	16	8
paid charges of a man sent to Alborowe to master Foxe, to bye his shippe flybote	0	6	8
paid to master Frobiser in accompte as followith			
for Nicholas Thornton carpentar 9 dayes	0	16	6
for Christofer Backer carpentar 9 dayes	0	16	6
for Petar Mogar carpentar	0	15	0

	li	s	d
for ij sawyers for j daye	0	2	4
for vij carpentares more for vj dayes apece	2	15	6
for ij calcares viij dayes apece	1	10	4
Some this side	122	19	6

	li	s	d
paid a joynar for selinge the Cabyne of the Gabriell, & makinge a bytackle and other worke	1	5	4
for bread and drinke & brekfastes to the carpentares to hasten their workes	2	0	0
for bote heyre of master Furbiser followinge his bussynes att this tyme	10	10	0
all thes charges paid to master Frobiser li 20. 11. 6.			
for brymestone to bryme the shipps, paid to master Lee of redryfe	1	4	0
paid to Richard Estwood carpentar for tymbar & worke on the ij ships Gabriell and Michaell, many dayes	3	6	0
paid Richard Lane smythe, for yron workes, boltes, spykes, nayles & other worke, by bylle	8	8	0
paid Leryges Smythe of Ratlyfe for pykes nayles and others	0	16	0
Thomas Bewell smythe, for yron worke boltes, spykes, and others	1	14	6
	29	0	10
	122	19	9
Some of this parcell which is for ships buyldinge & reparinge	152	0	4

	li	s	d
Paid Christopher Andrewes, & Robart Martine for a shippe called the Michaell burden 30. tone, with apparell, takell, and furnyture redy made Summe	120	0	0

	li	s	d
paid for divers takelinge, apparelle, and implementes & furniture for ryggynge of the ij shipps Gabriell & Michaell aforsaid & their pynaces paid li. 172. 5. 6. as followith			
paid to Adrian Prussom, for the makinge & workynge of all the saylles	5	4	8
paid to master Frobiser in accompt as followith			
for iiij mastes for the gabriell	2	5	0
for ij topes for her	0	14	6
for 9 baskattes	0	2	6
for spyninge of ockam to ij boyes	0	1	0

	li	s	d
for carvinge of the dragones hed	0	10	0
for ij smalle mastes	0	16	0
for sawinge of fyve anker stokes	0	2	6
for a new skyffe bote	3	0	0
for the paynter part of his worke in paynting of the shippe gabriell	2	0	0
for hopes to the coper	0	4	0
for schopper letheres to the boteswane	0	4	0
poudar & otheres frome towar	0	3	0

Sume paid master frobiser li 10. 2. 6.

	li	s	d
paid to Clement Fase turner for pulleys for ij shippes apperinge particulerlye in pursers boke	4	18	0
paid by N. Chaunseler purser for divers thinges necessarye for the furniture of the shipps apperinge particulerlye in his booke of accompt	15	17	1
paid to Robarte Crokey for vij ankeres for ships weyinge 7ᶜ. 3 qr. 24ˡˡ. at 22s. the C. amounteth	8	15	0
paid to Thomas Paynter for reste of paynting all yᵉ ships	2	5	0
paid to Ducke upholster for beddinge for master Captayne Frobiser	3	16	5
paid for iiij dosen owares & ij bordes	4	18	0
paid for j anker, jᶜ. jqr. 16ˡˡ.	1	10	8
Some of this side	57	7	4

	li	s	d
Paid to Clement Drapar, as Followithe.			
for .6. cables, for the shippes			
for .40. ropes for the shippes all weyinge 42ᶜ. at 21.s. the C.	44	4	0
for 9. barrelles of puche & tarre	5	10	0
for 3.ᶜ· weight of Rossen	1	10	0
for latchet lyne, marlyne, twyne, ockame	6	1	6

Sume paid Clement Drapar li. 57. 5. 0.

	li	s	d
paid to master Hawlle for 16. peces of poldavises & vandelowes, for sayles for the ships at divers times	49	6	0
paid for vᶜ. of yron stones of Russia at iiijᵈ pece li beinge vj tons for balliste for the Gabriell bought of master Patrik & R. Hopton	8	6	8
Some above	114	18	2
on thother syde	57	7	4
Som paid for takelinge and Implementtes and necessaryes for furnitur of the ships	172	5	6

paid for divers Ordinaunce, Munition and armour for furniture of the shipps as followith
paid to ghert Leke smythe, by bylle for 24 Calibres, with flaske & furniture — 12 0 0
for a longe musket, with a fyerloke — 1 6 0
for a flaske and tucheboxe of horne — 0 3 0
for a lether case for the musket — 0 2 6
for 24li leade for pelletes shotte — 0 2 6
for casting the pelletes of leade — 0 1 6
for a castinge ladell yron — 0 0 8
for a Ruler & square of yron — 0 2 0
for 2 Bages of leather — 0 0 8
for 120 stones of flynte for dages — 0 1 0

Some above — 13 19 10

paid for 20 crosbare shotte and 40 Round shott of fauconettes paid master frobiser — 0 10 0
per bill for these parcels
for 3 rapyers & 3 daggares — 0 15 0
for 1 armoringe sworde — 0 10 0
for 4 targattes — 0 12 0
for a masse of yrone — 0 5 0
for 2 cottes of plate — 1 6 8
for a manackell & a shackell of yrone — 0 5 4

Some paid li. 4. 4. 0.

paid for Munition had out of the towar followith
for corne poudare vjc. at 5li. C — 30 0 0
for serpeyntine pouder ijc. at 4li. 3s. 4d. — 8 6 8
per bill for partizens gilte .6. at s. 13. 4. — 4 0 0
for bowes 16 at s. 4. 2. — 3 6 8
for arrowes 20 sheffes at s. 2. — 2 0 0
for longe pykes 7. at s. 2. 6. — 0 17 6
for shippykes 14. at s. 2. — 1 8 0

Some paid li. 49. 18. 10.

paid for 30li. maches at 4d. pece paid N. Angere — 0 10 0
for a drome of William Aborrowe — 1 10 0
for a fawkenet caste yrone poiz. 4c. 3qr. 14li. at s. 13. the C Paid Roberte Croskey and with s. 18. for the carriage — 4 1 4
for 22. shot of yron fawconet — 0 3 8

Some paid li. 4. 5. 0.

paid Richard Ducke upholster for 2 newe flagges of bowtar with makinge — 3 12 10

for making of an aunchent of silke — 1 3 0
Some paid Duke li. 4. 15. 10.

paid to Ambrose Smythe for 18½ elles sarcenet of diveres collores at s. 5. 8d. & for an ancient — 5 4 10
paid to John and Thomas Castelyn for 4. faukonettes of cast yrone weinge 20c at s. 13. 4d the C amount — 13 6 8
for .4. carrages & ther furniture — 2 13 4
Some paid John & Thomas Castelen li. 16. 0. 0.

Some above — 86 8 6
on the other syde — 13 19 10
— 100 8 4

paid for dyvers vytells for furniture of the said ships as followithe
paid to Owine Gryffen, master of the shippe Michaell for bord wages — 1 10 0
paid to Christofer Halle for borde wages — 1 10 0
paid to divers mariners for bord wages — 0 12 0
paid for a bottell of aquavite for master Frobiser paid it to his mane Borrowes — 0 10 0

Some mony paid li. 3. 12. 0.

paid to master Frobiser in accompte as Followithe.
for beare and breade at launchinge of the Gabriell & for maryners dyners then — 0 19 0
paid for borde wages of divers maryners alande before any vyttells was allowed in ye ship
for Owine Greffyn li. 1. 2. 6.
for the trompitor li. 0.18. 0.
for Richard Slyght the gonner, li. 0.18. 0.
for paule whiteheare li. 0.17. 0.
for Alexander Ertake li. 0. 8. 0.
for William Thomson li. 0.15. 0.
for John Wilmote li. 0.16. 0.
for John Lyumond, li. 0.16. 0.
for Richard Frynd botswane li. 0.10. 0.
for William Nenet li. 0.18. 0.
for William Deane li. 0.17. 0.
for the Cooke, li. 0. 5. 0.
for Thomas Bolde master bondesman li. 0. 5. 0.
for Richard Sleght li. 0. 5. 0.

	li	s	d
Sume of all the borde wages	9	11	6
paid for bread at severall tymes	0	5	0
paid for wood for storre fyer	0	5	0
paid for hoddinge vj barrells bysket to a cooper	0	1	0
Sume paid master Frobiser li. 11. 1. 6.			
paid to Arnold Langly surgine, for a chest full of surgery wares for the shipps provisione	2	13	4
paid to Nicholas Chaunclor at Gravesend at ships departure thens for ships store	2	0	0
some paid is li. 4. 13. 4.			
some of this side	19	6	10
paid by N. Chanselar purser for freshe vittells daly bought abord shipps	5	15	3
paid to Nicholas Chaunseler for his owne bord wages doinge shipps busynes	2	14	0
paid for .24. cople of grenefyshe and haberdine for ship at 16^{C}	1	12	0
paid to Nicholas Agar chaundlar Followith			
for candles .37. dossen lb. divers sortes	5	8	0
for peasen .40. busshills, at 2. s	4	0	0
for otmell .12. bushell, at 4 s	2	8	0
for mustarde sede .5½ bushell, at .6. s. 8^{d}	1	16	8
for vinigare .2. hogshedes	2	0	0
for soppe .2. fyrkines	1	11	0
for caske and packinge all the same	1	12	5
Some paid Nicholas Angar li. 18. 16. 10.			
paid to Fraunces Green Bucher for xj oxen weinnge net 52^{C}. 3^{qr}. 17^{li}. beefe	45	0	0
paid to Henry Payntor baker for bysket bread 76^{C}. j^{qr}. 17^{li}. at .9. s the C & 4. s. for 4. dosen bred	34	11	6
paid to Nicholas Cooke for aquavite 3 hogshedes	13	18	0
paid to Anthony Duffilde breuer for .8. tonn Seabere at 40 s. tonne	16	0	0
for beare, dronke in the river.6. barrells	1	4	0
for sea colles ij chaudron at s. 13. 4. & carrag	1	8	0
Some paid Anthony Duffild .li. 18. 11. 0			
Paid Benjamen Clarke cooper as followith			

	li	s	d
for hoopes and caske for shipps store	1	7	0
paid to Clement Draper as Followith			
for 12 barrelles of mell for ships store	6	0	0
paid to Anthony Bleake cooper as Followith			
for divers Caske, & hoopes, & worke one them for the befe, bread, ryse, meale, wyne & other thinges, & 24 water barrelles had of him	10	19	0
paid for .v. tonne of Beare at .s. 42. bought of my Lord Admirall, by Artter Pett	10	10	0
Some paid one this side	169	7	7
The vittells for our shipps Gabrill & Michaell paid to Thomas Bagshawe as Followithe			
for .v.^{C} stockefyshe at s.25. Land fyshe	6	5	0
for .C. codefyshe Nor. [blank] at	3	13	4
for $q^{tr.}$ Lynge Island	1	2	6
Some paid Tho. Bagshawe li. 11. 00. 10			
paid to John Harte grocer as Followithe			
for ryse a but wayinge net .13.^{C} .2.10 at 24.^{s} C	16	6	1
paid to [blank] Mansfyld as Followithe			
for 5 barrells butter at 56.s. a barrell	14	0	0
for chese suffoke .v. wayes at 37.s.	9	5	0
Some paid [blank] Mansfyld li.23. 5. 0.			
paid Thomas Marvill as Followithe			
for baye salte ij wayes for ships store	8	1	8
for salte .38. bushells for beefe	4	8	2
for wheat meale 26. bushells at s .38.	4	15	4
for yron hoops .32. weinge 260^{li} at 3.^{d}½	3	15	4
Some paid Tho. Marville li 21. 0. 6.			
paid Davye Hasse for bacon .27. flyches at s. 5. 4.	8	10	0
paid to master alderman Bond for .v. tonne wyne sace	100	0	0
paid to Thomas Cordall for .2. hogsheds swet oyle .126. gallones at .s. 3. 0. gallone	18	18	0
some above	199	0	5
	169	7	7
	19	6	10
sum paid for vytelles	387	14	10

	li	s	d
theis Instrumentes to be restored.			
paid for divers Instrumentes for navigation as followithe.			
for ij paper bookes for Accomptes	0	9	0
paid for a booke of Cosmografie in frenche of Andreas Thevet makinge	2	4	0
paid to Humfrye Cole and others, as followithe			
for a great globe of metall in blanke in a case of Leather	7	13	4
for a great instrument of brasse named Armilla Tolomaej, or hemisperium, with a case	4	6	8
Somme is	14	13	0
paid for an Instrument of brasse named Sphera Nautica with a Case	4	6	8
for a great Instrument of brasse named Compassum Meridianum, with a case	4	6	8
for a great Instrument of brase named Holometrum Geometricum with a Case	4	0	0
for a great instrument of brase named Horologium Universale, with a case	2	6	8
for a ringe of brase named Annalus Astronomicus	1	10	0
for a littell standinge levell of brase		6	8
for a case with smalle instrumentes for geometrie, of yron	0	6	8
for an Instrument of wood, a stafe named Balistella, with a case	0	13	4
for a verye great Carte of Navigacon	5	0	0
for a great mappe universall of Mercator in prente	1	6	8
for iij other small mapps prented	0	6	8
for vj Cartes of navigacon written in blacke parchment wherof 4 ruled playne and 2 rounde	2	0	0
for a bible englishe, great volume	1	0	0
for a Cosmografical glasse & castell knowleg	0	10	0
for a newe world of Andreas Thevett englishe and frenche bookes ij smalle	0	6	8
for a regiment of Medina, spanishe	0	3	4
for Sir John Mandevylle, englishe	0	1	0
for a Carte of Orelius, prynte	[blank]		
paid to William Thomas compasse maker for 20 Compasses of divers sortes	3	3	0
for 18 hower glasses	0	17	0
some paid him li. 4. 0. 0.			

	li	s	d
paid for a Astrolabium, of William Burowe	3	10	0
some this side	36	1	0
some of the other side	14	13	0
some paid for Instrumentes	50	14	0
paid for wages, of men & maryners uppon the voyage beforehand as followithe			
paid to James Aldaye, uppon wages	5	0	0
paid to Owine Griffyne uppon wages	5	0	0
paid to Christofer Halle master of the Gabriell for 3. monthes wages before hand hired .j. may at 6. li	18	0	0
paid to Owine Griffyne master of the Michaell for rest of iij monthes wages befor hand he was highered the .j. maye at 5ᵘ· the monthe	10	0	0
paid to Richard Slight, master gonner for .2. monthes wages beforhand he was highered the .j. maye at 33 s. 4ᵈ per monthe	3	6	8
paid to Richard Purdye trompeter, for ij monthes wages .li. 3. 6. 8. & more s. 13. 4. payd before hand he was highered the .j. may at 33. 4d	4	0	0
paid to Richard Millar maryner, for ij monthes wages .li. 2. 13. 4. & more .li. 0. 6. 8. & .10. s paid he was highered the .5. June at 26 s. 8d. per moneth	3	10	0
paid to Robarte Garrat maryner, for ij monthes wages he was highered the .5. June at 26. s 8. per monthe	2	13	4
paid to William Denye maryner, for ij monthes wages he was highered the .j. maye at 26 s. 8. per monthe	2	13	4
paid to Pawle Whithere mariner for ij monthes wages he was highered the .j. maye at 26 s. 8. per monthe	2	13	4
paid to Alexander Creake maryner for ij monthes wages he was highered the .j. maye at .26s 8. per monthe	2	13	4
paid to Richard Frynde botswane, for ij monthes wages he was highered the .j. maye at 34.s per monthe	3	8	0
paid to John Hamond of pynas, for ij monthes wages he was highered the .j. maye at 28s per month	2	16	0
paid to Thomas Peke Marynar for ij monthes wages he was highered the .j. June at 26s 8. per month	2	13	4

	li	s	d
paid to William Priar marynar for ij monthes wages he was highered the .j. maye at 20s per monthe	2	0	0
paid to Renold Crespe marynar, for ij monthes wages he was highered the .j. June at 20s per monthe	2	0	0
paid to John Smythe, cooke, for ij monthes wages he was highered the 24. maye at 24s per month	2	8	0
paid to John Cominge gonner, for ij monthes wages he was highered the .j. maye at 20s per month	2	0	0
Some one this side paid	76	15	4

	li	s	d
paid to Edward Clothier Cooper & Koke for ij monthes wages beforhand he was highered .21. may at 26s 8. m.	2	13	4
paid to Peter Mogare, carpentar, for ij monthes wages he was highered the .15. maye at 26s 8. per monthe	2	13	4
paid to John Jacobe smythe for ij monthes wages he was highered the .5. maye at 22s 6. per monthe	2	5	0
paid to William Thomson maryner, for ij monthes wages he was highered the .j. may at 25s per month	2	10	0
paid to John Wilmote marynar for ij monthes wages he was highered .21. maye at 29s 8. per monthe	4	0	0
paid to John Peele marynar for ij monthes wages he was highered the firste of June at 25s per month	2	10	0
paid to Josephe Colbroke, maryner, for ij monthes wages he was highered the .7. June at 30s the monthe	2	6	0
paid to Robarte Westone maryner, for ij monthes wages he was highered the 20. maye at 26s 8. per month	2	13	4
paid to Robart Hollowaye carpentar for 2 monthes wages he was highered the .7. June at 30s the monthe	3	0	0
paid to Thomas Bormane, marynar for 2 monthes wages he was highered the .7. June at 3.ll per monthe	6	0	0
paid to Edward Parkines maryner for ij monthes wages he was highered the 8 June at 40s the monthe	1	0	0
paid to Phillipe Bocket surgion, for vj weekes wages he was highered the 8 June at 40s per monthe	3	0	0
paid to John Burche carpentar for parte of a monthe he was highered			

	li	s	d
the 12 June, at 26s.8. per monthe	1	0	0
paid to Symon Person, maryner of Plymothe for ij monthes he was highered the .5. June and at 26s. 8. the monthe he is rone away with the mony	2	13	4
paid to Thomas More taylar, for ij monthes wages he was highered the .3. June at 20s the monthe he is gone awaye with the monye which master Frobisher had	2	0	0
paid to iij marynares which were highered & wer put away againe, and for their service paid	1	8	0
paid for trompeters passed in shippe by Carte	0	10	0
paid for reward to the Queens man of the garde that came a bord the shippe at Blackwale	0	10	0
paid master Frobiser for Lord Warike 20s & at Gravesend 30. s & to his mane William.40s.	4	10	0
Some paid one this side	47	2	4

	li	s	d
paid unto Nicholas Chaunseler purser for .v. monthes wages he was highered .j. maye, at 40s the monthe which amounthe unto	10	0	0
paid to master Frobiser at divers tymes for his paynes takeinge in this voyage and his endevor untill his retorne which was paid to clere him out of England one the voyage	80	0	0
some of this side	90	0	0
	47	2	4
	76	15	4
Some paid for wages	213	17	8

Paid for divers Implementes of howshold necessarye for the shippes furniture as followithe.
paid to John James as Followithe.

	li	s	d
for a great kettle pan brasse with yron balle	0	18	0
for a great bassone of brasse to bake one	0	6	8
for a bakinge pane of yron with cover	0	2	8
for a chaffinge dishe of brasse	0	4	0
for a skimar of brasse	0	1	4
for a great potte of yrone, for meat	0	6	8
for a little pane brasse with handle yrone	0	1	4

	li	s	d
for a tryvet yrone	0	1	4
for ij fringe panes	0	5	0
for a drippinge pan yron	0	2	0
for a grydryon	0	1	0
for ij spyttes	0	3	4
for a payre of potte hokes	0	0	8
for a slyse of yron	0	0	8
for a fleshoke of yron	0	0	8
for ij hokes yron Flat	0	0	8
for a clever great choppinge knyfe of yron	0	1	6
for iij wooden platters Muskovia painted	0	1	6
for a great bassone an ewar of pewtar	0	6	8
for iij pynte pottes of beare and wyne	0	5	4
for a salte seller of pewtar	0	1	0
Some above	3	12	0

for ij flagane bottels of pewtare	0	7	0
for .6. platters, 6. dishes, 3. dishes, 6 sausars pewtar all lb. 56. at d. 6.	1	8	0
Some paid John James for stufe li 5. 7. 0			

paid to Willson cooper as Followithe for 18 bere barrells, for byskett & other necesaryes for the ships, at s. 1. 4. per pece	1	4	0
paid to good wife Brighte smythe Followithe for a great pare of bellowes for smythes forge	0	15	0
paid to Anthony Blewe cooper, more by his byll for 2½. tonne wyne Caske pips & hoggshedes for the sake had of master Bonde	1	5	0
Some of this side	4	14	0
some of ye other side	3	12	0
Some paid for Implementes	8	11	0

Summe of all the said Charges of furnyture of the said shipps owtwardes Coste as Followithe			
For Implementtes howshold	8	11	0
for wages of men	213	17	8
for instrumentes of navigatione	50	14	0
for vyttelles	387	14	10
for ordonans mutiton	100	8	4
for tackelinge of shipps	172	5	6
for buyldinge the shippe Gabrill and the pynace newe	152	0	4
for the shipe Michaell, with furnitur of her bought	120	0	0
Somme owtwardes of shippinge	1205	11	8

	li	s	d
Paid for dyvers Marchaundyse bought for the furnitur of the said voyag as followithe			
paid to William Web, for .j. tone of yron of dyvers sortes	10	13	4
paid to Jhon Clypsen, for lead .4.^{C} 1.^{qr} 12^{li}	2	14	4
paid to Richard Luksome for Axes .60. and hattchettes .60.	5	0	0
paid to Sir Lionell Ducket, for leade weinge xj$^{C.}$ weight	5	15	6
paid to William Curtes pewterar for pewtar vessell and tyne	20	16	5
paid to Ambrose Smithe mercer for all sortes of mercerye wares	25	12	7
paid to Peter Harte stacioner for paper parchement	3	3	0
paid to John Malyn braysser for 25 Latten kettells	4	17	7
paid to William Gilborne, for 5 peces of hamsher kersyes	9	15	0
paid to the companye of Russia for 4. clothes, 2. cottones	24	13	4
paid to William Albanye for remnanttes of brode clothe, and for Remnanttes of Bayes,	19	18	6
paid to Jefferye Ducket for Lynen clothe	16	15	7
paid to Thomas Marstone for rybans, laces, & silkes	4	1	0
Sum paid	153	16	2

paid to Edward Olmore grocer for grocerye wares	3	15	4
paid to Howe Morgane potticarye for pottycarye ware, droges	4	11	4
paid to Richard Clarke goldsmithe for golde smithes wares	5	6	4
paid to George Donskone draper for Devonsher carseis and fryses	9	0	0
paid to Robart Cuttes yremonger for yremongare wares	5	8	11
paid to William Hobson haberdasher for haberdashers wares	7	4	7
	35	6	6
	153	16	2
And for charges in the next leffe	189	2	8
	24	3	0
Sum totall	213	5	8

Paid for charge of Marchaundyse and other busynes, as Followithe for the said first voyage outwardes.

	li	s	d
paid to Thomas Nycolles the clarke of the Company of Russia for writinge the privilege granted frome the said Company unto Michaell Lok & Martine Frobiser for the discovery of Cathay & by the northewest parte	1	0	0
paid to master Whorlstone for a Councellors Fee, for drawing a plate of a newe privilege	1	0	0
paid to master Charke for translatinge out of latine into greeke, the Quenes majesties Letter of Favour directed to all princes in the behalfe of Martyne Frobiser one his voyag of discovery	0	10	0
paid to master Wolley for penninge & makinge in lattine the Quenes Majesties letters of favour in the behalfe of Martine Frobiser, for his firste voyage of discoverye directed to all princes paid to him and his man	2	0	0
paid to Conradus, for Lymminge the said ij letteres of favour and to a paynter for culleringe the quenes Majesties pictures therin	1	18	4
parchement skynes for those letters & boxes to put them yn	0	4	8
charges of a man, which caried those letters from London to Lee after the ships were departed	0	12	4
the brode seale of England to those ij letters silke laces	1	15	0
J Broke scrivener, for makinge divers bills, & writtinges for mens stokes	1	18	8
Somme	10	19	4

	li	s	d
Paid for makinge writtinges, for the ship flybote bought of Lord Clynton & sould afterward to master Burde paid to master Parker, of Admiralte	1	1	0
for iij great Bookes of paper to kepe accountes	1	4	0
for fees of the billes of enterans of the merchandys in the Costome howse, but we paid no Custome & for the searchars fees at London for the dispache of the ij shippes Gabriell and Michaell	0	8	5
for wharfage & literage of divers thinges for the provisione of the ships	0	16	6

	li	s	d
porterage of the same	0	13	0
paid to N. Chauncelor purser for the charges of divers vitteles & other necesaries abord ships	2	4	6
charges of master Hogane, & his man aborde ships, & about receyt of sum mony of the venturares	0	9	6
bote hier of master Lok abord ships and places, about dyspache of his busynes, this halfe yeare	2	10	0
botehyer to Gravesends, with divers men to dispache the ships frome thens, and charges there ij dayes, of the masters and Companye of other maryners	2	7	0
postage of a letter sente to Harwiche after the shipps	1	10	0
some	13	4	0
	10	19	0
Sum these charges	24	3	0

		li	s	d
Summ totalis of all the paymentes before written amountethe as followithe				
for the hulle of the shippe Gabriell and buldinge a newe pynasse and reparinge the shipe Michaell fo. 3.		152	0	4
for the shipe Michaell, bought fo. 3.		120	0	0
for tackelinge and apparell fo. 4.		172	5	6
for ordinaunce and munitione fo. 4.		100	8	4
for vittelles fo. 6.		387	14	10
for Instrumentes of navigatione fo. 6		50	14	0
for wages beforhand fo. 8.		213	17	8
for Implementes fo. 8		8	11	0
Summ of the shippes		1205	11	8
for dyvers marchandyse so bought fo. 9.		213	5	8
Summ of all the charges of this voyage outwardes		1418	17	4

those shippes departed frome Gravesend, the 12 June 1576

the Michaell retorned to Blackewall, the j September

the Gabriell retorned to Harwyche, the 2 october 1576

the pynnasse, was loste by the way goynge

658. May to October, 1576. Martin
Frobisher's first expedition
in search of the Northwest Passage.

*This narrative, written by Christopher Hall who
was master of the* Gabriel, *is virtually the ship's
log. Its economy and repetitive nature are evidence, more eloquent than a discourse, of two
features of voyages of discovery to America.
Firstly, that the Atlantic had to be crossed in
weeks of ship's routine before discovery began;
and secondly, that the success of the voyage depended greatly on the skill of the ship's master,
whose duties, apart from the management of the
ship, were, especially in strange waters and new
latitudes, to take soundings, observe currents
and tides, and note the variation of the compass.
The account finishes with a vocabulary of the
Eskimo language, not given here.*

Printed in R. Hakluyt, Principall navigations
*(1589), pp. 615–622; reprinted in abbreviated
form in* Principal navigations, *III (1600), 57–60
(VII [1904], 204–211). The earlier version is reprinted here.*

Upon Munday the 13. of May the Barke was
launched at Redriffe, and upon the 27. day following she saled from Redriffe to Ratcliffe.

The 7. of June being Thursday, the two barkes,
viz. the *Gabriel,* the *Michael,*[1] and our pinnesse
set saile at Ratcliffe, and bare downe to Detford,
and there we ancred: the cuase was, that our
pinnesse burst her boultsprit, and foremast
aboard of a shippe that rode at Detford, else wee
ment to have past that day by the Court then at
Greenewiche.

The 8. day being Friday, about 12, of the clocke
we wayed at Detford, and set saile all three of us,
and bare downe by the Court, where we shotte off
our ordinance, and made the best shewe wee
could: Her Maiestie beholding the same commended it, and bade us farewell with shaking her
hand at us out of the windowe. Afterward she
sent a Gentleman a boorde of us, who declared
that her Maiestie had good liking of our doings,
and thanked us for it, and also willed our Captaine

1. Sidenote: "Master Matthew Kinderslye was Captaine of the Michael."

to come the next day to the Court to take his leave
of her.

The same day towards night Master Secretarie
Woolly came aboorde of us, and declared to the
companie, that her Maiestie had appointed him to
give them charge to be obedient, and diligent to
their Captaine, and governours in all things, and
wished us happie successe.

The ninth day about noone the winde being
Westerly, having our ancres abborde ready to set
saile to depart, wee wanted some of our companie, and therefore stayed, and moared them
againe.

Sunday the 10. of June, wee set saile from
Blackewall at a Southwest, and by West sunne,
the winde being at North Northwest, and sailed
to Gravesend, and ancred there at a West north-
west sunne, the winde being as before.

The 12. day being over against Gravesend, by
the castle or blockehouse we observed the
latitude, which was 51. degrees 33. min. And in
that place the variation of the Compasse is 11.
degrees and a halfe. This day we departed from
Gravesend, at a West Southwest sunne, the
winde at North and by East a faire gale, and
sailed to the West part of Tilberie hope, & so
turned downe the Hope, and at a West sunne the
winde came to the East Southeast, and wee
ancred in 7. fathome beinge lowe water.

The 13. day wee set saile at a Northeast sunne,
the winde at West Southwest, and sailed downe
the Sweane and over the Spits, and at a South
southwest sunne, the winde came to the East
Northeast, then we turned downe to the Naze and
so over the Naze, & in the traling ground, and so
came to ancre.

The 14. day we wayed at 3. of the clocke afternoone, the winde at Southeast, and sailed down to
Orfordnesse, and there ancred being litle winde,
and the floud in hand.

The 15. we wayed at 2. a clocke in the morning
being litle winde at North northwest, and sailed
down to Alborough, and thwart Alborough the
wind came to the Northnortheast, we turned
downe to Solde, and there ancred at 9. a clocke in
5. fathoms, and rode all the floud, and at a high
water being a stiffe gale at North Northeast wee
wayed and put roome with Harwiche at a North-
west sunne, being 9. a clocke at night.

The 16. day wee wayed and set saile at 3. of the
clocke afternoone the winde at South southeast,

& sailed to Alborough. And at that present the winde came to the Northnorthwest, and North a stiffe gale. We put roome with Orfordnesse, and there rode all the night.

The 17. day we wayed at Orfordnesse at a Southeast, & by East sunne, the winde at Northeast, and by North, a good gale, and put roome with Harwich, and ancred there at a South, and by East sunne, and did observe the latitude of the place which was 51. deg. 54 min.

The 18. day wee wayed at Harwich, at a Northeast sunne, the winde at West southwest, and sailed out of Harwich Hause.

The 19. day wee set saile from Yarmouth roade at a Southwest sunne, the winde at East Southeast, and sailed betwixt the Cockle and the maine in three fathome, and a halfe at three quarters floud. From 7. to 10. a clocke at night the winde at South Southeast, the shippe sailed Northwest three leagues.

From tenne a clocke at night to 2. of the clocke in the morning the winde at South southeast, a faire gale, the shippe sailed Northwest 4. leagues.

The 20. day in the morning from 2. of the clocke to sixe a clocke, the winde at South Southeast a faire gale, the shippe sailed Northwest foure leagues. From 6. a clocke to tenne of the clocke in the forenoone, the winde at South Southeast a faire gale, the shippe sailed Northwest eight glasses, foure leagues. From tenne a clocke to two a clocke foure leagues more. And from two to eight sixe leagues: from eight to midnight we sailed North Northwest five leagues, we sounded having 30. fathome, and fine sande with blackes among and one shell. From midnight to 4. a clocke in the morning, the shippe sailed with all sailes 6. leagues, and that watch out we sounded having 37. fathomes, and fine gray sand.

From 4. a clocke in the morning to 8. in the forenoone, being the 21. day, the winde at South Southeast, a faire gale, the shippe sailed North Northwest 8. glasses, 5. leagues, then Northnorthwest, 6. leagues, the maine yard acrosse: we sounded having 40. fathome, and fine sand. And at that present we observed the latitude, which was 54. degr. 41. min.

The 22. day from 4. a clocke in the morning till 4. a clocke the next morning we sailed with a faire Southeast winde, 38. leagues. This day from 4. to 8. of the clocke the winde as before the shippe sailed, North Northwest sixe leagues, sounded

50. fathome, and fine sand. From 8. a clocke till 12. a clocke at noone, the winde at South litle winde with fogge, the ship sailed North Northwest 3. leagues. I sounded having 54. fathome, and fine sand like oze.

From 12. to foure of the clocke, the winde at South Southwest little winde, the shippe sailed North 1. league with great fogge. At the end of ye watch sounded, having 55. fathome & smal sand. From 4. to 8. a clocke the winde at West Northwest, litle winde with fogge, the ship went North 2. leagues. Sounded having 50. fathome, and browne sand. From 8. to midnight, the winde at Northwest litle wind & fog, the ship went Northnortheast 3. leagues. From midnight to 4. a clocke in the morning ye wind at Northwest, & by North, smooth waters, ye ship went Northeast 3. leagues.

The 24 day from 4. to 8. a clocke in the forenoone, the wind at North northwest, faire weather, the sea smoothe, the ship went West, 3. leagues and a halfe, and at the end of this watche sounded, having 60. fathome, and ozie sand, & litle white shels. From 8. to 12. a clocke at noone, the winde at Northwest and by North, a faire gale, the sea smooth, the ship went West 3. leagues and a halfe: sounded having 53. fathome, and streame ground with litle shels. From 12. to 4. in the afternoone the winde at North northwest, the ship went Northnortheast 4. leagues.

At 2. of the clocke after noone I had sighte of Faire yle, being from us 6. leagues North, and by East, and when I brought it Northwest and by North, it did rise at the Southermost ende with a little hommocke, and swampe in the middes.

From 4. a clocke at afternoone to 8. a clocke litle wind, ye ship sailed Northnortheast 2. leagues. I sounded having 60. fathomes, & streamie ground with shels, 4. leagues from the land. From 8. a clocke to midnight calme, and without accompt. From midnight to 4. a clocke in the morning, the winde Northwest, and by North litle winde, the ship sailed Northnortheast 1. league.

The 25. day from 4. to 8. a clocke in the forenoon, the winde at Northwest, and by North a fresh gale, I cast about to the Westward, the Southermost head of Shotland called Swinborne head Northnorthwest from me, and the land of Fare yle, West Southwest from me. I sailed directly to the Northhead of that said land sounding as I ranne in, having 60. 50. and 40. fathoms, and gray redde shels; and within halfe a mile of that Island, there are 36. fathoms, for I sailed to that Island to see whether there were any rodsteede for a Northwest winde, and I found by my sounding hard rockes, and foule ground, and deepe water, within two cables length of the shoare, 28. fathome, and so did not ancre but plied to and fro with my foresaile, and mizen till it was a high water under the Island. The tide setteth there Northwest and Southeast: the floud setteth Southeast, and the ebb Northwest.

The 26. day I having the winde at South a faire gale, sayling from Fare yle to Swinborne head, I did observe the latitude, being the Island of Fowlay West Northwest from me 6. leagues, and Swinborne head East southeast from me, I found my elevation to be 37. degr. and my declination 22. degr. 46 min. So that my latitude was 59. degr. 46 min. At that present being neere to Swinborne head, having a leake which did trouble us, as also to take in fresh water, I plyed roome with a sound, which is called S. Tronions, and there did ancre in seven fathoms water, and faire sande. You have comming in the sounds mouth in the entring 17. 15. 12. 10. 9. 8. and 7. fathoms, and the sound lyeth in North Northwest, and there roade to a West sunne, and stopped our leake, and having refreshed our selves with water, at a North Northwest sunne, I set saile from S. Tronions the winde at South Southeast, and turned out till wee were cleare of the sound, and so sailed West to go cleare of the Island of Fowlay. And running off toward Fowlay, I sounded, having fiftie fathome, and streamie ground, and also I sounded Fowlay, being North from mee one league off that Island, having fiftie fathome at the South head, and streamie grounde, like broken otmell, and one shell being redde and white like mackerell.

The 27. day at a South sunne I did observe the latitude, being the Islande of Fowlay, from mee two leagues east Northeast: I founde my selfe to be in latitude 59. degrees, 59. min. truely observed, the winde at South Southeast: I sailed West and by North.

From 12. to foure a clocke afternoone, the winde at South, a faire gale the shippe sailed West and by North 6. leagues, and at the ende of this watch, I sounded having 60. fathome, with little stones and shels, the Island from us 8. leagues East.

From 4. to 8. a clocke the winde at South a good gale, the shippe sailed West and by North 6. leagues.

From 8. a clocke to midnight, the winde at South Southeast, a good gale, the ship sailed west, and by North 7. leagues, I sounded having 65. fathoms. In halling up the lead the line brake, and so we lost our lead.

From midnight to 4. a clocke in the morning, the winde at Southeast a good gale, our maine saile ferled our maine topsaile, foresaile, and spreetsaile abroad, the ship sailed West and by North 8. leagues.

The 28. day from 4. to eight a clocke, the winde at Southeast a good gale, the shippe sailed West and by North eight leagues: from eight to 12. a clocke, the winde at East Southeast a fresh gale, the shippe sailed West and by North eight leagues.

From 12. to 4. a clocke at afternoone, the winde at East Southeast, a fresh gale, the ship sailed East and by North 8. leagues.

From 4. to 8. a clocke at night, the winde at East Southeast a fresh gale, the ship sailed West 8. leagues. I did sound, and could not get ground at 70 fathome.

From 8. to midnight the winde at East Southeast a good gale, the ship sailed West 8. leagues.

From midnight to 4. a clocke in the morning, the winde at East Northeast, a fresh gale the ship sailed West 8. leagues and a halfe.

From 4. to 8. a clocke the 29. day the winde at East Northeast a good gale, the shippe sailed West 8. leagues.

From 8. to 12. a clocke at noone, the winde at East Northeast, the ship sailed West 8. leagues.

From 12. to 4. a clocke in the afternoone the winde at East Northeast a faire gale, the ship sailed West 6. leagues, and at the ende of this watche I did sound, and could get no ground at 100 fathome.

From 4. to 8. a clocke at night, we sailed West 5. leagues.

From 8. to midnight 4. leagues.

From midnight to 4. a clocke in the morning 4. leagues West.

The 30. day from 4. to 8. a clocke in the forenoone, we sailed West 3. leagues.

From 8. to 12. a clocke 3. leagues.

From 12. to 4. a clocke at afternoone West 5.

leagues. And at the end of this watch I sounded, having 100. fathome and no ground.

From 4. to 8. a clocke 6. leagues.

From 8. to midnight, we sailed West 8. leagues.

From midnight to 4. a clocke in the morning 8. leagues.

The first of July, from 4. to 8. a clocke, we sailed West 4. glasses 4. leagues, and at that present we had so much winde that we spooned afore the sea Southwest 2. leagues.

From 8. to 12 at noone West and by North 6. leagues.

From 4. to 8. foure miles.

From 8. to midnight we sailed with 2 courses 4. leagues West.

From midnight to 4. a clocke in the morning 6. leagues.

The second day from 4. to 8. a clocke, 6 leagues and a halfe West.

From 8. to 12. West 7. leagues. From 12. to 4. at afternoone West 7 leagues more. And at the ende of this watch I sounded having 100. fathome, and no ground.

From 4. to 8. at night 7. leagues. From 8. to midnight West, and by North 7. leagues.

From midnight to 4. a clocke in the morning west and by North 6. leagues.

The 3. day we found our Compasse to bee varied one point to the Westwards: this day from 4. to 8. a clocke we sailed West, and by North 6. leagues.

From 8. to 12. a clocke at noone West, and by North 4. leagues. At that present I found our Compasse to be varied 11. deg. and one 4. part to the Westwards which is one point.

From 12. to 4. a clocke at afternoone West and by North, one league.

From 4. to 8. West, and by North, one league.

From 8. to midnight West. and by North 2. leagues.

From midnight to 4. a clocke in the morning West, and by North 3. leagues.

The 4. day from 4. to 8. the winde at Northwest and by North 4. leagues.

From 8. to 12. at noone West and by North 2. leagues. And at that present we sent off our pinnesse from the Gabriel to fish being calme.

From 12. to 4. a clocke at afternoone calme, and without accompt.

From 4. to 8. a clocke at night, West and by North 2. leagues.

From 8. to midnight West, and by North 7. leagues.

From midnight to 4. a clocke in the morning 9. leagues.

The 5. day from 4. to 8. a clocke West and by North 8. leagues.

From 8. to 12. having raine and fogge, West and by North 6. leagues.

From 12. to 4. at afternoone West and by North 5. leagues. From 4. to 8. North Northwest 6. leagues. From 8. to midnight North and by West 4. leagues.

From midnight to 6. a clocke in the morning wee hulled by the winde, and went West and by North 5. leagues.

From 12. to 4. a clocke West and by North 5. leagues.

From 8. at night to 8. in the morning 4. leagues.

From 12. to 4. a clocke at afternoone, North Northwest 4. leagues.

From 4. to 8. at night North Northwest 4. leagues.

From 8. to midnight, North two leagues.

From midnight to 8. a clocke calme, and without accompt.

The 8. day from 8. to 12. at noone, 3. leagues West.

From 12. to 4. a clocke West, 6. leagues.

From 4. to 8. eight leagues.

From 8. to midnight wee tooke in all our sailes, and spooned afore the sea because of our pinnesse, and at that present came fogge and miste, and so we lost sight of her. Wee sailed West five leagues.

From midnight to 4. a clocke, West southwest 4. leagues, with very much winde.

From 4. to 8. in the forenoone, the sea being mightily growne, 4. leagues.

From 8. to 12. Southwest afore the sea 4. leagues.

From 12. to 4. a clocke, West Southwest 5. leagues.

From that time to 8. a clocke the next day I layd the ship a hul, her way was south 4. leagues.

From 8. to 4. a clocke calme, and without accompt.

From 4. to 8. six leagues. From 8. to midnight 7. leagues.

From midnight to 4. a clocke, North 8. leagues.

From 4. to 8. a clocke, West and by south 5. leagues. From 8. to 12. a clocke at noone West, and by south 4. leagues, & at the southeast sunne we had sight of the land of Friseland bering from us West northwest 16. leagues, and rising like pinacles of steeples, and all covered with snow. I found my selfe in 61. degr. of latitude. We sailed to the shoare & could finde no ground at 150. fathome, we hoised out our boate, & the Captaine with 4. men rowed to the shoare to get on land, but the land lying full of yce they could not get on land, and so they came aboorde againe: Wee had much adoe to get cleare of the yce by reason of the fogge. Yet from Thursday 8. a clocke in the morning to Friday at noone we sailed Southwest 20 leagues.

The 13. day, a Northeast wind cleared us of the thicke miste, & we sailed southwest 5. leagues.

The 14. day the vehemencie of thewinde brake our foreyarde, and bore over boord our myssen maste, so we put our spreetsaile yard, with the spreetsaile coarse to our foremast, and spooned afore the sea Southwest 15. leagues, till it was Sunday.

This day from 4. in ye afternoone to 8. we sailed Southwest, we sailed 6. leagues. From thence to Munday morning 4. of the clocke, calme, and without accompt.

The 16. day from 4. to 8. the winde at South southwest, we sailed 6. leagues and a half. From 8. to 12. 5. leagues and a halfe, and from 12. to 4. 6 leagues. At the end of this watch, the head of our maine mast, maine topmaste, with the topsaile brake, and fel into the sea altogether.

From 4. to 8. we ranne somewhat a drift, because we layd up the ropes of our maine mast, and set our maine saile againe. From 8. to midnight, Northwest and by West 3. leagues.

The 17. day from 4. to 8. 3. leagues. From 8. to 12. two leagues, from 12. to 4. at afternoone 3. leagues, from 4. to 8. a clocke 3. leagues, in our old course: I prooved to sounde but founde no ground. From 8. to midnight, West and by South 2. leagues from midnight to 4. a clocke in the morning 2. leagues.

From 4. to 8. three leagues, from 8. to 12. at noone 3. leagues, and here at a Southeast sunne, I found the sunne to be elevated 33. deg. And at a Southsoutheast 40. deg. So I observed it till I founde it at the highest, and then it was elevated 52. degr. I judged the variation of the Compasse to be 2. points and a halfe to the Westward.

From 12. to 4. three leagues, from 4. to 8. three leagues, from 8. to midnight 2. leagues, From midnight to 4. a clocke one league, being litle winde.

From 4. to 8. North, 4. leagues, from 8. to 12. 8. leagues, from 12. to 4. foure leagues, from 4. to 8. 4. leagues, and at the end of this watch we cast about to the Eastwards. From 8. to midnight 3. leagues, from midnight 4. a clocke East and by North 3. leagues.

From 4. to 8. 3. leagues, from 8. to 12. 3. leagues, from 12. to 4. 4. leagues. From 4. to 8. three leagues, from 8. to midnight 4. leagues. From midnight to 4. a clocke 4. leagues. From 8. to 12. Northnortheast 4. leagues. From 12. to 4. 4. leagues, from 4. to 8. 4 leagues, from 8. to midnight foure leagues Northeast. From midnight to 4. a clocke, Northeast foure leagues, and at the ende of this watch we had sight of a great drift of yce, seeing a firme land, and we cast Westward to be cleare of it.

From 4. to 8. southwest 3. leagues, from 8. to 12. 2. leagues, from 12. to 6. 3. leagues, from 6. at night to sixe the next morning, northeast five leagues.

From 6. to 12. west five leagues, from 12. to 4. northnorthwest, 6. leagues: from 4. to 8. north northeast, 8. leagues: from 8. to midnight, 7. leagues: from midnight to 4. of the clocke, North northwest, 7. leagues.

From 4. to 8. 7. leagues: from 8. to 12. 7. leagues more: from 12. to 4. 5. leagues: from 4. to 8. 5. leagues: from thence to midnight, 6. leagues: from midnight to 4. of the clocke in the morning, west, northwest, 6. leagues.

From 4. to 8, 7. leagues: from 8. to 12. 7. leagues: from 12 to 4, 8. leagues: from 12. to 4, 8. leagues: from 4. to 8, 8. leagues: from 8. to midnight, 4. leagues, west, northwest, and with fogge: from midnight to 4. of the clocke, 4. leagues.

This day was litle wind, and we tried with both our courses: we had sight of a land of yce: the latitude was 62. degrees, two minuts. We ran from 12. to 4. 4. miles.

From 4. to 8, 4. miles: from 8. to 4. calme, and fogge: from thence to 4. of the clocke in the morninge calme, and foggie also.

From 4. to 8, 4. leagues: from 8. to 12, 3. leagues: from 12. to 4. northwest and by west, sixe leagues, but very foggie: from thence to 8. of the clocke in the morning, little wind: but at the clearing up of the fogge, we had sight of lande, which I supposed to be Labrador, with great store of yce about the land: I ran in towards it, and sounded, but could get no ground, at 100. fathom, and the yce being so thicke, I could not get to the shoare, and so lay off, and came cleare of the yce. Upon Munday, we came within a mile of the shoare, and sought a harborowe: all the sound was full of yce, and our boate rowing a shoare, could get no ground, at 100. fathom, within a Cables length of the shoare: then we sailed East northeast along the shoare, for so the lande lieth, and the currant is there great, setting northeast, and southwest: and if we could have gotten anker ground, we would have seen with what force it had runne, but I judge a ship may drive a league and a halfe, in one howre, with that tide.

This day, at 4. of the clocke in the morning, being faire and cleere, we had sight of a head land, as we judged, bearing from us north, and by East, and we sailed Northeast, and by North to that lande, and when wee came thither, wee could not gette to the lande for yce: for the yce stretched along the coaste, so that we could not come to the land, by five leagues.

Wensday the first of August, it calmed, and in the after noone, I caused my boate to be hoysed out, being hard by a great Island of yce, and I and foure men rowed to that yce, and sounded within two cables length of it, and had sixteene fathome, and little stones, and after that sounded againe within a Minion shotte, and had ground, at an hundreth fathome, and faire sand: we sownded the next day a quarter of a myle from it, and had sixtie fathome rough grounde, and at that present being aboord, that great Island of yce fell one part from another, making a noyce as if a great cliffe had fallen into the Sea. And at foure of the clocke, I sownded againe, and had 90. fathome, and small blacke stones, and little white stones, like pearles. The tide here did set to the shoare.

We sailed this day south southeast ofward, and layd it a trie.

The next day was calme and thicke, with a great sea.

The next day we sailed South, and by East, two leagues, and at eight of the clocke in the foore noone we cast about to the Eastwards.

The sixt day it cleered, and we ranne northwest into the shoare, to get a harborough, and being towards night, we notwithstanding kept at sea.

The seventh day we plied roome with the shoare, but being neere it, it waxed thicke, and we bare off againe.

The eight day we bended in towards the shoare againe.

The ninth day we sownded, but could gette no grounde at 130. fathome: the weather was calme.

The tenth I tooke foure men, and my selfe, and rowed to shoare to an Island one league from the maine, and there the floode setteth Southwest alongest the shoare, and it floweth as neere as I could judge so too, I could not tarry to proove it, because the shippe was a great way from me, and I feared a fogge: but when I came a shoare, it was a lowe water. I went to the toppe of the Island, and before I came backe, it was hied a foote water, and so without tarrying, I came aboord.

The 11. we found our latitude to be 63. degrees, and eight minutes, and this day entred the streight.

The 12. we set saile towardes an Island, called Gabriels Island, which was 10. leagues then from us.

We espied a sownd, and bare with it, and came to a sandie Baye, where we came to an anker, the lande bearing Eastsoutheast of us, and there we rode all night in 8. fathome water. It floweth there at a Southeast Moone. We called it Priors sownd, being from the Gabriels Island, tenne leagues.

The 14. we waied, and ranne into another sownde, where we ankered in 8. fathome water, faire sand, and blacke oaze, and there calked our ship, being weake from the wales upward, and tooke in fresh water.

The 15. day we waied, and sailed to Priors Baye, being a mile from thence.

The 16. day was calme, and wee rode still, without yce, but presently within two howres it was frozen round about the shippe, a quarter of an ynche thicke, and that daye very faire, and calme.

The 17. day we waied, and came to Thomas Williams Island.

The 18. day, we sailed north northwest, and ankered againe in 23. fathome, and tought oaze, under Butchers Island, which is from the former Island, ten leagues.

The 19. day in the morning, being calme, and no winde, the Captaine and I, tooke our boate, with eight men in her, to rowe us a shoare, to see if there were there any people, or no, and going to the toppe of the Island, we had sight of seven boates, which came rowing from the East side, toward that Island: whereupon we returned aboord againe: at length we sent our boate with five men in her, to see whither they rowed, and so with a white cloth brought one of their boates with their men along the shoare, rowing after our boate, till such time as they sawe our shippe, and then they rowed a shoare: then I went on shoare my selfe, and gave every of them a thredden point, and brought one of them aboord of me, where he did eate and drinke, and then carried him on shoare againe. Whereuppon all the rest came aboord with their boates, beeing nineteene persons, and they spake, but we understoode them not. They be like to Tartars, with long blacke haire, broad faces, and flatte noses, and tawnie in colour, wearing Seale skinnes, and so doe the women, not differing in the fashion, but the women are marked in the face with blewe streekes downe the cheekes, and round the eies. Their boates are made all of Seale skins, with a keele of wood within the skinne: the proportion of them is like a Spanish shallop, save only they be flat in the bottome, and sharpe at both endes.

The twentieth day, wee wayed, and wente to the East side of this Island, and I and the Captaine, with foure men more went on shoare, and there wee sawe their houses, and the people espying us, came rowing towardes our boate: whereuppon wee plied to our boate: and wee beeing in our boate, and they ashoare, they called to us, and wee rowed to them, and one of their companie came into our boate, and wee carried him aboord, and gave him a Bell, and a knife: so the Captaine and I willed five of our men to set him a shoare at a rocke, and not among the companie, which they came from, but their wilfulnes was such, that they would goe to them, and so were taken themselves, and our boate lost.

The next daye in the morning, wee stoode in neere the shoare, and shotte of a fauconet, and sownded our trumpet, but wee coulde heare nothing of our men: this sownde wee called the five mens sownde, and plyed out of it, but ankered againe in thirtie fathome, and oaze: and riding there all night, in the morning, the snowe laye a foote thicke uppon our hatches.

The two and twentieth daye in the morning, we wayed, and went againe to the place where wee lost our men, and our boate. Wee had sight of

foureteene boates, and some came neere to us, but we coulde learne nothing of our men: among the rest, we intised one in a boate to our shippes side, with a Bell, and in giving him the Bell, wee tooke him, and his Boate, and so kept him, and so rowed downe to Thomas Williams Island, and there ankered all night.

The 26. day we waied, to come homeward, and by 12. of the clocke at noone, we were thwart of Trumpets Island.

The next day, we came thwart of Gabriels Island, and at 8. of the clocke at night, we had the Cape Labradore West from us, ten leagues.

The 28. day we went our course Southeast.

The first day of September in the morning, we had sight of the land of Friseland, being eight leagues from us, but we could not come neerer it, for the monstrous yce that lay about it. From this day, till the sixth of this Moneth, wee ranne along Island, and had the South part of it at eight of the clocke, east from us ten leagues.

The seventh day of this moneth, we had a very terrible storme, by force whereof, one of our men was blowen into the sea out of our waste, but he caught holde of the foresaile sheate, and there held, till the Captaine pluckt him againe into the ship.

The 25. day of this moneth, we had sight of the Island of Orknye, which was then East from us.

The first day of October, we had sight of the Sheld, and so sailed along the coast, and ankered at Yarmouth, and the next day we came into Harwiche.

659. May to October, 1577. The second Frobisher voyage for the discovery of the Northwest Passage.

This account was written by Dionyse Settle, one of the gentlemen who made the voyage. It was published as A true reporte of the last voyage ... by Capteine Frobisher *(London, 1577), and was dedicated to George Clifford, Earl of Cumberland. It was the first piece of American exploration literature to be translated and circulated widely in European countries.*

Reprinted in R. Hakluyt, Principall navigations *(1589), pp. 622–630, and* Principal navigations, *III (1600), 32–39 (VII [1904], 211—230).*

A true report of Capteine Frobisher his last voyage into the West and Northwest regions, this present yere 1577. With a description of the people there inhabiting.

On Whitsunday last past, being the 26. of May, in this present yeare of our Lorde God 1577. Capteine Frobisher departed from Blacke Wall, with one of the Queenes Majesties shippes, called The Aide, of nine score tunne, or there aboutes: and two other little Barkes likewise, the one called The Gabriel, whereof Maister Fenton a Gentleman of my Lord of Warwicks was Capteine: and the other, The Michael, whereof Maister Yorke a Gentleman of my Lorde Admerals was Captein, accompanied with seven score gentlemen, souldiers and saylers, well furnished with victuals, and other prouision necessarie for one halfe yere, on this his seconde voyage, for the further discovering of the passage to Cataia, and other countries thereunto adjacent, by West and Northwest Navigations: whiche passage, or way, is supposed to be on the North and Northwest partes of America: and the sayd America to be an Islande invironed with the sea, wherethrough our Merchaunts might haue course and recourse with their merchandize, from these our Northernmost parts of Europe, to those oriental coasts of Asia, in much shorter time, and with greater benefit then any others, to their no little commoditie and profite that doe traffique the same. Oure sayde Capteine and Generall of this present voyage and companie, having the yere before, with two little Pinnisies, to his great daunger and no small commendations, given a worthy attempt towardes the performaunce thereof, is also prest (when occasion shall be ministred, to the benefite of his Prince and native countrie) to adventure him selfe further therein. As for this second voyage, it seemeth sufficient, that he hath better explored and searched the commodities of those people and countries, with sufficient commoditie unto the adventurers, which in his first voyage the yeare before he had found out.

Upon which considerations, the day and yeare before expressed, we departed from Blacke Wall to Harwiche, where making an accomplishment of thinges necessarie, the last of Maye we hoysed up sailes, and with a mery winde the 7. therof we arrived at the Islands called Orchades, or vulgarly Orkney, being in number 30. subject and adjacent to Scotland, where we made provision of freshe water: in the doing whereof, our Generall licenced the Gentlemen and Souldiers, for their recreation, to go on shoare. At our landing, the people fled from their poore cotages, with shrikes and alarums, to warne their neighbors of enimies: but by gentle persuasions we reclaimed them to their houses. It seemeth they are often frighted with Pirates, or some other enimies, that moveth them to such souden feare. Their houses are very simplie builded with pibble stone, without any chimneys, the fire being made in the midde thereof. The good man, wife, children, and other of their familie, eate and sleepe on the one side of the house, and their cattell on the other, very beastly and rudely, in respect of civilitie. They are destitute of wood, their fire is turffes and Cowe shardes. They have corne, bigge, and oates, with whiche they paye their Kinges rente, to the maintenance of his house. They take great quantitie of fishe, which they drie in the winde and Sunne. They dresse their meate very filthily, and eate it without salt. Their apparell is after the rudest sort of Scotland. Their money is all base. Their churche and religion is reformed according to the Scots. The fisher men of England, can better declare the dispositions of those people than I: wherfore, I remit other their usages to their reportes, as yearely repairers thither, in their course to and from Island for fish.

Wee departed herehence, the 8. of June, and followed our course betweene West and Northwest, untill the 4. of Julie: all which time, we had no night, but that easily, and without any impediment, we had when we were so disposed, the fruition of our bookes, and other pleasures to passe awaye the time: a thinge of no small moment, to such as wander in unknowen seas and longe Navigations, especially, when both the winds, and raging surges, do passe their common and wonted course. This benefite endureth in those partes not six weekes, whilest the Sunne is neere the Tropike of Cancer: but where the Pole is raised to 70. or 80. degrees, in continueth the longer.

All along these seas, after we were 6. dayes sayling from Orkney, we met floting in the sea, great Firre trees, which as wee judged, were with the furie of great floudes roote up, and so driven into the sea. Island hath almost no other wood nor fewel, but such as they take up upon their coastes. It seemeth, that these trees are driven from some parte of the New found land, with the Current that setteth from the West to the East.

The 4. of Julie, we came within the making of Freeseland. From this shoare 10. or 12. leagues, we met great Islands of yce, of halfe a mile, some more, some lesse in compasse, shewing above the sea 30. or 40. fathomes; and as we supposed, fast on ground, where, with oure leade wee could scarse sound the bottome for deapth.

Here, in place of odoriferous and fragrant smelles of sweete gummes, and pleasant notes of musicall birdes, which other Countries in more temperate Zone do yeeld, we tasted the most boisterous Boreall blasts, mixt with snow and haile, in the moneth of June and Julie, nothing inferiour to oure untemperate Winter: a soudeine alteration, and especially in a place or Paralele, where the Pole is not elevate above 61. degrees: at which height other countries more to the North, yea, unto 70. degrees, shewe themselves more temperat than this doth.

All along this coast yce lyeth, as a continuall bullworke, and so defendeth the countrie, that those whiche would land there incurre great daunger. Our Generall three dayes together, attempted with the shippboate to have gone on shoare, whiche, for that without great daunger he could not accomplishe, he deferred it until a more convenient time. All along the coast lye very highe mounteines covered with snowe, excepte in such places, where, through the steepenesse of the mounteines, of force it must needes fall.

Foure dayes coastinge along this Land, we found no signe of habitation. Little birdes, whiche we judged to have lost yᵉ shoare, by reason of thicke fogges, which that countrie is much subiect unto, came fleeting to oure shippes, whiche causeth us to suppose, that the countrie is both more tollerable, and also habitable within, then the outward shoare maketh shewe or signification.

From hence we departed the eight of Julie: and the 16. of the same, we came within the making of land, whiche land our Generall, the yeare before, had named The Queenes foreland, beeing an Island, as we judge, lying neere the supposed continent with America: & on the other side, opposite to yᵉ same, one other Island called Halles Isle, after the name of the Maister of our shippe, neere adjacent to the firme land, supposed continent

with Asia. Betweene the which two Islandes, there is a large entrance or streight, called Frobishers streight, after the name of oure Generall, the first finder thereof. This said streight, is supposed to have passage into the Sea of Sur, which I leave unknowne as yet.

It seemeth, that either here, or not farre hence, the Sea should have more large entraunce, than in other partes, within the frosen or untemperate Zone: and that some contrarie tide, either from the East or West, with maine force casteth out that great quantitie of yce, which commeth floating from this coast, even unto Freesland, causing that contrie to seeme more untemperate than others, muche more Northerly than they are.

I cannot judge, that any temperature under the Pole, beeing the time of the Sunnes Northerne declination, halfe a yeare together and one whole day, (considering, that the Sunnes elevation surmounteth not 23. degrees and 30. minutes,) can have power to dissolve such monstruous and huge yce, comparable to great mounteines, excepte by some other force, as by swift Currents and tydes, with the helpe of the said day of halfe a yeare.

Before we came within the making of these Landes, we tasted cold stormes, insomuch that it seemed, we had chaunged Summer with winter, if the length of the dayes had not removed us from that opinion.

At our first comming, the streightes seemed to be shutt up with a long mure of yce, whiche gave no little cause of discomfort unto us all: but our Generall, (to whose diligence, imminent daungers, and difficult attemptes seemed nothing, in respect of his willing mind, for the commoditie of his Prince and countrie,) with two little Pinnises prepared of purpose, passed twise thoroughe them to the East shoare, and the Islands there unto adjacent: and the shippe, with the two barks, lay off and on something further into the sea, from the daunger of the yce.

Whilest he was searching the countrie neere the shoare, some of the people of the countrie shewed themselves, leaping and dauncing, with straunge shrikes and cryes, whiche gave no little admiration to our men. Our Generall desirous to allure them unto him by faire meanes, caused knives, & other thinges, to be preferred unto them, whiche they would not take at our handes: but beeing layd on the ground, & the partie going away, they came and tooke up, leaving something of theirs to countervaile ye fame. At the length, two of them leaving their weapons, came downe to our Generall and Maister, who did the like to them, commaunding the companie to stay, and went unto them: who, after certeine dumbe signes and mute congratulations, began to lay handes upon them, but they deliverly escaped, and ranne to their bowes and arrowes, and came fiercely uppon them, (not respecting the rest of our companie, which were readie for their defence) but with their arrowes hurt diverse of them: we tooke the one, and the other escaped.

Whilest our Generall was busied in searching the countrie and those Islands adjacent on the East shoare, the ship and barckes having great care, not to put farre into the sea from him, for that he had small store of victuals, were forced to abide in a cruell tempest, chancing in the night, amongst and in the thickest of the yce, which was so monstruous, that even the least of a thousand had beene of force sufficient, to have shivered oure shippe and barkes into small portions, if God (who in all necessities, hath care upon the infirmitie of man) had not provided for this our extremitie a sufficient remedie, through the light of the night, whereby we might well discerne to flee from such imminent daungers, whiche wee a-voyded with 14. Bourdes in one watch the space of 4. houres. If we had not incurred this danger amongst these monstrous Islandes of yce, wee should have lost our Generall and Maister, and the most of our best sailers, which were on the shoare destitute of victualls: but by the valure of our Maister Gunner [*Richard Coxe*], being expert both in Navigation and other good qualities, we were all content to incurre the dangers afore rehearsed, before we would, with oure owne safetie, runne into the Seas, to the destruction of oure said Generall and his companie.

The day following, being the 19. of Julie, oure Capteine returned to the shippe, with good newes of great riches, which shewed it selfe in the bowelles of those barren mounteines, wherewith we were all satisfied. A souden mutation. The one parte of us being almost swallowed up the night before, with cruell Neptunes force, and the rest on shoare, taking thought for their greedie paunches, how to find the way to New found land: at one moment we were all rapt with joye, forgetting, both where we were, and what we had

suffred. Behold the glorie of man, to night contemning riches, and rather looking for death than otherwise: and to morrowe devising howe to satisfie his greedie appetite with Golde.

Within foure days after we had ben at the entraunce of the Streightes, the Northwest and West windes dispersed the yce into the Sea, and made us a large entrance into the Streights, that without any impediment, on the 19. of Julie, we entred them, and the 20. therof oure Generall and Maister, with great diligence, sought out and sounded the West shoare, and found out a fayre Harborough for the ship and barkes to ride in, and named it after our Maisters mate, Jackmans found, and brought the ship, barkes, and all their companie to safe anchor, except one man, whiche dyed by Gods visitation.

Who so maketh Navigations to these contries, hath not only extreme winds, and furious Seas, to encounter withall, but also many monstrous and great Islands of yce: a thing both rare, wonderfull, and greatly to be regarded.

We were forced, sundrie times, while the ship did ride here at anchor, to have continuall watch, with boates and men readie with Halsers, to knit fast unto such yce, which with the ebbe and floud were tossed to and fro in the Harboroughe, and with force of oares to hale them away, for endaungering the ship.

Our Generall; certeine dayes searched this supposed continent with America, and not finding the commoditie to aunswere his expectation, after he had made tryall thereof, he departed thence with two little barkes, and men sufficient, to the East shoare, being the supposed continent of Asia, & left the ship with most of the Gentlemen, Souldiers, and Saylers, untill such time as he, eyther thought good to send, or come for them.

The stones of this supposed continent with America, be altogether sparkled, and glister in the Sunne like Gold: so likewise doth the sande in the bright water, yet they verifie the olde Proverbe: All is not golde that glistereth.

On this West shoare we found a dead fishe floating, whiche had in his nose a horne streight & torquet, of lengthe two yardes lacking two ynches, being broken in the top, where we might perceive it hollowe, into which some of our Saylers putting Spiders, they presently dyed. I sawe not the tryall hereof, but it was reported unto me of a trueth: by the vertue whereof, we supposed it to be the sea Unicorne.

After our Generall had founde out good harborough for the Ship and Barkes to anchor in: and also suche store of Golde oare as he thought him selfe satisfied withall, he sent backe oure Maister with one of the Barkes, to conducte the great Ship unto him, who coasting along the West shoare, perceived a faire harborough, and willing to sound the same, at the enterance thereof they espyed two tentes of Seale skinnes.

At the sight of oure men, the people fled into the mounteines: neverthelesse, our sayde Maister went to their tents, and left some of our trifles, as Knives, Bels, and Glasses, and departed, not taking any thing of theirs, excepte one Dogge to our Shippe.

On the same day, after consultation had, we determined to see, if by fayre meanes we could eyther allure them to familiaritie, or otherwise take some of them, and so atteine to some knowledge of those men, whome our Generall lost the yeare before.

At our comming backe againe, to the place where their tentes were before, they had removed their tentes further into the said Bay or Sound, where they might, if they were driven from the land, flee with their boates into the sea. Wee parting our selves into two companies, and compassing a mounteine, came soudeinly uppon them by land, who espying us, without any tarying fled to their boates, leaving the most part of their oares behind them for hast, and rowed downe the Bay, where our two Pinisses met them, & drove them to shoare: but, if they had had all their oares, so swift are they in rowing, it had bene lost time to have chased them.

When they were landed, they fiercely assaulted oure men with their bowes and arrowes, who wounded three of them with our arrowes: and perceyving them selves thus hurt, they desperately leapt off the Rocks into the Sea, and drowned them selves: which if they had not done, but had submitted them selves: or if by any meanes we could have taken them alive, (being their enimies as they judged) we would both have saved them, and also have sought remedie to cure their woundes received at our handes. But they, altogether voyde of humanitie, and ignorant what

mercy meaneth, in extremities looke for no other then death: and perceiving they should fall into our hands, thus miserably by drowning rather desired death, then otherwise to be saved by us: the rest, perceiving their fellowes in this distresse, fled into the highe mounteines. Two women, not being so apt to escape as the men were, the one for her age, and the other being incombred with a yong childe, we tooke. The olde wretch, whome divers of oure Saylers supposed to be eyther a Divell, or a Witche, plucked off her buskins, to see, if she were cloven footed, and for her ougly hewe and deformitie, we let her goe: the young woman and the childe, we brought away. We named the place where they were slayne, Bloudie point: and the Bay or Harborough, Yorkes sound, after the name of one of the Capteines of the two Barkes.

Having this knowledge, both of their fiercenesse and crueltie, and perceiving that fayre meanes, as yet, is not able to allure them to familiaritie, we disposed our selves, contrarie to our inclination, something to be cruel, returned to their tentes, and made a spoyle of the same. Their riches are neyther Gold, Silver, or precious Draperie, but their sayde tentes and boates, made of the skinnes of red Deare and Seale skinnes: also, Dogges like unto Woolves, but for the most part black, with other trifles, more to be wondred at for their strangenesse, then for any other commoditie needeful for our use.

Thus returning to our Ship, the 3. of August, we departed from the West shoare, supposed firme with America, after we had anchored there 13. dayes: and so, the 4. thereof, we came to our Generall on the East shoare, and anchored in a fayre Harborough named Anne Warrwickes sound, unto whiche is annexed an Islande both named after the Countesse of Warrwicke, Anne Warrwickes sound and Isle.

In this Isle, our Generall thought good, for this voyage, to frayght both the Ship and Barkes, with suche Stone or Gold minerall, as he judged to countervaile the charges of his first, and this his second Navigation to these contries, with sufficient interest to ye venturers, wherby they might bothe be satisfied for this time, and also in time to come, (if it please God and our Prince,) to expect a much more large benefite, out of the bowells of those Septentrionall Paralels, which long time hath concealed it self, til at this present, through the wonderfull diligence, & great danger of our Generall and others, God is contented with the revealing thereof. It riseth so aboundantly, that from the beginning of August, to the 22. thereof. (every man following the diligence of our General) we raysed above grounde 200. tunne, which we judged a reasonable fraight for the Shippe and two Barkes, in the sayde Anne Warrwicks Isle.

In the time of our abode here, some of the countrie people, came to shewe them selves unto us, sundrie times on ye maine shoare, neere adjacent to the sayd Isle. Our Generall, desirous to have some newes of his men, whome he lost the yeare before, with some companie with him repayred with the Ship boat, to common, or signe with them for familiaritie, whereunto he is persuaded to bring them. They, at the first shewe, made tokens, that three of his five men were alive, and desired penne, ynck, and paper, and that within three or foure dayes, they could returne, and (as we judged) bring those of our men, whiche were living, with them.

They also made signes or tokens of their King, whom they called Cacough, and how he was carried on mens shoulders, and a man farre surmounting any of our companie, in bignesse and stature.

With these tokens and signes of writing, penne, yncke, and paper was delivered them, which they woulde not take at our handes: but being layde upon the shoare, and the partie gone away, they tooke up: which likewise they doe, when they desire any thing for chaunge of theirs, laying for that which is left, so much as they think will countervaile the same, and not comming neare together. It seemeth they have bene used to this trade or traffique, with some other people adjoyning, or not farre distant from their Countrie.

After 4. dayes, some of them shewed themselves upon the firme land, but not where they were before. Our General, very glad thereof, supposing to heare of our men, went from the Islande, with the boate, and sufficient companie with him. They seemed very glad, and allured him, about a certeine point of the land: behind which they might perceive a companie of the craftie villains to lye lurking, whome our Generall woulde not deale withall, for that he knewe not what companie they were, and so with fewe

signes dismissed them, and returned to his companie.

An other time, as our said Generall was coasting the contrie, with two litle Pinisses, whereby at oure returne hee might make the better relation thereof, three of the craftie villains, with a white skin allured us to them. Once againe, our Generall, for that he hoped to heare of his men, went towardes them: at oure comming neere the shoare, wheron they were we might perceive a number of them lie hidden behind great stones, & those three in sight labouring by all meanes possible, that some woulde come on land: & perceyving wee made no hast by words nor friendly signes, which they used by clapping of their handes, and beeing without weapon, and but three in sighte, they sought further meanes to provoke us thereunto. One alone layd flesh on the shoare, whiche we tooke upp with the Boate hooke, as necessarie victualls for the relieving of the man, woman, & child, whom we had taken: for that as yet, they could not digest oure meate: whereby they perceived themselves deceived of their expectation, for all their craftie allurements. Yet once againe, to make (as it were) a full shewe of their craftie natures, and subtile sleightes, to the intent thereby to have intrapped and taken some of our men, one of them counterfeyted himselfe impotent and lame of his legges, who seemed to descend to the water side, with great difficultie: and to cover his crafte the more, one of his fellowes came down with him, and in such places, where he seemed unable to passe, hee tooke him on his shoulders, set him by the water side, and departed from him, leaving him (as it should seeme) all alone, who playing his counterfeite pageant very well, thought thereby to provoke some of us to come on shoare, not fearing, but that any one of us might make oure partie good with a lame man.

Our Generall, having compassion of his impotencie, thought good (if it were possible) to cure him therof: wherfore, hee caused a souldiour to shoote at him with his Caleever, which grased before his face. The counterfeite villeine deliverly fled, without any impediment at all, and gott him to his bowe and arrowes, and the rest from their lurking holes, with their weapons, bowes, arrowes, slings, and darts. Our Generall caused some Caleevers to be shot off at them, whereby some being hurt, they mighte hereafter stand in more feare of us.

This was all the aunswere, for this time, wee could have of our men, or of our Generalls letter. Their craftie dealing, at these three severall times, being thus manifest unto us, maye plainely shewe, their disposition in other thinges to be correspondent. We judged, that they used these stratagemmes, thereby to have caught some of us, for the delivering of the man, woman, & child whome we have taken.

They are men of a large corporature, and good proportion: their colour is not much unlike the Sunne burnte Countrie man, who laboureth daily in the Sunne for his living.

They weare their haire somethinge long, and cut before, either with stone or knife, very disorderly. Their women weare their haire long, and knit up with two loupes, shewing forth on either side of their faces, and the rest foltred up on a knot. Also, some of their women race their faces proportionally, as chinne, cheekes, and forehead, and the wristes of their handes, whereupon they lay a colour, which continueth darke azurine.

They eate their meate all rawe, both fleshe, fishe, and foule, or something perboyled with bloud & a little water, whiche they drinke. For lacke of water, they wil eate yce, that is hard frosen, as pleasantly as we will doe Sugar Candie, or other Sugar.

If they, for necessities sake, stand in neede of the premisses, such grasse as the countrie yeeldeth they plucke uppe, and eate, not deintily, or salletwise, to allure their stomaches to appetite: but for necessities sake, without either salt, oyles, or washing, like brutish beasts devoure the same. They neither use table, stoole, or table cloth for comelinesse: but when they are imbrued with bloud, knuckle deepe, and their knives in like sort, they use their tongues as apt instruments to licke them cleane: in doeing whereof, they are assured to loose none of their victuals.

They franck or keep certeine doggs, not much unlike Wolves, whiche they yoke together, as we do oxen and horses, to a sled or traile: and so carrie their necessaries over the yce and snowe, from place to place: as the captive, whom we have, made perfecte signes. And when those Dogges are not apt for the same use: or when with hunger they are constreyned, for lacke of other

victuals, they eate them: so that they are as needefull for them, in respect of their bignesse, as our oxen are for us.

They apparell themselves in the skinnes of such beasts as they kill, sewed together with the sinewes of them. All the fowle which they kill, they skin, and make thereof one kinde of garment or other, to defend them from the cold.

They made their apparell with hoods and tailes, which tailes they give, when they thinke to gratifie any friendshippe shewed unto them: a great signe of friendshippe with them. The men have them not so syde as the women.

The men and women weare their hose close to their legges, from the wast to the knee, without any open before, as well the one kinde as the other. Uppon their legges, they weare hose of lether, with the furre side inward, two or three paire on at once, and especially the women. In those hose, they put their knives, needles, and other thinges needefull to beare about. They put a bone within their hose, whiche reacheth from the foote to the knee, whereupon they drawe their said hose, and so in place of garters, they are holden from falling downe about their feete.

They dresse their skinnes very softe and souple with the haire on. In cold weather or Winter, they weare ye furre side inward: and in Summer outward. Other apparell they have none, but the said skinnes.

Those beastes, flesh, fishes, and fowles, which they kil, they are both meate, drinke, apparel, houses, bedding, hose, shooes, thred, saile for their boates, with many other necessaries, whereof they stande in neede, and almost all their riches.

Their houses are tentes, made of Seale skinns, pitched with foure Firre quarters, foure square, meeting at the toppe, and the skinnes sewed together with sinowes, and layd thereuppon: so pitched they are, that the entraunce into them, is alwayes South, or against the Sunne.

They have other sortes of houses, whiche wee found, not to be inhabited, which are raised with stones and Whal bones, and a skinne layd over them, to withstand the raine, or other weather: the entraunce of them beeing not much unlike an Ovens mouth, whereto, I thincke, they resort for a time, to fishe, hunt, and fowle, and so leave them for the next time they come thether againe.

Their weapons are Bowes, Arrowes, Dartes, and Slinges. Their Bowes are of a yard long of wood, sinewed on the back with strong veines, not glued too, but fast girded and tyed on. Their Bowe stringes are likewise sinewes. Their arrowes are three peeces, nocked with bone, and ended with bone, with those two ends, and the wood in the middst, they passe not in lengthe halfe a yard or little more. They are fethered with two fethers, the penne end being cutte away, and the fethers layd uppon the arrowe with the broad side to the woode: in somuch that they seeme, when they are tyed on, to have foure fethers. They have likewise three sortes of heades to those arrowes: one sort of stone or yron, proportioned like to a heart: the second sort of bone, much like unto a stopte head, with a hooke on the same: the thirde sort of bone likewise, made sharpe at both sides, and sharpe pointed. They are not made very fast, but lightly tyed to, or else set in a nocke, that uppon small occasion, the arrowe leaveth these heades behinde them: and they are of small force, except they be very neere, when they shoote.

Their Darts are made of two sorts: the one with many forkes of bone in the fore ende, and likewise in the middest: their proportions are not muche unlike our toasting yrons, but longer: these they cast out of an instrument of wood, very readily. The other sorte is greater then the first aforesayde, with a long bone made sharp on both sides, not much unlike a Rapier, which I take to be their most hurtfull weapon.

They have two sorts of boates, made of Lether, set out on the inner side with quarters of wood, artificially tyed together with thongs of the same: the greater sort are not much unlike our Wherries, wherein sixteene or twentie men may sitte: they have for a sayle, drest the guttes of such beastes as they kyll, very fine and thinne, which they sewe together: the other boate is but for one man to sitte and rowe in, with one oare.

Their order of fishing, hunting, and fowling, are with these sayde weapons: but in what sort, or how they use them, we have no perfect knowledge as yet.

I can not suppose their abode or habitation to be here, for that neither their houses, or apparell, are of no such force to withstand the extremitie of colde, that the countrie seemeth to be infected with all: neyther doe I see any signe likely to performe the same.

Those houses, or rather dennes, which stand there, have no signe of footway, or any thing else troden, whiche is one of the chiefest tokens of habitation. And those tents, which they bring with them, when they have sufficiently hunted and fished, they remove to other places: and when they have sufficiently stored them of suche victuals, as the countrie yeldeth, or bringeth foorth, they returne to their Winter stations or habitations. This conjecture do I make, for the infertilitie, whiche I perceive to be in that countrie.

They have some yron, whereof they make arrowe heades, knives, and other little instrumentes, to woorke their boates, bowes, arrowes, and dartes withal, whiche are very unapt to doe anything withall, but with great labour.

It seemeth, that they have conversation with some other people, of whome, for exchaunge, they should receive the same. They are greatly delighted with any thinge that is brighte, or giveth a sound.

What knowledge they have of God, or what Idol they adore, wee have no perfect intelligence. I thincke them rather Anthropophagi, or devourers of mans fleshe, then otherwise: for that there is no flesh or fishe, which they finde dead, (smell it never so filthily) but they will eate it as they finde it, without any other dressing. A loathsome spectacle, either to the beholders, or hearers.

There is no maner of creeping beast hurtful, except some Spiders (which, as many affirme, are signes of great store of Golde:) and also certeine stinging Gnattes; which bite so fiercely, that the place where they bite, shortly after swelleth, and itcheth very sore.

They make signes of certeine people, that weare bright plates of Gold in their forheads, and other places of their bodies.

The Countries, on both sides the streightes, lye very highe with roughe stonie mounteynes, and great quantitie of snowe thereon. There is very little plaine ground, and no grasse, except a litle, whiche is much like unto mosse that groweth on soft-ground, such as we gett Turfes in. There is no wood at all. To be briefe, there is nothing fitte, or profitable for ye use of man, which that Countrie with roote yeeldeth or bringeth forth: Howbeit, there is great quantitie of Deere, whose skinnes are like unto Asses, their heads or hornes doe farre exceed, as wel in length as also in breadth, any in these oure partes or Countrie: their feete likewise, are as great as oure oxens, whiche we measured to be seven or eight ynches in breadth. There are also Hares, Wolves, fishing Beares, and Sea foule of sundrie sortes.

As the Countrie is barren and unfertile, so are they rude and of no capacitie to culture the same, to any perfection: but are contented by their hunting, fishing, and fowling, with rawe flesh and warme bloud, to satisfie their greedie panches, whiche is their onely glorie.

There is great likelyhood of Earthquakes, or thunder: for that huge and monstruous mounteynes, whose greatest substaunce are stones, and those stones so shaken with some extraordinarie meanes, that one is separated from another, whiche is discordant from all other Quarries.

There are no rivers, or running springes, but such, as through the heate of the Sunne, with such water as descendeth from the mounteines and hills, whereon great driftes of snowe doe lie, are ingendred.

It argueth also, that there should be none: for that the earth, which with the extremitie of the Winter, is so frosen within, that that water, whiche should have recourse within the same, to mainteine Springes, hath not his motion, whereof great waters have their originall, as by experience is seene otherwhere. Such valleies, as are capable to receive the water, that in the Summer time, by the operation of the Sunne, descendeth from great abundance of snow, whiche continually lyeth on the mounteines, and hath no passage, sinketh into the earth, and so vanisheth awaye, without any runnell above the earth, by which occasion, or continual standing of the said water, the earth is opened, and the great frost yeldeth to the force thereof, whiche in other places, foure or five fathoms within the ground, for lacke of the said moysture, (the earth, even in the very Summer time,) is frosen, and so combineth the stones together, that scarcely instruments, with great force, can unknitte them.

Also, where the water in those vallies can have no such passage away, by the continuaunce of time, in such order as is before rehearsed, the yearely descent from the mounteines, filleth them ful, that at the lowest banck of the same, they fall into the next vallie, and so continue, as fishing Pondes or Stagnes in the Summer time full of water, and in the Winter hard frosen: as by skarres that remaine thereof in Summer, may easily be perceived: so that, the heate of Summer, is nothing comparable, or of force, to dissolve the extremitie of colde, that commeth in Winter.

Neverthelesse, I am assured, that belowe the force of the frost, within the earth, the waters have recourse, and emptie themselves out of sighte into the sea, which through the extremitie of the frost, are constreyned to doe the same, by which occasion, the earth within is kept the warmer, and springes have their recourse. which is the onely nutriment of Gold and Minerals within the same.

There is much to be said of the commodities of these Countries, which are couched within the bowels of the earth, which I let passe till more perfect trial be made thereof.

Thus conjecturing, till time, with the earnest industrie of our Generall and others (who by al diligence remaine prest to explore the truth of that which is unexplored, as he hath to his everlasting praise found out that whiche is like to yeelde an innumerable benefite to his Prince & countrie:) after further triall, I conclude.

The 23. of August, after wee had satisfied our mindes with frayght sufficient for oure vessels, though not our covetous desires, with such knowledge of the countrie people and other commodities as are before rehearsed, the 24. therof wee departed therehence: the 17. of September we fell with yᵉ lands end of England, and so to Milford haven, from whence our General rode to the Court, for order, to what port or haven to conduct the shippe.

We lost our two Barkes in the way homeward, the one, the 29. of August, the other, the 31. of the same moneth, by occasion of great tempest and fogge. Howbeit, God restored the one to Bristowe, and yᵉ other making his course by Scotland to Yermouth. In this voyage wee lost two men, one in the waye by Gods visitation, and the other homewarde cast over borde with a surge of the sea.

I could declare unto your Honour, the Latitude and Longitude of such places and regions, as wee have beene at, but not altogether so perfect as our maisters and others, with many circumstances of tempests and other accidents incident to sea faring men, which seeme not altogether straunge, I let passe to their reportes as men most apte to sett forth and declare the same. I have also left the names of the countries on both the shoares untouched, for lacke of understanding the Peoples language: as also for sundrie respectes, not needfull as yet to be declared.

Countries new explored, where commoditie is to be loked for, doe better accord with a new name given by the explorers, then an uncerteine name by a doubtfull Authour.

Our General named sundrie Islands, Mounteines, Capes, and Harboroughs after the names of divers Noble men, and other gentlemen his friends, as wel on the one shoare, as also on the other: not forgetting amongest the reste your Lordship: whiche hereafter (when occasion serveth) are to be declared in his own Mapps or Charts.

THE ESKIMO BROUGHT BY FROBISHER IN 1576 AND 1577

THE MAN brought to London by Frobisher in 1576 caused great interest as his somewhat Asiatic features appeared to imply that indeed Frobisher had been on the way to Asia. He soon died, however. In 1577 another "catch" of Eskimo was obtained. Three Thule Eskimo—a man, a woman, and a child—were taken at Baffin Island together with a kayak. It was assumed that the man and woman were man and wife, but they were in fact strangers. At Bristol, the man was put through various athletic exercises in handling his kayak, but it is clear that he had a broken rib that ultimately penetrated his lung and caused his death. The woman died soon after. The child was brought to London as the only surviving curiosity, but she soon died also. The man, woman, and child were painted by John White, who was a member of the 1577 expedition (Paul Hulton and David B. Quinn, *The American Drawings of John White*, 2 vols. [London and Chapel Hill, 1964]). An important postmortem report on the man was made by Dr. Edward Dodding, in Latin, which Neil M. Cheshire (with the help of Dr. H. A. Waldron of the University of Birmingham Medical School) has managed to elucidate. It is in P.R.O., State Papers, Domestic, SP 12/118, 40, I.; printed in Richard Coelinson, *The Three Voyages of Martin Frobisher* (London, Hakluyt Society, 1867), pp. 189–191, and V. Stefansson, ed., *Three Voyages of Martin Frobisher*, 2 vols. (London, 1938), II, 135–137 (660).

In 1965 Alison M. Quinn found the record of the burial of both man and woman in St. Stephen's Parish Register, 1559–1663 (now in Bristol City Record Department) (661).

660. November 8, 1577. Postmortem report by Dr. Edward Dodding, at Bristol, on the Thule Eskimo man brought by Frobisher.

When the body had been dissected, the first thing to claim my attention was two ribs; these had been badly broken, in sustaining a fall of some force and impact, and were still gaping apart without having knit together. Either the care of them had been neglected, as tends to happen in such very hectic circumstances and restricted ship-board conditions, or (which I suspect is more likely) some contamination, which nobody noticed, had excited inflammation and the contusion of the lung had, in the course of time, become putrified as a result.

This condition, aggravated by the harmful cold outside and intensified by poor diet, was in the meantime neither put right from outside by surgery nor arrested from within by medicines, so that it rapidly developed unchecked day by day into an incurable ulcer of the lung. The disease spread and invaded healthy areas, with a great deal of clammy and sticky material flowing away from the same putrid region. The left part of the lung was so completely congested that it expelled nothing at all throughout the whole course of the illness, and his breath was virtually held in as a result of the constriction; consequently, the virulence of the malignant disease was resisted by a considerably weakened constitution.

When he was among us, his diet was too liberal either for the severity of the disease to tolerate or the man's habitual daily way of life to sustain. This situation was brought about by the utmost solicitousness on the part of that great man, the Captain, and by boundless generosity from those with whom he lodged. Everyone's judgement was deceived rather by the hidden nature of the disease, and by misguided kindness, than by ill-will; but when, shortly before his death, the nature of his illness expressed itself in the rather obvious symptom of breathlessness, he was already a victim of dropsy. For in the left thoracic cavity a great quantity of liquid (such as is rarely revealed to anatomical scrutiny and investigation) was obviously flowing. This was disturbed by any movement of the body (as one may be fairly sure from the outcome) and obstructed the expiration of the lung, and the lung itself in the end stuck to the ribs more firmly than anyone would think.

Innumerable indications of cerebral injury and ulceration (so to speak) remain and are coming very openly to light, quite apart from the deafness and intense head-pains with which he was continuously afflicted, but for brevity's sake I must pass over these in silence. However much of its appropriate volume nature had subtracted from this tiny spleen she had evidently added with interest to his enormous stomach, which, being flooded with liquid and swollen out, seemed much larger than is the case with our people; a consequence, I think, of his unhealthy voraciousness.

Elsewhere there was, you might say, an "Anglophobia," which he had from when he first arrived, even though his fairly cheerful features

and appearance concealed it and gave a false impression with considerable skill. His own actions, however, either betrayed it openly and exposed it (as it seemed to me when I was looking into individual things more closely and mistrusting everything), or else betokened an incipient fatal illness (as I declared often enough, but nobody would listen). These signs became more clearly recognisable and confirmed from the state of his pulse rather than from himself: for this was all the time too small, too sluggish and too weak rather than too slow, although it was also slower than either his youth or his bilious temperament would require.

In the early onset of the illness, I was summoned when his strength was still unimpaired; with much argument I recommended blood-letting, in order that, by quenching the fire of the inflammation and reducing the quantity of matter, they might both subside. But the foolish, and only too uncivilised, timidity of this uncivilised man forbade it, and the judgement of those with whom he was sailing prevailed with me.

In the end, having been called the hour before the one in which he died, I found everything threatening imminent death,—and no wonder, for his speech was impaired and almost cut off, his appetite faded and pulse non-existent. Quite enough! He summoned up to a certain extent all the energies and faculties which he had abandoned, came back to himself as if from a deep sleep and recognised us as people he knew. But I turned my attention to medication, and he spoke those words of ours which he had learned, the few that he could, and in turn replied quite relevantly to questions. And he sang clearly that same tune with which the companions from his region and rank had either mourned or ceremonially marked his final departure when they were standing on the shore (according to those who heard them both): just like the swans who foresee what good there is in death, and die happily with a song. I had scarcely left him when he moved from life to death, forcing out as his last words, given in our language, "God be with you."

I was bitterly grieved and saddened, not so much by the death of the man himself as because the great hope of seeing him which our most gracious Queen had entertained had now slipped through her fingers, as it were, for a second time. But the heroes of these new and substantial acts of gallantry are affected by a much greater sadness, for they have been deprived of the rewards and prizes for the truly Herculean labour which they have carried out. To express my opinion, these men can in all justice expect the highest recognition on our part, for they have triumphantly survived these expeditions by sea,—tortuous and comfortless that they indeed were, and obviously unachieved before this time. They have undertaken enormous tasks, bringing to the kingdom and posterity advantages greater than the hazards, and to their own names supreme glory; and they have demonstrated that what he has undertaken to do he has succeeded in.

Consequently we may retain these nerves and life-blood of kingdom and state (which is how the theorists appositely describe economic resources) as easily as we have sought them out. But let us not, before we take them over, lose sight in our ingratitude (for I don't see what else there is to fear) of what we should repay to God for all that he has made over to us from foreign kings. Let us not hope for any goodwill, because they do not wish it; and let us not fear any evil, because they do not venture it.

I am not saying this, however, to encourage anyone lurking in criminal shame to be of a quiet mind; but that I may shift particular individuals from dishonourable activity, and that I may press everyone in general toward a keener cultivation of sacred things. For what can be more absurd to say or think than that the quicker and more ready our Good and Supreme God is in giving, the slower we are at being deserving. And yet there will always be that true voice of the True God to be recognised: "Not because you are worthy, but because I am merciful." If the libation-vessels of incantation-makers; begged-for effigies, vacuous rituals and magic charms had been of any avail in overcoming disease, this man Calichoughe (for that was his name) would, while he was still alive, have hacked it off quivering like a hydra-head and then thrown it away. For nobody was more practised than he in this art, and (unless I am mistaken) nobody trusted more deeply in those very superstitions; he made an incantation for every time his pain abated.

I showed the body to the woman, who was troubled at the time with boils (which broke out very densely on her skin next day, when this was written); and at my persuasion she was led with me, albeit unwillingly, to the burial,—which I purposely wanted to be carried through without ceremony, lest there be implanted in her any fears about human sacrifice among us. She was kept there all the time until the body had been completely covered over with earth; I showed her human bones which had been dug up, and made her understand that we all were to be buried in the same way. This I did in order to remove from her mind all anxiety about human flesh being eaten (a practice which had become deeply rooted among them), and that she might learn to put aside the fear henceforward.

But that woman either excelled all our people in decorum and stoicism or else was far outstripped in human sensitivity by the wild animals themselves. For she was not in any way disturbed by his death, and, as far as we gathered from her expression, it did not distress her. So much so that, by this most recent behaviour of hers, she has expressed quite clearly what we had long before arrived at by conjecture: that she had regarded him with an astonishing degree of contempt, and that although they used to sleep in one and the same bed, yet nothing had occurred between them apart from conversation,—his embrace having been abhorrent to her.

Goodbye.
Yours, as you know,
    Edward Dodding

Bristol, November 8th [1577]

[Postscript:] "Had hardy Ulysses not seen
        Such danger-ridden days,
    How happy for Penelope;
        And yet how little praise!"

661. 1577. Burial record of two Thule Eskimo in register of St. Stephen's Church, Bristol.

Burials in 1577...
Collichang a heathen man buried the 8th of November
Egnock a heathen woman buried the 12th of November

662. May to October, 1578. The third Frobisher voyage to Baffin Island to load the presumed gold-bearing rock.

This account is by Thomas Ellis, who was on the voyage, and was published as A true report of the third voyage *(London, 1578); reprinted in R. Hakluyt,* Principall navigations *(1589), pp. 630–635, and* Principal navigations, *III (1600), 39–44 (VII [1904], 231–242). The narrative below is from the 1578 edition, with the last paragraph and the complimentary poems which follow omitted.*

The Preface.

For as muche (right noble & worthie Countrimen) as I am assured, that at this our safe arrivall and returning from the Northwest partes, nowe called by the Queenes most excellent Majestie, Meta incognita, and lately found out by the travell and industrie of the right worthie & adventurous Capteine, Maister Martine Frobisher Esquire, that you will be no lesse earnest and desirous, to learne & enquire, than attentive to knowe and heare, as well of our travelles, troubles, toyles, and daungers, as of our labours, adventures, happes, and good successes, together with the prowesse and industrie, of our Generall, with the residue of his companie, and also the order of our voyage, the commoditie of our Contrie, the fashion of the people, with the use & orders of the same, with all others thinges thereto apperteining or belonging: then we will be readie and willing to declare and make manifest the same, with the circumstances unto you.

I therefore, as one not of the best learned, or ablest: whose knowledge I confesse to be small, and of none accompt, in respect of others that were present: but as one most prone and willing to satisfie and answeare your desire and expectation, seeing that it is our chaunce and fortune, to be one of the first arrived, and hearing that those which landed before us, have hitherto sette forth nothing, whereby your serious affection might be satisfied, thought it not amisse, but rather meete and convenient, with all expedition to accomplish the same, knowing, that the nature of man is always desirours of newes: although I know right well, that manie learned and skilfull Gentlemen were present in our companie, whose bookes, as well for eloquence, as sound judgement, I am not worthie to beare: yet because I know not the time of their arrivall and returne, because the Seas are various, the windes fickle, the tempestes rigorous, & the passage dangerous, that nothing can bee brought to effect, or done, before the appointed time assigned from the celestiall throne. And though perchance there be some men, that will say, my judgement was to small, and my learning to simple, to take in hand a matter of such weight and importance: I will geve place and agree unto them. For why? my simple wit and judgement, cannot attaine and reache unto the flowing style of grave Plutarch, nor yet the eloquence of the noble Tullie: I being a Sailer, more studied and used in my Charde and Compasse, and other thinges belonging to Navigation, than trayned up in Minervas Court, or taught by the sage Philosophers the fathers of eloquence, whose sweete and sacred sappe I never sucked. But yet, because I knowe, that the best part of men, will weigh my good will, rather than finde fault with my simple skill. For them, and not for the other, I thought good to take in hand to write these fewe lines, conteining in breefe the summe & effect of all the accidences and chances that happened and befell, from the beginning of this our voyage, (being nowe the thirde, that our worthie Generall hath made, unto those parts,) unto this our arrivall againe in our native countrie.

Thomas Ellis.

The third and last voyage into
Meta Incognita.

These are to let you knowe, that upon the 25. of Maie, The Thomas Alline, being the Viceadmerall, whose Captein was M. Yorke, M. Gibbes Maister, Christopher Hall Pilot, accompanied with the Reareadmerall named The Hopewell, whose Capteine was Maister Henrie Carewe, the Maister Andrew Dier, and certaine other shippes, came to Graves end, where we anchored & abode the comming of certaine other of our fleete, which were not yet come.

The 27. of the same Moneth, our fleete being nowe gone together, and all thinges prest in a redinesse, the winde favouring, and Tide serving, we being of sailes in number 8. waide anchors, and hoised our sailes toward Harwich, to meet with our Admerall, and the residue, which then and there abode our arrivall: where we safely arrived, the 28. thereof, finding there our Admerall, where we, with the discharge of certeine peeces, saluted (according to order and dutie) and were welcomed with the like courtesie: which being finished, we landed: where our Generall continued mustring his Souldiers and Miners, and setting thinges in order apperteining to the voyage, untill the last of the saide Moneth of Maie, which day we hoised our sailes, and committing our selves to the conducting of almightie God, we set forward toward the West Countrie, in such luckie wise, and good successe, that by the .5. of June, we passed the Dursies, being the utmost part of Ireland, to the Westward.

And here it were not much amisse, nor farre from our purpose, if I shoulde a little discourse and speake of our adventures and chance by the way, at our landing at Plimmouth, as also the meeting of certeine poore men, which were robbed and spoiled of all that they had, by Pirates and Rovers: amongst whom was a man of Bristowe, on whom our Generall used his liberalitie, and sent him away with letters into England.

But because such thinges are impertinent to the matter, I will returne (without any more mentioning of the same) to that, from the which I have digressed, and swarved, I meane our shippes nowe sailing on the sourging seas, sometime passing at pleasure with a wished Easterne winde, sometime hindered of our course againe by the Westerne blastes, untill the .20. day of the foresaid Moneth of June, on which day in the morning we fell with Frizeland, which is a very high and cragged land, & being almost cleane covered with snowe, so that we might see nought but the craggie rockes, and the toppes of high and huge hilles, sometimes (and for the most part) all covered with foggie mistes. There might we also perceive the great Isles of yce lying on the seas, like mountaines, some small, some bigge, of sundrie kindes of shapes, and such a number of them, that we coulde not come neere the shoare for them.

Thus sailing alongest the coast, at the last we sawe a place somewhat voyde of yce, where our Generall, (accompanied with certaine other) went a shoare, where they sawe certaine tentes made of beastes skinnes, and boates much like unto theirs of *Meta incognita*. The tentes were furnished with fleshe, fishe, skinnes, and other

trifles: amongst the which was found a boxe of nailes: whereby we did conjecture, that they had either Artificers amongst them, or else a trafficke with some other nation. The men ranne away, so that we could have no conferrence or communication with them. Our Generall (because he would have them no more to flee, but rather incouraged to stay through his courteous dealing) gave commaundement, that his men should take nothing away with them, saving onely a couple of white Dogges, for which he left pinnes, pointes, knives, and other trifling thinges, and departed, without taking or hurting any thing, and so came a boord, and hoised sailes, and passed forwardes.

But beeing scarse out of the sight thereof, there fell such a fogge and hidious mist, that we coulde not see one another: wherupon we stroke our drummes, and sounded our trumpets, to the ende we might keepe together: and so continued all that day and night, till the next day, that the mist brake up: so that we might easily perceive all the shippes thus sailing together all that day, untill the next day, being the .22. of the same: on which day we sawe an infinite number of yce, from the which we cast about to shun the daunger thereof.

But one of our small barkes, named The Michael, whose Captein was Maister Kinderslie, the Master Bartholomew Bull, lost our companie, insomuche that we coulde not obteine the sight of her many dayes after, of whom I purpose to speake further anon, when occasion shalbe ministred, and opportunitie serve. Thus we continued on our course, untill the .2. of Julie, on which day we fell with The Queenes foreland, where we sawe so much yce, that we thought it unpossible to get into the Streightes: yet at the last we gave the adventure, and entered the yce.

Being in amongst it, we sawe The Michael, of whom I spake before, accompanied with The Judith, whose Captaine was Maister Fenton, the Maister Charles Jackman, bearing into the foresaid yce, farre distant from us, who in a storme that fell that present night, (whereof I will at large, God willing, discourse hereafter) were severed from us, & being in, wandered up and downe the Streightes, amongst the yce, many dayes, in great perill, till at the last, (by the providence of GOD) they came safely to harbour in their wished port, in The Countesse of Warwickes sound, the .20. of Julie aforesaid, 10. dayes before any of the other shippes: who going on shoare found where the people of the Countrie had bene, and had hid their provision in great heapes of stones, being both of fleshe, and fishe, which they had killed: whereof we also found great store in other places after our arrivall. They found also diverse engines: as bowes, slings, & dartes. They found likewise certeine peeces of the Pinnisse which our Generall left there the yeare before, which Pinnisse he had soonke, minding to have him againe the next yeare.

Now, seeing I have entreated so much of The Judith, and The Michael: I will returne to the rest of the other shippes, and will speake a little of the storme which fell, with the missehappes that we had, the night that we put into the yce: whereof I made mention before.

At the first entrie into the yce, in the mouth of the Streightes, our passage was very narrowe, and difficill: but being once gotten in, we had a faire open place without any yce, for the most part: being a league in compasse, the yce being round about us, and inclosing us, as it were within the pales of a Parke. In which place, (because it was almost night) we minded to take in our sailes, and lie a hull at that night. But the storme so increased, and the waves began to mount aloft, which brought the yce so neere us, and comming on so fast upon us, that we were feigne to beare in and out, where we might espie an open place. Thus the yce comming on us so fast, we were in great danger, looking everie houre for death. And thus passed we on in that great danger, seeing both our selves, and the rest of our ships so troubled and tossed amongst the yce, that it woulde make the strongest heart to relent.

At the last, the Barke Dionyse, being but a weake shippe, & brused afore amongst the yce, being so leake that she no longer could tarrie above the water, sanke without saving any of the goodes which were within her: which sight so abashed the whole fleete, that we thought verily we should have tasted of the same sauce. But neverthelesse, we seeing them in such daunger, manned out boates, and saved all the men, in such wise, that not one perished, (God be thanked.)

The storme still increased, and the yce inclosed us, that we were faine to take downe toppe and toppe mastes: for the yce had so environed us, that we could see neither land, nor Sea, as farre as we could kenne: so that we were faine to cutte our gables, to hang over boorde for fenders, some-

what to ease the shippes sides, from the great and drierie strokes of the yce: some Capstan barres, some fending off with Oares, some with planckes of .2. ynches thicke, which were broken immediatly with the force of the yce, some going out upon the yce to beare it off with their shoulders from the shippes. But the rigorousnesse of the tempest was suche, and the force of the yce so great, that not only they burst and spoiled the foresaid provision: but likewise so raced the sides of the shippes, that it was pitifull to behold, and caused the heartes of many to faint.

Thus continued we all that dismall and lamentable night, plunged in this perplexitie, looking for instant death: but our God, (who never leaveth them destitute which faithfully call upon him,) although he often punisheth, for amendments sake, in the morning he caused the windes to cease: and the fogge which all that night lay on the face of the water to cleare: so that we might perceive, about a mile from us, a certaine place cleare from any yce, to the which with an easie breath of winde, which our God sent us, we bent our selves. And furthermore, he provided better for us than we deserved, or hoped for: for when we were in the foresaid cleare place, he sent us a fresh gale at West, or at West Southwest, which set us cleare without all the yce. And further, he added more: for he sent us so pleasant a day, as the like we had not of a long time before, as after punishment, consolation.

Thus we joyfull wightes, being at libertie, tooke in all our sailes, and lay a hull, praising God for our deliverance: and staide to gather together our fleete, which once being done, we seeing that none of them had any great hurt, neither any of them wanted, saving onely they of whom I spake before, & the shippe which was lost, then at the last we hoised our sailes, and lay bulting off and on, till such time as it would please God to take away the yce, that we might get into the Streightes.

And as we thus lay off and on, we came by a marvellous huge mountaine of yce, which surpassed all the rest that ever we sawe: for we judged him to be neere a foure score fadams above water, and we thought him to be a ground for any thing that we could perceve, being there nine score fadams deepe, and of compasse about halfe a mile, of which Island I have, as neere as I coulde, drawne and here set downe the true proportion, as he appeared in diverse shapes passing alongest by him. [Sketches omitted.]

> These foure being but one Island of yce, and as we came neere unto it, and departed from it, in so many shapes it appeared.

Also the .5. of Julie, there fell a hidious fogge and mist, that continued till the .19. of the same: so that one shippe could not see another. Therefore, we were feigne to beare a small saile, and to observe the time: but there ranne such a current of a Tide, that it set us to the Northwest of the Queenes forelande: the backeside of all the Streightes: where (through the contagious fogge having no sight either of Sun or Starre) we scarse knewe where we were. In this fogge the .10. of Julie, we lost the companie of The Viceadmerall, the Anne Francis, the Busse of Bridgewater, and the Francis of Foy. The .16. day, one of our small Barks, named The Gabriel, was sent by our Generall to beare in with the land, to descrie it, where being on lande, they mette with the people of the contrie, which seemed very humane and civil, and offered to trafficke with our men, proffering them foules, and skinnes, for knives, and other trifles: whose courtesie caused us to thinke, that they had small conversation with the other of the Streightes.

Then we bare backe againe, to goe with The Queenes forelande: and the .18. day we came by .2. Islandes, whereon we went on shoare, and founde where the people had bene: but we sawe none of them. This day we were againe in the yce, and like to be in as great perill as wee were at the first. For through the darkenesse and obscuritie of the foggie mist, we were almost runne on rockes and Islandes, before we sawe them: But God (even miraculously) provided for us, opening the fogges, that we might see clearely, both where, and in what daunger we presently were, and also the way to escape: or else, without faile, we had ruinously ranne upon the rockes.

When we knewe perfectly our instant case, we cast about, to get againe on Sea boorde, which (God be thanked) by night we obteined and praised God. The cleare continued scarse an houre, but the fogge fell againe as thicke as ever it was.

Then The Reareadmerall, and The Beare got themselves cleare without danger of yce and rockes, stroke their sailes, and lay at hull, staying to have the rest of the fleete come foorth: which as yet had not found the right way to cleare themselves, from the danger of rockes and yce, untill the next morning, at what time The Rereadmerall discharged certeine warning peeces to geve notice that she had escaped, and that the rest (by following of her) might set them selves free, which they did that day.

Then having gathered our selves together, we proceeded on our purposed voyage, bearing off, and keeping our selves distant from the coast, till the .19. day of Julie: at which time the fogges brake up and dispersed, so that we might plainely and clearely beholde the pleasant aire, which so long had bene taken from us, by the obscuritie of the foggie mistes: and after that time, wee were not much encombred therewith, untill we had left the confines of the countrie.

Then we espying a faire sound, supposed it to go into the Streightes, betweene The Queenes foreland, and Jackemans sound, which proved, as we imagined. For our Generall sent forth again The Gabriel, to discover it, who passed through with much difficultie: for there ran such an extreme current of a Tide, with so horrible a gulfe, that with a fresh gale of winde they were scarse able to stemme it: yet at the length with greate travell they passed it, and came to the Streights, where they met with The Thomas Alline, The Thomas of Ipsewich, and the Busse of Bridgwater: who all together adventured to beare into the yce againe, to see if they could obteine their wished port. But they were so encombred, that with muche difficultie they were able to get out againe, yet at the last they escaping, The Thomas Alline, and the Gabriel bare in with the Westerne shore, where they founde harbour, and there mored their shippes, untill the 4. of August, at whiche time they came to us in The Countesse of warwiks sound. The Thomas of Ipsewich caught a great leake, which caused her to cast againe to Sea boorde, and so was mended.

We sailed along still by the coast, untill wee came againe to The Queenes foreland, at the point wherof we met with part of the gulfe aforesaid, which place or gulfe (as some of our Masters do credibly report) doeth flowe .9. houres, and ebbes but 3. At that point we discovered certeine lands Southwarde, to the which neither time nor opportunitie would serve to search. Then being come to the mouth of the Streights, we met with the Anne Francis, who had laine bulting up and downe ever since her departure alone, never finding any of her companie. Wee met then also The Francis of Foy, with whome againe wee intended to venter and get in: but the yce was yet so thicke, that we were compelled againe to retire and gett us on Sea boord.

There fell also the same day, being the 26. day of Julie, such an horrible snowe, that it laye a foote thicke upon the hatches, which frose as fast as it fell.

We had also at other times, divers cruell stormes, both of snowe and haile, which manifestly declared the distemperature of the Countrie: yet for all that, we were so many times repulsed and put backe from our purpose, knowing that long lingering delay was not profitable for us, but hurtfull to our voyage, we mutually consented to our valiant Generall once againe, to geve the onset.

The 28. day therefore of the same Julie wee assaid, and with little trouble (God be praised) we passed the dangers, by day light. Then night falling on the face of the earth, we hull in the cleare, till the chearefull light of the day had chased away the noysome darkenesse of the night: at which time wee set forward towards our wished port: by the 30. day we obteined our expected desire, where we found The Judith, and the Michael: which brought no small joy unto our Generall, and great consolation to the hevie heartes of those wearied wightes.

The 30. day of Julie wee brought our shippes into The Countesse of Warwickes sounde, and mored them, namely these ships, The Admerall, The Reareadmerall, The Francis of Foy, The Beare, Armenell, The Salomon, & The Busse of Bridgwater which being done, our Generall commaunded us all to come a shore, upon The Countesse Island, where he set his miners to work upon the mine, geving charge with expedition to dispatche with their lading.

Our Generall himselfe, accompanied with his Gentlemen, diverse times made rodes into sundrie partes of the Countrie, as well to finde newe mines, as also to finde out and see the people of the Countrie. He found out one mine, uppon an Island by Beares sound, and named it The Countesse of Sussex Island. One other was founde in Winters Fornace, with divers others, to which the shippes were sent sunderly, to be laden. In the same rodes he mette with diverse of the people of the Countrie, at sundrie times, as once at a place called Davids sound: who shotte at our men, and very desperately gave them the onset, being not above three or foure in number, there being of our Countrimen above a dozen: but seeing themselves not able to prevaile, they tooke themselves to flight: whom our men pursued, but being not used to suche craggie cliffes, they soone lost the sight of them, and so in vaine returned.

We also sawe of them at Beares sounde, both by Sea and Land, in great companies: but they would at all times keepe the water betweene them and us. And if any of our ships chaunced to bee in the sound, (as they came divers times,) because the harbor was not verie good, the ship laded, and departed again then so long as any ships were in sight, the people would not be seene. But when as they perceived the ships to be gone, they would not onely shew them selves standing uppon highe cliffes, and call us to come over unto them: but also would come in their botes, very neere to us, as it were to bragge at us: whereof our Generall having advertisement, sent for the Capteines and Gentlemen of the shippes, to accompanie and attende upon him, with the Capteine also of the Anne Francis, who was but the night before come unto us. For they, and The fleebote having lost us the 26. day, in the great snowe, put into an harbour in the Queenes foreland, where they found good oare, wherwith they laded them selves, and came to seeke the Generall: so that nowe we had all our shippes, saving one Barke, which was lost, and the Thomas of Ipsewiche, who compelled (by what furie I knowe not,) forsooke our companie, and returned home without lading.

Our Generall acompanied, with his Gentlemen, (of whom I spake) came altogether to The Countesse of Sussex Island, neare to Beares sound. where he manned out certein Pinnisses, and went over to the people: who perceiving his arrivall, fled away with all speede, and in hast left certeine dartes and other engines behind them, which we found: but the people we could not finde.

The next morning, our Generall perceiving certeine of them in bote upon the Sea, gave chase to them, in a Pinnisse under saile, with a fresh gale of wind, but could by no meanes come neere unto them: for the longer he sailed, the further off he was from them: which well shewed their cunning

& activitie. Thus time wearing away, and the day of our departure approching, our Generall commanded to lade with all expedition, that we might be againe on Sea boord with our ship: for whilest we were in the countrie, we were in continuall danger of frising in: for often times we had stormes and tempests, often snow and haile, often the water was so much frosen and congeled in the night, that in the morning we could scarse rowe our botes or Pinnisses, especially in Diers sound, which is a calme and still water: which caused our Generall to make the more haste, so that by the 30 day of August we were all laden, and made all thinges readie to depart.

But before I proceed any further herein, to shewe what fortune befell at our departure, I will turne my penne a little to M. Capteine Fenton, and those Gentlemen, which should have enhabited all the yeare in those countries, whose valiant minds were much to be commended, that neither feare of force, nor the cruell nipping stormes of the raging winter, neither the intemperature of so unhealthsome a Countrie, neither the savagenesse of the people, neither the sight and shewe of suche and so many straunge Meteores, neither the desire to returne to their native soile, neither regarde of friendes, neither care of possessions and inheritances: finally, not the love of life (a thing of all other most sweete) neither the terrour of dreadfull death it selfe, might seeme to bee of sufficient force, to withdrawe their pronesse, or to restraine from that purpose, thereby to have profited their countrie: but that with most willing heartes, venturous mindes, stoute stomachs, & singular, manhod they were content there to have tarried, and for the time (among a barbarous and uncivill people, Infidels and miscreantes) to have made their dwelling, not terrified with the manifolde and imminent daungers which they were like to runne into: & seeing before their eyes so many casualties, whereto their life was object, the least whereof would have made a milksoppe Thersites astonished and utterly discomfited: being I say thus minded and purposed, they deserve speciall commendation: For doubtlesse, they had done as they intended, if lucke had not withstood their willingnesse, & if that fortune had not so frowned upon their intentes.

For the Barck Dionyse, which was lost, had in her much of their house, which was prepared and should have bene builded for them, with many other implementes. Also The Thomas of Ipsewich, which had moste of their provision in her, came not into the Streightes at all: neither did we see her, since the day we were separated in the great snowe, (of which I spake before.) For these causes, having not their house, nor yet provision, they were disapointed of their pretence to tarie, and therefore laded their shippes, and so came away with us.

But before we toke shipping, we built a iitle house in The Countesse of Warwickes Island, & garnished it with many kindes of trifles, as Pinnes, Pointes, Laces, Glasses, Kombes, Babes on horsebacke and on foote, with innumerable other such fansies & toyes: thereby to allure & entice the people to some familiaritie against other yeares.

Thus having finished all things, we departed the contrie, (as I said before:) but becase The Busse had not lading enough in her, she put into Beares sound to take in a litle more. In the meane while, The Admerall, and the rest, without in the Sea, stayed for her. And that night fell such an outragious tempest, beating on our shipps, with such vehement rigor, that anchor and gable availed naught: for we were driven on rockes and Islandes of yce insomuch that (had not the great goodnesse of God bene miraculously shewed to us,) we had bene cast away every man. This daunger was more doubtfull and terrible, than any that preceded or went before: for there was not any one ship, (I thinke) that escaped without damage. Some lost anchor and also gables, some botes, some Pinnisses: some anchor, gables, botes, and Pinnisses.

This boysterous storme so severed us, one from another, that one ship knewe not what was becom of another. The Admerall knew not where to finde the Viceadmerall of Reareadmerall, or any other shippe of our companie. Our Generall being on lande in Beares sounde, coulde not come to his shippe, but was compelled to goe a boorde The Gabriel, where he continued al the way homewarde: for the boysterous blastes continued so extreamly and so long a time, that it sent us homewarde: (which was Gods favour towardes us,) will we, nill we, in such hast, as not any one of us were able to keepe in companie of other, but were separated. And if by chaunce, any one shippe did overtake other, by swiftnesse of Saile, or mette (as they often did:) yet was the rigour of the winde so hidious, that they could not continue companie together the space of one whole night.

Thus, our journey outwarde was not so pleasaunt, but our comming thither, entering the coastes and countrie, by narrowe Streightes, perillous yce, and swift tides, our time of aboade there in snowe, and stormes, and our departure from thence, the .3. of August, with daungerous blustering windes and tempestes, whiche that night arose, was as uncomfortable: Separating us so, as we sailed, that not any of us mette together, untill the 28. of September, whiche day we fell on The Englishe coastes, betweene Scylla and The landes ende, and passed the channell, untill our arrivall, &c.

663. 1578. Charges and countercharges arising out of the Frobisher voyages.

Michael Lok went bankrupt as a result of the Frobisher failure. He was accused of siphoning off money from the Company of Cathay for his own purposes. He volubly attacked his associates. This is a good example of his style of controversy. While what he says about Frobisher is not substantiated in detail, there are indications that the men under him did not respect his judgment.

P.R.O., State Papers, Domestic, Elizabeth I, SP 12/130, 17; printed in Richard Coelinson (ed.), The Three Voyages of Martin Frobisher, (London, Hakluyt Society, 1867), pp. 359-363, and V. Stefansson, The Three Voyages of Martin Frobisher, II (1938), 208-212.

[a] The Abuses of Captayn Furbusher agaynst the Companye. Anno 1578.

In the first voyage he brought home by chaunce a stoane of riche ewre, and being examyned by Sir William Wynter, Master Randall, Master Hogan, and the rest of the Comissioners, what quantitie was to be had, he said that in that countrie was inoughe therof to lade all the Quenes shippes, and promised to lade the shippes of the seconde voiage ther withall, wheruppon the seconde voiage was prepared, and comyssion geven him to bringe of the same. And Jonas, Denham, and Grigorie were

sent with him for the same; but he performed nothinge at all, & brought not so muche as one stoane therof; for ther was none to lade, as Jonas and the rest do witnes, but laded the ships with other mynes founde by chaunse.

In the seconde voyag he retorned the shipps laden with stoanes of strainge ewr found by chaunce there, sainge they were of gold myne worth iiii[xx] poundes a tonne, which is not yet so founde; and also he brought some stoanes of redde ewre and yellow ewer of Jonas mount, verye riche of gold, as D. Burcot witnessed, and the stoanes are yett to be seen. And promised to the comissioneres that ther was mountaynes therof, and he would lade all the shippes therwithal in the thirde voiage wheruppon the thirde voiage was prepared with so great chardg; but he brought home not one stoane therof afterwards that is yet found.

In the thirde voiage he promised to lade all the shippes with the ewr of Jonas mount, and other so riche ewre as the best of the second voiage was, and carried owt a number of ships for that purpose, and a c. men to inhabit there under culler of the Frenche mens preparacon to that countrie, and besydes the nomber appoynted to him by the Comissioners, he carried mor 4 shippes and a c. men more for his owne purpose, without the knowledge of the Comissioners, which now rest uppon the charge of the Companye, and he brought home those ships laden with none of the ewre that he promised, but with other strainge ewr, wher he could fynd yt. which he said was better then the best that was brought the yeare befor, which is not yt so found.

Also he promised to the Comissioners and had speciall charge by comissione first to plant C. Fenton and the c. men to inhabit in that new land, wheruppon the great preparacon was made; but afterwards, before his departure from London, he dislyked that enterprice, and diswaded the same cullerablie, and when he came there he would not helpe them therin one jote, not so muche as for 50 men wherwithall C. Fenton would have tarried there, he feringe that C. Fentons deede therin would dashe his glorye, and because he toke the victualls of that provicion to victuall his owne 4 shippes taken with him extraordinare, which went from hens envictualled uppon his promisse made them to victuall them, as Captayn Fenton and others witnes.

He promised and had comission to send the two barks this yere to make some discoverie of the passage for Cathai, which he might have donne; but when he came at Meta Incognita, he would do nothinge at all therin as Hawll & Jakman wytenes, but made all his endevour to lade his owne shippes, and the rest home agayne with ewre.

He hathe byn still verrie costlye and prodigall in the furniture of the shippes and men for the voyage, and his owne men being shipped for officieres of the shippes have made verie great spoile, wast, and pilfrye of the goods in the shippes, for the whiche he must give account.

He did practyse to advaunce D. Burcot into the place of Jonas, & mayntan Burcots false proffes made of the ewre, to thend he might be sett on agayn in this third voyage, as the Comissioneres and Denham canne witnes.

He was sent to Bristowe to dispatche the ships, the *Ayde* on the thirde voyage, wherin he was made victualler of the shippe, for the whiche sarvice he had money before hand, but he dide so evell vittell the same, as wheras the Companye allowed him to vittell her with fleshe 4 daye in the weke, he sarved the men therof onlye 3 dayes, and 2 dayes in the weke, and the rest of the weke with evill fishe, and that with scarsetie wherbye manye of them died, as the men do reporte.

He was sent into the west countrie to provide the 120 myners for the voiage, for whose furniture he received money of the Companye by fore hande, for their wags *li*240, and for their weapons *li*120, but therof he paid these men upon their wags, to some xx^s, to some xiii^s iiii^d, and to some nothinge the man, as the accounts declare. And what weapones they had, or he for them, as yet is unknoune. But in the west countrie is spreade agreat clamor that those mynares beinge prest by comissione many of them were afterwards chaunged by favour for showmakeres, taylores, and other artificers, no workemen, and were furnished to see at the charge of the townes and villages in maner of a subsedye as it is reported openlye.

He toke the shipe the *Sallomon* of Weymoth, in the west countrie, without knowledge of the comissioneres, by force of Her Majesties generall comission to him geven, and therby caused the owner, Hew Randall, to furnishe her, and to be with him

in this sarvice of the thirde voyage, promisinge hime victualls and other great matters, which he performed not, as Hewe Randall dothe saye.

He led all the shipps this yere to a wronge place of Meta Incognita, throughe his obstinate ignorance, wherby they were all in great danger to perrishe, as Hawll, Davis, and the rest of the shipps masters will witnes.

He, beinge at Meta Incognita, did refuse conference and counsell of all others, and said his instructiones, geven by her Majesties Honourable Privie Councell, were but the device of Fenton and Lok, and never reade by the Councell, though their hands were at the same, as Captayn Fenton and the other captaynes, and Hawell do witnes.

And when the shippes were mored salf in harbor in the countey of Warwicks Sounde, where they should lade, and from whence they should have departed orderlye, he beinge at Beares Sound, comaunded all the shippes (without anney advice or discretion) to come thether to take him and his men in, which place beinge no harbor, but wilde see, a Storme of weather happened which put all the shippes to see to save them selves, with losse of all their boates and pynnesses, and other spoile, leavinge him there behind them in the barke *Gabriell*. And so they came home in suche disorder as is openlye knowne.

He is so arrogant in his governement, as Hawle, Jakman, Davis, nor the other of the masters wille no more take charge of ships under him, and so imperious in his doinges as some of the comissioners are werie of his company, and manney of the venturares mynded to medle no more with him.

He drew his dagger and furiouslye ranne upon Jonas, beinge in his worke at Tower hill, and threatned to kill him yf he did not finishe his worke owt of hand, that he might be sett owt againe on the thirde voiage, wheruppon Jonas did conseave so eavell nature in him, that he made a sollempe vowe he would never go to see any more with him, which hath byn no small domage to the Company in the ewre brought home the thirde voyage.

He drew his dager on Captayne Fenton at Darteford, upon a quarrelous humor, and wolde haue mischefed him uppon the sodayne, yf Master Pelham and others had not bine present.

He is so full of lyinge talke as no man maye

credit anye thinge that he doth speake, and so impudent of his tonge as his best frindes are most sclanndered of him when he cannot have his wille.

He hath raysed lately such sclannderous reportes against Master Lok, and geven suche vehement false informaciones of iii^mli. and other greate somes of money to remayne in his hands dew to the Company, to paye the shipps fraights and mens wages, as hath well lyked some of the venturares, which hoaped therby to be forborne of the payment of their owne parts of money dewe for that purpose, wherby littell money cane yett be had of them of the li3,400 dewe by them to dyscharg that dutye whiche hath caused the Company to spent mli of monye in vayne, for chardgs of the shippes and men synes they came home, and by that meanes for lake of payment of their dewtye, a sclanderous rumoor is spreade over all the realme, to the great discredite of the Company.

He did paye wages to the men of the shipe *Thomas* of Ipswiche for v monthes, wheras the Comissioners did agree and comannd to paye them but for iiij monthes.

He hathe brought into wages of the Companye so many men, and suche men as he lyste, and many of them at suche wages as he lyste, without regard of their sarvyce or deserts wherof he is to geve accountt for that many of them are dead, and gone awaye.

He hath plased styll in the shippe *Ayde*, now in the Tames, a number of men at the Companyes charges, wherof many are suche disordered men, bothe of their tonges and of their hands, as are the cause of moche sclander to the Company, and great spoyle done in their shippes, and yt have but small dutye of wages owinge to them, when their accounts shalbe examined particulerlie.

He receaved cli of mony by Her Majesties order, at retorne of the seconde voiage, as of Her Majesties gyfte and reward to be distrybuted amonge the marineres and other men which sarved in that voyage, but no distribution is made therof as yett, as the men doo complayne.

To conclude, yf his doinges in thes iij voyages be well looked into, parchanse he wilbe found the most unproffitable sarvante of all that have sarved the Companye therin.

[b] The sclanderous Clamors of Captaine Furbusher against Michael Lok. 1578.

He hathe made false accountts to the Companye, and hathe cossened them of iii^mli of money.

He hathe cossened my Lord of Oxford of mli.

He hathe not one grote of venture in these voiages.

He is a bankerot knave.

[c]   The Answers of Michael Lok.

All these forsaid clamors are proved to be false sclanders, aswell by the new awdyte made of Master Loks accountts as also by the open knowledge had of all his doinges certiffied to Her Majesties Honorable Privie Councell.

And now, yf any evell successe should happen in the work of the ewr now layd at Dartford, which I trust shall not happen, yet wear not that to be imputed anye wayes unto Master Lok, whose innocentie therein is proved by his great goodes beinge ij^{m}vi^cli of money bestowed and ventured therin, and by the testimonie of the Comyssioners certiffienge the first proffe of the work made in the second voiage, but rather yf any such myschyef should happen, which God forbyd, the fame wear to be layed on Captaine Furbusher, whose great abusses therin are before declared and on Jonas and Denam, being the workmen therof, as men who have byn the fyndars and bringars of that ewr which is brought, and causars of the cost bestowed for the fetchinge and workinge of the same, and on them the same weare to be punished sharplie, but I trust no suche cause shalbe gyven.

[Endorsed:] 1578. The Abusses of Captayne Furbusher against the Companie.

Chapter Eighty-one
The Northwest Voyages of John Davis

THESE ORIGINATE in the assignment by Sir Humphrey Gilbert, under his patent of 1578, of rights north of 50°N to Dr. John Dee. Dee teamed up with Adrian Gilbert, Sir Humphrey Gilbert's brother, to exploit them, but Dee left England in 1583 and gave up his interest. This bore fruit in a patent of February 6, 1584, to Adrian Gilbert of Sandridge, Devon, who enlisted the aid of the pilot John Davis of the same place. It was, however, the London merchant William Sanderson, with some help from Exeter citizens, who mounted and maintained the voyages of 1585, 1586, and 1587, which considerably enlarged geographical knowledge even if they did not lead to the discovery of the Northwest Passage. Davis, in his book *The worldes hydrographicall discription* (1595), tried to put the Northwest Passage question and his own voyages into some sort of perspective.

664. February 6, 1584. Adrian Gilbert's patent.

P.R.O., Patent Roll, 26 Elizabeth, part 8, C. 66/1243; printed in R. Hakluyt, Principall navigations *(1589), pp. 774–776, and* Principal navigations, *III (1600), 96–98 (VII [1904], 375–381).*

The Letters patents of the Queenes Majestie, granted to Master Adrian Gylbert and others, for the search and discovery of the Northwest Passage to China.

Elizabeth by the grace of God of England, France, and Ireland Queene, defender of the faith, &c. To all, to whome these presents shall come, greeting: Forasmuch as our trustie and welbeloved subject Adrian Gylbert of Sandridge in the Countie of Devon, Gentleman, to his great costes and charges, hath greatly and earnestly travelled and sought, and yet doth travell and seeke, and by divers meanes indevoureth and laboureth, that the Passage unto China and the Iles of the Moluccas, by the Northwestward,

Northeastward, or Northward, unto which part or partes of the world, none of our loyall Subjects have hither to had any traffique or trade, may be discovered, knowen, and frequented by the Subjects of this our Realme: Knowe yee therefore that for the considerations aforesayd and for divers other good considerations us thereunto specially mooving. We of our grace especiall, certaine knowledge, and meere motion, have given and granted, and by these presents for us, our heires and successors, doe give and grant free libertie, power, and full authoritie to the sayd Adrian Gylbert, and to any other person by him or his heires to be assigned, and to those his associates and assistants, whose names are written in a Scedule hereunto annexed, and to their heires, and to one assignee of each of them, and each of their heires at all times, and at any time or times after the date of these presents, under our Banners and Ensignes freely, without let, interruption, or restraint, of us, our heires or successors, any law, statute, proclamation, patent, charter, or proviso to the contrary notwithstanding, to saile, make voyage, and by any maner of meanes to passe and to depart out of this our Realme of

228

England, or any our Realmes, Dominions, or Territories into all or any Isles, Countreys, Regions, Provinces, Territories, Seas, Rivers, Portes, Bayes, Creekes, armes of the Sea, and all Havens, and all maner of other places whatsoever, that by the sayde Northwestward, Northeastward, or Northward, is to be by him, his associates or assignes discovered, and for and in the sayde sayling, voyage, and passage, to have and use so many shippes, Barkes, Pinnesses, or other vessels of any quantitie or burthen, with all the furniture of men, victuals, and all maner of necessary provision, armour, weapons, ordinance, targets, and appurtinances whatsoever, as to such a voyage shall or may be requisite, convenient or commodious, any lawe, statute, ordinance or proviso to the contrary thereof notwithstanding. And also we doe give and grant to the sayde Adrian Gylbert, and his sayde associates, and to such assignee of him, and his heires, and to the heires and one assignee of every of his sayde associates for ever, full power and absolute authoritie to trade and make their resiance in any of the sayde Isles, Countreys, Regions, Provinces, Territories, Seas, Rivers, Portes, Bayes, and Havens, and all maner of other places whatsoever with all commodities, profites, and emoluments in the sayde places or any of them, growing and arising, with all maner of priviledges, prerogatives, jurisdictions and royalties both by sea and land whatsoever, yeelding and paying therefore unto us, our heires and successors, the tenth part of all such golde and silver oare, pearles, jewels, and precious stones, or the value thereof, as the sayd Adrian Gylbert and his sayd associates, their heires and assignes, servants, factors, or workemen, and every or any of them shall finde, the sayd tenth to bee delivered duely to our Customer, or other officers by us, our heires or successors thereunto assigned, in the Portes of London, Dartmouth, or Plimmouth, at which three places onely the sayde Adrian Gylbert, and his sayde associates, their sayde heires and assignes, shall lade, charge, arrive, and discharge all maner of wares, goods, and merchandizes whatsoever to the sayde voyage, and newe trade belonging or appertaining. And moreover, wee have given, granted, and authorized, and by these presents for us, our heires and successors, of our grace especiall, certaine knowledge, and meere motion, doe give, graunt, and authorize the sayd Adrian Gilbert, and his sayd associats for ever, their heires and their said assignes & every of them, that if the aforesayd Iles, Countreys, Regions, Provinces, Territories, Seas, Rivers, Ports, Bayes, or Havens, or any other of the premisses by the sayd Adrian Gylbert or his associats, their heires and their said assignes or any of them, to be found by them, discovered and traffiqued unto by any trade as aforesayd, shall be by any other our subjects visited, frequented, haunted, traded unto or inhabited by the wayes aforesayd, without the special licence in writing of the said Adrian Gylbert and his associats, and their heires and assignes for ever, or by the most part of them, so that the sayd Adrian Gilbert, his heires or assignes be one of them, that then aswell their ship, or ships in any such voyage or voyages be used, as all and singuler their goods, wares, and marchandizes, or any other things whatsoever, from or to any of the places aforesayd transported, that so shall presume to visit, frequent, haunt, trade unto, or inhabite, shall be forfaited and confiscated, ipso facto, the one halfe of the same goods and marchandizes, or other things whatsoever, or the value thereof to be to the use of us, our heires or successours, and the other moytie thereof to be to the use of the sayd Adrian Gylbert and his sayd associats, their heires and assignes for ever: and unto the sayd Adrian Gylbert and his sayd associats, their heires and assignes wee impose, give, assigne, create and confirme this name peculiar to be named by, to sue and to be sued by, that is to wit, by the name of the Colleagues of the fellowship for the discoverie of the Northwest passage, and them for us, our heires and successours by that name doe incorporate, and doe erect and create as one body corporate to have continuance for ever. Moreover unto the sayd Adrian Gylbert, and his said associats, and unto their heires and their sayd assignes for ever, by name of the Colleagues of the fellowship, for the discoverie of the Northwest passage, we have given, granted, and confirmed, and doe by these presents give, grant, and confirme full power and authoritie from time to time, and at all times hereafter, to make order, decree and enact, constitute and ordeine, and appoynt all such ordinances, orders, decrees, lawes, and actes, as the sayd new corporation or body politique, Colleagues of the fellowship for the discoverie of the

Northwest passage, shall thinke meete, necessary, and convenient, so that they or any of them be not contrary to the lawes of this realme, and of this our present graunt.

And we by our Royall prerogative, and fulnesse of our authority, of our grace especiall, certaine knowledge and meere motion, do establish, confirme & ratifie all such ordinances, orders, decrees, lawes and acts to be in so full and great power and authority, as we, our heires or successours may or can in any such case graunt, confirme, or ratifie. And further for the better incouragement of our loving subjects in this discoverie, we by our Royall prerogative, and fulnesse of authority for us, our heires and successours, doe give, graunt, establish, confirme, ordeine, ratifie and allow by these presents, to the sayd Adrian Gylbert and to his associates, and to the heires and assignes of them and every of them for ever, and to all other person or persons of our loving subjects whatsoever that shall hereafter travaile, sayle, discover, or make voyage as aforesayd to any the Iles, Mainelands, Countreys or Territories whatsoever, by vertue of this our graunt to be discovered, that the heires and assignes of them and every of them being borne within any of the Iles, Mainelands and Countreys, or Territories whatsoever before mentioned, shall have and injoy all the privileges of free Denizens, as persons native borne within this our Realme of England, or within our allegiance for ever, in such like ample maner and forme, as if they were or had bene borne and personally resiant within our sayd Realme, any law, statute, proclamation, custome or usage to the contrary hereof in any wise notwithstanding.

Moreover, for the consideration aforesayd by vertue hereof, we give and graunt unto the sayd Adrian Gylbert, his heires and assignes for ever, free libertie, licence and privilege, that during the space of five yeeres next and immediatly ensuing the date hereof, it shall not be lawfull for any person or persons whatsoever, to visit, haunt, frequent, trade, or make voyage to any Iles, Mainelands, Countreys, Regions, Provinces, Territories, Seas, Rivers, Ports, Bayes, and Havens, nor to any other Havens or places whatsoever hitherto not yet discovered by any of our subjects by vertue of this graunt to be traded unto, without the special consent and good liking of the said Adrian Gylbert, his heires or assignes first had in

writing. And if any person or persons of the associats of the sayd Adrian, his heires or assignes, or any other person or persons whatsoever, free of this discovery, shall do any act or acts contrary to the tenour and true meaning hereof, during the space of the sayd five yeeres, that then the partie and parties so offending, they and their heires for ever shall loose (ipso facto) the benefite and privilege of this our graunt, and shall stand and remaine to all intents and purposes as persons exempted out of this graunt.

And further by vertue hereof wee give and graunt, for us, our heires and successours at all times during the space of five yeers next ensuing the date hereof, libertie and licence, and full authority to the sayd Adrian Gylbert, and his heires and assignes, that if it shall happen any one or more in any ship or ships sayling on their sayd voyage, to become mutinous, seditious, disordered, or any way unruly to the prejudice or hinderance of the hope for the successe in the attempt or prosecuting of this discoverie or trade intended, to use or execute upon him or them so offending, such punishment, correction, or execution, as the cause shall be found in justice to require by the verdict of twelve of the companie sworne thereunto, as in such a case apperteineth: That expresse mention of the certaintie of the premisses, or of other gifts or graunts by us to the sayd Adrian Gylbert and his associats before this time made is not mentioned in these presents, or any other lawe, act, statute, proviso, graunt, or proclamation heretofore made or hereafter to be made to the contrary hereof in any wise notwithstanding. In witnesse whereof we have made these our Letters to bee made patents: Witnesse our selfe at Westminster, the sixt day of Februarie, in the sixe and twenty yeere of our reigne.

665. 1595. John Davis on the search for the Northwest Passage.

This report is excerpted from John Davis, The worldes hydrographicall discription *(London, 1595), a treatise on navigation. It was reprinted in R. Hakluyt,* Principal navigations, *III (1600), 119–120 (VII [1904], 440–445).*

A report of Master John Davis of his three Voyages made for the discovery of the Northwest passage, taken out of a Treatise of his, Intituled the worlds Hydrographicall description.

Now there onely resteth the North parts of America, upon which coast my selfe have had most experience of any in our age: for thrise I was that waye imployed for the discovery of this notable passage, by the honourable care and some charge of Syr Francis Walsingham knight, principall secretary to her Majestie, with whom divers noble men and worshipfull marchants of London joyned in purse and willingnesse for the furtherance of that attempt, but when his honour dyed the voyage was friendlesse, and mens mindes alienated from adventuring therein.

In my first voyage not experienced of the nature of those climates, and having no direction either by Chart, Globe, or other certaine relation in what altitude that passage was to be searched, I shaped a Northerly course and so sought the same toward the South, and in that my Northerly course I fell upon the shore which in ancient time was called Groenland, five hundred leagues distant from the Durseys Westnorthwest Northerly, the land being very high and full of mightie mountaines all covered with snow, no viewe of wood, grasse or earth to be seene, and the shore two leagues off into the sea so full of yce as that no shipping could by any meanes come neere the same. The lothsome view of the shore, and irksome noyse of the yce was such, as that it bred strange conceites among us, so that we supposed the place to be wast and voyd of any sensible or vegitable creatures, whereupon I called the same Desolation: so coasting this shore towards the South in the latitude of sixtie degrees, I found it to trend towards the West, I still followed the leading therof in the same height, and after fifty or sixtie leagues it fayled and lay directly North, which I still followed, and in thirtie leagues sayling upon the West side of this coast by me named Desolation, we were past al the yce and found many greene & pleasant Isles bordering upon the shore, but the hils of the maine were still covered with great quantities of snow, I brought my ship among those Isles and there mored to refresh our selves in our weary travell, in the latitude of sixtie foure degrees or there about. The people of the

countrey having espyed our shippes came downe unto us in their Canoas, & holding up their right hand to the Sunne and crying Yliaout, would strike their breasts: we doing the like the people came aboard our shippes, men of good stature, unbearded, small eyed and of tractable conditions, by whome as signes would permit, we understood that towards the North and West there was a great sea, and using the people with kindenes in giving them nayles and knives which of all things they most desired, we departed, and finding the sea free from yce supposing our selves to be past al daunger we shaped our course Westnorthwest thinking thereby to passe for China, but in the latitude of sixtie sixe degrees we fell with another shore, and there found another passage of twenty leagues broad directly West into the same, which we supposed to be our hoped straight, we entered into the same thirty or fortie leagues, finding it neither to wyden nor streighten, then considering that the yeere was spent (for this was the fine of August) not knowing the length of the straight and dangers thereof, we tooke it our best course to returne with notice of our good successe for this small time of search. And so returning in a sharpe fret of Westerly windes the 29. of September we arived at Dartmouth. And acquainting master Secretary Walsingham with the rest of the honourable and worshipfull adventurers of all our proceedings, I was appointed againe the second yere to search the bottome of this straight, because by all likelihood it was the place and passage by us laboured for. In this second attempt the marchants of Exeter, and other places of the West became adventurers in the action, so that being sufficiently furnished for six moneths, and having direction to search these straights, untill we found the same to fall into another sea upon the West side of this part of America, we should againe returne: for then it was not to be doubted, but shipping with trade might safely be conveied to China, and the parts of Asia. We departed from Dartmouth, and ariving upon the South part of the coast of Desolation coasted the same upon his West shore to the latitude of sixtie sixe degrees, and there ancored among the Isles bordering upon the same, where we refreshed our selves, the people of this place came likewise unto us, by whom I understood through their signes that towards the North the sea was large. At this place the chiefe ship whereupon I trusted, called the Mermayd of Dartmouth, found many occasions of discontentment, and being unwilling to proceed, shee there forsook me. Then considering how I had given my faith and most constant promise to my worshipfull good friend master William Sanderson, who of all men was the greatest adventurer in that action, and tooke such care for the performance thereof, that he hath to my knowledge at one time disbursed as much money as any five others whatsoever, out of his owne purse, when some of the companie have bene slacke in giving in their adventure: And also knowing that I should loose the favor of M. Secretary Walsingham, if I should shrink from his direction; in one small barke of 30 Tunnes, whereof M. Sanderson was owner, alone without farther company I proceeded on my voyage, and arriving at these straights followed the same 80. leagues, untill I came among many Islands, where the water did ebbe and flow sixe fadome upright, and where there had bene great trade of people to make traine. But by such things as there we found, wee knew that they were not Christians of Europe that had used that trade: in fine by searching with our boat, we found small hope to passe any farther that way, and therefore recovered the sea and coasted the shore towards the South, and in so doing (for it was too late to search towards the North) we found another great inlet neere 40 leagues broad, where the water entred in with violent swiftnesse, this we also thought might be a passage: for no doubt the North partes of America are all Islands by ought that I could perceive therein: but because I was alone in a small barke of thirtie tunnes, and the yeere spent, I entred not into the same, for it was now the seventh of September, but coasting the shore towardes the South wee saw an incredible number of birds: having divers fishermen aboord our barke they all concluded that there was a great skull of fish, we being unprovided of fishing furniture with a long spike nayle made a hooke, and fastened the same to one of our sounding lines, before the baite was changed we tooke more then fortie great Cods, the fish swimming so abundantly thicke about our barke as is incredible to bee reported, of which with a small portion of salt that we had, we preserved some thirtie couple, or thereaboutes, and so returned for England. And having reported to M. Secretarie

Walsingham the whole successe of this attempt, he commanded me to present unto the most honourable Lord high Treasurour of England, some part of that fish: which when his Lordship saw, & heard at large the relation of this second attempt, I received favourable countenance from his honour, advising me to prosecute the action, of which his Lordship conceived a very good opinion. The next yere, although divers of the adventurers fell from the Action, as all the Westerne marchants, and most of those in London: yet some of the adventurers both honorable & worshipfull continued their willing favor and charge, so that by this meanes the next yere two shippes were appointed for the fishing and one pinnesse for the discoverie.

Departing from Dartmouth, through Gods mercifull favour, I arrived at the place of fishing, and there according to my direction I left the two ships to follow that busines, taking their faithfull promise not to depart untill my returne unto them, which should be in the fine of August, and so in the barke I proceeded for the discoverie: but after my departure, in sixteene dayes the two shippes had finished their voyage, and so presently departed for England, without regard of their promise: my selfe not distrusting any such hard measure proceeded for the discoverie, and followed my course in the free and open sea betweene North and Northwest to the latitude of 67 degrees, and there I might see America West from me, and Gronland, which I called Desolation, East: then when I saw the land of both sides I began to distrust it would proove but a gulfe: notwithstanding desirous to know the full certainty I proceeded, and in 68 degrees the passage enlarged, so that I could not see the Westerne shore: thus I continued to the latitude of 73 degrees, in a great sea, free from yce, coasting the Westerne shore of Desolation: the people came continually rowing out unto me in their Canoas, twenty, forty, and one hundred at a time, and would give me fishes dryed, Salmon, Salmon peale, Cod, Caplin, Lumpe, Stone-base and such like, besides divers kinds of birds, as Partrige, Fesant, Guls, Sea birds and other kindes of flesh: I still laboured by signes to know from them what they knew of any sea toward the North, they still made signes of a great sea as we understood them, then I departed from that coast, thinking to discover the North parts of America: & after I had sailed towards the West 40 leagues, I fel upon a great banke of yce: the winde being North and blew much, I was constrained to coast the same toward the South, not seeing any shore West from me, neither was there any yce towards the North, but a great sea, free, large very salt and blew, & of an unsearchable depth: So coasting towards the South I came to the place where I left the ships to fish, but found them not. Then being forsaken & left in this distresse referring my self to the mercifull providence of God, I shaped my course for England, & unhoped for of any, God alone releeving me, I arrived at Dartmouth. By this last discovery it seemed most manifest that the passage was free & without impediment toward the North: but by reason of the Spanish fleet & unfortunate time of M. Secretaries death, the voyage was omitted & never sithens attempted. The cause why I use this particular relation of all my proceedings for this discovery, is to stay this objection, why hath not Davis discovered this passage being thrise that wayes imploied? How far I proceeded & in what forme this discovery lieth, doth appeare upon the Globe which M. Sanderson to his very great charge hath published, for the which he deserveth great favor & commendations.

666. June 13 to September 30, 1586. John Janes's narrative of the first Northwest Passage voyage of John Davis.

Printed in R. Hakluyt, Principall navigations *(1589), 776–781; Principal navigations, III (1600), 98–102 (VII [1904], 381–393).*

The first voyage of Master John Davis, undertaken in June 1585. for the discoverie of the Northwest passage, Written by Master John Janes Marchant, sometimes servant to the worshipfull Master William Sanderson.

Certaine Honourable personages and worthy Gentlemen of the Court & Countrey, with divers worshipful Marchants of London and of the West Countrey, mooved with desire to advance Gods glory and to seeke the good of their native Countrey, consulting together of the likelyhood of the Discoverie of the Northwest passage, which heretofore had bene attempted, but unhappily given over by accidents unlooked for, which turned the enterprisers from their principall purpose, resolved after good deliberation, to put downe their adventures to provide for necessarie shipping, and a fit man to be chiefe Conductour of this so hard an enterprise. The setting forth of this Action was committed by the adventurers, especially to the care of M. William Sanderson Marchant of London, who was so forward therein, that besides his travaile which was not small, hee became the greatest adventurer with his purse, and commended unto the rest of the companie one M. John Davis, a man very well grounded in the principles of the Arte of Navigation, for Captaine and chiefe Pilot of this exployt.

Thus therefore all things being put in a readines, wee departed from Dartmouth the seventh of June, towards the discoverie of the aforesayd Northwest passage, with two Barkes, the one being of 50. tunnes, named the Sunneshine of London, and the other being 35. tunnes, named the Mooneshine of Dartmouth. In the Sunneshine we had 23. persons, whose names are these following, Master John Davis Captaine, William Eston Master, Richard Pope Masters mate, John Jane Marchant, Henry Davie gunner, William Crosse boatswayne, John Bagge, Walter Arthur, Luke Adams, Robert Coxworthie, John Ellis, John Kelley, Edward Helman, William Dicke, Andrew Maddocke, Thomas Hill, Robert Wats Carpenter, William Russell, Christopher Gorney boy: James Cole, Francis Ridley, John Russell, Robert Cornish Musicians.

The Mooneshine had 19. persons, William Bruton Captaine, John Ellis Master, the rest Mariners.

The 7. of June the Captaine and the Master drewe out a proportion for the continuance of our victuals.

The 8. day the wind being at Southwest and West southwest, we put in for Falmouth, where we remained untill the 13.

The 13. the wind blew at North, and being faire weather we departed.

The 14. with contrary wind we were forced to put into Silley.

The 15. wee departed thence, having the wind North and by East moderate and faire weather.

The 16. wee were driven backe againe, and were constrained to arrive at newe Grymsby in Silley: here the winde remained contrary 12. dayes, and in that space the Captaine, the Master and I went about all the Ilands, and the Captaine did plat out and describe the situation of all the Ilands, rocks and harboroughs to the exact use of Navigation, with lines and scale thereunto convenient.

The 28. in Gods name we departed the wind being Easterly but calme.

The first of July wee sawe great store of Porposes; The Master called for an harping yron, and shot twise or thrise: sometimes he missed, and at last shot one and strooke him in the side, and wound him into the ship: when we had him aboord, the Master sayd it was a Darlie head.

The 2. we had some of the fish sodden, and it did eat as sweete as any mutton.

The 3. wee had more in sight, and the Master went to shoote at them, but they were so great, that they burst our yrons, and we lost both fish, yrons, pastime and all: yet neverthelesse the Master shot at them with a pike, and had welnigh gotten one, but he was so strong that he burst off the barres of the pike and went away: then he tooke the boat-hooke, and hit one with that, but all would not prevaile, so at length we let them alone.

The 6. we saw a very great Whale, and every day we saw whales continually.

The 16. 17. and 18. we saw great store of Whales.

The 19. of July we fell into a great whirling and brustling of a tyde, setting to the Northwards: and sayling about halfe a league wee came into a very calme Sea, which bent to the Southsouthwest. Here we heard a mighty great roaring of the Sea, as if it had bene the breach of some shoare, the ayre being so foggie and full of thicke mist, that we could not see the one ship from the other, being a very small distance asunder: so the Captaine and the Master being in distrust how the tyde might set them, caused the Mooneshine to hoyse out her boate and to sound, but they could not finde ground in 300. fathoms and better. Then the Captaine, Master, and I went towards the breach, to see what it should be, giving charge to our gunners that at every glasse they should shoote off a musket-shot, to the intent we might keepe our selves from loosing them. Then com-

ming nere to the breach, we met many Ilands of yce floting, which had quickly compassed us about: then we went upon some of them, and did perceive that all the roaring which we heard, was caused onely by the rowling of this yce together: Our companie seeing us not to returne according to our appoyntment, left off shooting muskets, and began to shoote falkonets, for they feared some mishap had befallen us, but before night we came aboord againe with our boat laden with yce, which made very good fresh water. Then wee bent our course toward the North, hoping by that meanes to double the land.

The 20. as we sayled along the coast the fogge brake up, and we discovered the land, which was the most deformed rockie and mountainous land that ever we saw: The first sight whereof did shew as if it had bene in forme of a sugar-loafe, standing to our sight above the cloudes, for that it did shew over the fogge like a white liste in the skie, the tops altogether covered with snow, and the shoare beset with yce a league off into the Sea, making such yrkesome noyse as that it seemed to be the true patterne of desolation, and after the same our Captaine named it, The land of Desolation.

The 21. the winde came Northerly and over-blew, so that we were constrained to bend our course South againe, for we perceived that we were runne into a very deepe Bay, where wee were almost compassed with yce, for we saw very much toward the Northnortheast, West, and Southwest: and this day and this night wee cleared our selves of the yce, running Southsouthwest along the shoare.

Upon Thursday being the 22. of this moneth, about three of the clocke in the morning, wee hoysed out our boate, and the Captaine with six saylers went towards the shoare, thinking to find a landing place, for the night before we did perceive the coast to be voyde of yce to our judgement, and the same night wee were all perswaded that we had seene a Canoa rowing along the shoare, but afterwards we fell in some doubt of it, but we had no great reason so to doe. The Captaine rowing towards the shoare, willed the Master to beare in with the land after him, and before he came neere the shoare by the space of a league, or about two miles, hee found so much yce, that hee could not get to land by any meanes. Here our mariners put to their lines to see if they could get any fish, because there were so many seales upon the coast, and the birds did beate upon the water, but all was in vaine: The water about this place was very blacke and thicke like to a filthy standing poole, we sounded and had ground in 120. fathoms. While the Captaine was rowing to the shoare, our men sawe woods upon the rocks like to the rocks of Newfoundland, but I could not discerne them, yet it might be so very well: for we had wood floting upon the coast every day, and the Mooneshine tooke up a tree at Sea not farre from the coast being sixtie foote of length and foureteene handfuls about, having the roote upon it: After this the Captaine came aboord, the weather being very calme and faire we bent our course toward the South, with intent to double the land.

The 23. we coasted the land which did lie Eastnortheast and Westsouthwest.

The 24. the winde being very faire at East, we coasted the land which did lie East and West, not being able to come neere the shoare by reason of the great quantitie of yce. At this place, because the weather was somewhat colde by reason of the yce, and the better to encourage our men, their allowance was increased: the captaine and the master tooke order that every messe, being five persons, should have halfe a pound of bread and a kan of beere every morning to breakfast. The weather was not very colde, but the aire was moderate like to our April-weather in England: when the winde came from the land, or the ice, it was some what colde, but when it came off the sea it was very hote.

The 25 of this moneth we departed from sight of this land at sixe of the clocke in the morning, directing our course to the Northwestward, hoping in Gods mercy to finde our desired passage, and so continued above foure dayes.

The 29 of July we discovered land in 64 degrees 15 minutes of latitude, bearing Northeast from us. The winde being contrary to goe to the Northwestwards, we bare in with this land to take some view of it, being utterly void of the pester of yce and very temperate. Comming neere the coast, we found many faire sounds and good roads for shipping, and many great inlets into the land, whereby we judged this land to be a great number of Islands standing together. Heere having mored our barke in good order, we went on shoare upon a small Island to seeke for water and wood.[1] Upon this Island we did perceive that there had bene people: for we found a small shoo and pieces of leather sowed with sinewes, and a piece of furre, and wooll like to Bever. Then we went upon another Island on the other side of our shippes: and the Captaine, the Master, and I, being got up to the top of an high rocke, the people of the countrey having espied us, made a lamentable noise, as we thought, with great outcries and skreechings: we hearing them, thought it had bene the howling of wolves. At last I hallowed againe, and they likewise cried. Then we perceiving where they stood, some on the shoare, and one rowing in a Canoa about a small Island fast by them, we made a great noise, partly to allure them to us, and partly to warne our company of them. Whereupon M. Bruton and the Master of his shippe, with others of their company, made great haste towards us, and brought our Musicians with them from our shippe, purposing either by force to rescue us, if need should so require, or with courtesie to allure the people. When they came unto us, we caused our Musicians to play, our selves dancing, and making many signes of friendship. At length there came tenne Canoas from the other Islands, and two of them came so neere the shoare where we were, that they talked with us, the other being in their boats a pretty way off. Their pronunciation was very hollow thorow the throat, and their speech such as we could not understand: onely we allured them by friendly imbracings and signes of curtesie. At length one of them pointing up to the Sunne with his hand, would presently strike his breast so hard that we might heare the blow. This hee did many times before he would any way trust us. Then John Ellis the Master of the Mooneshine was appointed to use his best policie to gaine their friendship; who strooke his breast, and pointed to the Sunne after their order: which when he had divers times done, they beganne to trust him, and one of them came on shoare, to whom we threw our cappes, stockings and gloves, and such other things as then we had about us, playing with our musicke, and making signes of joy, and dauncing. So the night comming, we bade them farewell, and went aboord our barks.

The next morning being the 30 of July there

1. Sidenote: "The sound where our ships did ride was called Gilberts sound."

came 37 Canoas rowing by our ships, calling to us to come on shoare: we not making any great haste unto them, one of them went up to the toppe of the rocke, and leapt and daunced as they had done the day before, shewing us a seales skinne, and another thing made like a timbrell, which he did beat upon with a sticke, making a noise like a small drumme. Whereupon we manned our boats and came to them, they all staying in their Canoas: we came to the water side were they were: and after we had sworne by the Sunne after their fashion, they did trust us. So I shooke hands with one of them, and he kissed my hand, and we were very familiar with them. We were in so great credit with them upon this single acquaintance, that we could have any thing they had. We bought five Canoas of them: we bought their clothes from their backs, which were all made of seales skinnes & birds skinnes; their buskins, their hose, their gloves, all being commonly sowed and well dressed: so that we were fully perswaded that they have divers artificers among them. We had a paire of buskins of them full of fine wooll like bever. Their apparell for heat was made of birds skinnes with their feathers on them. We saw among them leather dressed like Glovers leather, and thicke thongs like white leather of a good length. We had of their darts and oares, and found in them that they would by no meanes displease us, but would give us whatsoever we asked of them, and would be satisfied with whatsoever we gave them. They tooke great care one of another: for when we had bought their boats, then two other would come and cary him away betweene them that had solde us his. They are very tractable people, void of craft or double dealing, and easie to be brought to any civility or good order: but we judge them to be idolaters and to worship the Sunne.

During the time of our abode among these Islands we found reasonable quantity of wood, both firre, spruse and juniper; which whether it came floting any great distance to these places where we found it, or whether it grew in some great Islands neere the same place by us not yet discovered, we know not; but we judge that it groweth there further into the land then we were, because the people had great store of darts and oares which they made none account of, but gave them to us for small trifles, as points and pieces of paper. We saw about this coast marveilous great abundance of seales skulling together like skuls of small fish. [2] We found no fresh water among these Islands, but onely snow water, whereof we found great pooles. The cliffes were all of such oare as M. Frobisher brought from Meta incognita. We had divers shewes of Study or Muscovy glasse shining not altogether unlike to Christall. We found an herbe growing upon the rocks, whose fruit was sweet, full of red juice, and the ripe ones were like corinths. We found also birch and willow growing like shrubbes low to the ground. These people have great store of furres as we judge. They made shewes unto us the 30 of this present, which was the second time of our being with them, after they perceived we would have skinnes and furres, that they would go into the countrey and come againe the next day with such things as they had: but this night the winde comming faire, the captaine and the master would by no meanes detract the purpose of our discovery. And so the last of this moneth about foure of the clocke in the morning in Gods name we set saile, and were all that day becalmed upon the coast.

The first of August we had a faire winde, and so proceeded towards the Northwest for our discovery.

The sixt of August we discovered land in 66 degrees 40 minuts of latitude, altogether void from the pester of ice: we ankered in a very faire rode under a brave mount, the cliffes whereof were as orient as golde. This mount was named Mount Raleigh. The rode where our ships lay at anker was called Totnes rode. The sound which did compasse the mount was named Exeter sound. The foreland towards the North was called Diers cape. The foreland towards the South was named Cape Walsingham. So soone as we were come to an anker in Totnes rode under Mount Raleigh, we espied foure white beares at the foot of the mount: we supposing them to be goats or wolves, manned our boats and went towards them: but when we came neere the shore, we found them to be white beares of a monstrous bignesse: we being desirous of fresh victuall and the sport, began to assault them, and I being on land, one of them came downe the hill right against me: my piece was charged with

2. Sidenote: "They may make much traine, if they had meanes how to use it."

hailshot & a bullet: I discharged my piece and shot him in the necke; he roared a litle, and tooke the water straight, making small account of his hurt. Then we followed him with our boat, and killed him with boare-speares, & two more that night. We found nothing in their mawes; but we judged by their dung that they fed upon grasse, because it appeared in all respects like the dung of an horse, wherein we might very plainly see the very strawes.

The 7 we went on shore to another beare which lay all night upon the top of an Island under Mount Raleigh, and when we came up to him he lay fast asleep. I levelled at his head, and the stone of my piece gave no fire: with that he looked up, and layed downe his head againe: then I shot being charged with two bullets, and strooke him in the head: he being but amazed fell backwards: whereupon we ran all upon him with boare-speares, and thrust him in the body: yet for all that he gript away our boare-speares, and went towards the water; and as he was going downe, he came backe againe. Then our Master shot his boare-speare, and strooke him in the head, and made him to take the water, and swimme into a cove fast by, where we killed him, and brought him aboord. The breadth of his forefoot from one side to the other was foureteene inches over. They were very fat, so as we were constrained to cast the fat away. We saw a raven upon Mount Raleigh. We found withies also growing like low shrubs & flowers like Primroses in the sayd place. The coast is very mountainous, altogether without wood, grasse, or earth, and is onely huge mountaines of stone; but the bravest stone that ever we saw. The aire was very moderate in this countrey.

The 8 we departed from Mount Raleigh, coasting along the shoare, which lieth Southsouthwest, and Eastnortheast.

The 9 our men fell in dislike of their allowance, because it was too small as they thought: wherupon we made a new proportion; every messe being five to a messe should have foure pound of bread a day, twelve wine quarts of beere, six Newland fishes; and the flesh dayes a gill of pease more: so we restrained them from their butter and cheese.

The 11 we came to the most Southerly cape of this land, which we named The Cape of Gods mercy, as being the place of our first entrance for the discovery. The weather being very foggy we coasted this North land; at length when it brake up, we perceived that we were shot into a very faire entrance or passage, being in some places twenty leagues broad, and in some thirty, altogether void of any pester of ice, the weather very tolerable, and the water of the very colour, nature and quality of the maine ocean, which gave us the greater hope of our passage. Having sailed Northwest sixty leagues in this entrance we discovered certaine Islands standing in the midst thereof, having open passage on both sides. Wherupon our ships divided themselves, the one sailing on the North side, the other on the South side of the sayd Isles, where we stayed five dayes, having the winde at Southeast, very foggy and foule weather.

The 14 we went on shoare and found signes of people, for we found stones layed up together like a wall, and saw the skull of a man or a woman.

The 15 we heard dogs houle on the shoare, which we thought had bene wolves, and therefore we went on shoare to kill them. When we came on land the dogges came presently to our boat very gently, yet we thought they came to pray upon us, and therefore we shot at them, and killed two: and about the necke of one of them we found a leatherne coller, wherupon we thought them to be tame dogs. There were twenty dogs like mastives with prickt eares and long bush tailes: we found a bone in the pizels of their dogs. Then we went farther, and found two sleads made like ours in England: the one was made of firre, spruse and oken boords sawen like inch boords: the other was made all of whale bone, & there hung on the tops of the sleads three heads of beasts which they had killed. We saw here larks, ravens, and partridges.

The 17 we went on shoare, and in a little thing made like an oven with stones I found many small trifles, as a small canoa made of wood, a piece of wood made like an image, a bird made of bone, beads having small holes in one end of them to hang about their necks, & other small things. The coast was very barren without wood or grasse: the rocks were very faire like marble, full of vaines of divers colours. We found a seale which was killed not long before, being fleane, and hid under stones.

Our Captaine and Master searched still for probabilities of the passage, and first found, ‖ that this place was all Islands, with great sounds passing betweene them.

Secondly, the water remained of one colour with the maine ocean without altering.[3]

Thirdly, we saw to the West of those Isles three or foure whales in a skull, which they judged to come from a Westerly sea, because to the Eastward we saw not any whale.

Also as we were rowing into a very great sound lying Southwest, from whence these whales came, upon the sudden there came a violent counter-checke of a tide from the Southwest against the flood which we came with, not knowing from whence it was mainteined.

Fiftly, in sailing twenty leagues within the mouth of this entrance we had sounding in 90 fadoms, faire grey osie sand, and the further we ran into the Westwards the deeper was the water; so that hard aboord the shoare among these Isles we could not have ground in 330 fadoms.

Lastly, it did ebbe and flow sixe or seven fadome up and downe, the flood comming from divers parts, so as we could not perceive the chiefe maintenance thereof.

The 18 and 19 our Captaine and Master determined what was best to doe, both for the safegard of their credits, and satisfying of the adventurers, and resolved, if the weather brake up, to make further search.

The 20 the winde came directly against us: so they altered their purpose, and reasoned both for proceeding and returning.

The 21 the winde being Northwest, we departed from these Islands; and as we coasted the South shoare we saw many faire sounds, whereby we were perswaded that it was no firme land but Islands.

The 23 of this moneth the wind came Southeast, with very stormy and foule weather: so we were constrained to seeke harborow upon the South coast of this entrance, where we fell into a very faire sound, & ankered in 25 fadoms greene osie sand. Here we went on shore, where we had manifest signes of people where they had made their fire, and layed stones like a wall. In this place we saw foure very faire faulcons; and M. Bruton tooke from one of them his prey, which we

judged by the wings and legs to be a snite, for the head was eaten off.

The 24 in the afternoone, the winde comming somewhat faire, we departed from this road, purposing by Gods grace to returne for England.

The 26 we departed from sight of the North land of this entrance, directing our course homewards untill the tenth of the next moneth.

The 10. of September wee fell with The land of desolation, thinking to goe on shoare, but we could get never a good harborough. That night wee put to sea againe thinking to search it the next day: but this night arose a very great storme, and separated our ships, so that we lost the sight of the Mooneshine.

The 13. about noone (having tried all the night before with a goose wing) we set saile, & within two houres after we had sight of the Mooneshine againe: this day we departed from this land.

The 27. of this moneth we fell with sight of England. This night we had a marveilous storme and lost the Mooneshine.

The 30. of September wee came into Dartmouth, where wee found the Mooneshine being come in not two houres before.

667. May 7 to October 8, 1587. The second Davis voyage in search of the Northwest Passage.

The documentation comprises (a) the journal of the four vessels, Mermaid, Sunshine, Moonshine, North Star, *and a pinnace, from May 7 until June 7, when Davis divides the little fleet at 60° N. Davis, with* Moonshine *and* Mermaid, *proceeds, but leaves* Mermaid *on August 2 to return home alone, so that from this point the journal is that of the* Moonshine *alone; (b) October 14, 1587, John Davis wrote to his principal backer, William Sanderson, giving his impression of the result of the voyage; (c) the journal by Henry Morgan of the* Sunshine *and* North Star *from June 7 until October 6.*

R. Hakluyt, Principall navigations *(1589), pp. 776–789, and* Principal navigations, *III (1600), 103–111 (VII [1904], 393–413).*

---

3. Sidenote: "Wee never came into any bay before or after, but the waters colour was altered very blackish."

The second voyage attempted by Master John Davis with others, for the discovery of the Northwest passage, in Anno 1586.

[a] The 7. day of May, I departed from the port of Dartmouth for the discovery of the Northwest passage, with a ship of an hundred and twentie tunnes named the Mermayd, a barke of 60. tunnes named the Sunneshine, a barke of 35. tunnes named the Mooneshine, and a pinnesse of tenne tunnes named the North starre.

And the 15. of June I discovered land in the latitude of 60. degrees, and in longitude from the Meridian of London Westward 47. degrees, mightily pestered with yce and snow, so that there was no hope of landing: the yce lay in some places tenne leagues, in some 20. and in some 50. leagues off the shore, so that wee were constrained to beare into 57. degrees to double the same, and to recover a free Sea, which through Gods favourable mercy we at length obtained.

The 29. of June after many tempestuous storms we againe discovered land, in longitude from the Meridian of London 58. degr. 30. min. and in latitude 64. being East from us: into which course sith it please God by contrary winds to force us, I thought it very necessary to beare in with it, & there to set up our pinnesse, provided in the Mermayd to be our scout for this discovery, and so much the rather because the yere before I had bene in the same place, and found it very convenient for such a purpose, wel stored with flote wood, & possessed by a people of tractable conversation: so that the 29. of this moneth we arrived within the Isles which lay before this land, lying North northwest, and South southeast, we know not how farre. This land is very high & mountainous, having before it on the West side a mighty company of Isles full of faire sounds, and harboroughs. This land was very litle troubled with snow, and the sea altogether voyd of yce.

The ships being within the sounds wee sent our boates to search for shole water, where wee might anker, which in this place is very hard to finde: and as the boat went sounding and searching, the people of the countrey having espied them, came in their Canoas towards them with many shoutes and cries: but after they had espied in the boat some of our company that were the yeere before here with us, they presently rowed to the boate, and tooke hold on the oare, and hung about the boate with such comfortable joy, as would require a long discourse to be uttered: they came with the boates to our ships, making signes that they knewe all those that the yeere before had bene with them.[1] After I perceived their joy and small feare of us, my selfe with the Merchants & others of the company went a shoare, bearing with me twentie knives: I had no sooner landed, but they lept out of their Canoas and came running to mee and the rest, and embraced us with many signes of heartie welcome: at this present there were eighteene of them, and to eche of them I gave a knife: they offred skinnes to me for reward, but I made signes that they were not solde, but given them of courtesie: and so dismissed them for that time, with signes that they should returne againe after certaine houres.

The next day with all possible speede the pinnesse was landed upon an Isle there to be finished to serve our purpose for the discoverie, which Isle was so convenient for that purpose, as that we were very wel able to defend our selves against many enemies. During the time that the pinnesse, was there setting up, the people came continually unto us sometime an hundred Canoas at a time, sometime fourtie, fiftie, more and lesse, as occasion served. They brought with them seale skinnes, stagge skinnes, white hares, Seale fish, samon peale, smal cod, dry caplin, with other fish, and birds such as the countrey did yeeld.

My selfe still desirous to have a further search of this place, sent one of the shipboates to one part of the lande, and my selfe went to another part to search for the habitation of this people, with straight commandement that there should be no injurie offered to any of the people, neither any gunne shot.

The boates that went from me found the tents of the people made with seale skinnes set up upon timber, wherein they found great store of dried Caplin, being a litle fish no bigger then a pilchard: they found bags of Trane oyle, many litle images cut in wood, Seale skinnes in tan-tubs, with many other such trifles, whereof they diminished nothing.

They also found tenne miles within the snowy mountaines a plaine champion countrey, with

1. Sidenote: "Gentle and loving Savages."

earth and grasse, such as our moory and waste grounds of England are: they went up into a river (which in the narrowest place is two leagues broad) about ten leagues, finding it still to continue they knewe not howe farre: but I with my company tooke another river, which although at the first it offered a large inlet, yet it proved but a deepe bay, the ende whereof in foure houres I attained, and there leaving the boat well manned, went with the rest of my company three or foure miles into the countrey, but found nothing, nor saw any thing, save onely gripes, ravens, and small birds, as larkes and linnets.

The third of July I manned my boat, and went with fifty Canoas attending upon me up into another sound where the people by signes willed mee to goe, hoping to finde their habitation: at length they made signes that I should goe into a warme place to sleepe, at which place I went on shore, and ascended the toppe of an high hill to see into the countrey, but perceiving my labor vaine, I returned againe to my boat, the people still following me, and my company very diligent to attend us, and to helpe us up the rockes, and likewise downe: at length I was desirous to have our men leape with them, which was done, but our men did overleape them: from leaping they went to wrestling, we found them strong and nimble, and to have skil in wrestling, for they cast some of our men that were good wrestlers.

The fourth of July we lanched our pinnesse, and had fortie of the people to helpe us, which they did very willingly: at this time our men againe wrestled with them, and found them as before, strong and skilfull. This fourth of July the Master of the Mermayd went to certaine Ilands to store himselfe with wood, where he found a grave with divers buried in it, only covered with seale skinnes, having a crosse laid over them. The people are of good stature, wel in body proportioned, with small slender hands and feet, with broad visages, and smal eyes, wide mouthes, the most part unbearded, great lips, and close toothed.[2] Their custome is as often as they go from us, still at their returne to make a new truce, in this sort, holding his hand up to the Sun with a lowd voice he crieth Ylyaoute, and striketh his brest with like signes, being promised safety, he giveth credit. These people are much given to bleed, and

therefore stop their noses with deeres haire, or the haire of an elan. They are idolaters and have images great store, which they weare about them, and in their boats, which we suppose they worship. They are witches, and have many kinds of inchantments, which they often used, but to small purpose, thankes be to God.

Being among them at shore the fourth of July, one of them making a long oration, beganne to kindle a fire in this maner: he tooke a piece of a board wherein was a hole halfe thorow: into that hole he puts the end of a round stick like unto a bedstaffe, wetting the end thereof in Trane, and in fashion of a turner with a piece of lether, by his violent motion doeth very speedily produce fire[3]: which done, with turfes he made a fire, into which with many words and strange gestures, he put diverse things, which wee supposed to be a sacrifice: my selfe and divers of my company standing by, they were desirous to have me go into the smoke, I willed them likewise to stand in the smoke, which they by no meanes would do. I then tooke one of them, and thrust him into the smoke, and willed one of my company to tread out the fire, & to spurne it into the sea, which was done to shew them that we did contemne their sorcery. These people are very simple in all their conversation, but marveilous theevish, especially for iron, which they have in great account. They began through our lenitie to shew their vile nature: they began to cut our cables: they cut away the Moonelights boat from her sterne, they cut our cloth where it lay to aire, though we did carefully looke unto it, they stole our oares, a caliver, a boare speare, a sword, with divers other things, wherat the company and Masters being grieved, for our better securitie, desired me to dissolve this new friendship, and to leave the company of these theevish miscreants: whereupon there was a caliver shot among them, and immediatly upon the same a faulcon, which strange noice did sore amaze them, so that with speed they departed: notwithstanding their simplicitie is such, that within ten houres after they came againe to us to entreat peace; which being promised, we againe fell into a great league. They brought us Seale skinnes, and sammon peale, but seeing iron, they could in no wise

---

2. Sidenote: "The Tartars and people of Japon are also smal eyed."

3. Sidenote: "Their maner of kindling fire like to theirs in America. A fire made of turfes."

forbeare stealing: which when I perceived, it did but minister unto mee an occasion of laughter, to see their simplicitie, and I willed that in no case they should bee any more hardly used, but that our owne company should be the more vigilant to keepe their things, supposing it to be the very hard in so short time to make them know their evils. They eate all their meat raw, they live most upon fish, they drinke salt water, and eate grasse and ice with delight: they are never out of the water, but live in the nature of fishes, save only when dead sleepe taketh them, and then under a warme rocke laying his boat upon the land, hee lyeth downe to sleepe. Their weapons are all darts, but some of them have bow and arrowes and slings. They make nets to take their fish of the finne of a whale: they do all their things very artificially: and it should seeme that these simple theevish Islanders have warre with those of the maine, for many of them are sore wounded, which wounds they received upon the maine land, as by signes they gave us to understand. We had among them copper oare, black copper, and red copper: they pronouce their language very hollow, and deepe in the throat: these words following we learned from them.

Kesinyoh, Eate some.
Madlycoyte, Musicke.
Aginyoh, go fetch.
Yliaoute, I meane
  no harme.
Ponameg, A boat.
Blete, An eye.
Unuicke, Give it.
Tuckloak, A stagge
  or ellan.
Panygmah, A needle.
Aob, The Sea.
Mysacoah, Wash it.
Lethicksaneg, A seale
  skinne.
Canyglow, Kisse me.
Ugnera, My sonne.
Acu, Shot.
Conah, Leape.
Maatuke, Fish.
Sambah, Below.
Maconmeg, Wil you
  have this.

Paaotyck, An oare.
Asanock, A dart.
Sawygmeg, A knife.
Uderah, A nose.
Aoh, Iron.
Cocah, Go to him.
Aba, Fallen downe.
Icune, Come hither.
Awennye, Yonder.
Nugo, No.
Tucktodo, A fogge.
Lechiksah, A skinne.
Maccoah, A dart.
Sugnacoon, A coat.
Gounah, Come downe.
Sasobneg, A bracelet.
Ugnake, A tongue.
Ataneg, A seale.
Macuah, A beard.
Pignagogah, A threed.
Quoysah, Give it to me.

The 7. of July being very desirous to search the habitation of this countrey, I went myselfe with our new pinnesse into the body of the land, thinking it to be a firme continent, and passing up a very large river, a great flaw of winde tooke me, whereby wee were constrained to seeke succour for that night, which being had, I landed with the most part of my company, and went to the top of a high mountaine, hoping from thence to see into the countrey: but the mountaines were so many and so mighty as that my purpose prevailed not: whereupon I againe returned to my pinnesse, and willing divers of my company to gather muscles for my supper, whereof in this place there was great store, my selfe having espied a very strange sight, especially to me that never before saw the like, which was a mighty whirlewinde taking up the water in very great quantitie, furiously mounting it into the aire, which whirlewinde, was not for a puffe or blast, but continual, for the space of three houres, with very little intermission, which sith it was in the course that I should passe, we were constrained that night to take up our lodging under the rockes.

The next morning the storme being broken up, we went forward in our attempt, and sailed into a mighty great river directly into the body of the land, and in briefe, found it to be no firme land, but huge, waste, and desert Isles with mighty sounds, and inlets passing betweene Sea and Sea. Whereupon we returned towards our shippes, and landing to stoppe a floud, wee found the burial of these miscreants; we found of their fish in bagges, plaices, and caplin dried, of which wee tooke onely one bagge and departed. The ninth of this moneth we came to our ships, where wee found the people desirous in their fashion, of friendship and barter, our Mariners complained heavily against the people, and said that my lenitie and friendly using of them gave them stomacke to mischiefe: for they have stollen an anker from us, they have cut our cable very dangerously, they have cut our boats from our sterne, and nowe since your departure, with slings they spare us not with stones of halfe a pound weight: and wil you stil indure these injuries? It is a shame to beare them. I desired them to be content, and said, I doubted not but al should be wel. The 10. of this moneth I went to the shore, the people following mee in their Canoas: I tolled them on shore, and used them with much courtesie, and then departed aboord, they following me, and my company. I gave some of them bracelets, & caused seven or eight of them to come aboord, which they did willingly, and some of them went into the top of the ship: and thus curteously using them, I let them depart: the Sunne was no sooner downe, but they began to practise their devilish nature, and with slings threw stones very fiercely into the Moonelight, and strake one of her men then boatswaine, that he overthrew withall: whereat being moved, I changed my curtesie, and grew to hatred, my self in my owne boate well manned with shot, and the barks boat likewise pursued them, and gave them divers shot, but to small purpose, by reason of their swift rowing: so smally content we returned.

The 11. of this moneth there came five of them to make a new truce: the master of the Admiral came to me to shew me of their comming, and desired to have them taken and kept as prisoners untill we had his anker againe: but when he sawe that the chiefe ringleader and master of mischiefe was one of the five, he then was vehement to execute his purpose, so it was determined to take him: he came crying Iliaout, and striking his brest offered a paire of gloves to sell, the master offered him a knife for them: so two of them came to us, the one was not touched, but the other was soone captive among us: then we pointed to him and his fellowes for our anker, which being had, we made signes that he should be set at libertie: within one houre after he came aboord the winde came faire, whereupon we weyed and set saile, and so brought the fellow with us: one of his fellowes still following our ship close aboord, talked with him and made a kinde of lamentation, we still using him wel with Yliaout, which was the common course of curtesie.[4] At length this fellow aboord us spake foure or five words unto the other and clapped his two hands upon his face, whereupon the other doing the like, departed as we suppose with heavie chere. We judged the covering of his face with his hands and bowing of his body downe, signified his death. At length he became a pleasant companion among us. I gave him a new sute of frize after the English fashion, because I saw he could not indure the colde, of which he was very joyfull, he trimmed up his darts, and all his fishing tooles, and would make okam, and set his hand to a ropes end upon occasion. He lived with the dry

4. Sidenote: "One of the people taken which after dyed."

Caplin that I tooke when I was searching in the pinnis, and did eate dry Newland fish.

All this while, God be thanked, our people were in very good health, onely one young man excepted, who dyed at sea the fourteenth of this moneth, and the fifteenth, according to the order of the sea, with praise given to God by service, was cast overboord.

The 17 of this moneth being in the latitude of 63. degres 8. minuts, we fell upon a most mighty and strange quantitie of yce in one intire masse, so bigge as that we knew not the limits thereof, and being withall so very high in forme of a land, with bayes and capes and like high cliffe land, as that we supposed it to be land, and therefore sent our pinnesse off to discover it: but at her returne we were certainely informed that it was onely yce, which bred great admiration to us all considering the huge quantitie thereof, incredible to be reported in trueth as it was, and therefore I omit to speake any further thereof. This onely I thinke, that the like before was never seene: and in this place we had very stickle and strong currents.

We coasted this mightie masse of yce untill the 30 of July, finding it a mighty barre to our purpose: the ayre in this time was so contagious and the sea so pestered with yce, as that all hope was banished of proceeding: for the 24 of July all our shrowds, ropes and sailes were so frosen, and compassed with yce, onely by a grosse fogge, as seemed to me more then strange, sith the last yeere I found this sea free and navigable, without impediments.

Our men through this extremity began to grow sicke and feeble, and withall hopelesse of good successe: whereupon very orderly, with good discretion they intreated me to regard the state of this busines, and withall advised me, that in conscience I ought to regard the saftie of mine owne life with the preservation of theirs, and that I should not through my overboldnes leave their widowes and fatherlesse children to give me bitter curses. This matter in conscience did greatly move me to regard their estates: yet considering the excellencie of the businesse if it might be attained, the great hope of certaintie by the last yeeres discovery, and that there was yet a third way not put in practise, I thought it would growe to my great disgrace, if this action by my negligence should grow into discredite: whereupon seeking helpe from God, the fountaine of all mercies, it pleased his divine majestie to move my heart to prosecute that which I hope shal be to his glory, and to the contentation of every Christian minde. Whereupon falling into consideration that the Mermaid, albeit a very strong & sufficient ship, yet by reason of her burthen was not so convenient and nimble as a smaller bark, especially in such desperate hazzards: further having in account her great charge to the adventurers being at 100.li. the moneth, and that in doubtfull service: all the premisses considered with divers other things, I determined to furnish the Moonelight with revictualling and sufficient men, and to proceede in this action as God should direct me. Whereupon I altered our course from the yce, and bare Eastsoutheast to recover the next shore where this thing might be performed: so with favourable winde it pleased God that the first of August we discovered the land in Latitude 66. degrees, 33. min. and in longitude from the Meridian of London 70. degrees voyd of trouble without snow or ice.

The second of August wee harboured our selves in a very excellent good road, where with all speed we graved the Moonelight, and revictualled her: wee searched this countrey with our pinnesse while the barke was trimming, which William Eston did: he found all this land to be onely Ilands, with a Sea on the East, a Sea on the West, and a Sea on the North. In this place wee found it very hot, and wee were very much troubled with a flie which is called Muskyto, for they did sting grievously. The people of this place at our first comming in caught a Seale, and with bladders fast tied to him sent him unto us with the floud, so as hee came right with our shippes, which we tooke as a friendly present from them.

The fift of August I went with the two Masters and others to the toppe of a hill, and by the way William Eston espied three Canoas lying under a rocke, and went unto them: there were in them skinnes, darts, with divers superstitious toyes, whereof wee diminished nothing, but left upon every boat a silke point, a bullet of lead, and a pinne. The next day being the sixt of August, the people came unto us without feare, and did barter with us for skinnes, as the other people did: they differ not from the other, neither in their Canoas nor apparel, yet is their pronuntiation more

plaine then the others, and nothing hollow in the throat. Our Savage aboord us kept himselfe close, and made shew that he would faine have another companion. Thus being provided, I departed from this lande the twelft of August at six of the clocke in the morning, where I left the Mermayd at an anker: the foureteenth sailing West about fiftie leagues, we discovered land, being in latitude 66. degrees 19 minuts: this land is 70. leagues from the other from whence we came. This fourteenth day from nine a clocke at night till three a clocke in the morning, wee ankered by an Iland of yce, twelve leagues off shore, being mored to the yce.

The fifteenth day at three a clocke in the morning we departed from this land to the South, and the eighteenth of August we discovered land Northwest from us in the morning, being a very faire promontory, in latitude 65. degrees, having no land on the South. Here wee had great hope of a through passage.

This day at three a clocke in the afternoone wee againe discovered lande Southwest and by South from us, where at night wee were becalmed. The nineteenth of this moneth at noone, by observation, we were in 64. degrees 20. minuts. From the eighteenth day at noone unto the nineteenth at noone, by precise ordinary care, wee had sailed 15. leagues South and by West, yet by art and more exact observation, we found our course to be Southwest, so that we plainely perceived a great current striking to the West.

This land is nothing in sight but Isles, which increaseth our hope. This nineteenth of August at six a clocke in the afternoone, it began to snow, and so continued all night with foule weather, and much winde, so that we were constrained to lie at hull all night five leagues off the shore: In the morning being the twentieth of August, the fogge and storme breaking up, we bare in with the lande, and at nine a clocke in the morning wee ankered in a very faire and safe road and lockt for all weathers. At tenne of the clocke I went on shore to the toppe of a very high hill, where I perceived that this land was Islands: at foure of the clocke in the afternoone wee weyed anker, having a faire North northeast winde, with very faire weather; at six of the clocke we were cleare without the land, and so shaped our course to the South, to discover the coast, whereby the passage may be through Gods mercy found.

We coasted this land till the eight and twentieth of August, finding it still to continue towards the South, from the latitude of 67. to 57. degrees: we found marveilous great store of birds, guls and mewes, incredible to be reported, whereupon being calme weather, we lay one glasse upon the lee, to prove for fish, in which space we caught 100. of cod, although we were but badly provided for fishing, not being our purpose. This eight and twentieth having great distrust of the weather, we arrived in a very faire harbour in the latitude of 56. degrees, and sailed 10. leagues into the same, being two leagues broad, with very faire woods on both sides: in this place wee continued until the first of September, in which time we had two very great stormes. I landed & went sixe miles by ghesse into the countrey, and found that the woods were firre, pineapple, alder, yew, withy, and birch: here wee saw a blacke beare: this place yeeldeth great store of birds, as fezant, partridge, Barbary hennes or the like, wilde geese, ducks, black birdes, jeyes, thrushes, with other kinds of small birds. Of the partridge and fezant we killed great store with bow and arrowes: in this place at the harborough mouth we found great store of cod.

The first of September at tenne a clocke wee set saile, and coasted the shore with very faire weather. The thirde day being calme, at noone we strooke saile, and let fall a cadge anker, to prove whether we could take any fish, being in latitude 54. degrees 30. minuts, in which place we found great abundance of cod, so that the hooke was no sooner overboord, but presently a fish was taken. It was the largest and the best fed fish that ever I sawe, and divers fisher men that were with me sayd that they never saw a more suavle or better skull of fish in their lives: yet had they seene great abundance.

The fourth of September at five a clocke in the afternoone we ankered in a very good road among great store of Isles, the countrey low land, pleasant and very full of fayre woods. To the North of this place eight leagues, we had a perfect hope of the passage, finding a mightie great sea passing betweene two lands West.[5] The South land to our judgement being nothing but Isles: we greatly desired to goe into this sea, but the winde was directly against us. We ankered in foure fathome fine sand. In this place is foule and fish mightie store.

The sixt of September having a faire Northnorthwest winde, having trimmed our Barke we purposed to depart, and sent five of our sailers yong men a shore to an Island, to fetch certaine fish which we purposed to weather, and therefore left it al night covered upon the Isle: the brutish people of this countrey lay secretly lurking in the wood, and upon the sudden assaulted our men: which when we perceived, we presently let slip our cables upon the halse, and under our foresaile bare into the shoare, and with all expedition discharged a double musket upon them twise, at the noyse whereof they fled: notwithstanding to our very great griefe, two of our men were slaine with their arrowes, and two grievously wounded, of whom at this present we stand in very great doubt, onely one escaped by swimming, with an arrow shot thorow his arme. These wicked miscreants never offered parly or speech, but presently executed their cursed fury.

This present evening it pleased God further to increase our sorrowes with a mighty tempestuous storme, the winde being Northnortheast, which lasted unto the tenth of this moneth very extreme. We unrigged our ship, and purposed to cut downe our masts, the cable of our shutanker brake, so that we onely expected to be driven on shoare among these Canibals for their pray. Yet in this deepe distresse the mightie mercie of God, when hope was past, gave us succour, and sent us a faire lee, so as we recovered our anker againe, and newe mored our ship: where we saw that God manifestly delivered us: for the straines of one of our cables were broken, and we only roade by an olde junke. Thus being freshly mored a new storme arose, the winde being Westnorthwest, very forcible, which lasted unto the tenth day at night.

The eleventh day with a faire Westnorthwest winde we departed with trust in Gods mercie, shaping our course for England, and arrived in the West countrey in the beginning of October.

[b] Master Davis being arrived, wrote his letter to Master William Sanderson of London, concerning his voyage as followeth.

Sir, the Sunneshine came into Dartmouth the fourth of this moneth: she hath bene at Island, and

---

5. Sidenote: "A perfect hope of the passage about 54. degrees and an halfe."

from thence to Groenland, and so to Estotiland, from thence to Desolation, and to our Marchants, where she made trade with the people, staying in the countrey twentie dayes. They have brought home five hundred seale skinnes, and an hundred and fortie halfe skinnes and pieces of skinnes. I stand in great doubt of the pinnesse, God be mercifull unto the poore men, and preserve them, if it be his blessed will.

I have now experience of much of the Northwest part of the world, & have brought the passage to that likelihood, as that I am assured it must bee in one of foure places, or els not at all. And further I can assure you upon the perill of my life, that this voyage may be performed without further charge, nay with certaine profite to the adventurers, if I may have but your favour in the action. I hope I shall finde favour with you to see your Card. I pray God it be so true as the Card shal be which I will bring you: and I hope in God, that your skill in Navigation shall be gainefull unto you, although at the first it hath not proved so. And thus with my humble commendations I commit you to God, desiring no longer to live, then I shall be yours most faithfully to command. Exon this fourteenth of October. 1586.
Yours to command
John Davis.

[c] The relation of the course which the Sunshine a barke of fiftie tunnes, and the Northstarre a small pinnesse, being two vessels of the fleete of Master John Davis, helde after hee had sent them from him to discover the passage betweene Groenland and Island, written by Henry Morgan servant to Master William Sanderson of London.

The seventh day of May 1586. wee departed out of Dartmouth haven foure sailes, to wit, the Mermaid, the Sunshine, the Mooneshine, & the Northstarre. In the Sunshine were sixteene men, whose names were these: Richard Pope Master, Marke Carter Masters mate, Henry Morgan Purser, George Draward, John Mandie, Hugh Broken, Philip Jane, Hugh Hempson, Richard Borden, John Philpe, Andrew Madock, William Wolcome, Robert Wag carpenter, John Bruskome, William Ashe, Simon Ellis.
Our course was Westnorthwest the seventh and eight dayes: and the ninth day in the morning we were on head of the Tarrose of Silley. Thus coasting along the South part of Ireland the 11. day, we were on head of the Dorses: and our course was Southsouthwest untill six of the clocke the 12. day. The 13. day our course was Northwest. We remained in the company of the Mermaid and the Mooneshine until we came to the latitude of 60. degrees: and there it seemed best to our Generall M. Davis to divide his fleete, himself sayling to the Northwest, and to direct the Sunshine, wherein I was, and the pinnesse called the Northstarre, to seeke a passage Northward betweene Groenland and Island to the latitude of 80. degrees, if land did not let us. So the seventh day of June wee departed from them: and the ninth of the same we came to a firme land of yce, which we coasted along the ninth, the tenth, and the eleventh dayes of June: and the eleventh day at six of the clocke at night we saw land which was very high, which afterward we knew to be Island: and the twelft day we harboured there, and found many people: the land lyeth East and by North in 66. degrees.

Their commodities were greene fish, and Island lings, and stockfish, and a fish which is called Scatefish: of all which they had great store. They had also kine, sheep and horses, and hay for their cattell, and for their horses. Wee saw also their dogs. Their dwelling houses were made on both sides with stones, and wood layd crosse over them, which was covered over with turfes of earth, and they are flat on the tops, and many of these stood hard by the shore. Their boates were made with wood and yron all along the keele like our English boates: and they had nayles for to naile them withall, and fish-hookes and other things for to catch fish as we have here in England. They had also brasen kettles, and girdles and purses made of leather, and knoppes on them of copper, and hatchets, and other small tooles as necessary as we have. They drie their fish in the Sun, and when they are dry, they packe them up in the top of their houses. If we would goe thither to fishing more then we doe, we should make it a very good voyage: for wee got an hundreth greene fish in one morning. Wee found heere two English men with a shippe, which came out of England about Easter day of this present yeere 1586, and one of them came aboord of us, and brought us two lambs. The English mans name was Master John Roydon of Ipswich marchant:

hee was bound for London with his ship. And this is the summe of that which I observed in Island. We departed from Island the sixteenth day of June in the morning, and our course was Northwest, and we saw on the coast two small barkes going to an harborough: we went not to them, but saw them a farre off. Thus we continued our course unto the end of this moneth.

The third day of July we were in betweene two firme lands of yce, and passed in betweene them all that day untill it was night: and then the Master turned backe againe, and so away we went towards Groenland. And the seventh day of July we did see Groenland, and it was very high, and it looked very blew: we could not come to harborough into the land, because we were hindered by a firme land as it were of yce, which was along the shoares side: but we were within three leagues of the land, coasting the same divers dayes together. The seventeenth day of July wee saw the place which our Captaine M. John Davis the yeere before had named The land of Desolation, where we could not goe on shore for yce. The eighteenth day we were likewise troubled with yce, and went in amongst it at three of the clocke in the morning. After wee had cleared our selves thereof, wee ranged all along the coast of Desolation untill the ende of the aforesayd moneth.

The third day of August we came in sight of Gilberts sound in the latitude of 64. deg. 15 min. which was the place where wee were appoynted to meete our Generall and the rest of our Fleete. Here we came to an harborough at 6. of the clocke at night.

The 4. day in the morning the Master went on shore with 10. of his men, and they brought us foure of the people rowing in their boats aboord of the ship. And in the afternoone I went on shore with 6. of our men, and there came to us seven of them when we were on land. We found on shore three dead people, and two of them had their staves lying by them, and their olde skinnes wrapped about them and the other had nothing lying by, wherefore we thought it was a woman. We also saw their houses neere the Sea side, which were made with pieces of wood on both sides, and crossed over with poles and then covered over with earth: we found Foxes running upon the hilles: as for the place it is broken land all the way that we went, and full of broken Islands.

The 21. of August the Master sent the boate on shore for wood with six of his men, and there were one and thirtie of the people of the countrey which went on shore to them, & they went about to kill them as we thought, for they shot their dartes towards them, and we that were aboord the ship, did see them goe on shore to our men: whereupon the Master sent the pinnesse after them, and when they saw the pinnesse comming towards them, they turned backe, and the Master of the pinnesse did shoote off a caliver to them the same time, but hurt none of them, for his meaning was onely to put them in feare. Divers times they did wave us on shore to play with them at the football, and some of our company went on shore to play with them, and our men did cast them downe as soone as they did come to strike the ball. And thus much of that which we did see and do in that harborough where we arrived first.

The 23. day wee departed from the Merchants Isle, where wee had beene first, and our course from thence was South & by West, and the wind was Northeast, and we ran that day and night about 5. or 6. leagues, untill we came to another harborough.

The 24. about eleven of the clocke in the forenoone wee entred into the aforesayd new harborow, and as wee came in, we did see dogs running upon the Islands. When we were come in, there came to us foure of the people which were with us before in the other harborough, and where we rode, we had sandie ground. We saw no wood growing, but found small pieces of wood upon the Islands, & some small pieces of sweete wood among the same. We found great Harts hornes, but could see none of the Stagges where we went, but we found their footings. As for the bones which we received of the Savages I cannot tell of what beasts they be.

The stones that we found in the countrey were black, and some white, as I thinke they be of no value, neverthelesse I have brought examples of them to you.

The 30. of August we departed from this harborough towards England, & the wind tooke us contrary, so that we were faine to go to another harborough the same day at 11. of the clocke. And there came to us 39. of the people, and brought us 13. Seale skins, and after we received these skins of them, the Master sent the carpenter to change one of our boates which wee had bought of them before, and they would have taken the boate from him perforce, and when they sawe they could not take it from us, they shot with their dartes at us, and stroke one of our men with one of their dartes, and John Filpe shot one of them into the brest with an arrow.[6] And they came to us againe, and foure of our men went into the shipboate, and they shot with their dartes at our men: but our men tooke one of their people in his boate into the shipboate, and he hurt one of them with his knife, but we killed three of them in their boates: two of them were hurt with arrowes in the brests, and he that was aboord our boat, was shot in with an arrow, and hurt with a sword, and beaten with staves, whome our men cast overboord, but the people caught him and carried him on shore upon their boates, and the other two also, and so departed from us. And three of them went on shore hard by us, where they had their dogs, and those three came away from their dogs, and presently one of their dogs came swimming towards us hard aboord the ship, whereupon our Master caused the Gunner to shoote off one of the great pieces towards the people, and so the dog turned backe to land and within an houre after there came of the people hard aboord the ship, but they would not come to us as they did come before.

The 31. of August we departed from Gylberts sound for England, and when we came out of the harborough there came after us 17. of the people looking which way we went.

The 2. of September we lost sight of the land at 12. of the clocke at noone.

The third day at night we lost sight of the Northstarre our pinnesse in a very great storme, and lay a hull tarying for them the 4. day, but could heare no more of them.[7] Thus we shaped our course the 5. day Southsoutheast, and sayling untill the 27. of the sayd moneth, we came in sight of Cape Clere in Ireland.

The 30. day we entred into our owne chanell.

The 2. of October we had sight of the Isle of Wight.

The 3. we coasted all along the shore, and the 4. and 5.

The 6. of the said moneth of October wee came

6. Sidenote: "A skirmish between the Savages and our men."
7. Sidenote: "The pinnesse never returned home."

into the river of Thames as high as Ratliffe in safetie God be thanked.

668. May 19 to September 15, 1587. The third voyage by John Davis in search of the Northwest Passage.

Printed in R. Hakluyt, Principall navigations *(1589), pp. 789–792, and* Principal navigations, *III (1600), 96–100 (VII [1904], 414–422).*

The third voyage Northwestward, made by Master John Davis Gentleman, as chiefe captaine & Pilot generall, for the discovery of a passage to the Isles of the Moluccas, or the coast of China, in the yeere 1587. Written by Master John Janes.

May.

The 19. of this present moneth about midnight wee weyed our ankers, set sayle, and departed from Dartmouth with two Barkes and a Clincher, the one named the Elizabeth of Dartmouth, the other the Sunneshine of London, and the Clincher called the Helene of London: thus in Gods name we set forwards with the wind at Northeast a good fresh gale. About 3. houres after our departure, the night being somewhat thicke with darknesse, we had lost the pinnesse: the Captaine imagining that the men had runne away with her, willed the Master of the Sunshine to stand to Seawards, and see if we could descry them, we bearing in with the shore for Plimmouth. At length we descried her, bare with her, and demanded what the cause was: they answered that the tiller of their helme was burst. So shaping our course Westsouthwest, we went forward, hoping that a hard beginning would make a good ending, yet some of us were doubtfull of it, falling in reckoning that she was a Clincher; neverthelesse we put our trust in God.

The 21. we met with the Red Lion of London, which came from the coast of Spaine, which was afrayed that we had bene men of warre, but we hailed them, and after a little conference, we desired the Master to carie our letters for London directed to my uncle Sanderson, who promised us a safe deliverie. And after wee had heaved them a lead and a line, whereunto wee had made fast our letters, before they could get them into the ship, they fell into the Sea, and so all our labour and theirs also was lost; notwithstanding they promised to certifie our departure at London, and so we departed, and the same day we had sight of Silley. The 22. the wind was at Northeast by East with faire weather, and so the 23. and 24. the like. The 25. we layd our ships on the Lee for the Sunneshine, who was a romaging for a leake, they had 500. strokes at the pumpe in a watch, the wind at Northwest.

The 26. and 27. wee had faire weather, but this 27. the pinnesses foremast was blowen overboord. The 28. the Elizabeth towed the pinnesse, which was so much bragged off by the owners report before we came out of England, but at Sea she was like a cart drawen with oxen. Sometimes we towed her because she could not saile for scant wind.

The 31. day our Captaine asked if the pinnesse were stanch, Peerson answered that she was as sound and stanch as a cup. This made us something glad, when we sawe she would brooke the Sea, and was not leake.

June.

The first 6. dayes wee had faire weather: after that for 5. dayes wee had fogge and raine, the winde being South. The 12. wee had cleare weather. The Mariners in the Sunneshine and the Master could not agree: the Mariners would goe on their voyage a fishing, because the yeere began to waste: the Master would not depart till hee had the companie of the Elizabeth, whereupon the Master told our Captaine that hee was afrayd his men would shape some contrary course while he was asleepe, and so he should lose us. At length after much talke and many threatnings, they were content to bring us to the land which we looked for daily.

The 14. day we discovered land at five of the clocke in the morning, being very great and high mountaines, the tops of the hils being covered with snow. Here the wind was variable, sometimes Northeast, Eastnortheast, and East by North: but we imagined ourselves to be 16. or 17. leagues off from the shore.

The 16. we came to an anker about 4. or 5. of the clocke after noone, the people came presently to us after the old maner, with crying Ilyaoute, and shewing us Seales skinnes. The 17. we began to set up the pinnesse that Peerson framed at Dartmouth, with the boords which hee brought from London.

The 18. Peerson and the Carpenters of the ships began to set on the plankes. The 19. as we went about an Island, were found blacke Pumise stones, and salt kerned on the rockes, very white and glistering. This day also the Master of the Sunneshine tooke of the people a very strong lusty yoong fellow.

The 20. about two of the clocke in the morning, the Savages came to the Island where our pinnace was built readie to bee launched, and tore the two upper strakes, and carried them away onely for the love of the yron in the boords. While they were about this practise, we manned the Elizabeths boate to goe a shore to them: our men being either afrayd or amazed, were so long before they came to shore, that our Captaine willed them to stay, and made the Gunner give fire to a Saker, and layd the piece levell with the boate which the Savages had turned on the one side because wee should not hurt them with our arrowes, and made the boate their bulwarke against the arrowes which we shot at them. Our Gunner having made all things readie, gave fire to the piece, and fearing to hurt any of the people, and regarding the owners profite, thought belike hee would save a Sakers shot, doubting wee should have occasion to fight with men of warre, and so shot off the Saker without a bullet: we looking stil when the Savages that were hurt should run away without legs, at length wee could perceive never a man hurt, but all having their legges could carrie away their bodies: wee had no sooner shot off the piece, but the Master of the Sunneshine manned his boate, and came rowing toward the Island, the very sight of whom made each of them take that hee had gotten, and flee away as fast as they could to another Island about two miles off, where they tooke the nayles out of the timber, and left the wood on the Isle. when we came on shore, and saw how they had spoiled the boat, after much debating of the matter, we agreed that the Elizabeth should have her to fish withall: whereupon she was presently caryed aboord, and stowed.

Now after this trouble, being resolved to depart with the first wind, there fell out another matter worse then all the rest, and that was in this maner. John Churchyard one whom our Captaine had appoynted as Pilot in the pinnace, came to our Captaine, and master Bruton, and told them that the good ship which we must all hazard our lives in, had three hundred strokes at one time as she rode in the harbour: This disquieted us all greatly, and many doubted to goe in her. At length our Captaine by whom we were all to be governed, determined rather to end his life with credite, then to returne with infamie and disgrace, and so being all agreed, wee purposed to live and die together, and committed our selves to the ship. Now the 21. having brought all our things aboord, about 11. or 12. of the clocke at night, we set saile and departed from those Isles, which lie in 64. degrees of latitude, our ships being all now at Sea, and wee shaping our course to goe, coasting the land to the Northwards upon the Easterne shore, which we called the shore of our Marchants, because there we met with people which traffiqued with us, but here wee were not without doubt of our ship.

The 24. being in 67. degrees, and 40. minutes, wee had great store of Whales, and a kinde of sea birds which the Mariners call Cortinous. This day about six of the clocke at night, we espied two of the countrey people at Sea, thinking at the first they had bene two great Seales, untill wee sawe their oares glistering with the Sunne: they came rowing towardes us, as fast as they could, and when they came within hearing, they held up their oares, and cryed Ilyaoute, making many signes: and at last they came to us, giving us birdes for bracelets, and of them I had a darte with a bone in it, or a piece of Unicorns horne, as I did judge. This dart he made store of, but when he saw a knife, he let it go, being more desirous of the knife then of his dart: these people continued rowing after our ship the space of 3. howres.

The 25. in the morning at 7. of the clocke we descried 30. Savages rowing after us, being by judgement 10. leagues off from the shore: they brought us Salmon Peales, Birdes, and Caplin, and we gave them pinnes, needles, bracelets, nailes, knives, bels, looking glasses, and other small trifles, and for a knife, a naile or a bracelet, which they call Ponigmah, they would sell their boate, coates, or any thing they had, although they were farre from the shore. Wee had but few

skinnes of them, about 20. but they made signes to us that if wee would goe to the shore, wee should have more store of Chichsanege: they stayed with us till 11. of the clocke, at which time wee went to prayer, and they departed from us.

The 28. and 29. were foggie with cloudes, the 30. day wee tooke the heigth, and found our selves in 72. degrees and 12 minutes of latitude both at noone and at night, the Sunne being 5. degrees above the Horizon. At midnight the compasse set to the variation of 28. degrees to the Westward. Now having coasted the land, which wee called London coast, from the 21. of this present, till the 30. the Sea open all to the Westwards and Northwards, the land on starboord side East from us, the winde shifted to the North, whereupon we left that shore, naming the same Hope Sanderson, and shaped our course West, and ranne 40. leagues and better without the sight of any land.

July.

The second of July wee fell with a mightie banke of yce West from us, lying North and South, which banke wee would gladly have doubled out to the Northwards, but the winde would not suffer us, so that we were faine to coast it to the Southwards, hoping to double it out, that wee might have run so farre West till wee had found land, or els to have beene thorowly resolved of our pretended purpose.

The 3. wee fell with the yce againe, and putting off from it, we sought to the Northwards, but the wind crossed us.

The 4. was foggie: so was the 5. also with much wind at the North.

The 6. being very cleare, we put our barke with oares through a gap in the yce, seeing the Sea free on the West side, as we thought, which falling out otherwise, caused us to returne after we had stayed there betweene the yce. The 7. and the 8. about midnight, by Gods helpe we recovered the open Sea, the weather being faire and calme, and so was the 9. The 10. we coasted the yce. The 11. was foggie, but calme.

The 12. we coasted againe the yce, having the wind at Northnorthwest. The 13. bearing off from the yce, we determined to goe with the shoare and come to an anker, and to stay 5. or 6. dayes for the dissolving of the yce, hoping that the Sea continually beating it, and the Sunne with the extreme force of heat which it had alwayes shining upon it, would make a quicke dispatch, that we might have a further search upon the Westerne shore. Now when we were come to the Easterne coast, the water something deepe, and some of our companie fearefull withall, we durst not come to an anker, but bare off into the Sea againe. The poore people seeing us goe away againe, came rowing after us into the Sea, the waves being somewhat loftie. We truckt with them for a few skinnes and dartes, and gave them beads, nailes, pinnes, needles and cardes, they poynting to the shore, as though they would shew us some great friendship: but we little regarding their curtesie, gave them the gentle farewell, and so departed.

The 14. wee had the wind at South. The 15. there was some fault either in the barke, or the set of some current, for wee were driven sixe points beyond our course West. The 16. wee fell with the banke of yce West from us. The 17. and 18. were foggie. The 19. at one a clocke after noone, wee had sight of the land which we called Mount Raleigh, and at 12. of the clocke at night, we were thwart the streights which we discovered the first yeere. The 20. wee traversed in the mouth of the streight, the wind being at West, with faire and cleare weather. The 21. and 22. wee coasted the Northerne coast of the streights. The 23. having sayled threescore leagues Northwest into the streights, at two a clocke after noone wee ankered among many Isles in the bottome of the gulfe, naming the same The Earle of Cumberlands Isles, where riding at anker, a Whale passed by our ship and went West in among the Isles. Heere the compasse set at thirtie degrees Westward variation. The 23. wee departed, shaping our course Southeast to recover the Sea. The 25. wee were becalmed in the bottome of the gulfe, the ayre being extreme hot. Master Bruton and some of the Mariners went on shoare to course dogs, where they found many Graves and Trane spilt on the ground, the dogs being so fat that they were scant able to run.

The 26. wee had a prety storme, the winde being at Southeast. The 27. and 28. were faire. The 29. we were cleare out of the streights, having coasted the South shore, and this day at noone we were in 62. degrees of latitude. The 30. in the afternoone wee coasted a banke of yce, which lay on the shore, and passed by a great banke or Inlet, which lay between 63. and 62. degrees of latitude, which we called Lumlies In-

let. We had oftentimes, as we sailed alongst the coast, great ruttes, the water as it were whirling and overfalling, as if it were the fall of some great water through a bridge.

The 31. as we sayled by a Headland, which we named Warwicks Foreland, we fell into one of those overfals with a fresh gale of wind, and bearing all our sailes, wee looking upon an Island of yce betweene us and the shoare, had thought that our barke did make no way, which caused us to take markes on the shoare: at length wee perceived our selves to goe very fast, and the Island of yce which we saw before, was carried very forcibly with the set of the current faster then our ship went. This day and night we passed by a very great gulfe, the water whirling and roaring as it were the meetings of tydes.

August.

The first of August having coasted a banke of ice which was driven out at the mouth of this gulfe, we fell with the Southermost cape of the gulfe, which we named Chidleis cape, which lay in 61 degrees and 10 minutes of latitude. The 2 and 3 were calme and foggie, so were the 4, 5, and 6. The 7 was faire and calme: so was the 8, with a litle gale in the morning. The 9 was faire, and we had a litle gale at night. The 10 we had a frisking gale at Westnorthwest. The 11 faire. The 12 we saw five deere on the top of an Island, called by us Darcies Island. And we hoised out our boat, and went ashore to them, thinking to have killed some of them. But when we came on shore, and had coursed them twise about the Island, they tooke the sea and swamme towards Islands distant from that three leagues. When we perceived that they had taken the sea we gave them over because our boat was so small that it could not carrie us, and rowe after them, they swamme so fast: but one of them was as bigge as a good pretty Cow, and very fat, their feet as bigge as Oxe feet. Here upon this Island I killed with my piece a gray hare.

The 13 in the morning we saw three or foure white beares, but durst not go on shore to them for lacke of a good boat. This day we stroke a rocke seeking for an harborow, and received a leake: and this day we were in 54 degrees of latitude.

The 14 we stopt our leake in a storme not very outragious, at noone.

The 15 being almost in 52 degrees of latitude,

and not finding our ships, nor (according to their promise) any kinde of marke, token, or beacon, which we willed them to set up, and they protested to do so upon every head land, Island or cape, within twenty leagues every way off from their fishing place, which our captaine appointed to be betweene 54 and 55 degrees: This 15 I say we shaped our course homewards for England, having in our ship but litle wood, and halfe a hogshead of fresh water. Our men were very willing to depart, and no man more forward then Peerson, for he feared to be put out of his office of stewardship: but because every man was so willing to depart, we consented to returne for our owne countrey: and so we had the 16 faire weather, with the winde at Southwest.

The 17 we met a ship at sea, and as farre as we could judge it was a Biskaine: we thought she went a fishing for whales; for in 52 degrees or thereabout we saw very many.

The 18 was faire, with a good gale at West.

The 19 faire also, with much winde at West and by South.

And thus after much variable weather and change of winds we arrived the 15 of September in Dartmouth anno 1587, giving thanks to God for our safe arrivall.

Chapter Eighty-two
The Continued Search
for the Northwest Passage, 1602–1613

At THE TURN of the seventeenth century, despite the efforts of Martin Frobisher and John Davis, the English were no nearer to finding the coveted Northwest Passage to China. Although they were now able to sail east by way of the Cape of Good Hope, it was obvious that the route to the north of America would provide a speedier passage. This was of especial value to mercantile interests, and most of the voyages to the area in the period were sponsored by trading companies. The East India Company, formed in 1600, soon expressed an interest and in 1602 under their auspices, George Waymouth took two ships to the northwest. He sailed along the coast of Labrador between 55° and 63°N and, despite being beset by storms and ice, managed to penetrate the mouth of Hudson Strait, although his abbreviated journal makes it almost impossible to follow his exact course. The cold, foggy weather proved a discouragement to the two crews, who decided they could go no further and turned the ship toward home. Waymouth was powerless to do anything. He was exonerated by the company for the failure of the expedition to follow up the discoveries of Frobisher and Davis. The company planned a voyage for 1603, but the idea was abandoned and Waymouth next appears in 1605 off the New England coast. Undeterred, the company joined with the Muscovy Company and formed the Company of English Merchants Trading to the North West. In 1606 they sent out the *Hopewell* commanded by John Knight, who had been in the Danish service the previous year. Knight met with high winds and heavy ice and was forced to ground the boat to repair leaks. He and five other men disappeared during an expedition to a nearby island, and two days later the rest of the crew was attacked by Eskimos. Repairs were hastily completed and the ship refloated. Although it was still leaking badly, the vessel managed to limp into Newfoundland where further repairs were undertaken to enable them to cross the Atlantic.

England was not the only nation to express an interest in the northwest. Both Denmark and Holland sent out expeditions in the period. Between 1605 and 1607 Christian IV of Denmark sponsored three voyages in which the Englishmen John Knight and James Hall, who had been on one of the voyages of Davis, played prominent parts. Rather than a passage, the purpose of the voyages was to find the lost Scandinavian colonies in Greenland, but they did add a little to the geographical knowledge of the area. The first expedition was the most successful. The three ships sailed north up Davis Strait until they were prevented from making any further progress by the thick pack ice. They then turned east and coasted down the west side of Greenland. Hall, the chief pilot, made detailed maps and reports based on his observations. No discoveries were made on the 1606 venture, the men being diverted by hopes of rich mineral ore in Greenland. The 1607 expedition was forced to turn back before reaching Iceland. The Dutch appeared in North American waters later than the other maritime powers. For much of the sixteenth century they were fighting against Spanish occupation of their lands, which left them little chance to enter into schemes for the expansion of trade or colonization. With the conclusion of the war with Spain, Dutch merchants began to cast around for new markets for their goods. In 1602 the Dutch East India Company was formed. It merged all the different trading interests in Holland and was given a monopoly of trade by the state. Among the company's areas of interest was North America, where Dutch vessels were soon fishing and trading in furs. Like their English counterparts, many Dutch merchants believed that there was another prize to be found in these waters—a passage through to the East. Therefore, from the beginning the Dutch saw America more as a center for trade than a land ripe for colonization.

Among those with an interest in the trade was Emanuel Van Meteren, the Dutch consul in London, who became well-acquainted with the efforts of men like Frobisher, Davis, Waymouth, and Hudson to discover a sea route to the East. In 1607 Hudson, acting for the Muscovy Company, attempted to find a North or Northeast Passage and sailed as far as the northern end of Spitzbergen (discovered in 1596 by the Dutchman William Barents). The following year he was employed by the company on a second voyage, during which he landed on the coast of Novaya Zemlya, but was prevented from going any further by a frightened and potentially mutinous crew, a not uncommon occurrence. On his return to England, the directors of the Dutch East India Company, following the recommendation of Van Meteren, sent for him. Hudson impressed them with his theory that it was possible to sail right across the North Pole, and his view that the climate became warmer as one got closer to the pole. Hudson also believed that there was a passage just to the north of Virginia. This idea had been fostered by letters and maps he received from Captain John Smith, who had been led to the same conclusion by his exploration of the Chesapeake Bay and his discussions with the natives. Hudson knew that the area between 37° and 41°30′ had not been properly explored since 1524. He was more inclined to go for the westerly passage, but was ordered by the company to find one to the east. Therefore, in 1609, he steered his way up the west coast of Norway, but once more was threatened by the mutiny of his sailors who refused to go any further north and east. Hudson retraced his course and then decided to head west to the area north of the Chesapeake. The ship met the American coast north of Newfoundland and then sailed down to the region of Cape Hatteras, where Hudson turned north to explore the coast in more detail with the hope of finding the passage. After investigating the Delaware Bay, the *Halve Maen* anchored in New York harbor on September 11. The ship then went up the Hudson River as far as the site of present-day Albany. This point was reached on September 19. Here some of the crew were sent upstream in a small boat. On their return they reported that the river became progressively more narrow, and shallow. By now Hudson was convinced that this was not the passage he sought. Ignoring suggestions that they winter in Newfoundland and resume the search the following year, he returned to England and sent a proposal to the Dutch that he should go out again and search for a Northwest Passage. The English authorities, however, refused to let him leave for Holland. Since it obviously did not lead to the East, Hudson regarded his 1609 voyage as a failure, and it was some years before the importance of his discovery was realized. The Dutch made another attempt to find the elusive passage, and in 1611–1612 Captain Jan Cornelisoon May sailed along the Greenland coast but with no success.

The year 1610 saw Hudson again employed by the English to discover a northern passage. On this occasion he chose the northwest route, approaching Hudson Strait, which had been entered by Martin Frobisher in 1578 and conceivably by Portuguese navigators before 1575. Although the ice had not yet completely cleared, Hudson navigated the strait and entered Hudson Bay. There is no doubt that as he approached the great expanse of water, Hudson thought he had found the passage. He sailed the *Discovery* south along the eastern shore of the bay and into James Bay at the southern end. Here he and his crew spent the winter of 1610–1611, frozen in by the thick ice. Food was in short supply, and many of the crew began to distrust Hudson. The rumor quickly spread that the captain had no idea where he was going. On June 12, 1611, the ship managed to break clear of the ice and Hudson ordered a further search to the west, but the doubts remained among the crew and several men mutinied, setting Hudson, his son John, and seven sailors adrift in a pinnace. It was later alleged that they had been abandoned because of the shortage of food, which necessitated the sacrifice of the infirm in order to enable the rest to survive and return to England to report what they had found. Conveniently for the mutineers, several of the survivors were attacked and killed by Eskimo while looking for food on Digges Island at the entrance to the bay. They were later to be blamed for the mutiny. The nine remaining crew members managed to bring the ship back to England. In October, 1611, an investigation into the mutiny was instituted at Trinity House. Depositions were taken from the men, and the Master and Wardens arrived at the conclusion that "they deserve to be hanged." Nothing more was done until 1616 when Robert Bylot, Abacuk Pricket, and others were summoned before the High Court of Admiralty to answer charges of murder and mutiny. After hearing the evidence of the men, no verdict was reached, though they were cleared in July, 1618. One of the reasons for the delay in bringing the men to trial was the involvement of Bylot, Prickett, and Edward Wilson in the newly formed company, the Discoverers of the North West Passage. On their return to England, they announced that they had found, for all practical purposes, the Northwest Passage. They produced a chart drawn by Hudson that showed the strait and the eastern part of the bay and was by far the most accurate survey of the region that had thus far appeared. However, it contained no details of the western coast of the bay, and it was in this area that the merchants' hopes for a passage now centered. In 1612 Bylot and Prickett were members of the first of many expeditions sent out to find the passage. The discoveries of Hudson overshadowed the circumstances of his disappearance, much to the relief of the nine men who managed to survive both the mutiny and the Eskimo attack.

Meanwhile, efforts had been made to follow up the earlier discoveries of Hudson and James Hall. The Muscovy Company had been encouraged by Hudson's reports on the number of whales in Spitzbergen and was determined to start a whaling industry there. In 1610 it sent out a ship under the command of Jonas Poole, a man who had been active in Virginia. He explored the western bays and anchored there for some time, making forays on land to hunt bear, deer, and other animals, including walrus that strayed too close to the boat. The following year the company was given a charter that granted it sole rights to the Spitzbergen fishery, and it again sent out Poole, but this time with full whaling equipment and a number of expert Basque whalers. They made their headquarters in Foreland Sound, the chief station being at English Bay. However, the expedition ran into trouble while trying to leave for Greenland and had to be rescued by an interloper from Hull who was there hunting walrus. Undaunted, the company sent out other ships in the next few years to fish and to drive out foreign vessels. At the same time interest was still being shown further to the west in Greenland, of which Spitzbergen was then thought to be part. In 1612 James Hall led two ships to the west coast on behalf of the Merchant Adventurers of London. There is some doubt as to the object of the expedition, but it seems clear that Hall was still interested in the mineral ore that had sidetracked him in 1606 and had been proved to be worthless. While they were anchored on the coast, Hall was killed by an Eskimo, who obviously had a grudge against him from one of the earlier visits, and who singled him out, leaving the rest of the party unmolested. After some argument about who should take over command, the ships returned to England. Apart from the murder of Hall, the voyage is only noteworthy for giving the first taste of Arctic travel to William Baffin, who later went on several trips that led him beyond the area penetrated by John Davis and discovered the bay and gave the land that bears it his name. Although the passage was not found by the expeditions of the early seventeenth century, they did serve to increase knowledge of the geography of the northwest and opened up new possibilities for exploration, notably Hudson Bay.

For the sources on the Northwest Passage voyages of 1602–1611 we are almost wholly dependent on those printed in Samuel Purchas, *Pilgrimes*, III (1625), who, in turn, made use of the manuscripts collected by Richard Hakluyt for his never-completed third edition of his *Principal navigations* (see Colin R. Steele, "From Hakluyt to Purchas," *The Hakluyt Handbook*, edited by D. B. Quinn, 2 vols. [Cambridge, England, 1974], I, 88–91). G. M. Asher, ed., *Henry Hudson the Navigator* (London, Hakluyt Society, 1860), was not able to add to Purchas. The earliest published source on Henry Hudson's last voyage was a brief note on the back of the chart in Hessel Gerritz, *Descriptio et delineatio geographica detectionis freti ab H. Hudsono inventi* (Amsterdam, 1612), versions in both Dutch and Latin appearing in 1612 and 1613.

It has been possible to add a certain amount from the Public Record Office, London. Thus, the death of John Knight on his voyage of 1606 produced an examination in a case on the civil side of the High Court of Admiralty, the depositions in which are of value (672). Similarly the death of Henry Hudson produced long-delayed proceedings on the criminal side of the High Court of Admiralty in 1617 (676–677), while an informal examination of those who returned, in the archives of Trinity House, London (675), gives a much earlier (1611) picture of the situation as seen through their eyes.

669. May 2 to [October 4], 1602. George Waymouth scouts Baffin Island and Labrador.

The Discovery *and* Godspeed *reached the coast of Labrador at 57° 35' and ran up a little beyond the islands off Frobisher Inlet at 62° 30'. Turning south George Waymouth reached the place "where the great Current setteth to the West," which he hoped would prove to be the passage. Contrary winds held him back in July, sailing somewhat south of 60° and then north to 63° 53', but finally he gave up hope of making progress that season. He made a last attempt in which "I did reckon my self to be in the entering of an Inlet, which standeth in the latitude of 61. degrees and 40. minutes." Whether this was Hudson Strait or not,* *his men would not make a further attempt to enter. They worked down the coast of Labrador and thence homeward. The box containing the queen's letters to the Emperor of China, sent with Waymouth, is now in Lancashire County Record Office, Preston.*

S. Purchas, Pilgrimes, III (1625), 809–814 (XIV [1906], 306–318), provides the only text.

The voyage of Captaine George Weymouth, intended for the discoverie of the Northwest Passage toward China, with two flye Boates.

On Sunday the second day of May, 1602. in the afternoone, I weighed anchor and set saile from

Redcliffe with two Fly-boates, the one called the Discovery, of seventie Tunnes; and the other called the God speed, of sixtie Tunnes, to discover the North-west passage, having in my ships five and thirtie men and boyes, throughly victualled and abundantly furnished with all necessaries for a yeere and an halfe, by the right Worshipfull Merchants of the Moscovie and Turkie Companies: who for the better successe of the voyage provided mee of a great travailer and learned Minister one Master John Cartwright. The Master under mee in the Discoverie was one William Cobreth, a skilfull man in his profession; and in the God speed, one John Drewe, and Mate in the said ship one John Lane.

The first of June, we descried Buquhamnes in the Latitude of 57. degrees. The second day we saw the Point of Buquhamnes North-west from us, being a very smooth land; and the land by it to the Southward riseth with many Homocks. There lyeth a ledge of Rockes hard by the Nesse, in a sandie Bay faire by the shore. When we came neer the land, we met with a fisher Boat, and I agreed with one of the fisher men to carry me betweene the Isles of Orkney, because I was not acquainted with the coast. The fourth day, at ten of the clocke, wee descried the Isles of Orkney. Some of those Southerne Ilands are prettie high land; but the Northerne Iland, which is called the Start, is very low land. There is no danger, giving the shore a good birth, unlesse it be by the Norther point of the Start: there doth a ledge of Rockes lye a mile from the shoare. At noone I found my selfe to be in the latitude of 59. degrees and 30. minutes, the point of the Start bearing West: and at one of the clocke in the afternoone, we saw a faire Ile, which bare North-east and by North from us: and at eight of the clocke at night, wee were North of the Start: Then I directed my course West and by North. The fifth day about ten of the clocke in the morning, we ranne some tenne leagues, and then we saw two small Ilands, some two leagues off: and at eight and nine of the clocke we saw foure or five Boats of Fisher-men, and spake with one of them, and they were Scottish-men. The sixt, in the morning fell much raine, and lasted till nine of the clocke: and at ten of the clocke it cleared up, and became very faire weather, and very temperate and warme, and our course was West. The seaventh, the winde was at East and by North, faire weather, and our course

West. The eight, at noone I observed the Sunne, and found us to be in 59. degrees and fortie seven minutes, and we ran West South-west.

The twelfth day we held our course West, the winde at East North-east, with fogge in the morning: at noone I observed the Sunne, and found my selfe in 57. degrees, and 55. minutes. the variation here was nothing at all. The thirteenth at noone, our course was West and by North, the winde at North-east, with fogge some three or foure houres, and then cleare againe: the ayre very warme, as in England in the moneth of May. The foureteenth was faire weather, and the winde at East North-east, and our course West and by North. The fifteenth much raine all the forenoone, our course West, the winde at East and by North. The sixteenth, the winde was at North North-east, with much raine, winde and fogge. In the forenoone, being very cold, and at noone, I observed the Sun, and found us to be in 57. degrees and 35. minutes: we found the variation to be eleven degrees Westward; and by that meane I found my selfe to be one degree more to the Southward, then we should have bin by our course; for we could not see the Sunne in 96. houres before this day at noone, and at our last observation before this, which was the twelfth day, we could not finde any variation at all. Then we stood close by a winde to the Westward, the winde being at North North-east. The seaventeenth wee ranne North and by West, the winde at North North-east, faire weather. This day we saw many gray Gulles, and some Pigions. The eighteenth at noone I observed the Sunne, and found our selves to be in the latitude of 59. degrees, and 51. minutes. And then we first descried a great Iland of Ice, which lay North from us, as farre as we could ken it from the head of our maine topmast: and about two of the clocke in the afternoone, we saw the South part of Groneland, North from us some ten leagues. As we coasted this Ice to the Northward, we found it to be a maine banke of Ice; for we saw the other end of it to beare West North-west from us; the winde being at South South-west, little winde: Then we ranne West South-west, to cleere us of the Ice. The nineteenth, the winde was at East South-east, with some small raine. The twentieth, our course was West North-west, the winde being at North and by East, little winde. This day sometimes we came into blacke water as thicke as puddle, and in sailing a little space the water would be cleare againe. Seeing this change of water, so often to be thick, and cleare againe so suddenly, we imagined it had beene shallow water: then we sounded, and could fetch no ground in one hundred and twenty fathomes: and the Sea was so smooth, that we could discerne no current at all. At this time I reckoned the Cape of desolation to beare North North-east twentie foure leagues from us. The one and twentieth, the winde was variable. The two and twentieth, we were in the latitude of 60. degrees and 37. minutes: the winde being at West, wee ranne North and by West. The seaven and twentieth, the winde was at West South-west: then our course was North-west and by North, the weather faire and warme, as in England, in the moneth of May. This day we saw great store of Gulles, which followed our Ship sundry dayes.

The eight and twentieth, the winde being at North and by West, wee directed our course to the Westward; and about twelve of the clocke the same night, we descried the land of America, in the latitude of 62. degrees and 30. minutes; which we made to be Warwicks foreland. This Headland rose like an Iland. And when we came neere the Foreland, we saw foure small Ilands to the Northwards, and three small Ilands to the Southward of the same Foreland. The Foreland was high land: all the tops of the hils were covered with Snow. The three small Ilands to the Southward were also white, that we could not discerne them from Ilands of Ice: also there was great store of drift Ice upon the Eastside of this Foreland: but the Sea was altogether voide of Ice: the Land did lye North and by East, and South and by West, being six leagues of length.

The nine and twentieth, at six of the clocke in the morning, wee were within three leagues of this Foreland: then the winde came up at Northeast and by East, a good stiffe gale with fogge: and wee were forced to stand to the Southward, because wee could not wether the Land to the Northward: and as wee stood to the Southward along by Warwicks Foreland, we could discerne none otherwise, but that it was an Iland. Which if it fall out to be so, then Lumleys Inlet, and the next Southerly Inlet, where the great Current setteth to the West, must of necessitie be one Sea; which will be the greatest hope of the passage that way. The thirtieth, the winde was at North-

east, with fogge and Snow. This day wee came into a great whirling of a Current, being in the latitude of 61. degrees, and about twelve leagues from the coast of America.

The first day of July, the winde was at West, with fogge and Snow; the ayre being very cold. This day wee came into many Overfals, which seemed to runne a great current; but which way it did set, wee could not well discerne. The greatest likelihood was, that it should set to the West. But having contrary windes some sixteene or seventeene dayes, we alwayes lay in traverse among these overfals; but could never finde any great current by our courses: wee sounded sometimes, but could get no ground in one hundred and twentie fathomes.

The second day, wee descried a maine Banke of Ice in the latitude of 60. degrees: the winde was at North North-west, and very faire weather. Wee wanting fresh water did sayle close to this Land of Ice, and hoysed out our Boate, and loaded her twice with Ice, which made us very good fresh water. Within twenty leagues of the coast of America, wee should oftentimes come into many great overfals. Which doth manifestly shew, that all the coast of America is broken Land.

The third, the winde was at South-west, very foggie: and as wee stood toward the coast of America, wee met with another maine Banke of Ice. The fogge was so thicke, that we were hard by the Ice, before wee could see it. But it pleased God that the winde was faire to put us cleare from this Ice againe; and presently it began to cleare up, so that wee could see two or three leagues off; but we could see no end of the Ice. Wee judged this Ice to be some tenne leagues from the coast of America. We found the water to be very blackish and thicke, like puddle water.

The eight, the winde was at North North-west, very faire weather; wee standing to the Westwards met with a mighty maine Banke of Ice, which was a great length and breadth, and it did rest close to the shoare. And at eleven of the clocke in the forenoone, wee descried againe the Land of America, in the latitude of 63. degrees and 53. minutes, being very high Land: and it did rise as Ilands, the toppes being covered with Snow. This Land was South-west and by West, some five leagues off us: we could come no neerer it for the great quantitie of Ice, which rested by the shoare side.

The ninth, the winde being at North-east and by East, blew so extremely, that we were forced to stand to the Southward, both to cleare our selves of the Land, and of the Ice: for the day before we passed a great banke of Ice, which was some foureteene leagues to the Eastward of us, when the storme began; but thankes be to God, we cleared our selves both of the Land and of the Ice. This day in the afternoone the storme grew so extreame, that we were forced to stand along with our forecourse to the Southward.

The seventeenth was very foggie, the winde being at East: and about two of the clocke in the afternoone, wee saw foure great Ilands of Ice, of a huge bignesse: and about foure of the clocke we came among some small scattered Ice, and supposed our selves to be neere some great Banke. The fogge was very thicke, but the winde large to stand backe the same way wee came in; or else it would have indangered our lives very much. And at nine of the clocke at night we heard a great noyse, as though it had bin the breach of some shoare. Being desirous to see what it was, we stood with it, and found it to be the noyse of a great quantity of Ice, which was very loathsome to be heard. Then wee stood North North-west, and the fogge continued so thicke, that wee could not see two Shippes length from us: whereupon we thought good to take in some of our sayles; and when our men came to hand them, they found our sayles, ropes, and tacklings, so hard frozen, that it did seeme very strange unto us, being in the chiefest time of Summer.

The eighteenth day, the winde was at North-east and by North, the ayre being very cleere and extreame cold, with an exceeding great frost; and our course was North-west. This day in the forenoone, when we did set our sayles, we found our ropes and tacklings harder frozen then they were the day before: which frost did annoy us so much in the using of our ropes and sayles, that wee were enforced to breake off the Ice from our ropes, that they might runne through the blockes. And at two of the clocke in the afternoone, the winde began to blow very hard, with thicke fogge, which freezed so fast as it did fall upon our sayles, ropes, and tackling, that we could not almost hoyse or strike our sayles, to have any use of them. This extreame frost and long continuance thereof, was a maine barre to our proceedings to the Northward, and the discouraging of all our men.

The nineteenth day, the winde was at North and by East, and our course to the Eastwards. The same night following, all our men conspired secretly together, to beare up the helme for England, while I was asleepe in my Cabin, and there to have kept mee by force, untill I had sworn unto them that I would not offer any violence unto them for so doing. And indeede they had drawn in writing, the causes of their bearing up of the helme, and thereunto set their hands, and would have left them in my Cabin: but by good chance I understood their pretence, and prevented them for that time.

The twentieth day, I called the chiefest of my Company into my Cabin, before Master John Cartwright our Preacher, and our Master, William Cobreth, to heare what reasons they could alleadge for the bearing up of the Helme, which might be an overthrow to the Voyage, seeing the Merchants had bin at so great a charge with it. After much conference, they delivered mee their reasons in writing:

Concluding, that although it were granted, that we might winter betweene 60. and 70. degrees of latitude, with safetie of our lives and Vessels, yet it will be May next before wee can dismore them, to lanch out into the Sea. And therefore if the Merchants should have purpose to proceede on the discoverie of these North-west parts of America; the next yeare you may be in the aforesaid latitudes for England, by the first of May, and so be furnished better with men and victuals, to passe and proceede in the aforesaid action.

Seeing then that you cannot assure us of a safe harbour to the Northward, wee purpose to beare up the Helme for England, yet with this limitation, that if in your wisedome, you shall thinke good to make any discovery, either in 60. or 57. degrees, with this faire Northerly winde, we yeelde our lives with your selfe, to encounter any danger. Thus much we thought needefull to signifie, as a matter builded upon reason, and not proceeding upon feare or cowardise.

Then, wee being in the latitude of 68. degrees and 53. minutes: the next following, about eleven of the clocke, they bare up the Helme, being all so bent, that there was no means to perswade them to the contrary. At last understanding of it, I came forth of my Cabin, and demanded of them, who bare up the Helme? They answered me, One and All. So they hoysed up all the sayle they could, and directed their course South and by West.

The two and twentieth, I sent for the chiefest of those, which were the cause of the bearing up of the Helme, and punished them severely, that this punishment might be a warning to them afterward for falling into the like mutinie. In the end, upon the intreatie of Master Cartwright our Preacher, and the Master, William Cobreath, upon their submission, I remitted some part of their punishment. At twelve of the clocke at noone, wee came hard by a great Iland of Ice: the Sea being very smooth and almost calme, wee hoysed out the Boates of both our Shippes: being in want of fresh water, and went to this Iland to get some Ice to make us fresh water. And as wee were breaking off some of this Ice (which was verie painefull for us to doe; for it was almost as hard as a Rocke:) the great Iland of Ice gave a mightie cracke two or three times, as though it had bin a thunder-clappe; and presently the Iland began to overthrow, which was like to have sunke both our Boates, if wee had not made good haste from it. But thankes be to God, we escaped this danger very happily, and came aboord with both our Boates, the one halfe laden with Ice. There was great store of Sea Foule upon this Iland of Ice.

The five and twentieth and six and twentieth, the winde being at East, did blow a hard gale, and our course was West and by South, with fogge. This day in the afternoone I did reckon my selfe to be in the entering of an Inlet, which standeth in the latitude of 61. degrees and 40. minutes.

The seven and twentieth, the winde was at South South-east, and blew very hard, our course was West. The eight and twentieth and nine and twentieth, our course was West and by South, the winde blowing very hard at East South-east, with fogge and raine. The thirtieth, the winde came up in a showre by the West North-west, blowing so hard, that wee were forced to put a fore the Sea. Now because the time of the yeare was farre spent, and many of our men in both Shippes sicke, wee thought it good to returne with great hope of this Inlet, to bee a passage of more possibilitie,

then through the Straight of Davis: because I found it not much pestered with Ice, and to be a straight of fortie leagues broad. Also I sayled an hundred leagues West and by South, within this Inlet: and there I found the variation to be 35. degrees to the Westward, and the needle to decline, or rather incline 83. degrees and an halfe.

The fifth of August (the winde all that while Westerly) wee were cleare of this Inlet againe. The sixth the winde was at East South-east with fogge. The seaventh, eight, and ninth, we passed by many great Ilands of Ice. The ninth day at night, we descried the land of America, in the latitude of 55. degrees, and 30. minutes. This Land was an Iland, being but low land and very smooth: then the night approaching, and the weather being something foggie and darke, we were forced to stand to the Northward againe. This night we passed by some great Ilands of Ice, and some bigge peeces which did breake from the great Ilands: and we were like to strike some of them two or three times: which if we had done, it might have endangered our Shippes and lives. Our consort, the Godspeede, strooke a little piece of Ice, which they thought had foundred their Shippe; but thankes be to God they received no great hurt, for our Shippes were very strong.

The tenth day, the winde was at North-east and by North, with fogge and raine; and our course was to the South-eastward: for we could by no meanes put with the shoare, by reason of the thicknesse of the fogge, and that the winde blew right upon the shoare, so that we were forced to beare saile to keepe our selves from the land, untill it pleased God to send us a cleare, which God knoweth we long wanted. At six of the clocke in the afternoone, it was calme; and then I judged my selfe, by mine account, to be neere the Land: so I sounded, and had ground in 160. fathomes, and fine grey Osie Sand: and there was a great Iland of Ice, a ground within a league of us, where we sounded, and within one houre it pleased God to send us a cleere. Then we saw the land some foure leagues South-west and by South from us. This land lyeth East and by South, and West and by North, being good high land, but all Ilands, as farre as wee could discerne. This calme continued untill foure of the clocke in the afternoone of the eleventh day: the weather being very cleere, we could not discerne any Current to goe at all by this

Land. This day the Sea did set us in about a league neerer the Land, so that wee judged our selves three leagues off. Here we sounded againe, and had but eightie fathoms.

The variation of the Compasse we found to be 22. degrees and 10. minutes Westward. At five of the clocke there sprung up a fine gale of winde, at East South-east, and being so neere night, wee stood to the Southward, thinking the next day to seeke some harbour. But it pleased God, the next day, being the twelfth, to send us a storme of foule weather, the winde being at East and by South, with fogge: so that we could by no meanes get the shoare. Thus wee were forced to beate up and downe at Sea, untill it should please God to send us better weather.

The foureteenth, I thought good to stand to the Westward to search an Inlet, in the latitude of 56. degrees. I have good hope of a passage that way, by many great and probable reasons.

The fifteenth the winde continued at the South, with exceeding faire weather, and our course was West. We were this day at noone in the latitude of 55. degrees and 31. minutes: and I found the variation to be 17. degrees and 15. minutes, to the Westward. And about seven of the clocke at night, we descried the Land againe, being tenne leagues to the Eastward of this Inlet. This Land did beare from us South-west, some eight leagues off: and about nine of the clocke the same night, the winde came to the West; which blew right against us for our entring into this Inlet.

The sixteenth, the winde was at West North-west, and was very faire weather, and our course South-west: about nine of the clocke in the forenoone, we came by a great Iland of Ice; and by this Iland we found some peeces of Ice broken off from the said Iland: And being in great want of fresh water, wee hoysed out our Boates of both Shippes, and loaded them twice with Ice, which made us very good fresh water. This day at noone wee found our selves to be in the latitude of 55. degrees and twentie minutes: when we had taken in our Ice and Boates, the weather being very faire and cleare, and the winde at West North-west, we bent our course for the Land, and about three of the clocke in the afternoone, we were within three leagues of the shoare. It is a very pleasant low Land; but all Ilands, and goodly sounds going betweene them, toward the South-west. This Land doth stand in the latitude

of 55. degrees; and I found the variation to be to the West 18. degrees and 12. minutes. This coast is voide of Ice, unlesse it be some great Ilands of Ice, that come from the North, and so by windes may be driven upon this coast. Also we did finde the ayre in this place to be very temperate. Truely there is in three severall places great hope of a passage, betweene the latitude of 62. and 54. degrees; if the fogge doe not hinder it, which is all the feare I have. At six of the clocke, wee being becalmed by the shoare, there appeared unto us a great ledge of rockes, betweene us and the shoare, as though the Sea did flye over it with a great height. As we all beheld it, within one houre, upon a sudden it vanished cleane away; which seemed very strange unto us all. And to the Eastward of us, some two leagues, we saw a great Rocke, lying some three leagues off the Land: we then supposing it to be shoald water, by this broken ground, sounded, but could get no ground in one hundred and sixtie fathoms. About seven of the clocke, there sprung up a gale of winde, by the South South-east, which was a very good winde to coast this Land.

But the seventeenth in the morning, the winde being at the South, it began to blow so extreamely, that we durst not stay by the shoare, for it was like to be a great storme: then our course was East North-east, to get us Sea roome. This storme still increasing, our flye-boates did receive in much water; for they wanted a Sparre-decke, which wee found very dangerous for the Sea. About twelve of the clocke at noone, this day there rose up a great showre in the West, and presently the winde came out of that quarter with a whirle, and taking up the Sea into the ayre, and blew so extreamely, that we were forced alwayes to runne before the Sea, howsoever the winde did blow. And within twelve houres after this storme beganne, the Sea was so much growen, that we thought our flye Boates would not have beene able to have endured it.

The eighteenth, the winde was at North-west, and the storme increased more extreame, and lasted untill eight of the clocke in the morning of the nineteenth day, so furious, that to my remembrance, I never felt a greater; yet when we were in our greatest extremities, the Lord delivered us his unworthy servants. And if the winde, with so great a storme, had bin either Northerly, or Southerly, or Easterly but one day, we had all perished against the Rocks, or the Ice: for wee were entred thirty leagues within a Head-land of an Inlet, in the latitude of 56. degrees. But it pleased God to send us the winde so faire, as we could desire, both to cleare our selves of the Land and Ice. Which opportunitie caused us for this time to take our leaves of the coast of America, and to shape our course for England.

The fourth [October ?], in the morning, wee descried the Iland of Silly North-east and by East, some foure leagues off us. Then wee directed our course East and by North: and at tenne of the clocke in the forenoone, wee descried the Lands end, and next day were forced to put into Dartmouth.

[Note] This book was also subscribed by W. Cobreth and John Drew.

670. May 2 to August 10, 1605. The Danish Lindenov expedition to Greenland.

Under the auspices of Christian IV of Denmark, John Cunningham and James Knight, two English captains, with the Danish nobleman Godske Lindenov in command, went to search the west coast of Greenland. The pilot, James Hall, gave a full account of the voyage of the Røde Løve, Trost, *and* Marekatten. *While not of much value for the Northwest Passage search, Hall's narrative does clarify the topography of the eastern side of Davis Strait. No trace was found of the old Norse settlements.*

Hall's abbreviated narrative is in S. Purchas, Pilgrimes, III (1625), 814–821 (XIV [1906], 318–338). It is in two parts (a) his journal and (b) his topographical description.

[a] James Hall his Voyage forth of Denmarke for the discovery of Greenland, in the yeare 1605. abbreviated.

In the name of God Amen, we set sayle from Copeman-haven in Denmarke, the second day of May, in the yeare of our redemption 1605. with two Shippes and a Pinnace: The Admirall, called the Frost, a shippe of the burthen of thirty or fortie lasts, wherein was Captaine, and chiefe

commander of the whole Fleet, Captaine John Cunningham, a Scottish Gentleman, servant unto the Kings Majestie of Denmarke, my selfe being principall Pilot. The Lyon Viceadmirall, being about the foresaid burthen, wherein was Captaine, one Godscaio Lindenose, a Danish Gentleman, and Steereman of the same, one Peter Kilson of Copeman-haven. The Pinnace, a Barke of the burthen of twelve Lasts, or thereabouts: wherein was Steereman or commander, one John Knight, my Countrie-man. So setting sayle from Copeman-haven, with a faire gale of winde Easterly, wee came unto Elsonure, where we anchored, to take in our water.

The third day we tooke in our water, at which time, the Captaines, my selfe, with the Lieutenants, and the other Steeremen, did thinke it convenient to set downe certaine Articles, for the better keeping of company one with another, to which Articles or covenants wee were all severally sworne, setting thereunto our hands.

The sixt we came to Flecorie, into which harbour, by Gods helpe, we came at two a clocke in the afternoone. The seaventh day we supplied our wants of wood and water. The eight day, about two a clocke in the afternoone, we set sayle forth of the harbour of Flecorie, about six a clock it fell calme, till about eight, about which time, the Nase of Norway, by the Danish men, called Lyndis-nose, bare next hand North-west of us, six leagues off; at which time I directed my course West Northwest, finding the compasse varied 7. degrees 10. minutes, to the Eastwards of the true North.

The thirteenth, we had sight of the Iland of Faire Ile, and also of the South-head of Shotland, called Swimborne head, which are high Lands; at noone, the Iland of Faire Ile bearing West halfe a point Northerly: foure leagues off I made observation, and found us in the latitude of 59. degrees 20. minutes. This night about seven a clocke, wee came about an English league to the Northwards of the North-west end of Faire Ile, wee met with a great race of a tyde, as though it had beene the race of Portland, it setting North North-west. Being out of the said race, I directed my course West and by North, having the winde North-east and by North: this evening Faire Ile bearing East South-east foure leagues; Swimborne head, North-east and by North eight leagues: the Iland of Foole, North-east and by East, seven leagues.

I found by exact observation, the compasse to be varied to the East-ward of the true North 60. degrees 10. minutes.

The fourteenth in the morning, the winde came to the East South-east, wee steering West and by North away: this morning the Iland of Faire Ile did shew in my sight to bee about ten leagues off, at which time we did descrie two of the Westermost Ilands of Orkney, which did beare Southwest and by South.

The eighteenth, the winde at North-west and by West, wee laid it away South-west and by West, and sometimes South-west. This day at noone wee were in the Latitude of 58. degrees 40. minutes. The nineteenth day, the winde at South-west and South-west and by West, wee lying as the night before, being at noone in the Latitude of 59. degrees and a halfe. The foure and twentieth day, the winde at North-east and by East, we steering still with a fresh gale West South-west, this evening we looked to have seene Busse Iland, but I doe verily suppose the same to be placed in a wrong Latitude in the Marine Charts. The sixe and twentieth at noone, wee were in the latitude of 57. degrees 45. minutes. The thirtieth day in the morning betweene seven and eight, the weather began to cleere, and the Sea and winde to waxe lesse, wee looking for the Lion and the Pinnasse, could have no sight of them, we supposing them to bee asterne off us, we standing still under our courses. This day the winde came to the North-east and by East, being very cold weather, we lying North North-west away. Making my observation at noone, I found us in the latitude of 59. degrees 15. minutes, our way North North-west fortie leagues. This afternoone between one and two a clock we descried Land, it bearing North North-east off us about ten leagues off North-east & by North off us about ten leagues, it being a very high ragged land, lying in the latitude of 59. degrees 50. minutes, lying alongst South-east and by South, and North-west and by North.

This Head-land wee named after the Kings Majesties of Denmarke, because it was the first part of Groenland, which we did see. This afternoone about one a clock, bearing in for the shoare we saw an Iland of Ice, which bore West Southwest of us three leagues off, so having the wind at East South-east, we bore in for the shoare, where wee found so much Ice that it was impossible either for us or any other ship to come into the shoare without great danger: yet wee put our selves into the Ice as wee thought convenient, being incumbred and compassed about with the same in such sort, as the Captaine, my selfe, the Boatswaine with another of our companie, were forced to goe overboord upon an Iland of Ice, to defend it from the ship, at which time I thought it convenient to stand off into the Sea againe, and so being cleere of the Ice, to double Cape Desolation, to the North-westwards of which I doubted not but to find a cleer coast, so standing away all this night West South-west, to cleere us of the Ice, which lay farre from the shoare, being very thicke towards the Land with great Ilands of Ice that it is wonderfull. This evening, the Cape Christian bearing North-east and by East five leagues, I found the Compasse varied 12. degrees 15. minutes to the North-westwards. Moreover, standing to Seaward from the foresaid Cape, we came in blacke water, as thicke as though it had beene puddle water, we sayling in the same for the space of three houres.

The one and thirtieth in the morning faire weather, with the winde somewhat variable, wee steering away North-west and by West, betweene foure and five in the morning we had sight of the Lion againe, but not of the Pinnasse. They being a Sea-boord off and having espied us, they stood with us, at which time the Captaine, Lieutenant, and Steereman came aboord us, earnestly intreating mee to bestow a Sea Chart of the Steerman, and to give him directions if by tempestuous weather they should lose us, they protesting and swearing that they would never leave us as long as winde and weather would permit them to keepe companie with us. By whose speeches I being perswaded did give them a Sea Chart for those Coasts, telling them that if they would follow me, that by Gods assistance I would bring them to a part of the Land void without pester of Ice, and also harbour the ships in good Harbour, by Gods helpe; they swearing and protesting, that they would follow mee so long as possibly they could, with which oathes and faire speeches I rested satisfied, thinking they had thought as they had sworne, but it fell out otherwise. So having made an end with us about noone, they went aboord againe, wee being this day in the latitude of 59. degrees 45. minutes, having stood all the night before, and this forenoone also, so nigh the shoare as wee could for Ice, the Cape Christian South South-east and North North-west, and from the Cape to Cape Desolation, the Land lyeth East and by South, and West and by North about fiftie leagues. This day betweene one and two a clocke, the Vice-admirals Boat, being newly gone aboord, it fell very hasie and thicke, so that wee could not see one another by reason of the fog, therefore our Captaine caused to shoote off certaine Muskets with a great peece of Ordnance, to the intent the Lion might heare us, which heard of them they presently stood with us, at which time the fogge began somewhat to cleere, wee having sight one of another and so stood alongst the shoare, as nigh as we could for Ice.

The first of June, wee had a fresh gale of winde at South-west, wee steering North-east and by North into the shoare, about three in the morning there fell a mightie fogge, so that we were forced to lye by the lee, for the Lion playing upon our Drum to the intent for them to heare us, and to keepe companie with us, they answering us againe with the shooting of a Musket, wee trimming our sailes, did the like to them, and so stood away North-east and by East: larboord tackt aboord halfe a glasse, when we were hard incumbred amongst mightie Ilands of Ice, being very high like huge Mountaines, so I caused to cast about and stand to the Westwards North-west and by West. About twelve of the clocke this night it being still calme, wee found our selves suddenly compast round about with great Ilands of Ice, which made such a hideous noyse as was most wonderfull, so that by no meanes wee could double the same to the Westward: wherefore wee were forced to stand it away to the Southwards, South South-West, stemming the Current, for by the same Current wee were violently brought into this Ice, so being incumbred and much to doe to keepe cleere of the mightie Ilands of Ice, there being as both I and others did plainly see upon one of them a huge rocke stone, of the weight of three hundred pounds or thereabouts, as wee did suppose. Thus being troubled in the Ice for the space of two or three houres, it pleased God that we got thorow the same.

The second day in the morning about three a clocke, I came forth of my Cabin, where I found that the Shipper whose name was Arnold had altered my course which I had set, going contrarie to my directions North North-west away, whereupon hee and I grew to some speeches, both for at this time and other times hee had done the like. The Captaine likewise seeing his bad dealing with me, did likewise roundly speake his minde to him, for at this instant wee were nigh unto a great banke of Ice, which wee might have doubled if my course had not beene altered, so that we were forced to cast about to the South-wards, South and by East and South South-east, with the winde at South-west and by South or South-west till ten a clocke, when we stood againe to the Westwards, lying West North-west and North-west and by West, being at noone in the latitude of 60. degrees 18. minutes, Cape Desolation is, I did suppose, bearing North and by West three or foure leagues off, the weather being so thicke and hasie that wee could never see the Land.

The fourth day betweene one and two a clocke in the morning, it began to blow a fresh gale Easterly, we steering away North and North and by West, we being at noone in the latitude of 59. degrees 50. minutes, having made a West and by North way foure and twentie leagues. This evening about seven a clocke we had very thicke water, and continued so about halfe an houre: about nine a clocke we did see a very high Iland of Ice to the windward of us, and about halfe an houre after with some drift Ice, they in the Lion thorow the fearefulnesse of their Commanders presently cast about standing away larboord tackt, till they did perceive that I stood still away as I did before, without impediment of the Ice, they cast about againe and followed us.

The fift in the morning, being very faire weather with the winde at East South-east, our course North North-west, some of our people supposed they had seene the Land: our Captaine and I went aboord the Pinnasse, when after an houre of our being there wee did see the supposed Land to be an hasie fogge, which came on us so fast that wee could scarce see one another. But the Lion being very nigh unto us, and it being very calme, wee laid the Pinnasse aboord of her, and so the Captaine and I went aboord of them.

The ninth day about foure a clocke, it began to blow an easie gale at South-east and by South, I directing my course still North North-west, when some of our people would not be perswaded but they did see Land, and therefore I stood in North and by East and North North-east, till about three a clocke in the afternoone, when wee met with a huge and high Iland of Ice, wee steering hard to board the same, and being shot a little to Northwards of it, there fell from the top thereof some quantitie of Ice, which in the fall did make such a noyse as though it had beene the report of five Cannons. This evening wee came amongst much drift Ice, being both windwards and to leewards of us, yet by Gods helpe we got very well through the same, when being cleere I directed my course againe North North-west.

The tenth day the winde at South-west and by West, I steering still North-west and by North. This forenoone also wee met with great Ilands of Ice, it being very hasie and thicke weather, the which did drive them in the Lion into great feare, and calling to us very fearfully perswaded me to alter my course and to returne homeward, saying that it was impossible for us by any working, and course keeping to sease upon the Land, which did drive all our companie into such a feare, that they were determined, whether I would or not, to have returned home, had not the Captaine as an honest and resolute Gentleman stood by mee, protesting to stand by me so long as his blood was warme, for the good of the Kings Majestie, who had set us forth, and also to the performing of the Voyage. Which resolution of his did mitigate the stubbornenesse of the people: yet nothing would perswade those fearfull persons in the Lion, especially the Steerman, who had rather long before this time have returned home, then to have proceeded on the action, as before the said Steerman had done when he was imployed eight yeeres before in the said action or discoverie. Therefore our Captaine and my selfe seeing their backwardnesse now, as before we had done, went our selves the same evening into the Pinnasse, having a mightie banke of Ice of our larboord side, and spake to them very friendly, giving order both to our owne ship and to them, that they should keepe a Seaboord of us (for I did suppose this banke of Ice to lye in the narrowest of the Streight, betweene America and Groenland, as indeed by experience I found the same to be) therefore I determined to coast the Ice alongst till I found it to bee driven and fall away, by reason of the swift current that setteth very forcibly through the said Strait, and then by the grace of God to set over for a cleere part of the coast of Groenland, so all this night we coasted the Ice as close aboord as

we could East North-east and North-east and by East, till about midnight, when we found the said banke to fall away.

The eleventh day, being cleere of the Ice, I stood away North North-east till sixe a clocke, when we met with another great banke of Ice, at which time the Commanders of the Lion being now againe very fearfull as before, came up to our ship, perswading the Shipper and Companie to leave us, and to stand to Seaboord with them. But the Shipper who was also Lieftenant of the ship, being more honestly minded, said, that he would follow us so long as he could: with which answere they departed, using many spitefull wordes, both of the Captaine and mee, saying we were determined to betray the Kings ships, at which time they shot off a peece of Ordnance, and so stood away from us. I seeing their perverse dealing let them goe, wee coasting alongst the Ice North North-east with a fresh gale, it being extreme cold with snow and hayse, the Sea also going very high by reason of a mightie current, the which I found to set very forceably through this Strait, which being nigh unto America side, setteth to the Northwards, and on the other side to the contrarie, as by proofe I found. So coasting alongst this mayne banke of Ice, which seemed as it had beene a firme Continent till about eleven a clocke, when wee espyed the Ice to stretch to windward, on our weather bow wee setting our starboord takes aboord, stood away East and by South with the winde at South and by East, till wee had doubled a Seaboord the Ice, at which time I directed my course directly over for the cleere coast of Groineland, East and by North, which course I directed all the Frost to goe, wee standing away our course all this night, it being very much snow and sleete.

The twelfth day in the morning about foure a clocke, we espyed the Land of Groenland, being a very high ragged Land, the tops of the Mountaines being all covered with snow, yet wee found all this coast utterly without Ice, wee standing into the Land espyed a certaine Mount above all the rest, which Mount is the best marke on all this Coast, the which I named Mount Cunningham after the name of my Captaine. We comming into the shoare betweene two Capes or Head-lands, the Land lying betweene them North and by East, and South and by West, the Southmost of which Forelands I named Queene

Annes Cape, after the name of the Queenes Majestie of Denmarke, and the Northermost of the two I called Queene Sophias Cape, after the name of the Queene Mother.

So standing into the Land, we came amongst certaine Ilands, where sayling in still amongst the same unto the Southermost foot of the foresaid Mount, wee came into a goodly Bay, which wee did suppose to be a River, being on both sides of the same very high and steepe Mountaines, wee named the same King Christianus Foord, after the name of the Kings Majestie of Denmarke. So sayling up this Bay, which wee supposed to bee a River, the space of sixe or seven English leagues, finding in all that space no anchoring, being marvellous deepe water, till at the length we had sayled up the Bay the foresaid distance, at length I brought the Ship and Pinnasse to an anchor in sixteene fathom shelly ground, at which time our Captaine and I went aland, giving thankes unto God for his unspeakable benefits, who had thus dealt with us as to bring us to this desired Land into so good an Harbour; which done, the Captaine and I walked up the Hills, to see if wee could see any of the people, having our Boat to row alongst with us. Having gone alongst the River side upon the tops of the Hills the space of three or foure English miles; at length looking towards our Boat, wee saw upon the River side foure of the people standing by their Houses or rather Tents, covered over with Seale-skins. Wee comming downe the Hills towards them (they having espyed us) three of them ranne away upon the Land, and the other tooke his Boat and rowed away leaving their Tents. Wee being come downe the Hills called to our men in the Boat, and entring into her rowed towards the Savage who was in his Boat made of Seale-skins. Hee holding up his hands towards the Sunne, cryed Yota; wee doing the like, and shewing to him a knife, hee presently came unto us and tooke the same of the Captaine. When hee had presently rowed away from us, wee rowed a little after him, and seeing it was but in vaine wee rowed aland againe and went into their Tents, which wee found covered (as is aforesaid) with Seale-skins. Wee finding by the houses two Dogs being very rough and fat, like in shape to a Foxe, with very great abundance of Seale fish, lying round about their Tents a drying, with innumerable quantities of a little fish unto a Smelt (which fish are commonly called Sardeenes)

of which fish in all the Rivers are wonderfull skuls, these fishes also lay a drying round about their Tents in the Sunne in great heapes, with other sundrie kindes. Then entring into their Tents, wee found certaine Seale skins and Foxe skins very well drest; also certaine Coates of Seale skins and Fowle skins with the feather side inward: also certaine Vessels boyling upon a little Lampe, the Vessell being made after the manner of a little Pan, the bottome whereof is made of stone, and the sides of Whales finnes; in which Vessell was some little quantitie of Seale fish boyling in Seale oyle; and searching further, wee did finde in another of their Vessels a Dogs head boyled, so that I perswaded my selfe that they eate Dogs flesh. Moreover, by their houses there did lye two great Boates, being covered under with Seales skins, but aloft open after the forme of our Boates, being about twentie foote in length, having in each of them eight or ten tosts or seates for men to sit on, which Boates, as afterwards I did perceive, is for the transporting of their Tents and baggage from place to place, and for a saile they have the guts of some beast, which they dresse very fine and thin, which they sow together.

Also the other sorts of their Boats are such as Captaine Frobisher, and Master John Davis brought into England, which is but for one man, being cleane covered over with Seale skins artificially dressed except one place to sit in,[1] being within set out with certaine little ribs of Timber, wherein they use to row with one Oare more swiftly, then our men can doe with ten, in which Boates they fish being disguised in their Coates of Seale skinnes, whereby they deceive the Seales, who take them rather for Seales then men; which Seales or other fish they kill in this manner. They shoot at the Seales or other great fish with their Darts, unto which they use to tye a bladder, which doth boy up the fish in such manner that by the said means they catch them. So comming aboord our ships having left certaine trifles behind us in their Tents, and taking nothing away with us, within halfe an houre after our comming aboord, the Savage to whom wee had given the Knife with three others, which we did suppose to be them which we saw first, came rowing to our

1. Sidenote: "Of the other sort of Boats. There is one of these Boats in Sir Thomas Smiths Hall."

ships in their Boats, holding up their hands to the Sunne, and striking of their brests, crying Yota. We doing the like, they came to our shippe or Captaine: giving them bread and Wine, which, as it did seeme, they made little account of; yet they gave us some of their dryed fishes, at which time there came foure more, who with the other bartered their Coats, and some Seale skinnes, with our folke for old Iron Nailes, and other trifles as Pinnes and Needles, with which they seemed to be wonderfully pleased, and having so done, holding their hands towards the Sunne they departed.

The thirteenth, there came fourteene of them to our ship, bringing with them Seale skinnes, Whale Finnes, with certayne of their Darts and Weapons, which they bartered with our people, as before. This day I made observation of the latitude, and found this Roadsted in the latitude of 66. degrees 25. minutes, and the mouth of this Bay or Sound, lyeth in the latitude of 66. degrees 30. minutes. Also here I made observation of the tydes, and found an East and West Moone to make a full Sea, upon the Full and Change, more it floweth, three fathome and an halfe water, right up and downe.

The fourteenth and fifteenth dayes we rode still, the people comming to us, and bartering with us for pieces of old Iron, or Nailes, Whale Finnes, Seales Skinnes, Morse Teeth, and a kind of Horne which we doe suppose to be Unicornes Horne, at which time the Captaine went with our Boat, to the place where we had seene their Tents, but found them removed; and the other fish and the Seale fish lying still a drying: the Captaine taking a quantitie of the Sea fish into the Boat, caused some of the Mariners to boyle it ashoare, the Savages helping our men to doe the same, the Captaine using them very friendly, they having made about a barrell and an halfe of Oyle, leaving it aland all night, thinking to bring the same aboord in the morning. But the Savages the same night let the same forth. Yet notwithstanding, the Captaine shewed no manner of discontent towards them.

The sixteenth day, I went into the Pinnasse, to discover certaine Harbours to the Northwards, the wind being at East South-east, I loosed and set saile, but instantly it fell calme, and so continued about an houre. When the wind came opposite at the West North-west a stiffe gale, we spending the tide till the floud being come, I put

roome againe, and came to an Anchor a little from the Frost in twelve fathomes sandie ground. About one in the afternoone, the Frost departed from us further up the Bay, which we did suppose to be a River, promising to abide our returne two and twentie dayes.

The seventeenth day, the wind continuing at the West North-west blowing very hard, wee rode still, the people comming and bartering with us.

The eighteenth day, the winde and weather as before, wee riding still. This forenoone there came to the number of thirtie of them, and bartered with us as they had done before, which done, they went ashoare at a certaine point about a flight-shot off us, and there upon a sudden began to throw stones with certaine Slings which they had without any injury offered at all; yea, they did sling so fiercely, that we could scarce stand on the hatches. I seeing their brutish dealing, caused the Gunner to shoot a Falcon at them, which lighted a little over them, at which time they went to their Boates, and rowed away. About one a clocke in the afternoone, they came againe to us crying in their accustomed manner, Yliont, they being sixtie three in number, the shipper inquired of me whether they should come to us or not, I willed him to have all things in a readinesse, they comming in the meane time nigh to the Pinnasse, I did perceive certaine of them to have great bagges full of stones, they whispered one with another began to sling stones unto us. I presently shot off a little Pistol which I had for the Gunner, and the rest of the folke to discharge, which indeed they did, but whether they did hurt or kill any of them or not, I cannot certainly tell, but they rowed all away making a howling and hideous noise: going to the same point, whereas in the forenoone they had beene, being no sooner come on Land, but from the Hils they did so assaile us with stones, with their slings, that it is incredible to report, in such sort that no man could stand upon the Hatches, till such time as I commanded for to lose sailes and bonnets two mens height, to shield us from the force of the stones, and also did hide us from their sight; so that we did ply our Muskets and other Peeces such as wee had at them: but their subtiltie was such, that as soone as they did see fire given to the Peeces, they would suddenly ducke downe behind the Cliffes, and when they were discharged, then sling their stones fiercely at us againe. Thus having continued there till foure a clocke, they departed away.

The nineteenth day in the morning, about foure a clocke it beeing calme, I departed from this Roadsted, so causing our men to row alongst the shoare, till the tide of the ebbe was bent, at which time it began to blow a fresh gale at North-west and by West, we turning downe till about two a clocke, when the tide of floud being come: when I came to an Anchor in an excellent Haven, on the South side of Cunninghams Mount, which for the goodnesse thereof, I named Denmarkes Haven.

The twentieth day, in the morning the weather beeing very rainie with a little aire of wind, I loosed and caused to row forth of the foresaid Harbour, and comming forth betweene the Ilands and the maine, the people being as it seemed looking for us espied us: making a hideous noise, at which time at an instant were gathered together about seventie-three Boats with men rowing to us. I seeing them, thought it best to prevent the worst, because we were to come hither againe: therefore to dissemble the matter, I thought it best to enter into barter with them for some of their Darts, Bowes and Arrowes, wee finding every one of them to bee extraordinarily furnished therwith: so rowing forth to Sea amongst the Ilands, there stil came more Boats to the number of one hundred and thirtie persons, they still rowing by us, made signes to us to goe to anchor amongst some of the Ilands: but I preventing their devices, made certaine Skonces with our sailes, to defend us from their Stones, Arrowes and Darts. They seeing this, went certaine of them from us rowing to certaine Ilands, to which they did thinke wee would come: leaving no more but about ten men and Boates about us, who rowed alongst the space of an houre with us, making signes of friendship to us. At length perceiving, that wee were not minded to goe forth amongst these Ilands, upon which the rest of their folke were, they threw certaine shels and trifles into the Boat, making signes and tokens to fetch them, the which my Boy called William Huntries did. He being in the Boat, they presently shot him through both the buttockes with a Dart, at which time they rowed from us, they mustering upon the Ilands to the number of three hundred persons, keeping themselves farre enough from our danger. About six a clocke this Evening it began to blow a faire gale Easterly, we getting off to

Sea, stood all this night North and by East alongst the Land.

[b]A Topographicall Description of the Land as I did discover the same.

Now having proceeded for the discoverie of the Coast and Harbours so farre, and so long time as the time limited to me, therefore I thinke it convenient, to make a briefe description of the same, according as by my short experience I found the same to be.

The Land of Groenland is a very high, ragged and mountainous Countrey, being all alongst the Coast broken Ilands, making very goodly Sounds and Harbours, having also in the Land very many good Rivers and Bayes, into some of which I entred sayling up the same the space of ten or twelve English leagues, finding the same very navigable, with great abundance of fish of sundrie sorts. The Land also in all places wheresoever I came, seemed to be very fertile, according to the Climate wherein it lyeth: for betweene the Mountaynes was most pleasant Plaines and Valleyes, in such sort as if I had not seene the same, I could not have beeleved, that such a fertile Land in shew could bee in these Northerne Regions. There is also in the same great store of Fowle, as Ravens, Crowes, Partridges, Pheasants, Seamewes, Gulles, with other sundry sorts. Of Beasts I have not seene any, except blacke Foxes, of which there are very many. Also as I doe suppose there are many Deere, because that comming to certaine places where the people had had their Tents, we found very many Harts Hornes, with the bones of other beasts round about the same. Also going up into the Land wee saw the footing and dunging of divers beasts, which we did suppose to be deere, and other beasts also, the footing of one which wee found to be eight inches over, yet, notwithstanding we did see none of them: for going some two or three miles from the Pinnasse we returned againe to goe aboord. Moreover, in the Rivers we found sundry sorts of Fishes, as Seales, Whales, Salmons, with other sorts of fishes in great abundance. As concerning the Coast, all alongst it is a very good and faire Land, having very faire shoalding of the same: for being three English leagues off the same, I found very faire shoalding in fifteene fathomes, and comming neerer the same fourteene, twelve, and tenne fathomes very faire sandie ground. As concerning the people, they are (as I doe suppose) a kinde of Samoites, or wandring Nation travelling in the Summer time in Companies together, first to one place, and having stayed in that place a certayne time in hunting and fishing for Deere and Seales with other fish, streight they remove themselves with their Tents and baggage to another. They are men of a reasonable stature, being browne of colour, very like to the people of the East and West Indies. They be very active and warlike, as we did perceive in their Skirmishes with us, in using their Slings and Darts very nimbly. They eat their meate raw, or a little perboyled either with bloud, Oyle, or a little water, which they doe drinke. They apparell themselves in the skinnes of such beasts as they kill, but especially with Seales skins and fowle skins, dressing the skins very soft and smooth, with the haire and feathers on, wearing in Winter the haire and feather sides inwards, and in Summer outwards. Their Weapons are Slings, Darts, Arrowes, having their Bowes fast tyed together with sinewes; their Arrowes have but two feathers, the head of the same being for the most part of bone, made in manner and forme of a Harping Iron. As concerning their Darts, they are of sundry sorts and fashions. What knowledge they have of God I cannot certainly say, but I suppose them to bee Idolaters, worshipping the Sunne. The Countrey (as is aforesaid) seemeth to be very fertile, yet could I perceive or see no wood to grow thereon. Wee met all alongst this Coast much Drift-wood, but whence it commeth I know not. For coasting all this Coast alongst from the latitude of 66. degrees and an halfe, untill the latitude of 69. degrees, I found many goodly Sounds, Bayes, and Rivers: giving names unto divers of them, and purposing to proceed further, the folke in the Pinnasse with me did earnestly intreate me to returne to the ship againe, alleaging this, that if we came not in convenient time, the people in the ship would mutinie: and so returne home before we came: the which indeed had fallen forth, if the Captaine as an honest Gentleman had not by severe meanes withstood their attempts, who would needes contrarie to their promises have beene gone home within eight dayes after my departure from them. But the Captaine respecting his promise to mee, would by no meanes consent, but withstood them both by faire meanes and other wayes. So that upon the seventh day of July, I returned again

into the Kings Foord, which they in the ship had found to be a Bay, and comming to the place where wee had left the ship hoping to have found them there, I saw upon a certaine point a Warlocke of stones, whereby I did perceive that they were gone downe the Ford. So the tide of ebbe being come, it being calme we rowed downe the Foord, finding in the mouth of the same amongst the Ilands, many good Sounds and Harbours.

The tenth day of July the wind being at North North-west, I beeing in a certaine Sound amongst the Ilands, it being high water I weighed, stood West forth of the Foord going to Sea on the South side between a little Iland and the Maine, which Iland at our first comming, we called Frost Iland, after the name of the ship: we espied on the South sides certaine Warlockes set up, whereupon I suspected that the Frost might be there, commanded the Gunner to shoot off a Peece of Ordnance, they presently answered us againe with two other. We seeing the smoake (but heard no report) bore in to them, comming to an Anchor in a very good Sound by them, and found them all in health: the Captaine being very glad of our comming, forasmuch as hee had very much trouble with the company for the cause aforesaid. Also in the time of our absence the people did very much villanie to them in the ship, so that the Captaine tooke three of them; other of them also he slew, but the three which he tooke he used with all kindnesse, giving them Mandillions and Breeches of very good cloth, also Hose, Shoes, and Shirts off his own backe. This afternoone, I with my Boy came againe aboord the ship, taking in this Evening all our provision of water.

The eleventh day, the wind being at North North-east, we set saile forth of the Sound which we named Frost Sound, but before our comming forth of the same our Captaine commanded a young man whose name was Simon, by the expresse commandement of the State-holder of Denmarke to bee set aland, wee also in the Pinnasse set another aland, they both being Malefactors, the which was done before our comming away, we giving to them things necessarie, as victuall and other things also. Thus having committed both the one and the other to God, wee set saile homewards, we standing forth to Sea South-west, and South-west and by West till noone, when making observation, Queene Annes Cape bearing South and by East halfe Easterly some ten leagues, I found my selfe in the latitude of 66. degrees 10.

minutes, when I directed my course South South-west till sixe aclocke when wee were amongst much Drift Ice, being to leeward two points upon our lee-bow, so that I was forst to lie off West North-west till we were cleere of the same, at which time I directed my course South-west and by South, wee sayling so all the night following.

The twelfth day, the wind at North North-east, wee went away South-west and by South till ten a clocke, when we were amongst more Drift Ice, wee being againe to lie West North-west, to get cleere of the same, which we did about noone, we having this day and the Evening before a mightie hollow Sea, which I thought to be a current, the which setteth thorow Fretum Davis to the Southwards, as by experience I proved: for making observation this day at noone, we found our selves in the latitude of 62. degrees 40. minutes, whereas the day before we were but in the latitude of 66. degrees 10. minutes, having made by account a South and by West way about ten leagues. This afternoone I directed my course South South-west.

The thirteenth day, the wind as before, we steered still South and by West, being at noone in the latitude of 60. degrees 17. minutes, going at the same time away South and by East. This foresaid current I did find to set alongst the Coast of Gronland South and by East. The fourteenth day, close weather, being an easie gale we steering South-east and by East. The fifteenth day, stil close weather til noone, we steering as before, being in the latitude of 59. degrees. This day at noone I went away East South-east; this afternoone it was hasie and still weather, when we had sight of some Drift Ice. The 16. day, close weather with the wind at North-west and by West, our course East South-east til about ten aclock, when we met with a mightie bank of Ice to windward of us, being by supposition seven or eight leagues long, wee steering South South-east to get cleere of the same. We met all alongst this Ice a mightie scull of Whales. Moreover, wee light with a great current, which as nigh as we could suppose, set West North-west over for America. This day at noone, the weather being very thicke, I could have no observation, this Evening by reason of the Ice, wee were forced to lye South and by West, and South South-west, to get cleere of the same, amongst which we came by divers huge Ilands of Ice.

The seventeenth day, being cleere of the Ice, about foure in the morning, I directed my course South-east by South till noone, at which time I went away East and by South, the weather being very haysie and thicke: about midnight it fell calme, the wind comming up Easterly.

The eighteenth day, the wind still Easterly, we lying East South-east, away under a couple of courses larboord tackt. This day in the forenoone, we saw certayne Ilands of Ice. The nineteenth day, the wind still Easterly with the weather very hasie.

The first day of August also it was very thicke weather, with a faire gale at South-west and by West. This forenoone wee met with a scull of Herrings, so that I knew wee were not farre from the Iles of Orkney, so having a shrinke at noone, I found us in the latitude of 58. degrees 40. minutes, at which time I sounded with the deepest Lead, finding 42. fathomes redde sandie ground, with some blacke dents. This Evening betweene five and sixe a clocke wee sounded againe, when we had no more but twentie fathomes dent ground, whereby I knew that we were faire by the shoare, when some of our men looking forth presently, espied one of the Ilands of Orkeney, it being very thicke, wee cast about, and stood with a small sayle to Seaboord againe, we lying West North-west off all this night.

The tenth day, about five in the morning, we came thwart of the Castle of Elsonvere, where we discharged certaine of our Ordnance, and comming to an Anchor in the Road, the Captaine with my selfe went ashoare, and hearing of his Majesties being at Copeman-Haven, wee presently went aboord againe, and set sayle comming thither about two a clocke. The Pinnasse also which he had lost at Sea, in which my Countreyman John Knight was Commander, came also the same night about foure a clocke, both they and we being all in good health, praised bee Almightie God. Amen.

671. April 18 to September 24, 1606. John Knight's voyage in the *Hopewell*.

John Knight, who had been on the Lindenov voyage of 1605, was commissioned by a syndicate formed jointly by the Muscovy Company and the East India Company to make a further Northwest Passage voyage in 1606. The Hopewell *sailed up and down the coast of Labrador, not making a latitude higher than 58°. The ship grounded on the Labrador coast, and the men were busy putting their shallop together and salvaging goods when Knight went off with three men to prospect for a harbor in which they might repair the ship. They disappeared and were presumably killed by Eskimo. Afterward, the Eskimo attacked the remaining eight men, who beat them off with the aid of their dog. They managed to refloat and roughly repair their ship, made their way to Fogo Island where they got help from codfishermen, and were able to sail home.*

The journal by John Knight, continued by Oliver Brown, is in S. Purchas, Pilgrimes, *III (1625), 827–831 (XIV [1906], 353–365).*

The Voyage of Master John Knight, (which had beene at Groenland once before 1605. Captaine of a Pinnasse of the King of Denmarke) for the Discovery of the Northwest Passage, begun the eighteenth of Aprill 1606.

I set sayle from Gravesend in a Barke of fortie tunnes, called the Hope-well, well victualled and manned at the cost of the Worshipfull Companies of Moscovie, and the East Indie Merchants, for the Discoverie of the North-west Passage the eighteenth of Aprill 1606. and arrived the sixe and twentieth of the same moneth in the Ile of Orkney, in a Sound called Pentlefrith. Heere wee were stayed with contrary winds at West and North-west, and with much storme and foule weather above a fortnight. In which meane space, I entertained two men of this Countrey, which are both lustie fellowes at Sea and Land, and are well acquainted with all the Harbours of these North parts of Scotland. These men brought us into a very good Harbour, called Saint Margarites Hope, where we had the Sea open to us for all winds that are good for us to proceed on our Voyage. In this Countrey we found little worthy of Relation. For it is poore, and hath no wood growing upon it. Their Corne is Barley and Oates. Their fire is Turffe, their houses are low and unseemely without, and as homely within.

Upon Munday the twelfth of May, I set sayle from Saint Margarites Sound or Hope in Orkney, at nine of the clocke in the morning, our course being West and by South: and at eight of the clocke at night, the Hill called Hoyce, did beare West Southerly eleven or twelve leagues, and the Stacke South and by East Easterly three leagues and an halfe, the winde beeing at East Southeast.

This day was for the most part calme, and sometimes wee had a fresh gale of winde: our course was West and by South, halfe a point Southerly. This day I passed by two small Ilands. The one of them is called, the Clete, and the other the Run. They are distant foure leagues the one from the other. The course betweene them is South-west and North-east. The Southermost is called the Clete, and is the lesser of the twaine: it is distant from the North-east part of Lewis, called the Bling-head, seven leagues: and the course betwixt them is North-west and South-east. Also this Bling-head is distant from the Farro Head, of the Hieland of Scotland West and by North halfe a point Westerly, and is distant seventeene leagues. Also the course betweene Bling-head and the North-west part of Lewis, is West and by South halfe a point Westerly, and faire low Land without Wood. There is good riding all along the shoare, the winde beeing off the Land, and in some places are very good Harbours for all winds. From eight to twelve at night, we ran six leagues West South-west.

This morning we had a fresh gale of wind at East North-east: our course was South-west and by West two houres five leagues. From two to ten South-west, and by South 20. leagues. From ten to twelve West South-west six leagues. The latitude at noone was 58. degrees 27. minutes.

From Wednesday at noone till Thursday at noone, was for the most part raine and fogge, the wind at North-east and by East: our course was West halfe a point Southerly: our latitude at noone being Thursday, 58. degrees 23. minutes. From Thursday at noone till Friday at noone, being the sixteenth, our way was West Southerly about twentie leagues: the latitude at noone was 58. degrees 19. minutes. This night the wind was sometimes variable betweene the South and by West and South-east, with faire weather, the Magneticall Declination 18. degrees: the height of the Pole was 58. degrees 10. minutes. Also in the morning the Sunne beeing tenne degrees above the Horizon, was distant from the East to the North-wards of the East twentie two degrees.

From Friday at noone untill midnight was little wind Southerly, and sometimes calme, and from midnight till twelve at noone the next day a stiffe gale of wind at East North-east. This foure and twentie houres I judged our way to be made good West, something Southerly thirtie leagues. The latitude at noone was 58. degrees 10. minutes. Also the sunne did rise fiftie degrees to the Northward of the East.

From Saturday at noone being the seventeenth, till Sunday at noone being the eighteenth, our course was West and by South a stiffe gale of wind fiftie leagues, being close weather, we made no observation of latitude.

From Sunday at noone till Munday at noone I steered away West and West and by South, having a storme at East and by North: our course was West and Southerly fiftie leagues.

From Munday at noone till midnight, our course was West and Southerly: and from that time till noone West and by North and West among. I judged wee sayled fortie leagues these foure and twentie houres, being for the most part foggie. The latitude at noone was 57. degrees 50. minutes.

From Tuesday at noone till noone on Wednesday, our course was West and by North fortie five leagues, being foggie weather without observation. Here wee had a current, which I judge setteth to the Northwards.

From Wednesday at noone till Thursday at noone, being the two and twentieth, our course was West and by North fiftie leagues with much fogge and close weather, and much winde at North-east and by East.

From Thursday at noone till midnight, our course was West and by North. Then the winde came to the North: wee tooke in our mayne course, and I spooned away with our fore-saile till Friday, the winde being at North North-east, I judged our way West South-west, the twelve houres that I spooned about fifteene leagues, the other twelve houres West Northerly five and twentie leagues. This three and twentieth day, wee saw many Gulles and much Rock-weed.

From Friday at noone till Saturday at noone, I judged our way to bee made South-west and by West, but it proved West and by South, rather Westerly, twentie leagues by reason of a current, that I judge setteth to the North-eastward. The latitude at noone was 57. degrees 53. minutes. The variation of the Compasse was about a point

to the Westward. This forenoone and all night the wind was at North a very hard gale; wee spooned with our fore-sayle. Also this forenoone, we saw much Sea Tange and Rock-weed.

From Saturday at noone till Sunday at noone, our course was Southward about twentie leagues, the wind being Northerly. This day we saw much Rock-weed and Drift-wood. The latitude was fiftie seven degrees. The variation was to the Westward thirteene degrees or thereabout. The sunne being five degrees high in the morning, was twentie foure degrees to the Northward of the East.

From Sunday at noone till two of the clocke the next day in the morning, beeing Munday, our course was West North-west, we made our way West and by North twentie leagues, having a fresh gale at South-east and by East: it fell calme till foure of the clocke: then it blew an easie gale at West South-west, wee stemming North-west, &c. betweene that and North North-east the wind being variable. The wind freshed toward noone. This morning we saw an Owle.

The latitude at noone the eight and twentieth, was 57. degrees 57. minutes. The variation of the Compasse was fourteene degrees and an halfe to the West. This day wee had blacke water, and many over-falls, streame leeches, and sets of currents, as it seemed to the Northward, and some to the Westward.

The thirtieth, we found our latitude to be fiftie eight degrees. Heere it seemed that we were in a tyde gate, which I judged to set North and South, or that it was the Eddie of the currents, which we saw the other day. Also wee saw white Fowles, which cheeped like Sparhawkes. Also we saw driving many dead Cowes.

The one and thirtieth, the sunne being fiftie degrees above the Horizon, I found it to bee twentie seven degrees to the Eastward of the South: againe in the afternoone, the sunne beeing fiftie degrees high, it was distant from the South to the Westward fiftie one degrees: at noone it was 55. degrees 6. minutes, the height of the Pole was 58. degrees 3. minutes. The variation of the Compasse was twentie foure degrees toward the North-west. Our way made these twentie foure houres was not above six leagues West, being little wind for the most part.

From Saturday at noone till two of the clocke it was calme: then it began to blow an easie gale at North. At night I observed the sunne setting, and found it to set twentie one degrees to the West-ward of the North, the winde continuing variable betweene the North and the West North-west till noone, being the first of June. Then I found my selfe by observation to be in the latitude of 57. degrees 35. minutes. I judged our way from noone to noone West and by South or thereabout thir-teene leagues.

From Sunday at noone till ten of the clocke the same Evening, it was calme. Then it began to blow a stiffe gale of wind at South South-east. Our course was West till noone, the next day being Munday, twentie three leagues. This day wee saw many blacke Fowles like Willockes flying in flockes together.

The fourth my latitude at noone, was 56. de-grees 40. minutes. The latitude next day at noone was fiftie sixe degrees. The variation of the Com-passe by the Scale was twentie degrees, and by my other Instrument twentie foure degrees to the West. The sunne was twentie two degrees and an halfe high, and to the North of the West thirtie degrees by the Instrument, and twentie sixe de-grees by the Scale.

Our latitude at noone the eleventh, was fiftie eight degrees. And at night the sunne did set fourteene degrees to the Westward of the North, and did rise fiftie degrees to the Eastward of the North.

The thirteenth, the Ice seemed to be dispersed thinner with the wind, or some other accident: then I set sayle with our two courses, but was forced to take them in againe, and moored to another great Iland of Ice, about a mile to the Westward of the other. Here setteth some smal current to the South-westward. For the great flakes of Ice that were somewhat deep, drave to the Southward, and the other small Ice which was flotie drave with the wind, which was variable betwixt the North-west and the North. Here we were in sight of Land, which bore West South-west from us, shewing in some parts like Ilands. Our latitude at noone was 57. degrees 25. min-utes.

From Friday at noone till eight of the clocke at night, wee continued moored to the aforesaid Ice: then it fell calme, and I loosed and rowed to the West-ward with our Oares, hoping to get thorough, till twelve of the clocke, then the Ice grew very thicke. I moored againe till foure of the clocke the next morning. Then we rowed and

sayled with an easie gale of wind till eight of the clocke the next morning being Saturday. Then it began to blow a fresh gale Easterly, and we cunned the ship among the Ice with our Oares till noone. Our latitude was fiftie eight degrees. From Saturday at noone till midnight wee guided our shippe to the Westward among the Ice with our Oares, hoping to get thorough: but wee were suddenly compassed about with many great Ilands of Ice, and continued so distressed with a sore storme of wind at South-east, being foggie and thicke weather: we were so bruised betweene mightie great Ilands of Ice, that we were in danger every minute to be crushed in pieces with force of the heaving and setting of the said Ice with the great Sea that the wind made, had not God of his mercie provided for us: for our owne endevours did little availe to our helpe, though wee employed all our industries to the uttermost of our powres.

The nineteenth, we descryed the Land of America, which riseth like eight Ilands: the Northermost part of it did beare North and by West about fifteene leagues from us. I observed the latitude, and found my selfe to be in 56. degrees and 48. minutes. The variation of the Compasse was twentie five degrees to the West-ward. All this Coast sheweth like broken Land or Ilands; and the tyde of floud commeth from the Northward.

Tuesday the foure and twentieth all the morn-ing, there blew a storme Northerly, and such a suffe of the Sea, and so much Ice came in, that our fasts brake that were fast on shoare, and our Rudder was driven from our sterne with the force of mightie Ilands of Ice; so that we were forced to hale close into the bottome of the Cove to save our clothes, furniture and victuals: wee did our best, but before we had done, our ship was halfe full of water: the night comming upon us being wearie, we tooke a little rest.

On Wednesday, we went hard to worke when the ship was on ground, to get the water out of her, and to stop so many of her leakes as we could come by, and to save so much of our bread as we could; and some went to building our shallop. Also I caused our Boate to be lanched over the Iland; and sent my Mate Edward Gorrell, with three others, to seeke for a better place where to bring our ship on ground, if it were possible, to mend her againe. But they returned without any certaintie by reason of the abundance of Ice, which choked every place. They found wood growing on the shoare.

Thursday being faire weather.

Here Master John Knight ended writing in this Journall. On this Thursday the sixe and twentieth of June in the morning, our Master caused some of our men to goe aboord our ship, to save what things they could. And hee and Edward Gorrell his Mate, and his brother, and three more of our Company tooke the Boate, carrying with them foure Pistols, three Muskets, five Swords, and two halfe Pikes for to goe over to a great Iland, which was not above a mile from our ship, to looke if they could find any Harbour or any Cove, to get our ship into for to mend her. Also he carried an Equinoctiall Diall with him, and paper to make a Draught of the Land. When they were passed over to the other side, our Master, his Mate, and his brother, and one more went on shoare, leaving two of us in the Boate with one Musket, one Sword, and an halfe Pike to keepe it: which two stayed in the Boate from ten of the clocke in the morning, untill eleven of the clocke at night, but could heare no newes of them after their departure up into the top of the Hill. Then did the Trumpettor sound two or three times, and the other did discharge his Musket two or three times, and so they came away to the other side to the West of the Company, where the ship was: where they were watching for our comming; who seeing us two comming and no more, they marvelled where the rest of the company were. When wee came on shoare, they enquired for our Master and the rest of our company. But we could tell them no newes of them after their departure out of the Boat, but that we did see them goe up to the top of the Iland. Which report did strike all our men into a great feare to thinke in what extremitie we were, because we did want our Master and three of our best men, and our Ship lay sunke, and we had nothing to trust to but our Shallop, which was not at that time halfe finished. This night lying on shoare in our Tent, which was betweene two Rockes, we kept very good watch, for feare of any peoples sudden assaulting of us: or if our Master and his company had travailed so farre, that they could not come againe that night, and would shoote a Musket, that wee might heare them. But they came not at all.

The next day being Friday, and the seven and twentieth of June, wee consulted to goe over seven of us with our Boate, to try if we could see or learne any news of our Master, or any of our men; for we were afraid that they were either surprised by the Savages of the Countrie, or else devoured by the wilde Beasts. So we tooke with us seven Muskets, and Swords, and Targets, and such provision as we had in the Ship, and went downe to the Sea-side, but wee could not get over for Ice. At length we returned, with much adoe to get on shoare, and went to our Ship, to save what things we could all that day.

On Saturday, the eight and twentieth, we did likewise save what things we could, and gat all our things out of our Ship, and made her cleane in hold, having faire weather, hoping in God to save her, and to mend all things, as well as we could; for she lay upon hard rocks: wherefore we kept her as light as we could, for beating and bruising of her hull. That night about nine of the clocke, it began to raine very sore, and so continued all night: and about one of the clocke at night, our Boate-Swaine and our Steward being at watch, and their watch almost out, the Steward went aboord the Ship to pumpe, leaving the Boate-Swaine at watch some Musket shot length from our Tent: while he was in pumping, there came over the rocks a great sort of the Countrey people toward the place where the Boate-Swaine was: who when they saw him, they shot their arrowes at him, running toward him as fast as they could. Whereupon hee discharged his Musket at them, and fled to our Tent as fast as hee could, thinking they had beset us, they were so many of them in sight. The Steward hearing his Musket goe off, came out of the Ship, and as he was comming, saw the Savages running to our Shallop, and cryed out to us that were asleepe in our Tent, to come to rescue the Boate-Swaine, and the Shallop. We made what haste we could; when we came towards them, and saw so many of them in our Shallop, we were afraid we were betraid. At this time it rained very sore; yet calling our wits together, we sent two of our men backe unto our Tent, the rest of us made toward them, and shot at them some three or foure Muskets: who when they saw us shoote, they stood in our Shallop, and held up their hands unto us, calling one to another. Then thought we with our selves, that we were better to dye in our defence in pursuing of them, then they us, being but eight Men and a great Dogge. When they saw us marching toward them so fiercely, our Dogge being formost, they ranne away: but we durst not pursue them any further, for it was in the night, and they were in sight above fiftie men. Thus we recovered our Shallop. Then we sent some more of our men to our Tent to keepe it; and the rest followed toward the place whither they fled. But before we could overtake them, they were gotten into their Boates, and were rowing away through the Ice; which was so thicke, that they could not passe away, but stucke fast; for their Boates were very great: wee seeing them sticke fast in the Ice, some setting with Oares, and some rowing, came so neere them, as we could, and shot at them some dozen shot, before they could get cleere: which shot caused them to cry out very sore one to another; for their Boates were full of men. As farre as we could judge, they be very little people, tawnie coloured, thin or no beards, and flat nosed, and Man-eaters.

On Sunday, the nine and twentieth, all day long we gat such things as we could aboord our Shippe, for feare they should come over with more men, and beset us, our Ship lying betweene two great Rocks, and all without so full of Ice, that we could not passe any way to Sea, no not with a Boate. That day, two of our men kept watch upon the Rocks, to give us warning, if they did come over with Boats. Then did our Carpenter make what shift hee could with our Shallop, and did tench her in some places, but neither calked her, nor pitched her. Then did wee take her, and bring her downe close to the Shippe, and there shee did stand all night.

On Munday, the thirtieth day in the morning we went to worke to cut the Ice with Axes and Pick-axes, to get our Shippe; for all about the Iland was nothing but Ice, and no place to ride free neither with Shippe nor Boate. That night it pleased God, that wee got her out, and came away rowing with our Oares; but she was exceeding leake, and our Shallop too: and, which was worse, we had never a Rudder to stirre our Ship withall. Wee rowed all that night among the Ice.

The first and second dayes of July, we continued also rowing up and downe among the floting and driving Ice, with little hope of recovering our Countrey.

The third of July, we had a gale of winde at

North, and a great current setting to the Southward: Then made we fast our Ship to an Iland of Ice, and went to worke, and to stow her things within boord, to make her stiffe; for wee had never a whit of balast in her. Then did our Carpenter make what shift he could, to hang our Rudder, having nothing convenient in our Ship to make Gudgins, nor Pintels. Then were we forced to breake open our Masters Chest, and to take all the Iron bands off it, to make fast two Pick-axes, for two Pintels, and to binde our Rudder withall. So, as it pleased God, that night we hanged our Rudder, having but two Pintels and a Cable through the middle of it, to keepe it to with two tacks. Then were we in good hope to get cleare of the Ice, because wee had some steerage, though it was but bad: for before, we durst beare but little sayle, our Ship being so leake, and her stemme so sore beaten with the rocks and Ice, and having no steerage, but were forced to rowe with our Oares, till wee were all sore and weary.

The next day about tenne of the clocke in the morning, the winde came to the West Northwest, and was faire weather: so we steered away East and by North, to get us out of the Bay: And at noone, the watch being out, which was the third watch that we had after we came out of the Countrey (for before, continually we did watch all, to keepe our Shippe cleare of the Ice, as neere as we could) we began to Pumpe our Shippe, but could not make her sucke in a thousand stroakes, if she had stood but one halfe houre unpumped. Then were wee forced to unromage our Ship, to see if we could finde our leakes. We soone found a great many of leakes, but not that which caused us to Pumpe so sore. At the last, we found it close abaft our forefoot, where her keele was splintred in two or three places, where the Sea came running in so fast, that it was not possible to keepe her free with both our Pumps, and wee could not come to it to stop it; for it was under the timbers. Then did wee take our maine Bonnet, and basted it with Occom, and put it overboord, right against our leake, which eased us some foure or five hundred strokes in an houre. Then upon consultation had among our selves, wee resolved to shape our course towards Newfound Land, to see if we could get any place to mend our Ship, hoping there to meete with some English or French men. At this time we had one of our men very sicke, and another had his hand very sore splitted; and most of us all were so sore with rowing and pumping, that we were scarce able to stirre, but that we must perforce.

The fift of Julie, wee shaped our course for New found Land, with the winde at West South-west.

The one and twentieth, the winde was at South South-west; and we fell with the Land, being nothing but broken Ilands. Then we stood to the Westward, being in the latitude of 49. degrees and an halfe.

The two and twentieth was faire weather, and the winde very variable: and about sixe of the clocke at night, the winde came to the West North-west. Then we steered in among the Ilands, to see if we could finde any harbour to mend our Shippe; for she was very leake. When we were come in among them, we found nothing but broken Ilands, and a great current, which did set from Iland to Iland, and had no ground at an hundred fathoms. That night we were very sore intangled with sunken Rocks, and in great danger of casting away our Ship, having very thicke weather: wherefore we kept to and fro all that night.

The foure and twentieth of July, in the morning, we spied some dozen Shallops, which were fishing some two leagues from us. Then wee made what way wee could toward them, &c. We remained in this Bay of Fogo, in repairing our Shippe, and refreshing of our selves untill the two and twentieth of August. Then taking our leaves of our kinde and loving friends, with giving them most heartie thankes for their goodnesse towards us, we put forth to the Sea, and with an indifferent and reasonable good passage we arrived safely in Dartmouth in Devonshire, and sent word to London unto our owners, of the losse of our Master and his three companions, and of the dolefull successe of our Voyage, the foure and twentieth day of September, 1606.

The rest of this Journall, from the death of Master John Knight, was written by Oliver Browne, one of the Company.

672. November 15, 1606. Examinations of the members of the crew of the *Hopewell.*

When the ship returned, minus its master and

three of his men, an inquiry was held in the High Court of Admiralty at the instance of the syndicate (describing itself as the Society of English Merchants for the Discovery of New Trades) that sent the vessel out. The interrogatories are not available, but the answers of the men make clear that the loss was an accident and not the result of mutiny or desertion. The main examination is that of Abraham Wynam, with those of Henry Scott, Oliver Brown, Henry West, William Lockier, Richard Collins, Ralph Hearne, and Thomas Homes, the remaining survivors, corroborating him.

P.R.O., HCA 13/38, November 15–17, 1606.

[a] Die sabbato XV Novembris 1606.

Abraham Wynan of St Katherins marriner aged XXIX^{te} yeres or thereabouts Sworne & examined before the righte worshipfull Sir Thomas Crampton Knight judge of his majesties Courte of the Admiraltie uppon certaine articles geven in the said Courte on the behalfe of the companie of englishe merchants tradeinge for the North west passage, Saith thereunto as followeth.

To the firste and second Articles he saith he did knowe John Knighte late master of the Hopewell in the late viadge to the North West parts for this examinate was boatswaine of the said shippe the same viadge.

To the thirde he saith That the conferance & resolution of the master & companie of the said shippe when she was on grounde at America was to forsake the shippe, because she was full of water which spoiled their victualls & out of all hope to recover the shippe, the rather for that the rudder was beaten from her, the keele and stern broken & everie hower in perill to sinke amongst the yce.

To the fourth he saith that the resolution of the master & companie was if this misfortune had not happened to the shippe to have discoverie as farre as they coulde, and then to have lade upp the shippe & wintered uppon some shore for that they had victualls sufficient in the shippe.

To the vth he saith that all the companie did agree & consent to suche directions & purposes as the master thoughte fitt to give & appointe, & never a man in the said shippe to his knowledge did disconsent from the same.

To the vith he saith there was not anie discontents differences or disagreements betwene the master or anie of his companie neyther did anie of his companie shewe themselves unwilling to followe the masters directions to his knowledge.

To the vii[th] he saith that the said master with fyve of his companie went from the shippe in theire boats to an other Iland from the place where the shippe laie aboute viii of the clocke in the morneinge on a Thursdaie beinge the xxvi[th] of June laste with intent to make a draughte of the lande, and saith that Edward Gorrye, Gabriell Knighte, Oliver Browne, Richard Collins & Richard Ambler went on shore with the master.

To the viii[th] he saith the boate staied a shore untill midnighte followeinge, and then Oliver Browne & Richard Collins came backe with the boate, & tould this examinate the rest of the companie that the master with the other three were gone upp to the toppe of a highe hill & willed them to staye untill theye came downe againe, sayeinge theye would be backe by two or thre a clocke in the afternoone, & the said Collins & Browne staieinge untill midnight & seeinge theye did not come backe did retorne to the shippe.

To the ix[th] he saith that the said Collins & Browne reported that they sawe the master & the other three with him wave theire Capps unto them when theye were almost at the topp of the hill & afterwards theye sawe them not as theye saide, & otherwise it is answered aforesaid.

To the xth it is answered before.

To the xi[th] he saith that viii of the companie with the boate the next daie & the thirde daie followeinge went out & endeavored to goe to the said Iland to seeke the said master but could not possibleye gett over by reason of the Ise, althoughe theye did use all meanes possible to doe the same.

To the xii[th] he saith that upon the xxix[th] of June laste in the nighte time 30 or 40 of the Salvagions sett upon this examinate & the rest of the marriners that were ashore haveinge forsaken the shippe & there shott manie arrowes at this examinate beinge then at the watche and the rest beinge a sleepe, And the saide Salvagions landed on the other side of the Islande & came over the Iland to them & carried awaie their pitchepott, & most of there Carpenters tooles, And this exam-inate & the rest of his companie sett uppon the Salvagions with the helpe of a greate dogge & drove them backe to the place where theye landed, And this examinate & the rest of his companie beinge but a fewe in number durst not followe the Salvagions anie farther for feare of treacherie, & left their tent should have byn betraied wherein all theire provision was, and saith that this examinate & companie persued them soe faste that theye made them leave a bowe, a dorke & some arrowes behinde them, & shott some twentie shott at them whilest they were in theire boate & within shott, whether theye killed anie of them or noe he knoweth not.

To the xiii[th] he saith there was noe merchandises in the said shippe but onlye one boxe & a little drifatt whiche theye carried forth in the said shippe & broughte backe againe in the same. What is in them he knoweth not, And denieth that this examinate or anie the companie made awaie anie thinge out of the said shippe belongeinge to the said merchants or master, but broughte all suche thinges as were saved and lefte unspent backe againe in the said shippe & restored the same againe to the said merchants, saveinge that this examinate & companie did bestawe some fewe peices of beefe, a case of boltes [or botles] & some other trifles uppon a Frenche Man to have his good will to have his boate to towe them into a harbor in Newefoundelande. And further this examinate saith that theye were forced to leave manie thinges in the Salvagions Countrie beinge forced away by the salvagions for feare least theye should have come downe in the nighte time & spoiled them.

[Signed:] Abraham Wynan

[b]   November 15. Depositions of Henry Scott (who says that after the wreck it was decided to build up the shallop and go in her for Newfoundland), Oliver, Browne, Henry West, and William Lockier.

November 17. Depositions of Richard Collins (who says that the master's purpose in going on land and to the top of the hill was to find the meridian of the sun so as to know their position), Ralph Hearne, Thomas Homes.

Chapter Eighty-three
The Discovery of Hudson Bay

673. April 17 to August 7, 1610. Henry Hudson's journal records the discovery of Hudson Strait.

The abstract of Hudson's journal, as it still exists, was probably truncated by the members of his crew after the winter stay at James Bay, but it records the voyage of the Discovery *from its departure. By this time it was fairly clear that if there was a passage, it was situated at or near 60° N. Hudson kept his ship moving between 58° 50' and 63° until he could make a clear run westward. This he was able to do at the beginning of August, sending his men ashore to make certain that he was going through a passage. By August 3, when the surviving version of the journal ends, they had cleared the strait and were in 61° 20' with "a Sea to the Westward."*

Printed in S. Purchas, Pilgrimes, *III (1625), 596–597 (XIV [1906], 374–377).*

An Abstract of the Journall of Master Henry Hudson, for the Discoverie of the Northwest Passage, begunne the seventeenth of Aprill, 1610. ended with his end, being treacherously exposed by some of the Companie.

The seventeenth of Aprill, 1610. we brake ground, and went downe from Saint Katharines Poole, and fell downe to Blacke-wall: and so plyed downe with the ships to Lee, which was the two and twentieth day.

The two and twentieth, I caused Master Coleburne to bee put into a Pinke, bound for London, with my Letter to the Adventurers, importing the reason wherefore I so put him out of the ship, and so plyed forth.

The second of May, the wind Southerly, at Eeven we were thwart of Flamborough Head.

The fift, we were at the Iles of Orkney, and here I set the North end of the Needle, and the North of the Flie all one.

The sixt, wee were in the latitude of 59. degrees 22. minutes, and there perceived that the North end of Scotland, Orkney, and Shotland are not so Northerly, as is commonly set downe. The eight day, wee saw Farre Ilands, in the latitude of 62. degrees 24. minutes. The eleventh day, we fell with the Easter part of Island, and then plying along the Souther part of the Land, we came to Westmony, being the fifteenth day, and still plyed about the mayne Iland, untill the last of May with contrary winds, and we got some Fowles of divers sorts.

The first day of June, we put to Sea out of an Harbour, in the Westermost part of Island, and so plyed to the Westward in the latitude of 66. degrees 34. minutes, and the second day plyed and found our selves in 65. degrees 57. minutes, with little wind Easterly.

The third day, wee found our selves in 65. degrees 30. minutes, with winde at North-east, a little before this we sayled neere some Ice.

The fourth day, we saw Groneland over the Ice perfectly, and this night the Sunne went downe due North, and rose North North-east. So plying the fift day, we were in 65. degrees, still encombred with much Ice, which hung upon the Coast of Groneland.

The ninth day, wee were off Frobishers Streights with the winde Northerly, and plyed unto the South-westwards untill the fifteenth day.

The fifteenth day, we were in sight of the land, in latitude 59. degrees 27. minutes, which was called by Captayne John Davis, Desolation, and found the errour of the former laying downe of that Land: and then running to the Northwestward untill the twentieth day, wee found the ship in 60. degrees 42. minutes, and saw much

Ice, and many Riplings or Over-fals, and a strong streame setting from East South-east, to West North-west.

The one and twentie, two and twentie, and three and twentie dayes, with the winde variable, we plyed to the North-westward in sight of much Ice, into the height of 62. degrees 29. minutes.

The foure and twentie, and five and twentie dayes, sayling to the West-ward about midnight, wee saw Land North, which was suddenly lost againe. So wee ranne still to the West-ward in 62. degrees 17. minutes.

The fift of July, wee plyed up upon the Souther side, troubled with much Ice in seeking the shoare untill the fift day of July, and we observed that day in 59. degrees 16. minutes. Then we plyed off the shoare againe, untill the eight day, and then found the height of the Pole in 60. degrees no minutes. Here we saw the Land from the North-west by West, halfe Northerly unto the South-west by West, covered with snow, a Champaigne Land, and called it, Desire provoketh.

We still plyed up to the Westward, as the Land and Ice would suffer untill the eleventh day; when fearing a storme, we anchored by three Rockie Ilands in uncertayne depth, betweene two and nine fathomes; and found it an Harbour unsufficient by reason of sunken Rockes, one of which was next morning two fathomes above water. Wee called them the Iles of Gods Mercies. The water floweth here better then foure fathomes. The Floud commeth from the North, flowing eight the change day. The latitude in this place is 62. degrees 9. minutes. Then plying to the South-westward the sixteenth day, wee were in the latitude of 58. degrees 50. minutes, but found our selves imbayed with Land, and had much Ice: and we plyed to the North-westward untill the nineteenth day, and then wee found by observation the height of the Pole in 61. degrees 24. minutes, and saw the Land, which I named, Hold with Hope. Hence I plyed to the North-westward still, untill the one and twentieth day, with the wind variable. Heere I found the Sea more growne, then any wee had since wee left England.

The three and twentieth day, by observation the height of the Pole was 61. degrees 33. minutes. The five and twentieth day, we saw the Land; and named it Magna Britannia. The sixe and twentieth day, wee observed and found the latitude in 62. degrees 44. minutes. The eight and twentieth day, we were in the height of 63. degrees 10. minutes, and plyed Southerly of the West. The one and thirtieth day, plying to the Westward, at noone wee found our selves in 62. degrees 24. minutes.

The first of August, we had sight of the Northerne shoare, from the North by East to the West by South off us: the North part twelve leagues, and the Wester part twentie leagues from us: and we had no ground there at one hundred and eightie fathomes. And I thinke I saw Land on the Sunne side, but could not make it perfectly, bearing East North-east. Here I found the latitude 62. degrees 50. minutes.

The second day, we had sight of a faire Headland, on the Norther shoare six leagues off, which I called Salisburies Fore-land: we ranne from them West South-west, fourteene leagues: In the mid-way of which wee were suddenly come into a great and whurling Sea, whether caused by meeting of two streames, or an Over-fall, I know not. Thence sayling West and by South seven leagues farther, we were in the mouth of a Streight and sounded, and had no ground at one hundred fathomes: the Streight being there not above two leagues broad, in the passage in this Wester part: which from the Easter part of Fretum Davis, is distant two hundred and fiftie leagues there abouts.

The third day, we put through the narrow passage, after our men had beene on Land, which had well observed there, That the Floud did come from the North, flowing by the shoare five fathomes. The head of this entrance on the South side I named Cape Worsenholme; and the head on the North-wester shoare, I called Cape Digs. After wee had sailed with an Easterly winde, West and by South ten leagues, the Land fell away to the Southward, and the other Iles and Land left us to the Westward. Then I observed and found the ship at noone in 61. degrees 20. minutes, and a Sea to the Westward.

674. April 17, 1610 to [   ] 1611. The discourse of Abacuk Pricket on Henry Hudson's last voyage.

Abacuk Pricket (Habacuk Pricket), a represent-

ative of the company and not a sailor, was the most vocal of the survivors who at last reached England. His journal covers the early part of the voyage (stressing, as Hudson's journal does not, the many icebergs that obstructed his passage), until at last he had "a cleere Sea." By November 10 they were frozen in at the foot of James Bay. He blamed the abandoning of Hudson, his son, the carpenter, and the sick men in the shallop on Henry Green and William Wilson, the bosun, who were conveniently killed by Eskimo after the Discovery emerged from Hudson Strait. The miserable voyage homeward of the remaining handful is told in detail. Pricket's narrative shows him to have been at the least a timid trimmer, at worst a clever associate of the mutineers. Purchas added a skeptical note (not printed) about Pricket but said he presented the evidence as he found it.

S. Purchas, Pilgrimes, III (1625), 597–609 (XIII [1906], 377–410).

A larger Discourse of the same Voyage, and the successe thereof, written by Abacuk Pricket.

We began our Voyage for the North-west passage; the seventeenth of April, 1610. Thwart of Shepey, our Master sent Master Colbert backe to the Owners with his Letter. The next day we weighted from hence, and stood for Harwich, and came thither the eight and twentieth of Aprill. From Harwich we set sayle the first of May, along the Coast to the North, till we came to the Iles of Orkney, from thence to the Iles of Faro, and from thence to Island: on which we fell in a fogge, hearing the Rut of the Sea, ashoare, but saw not the Land whereupon our Master came to an Anchor. Heere we were embayed in the South-east part of the Land. Wee weighed and stood along the Coast, on the West side towards the North: but one day being calme, we fell a fishing, and caught good store of fish, as Cod and Ling, and Butte, with some other sorts that we knew not. The next day, we had a good gale of wind at South-west, and raysed the Iles of Westmonie, where the King of Denmarke hath a Fortresse, by which we passed to rayse the Snow Hill foot, a Mountayne so called on the North-west part of the Land. But in our course we saw that famous

Hill, Mount Hecla, which cast out much fire, a signe of foule weather to come in short time. Wee leave Island a sterne of us, and met a Mayne of Ice, which did hang on the North part of Island, and stretched downe to the West, which when our Master saw, he stood backe for Island to find an Harbour, which we did on the North-west part, called Derefer, where wee killed good store of Fowle. From hence wee put to Sea againe, but (neither wind nor weather serving) our Master stood backe for this Harbour againe, but could not reach it, but fell with another to the South of that, called by our Englishmen, Lousie Bay: where on the shoare we found an hot Bath, and heere all our Englishmen bathed themselves: the water was so hot that it would scald a Fowle.

From hence the first of June we put to Sea for Groneland, but to the West wee saw Land as we thought, for which we beare the best part of a day, but it proved but a foggie banke. So wee gave it over, and made for Gronland, which we raysed the fourth of June. Upon the Coast thereof hung good store of Ice, so that our Master could not attayne to the shoare by any meanes. The Land in this part is very Mountaynous, and full of round Hils, like to Sugar-loaves, covered with snow. We turned the Land on the South side, as neere as the Ice would suffer us. Our course for the most part was betweene the West and North-west, till we raysed the Desolations, which is a great Iland in the West part of Groneland. On this Coast we saw store of Whales, and at one time three of them came close by us, so as wee could hardly shunne them: then two passing very neere, and the third going under our ship, wee received no harme by them, praysed bee God.

From the Desolations our Master made his way North-west, the wind being against him, who else would have gone more to the North: but in this course we saw the first great Iland or Mountayne of Ice, whereof after we saw store. About the latter end of June, we raysed Land to the North of us, which our Master tooke to bee that Iland which Master Davis setteth downe in his Chart. On the West side of his Streight, our Master would have gone to the North of it, but the wind would not suffer him: so we fell to the South of it, into a great Rippling or over-fall of current, the which setteth to the West. Into the current we went, and made our way to the North of the West, till we met with Ice which hung on this Iland.

Wherefore our Master casting about, cleered himselfe of this Ice, and stood to the South, and then to the West, through store of floting Ice, and upon the Ice store of Seales. We gained a cleere Sea, and continued our course till wee meete Ice; first, with great Ilands, and then with store of the smaller sort. Betweene them we made our course North-west, till we met with Ice againe. But, in this our going betweene the Ice, we saw one of the great Ilands of Ice overturne, which was a good warning to us, not to come nigh them, nor within their reach. Into the Ice wee put ahead, as betweene two Lands. The next day we had a storme, and the wind brought the Ice so fast upon us, that in the end we were driven to put her into the chiefest of the Ice, and there to let her lie. Some of our men this day fell sicke, I will not say it was for feare, although I saw small signe of other griefe.

The storme ceasing, we stood out of the Ice, where wee saw any cleere Sea to goe to: which was sometime more, and sometime lesse. Our course was as the Ice did lye, sometime to the North, then to the North-west, and then to the West, and to the South-west: but still inclosed with Ice. Which when our Master saw, he made his course to the South, thinking to cleere himselfe of the Ice that way: but the more he strove, the worse he was, and the more inclosed, till we could goe no further. Here our Master was in despaire, and (as he told me after) he thought he should never have got out of this Ice, but there have perished. Therefore hee brought forth his Card, and shewed all the company, that hee was entred above an hundred leagues further then ever any English was: and left it to their choice, whether they would proceed any further; yea, or nay. Whereupon, some were of one minde, and some of another, some wishing themselves at home, and some not caring where, so they were out of the Ice: but there were some who then spake words, which were remembred a great while after.

There was one who told the Master, that if he had an hundred pounds, hee would give fourescore and ten to be at home: but the Carpenter made answere, that if hee had an hundred, hee would not give ten upon any such condition, but would thinke it to be as good money as ever he had any, and to bring it as well home, by the leave of God. After many words to no purpose, to worke

we must on all hands, to get our selves out, and to cleere our ship. After much labour and time spent, we gained roome to turne our ship in, and so by little and little, to get cleere in the Sea a league or two off, our course being North and North-west.

In the end, we raysed Land to the South-west, high Land and covered with Snow. Our Master named this Land, Desire provokes. Lying here, wee heard the noyse of a great over-fall of a tyde, that came out of the Land: for now we might see well, that wee had beene embayed before, and time had made us know, being so well acquainted with the Ice, that when night, or foggie, or foule weather tooke us, we would seeke out the broadest Iland of Ice, and there come to anchor and runne, and sport, and fill water that stood on the Ice in Ponds, both sweete and good. But after we had brought this Land to beare South of us, we had the tyde and the current to open the Ice, as being carried first one way, and then another: but in Bayes they lye as in a pond without moving. In this Bay where wee were thus troubled with Ice, wee saw many of those Mountaynes of Ice a-ground, in sixe or sevenscore fathome water. In this our course we saw a Beare upon a piece of Ice by it selfe, to the which our men gave chase with their Boat: but before they came nigh her, the tyde had carried the Ice and the Beare on it, and joyned it with the other Ice: so they lost their labour, and came aboord againe.

We continued our course to the North-west, and raysed Land to the North of our course, toward which we made, and comming nigh it, there hung on the Eastermost point, many Ilands of floting Ice, and a Beare on one of them, which from one to another came towards us, till she was readie to come aboord. But when she saw us looke at her, she cast her head betweene her hinder legges, and then dived under the Ice: and so from one piece to another, till she was out of our reach. We stood along by the Land on the Southside ahead of us, wee met with Ice that hung on a point of Land that lay to the South, more then this that we came up by: which when our Master saw, he stood in for the shoare. At the West end of this Iland (for so it is) we found an Harbour, and came in (at a full Sea) over a Rocke, which had two fathome and an halfe on it, and was so much bare at a low water. But by the great mercie of God, we came to an Anchor cleere of it: and close by it, our

Master named them, the Iles of Gods Mercie. This is an Harbour for need, but there must be care had how they come in. Heere our Master sent me, and others with me, to discover to the North and North-west: and in going from one place to another, we sprung a Covey of Partridges which were young: at the which Thomas Woodhouse shot, but killed only the old one. This Iland is a most barren place, having nothing on it but plashes of water and riven Rockes, as if it were subject to Earthquakes. To the North there is a great Bay, or Sea (for I know not what it will prove) where I saw a great Iland of Ice aground, betweene the two Lands, which with the Spring-tide was set afloat, and carried into this Bay or Sea to the North-westward, but came not backe againe, nor within sight. Here wee tooke in some Drift wood that we found ashoare.

From hence we stood to the South-west, to double the Land to the West of us, through much floting Ice: In the end wee found a cleere Sea, and continued therein, till wee raysed Land to the North-west. Then our Master made his course more to the South then before: but it was not long ere we met with Ice which lay ahead of us. Our Master would have doubled this Ice to the North, but could not; and in the end put into it downe to the South-west through much Ice, and then to the South, where we were embayed againe. Our Master strove to get the shoare, but could not, for the great store of Ice that was on the coast. From out of this Bay, we stood to the North, and were soone out of the Ice: then downe to the South-west, and so to the West, where we were enclosed (to our sight) with Land and Ice. For wee had Land from the South to the North-west on one side, and from the East to the West on the other side: but the Land that was to the North of us, and lay by East and West, was but an Iland. On we went till we could goe no further for Ice: so we made our ship fast to the Ice which the tide brought upon us, but when the ebbe came, the Ice did open, and made way; so as in seven or eight houres we were cleere from the Ice, till we came to weather; but onely some of the great Ilands, that were carried along with us to the North-west.

Having a cleere Sea, our Master stood to the West along by the South shoare, and raysed three Capes or Head-lands, lying one above another. The middlemost is an Iland, and maketh a Bay or Harbour, which (I take) will prove a good one. Our Master named them Prince Henries Cape, or Fore-land. When we had layd this we raised another, which was the extreme point of the Land, looking towards the North: upon it are two Hills, but one (above the rest) like an Hay-cocke; which our Master named, King James his Cape. To the North of this, lie certaine Ilands, which our Master named, Queene Annes Cape, or Fore-land. Wee followed the North shoare still. Beyond the Kings Cape there is a Sound or Bay, that hath some Ilands in it: and this is not to be forgotten, if need be. Beyond this, lieth some broken Land, close to the Mayne, but what it is I know not: because we passed by it in the night.

Wee stood to the North to double this Land, and after to the West againe, till wee fell with Land that stretched from the Mayne, like a shewer from the South to the North, and from the North to the West, and then downe to the South againe. Being short of this Land, a storme tooke us, the wind at West, we stood to the North, and raised Land: which when our Master saw, he stood to the South againe; for he was loath at any time that wee should see the North shoare. The storme continuing, and comming to the South shoare againe, our Master found himselfe shot to the West, a great way, which made him muse, considering his Leeward way. To the South-west of this Land, on the Mayne, there is an high Hill, which our Master named Mount Charles. To the North and beyond this, lieth an Iland, that to the East hath a faire head, and beyond it to the West other broken Land, which maketh a Bay within, and a good Road may be found there for ships. Our Master named the first, Cape Salsburie.

When we had left this to the North-east, we fell into a Rippling or Over-fall of a Current, which (at the first) we tooke to bee a Shoald: but the Lead being cast, wee had no ground. On we passed still in sight of the South shoare, till we raised Land lying from the Mayne some two leagues. Our Master tooke this to bee a part of the Mayne of the North Land; but it is an Iland, the North side stretching out to the West more then the South. This Iland hath a faire Head to the East, and very high Land, which our Master named Deepes Cape: and the Land on the South side, now falling away to the South, makes another Cape or Head-land, which our Master named, Worsenhams Cape. When wee were nigh the North or Iland

Cape, our Master sent the Boat ashoare, with my selfe (who had the charge) and the Carpenter, and divers others, to discover to the West and North-west, and to the South-west: but we had further to it then we thought; for the Land is very high, and we were overtaken with a storme of Raine, Thunder and Lightning. But to it we came on the North-east side, and up we got from one Rocke to another, till we came to the highest of that part. Here we found some plaine ground, and saw some Deere; as first, foure or five, and after, a dozen or sixteene in an Herd, but could not come nigh them with a Musket shot.

Thus, going from one place to another, wee saw to the West of us an high Hill above all the rest, it being nigh us: but it proved further off then we made account; for, when wee came to it, the Land was so steepe on the East and North-east parts, that wee could not get unto it. To the South-west we saw that wee might, and towards that part wee went along by the side of a great Pond of water, which lieth under the East side of this Hill: and there runneth out of it a streame of water, as much as would drive an over-shot Mill: which falleth downe from an high Cliffe into the Sea on the South side. In this place great store of Fowle breed, and there is the best Grasse that I had seene since we came from England. Here wee found Sorell, and that which wee call Scurvy-grasse, in great abundance. Passing along wee saw some round Hills of stone, like to Grasse cockes, which at the first I tooke to be the worke of some Christian. Wee passed by them, till we came to the South side of the Hill; we went unto them, and there found more; and being nigh them, I turned off the uppermost stone, and found them hollow within, and full of Fowles hanged by their neckes. Then [Henry] Greene, and I, went to fetch the Boat to the South side, while Robert Billet and hee got downe a Valley to the Sea side, where wee tooke them in.

Our Master (in this time) came in betweene the two Lands, and shot off some Peeces to call us aboord; for it was a fogge. Wee came aboord, and told him what we had seene, and perswaded him to stay a day or two in this place, telling him what refreshing might there bee had: but by no meanes would he stay, who was not pleased with the motion. So we left the Fowle, and lost our way downe to the South-west, before they went in sight of the Land, which now beares to the East

from us, being the same mayne Land that wee had all this while followed. Now, we had lost the sight of it, because it falleth away to the East, after some five and twenty or thirty leagues. Now we came to the shallow water, wherewith wee were not acquainted since we came from Island; now we came into broken ground and Rockes, through which we passed downe to the South. In this our course we had a storme, and the water did shoald apace. Our Master came to an anchor in fifteene fathoms water.

Wee weighed and stood to the South-east, because the Land in this place did lie so. When we came to the point of the West Land (for we now had Land on both sides of us) we came to an anchor. Our Master sent the Boat ashoare, to see what that Land was, and whether there were any way through. They soone returned, and shewed that beyond the point of Land to the South, there was a large Sea. This Land on the West side, was a very narrow Point. Wee weighed from hence, and stood in for this Sea betweene the two Lands, which (in this place) is not two leagues broad downe to the South, for a great way in sight of the East shoare. In the end we lost sight thereof, and saw it not till we came to the bottome of the Bay, into sixe or seven fathomes water. Hence we stood up to the North by the West shoare, till wee came to an Iland in 53. where we tooke in water and ballast.

From hence wee passed towards the North: but some two or three dayes after (reasoning concerning our comming into this Bay, and going out) our Master tooke occasion to revive old matters, and to displace Robert Juet from being his Mate, and the Boat-swaine from his place, for words spoken in the first great Bay of Ice. Then hee made Robert Billet his Mate, and William Wilson our Boat-swaine. Up to the North wee stood, till we raised Land, then downe to the South, and up to the North, then downe againe to the South: and on Michaelmasse day came in, and went out of certaine Lands: which our Master sets downe by the name of Michaelmasse Bay, because we came in and went out on that day. From hence wee stood to the North, and came into shoald water; and the weather being thicke and foule, wee came to an anchor in seven or eight fathome water, and there lay eight dayes: in all which time wee could not get one houre to weigh our anchor. But the eight day, the wind beginning to cease, our Master would have the anchor up, against the mind of all who knew what belonged thereunto. Well, to it we went, and when we had brought it to a peake, a Sea tooke her, and cast us all off from the Capstone, and hurt divers of us. Here wee lost our Anchor, and if the Carpenter had not beene, we had lost our Cable too: but he (fearing such a matter) was ready with his Axe, and so cut it.

From hence we stood to the South, and to the South-west, through a cleere Sea of divers sounding, and came to a Sea of two colours, one blacke, and the other white, sixteene or seventeene fathome water, betweene which we went foure or five leagues. But the night comming, we tooke in our Top-sayles, and stood afore the wind with our Maine-sayle and Fore-sayl, and came into five or six fathomes, and saw no Land for it was darke. Then we stood to the East, and had deepe water againe, then to the South and Southwest, and so came to our Westermost Bay of all, and came to an anchor neerest to the North shoare. Out went our Boat to the Land that was next us, when they came neere it, our Boat could not flote to the shoare it was so shallow: yet ashoare they got. Here our men saw the footing of a man and a Ducke in the snowy Rockes, and Wood good store, whereof they tooke some and returned aboord. Being at anchor in this place, we saw a ledge of Rockes to the South of us, some league of length; It lay North and South, covered at a full Sea; for a strong tide setteth in here. At mid-night wee weighed, and stood to goe out as we came in; and had not gone long, but the Carpenter came and told the Master, that if he kept that course he would be upon the Rockes: the Master conceived that he was past them, when presently wee ranne on them, and there stucke fast twelve houres: but (by the mercy of God) we got off unhurt, though not unscarred.

Wee stood up to the East and raysed three Hills, lying North and South: wee went to the furthermost, and left it to the North of us, and so into a Bay, where wee came to an anchor. Here our Master sent out our Boat, with my selfe and the Carpenter to seeke a place to winter in: and it was time; for the nights were long and cold, and the earth covered with Snow. Having spent three moneths in a Labyrinth without end, being now the last of October, we went downe to the East, to the bottome of the Bay: but returned without speeding of that we went for. The next day we went to the South, and the South-west, and found a place, whereunto we brought our ship, and haled her aground: and this was the first of November. By the tenth thereof we were frozen in: but now we were in, it behooved us to have care of what we had; for, that we were sure of; but what we had not, was uncertaine.

Wee were victualled for six moneths in good proportion, and of that which was good: if our Master would have had more, he might have had it at home and in other places. Here we were now, and therefore it behoved us so to spend, that wee might have (when time came) to bring us to the Capes where the Fowle bred, for that was all the hope wee had to bring us home. Wherefore our Master tooke order, first for the spending of that wee had, and then to increase it, by propounding a reward to them that killed either Beast, Fish, or Fowle, as in his Journall you have seene. About the middle of this moneth of November, dyed John Williams our Gunner: God pardon the Masters uncharitable dealing with this man. Now for that I am come to speake of him, out of whose ashes (as it were) that unhappy deed grew which brought a scandall upon all that are returned home, and upon the action it selfe, the multitude (like the dog) running after the stone, but not at the caster: therefore, not to wrong the living, nor slander the dead, I will (by the leave of God) deliver the truth as neere as I can.

You shall understand, that our Master kept (in his house at London) a young man, named Henrie Greene, borne in Kent, of Worshipfull Parents, but by his leud life and conversation hee had lost the good will of all his frinds, and had spent all that hee had. This man, our Master would have to Sea with him, because hee could write well: our Master gave him meate, and drinke, and lodging, and by meanes of one Master Venson, with much adoe got foure pounds of his mother to buy him clothes, wherewith Master Venson would not trust him: but saw it laid out himselfe. This Henrie Greene was not set downe in the owners booke, nor any wages made for him. Hee came first aboord at Gravesend, and at Harwich should have gone into the field, with one Wilkinson. At Island the Surgeon and hee fell out in Dutch, and hee beat him a shoare in English, which set all the company in a rage; so that wee had much adoe to get the Surgeon aboord. I told the Master of it, but hee bade mee let it alone, for (said hee) the

Surgeon had a tongue that would wrong the best friend hee had. But Robert Juet (the Masters Mate) would needs burne his finger in the embers, and told the Carpenter a long tale (when hee was drunke) that our Master had brought in Greene to cracke his credit that should displease him: which words came to the Masters eares, who when hee understood it, would have gone backe to Island, when he was fortie leagues from thence, to have sent home his Mate Robert Juet in a Fisher-man. But, being otherwise perswaded, all was well. So Henry Greene stood upright, and very inward with the Master, and was a serviceable man every way for manhood: but for Religion he would say, he was cleane paper whereon he might write what hee would. Now, when our Gunner was dead, and (as the order is in such cases) if the company stand in need of any thing that belonged to the man deceased, then is it brought to the Mayne Mast, and there sold to them that will give most for the same: This Gunner had a gray cloth gowne, which Greene prayed the Master to friend him so much as to let him have it, paying for it as another would give: the Master saith hee should, and thereupon hee answered some, that sought to have it, that Greene should have it, and none else, and so it rested.

Now out of season and time, the Master calleth the Carpenter to goe in hand with an house on shoare, which at the beginning our Master would not heare, when it might have beene done. The Carpenter told him, that the Snow and Frost were such, as hee neither could, nor would goe in hand with such worke. Which when our Master heard, hee ferreted him out of his Cabbin to strike him, calling him by many foule names, and threatning to hang him. The Carpenter told him that hee knew what belonged to his place better then himselfe, and that hee was no House Carpenter. So this passed, and the house was (after) made with much labour, but to no end. The next day after the Master and the Carpenter fell out, the Carpenter tooke his Peece and Henry Greene with him, for it was an order that none should goe out alone, but one with a Peece, and another with a Pike. This did move the Master so much the more against Henry Greene, that Robert Billet his Mate must have the gowne, and had it delivered unto him; which when Henry Greene saw, he challenged the Masters promise: but the Master did so raile on Greene, with so many words of

disgrace, telling him, that all his friends would not trust him with twenty shillings, and therefore why should he? As for wages he had none, nor none should have, if he did not please him well. Yet the Master had promised him to make his wages as good, as any mans in the ship; and to have him one of the Princes guard when we came home. But you shall see how the devil out of this so wrought with Green, that he did the Master what mischiefe hee could in seeking to discredit him, and to thrust him and many other honest men out of the Ship in the end. To speake of all our trouble in this time of Winter (which was so cold, as it lamed the most of our Company, and my selfe doe yet feele it) would bee too tedious.

But I must not forget to shew, how mercifully God dealt with us in this time; for the space of three moneths wee had such store of Fowle of one kinde (which were Partridges as white as milke) that wee killed above an hundred dozen, besides others of sundry sorts: for all was fish that came to the net. The Spring comming, this Fowle left us, yet they were with us all the extreame cold. Then in their places came divers sort of other Fowle, as Swanne, Geese, Duck, and Teale, but hard to come by. Our Master hoped they would have bred in those broken grounds, but they doe not: but came from the South, and flew to the North, further then we were this Voyage; yet if they be taken short with the wind at North, or Northwest, or North-east, then they fall and stay till the winde serve them, and then flye to the North. Now in time these Fowles are gone, and few or none to bee seene. Then wee went into the Woods, Hilles, and Valleyes, for all things that had any shew of substance in them, how vile soever: the mosse of the ground, then the which I take the powder of a post to bee much better, and the Frogge (in his ingendring time as loathsome as a Toade) was not spared. But amongst the divers sorts of buds, it pleased God that Thomas Woodhouse brought home a budde of a Tree, full of a Turpentine substance. Of this our Surgeon made a decoction to drinke, and applyed the buddes hot to them that were troubled with ach in any part of their bodies; and for my part, I confesse, I received great and present ease of my paine.

About this time, when the Ice began to breake out of the Bayes, there came a Savage to our Ship, as it were to see and to bee seene, being the first that we had seene in all this time: whom our Master intreated well, and made much of him, promising unto himselfe great matters by his meanes, and therefore would have all the Knives and Hatchets (which any man had) to his private use, but received none but from John King the Carpenter, and my selfe. To this Savage our Master gave a Knife, a Looking-glasse, and Buttons, who received them thankefully, and made signes that after hee had slept hee would come againe, which hee did. When hee came, hee brought with him a Sled, which hee drew after him, and upon it two Deeres skinnes, and two Beaver skinnes. Hee had a scrip under his arme, out of which hee drew those things which the Master had given him. Hee tooke the Knife and laid it upon one of the Beaver skinnes, and his Glasses and Buttons upon the other, and so gave them to the Master, who received them; and the Savage tooke those things which the Master had given him, and put them up into his scrip againe. Then the Master shewed him an Hatchet, for which hee would have given the Master one of his Deere skinnes, but our Master would have them both, and so hee had, although not willingly. After many signes of people to the North, and to the South, and that after so many sleepes he would come againe, he went his way, but never came more.

Now the Ice being out of the Sounds, so that our Boat might go from one place unto another, a company of men were appointed by the Master to go a fishing with our net; their names were as followeth: William Wilson, Henry Greene, Michael Perce, John Thomas, Andrew Moter, Bennet Matthewes, and Arnold Lodlo. These men, the first day they went, caught five hundred fish, as big as good Herrings, and some Troutes: which put us all in some hope to have our wants supplied, and our Commons amended: but these were the most that ever they got in one day, for many dayes they got not a quarter so many. In this time of their fishing, Henry Green and William Wilson, with some others, plotted to take the net and the shallop, which the Carpenter had now set up, and so to shift for themselves. But the shallop being readie, our Master would goe in it himselfe, to the South and South-west, to see if hee could meete with the people; for, to that end was it set up, and (that way) wee might see the Woods set on fire by them. So the Master tooke

the Sayve and the Shallop, and so much victuall as would serve for eight or nine dayes, and to the South hee went. They that remained aboord, were to take in water, wood, and ballast, and to have all things in a readinesse against hee came backe. But hee set no time of his returne; for he was perswaded, if he could meet with the people, hee should have flesh of them, and that good store: but hee returned worse then hee went forth. For, hee could by no meanes meete with the people, although they were neere them, yet they would set the woods on fire in his sight.

Being returned, hee fitted all things for his returne, and first, delivered all the bread out of the bread roome (which came to a pound a piece for every mans share) and delivered also a Bill of Returne, willing them to have that to shew, if it pleased God, that they came home: and he wept when hee gave it unto them. But to helpe us in this poore estate with some reliefe, the Boate and Sayve went to worke on Friday morning, and stayed till Sunday noone: at which time they came aboord, and brought fourescore small Fish, a poore reliefe for so many hungry bellies. Then we wayed, and stood out of our wintering place, and came to an Anchor without, in the mouth of the Bay: from whence we wayed and came to an anchor without in the Sea, where our bread being gone, that store of cheese we had was to stop a gap, whereof there were five, whereat the company grudged, because they made account of nine. But those that were left, were equally divided by the Master, although he had counsell to the contrarie: for there were some who having it, would make hast to bee rid thereof, because they could not governe it. I knew when Henrie Greene gave halfe his bread, which hee had for fourteene dayes, to one to keepe, and prayed him not to let him have any untill the next Munday: but before Wednesday at night, hee never left till hee had it againe, having eaten up his first weekes bread before. So Wilson the Boatswaine hath eaten (in one day) his fortnights bread, and hath beene two or three dayes sicke for his labour. The cause that moved the Master to deliver all the Cheese, was because they were not all of one goodnesse, and therefore they should see that they had no wrong done them: but every man should have alike the best and the worst together, which was three pounds and a halfe for seven dayes.

The wind serving, we weighed and stood to the

North-west, and on Munday at night (the eighteenth day of June) wee fell into the Ice, and the next day the wind being at West, we lay there till Sunday in sight of Land. Now being here, the Master told Nicholas Simmes, that there would be a breaking up of chests, and a search for bread, and willed him (if hee had any) to bring it to him, which hee did, and delivered to the Master thirty cakes in a bagge. This deed of the Master (if it bee true) hath made mee marvell, what should bee the reason that hee did not stop the breach in the beginning, but let it grow to that height, as that it overthrew himselfe and many other honest men: but there are many devices in the heart of man, yet the counsell of the Lord shall stand.

Being thus in the Ice on Saturday, the one and twentieth of June at night, Wilson the Boatswayne, and Henry Greene came to mee lying (in my Cabbin) lame, and told mee that they and the rest of their Associates, would shift the Company, and turne the Master, and all the sicke men into the shallop, & let them shift for themselves. For, there was not fourteen daies victual left for all the Company, at that poore allowance they were at, and that there they lay, the Master not caring to goe one way or other: and that they had not eaten any thing these three dayes, and therefore were resolute, either to mend or end, and what they had begun they would goe through with it, or dye. When I heard this, I told them I marvelled to heare so much from them, considering that they were married men, and had wives and children, and that for their sakes they should not commit so foule a thing in the sight of God and man, as that would bee; for why should they banish themselves from their native Countrie? Henry Greene bad me hold my peace, for he knew the worst, which was, to be hanged when hee came home, and therefore of the two he would rather be hanged at home then starved abroad: and for the good will they bare me, they would have mee stay in the Ship. I gave them thankes, and told them that I came into her, not to forsake her, yet not to hurt my selfe and others by any such deed. Henry Greene told me then, that I must take my fortune in the Shallop. If there bee no remedie (said I) the will of God bee done.

Away went Henry Greene in a rage, swearing to cut his throat that went about to disturbe them, and left Wilson by me, with whom I had some talke, but to no good: for he was so perswaded,

that there was no remedie now, but to goe on while it was hot, least their partie should faile them, and the mischiefe they had intended to others, should light on themselves. Henry Greene came againe, and demanded of him what I said. Wilson answered, He is in his old song, still patient. Then I spake to Henry Greene to stay three dayes, in which time I would so deale with the Master, that all should be well. So I dealt with him to forbeare but two dayes, nay twelve houres; there is no way then (say they) but out of hand. Then I told them, that if they would stay till Munday, I would joyne with them to share all the victuals in the ship, and would justifie it when I came home; but this would not serve their turnes. Wherefore I told them, it was some worse matter they had in hand then they made shew of, and that it was bloud and revenge hee sought, or else he would not at such a time of night undertake such a deed. Henry Greene (with that) taketh my Bible which lay before me, and sware that hee would doe no man harme, and what hee did was for the good of the voyage, and for nothing else; and that all the rest should do the like. The like did Wilson sweare.

Henry Greene went his way, and presently came Juet, who because hee was an ancient man, I hoped to have found some reason in him; but hee was worse then Henry Greene, for hee sware plainely that he would justifie this deed when he came home. After him came John Thomas, and Michel Perce, as birds of one feather: but because they are not living I will let them goe, as then I did. Then came Moter and Bennet, of whom I demanded, if they were well advised what they had taken in hand. They answered, they were, and therefore came to take their oath.

Now, because I am much condemned for this oath, as one of them that plotted with them, and that by an oath I should bind them together to performe what they had begun, I thought good heere to set downe to the view of all, how well their oath and deedes agreed: and thus it was. You shall sweare truth to God, your Prince and Countrie: you shall doe nothing, but to the glory of God, and the good of the action in hand, and harme to no man. This was the oath, without adding or diminishing. I looked for more of these companions (although these were too many) but there came no more. It was darke, and they in a readinesse to put this deed of darknesse in execution. I called to Henry Greene and Wilson, and prayed them not to goe in hand with it in the darke, but to stay till the morning. Now, everie man (I hope) would goe to his rest, but wickednesse sleepeth not; for Henry Greene keepeth the Master company all night (and gave mee bread, which his Cabbin-mate gave him) and others are as watchfull as he. Then I asked Henrie Greene, whom he would put out with the Master? he said, the Carpenter John King, and the sicke men. I said, they should not doe well to part with the Carpenter, what need soever they should have. Why the Carpenter was in no more regard amongst them, was; first, for that he and John King were condemned for wrong done in the victuall. But the chiefest cause was, for that the Master loved him, and made him his Mate, upon his returne out of our wintering place, thereby displacing Robert Billet, whereat they did grudge, because hee could neither write nor read. And therefore (said they) the Master and his ignorant Mate would carry the Ship whither the Master pleased: the Master forbidding any man to keepe account or reckoning, having taken from all men whatsoever served for that purpose. Well, I obtained of Henrie Greene and Wilson, that the Carpenter should stay, by whose meanes I hoped (after they had satisfied themselves) that the Master, and the poore man might be taken into the Ship againe. Or, I hoped, that some one or other would give some notice, either to the Carpenter John King, or the Master; for so it might have come to passe by some of them that were the most forward.

Now, it shall not bee amisse to shew how we were lodged, and to begin in the Cooke roome; there lay Bennet and the Cooper lame; without the Cooke roome, on the steere-board side, lay Thomas Wydhouse sicke; next to him lay Sydrack Funer lame, then the Surgeon, and John Hudson with him; next to them lay Wilson the Boatswaine, and then Arnold Lodlo next to him: in the Gun-roome lay Robert Juet and John Thomas; on the Lar-boord side, lay Michael Bute and Adria Moore, who had never beene well since wee lost our Anchor; next to them lay Michael Perce and Andrew Moter. Next to them without the Gun-roome, lay John King, and with him Robert Billet: next to them my selfe, and next to me Francis Clements: In the mid-ship, betweene the Capstone and the Pumpes, lay Henrie Greene

and Nicholas Simmes. This night John King was late up, and they thought he had been with the Master, but he was with the Carpenter, who lay on the Poope, and comming downe from him, was met by his Cabbin-mate, as it were by chance, and so they came to their Cabbin together. It was not long ere it was day: then came Bennet for water for the Kettle, hee rose and went into the Hold: when hee was in, they shut the Hatch on him (but who kept it downe I know not) up upon the Deck went Bennet.

In the meane time Henrie Greene, and another went to the Carpenter, and held him with a talke, till the Master came out of his Cabbin (which hee soone did) then came John Thomas and Bennet before him, while Wilson bound his armes behind him. He asked them what they meant? they told him, he should know when he was in the Shallop. Now Juet, while this was a doing, came to John King into the Hold, who was provided for him, for he had got a sword of his own, and kept him at a bay, and might have killed him, but others came to helpe him: and so he came up to the Master. The Master called to the Carpenter, and told him that he was bound; but, I heard no answere he made. Now Arnold Lodlo, and Michael Bute rayled at them, and told them their knaverie would shew it selfe. Then was the Shallop haled up to the Ship side, and the poore, sicke, and lame men were called upon to get them out of their Cabbins into the Shallop. The Master called to me, who came out of my Cabbin as well as I could, to the Hatch way to speake with him: where, on my knees I besought them, for the love of God, to remember themselves, and to doe as they would be done unto. They bad me keepe my selfe well, and get me into my Cabbin; not suffering the Master to speake with me. But when I came into my Cabbin againe, hee called to me at the Horne, which gave light into my Cabbin, and told mee that Juet would overthrow us all; nay (said I) it is that villaine Henrie Greene, and I spake it not softly.

Now was the Carpenter at libertie, who asked them, if they would bee hanged when they came home: and as for himselfe, hee said, hee would not stay in the Ship unlesse they would force him: they bad him goe then, for they would not stay him: I will (said hee) so I may have my chest with mee, and all that is in it: they said, hee should, and presently they put it into the Shallop. Then hee came downe to mee, to take his leave of mee, who perswaded him to stay, which if he did, he might so worke that all should bee well: hee said, hee did not thinke, but they would be glad to take them in againe. For he was so perswaded by the Master, that there was not one in all the ship, that could tell how to carrie her home; but (saith he) if we must part (which wee will not willingly doe, for they would follow the ship) hee prayed me, if wee came to the Capes before them, that I would leave some token that wee had beene there, neere to the place where the Fowles bred, and hee would doe the like for us: and so (with teares) we parted. Now were the sicke men driven out of their Cabbins into the Shallop; but John Thomas was Francis Clements friend, and Bennet was the Coopers, so as there were words betweene them and Henrie Greene, one saying, that they should goe, and the other swearing that they should not goe, but such as were in the shallop should returne. When Henrie Greene heard that, he was compelled to give place, and to put out Arnold Lodlo, and Michael Bute, which with much adoe they did.

In the meane time, there were some of them that plyed worke, as if the Ship had beene entred by force, and they had free leave to pillage, breaking up Chests, and rifling all places. One of them came by me, who asked me, what they should doe. I answered, hee should make an end of what hee had begun; for I saw him doe nothing but sharke up and downe. Now, were all the poore men in the Shallop, whose names are as followeth; Henrie Hudson, John Hudson, Arnold Lodlo, Sidrack Faner, Phillip Staffe, Thomas Woodhouse, or Wydhouse, Adam Moore, Henrie King, Michael Bute. The Carpenter got of them a Peece, and Powder, and Shot, and some Pikes, an Iron Pot, with some meale, and other things. They stood out of the Ice, the Shallop being fast to the Sterne of the Shippe, and so (when they were nigh out, for I cannot say, they were cleane out) they cut her head fast from the Sterne of our Ship, then out with their Top-sayles, and towards the East they stood in a cleere Sea. In the end they tooke in their Top-sayles, righted their Helme, and lay under their Fore-sayle till they had ransacked and searched all places in the Ship. In the Hold they found one of the vessels of meale whole, and the other halfe spent, for wee had but two; wee found also two firkins of Butter, some twentie seven piece of Porke, halfe a bushell of Pease, but

in the Masters Cabbin we found two hundred of bisket Cakes, a pecke of Meale, of Beere to the quantitie of a Butt, one with another. Now, it was said, that the Shallop was come within sight, they let fall the Main-sayle, and out with their Top-sayles, and flye as from an Enemy.

Then I prayed them yet to remember themselves: but William Wilson (more then the rest) would heare of no such matter. Comming nigh the East shoare they cast about, and stood to the West and came to an Iland, and anchored in sixteene or seventeene fathome water. So they sent the Boat, and the Net ashoare to see if they could have a Draught: but could not for Rocks and great stones. Michael Perse killed two Fowle, and heere they found good store of that Weede, which we called Cockle grasse in our wintering place, whereof they gathered store, and came aboard againe. Heere we lay that night, and the best part of the next day, in all which time we saw not the shallop, or ever after. Now Henrie Greene came to me and told mee, that it was the Companies will, that I should come up into the Masters Cabbin, and take charge thereof. I told him it was more fit for Robert Juet: he said, he should not come in it, nor meddle with the Masters Card, or Journals. So up I came, and Henrie Greene gave me the Key of the Masters Chest, and told me then, that he had laid the Masters best things together, which hee would use himselfe when time did serve: the bread was also delivered me by tale.

The wind serving, we stood to the North-east, and this was Robert Billets course, contrarie to Robert Juet, who would have gone to the North-west. We had the Easterne shoare still in sight, and (in the night) had a stout gale of wind, and stood afore it, till wee met with Ice, into the which we ranne from thinne to thicke, till we could goe no further for Ice, which lay so thicke ahead of us (and the wind brought it after us asterne) that wee could not stirre backward, nor forward: but so lay imbayed fourteene daies in worse Ice, then ever wee met to deale withall, for we had beene where there was greater store, but it was not so broad upon the water as this: for this floting Ice contained miles, and halfe miles in compasse, where we had a deepe Sea, and a Tide of flood and ebbe, which set North-west and South-east. Heere Robert Juet would have gone to the North-west, but Robert Billet was confident to go through to the North-east, which he did. At last, being cleere of this Ice, he continued his course in sight of the Easterne shoare, till he raised foure Ilands which lay North and South: but we passed them sixe or seven leagues, the wind took us so short. Then wee stood backe to them againe, and came to an Anchor betweene two of the most Northermost. We sent the Boat ashoare, to see if there were any thing there to be had, but found nothing, but cockle Grasse, whereof they gathered store, and so returned aboard. Before we came to this place, I might well see, that I was kept in the ship against Henry Greenes minde, because I did not favour their proceedings better then I did. Then hee began (very subtilly) to draw me to take upon me to search for those things, which himselfe had stolne: and accused me of a matter no lesse then Treason amongst us, that I had deceived the company of thirtie Cakes of bread. Now they began to talke amongst themselves, that England was no safe place for them, and Henry Greene swore, the shippe should not come into any place (but keepe the Sea still) till he had the Kings Majesties hand and Seale to shew for his safetie. They had many devices in their heads, but Henry Greene in the end was their Captaine, and so called of them.

From these Ilands we stood to the North-east and the Easter Land still in sight: wee raysed those Ilands, that our Master called Rumnies Ilands. Betweene these Ilands and the shallow ground to the East of them, our Master went downe into the first great Bay. We kept the East shoare still in our sight, and comming thwart of the low Land, wee ranne on a Rocke that lay under water, and strooke but once; for if shee had, we might have beene made Inhabitans of that place: but God sent us soone off without any harme that wee saw. Wee continued our course and raysed Land a head of us, which stretched out to the North: which when they saw, they said plainly, that Robert Billet by his Northerly course had left the Capes to the South, and that they were best to seeke downe to the South in time for reliefe, before all was gone: for we had small store left. But Robert Billet would follow the Land to the North, saying, that he hoped in God to find somewhat to releeve us that way, as soone as to the South. I told them that this Land was the Mayne of Worsenhome Cape, and that

the shallow rockie ground, was the same that the Master went downe by, when he went into the great Bay. Robert Juet and all said, it was not possible, unlesse the Master had brought the ship over Land, and willed them to looke into the Masters Card, and their course how well they did agree. We stood to the East, and left the mayne Land to the North, by many small Ilands into a narrow gut betweene two Lands, and there came to an Anchor. The Boat went ashoare on the North side, where wee found the great Horne, but nothing else. The next day wee went to the South side, but found nothing there, save Cockle grasse of which we gathered. This grasse was a great releefe unto us, for without it, we should hardly have got to the Capes for want of victuall. The wind serving we stood out, but before we could get cleane out, the wind came to the West, so that we were constrayned to anchor on the North side.

The next day wee weighed and doubled the point of the North Land, which is high Land, and so continueth to the Capes, lying North and South, some five and twentie or thirtie leagues. To the North we stood to see store of those Fowles that breed in the Capes, and to kill some with our shot, and to fetch them with our Boat. We raised the Capes with joy, and bare for them, and came to the Ilands that lie in the mouth of the streight: but bearing in betweene the Rockie Iles, we ranne on a Rocke that lay under water, and there stucke fast eight or nine houres. It was ebbing water when we thus came on, so the floud set us afloat, God guiding both wind and Sea, that it was calme, and faire weather: the ebbe came from the East, and the floud from the West. When wee were afloat, wee stood more neere to the East shoare, and there anchored.

The next day being the seven and twentieth of July, we sent the Boat to fetch some Fowle, and the ship should way and stand as neere as they could: for the wind was against us. They had a great way to row, and by that meanes they could not reach to the place where the Fowle bred: but found good store of Gulls, yet hard to come by, on the Rocks and Cliffes, but with their Peeces they killed some thirtie, and towards night returned. Now we had brought our ship more neere to the mouth of the Streights, and there came to an anchor in eighteen or twentie fathom water, upon a Riffe or shelfe of ground: which after they had weighed their Anchor, and stood more neere to the place where the Fowle bred, they could not find it againe, nor no place like it: but were faine to turne to and fro in the mouth of the Streight, and to be in danger of Rockes, because they could not find ground to let fall an Anchor in, the water was so deepe.

The eight and twentieth day, the Boat went to Digges his Cape for Fowle, and made directly for the place where the Fowle bred, and being neere, they saw seven Boates come about the Easterne point towards them. When the Savages saw our Boate, they drew themselves together, and drew their lesser Boats into their bigger: and when they had done, they came rowing to our Boate, and made signes to the West, but they made readie for all assayes. The Savages came to them, and by signes grew familiar one with another, so as our men tooke one of theirs into our Boate, and they tooke one of ours into their Boate. Then they carried our man to a Cove where their Tents stood toward the West of the place, where the Fowle bred: so they carried him into their Tents, where he remayned till our men returned with theirs. Our Boat went to the place where the Fowle bred, and were desirous to know how the Savages killed their Fowle: he shewed them the manner how, which was thus, They take a long Pole with a snare at the end, which they put about the Fowles necke, and so plucke them downe. When our men knew that they had a better way of their owne, they shewed him the use of our Peeces, which at one shot would kill seven or eight. To be short, our Boat returned to their Cove for our man, and to deliver theirs. When they came they made great joy, with dancing and leaping, and stroking of their brests: they offered divers things to our men, but they only tooke some Morses Teeth, which they gave them for a Knife, and two glasse buttons: and so receiving our man they came aboard, much rejoycing at this chance, as if they had met with the most simple and kind people of the World.

And Henry Greene (more then the rest) was so confident, that (by no meanes) we should take care to stand upon our Guard: God blinding him so, that where hee made reckoning to receive great matters from these people, he received more then he looked for, and that suddenly by being made a good example for all men: that make

no conscience of doing evill, and that we take heed of the Savage people, how simple soever they seeme to be.

The next day, the nine and twentieth of July, they made haste to be ashoare, and because the ship rid too farre off, they weighed and stood as neere to the place where the Fowle bred, as they could: and because I was lame, I was to go in the Boat, to carrie such things, as I had in the Cabbin of every thing somewhat: and so with more haste then good speed (and not without swearing) away we went, Henry Greene, William Wilson, John Thomas, Michael Perse, Andrew Moter, and my selfe. When we came neere the shoare, the people were on the Hils, dancing and leaping: to the Cove we came, where they had drawne up their Boates: wee brought our Boate to the East side of the Cove, close to the Rockes. Ashoare they went, and made fast the Boat to a great stone on the shoare, the people came, and every one had somewhat in his hand to barter: but Henry Greene swore they should have nothing, till he had Venison, for that they had so promised him by signes.

Now when we came, they made signes to their Dogges (whereof there were many like Mongrels, as bigge as Hounds) and pointed to their Mountaine, and to the Sunne, clapping their hands. Then Henry Greene, John Thomas, and William Wilson, stood hard by the Boate head, Michael Perse, and Andrew Moter were got up upon the Rocke, a gathering of Sorrell: not one of them had any weapon about him, not so much as a sticke, save Henry Greene only, who had a piece of a Pike in his hand: nor saw I any thing that they had wherewith to hurt us. Henry Greene and William Wilson had Looking-glasses, and Jewes Trumps, and Bels, which they were shewing the people. The Savages standing round about them, one of them came into the Boats head to me to shew me a Bottle: I made signes to him to get him ashoare, but he made as though he had not understood me, whereupon I stood up, and pointed him ashoare. In the meane-time, another stole behind me to the sterne of the Boat, and when I saw him ashoare, that was in the head of the Boat, I sate downe againe: but suddenly I saw the legge and foote of a man by mee. Wherefore I cast up my head, and saw the Savage with his Knife in his hand, who strooke at my brest over my head: I cast up my right arme to save my brest, he wounded my arme, and strooke me into the bodie under my right Pappe. He strooke a second blow which I met with my left hand, and then he strooke me into the right thigh, and had like to have cut off my little finger of the left hand. Now, I had got hold of the string of the Knife, and had woond it about my left hand, he striving with both his hands, to make an end of that he had begunne, I found him but weake in the gripe (God enabling me) and getting hold of the sleeve of his left arme, so bare him from me. His left side lay bare to me, which when I saw, I put his sleeve off his left arme into my left hand, holding the string of the Knife fast in the same hand: and having got my right hand at libertie, I sought for somewhat wherewith to strike him (not remembring my Dagger at my side) but looking downe I saw it, and therewith strooke him into the bodie, and the throate.

Whiles I was thus assaulted in the Boat, our men were set upon on the shoare. John Thomas and William Wilson had their bowels cut, and Michael Perse and Henry Greene being mortally wounded, came tumbling into the Boat together. When Andrew Moter saw this medley, hee came running downe the Rockes, and leaped into the Sea, and so swamme to the Boat, hanging on the sterne thereof, till Michael Perse tooke him in, who manfully made good the head of the Boat against the Savages, that pressed sore upon us. Now Michael Perse had got an Hatchet, wherewith I saw him strike one of them, that he lay sprawling in the Sea. Henry Greene crieth Coragio, and layeth about him with his Truncheon: I cryed to them to cleere the Boat, and Andrew Moter cryed to bee taken in: the Savages betooke them to their Bowes and Arrowes, which they sent amongst us, wherewith Henry Greene was slaine out-right, and Michael Perse received many wounds, and so did the rest. Michael Perse cleereth the Boate, and puts it from the shoare, and helpeth Andrew Moter in: but in turning of the Boat, I received a cruell wound in my backe with an Arrow: Michael Perse and Andrew Moter rowed the Boate away, which when the Savages saw, they ranne to their Boats, and I feared they would have launched them, to have followed us, but they did not, and our ship was in the middle of the channell, and could not see us.

Now, when they had rowed a good way from the shoare, Michael Perse fainted, and could row no more: then was Andrew Moter driven to stand in the Boat head, and waft to the ship, which (at the first) saw us not, and when they did, they could not tel what to make of us, but in the end they stood for us, and so tooke us up. Henry Greene was throwne out of the Boat into the Sea, and the rest were had aboard, the Savage being yet alive, yet without sense. But they died all there that day, William Wilson swearing and cursing in most fearefull manner: Michael Perse lived two dayes after, and then died. Thus you have heard the Tragicall end of Henry Greene and his Mates, whom they called Captaine, these foure being the only lustie men in all the ship.

The poore number that was left, were to ply our ship too and fro, in the mouth of the streight, for there was no place to anchor in neere hand: besides, they were to goe in the Boate to kill Fowle, to bring us home, which they did, although with danger to us all. For if the wind blew, there was an high Sea, and the eddies of the Tydes would carrie the ship so neere the Rockes, as it feared our Master, for so I will now call him. After they had killed some two hundred Fowle, with great labour on the South Cape, wee stood to the East: but when wee were six or seven leagues from the Capes, the wind came up at East. Then wee stood backe to the Capes againe, and killed an hundred Fowle more. After this, the wind came to the West, so wee were driven to goe away, and then our Master stood (for the most) along by the North shoare, till he fell into broken ground about the Queenes Foreland, and there anchored. From thence wee went to Gods Mercies, and from thence to those Ilands, which lye in the mouth of our Streight, not seeing the Land, till we were readie to runne our Bosprite against the Rockes in a fogge. But it cleered a little, and then we might see our selves inclosed with Rockie Ilands, and could find no ground to anchor in. There our Master lay atrie all night, and the next day the fogge continuing, they sought for ground to anchor in, and found some in an hundred and odde fathomes of water. The next day we weighed and stood to the East, but before wee came heere, we had put our selves to hard allowance, as halfe a foule a day with the pottage: for yet we had some meale left, and nothing else. Then they beganne to make triall of all whatsoever: wee had flayed our Fowle, for they wil not pull: and Robert Juet was the first, that made use of the skins by burning of the Feathers: so they became a great dish of meate, and as for the garbidge, it was not throwne away.

After we were cleere of these Ilands, which lie out with two points, one to the South-east, and the other to the North, making a Bay to the sight as if there were no way through, we continued our course East South-east, and South and by East, to raise the Desolations, from thence to shape our course for Ireland. Thus we continued divers dayes: but the wind comming against us, made us to alter our course, and by the meanes of Robert Juet, who perswaded the company, that they should find great reliefe in Newfound Land, if our Countrey-men were there, and if they were gone before we came, yet should we find great store of bread and fish left ashoare by them: but how true, I give God thankes, we did not trie. Yet we stood to the South-west, and to the West, almost to fiftie seven degrees: when (by the will of God) the winde came up at South-west. Then the Master asked me, if he should take the benefit of this wind, and shape his course for Ireland. I said it was best to goe, where we knew Corne grew, and not to seeke it, where it was cast away, and not to be found. Towards Ireland now wee stood, with prosperous winds for many dayes together: then was all our Meale spent, and our Fowle restie and dry: but (being no remedie) we were content with the Salt broth for Dinner, and the halfe Fowle for Supper. Now went our Candles to wracke, and Bennet our Cooke made a messe of meate of the bones of the Fowle, frying them with Candle-grease, till they were crispe, and with Vineger put to them, made a good dish of meate. Our Vinegar was shared, and to every man a pound of Candles delivered for a weeke, as a great daintie. Now Robert Juet (by his reckoning) saith, wee were within sixtie or seventie leagues of Ireland, when wee had two hundred thither. And sure our course was so much the longer, through our evill steeredge: for, our men became so weake, that they could not stand at the Helme, but were faine to sit.

Then Robert Juet dyed, for meere want, and all our men were in despaire, and said wee were past Ireland, and our last Fowle were in the steep-tub. So, our men cared not which end went forward, insomuch as our Master was driven to looke to

their labour, as well as his owne: for some of them would sit and see the fore-sayle, or mayne-sayle flie up to the tops, the sheetes being either flowne or broken, and would not helpe it themselves, nor call to others for helpe, which much grieved the Master. Now in this extremitie it pleased God to give us sight of Land, not farre from the place our Master said he would fall withal, which was the Bay of Galloway, and we fell to the West of the Derses, and so stood along by the coast, to the South-west. In the end, there was a joyful cry, a sayle, a sayle, towards which they stood, then they saw more, but to the neerest we stood, and called to him: his Barke was of Fowy, and was at anchor a Fishing: he came to us, and brought us into Bere Haven. Here we stayed a few dayes, and delt with the Irish, to supply our wants, but found no reliefe: for in this place there was neither Bread, Drinke, nor mony to be had amongst them. Wherfore they advised us to deale with our Countrymen, who were there a fishing, which we did: but found them so cold in kindnesse, that they would doe nothing without present money, whereof we had none in the Ship. In the end, we procured one John Waymouth, Master of the Barke that brought us into this Harbour, to furnish us with money, which hee did, and received our best Cable and Anchor in pawne for the same. With this money, our Master with the helpe of John Waymouth, bought Bread, Beere, and Beefe.

Now, as wee were beholding to Waymouth for his money, so were wee to one Captaine Taylor, for making of our contracts with Waymouth, by whose meanes hee tooke a Bill for our Cable and Anchor, and for the mens Wages, who would not goe with us, unlesse Waymouth wold passe his word for the same: for they made shew, that they were not willing to goe with us for any wages. Whereupon Captaine Taylor swore hee would presse them, and then, if they would not goe, hee would hang them.

In conclusion, wee agreed for three pound ten shillings a man, to bring our Ship to Plimouth, or Dartmouth, and to give the Pilot five pound: but if the winde did not serve, but that they were driven to put into Bristow, they were to have foure pound ten shillings a man, and the Pilot sixe pound. Omitting therefore further circumstances, from Bere Haven wee came to Plimouth, and so to an anchor, before the Castle: and from

Plimouth, with faire winde and weather without stop or stay, wee came to the Downes, from thence to Gravesend, where most of our men went a shoare, and from thence came on this side Erith, and there stopped: where our Master Robert Billet came aboord, and so had mee up to London with him, and so wee came to Sir Thomas Smiths together.

THE AFTERMATH OF THE HUDSON VOYAGE

THE STATUS of the *Discovery* and the men who brought it back, when the fate of Hudson was learned, remained ambiguous. It was felt that they had been guilty of mutiny, desertion, and perhaps of murder. Yet there was some sympathy for their plight. All had suffered. Abacuk Pricket, most eloquent of the survivors, was a representative of the syndicate that sent out the ship, not a member of the crew, and he threw the main blame for the mutiny on members of the crew who were dead. However, it was felt that an inquiry was necessary. This was made, in the first place, by the Masters of Trinity House, arbitrators of some standing in maritime issues. The inquiry was unfavorable to the survivors (675). But a Northwest Passage Company was being launched, and criminal proceedings would have clouded the campaign to exploit the new Hudson Strait as a possible passage to Asia. Criminal proceedings were begun only some five years later, when the newer northwest voyages and their promoting company had failed. All of the *Discovery* survivors were in peril of their lives for mutiny in the proceedings in the High Court of Admiralty. All testified, yet no verdict has been found. Responsibility for Hudson's treatment and death could not convincingly be pinned on those who survived. The case in the end could not be proved and was dropped.

675. October 24, 1611. Examination of the survivors of the *Discovery* on behalf of Trinity House.

Trinity House, London, Transactions, 1609–1625, fols. 11v.–12.

Robart Billet who came home Master sayeth that going into the Straightes they weare 5 weekes in ther passage to Cape Salisbury but in Comming to the East Ward they Weare Cleere of Cape Desolation in 16 dayes as he conceaves

Men turned out of the ship 23 June:
Henry Hudson Master
John Hudson his son
Arnold Ladley
John King quarter Master
Michall Butt Maried
Thomas Woodhowse a Mathematition put away
   in great distress

Adam Moore
Phillipp Staffe Carpenter
Syracke Farmer Maried

[Died:]
John Williams dyed in 9 october
Juet dyed comming home

Slaine:
Henry Greene
William Wilson
John Thomas
Michell Peerce

Men that came home:
Robart Billet Master.
Abecocke Pricket a landman put in by the Adventurers.
Edward Wilson Surgeon.
Frances Clemens Boteson.
Adrian Motter
Bennet Mathues a landman.
Nicholas Syms Boy:
Silvanus Bond Couper

The Company remaining on the Ship after the Master was put Owte made Choice of Billet for Master.

They departed from London 18 Aprill and fell with Cape Salsbery 2 August victled for 8 Monethes.

Abacuck Pricket sworne saith, that the Shipp began to retorne abowte 12 of June and abowt 22 or 25 they put away the Master.

Greene and Willson weare imployed to fishe for the Company and being at Sea, Combyned to steale away the Shaollope, but at last resolved to take away the Ship, and put the Master and other impotent men into the Shallope:

Upon his othe he cleers the now Master of any foreknowledge of this Complot but saith he assures him selfe they relyed on Juetts Judgement and Skill.

Silvanus Bond Sayth that the Certaine tyme of the Ships Comming owte of the wintring port he remembreth not, but that it was in June. But he saith that Wilson was the first, that plotted the putting away of the Master and saith that by the relation of William Wilson and Greene, the now Master was acquainted with the same, either the second or third man, and the rest that came home weare all likewise Consenting to it:

[Signed:] Silvanus Bond

Edward Wilson Surgeon saith that they Came owte of ther wintering port abowt the 12 of June: but this deponent knew not of the putting the Master owte of the Ship untill he sawe the Master brought pinioned downe beffore his Caben dore: Neither who weare to be put owte of the Ship with him.

[Signed:] Edward Wilson

Frances Clemens, Adrian Motter, Bennet Mathues all sworne saith that the Master was put owte of the Shipp by Consent of all that weare in health in regard that ther victells was much wasted by him, and so to preserve life in the rest. The Resolution was begun by William Wilson, Greene and others, and few or none against it, and some of thers that weare directly against the Master: and yet for Safety of the rest put away with him: and all by thos men that were slaine principally

[Signed:] Bennet Mathue, Fran: Clemence., Adrean Motter.

By Examination of Seaven of the Company of

that Shipp that endeavored the Northwest discovery: It plainly appeareth, that the Master and the rest of those men which are lost, weare put owte of the Ship, by Consent of all such as are come home and then weare in health, and also not with owte the approbation of some of them that went with him, as Michaell Butt who consented to ye same.

It appeareth further that the plot was begun by Henry Greene, and William Wilsonn, and that by the privity of Juet whome they presurved on for ther best Guide.

Some of them Confess that Robart Billet who came home Master was acquainted with the same in the beginning, But Pricket cleers him thereof And saith he was Chosen to take the Charge after the Master was put away:

They all Charge the Master to have wasted the victells by a scuttle made owte of his Cabin into the hold, and it appears that he Fedd his Favorites, as the Surgeon &c and kept others at only ordenary allowance, which made those that weare not favored to give the Attempt and to performe it so violently.

But all Conclude that to save some from Starving they weare Content to put away so many and that to most of those it was utterly unknowne who should goe or who tarry, but as affection or Rage did guide them in that fury that weare authors and Exectioners of that Plott.

676. February 7, 1617. Examination of Robert Bylot on Hudson's voyage of 1610–1611.

P.R.O., HCA 1/48, fols. 120–121v.

Die predicto February 7, 1617

Roberte Bileth of St Katherines mariner examined in his majestes High Courte of the Admiralty uppon the said articles Sayth thereunto as followeth:

To the first article he sayth that uppon a discontent amongst the company of the shipp Discovery in the finding out of the north west passadge, by occasion of the wante of victualls, Henry Grene beinge the principall togeather with John

Thomas, William Wilson Robert Juett & Michael Pearse determined to shifte the company, and thereuppon Henry Hudson the master was by force putt into the shallopp and VIII or nine more were commanded to goe into the Shallopp to the master, which they did, this deponent thinking this course was taken only to seach the masters cabin & the shipp for victualls which the said Grene & others thought the master concealed from the company to serve his own turne. But when they were in the said Shallopp the said Grene & the rest would not suffer them to come any more on bord the shipp and so the said Hudson & the rest in the Shallopp went away to the Southward, & the shipp came to the Eastward, and the one never saw the other since what is otherwise become of them he knoweth not.

To the second he sayth that after the departure of the shallopp, the shipp sayled to Didges Island, and there the said Grene, and fyve others goinge a shore to gett victualls were betrayed by the salvages and two of them had theire gutts cutt out, and all the rest wounded but one so as foure of them died shortly after they came on bord, and by that meanes & no other the cabins beds and clothes were made bluddye. To the third he sayth there was discontent amongst the company, but no mutiny to his knowledge untill the said Grene and his associattes turned the master and others with him into the Shallopp.

To the iiiith he sayth he heard of no mutiny untill one night, when Hudson & the rest were putt into the Shallopp the next-day, and this deponent and Master Prickett persuaded the said Grene to the contrary, and Grene answered, the Master was resolved to overthrowe all, and therefore he and his friends would shifte for them selves.

To the Vth and VIth he sayth that such clothes of the said Hudson and his associattes as were lefte behind them in the shipp were sould and worne by some of the company that wanted clothes.

To the VIIth he sayth he heard not neither knowe any such thinge as the article [ ] with.

To the VIIIth he sayth the shipp carpenter never used any such speeches to his knowledge.

To the ninth he sayth that Phillip Staffe the ship carpenter wente into the Shallopp of his owne accord without any compulsion, whether he be deade or alive, or what has since become of him he knoweth not.

To the Xth he sayth no man eyther drunke or sober can reporte, that the said Hudson and his associattes or any of them were shott at, after they were in the Shallopp: for as he sayth there was no such thinge done.

To the XIth he sayth he was under the deck when Henry Hudson was putt out of the shipp into the Shallopp, so as he saw him not putt out nether knoweth whether he was bound or no but sayth he heard he was pinnioned when he was putt out of the shipp.

To the XIIth he sayth Henry Grene & two or three others made a motion to turne piratte and this deponent beleveth they would have done so if they had lived.

To the XIIIth he hath not heard as he sayth of any such thinge putt into printe as is articulat.

To the XIIIIth he denieth that he tooke any ringe out of the said Hudsons pockett, nether ever saw yt except on his finger, nether knoweth what became of yt.

To the XVth he sayth such beds & clothes as were left in the shipp & not taken by Hudson & the rest into the Shallopp were brought into England because they lefte them behind them in the shipp.

To the XVIth he sayth there was not any watch word given to his knowledge, but the said Grene and others commanded the said Hudson & the rest into the Shallopp, and uppon that command they wente into the Shallopp.

To the XVIIth he sayth he tould Sir Thomas Smith the manner howe the said Hudson & the rest went from them, but what Sir Thomas sayd to theire wiffes he knoweth not.

To the XVIIIth he sayth he tould the masters of the Trinity House, howe this business was carried. But the said Masters used no such wordes as are articulate to his knowledge.

To the XIXth he sayth there was no mutiny but some discontent amongst the company, and sayth they were not victualled with any abundance of rabette or partridges all the viadge.

To the XXth he cannot depose.

To the XXIth he sayth that the said Grene & his associattes putt out the said Hudson & the rest for want of victualls.

To the XXIIth he denieth the same.

To the XXIIIth he sayth he doth not knowe the hand writinge of Thomas Widowes, nether what the said Widowes hath putt downe in writinge.

To the XXIIIIth he sayth the matter was deferred by meanes of Sir Thomas Smith Sir Dudley Digges and Master Worseman as he thinketh, who were well informed of all that proceeded in the said viadge.

[Signed:] Robert Byleth

677. May 13, 1617. Examination of Francis Clemence on Henry Hudson's voyage of 1610–1611.

*P.R.O., HCA 1/48, fols. 130–130*v.

Die martiis XIII May 1617

Frances Clemence of Wappinge mariner aged forty yeares or thereaboutes examined before Master Doctor Any deputy Judge of the Admiralty uppon certaine articles ministered against him on his majeste behalf Sayth there unto as followeth.

To the first article he sayth that Henry Hudson the master and eight persons more were putt out of the Discovery into the shallopp about XX leagues from the place where they wintered about the XXIIth of June shalbe six yeares in June next, by the rest of the company as he hath heard for this deponent had his nayles frozen of, and was verry sick, at that tyme & was not acquainted [with] what was done, neyther doth he know what is since become of the said men.

To the second he sayth that Henry Grene, William Wilson, John Thomas & Michael Pearse were slayne on shore by the Salvages at Sir Dudley Digges Island, and Robert Juett died at sea after they were slayne.

To the third he sayth that Phillipp Staffe the shipp carpenter, was one of them who was putt into the shallopp with the Master and the rest, but whether he be dead or alive he knoweth not.

To the IIIIth he sayth that the clothes which were brought home bloody were the clothes of them who were slayne by the salvages having their bellies ript up, then theire gutt hong out, when they came on bord, and died abord.

The Vth he sayth there were wounded at Sir Dudley Digges his Island goinge ashore to seeke victualls.

To the VIth he sayth the master displaced some of the company out of theire places, and putt others in theire roome, but theire was no mutiny in the shipp to his knowledge.

To the VIIth he sayth he was sick in his cabin, and knoweth not who gave the watch word, or whether any watchword was given.

To the VIIIth he was in his cabin, and not able to helpe himselfe, and did not any thinge in the said action.

To the ninth he sayth he knoweth nothinge of the contents of this article.

To the Xth he denieth the same for his parte, & cannot imagyn that any others could or would confesse that they which were putt into the shallop were slayne.

To the XIth he sayth there was no such intent that they would turne piratte to his knowledge.

To the XIIth he hath observed no such thinge.

To the XIIIth he confesseth that Henry Hudson was pinnioned when he was putt into the shallopp.

To the XIIIIth he knoweth nothing thereof.

[Signed:] Francis Clemence

678. 1612. Hessel Gerritz's brief note (on his chart of the Northwest Passage) on Hudson's discovery.

Hessel Gerritz, Descriptio et delineatio geographica detectionis freti ab H. Hudsono inventi (Amsterdam, 1612), translated in Henry Murphy, Hudson in Holland (The Hague, 1909), pp. 181–183.

Mr. Hudson, who has been repeatedly engaged in the search of a western passage, long intended to undertake an expedition for this same purpose through Lumley's Inlet, a channel leading out of Davis's Strait; as we ourselves have seen pointed out on his map, which is in Mr. Plancius' hands. He hoped thus to reach the Pacific by the west of Nova Albion, where another Englishman had, according to his drawings, passed through. Hudson found after many labours the way represented on our map, and he was only prevented from following it further up, by the resistance of his crew. This mutiny took place under the following circumstances. They had been absent from home about ten months, being provisioned only for eight, and during their whole voyage they had met but a single man, who brought them an animal which they ate; but having been badly treated, the man never returned. Having thus left the latitude of 52°, where they had wintered, and having sailed up to 60°, along the western shore of their bay, they fell in with a wide sea and with a great flood from the north-west. The commanders intended to proceed further. The crew then rose against him, and put all the officers out of the ship into a boat, and sailed home to England. For this cause they have, on their arrival at home, all been put in prison; and in the course of the present summer (1612) some ships have again been sent to those regions by order of the king and of the Prince of Wales, to discover a passage and to look for Mr. Hudson and his companions. These have received orders that, in case the passage be found, two of them shall pass through it, the third shall be sent home with the news, which we are expecting.

XIX

France in North America, 1577–1603

THIS IS a long and complex story. The period starts, for France, with a question mark. Apart from fishing off and near Newfoundland and Cape Breton, what were the French doing in the northeast between the 1540s and the late 1570s or early 1580s? Further question marks arise. Why should France have decided that New England was not desirable, that even Acadia was only marginally of interest? Why should it have concentrated on the St. Lawrence alone? Something of the answer emerges from the documents that follow, but not all. It is necessary to look at the transition from fish to fur, glanced at in connection with Newfoundland earlier in this volume. Diplomatic secrets will perhaps be found wrapped up in French changes of direction. In the earlier phase, 1577–1603, the personalities encountered are too vaguely defined, their motives too mixed to show us a clear way ahead. But once Samuel Champlain comes on the scene, first as the humble right arm of Aymar des Chastes and then of Pierre du Gua, Sieur de Monts, and finally as a leader in his own right, a guide exists to the mechanics and meaning of much of French enterprise. Only then New France emerges as an entity, after such a long cloud-covered existence.

Chapter Eighty-four
Laudonnière and Champlain on French Colonizing Objectives

ALTHOUGH FAR APART in time and out of strict context in this setting, the views of Laudonnière (in the early 1570s) and of Champlain (1613) reflect French views, rarely made explicit, on the purposes and advantages of colonization, in general, and in North America, in particular.

679. 1576. René de Laudonnière's views on the prospects for French overseas colonization.

We have few expressions of French opinion in the sixteenth century on the general question of the desirability of overseas colonization. Laudonnière prefaced L'histoire notable de la Floride *(1576) with such a brief general statement. It was retained in Richard Hakluyt's translation,* A notable history *(1587), sig. a6–a8, reprinted in* Principal navigations, *III (1600), 303–304 (VIII [1904], 446–448).*

The Preface of Master René Laudonnière.

There are two things, which according to mine opinion have bene the principall causes, in consideration whereof aswell they of ancient times, as those of our age have bene induced to travell into farre and remote regions. The first hath beene the naturall desire which wee have to search out the commodities to live happily, plentifully, and at ease: be it whither one abandon his naturall Countrey altogether to dwell in a better, or bee it that men make voyages thither, there to search out and bring from thence such things as are there to be found, and are in greatest estimation and in most request in our Countreys. The second cause hath bene the multitude of people too fruitefull in generation, which being no longer able to dwell in their native soyles, have entred upon their neighbours limites, and oftentimes passing further have pearced even unto the uttermost regions. After this sort the North climate, a fruitfull father of so many nations hath oftentimes sent foorth this way and that way his valiant people, and by this meane hath peopled infinite Countreys: so that most of the nations of Europe drawe their originall from these parts. Contrariwise the more Southerne regions, because they bee too barren by reason of their insupportable heate which raigneth in them, neede not any such sending forth of their inhabitants, and have bene oftentimes constrained to receive other people more often by force of armes then willingly. All Afrike, Spaine, and Italie can also testifie the same, which never so abounded with people that they had neede to send them abroad to inhabite elsewhere: as on the contrary Scythia, Norway, Gotland, and France have done. The posterity of which nations remaineth yet not only in Italy, Spaine & Afrike, but also in fruitful and faire Asia. Neverthelesse I find that the Romans proceeding further, or rather adding unto these two chiefe causes aforesaid, (as being most curious to plant not onely their ensignes and victories, but also their lawes, customes, & religion in those provinces which they had conquered by force of armes) have oftentimes by the decree of their soveraigne Senate sent forth inhabitants, which they called Colonies (thinking by this way to make their name immortall) even to the unfurnishing of their own Countrey of the forces which should have preserved the same in her perfection: a thing

301

which hindred them much more, then advanced them to the possession of the universal monarchy, whereunto their intention did aspire. For it came to passe that their Colonies here and there being miserably sacked by strange people did utterly ruin and overthrow their Empire. The brinks of the river of Rhene are yet red, those of Danubius are no lesse bloody, and our France became fat with their blood which they lost. These are the effects and rewards of al such as being pricked forward with this Romane and tyrannical ambition will goe about thus to subdue strange people: effects, I say, contrary to the profit which those shall receive, which onely are affectioned to the common benefite, that is to say, to the generall policie of all men, and endevour to unite them one with another as well by trafficke and civill conversations, as also by military vertues, and force of armes, when as the Savages will not yeeld unto their endevours so much tending unto their profit.

For this cause princes have sent forth out of their Dominions certaine men of good activity to plant themselves in strange Countreys, their to make their profite to bring the Countrey to civilitie, and if it might be, to reduce the inhabitants to the true knowledge of our God: an end so much more commendable, as it is farre from all tyrannicall and cruell governement: and so they have alwayes thrived in their enterprises, and by little and little gained the heartes of them which they have conquered or wonne unto them by any meanes. Hereof wee may gather that sometimes it is good, yea very expedient to send forth men to discover the pleasure and commoditie of strange Countreys: But so, that the Countrey out of which these companies are to passe remaine not weakned, nor deprived of her forces: And againe in such sort that the company sent forth be of so just & sufficient number, that it may not be defeated by strangers, which every foote endevour nothing else but to surprise the same upon the sudden. As within these few daies past the French have proved to my great griefe, being able by no means possible to withstand the same, considering that the elements, men, and all the favours which might be hoped for of a faithfull and Christian alliance fought against us: which thing I purpose to discover in this present historie with so evident trueth, that the Kings Majesty my soveraigne prince shall in part be satisfied of the diligence which I have used in her service, and

mine adversaries shall find themselves so discovered in their false reports, that they shall have no place of refuge. But before I begin, I will briefly set downe the situation and description of the land whereunto we have sailed and where we have inhabited from the yeere 1561. unto sixty five, to the ende that those things may the more easily be borne away, which I meane to describe in this discourse.

680. 1613. Champlain on motives for French colonization in Canada.

Champlain is almost as elusive as his precursors in providing clues to underlying French colonial objectives; perhaps we can extract a little from his opening remarks in Les voyages, *where he places his expedition, set out by the Sieur de Monts, in a historical perspective.*

Samuel de Champlain, Les voyages, *pp. 1–6; The Works of Samuel de Champlain, edited and translated by H. P. Biggar (and others), I (1922), 225–232.*

1

According to the diversity of their dispositions, men's inclinations vary, and each in his calling has a particular object. Some aim at profit, others at glory, and others at the public welfare. The greater number take to commerce, and especially that which is carried on by sea. Thence springs the people's principal source of comfort, with the wealth and honour of states. This it was that raised ancient Rome to the sovereignty and mastery of the whole world, and the Venetians to a height comparable with that of mighty kings. In all ages it has made maritime cities abound in riches, among which cities Alexandria and Tyre are so famous, and a host of others occupying the interiors of countries, while foreign nations have sent them whatever beautiful and remarkable things they possess. This is why many princes have striven to find a route to China by the north, in order to facilitate commerce with the peoples of the East, in the hope that this route might prove shorter and less dangerous.

In the year 1496 the king of England commissioned for this search John Cabot and Sebastian his son. About the same time Dom Manoel, king of Portugal, sent thither Gaspar Corte Real, who returned without having found what he hoped, and the following year on resuming the same path, he died during the expedition, as did Michael, his brother, who stubbornly continued the search. In the years 1534 and 1535 Jacques Cartier received a similar commission from King Francis I, but was checked in his course. Six years later the Sieur de Roberval, having renewed the attempt, sent Jean Alfonse of Saintonge farther to the northward, along the coast of Labrador; but he returned as wise as the others. In the years 1576, 1577, and 1578, Sir Martin Frobisher, an Englishman, made three voyages along the northern coasts. Seven years later Humfrey Gilbert, also an Englishman, set out with five ships but was cast away upon Sable island, where three of his vessels were lost. In the same and two following years John Davis, an Englishman, made three voyages for the same purpose, and penetrated to 72°, but did not sail beyond a strait which to this day is called by his name. And after him Captain Georges also made one in the year 1590, but was obliged on account of the ice to return without having discovered anything. As for the Dutch, they have not obtained any more exact knowledge at Nova Zembla.

So many voyages and explorations at the cost of so much effort and expense having been undertaken in vain, our Frenchmen were induced in these last few years to endeavour to effect a permanent settlement in those lands which we call New France, in the hope of attaining more easily to the completion of this enterprise, since the voyage would begin in this land beyond the ocean, along which the search for the desired passage is to be made. This consideration induced the Marquis de La Roche, in the year 1598, to obtain a commission from the king for settling the said country. To this end he landed men and supplies on Sable island; but the conditions accorded to him by his Majesty having been revoked, he was obliged to abandon his undertaking and to leave his men there. A year later Captain Chauvin obtained another commission to take out other men, but this having been shortly afterwards revoked, he followed the matter no further.

After them, notwithstanding all these vicissitudes and hesitations, the Sieur de Monts desired to attempt this desperate undertaking, and asked his Majesty for a commission for this purpose; for he realised that what had ruined the former undertakings had been a lack of assistance to the promoters, who, neither in a single year nor in two, had been able to become acquainted with the regions and the peoples who inhabit them, or to find harbours suitable for a settlement. He proposed to his Majesty a method of meeting the expenses without drawing anything from the royal exchequer, namely, that he be given a monopoly of the fur trade of that country. This having been granted to him, he contracted large and excessive expenditure, and took with him a considerable number of men of divers conditions, and had constructed there the dwellings necessary for his men. This expenditure he continued for three consecutive years, after which, in consequence of the jealousy and importunity of certain Basque and Breton merchants, his grant was revoked by the Council, to the great detriment of the said Sieur de Monts, who, in consequence of this revocation, was compelled to abandon everything, with the loss of his labour and of all the implements wherewith he had provided his settlement.

But as he had made a report to the king of the fertility of the soil, and I had made one upon the means of discovering the passage to China without the inconvenience of the northern icebergs, or the heat of the torrid zone through which our seamen, with incredible labours and perils, pass twice in going and twice in returning, his Majesty commanded the Sieur de Monts to prepare a fresh expedition and again to send men to continue what he had begun. This he did; and because of the uncertainty of his commission he changed the locality in order to deprive his rivals of the distrust he had aroused in them. He was influenced also by the hope of greater advantages in the interior, where the peoples are civilised, and where it is easier to plant the Christian faith and to establish such order as is necessary for the preservation of a country than along the seashore where the Indians usually dwell. Thus he hoped to bring it about that the king would derive therefrom a profit too great to be estimated; for it is easy to believe that the nations of Europe will rather seek to take advantage of this convenience than endure the envious and intractable dispositions of the peoples along the coasts and the barbarous nations.

Chapter Eighty-five
The Revival of French Activity in
Canada and Acadia, 1577–1603

THE REVIVAL of French activity in the St. Lawrence and along the shores of Acadia is inadequately documented. Much early knowledge derives from English sources and is indicative rather than comprehensive. In March, 1577, Troïlus de Mesgouëz, Sieur de Kermoalec, and Marquis de la Roche, a Breton nobleman, was given authority to occupy Newfoundland and adjacent lands for France, and on January 3, 1578, he was commissioned as "vice-roi des nouvelles terres." He held this office *en titre* until 1603. His own attempts to set out expeditions in 1578 and in 1584 were both failures (his ships suffered early damage and were forced to return). He was involved in the French internal struggle for many years and was imprisoned by the Leaguer Duke of Mercoeur until 1596. Henry IV endeavored to restore his position in New France and he was regranted, in 1597, authority as the king's lieutenant in Canada, Hochelaga, Terre Neuve, Labrador, Norumbega, and Sable Island.

Meanwhile, the revival of fur trading by the Bretons from at least 1581, with the subsequent participation of Channel Islanders, Normans, and French Basques, left the whole area open to competition. The Cardinal of Bourbon hoped in 1583 to combine fur trading and missionary activity in Acadia, but the Bellenger voyage of that year (682) produced furs but not settlement. In the 1580s the leading St. Lawrence traders and explorers were the nephew and grand nephews of Jacques Cartier (681), but a monopoly grant to one of them, Jacques Noël, and to a relative Étienne Châton de la Jannaye, in 1588, led to protests from free traders and it was withdrawn except for mineral deposits. Pierre de Chauvin, on November 22, 1599, and January 15, 1600, was authorized to establish settlements in Canada (nominally as La Roche's lieutenant, although La Roche was not satisfied that he had any control of him). His colony at Tadoussac, 1600–1601, was a failure. Meanwhile, in 1598, La Roche brought sturdy beggars and convicts to settle Sable Island (which he renamed Ile de Bourbon) (686). They lived on cattle left there much earlier by the Barcelos family and collected seal and walrus pelts (and walrus ivory) for La Roche. They were under military guard. Chefdhostel, for La Roche, brought supplies and took furs and other goods from them in 1599, 1600, and 1601. He failed to appear in 1602. In 1603 he found that they had killed their guards and a number of themselves. The survivors were repatriated and pardoned by Henry IV, to La Roche's disgust. In 1603, however, La Roche's authority had been revoked and a monopoly and authority as king's lieutenant was conferred on Pierre du Gua, Sieur de Monts.

M. Trudel, *Histoire de la Nouvelle France*, I (Montreal, 1962), and *The Beginnings of New France, 1524–1663* (Montreal, 1974), and Gustave Lanctot, *Réalisations françaises de Cartier à Montcalm* (Montreal, 1951), pp. 29–50, are the best secondary authorities.

681. 1583–1587. News of French discoveries in Canada.

As secretary and chaplain to the English ambassador in Paris (1584–1588), Richard Hakluyt collected narratives (incomplete) of the last Cartier-Roberval expeditions. He is likely to have obtained them indirectly from relatives of Cartier. Jacques Noël, Cartier's nephew, had a Cartier chart and had been himself to the foot of the rapids on the St. Lawrence and learned something of the great lake (Ontario) that lay beyond. This was in 1583 or 1585. He had a chart of his own that he gave to his sons, Michel and Jean, who were in Canada in 1587. Jacques Noël wished to get information on Hakluyt's map, published in his edition of Peter Martyr, De orbe novo decades (Paris, 1587), and contact was made indirectly with him by way of Jean Groute, who knew Hakluyt in Paris. Later, Hakluyt seems to have obtained a map through the Noël family, which showed the lake above the rapids, and it appeared in Edward Wright's map in R. Hakluyt's Principal navigations in 1599. The indirect correspondence of 1587 is (a) letter of June 19, 1587, Jacques Noël to Jean Groute; (b) part of a further letter (also of 1587?) from Noël to Groute. Hakluyt printed them in Principal navigations, III (1600), 236–237 (VIII [1904], 272–274).

On February 12, 1588, Jacques Noël, in partnership with Etienne Cháton de la Jannaye, received a monopoly of the fur trade and mines of Canada for twelve years. In the following year it was withdrawn and the syndicate was left with mineral rights only, which they are not known to have exploited (see Marcel Trudel, The Beginnings of New France [1974], p. 59).

[a] A letter written to M. John Growte student in Paris, by Jaques Noel of S. Malo, the nephew of Jaques Cartier, touching the foresaid discovery.

Master Growte, your brother in law Giles Walter shewed me this morning a Mappe printed at Paris, dedicated to one M. Hakluyt an English Gentleman: wherein all the West Indies, the kingdome of New Mexico, and the Countreys of Canada, Hochelaga and Saguenay are contained. I hold that the River of Canada which is described in that Mappe is not marked as it is in my booke,

which is agreeable to the booke of Jaques Cartier: and that the sayd Chart doth no marke or set downe The great Lake, which is above the Saults, according as the Savages have advertised us, which dwell at the sayd Saults. In the foresayd Chart which you sent me hither, the Great Lake is placed too much toward the North. The Saults or falles of the River stand in 44. degrees of latitude: it is not so hard a matter to passe them, as it is thought: The water falleth not downe from any high place, it is nothing else but that in the middest of the River there is bad ground. It were best to build boates above the Saults: and it is easie to march or travell by land to the end of the three Saults: it is not above five leagues journey. I have bene upon the toppe of a mountaine, which is at the foot of the Saults, where I have seene the sayd River beyond the sayd Saultes, which shewed unto us to be broader then it was where we passed it. The people of the Countrey advertised us, that there are ten dayes journey from the Saults unto this Great Lake. We know not how many leagues they make to a dayes journey. At this present I cannot write unto you more at large, because the messenger can stay no longer. Here therefore for the present I will ende, saluting you with my hearty commendations, praying God to give you your hearts desire. For S. Malo in haste this 19 day of June 1587.
Your loving Friend,
       Jaques Noel.

Cosin, I pray you doe me so much pleasure as to send mee a booke of the discovery of New Mexico, and one of those new Mappes of the West Indies dedicated to M. Hakluyt the English Gentleman, which you sent to your brother in law Giles Walter. I will not faile to informe my selfe, if there be any meane to find out those descriptions which Captaine Cartier made after his two last voyages into Canada.

[b] Underneath the aforesaid unperfite relation that which followeth is written in another letter sent to M. John Growte student in Paris from Jaques Noel of S. Malo, the grand nephew of Jaques Cartier.

I can write nothing else unto you of any thing that I can recover of the writings of Captaine Jaques Cartier my uncle disceased, although I have made search in all places that I could possibly in this

Towne: saving of a certaine booke made in maner of a sea Chart, which was drawne by the hand of my said uncle, which is in the possession of master Cremeur: which booke is passing well marked and drawne for all the River of Canada, whereof I am well assured, because I my self have knowledge thereof as farre as to the Saults, where I have bene: The height of which Saults is in 44. degrees. I found in the sayd Chart beyond the place where the River is divided in twaine in the midst of both the branches of the said river somewhat neerest that arme which runneth toward the Northwest, these words following written in the hand of Jaques Cartier.

By the people of Canada and Hochelaga it was said, That here is the land of Saguenay, which is rich and wealthy in precious stones.

And about an hundred leagues under the same I found written these two lines following in the said Carde enclining toward the Southwest. Here in this Countrey are Cinamon and Cloves, which they call in their language Canodeta.

Touching the effect of my booke whereof I spake unto you, it is made after the maner of a sea Chart, which I have delivered to my two sonnes Michael and John, which at this present are in Canada. If at their returne, which will be God willing about Magdalene tyde, they have learned any new thing worthy the writing, I will not faile to advertise you thereof.
Your loving Friend,
Jaques Noel.

682. 1583. The voyage of Étienne Bellenger to Acadia.

French activity on the coast southward from Cape Breton may well have been continuous in the latter half of the sixteenth century. Étienne Bellenger had been there three times before 1583. In 1583 he made a voyage to trade in furs, to establish a permanent fur-trading station, and to prepare it as a mission station (under the guidance of the Cardinal of Bourbon). He accomplished a substantial coasting from Cape Breton to the tip of Nova Scotia, up the Bay of Fundy (at the head of which he placed a cross), and down the mainland coast, perhaps as far south as Penobscot Bay. He collected a valuable cargo of furs, but lost his pinnace and some men to an Indian attack and did not establish his trading and mission station. Richard Hakluyt met him at Rouen, obtained his story, and also then or later acquired a copy of his map (part of which was incorporated into the 1599 map in Principal navigations*). Bellenger's 1584 voyage was planned to follow up his 1583 venture in association with some English merchants, but nothing is known of its outcome. The Reverend Richard Hakluyt sent the brief account to Dr. Julius Caesar, judge of the High Court of Admiralty.*

B.L., Additional MS 14027, fols. 289–290v., first printed in D. B. Quinn, "The Voyage of Étienne Bellenger to the Maritimes in 1583: A New Document," Canadian Historical Review, *LXIII (1962), 328–343.*

The Relation of master Stephen Bellanger dwelling in Roan in the street called Rue de Augustines at the syne of the golden tyle in frenche thuille deor of his late voiadge of discoverie of two hundreth leagues of coast from Cape Brittone nere Newfound Land West southwest at the charges of the Cardinall of Borbon this last yere 1583. With mention of some of the comodities fownde in those Cuntries and brought home into Fraunce by hym./

Master Stephen Bellanger nowe dwelling in Roan in the streete of the Augustines nexte howsse to the signe of the golden tyle in frenche thuille d'or; departed from Newhaven the 19th of Januarii 1583 in a barck of Fiftie Tons and a little Pinnesse loose within board accompanied with Master Cottee an excellent Pilott of Newhaven and thirtie men and boyes at the charges of the Cardinall of Burbon, and within lesse then a Moneth arrived at Cape Bryton a little to the sowthwest of Newefownde Land./

From thence he toke his course following the Coast along to the southwest for the space of Two hundreth Leagues the draught and particular discription whereof he shewed me/

He discovered all the Bayes, Harbors, Creekes, Rivers, Sandes, Rockes, Islandes, Flattes, with the depthes of Water along as he went which were in some places. 15.30.40.44.50.60. fathoms which he had dilligentlie noted downe in writing within. 50. or threescore Leagues to the west and by south of Cape Briton he had drawne the Iland of St. John which lieth east and west the space of Fiftie leagues, and lieth in forme of a Triangle/

In a great Bay of that Iland which at one place of the enteraunce is so narrowe that a Colverin shott can reache from one side to the other, and after you are passed that streight is xxv leagues upp and 20 leagues broad he planted the Cardinall of Burbons Armes in a mightie highe tree and gave names to many places/

To the west of that Iland about.20. leagues he fownde a great River into which he ran upp with his smale Pynnasse seaven Leagues and thincketh it is navigable three or fowrescore leagues/

He wente on shoare in Tenn or twelve places which he fownde verie pleasaunt. And the coast lieth in 42 43 44 degrees of Latitude more or lesse, and is as warme as Bayon, Bordeux, Rochell, and Nantes varieng a litle as it lieth more to the North or the south/

Salt. He thincketh verilie that verie good salte may be made there in great quantitie in divers places along the Coast seeing there wanteth no heate of the sonne nor lowe of flattes like those of Rochell fytt for the purpose/

Trees. He fownde the Countrey full of good trees to build Shipps withall and namely great plentie of oakes, Cypresses, Pynes, hasels etc and divers good herbes as sorrell etc.

Trafficke. In many places he had traffique with the people which are of verie good disposition and stature of Bodie

They weare their hayre hanging downe long before and behynde as lowe as their Navells which they cutt short only overthwart their browes

They go all naked saving their privities which they cover with an Apron of some Beastes skynn, and tye it unto them with a long buff gerdle that comes three times about them beeing made fast behynde and at boath the endes it is cutt into litle thynn thonges, which thonges they tye rownde about them with slender quils of birdes fethers wherof some are as red as if they had byn dyed in cuchanillo/

Their girdells have also before a litle Codd or Pursse of Buff wherein they putt divers thinges but especiallie their tinder to keepe fire in, which is of a dry roote and somewhat like a hard sponge and will quicklie take fyer and is hardlie put out./
Their weapons wherof he brought hoame store to the Cardinall are Bowes of two yardes long and arrowes of one yarde hedded with indented bones three or fower ynches long, and are tyed into a nocke at the ende with a thong of Lether/

In divers places they are gentle and tractable. But those about Cape Briton and threescore or fowerscore leagues Westward are more cruell and subtill of norture then the rest. And you are not to trust them but to stond upon your gard/ For among them he lost two of his men and his smale Pinesse which happned through their owne follye in trusting the salvadges to farr/

Commodities brought home. He had traffique with them in divers places and for trifles, as knyves belles, glasses, and suche like smale marchaundize which cost hym but Fortie livers which amount but to fower Poundes Englishe he had by waie of traffique comodities that he sould in Roan at his retourne. for Fower hundreth and Fortie Crownes/

Theis were some of the Comodities which he brought hoame from thence, & showed them me at his howsse./

1. Buff hides reddie dressed upon both sides bigger than an Oxe,

2. Deere skynes dressed well on the inner side, with the hayre on the outside/

3. Seale skynns exceding great dressed on the ynnerside/

4. Marterns enclyning unto Sables

5. Bevers skynes verie fayre as many as made 600 bever hattes

6. Otters skynnes verie faire and large

7. A kynde of liquide muske or sivet taken out of the Bevers stones/

8. The fleshe of Deere dried in the sunne in peeces a foote Long/

9. Divers excellent Cullors, as scarlet, vermillion, redd, tawny, yellowe, gray and watchett/

10. Fethers the quils wherof are redd as vermillion

11. Luserns, which the frenche call Loupcerviers Whereof twentie he gave to the Cardinall of Burbon for a present, and divers others to certaine of his frendes which I sawe, and was enformed that they were worth some 6.8.10.12.15 crownes a skynne/

12. A kynde of mynerall matter which as some that have seene thinck houldes sylver and tynn, whereof he gave me a peece/

Divers other comodities he fownde the secrites wherof he was loath to disclose unto me/

He affirmeth by his owne experience that fishe

of that Coast on the which he hath byn thrise, is bigger and better then that of New found Land; and that the havens are exceding good/

He was out upon his voiadge but Foure Moneths and a half

He hathe drawen a fayre Carde of all his discoverie which he presented latelie to the Cardinall of Burbon/

His first draught he shewed me at his howsse and all the comodities above mentioned and gave me parte of each of them for his kynnesmanns sake one Andrewe Mayer the Compasse maker of Roan. which made me acquaynted with hym/

He hath also made brief relation of his voiadge in the presences of divers Englishe men of Credit whome I brought into his Companie that they might here the same And namely of one Master Harvie of Lymehouse the owner of the Barck called the Thomas & John of Master Malym master of the barck called the Christian of one Moyser an englishe merchannt of Roan and one Howe a sayler & other honest men/

And this present yere 1584 he setteth fourth agayne for further Traffique in the same voiadge with a barck and a smale Pinesse which are in preparing ayenst the first of Marche at Homefleur upon the Coast of Normandy

Upon knowledge of this voiadge made by Master Stephen Bellanger divers Englishe merchauntes of Roan have conferred togeather to contribute to the furthering of the voiadge which is nowe to be sett forth in England namely theis/ Master Greene, Master Lacie, Master Grove, Master Martyn, Master Moyser, Master [ ] his chamber fellowe, Master Walbn, Master Smyth the owner of the Inne called the Diepe, Master Harvie of Lymehouse, Master Richardson of Hull, Master Malym, Master Bellpytt and Master Mychell both of Weymouth, Master Vyney, &c.

[Endorsed:] A discowrse of the newefound land. 1584.

683. January 12, 1598. Henry IV grants to the Marquis de la Roche the right to take criminals out to Canada.

Photostat, Public Archives of Canada, MG.18, 84, abstract.

Henry IV grants to the Marquis de la Roche "on the occasion of the voyage which he is going to make for our service to the Isles of Canada and adjacent" the right to levy those condemned and those to be condemned to take with him. Paris, January 12, 1598.

[Signed:] Henry Potier

684. March 1, 1598. Commission for raising a company of soldiers to accompany the Marquis de la Roche to Canada.

In virtue of letters from King Henry IV, the governor of Normandy ordered the raising of a company of 100 infantry (under a lieutenant yet to be named) to accompany the Marquis de la Roche to Canada, provided they do so within two weeks after the company is raised.

Original in H. I. Morse Collection, Houghton Library, Harvard University; printed and translated in H. I. Morse, Acadiensia Nova, *2 vols. (London, 1929), II, 28–30.*

Henry de Bourbon, Duke of Montpensier, Peer of France, Governor and Lieutenant General for my Lord the King in Normandy. Having seen His Majesty's Letters of Commission to which these presents are attached under our seal, signed Henry and lower down, for the King, Potier, by which his aforesaid Majesty, having recognized how useful the conquest of the Islands of Canada and others adjacent may be to the welfare and advancement of his affairs, has resolved to give charge of them to the Lord Marquis de la Roche, and wishing to give him the means of bringing to perfection such an enterprise according to the affection he bears to it, has decreed that he be assisted with the necessary number of soldiers, and to this end has appointed as Commissioner and Deputy Sieur de [ ] in order to raise a company of one hundred of the best and most experienced French infantry that can be found among the best and most proved soldiers that he can choose and select, to employ these in exploits of war, that may be met with for His Majesty's service under the said Lord Marquis de la Roche his Lieutenant-General in the conquest of the said islands during his voyage to the place whither he will by him be ordered, always on the condition of his embarking with the said company two weeks after the raising of the same without further tarrying in the country according as it is more fully set forth and contained in the said letters, to the effect and registration of which according to their form and tenour we consent, so far as concerns us, so that the raising of this company may be carried out on the charges and conditions hereinbefore stated, without tarrying in the country more than two weeks after the same, commanding to this end all Justiciars, Officers, Subjects of His Majesty to afford the said Sieur [   ] every comfort and assistance of which he may stand in need.

Given at Rouen, the first day of March, one thousand five hundred and ninety-eight.

[Signed:] Henry de Bourbon

For my Lord the aforesaid Governor and Lieutenant General
[Signed:] Gaveau

685. May 20, 1598. The Parlement of Normandy authorizes the transportation of 250 persons to Canada.

The Parlement of Normandy was prepared to transfer to the Marquis de la Roche 200 men and 50 women from among the sturdy beggars who could be rounded up in Rouen to be transported to Sable Island.

Rouen, Archives de la Seine-Inférieure, Parlement de Normandie, Archives Secrètes, 20 Mai 1598, fol. 189v., printed and translated in W. I. Morse, Acadiensia Nova, 2 vols. (London, 1929), II, 34–35.

20th May, 1598.

On the occurrence of several matters which were presented in the first place in reference to the thefts which are committed nightly in this town, and even during last night, Monsieur Eaufranc de Pylon, lieutenant general of the police of Rouen, was sent for and was brought in, and before him were laid the complaints of the said thefts and how that he in spite of them felt himself under no obligation to put into action any of the

investigations which other lieutenants were known to have made use of at other times in similar matters and how that vigilance seemed to have been relaxed at present; whereupon the said lieutenant declared that as soon as they received any information, either from the police or the detectives, they inform themselves of the matter and take all possible measures, but that they discover nothing from the information given, and that with reference to a burglary committed in a house of St. Etienne, they are holding a prisoner, on the trial of whom they are at present engaged: and that if it will please the Court to see what they have done, the Court will recognize the care they are taking. He was dismissed and recalled after the matter had been discussed, and he was enjoined to proceed at once to complete the trial on which he was engaged, and to make a careful investigation, both himself and his investigators, of the vagabonds and tramps, in order to take steps against them according to their position and reason given by those who are found; moreover the Court advised him to have a trumpet proclamation made in order to assemble in the four quarters of the town each and every one of the strong tramps and beggars, both men and women, and to choose and take from the said number as many as 200 men and 50 women to be sent to Canada, according to the will, and intention of the King, and for that purpose that they be handed over to the Marquis de la Roche, and that while waiting for the arrangement of the said voyage they be fastened in pairs and employed on public works and provided with bread and provisions, and that the said tramps be enjoined to obey without wandering or begging any more through the streets under penalty of the lash, whereupon the said lieutenant general [   ].

It was likewise ordered that Monseigneurs should travel through the parishes according to the division which was presently to be made, in order to inform themselves at the various houses of the position of those living there who did not belong to the household.

And this being done, the matter of helping the poor was discussed.

686. May 23, 1598. Sturdy beggars rounded up at Rouen to go to Canada.

The chief of police in Rouen rapidly rounded up 800 sturdy beggars and gave 250 of them the chance to go to Canada. He reckoned to get a sufficient number of the healthiest, if they were fed promptly and properly.

Rouen, Archives de la Seine-Inférieure, Parlement de Normandie, Archives Secrètes, 23 Mai 1598, fol. 192v.; printed and translated in W. I. Morse, Acadiensia Nova, II (1929), 36.

23rd May, 1598.

Monsieur Eaufranc, lieutenant general of the police of Rouen, was brought in and he declared that in pursuance of the order of the Court he had caused to assemble all the healthy poor in the four quarters of the town; of these there were found as many as 800 and more, both men and women and children, and he had let them know that it was the intention of the King and of the Court to take a certain number of the said poor, the strongest and healthiest, to make use of them in an expedition to Canada; some of them had declared that they preferred to return to their own country, others that they were ready to go on the voyage; he declared that most of them came from Neufbourg, Harcourt and near Bayeulz, and that in view of the declaration of the said poor people that they would do whatever was required, provided that they were fed, he had not imprisoned them. The lieutenant was told that the Court would make provision and he withdrew.

687. 1598. The Marquis de la Roche fails to get a criminal reprieved to go to Canada.

Rouen, Archives de la Seine-Inférieure, Registre de Parlement de Normandie, MG.18, B2, fol. 212 (copy in Public Archives of Canada, Ottawa), translated.

Jacques La Tainturier (otherwise Graumare) having been condemned to death by order of the Vacation Chamber of October 4, 1598, which confirmed the sentence given against him one year before, was returned to the Bailwick of Rouen for

the said Tainturier to be executed. The Marquis de la Roche presented himself to the same (or his lieutenant), and demanded that the said Tainturier should be delivered to be sent to the islands of Canada, Sable or Norembecque. On returning the matter to the Chamber the said Marquis de la Roche presented his request for the same according to the order of September 10, which without having regard to the said requisition of the Marquis de la Roche ordered that the said decree of October 14 ought to be confirmed and execution done against the said Tainturier who was accused of villainy in raping a girl.

688. 1606. The Marquis de la Roche recalls his settlement of Sable Island.

This document refers obliquely to his long formal connection with Canada, from 1577 to 1603, and protests that others have been given privileges due to himself. Its main importance is that in 1597 or 1598 he is said to have been given 12,000 crowns by Henry IV, that he kept his men on Sable Island from 1598–1603 (victualing them except in one year by Captain Chefdhostel), and that they finally turned on his lieutenant, Querbonyer, Captain Coussez, and others and killed them. When survivors were brought back to France in 1603 they were rewarded instead of being hanged. Since 1603 the Sieur de Monts had usurped his position and, it might appear, taken over Sable Island, which La Roche appears to hope will be returned to him.

Paris, Bibliothèque de L'Institut, Collection Godefroy, CCXCI; translated in W. I. Morse, Acadiensia Nova, II (1929), 31–33. Reprinted in French in Robert Le Blant and René Baudry, eds., Nouveaux documents sur Champlain et son époque (Ottawa, 1967), pp. 63–68.

Document sent by the Marquis Troïllus de Mesgouës de la Roche-Mesgouëz in Brittany to King Henry IV about the year 1598 or 1599 at the time of the Peace with the Duc de Mercoeur, chiefly on the subject of the trouble and opposition he met with in the Isle de Bourbon [situated] 25 leagues distant from Cape Breton towards New France

[= Sable Island], and in Florida in America, in the bay along the river towards Cadessart [= Tadoussac], possession of which [territories] was granted to him by Kings Henry III and IV....

Finding myself without commission from Your Majesty, I desired to withdraw from France to undertake the voyage to America, with which the late King Henry charged me, and I received from Your Majesty a like charge, which caused me to set out for the Isle de Bourbon [Sable Island] which lies 25 leagues from Cape Breton.

While I was absent from France Your Majesty made peace and declared me a prisoner to be ransomed for 3,000 crowns: this was paid out of my own money, without it pleasing Your Majesty to consider that Monsieur de Mercoeur was indebted to me for my imprisonment, the ruin of my lands, forests and houses which were burned and rased, and damages to the extent of more than 120,000 crowns.

Returning from there at the end of four months I came to find Your Majesty at Monceaux, where Your Majesty promised to have continued the payment to me of one crown per ton of merchandise coming and loading at the ports of Normandy. After coming to Paris Your Majesty had sent to me an order for 12,000 crowns on this account; this was sent and it was collected and controlled by the comptrollers.

In this waiting from year to year my men have lived there more than five years, during which time (except in one year) I sent the Captain Chefdhôtel de Voteuille to take to them supplies of wine and clothing.

Because of this length of time they set themselves to plot against a gentleman named Querbonyer, a Breton who lived there in my absence as Your Majesty's lieutenant; him they killed wickedly and treacherously while he slept. Afterwards they killed the Captain named Coussez, Master of the Magazine, and they went on to kill six or seven more. Nevertheless when they came to France, instead of being hanged for their misdeeds, they were rewarded with money, in spite of the fact that they had themselves confessed to the murders. During this time Monsieur Belinguant told me that to his belief Your Majesty gave to Captain Chauvin a similar commission to mine, and on coming to see you that you reduced Chauvin to having no other command than of being one of my lieutenants within a hundred leagues only in the bay along the river towards Cadessart.

The said Monsieur Belinguant told me, and he assured me that it was the truth, that in order to secure this commission Chauvin had shown the greatest effrontery there ever was in dealing with Your Majesty, declaring that he had been in the country and that he knew everything, as was false, inasmuch as he had never been there, and took to help him in his imposture a man named Le Pont [= François Gravé] from St Malo, who had been there, one who cheated his associates who were engaged in trade at St Malo. The said Chauvin knew that he had encroached more than he ought upon me, and having almost ruined all his extensive means for this purpose, he thereupon died of chagrin.

Monsieur de Monts, who had never been there or even at sea, proceeded to form a company with the late Chauvin, dead though he was; he purposed to encroach upon me and the commission which Your Majesty had given me. It is three years ago since this de Monts carried out his great exploits, and he has succeeded in putting himself behind five or six isles, whereby he protects himself. The isle [Isle of Bourbon, Sable Island] is of small extent and very thinly populated and has little likelihood of being of service to Your Majesty. Nevertheless through the support of those who maintain him and share his profits, many of your subjects suffer numerous misfortunes [at his hands].

[Signed:] Troïllus de Mesgouëz

New France—Acadia and the St. Lawrence, 1603–1612

BEFORE 1600 France had made several attempts to establish colonies in the eastern parts of North America, from Florida to the St. Lawrence. All had failed, due mainly to inexperience in the management of colonies and the hostility of Spain. However, the link with the New World was maintained by the yearly visits of French fishermen to the Newfoundland Banks and to the island harbors, and some of these men penetrated into the mouth of the St. Lawrence and established a trade in furs with the Indians. Although, through fear of interference, the traders and fishermen were reluctant to discuss their activities, inevitably their knowledge of America percolated through to people such as the Marquis de la Roche, François Gravé du Pont, and Jean de Biencourt, Sieur de Poutrincourt, men interested in exploration and colonization who became the prime movers in the new attempts at French settlement in America in the opening decade of the seventeenth century, when peace in Europe and the friendly attitude of Henry IV combined to create a favorable climate for French expansion.

The French chose Acadia and the St. Lawrence region as the areas for their activity in the New World. These areas were well known to many of the seamen, through the fishing link, and were sufficiently far removed from the Spanish possessions in Florida and the West Indies. Above all, the discovery by Cartier of the St. Lawrence had established a claim by France that was rarely challenged. However, the French government saw the establishment of a settlement in the St. Lawrence region as a means of securing its absolute authority in the area. To achieve this, a monopoly of the fur trade (under the Marquis de la Roche) was granted for ten years to Pierre Chauvin who, in return, was to send out colonists. However, his first attempt at settlement at Tadoussac on the St. Lawrence in 1600–1601 failed, and it was agreed that more information was needed on the area and on its native inhabitants before a successful colony could be established. In fact, beyond its mouth little advance in knowledge of the St. Lawrence had been made since the time of Cartier.

In 1603 a small expedition was sent to America. The vessel carried no colonists, since the chief aim was to explore the river to the point of Cartier's farthest penetration, and while doing this to choose a site suitable for settlement. The party was led by François Gravé and among its members was Samuel Champlain. He had traveled in the Spanish colonies between 1599 and 1601. In 1603, to reinforce his claim for a royal pension, he presented to the king an illustrated report on his observations in which he condemned much of the Spanish colonial policy, especially the treatment of the natives. His experiences in the Caribbean were to prove valuable in molding his own ideas on colonization and on the conversion of the Indians, which he was to put into practice in Canada. Champlain was offered a place on the 1603 expedition with specific orders to explore the St. Lawrence and bring back a full report, complete with maps. The ships landed at Tadoussac in May, and Champlain with Gravé and five sailors transferred to a small vessel and explored the river as far as the Lachine Rapids which, as in Cartier's time, was regarded as an obstacle to further progress. Champlain augmented his own observations with information obtained from the Indians. From them he learned of the existence of Lake George, the Hudson River, Lakes Ontario, Erie, and Huron, and Niagara Falls. He was very excited at the possibility that these lakes and rivers linked together to form the prized passage to China and the East. Indeed, the whole expedition proved successful for Champlain. He reported that the area was eminently suited for colonization and noted several possible sites for settlement. The fur trade was already organized and promised immediate profit, and the natives were friendly and willing to help the French.

The Indians encountered by Champlain were not of the same tribe as those who met Cartier. The Hurons, who inhabited the St. Lawrence in the mid-sixteenth century, had been driven away to the area around Lake Huron, most likely by the powerful Iroquois groups that lived in the region to the south, in what is now upper New York State. They had been replaced by Algonquin Indians, who had their headquarters on the Ottawa River, and by a branch of the Montagnais, a widely dispersed group of similar linguistic stock, who controlled the lower St. Lawrence. When Champlain arrived at Tadoussac the Algonquin and Montagnais were celebrating a victory against their traditional enemies, the Iroquois. By the beginning of the seventeenth century, the quarrels between the two groups were becoming exacerbated by an additional factor, the control of the trade in furs with the Europeans. The French, to ease trade and settlement in the St. Lawrence, wished to gain the friendship of the Indians of the river basin, and hence Champlain and Gravé promised the help of their nation against the Iroquois. It was a fateful decision since it created hostility between the French and the Iroquois, who were later to become the ally of the English and were to be instrumental in helping the latter drive out the French from Canada in the eighteenth century. But all this was in the future, and it was an optimistic Champlain who reported back to the king.

However, the colonists sent out to America the following year did not head for the St. Lawrence but for Acadia to the south. The leader of the enterprise, Pierre du Gua, Sieur de Monts, who now had control of the fur monopoly, had experience on the St. Lawrence in 1600 and appears to have believed that the winters in that region were too harsh. Champlain suggests that de Monts feared interference with the colony from illicit fur traders. Certainly de Monts, in choosing to go to the south, seems to have been more concerned with establishing a colony than with commercial profit. Two ships left France in March, 1604, with 120 colonists, consisting of workmen, gentlemen, Poutrincourt, and Champlain, whose special task was to make a survey of the area and report on his findings. They sailed up the Bay of Fundy and chose an island in the St. Croix River (now the boundary between Canada and the United States) as the site for settlement. However, after the colony endured an exceptionally hard winter, Champlain was sent out in June to find a better site. He sailed down the New England coast as far as a point beyond Cape Cod. No site was found, but Champlain did take the opportunity to explore the coast and to observe its inhabitants. On his return it was decided to move the colony across the bay to Port Royal (Annapolis Basin), which had been discovered the previous year. Although the winter was milder, twelve of the forty-five men died of scurvy. When the supply ships from France failed to arrive on time, it was decided to abandon the colony and go north in the fishing vessels to find a passage to Europe. Off the coast of Nova Scotia they encountered the relief ship that contained more colonists, including Marc Lescarbot, who later wrote of his experiences in New France, and who was to become a great propagandist for settlement in America. They all returned to Port Royal, and Champlain again set out to explore the coast to the south. He went as far as Nantucket Island before the onset of winter forced him to return north. Since the winter was mild, the French did not have to use all their energies in survival and were able to turn to other matters, such as cultivating the friendship of the local Micmac Indians. From the writings of Lescarbot and Champlain, it appears that relations between the two peoples were good. They tell of meals to which the chiefs were invited and of the Indians coming to live near the French settlement. In May, 1607, a supply ship arrived from France with the news that the monopoly held by de Monts had been revoked and trade had again been thrown open to all.

Most of the men, including Lescarbot and Champlain, decided to return to France, but some decided to come back to maintain a French presence at Port Royal; and Poutrincourt, for example, decided that he would bring his family over to settle. He eventually returned in 1610, accompanied by a parish priest who engaged in missionary work among the Indians—work that was so successful that within three weeks he had converted and baptized the chief and twenty others. However, one is left to wonder how genuine these "conversions" were. Poutrincourt applauded the efforts of the priest, because he was anxious to prove that Jesuit missionaries, who were being pressed on him by influential figures at Court, were not required at Port Royal. However, the following year Biencourt, his son, was forced to take out for financial reasons two Jesuits, Fathers Biard and Ennemond Massé. They were joined in 1612 by a lay brother, but their work was hampered by the attitude of Poutrincourt and by the difficulty they had in mastering the Indian languages. Thus, in 1613 the Jesuits in France sent out their own men to form another colony down the mainland coast on or near Mount Desert Island. Unfortunately, this was not to last long for in the same year an English expedition attacked the post, destroyed the colony, and took prisoners back to Virginia. Later, the colony of Poutrincourt suffered a similar fate. However, a few Frenchmen managed to remain in Acadia and ensured that the area would retain some of its Gallic character, something which has lasted down to the present.

Meanwhile, Champlain turned his attention back to the St. Lawrence. He had come to the conclusion that the area of the Bay of Fundy was not sufficiently favorable for the fur trade and, more importantly, his survey of the coast had revealed nothing that gave hope for a passage to the East. In January, 1608, helped by de Monts, he persuaded Henry IV to renew the fur monopoly. Later in the year, de Monts and his partners fitted out two ships for the St. Lawrence, which from that time on was to become the chief focus of French effort in America. Despite holding the fur monopoly and authority to settle, Champlain encountered great hostility from the established summer fur traders, who saw the colony as a threat to their livelihood. At Tadoussac the hostility erupted into fighting. Peace was restored only when it was agreed that the dispute should be settled in France. Champlain continued upriver and founded the settlement of Québec at a point where the river narrows to a width of less than one mile. After foiling a plot against his life by disgruntled associates, he organized the building of shelters and defense works and gathered in food for the winter (which passed with the loss of fifteen out of the twenty-eight men).

Undaunted, Champlain set out in June, 1609, to explore the land around Québec and took part with his Montagnais and Algonquin allies in a raiding party against the Iroquois. They sailed along the St. Lawrence to the mouth of the Richelieu River and then turned south along that river to Lake Champlain, where the battle took place. The Frenchman witnessed the victory of his allies and the subsequent victory celebrations that included the torture of Iroquois prisoners. The Montagnais Indians returned to Tadoussac with Champlain, who set sail for France to report on his progress in Canada, but he returned to Québec the following year. Some limited exploration was undertaken, but Champlain soon discovered that the natives in the interior, the Algonquin on the Ottawa River and the Huron on Lake Huron, were unwilling to allow a European to visit their lands. They regarded themselves as middlemen through whom the white men could trade in furs with the remoter tribes. However, Champlain persuaded an Algonquin chief to allow a French boy, Etienne Brûlé, to spend the winter with his people, and in return he took an Indian back with him to France. In 1611 Champlain again went to the St. Lawrence to find that the Indians had been scared by rumors that the French were to join with the Iroquois against them. As a result they were late in bringing their furs to the rapids to trade and were soon frightened away by the rough and unfair treatment meted out by the traders. Champlain went beyond the Lachine Rapids to the Indian camp to make peace. After the fears of the Indians had been quelled, they agreed to take two Frenchmen to spend the winter with them. One of these, Henry Vignau, went with the Algonquin as far north as Hudson's Bay. Champlain himself returned to France for a deep consideration of the progress of his colonizing enterprises.

It was obvious that unlicensed traders were a threat to any stability in the St. Lawrence area. Their ruthless search for furs had frightened the Indians and created a potentially dangerous situation that had been calmed only by the personal intervention of Champlain, at least that is how he presented the picture. The cooperation of the natives was necessary for peaceful exploration and colonization of the land, and it was for this reason that Champlain had allied France with the Montagnais and Algonquin against the Iroquois. Colonists and missionaries were not likely to be attracted to New France unless the activities of the traders could be curbed and peaceful relations established with the Indians. Throughout 1612 he worked to renew the monopoly that had been achieved, but only for trade west of Québec. However, he was able to return with plans to bring colonists and missionaries. In the years after 1613 he explored the Ottawa River and Lakes Nipissing, Huron, and Ontario and secured the French foothold in

Canada. Recollets and Jesuits soon began their missionary work, which was to last for over a century. An incidental result of their activities was an increased awareness of the area around the St. Lawrence and beyond. Jesuits were often the first white men to penetrate and to explore strange lands in their search for souls. Largely because of their efforts, French knowledge of North America was always far ahead of that of the English. However, the French settlements in America remained essentially trading posts. In the whole of Champlain's lifetime there were rarely more than one hundred French residents throughout Canada. This was not the fault of men of ideals like Champlain, who had a wider vision of the benefits of colonization, but they were unable to transmit their ideas to the French Crown or to convince the authorities of the need for permanent settlements like those the English had established to the south.

Information on French activity in Acadia and the St. Lawrence before 1612 can be gained from three main sources, all written by men who crossed the Atlantic and who were instrumental in creating New France. The most important of the three are the works of Samuel Champlain who saw himself not only as an explorer, but also as a propagandist for French colonization of the area. Instead of staying for any length of time in Canada, he returned home in the winters of 1609, 1610, and 1611 and spent the whole of 1612 in France. During these visits he worked tirelessly to promote his ideas among men of power and influence and wrote avidly to the king and the Chamber of Commerce. He was among those who persuaded the Crown to renew the fur monopoly in 1608 and 1612. To increase his knowledge of America he sent Frenchmen to winter with the Indians and brought back natives with him to France in exchange. The latter were used to encourage promoters and settlers. But his chief instruments of persuasion were his own writings.

It was his careful report on the West Indies that first brought him to the notice of the king and gained him the appointment as official geographer on the 1603 expedition to the St. Lawrence. On this trip Champlain explored the region of Tadoussac and went upriver as far as the rapids beyond Montreal. On his return he published an account of what he had seen under the title of *Des Sauvages*. However, he was unable to convince others of his belief that the St. Lawrence was an eminently suitable area for settlement, for the expedition mounted the following year went south to Acadia. Champlain, apparently undeterred by this rebuff to his views, went along again in the role of geographer. During his stay he explored and mapped the Bay of Fundy and the coast of New England as far south as Nantucket Sound. But his travels failed to shake his belief that the St. Lawrence held the best chance of colonial and commercial success for his country. Between 1608 and 1611 he visited the area three times, spending the winter of 1608–1609 in the infant colony at Quebec. He explored the St. Lawrence as far as the Lachine Rapids and went down the Richelieu River to the lake that now bears his name. On his return from a fourth visit in 1613, his writings on Acadia and the St. Lawrence were published, as *Les voyages*. He updated this work in 1619 to include a description of his travels in New France since 1613. In 1632 he published what was his last work, *Les voyages de la Nouvelle France occidentale, dicte Canada, faits par le Sieur de Champlain*. In this he gives a history of New France up to 1631 but, although he corrects a few errors made in his earlier writings, many details and even some important episodes are omitted. Although Champlain's works are not unique, since they cover much the same events as Marc Lescarbot, they were throughout the result of immediate experience and must rank as the greater in historical value and interest. Champlain relates the history of New France and, more importantly, describes the country and its inhabitants. For example, the work of 1603 includes the earliest description of the Algonkian Indians of eastern Canada. At present Champlain's work appeals principally as a history, but it was valued by his contemporaries more as a topographical study. Prior to his travels, the Atlantic coast of Canada and New England were known only through the largely inaccurate maps and loose narratives of earlier explorers. Champlain replaced these by accurate descriptions and maps based on proper scientific surveys. The most important of the maps was completed in 1607 (although it was not published) and shows the results of three years activity in Acadia. There are some discrepancies between the early maps and the narratives. This suggests to W. E. Ganong in his introduction to the work on Acadia that Champlain's descriptions were not always written directly from the journals he kept in America, but from written memoranda aided by memory. However, Champlain did not need notes to help him express his views on the whole concept of colonization, views which appear throughout his books. He was convinced that France should make a determined effort to explore and colonize Canada, a land that he believed had no equal anywhere else in the world. Colonization would give control of the lucrative fur trade to France and exploration, with the possibility of discovering a passage to the East, would not only result in financial reward to France but would also benefit the natives by bringing missionaries to convert and educate them, thus protecting them from the depredations that the Indians to the south had suffered in the hands of the Spaniards.

The writings of Champlain have long been acknowledged as having great value to any study of New France. His complete works were reprinted in French, edited by C. H. Lavadière, *Oeuvres de Champlain*, 3 vols. (Université Laval, Québec, 1870). Several English translations of pieces of his writings have been made; the earliest was of *Des Sauvages* by Samuel Purchas, which appeared in *Pilgrimes*, IV (1625), 1605-1619. The complete works were translated by a group led by H. P. Biggar for the Champlain Society, *The Works of Samuel de Champlain*, 7 vols. (Toronto, 1922–1926, reprinted 1971).

Marc Lescarbot, who wrote *L'histoire de la Nouvelle France*, at first glance appears to be a most unlikely recruit for colonization. A lawyer by profession, he had published some orations and translations from Latin. However, among his clients was the Sieur de Poutrincourt who asked Lescarbot if he would care to accompany him to Port Royal in 1606. Having just suffered some injustice, Lescarbot agreed and spent a year in Acadia, returning to France when news of the revocation of the fur monopoly was received. The next two years were spent preparing an account of French activity in New France, drawn largely from his own experiences. The book, dedicated to the king, Marie de Médicis, and other notables, aroused great public interest when it appeared in 1609. An English translation of part of the work (*Nova Francia*) was made in the same year. In addition Lescarbot wrote letters describing his experiences, such as the one penned at Port Royal in August, 1606, which relates the Atlantic voyage and his first impressions of the area. Although he was not to visit New France again, he maintained his interest in the progress of colonization there. New and enlarged editions of his history appeared in 1611, 1614, and 1618, along with shorter works on the need to convert the Indians and a description of events in the Acadia settlement after 1607. His work is of greater literary merit than that of Champlain and provides a good complement to it. For example, he gives much more vivid detail on events when both men were at Port Royal and on the Atlantic crossing since this was a completely new experience to Lescarbot, whereas by 1606 Champlain had traversed the ocean several times.

Lescarbot is very enthusiastic when discussing Port Royal and compares it with the promised land of the Israelites. He dwells at length on the problems of sustaining a colony, noting his belief that scurvy was caused by bad meat and could be cured by lemon juice. He also gives good and sympathetic descriptions of the Indians and was obviously deeply troubled by their ignorance of Christianity. He recommended that they should be converted by the French to prevent them from being exposed to Spain. However, at the same time he was strongly anti-Jesuit, blaming Father Biard for provoking the English attack on Port Royal, and believing that they had no part to play in missionary work. Above all, like Champlain, he was a champion of French colonization and he spends much time stressing the benefits of settlement, not for any riches that might accrue from the discovery of gold, but for the wealth that agriculture and trade would bring. His work can therefore be seen not only as a description of the land and natives of Acadia, but also as a passionate appeal for France to plant in the New World for her own advancement as well as for the benefit of the natives. In his books he laid down a program for the development of the French overseas empire. It was this program that Champlain strove to put into effect, and it was later adopted by the French government. Lescarbot's *L'histoire de la Nouvelle France* (1609) is now regarded as one of the classic works of the period of exploration but, curiously, no new complete French edition has appeared since 1866. However, a book of selections from it was published in 1968. The 1609 translation into English was reissued in 1745, and in 1928 it was edited by H. P. Biggar. Purchas translated the part that relates to the Acadia colony and published it in 1625. A new translation of the 1618 edition was made by W. L. Grant in three volumes for the Champlain Society in 1907–1914. Included in volume III of this work is the letter in French, probably written by Lescarbot from Port Royal in 1606, together with a translation of the letter. Lescarbot's minor works on colonization, *La conversion des sauvages qui ont esté baptizés en la Nouvelle France cette année 1610* and *Relation dernière qui s'est passé au voyage du sieur de Poutrincourt en La Nouvelle France*, appeared in print in 1610 and 1612, respectively. Both were reprinted by Lucien Campeau in *Monumenta Novae Franciae I. La première mission d'Acadie (1602–1616)* (Rome and Québec, 1967), having earlier been translated by Reuben G. Thwaites in his *Jesuit Relations*, vols. I and II (Cleveland, 1896).

The third major source on the history of New France between 1603 and 1612 can be found in the writings of the Jesuits who, by 1612, had just begun their valuable work among the Canadian Indians. As early as March, 1605, members of the order considered sending out missionaries to Acadia. It appears that they were worried by the strong Huguenot element in the colony, but they thought it best to wait to see how the settlement progressed. Meanwhile, the leaders of the colony, de Monts and Poutrincourt, with the help of Lescarbot, who printed a list of all the converts, were trying to prove that conversion and baptism were being carried out successfully without the help of the Jesuits. In fact, despite the presence of Catholics in the colony, little was done until Poutrincourt brought out a parish priest with him in 1610. Two years previously the Society of Jesus had induced the king to provide 100 livres a year for the support of two Jesuit priests in Acadia. In 1610 two missionaries were ready to sail, but they were hindered by the attitude of the Huguenot merchants and by Poutrincourt himself who left without them. But the following year, in order to gain essential financial support from the court, Poutrincourt's son, Biencourt, was forced to take over two Jesuits. The following year the Society equipped and sent out a ship of its own carrying forty-eight men and two more missionaries. Because of continuous harassment by the colonists, the fathers were forced to found their own settlement and there begin their work of conversion and exploration, which was to last in New France until their Order was removed from the continent. The letters written by these men provide a valuable insight into life in New France, especially into the customs of the Indians, and their opinions form a good contrast to those expressed by men like Poutrincourt and Lescarbot. Several collections of the letters have been published in French, the first edited by Auguste Carayon, *La Première Mission des Jésuits au Canada* (Paris, 1864). More recent is the collection edited by Lucien Campeau, *La première mission d'Acadie* (1967). Many of the letters had already been translated into English by Reuben Thwaites in the earlier volumes of *Jesuit Relations*, from 1896 onward.

Chapter Eighty-six
The Sieur de Monts and North America,
1603–1607

By 1603, HENRY IV was not confident that anything effective would be done by the Marquis de la Roche in Canada. He was approached by Pierre du Gua, Sieur de Monts, a Huguenot nobleman, who offered an interesting proposition. The 1603 voyage made under his auspices (703) had given him the idea that settlement (as distinct from commerce) was unlikely to be successful in the St. Lawrence Valley, but that successful settlement was possible in Acadia. On November 6 the king agreed in the main to his propositions: (a) he was to have a monopoly of the territory between 40° and 46°N, and to settle 100 persons every year, some of whom could be able-bodied beggars and reprieved criminals. He was himself (and his Rouen associates) to bear two-thirds of the cost while Monsieur de Danville, Admiral of Brittany, would be responsible for the remaining third; (b) in recompense he was to control the whole fur trade with the St. Lawrence River and issue licenses for its exploitation, which would provide him with revenue to carry on colonizing and trading in Acadia (689–690). The patent was issued on December 8, and a printed proclamation was circulated, warning all those engaged in trading that they could do so only under a Commission from the Sieur de Monts, with heavy penalties if they did not. A copy later came into Spanish hands (766). This was the basis for the French activities on the Acadia and New England coasts, 1603–1607, and the attempt to levy license money from the St. Lawrence River fur traders. Neither of these was in the end successful—the Sieur de Monts never obtained the capital that would enable him to plant sufficient settlers in Acadia, the trade with Acadia did not prove profitable, and the enforcement of the licensing system on the St. Lawrence fur traders proved impossible to implement effectively. The patent did lead to the exploration, under Champlain, of the whole coast from the Bay of Fundy to Nantucket Sound and to the establishment (after the 1604–1605 experience of Ste Croix) to the Port Royal *habitacion* from 1605 onward.

689. November 6, 1603. The propositions of the Sieur de Monts to Henry IV for his settlement of Acadia and Henry IV's replies.

W. I. Morse, Pierre du Gua, Sieur de Monts *(London, 1939), pp. 6–8, translated.*

Articles proposed to the King by the Sieur de Mons for the discovery and settlement of the coasts and lands of Acadia, with the decisions of his Majesty.

1. The Sieur de Mons, considering the commodity which could arise to the benefit and advancement of his Majesty's affairs by the discovery and settlement of the lands and coasts of Acadia [l'Acadie], for the reasons which He made clear to me, proposes and offers under his good pleasure and authority to proceed there and employ himself there in person so as to exert all effort and duty, and to the end that he can do so have the

more easily such authority to perform therein. Supplicates most humbly His Majesty to bestow upon him the title of Vice Roy and Captain General, as well by sea as by land, in all the coasts, lands and countries which will be granted to him by Him the King, with power to make war and alliances, grant pardons and privileges as well to those of the country as to persons who shall go to settle there, to distribute lands, and to assign titles and seigneuries.

[The King replies:] The King praises and approves of the good will and intention of the Sieur de Monts, desires the advancement and prompt execution of his plan and will supply willingly all the means which are within his power and authority for the enterprise, progress and conduct of the same. He accepts with pleasure the offer which M. Damphile [Danville], Admiral of France and of Brittany, makes to contribute a third of all the expenses which it will prove necessary to incur and that he brings there moreover all that will be necessary and requisite to the authority of his office and will deliver to this end to the Sieur de Monts on behalf of his Majesty and of the said Lord Admiral the commissions and powers requisite and necessary for this in conformity with those which at other times were granted to the Sieur de Roberval and Villegaignon for Florida and Terre Neuve.

2. That it please his Majesty to appoint him to discover and people all the extent of coasts and maritime countries of the land of Acadia from 40° to 46°, in the same way he will be able to accomplish in these lands, the said Sieur de Mons promises to carry artizans and other persons into this said land from the first voyage which he makes there and likewise to continue the other years, living there and having necessary things brought.

[The King replies:] Agreed for the cost of transport and leaving in the said country a hundred persons the first year and continuing every one following, of bringing there equal numbers at the least, notably artizans, architects and other expert men for the buildings and fortifications as much as can be done and lodging, feeding and maintaining them there.

3. That he be permitted for this purpose to take sturdy beggars [vagabonds] which are to be found as well in the towns as in the countryside.

[The King replies:] Agreed and also orders will be given by his Majesty to the Court and other judges to convert the pains and condemnations of banishment and other similar punishments to service which they can do, as it were for the peopling, inhabiting and living in the said land and countries of Acadia.

4. That he have power to build forts and fortresses and establish garrisons and perform all other necessary things for the said establishments in all the places which the Sieur de Mons judges to be necessary.

[The King replies:] Agreed and the said Sieur de Monts will show all duty and diligence to build a fort in the place most advantageous and commodious which he can make.

5. That all the arrangements which he will make by reason of the said voyage will be recorded by the King's Privy Council and instructions given to all other Courts to take cognizance of them.

[The King replies:] The cognizance appertains in the first instance to the officers established at the Marble Table of the Palace of Rouen to avoid costs and expenses for many matters of slight importance which could arise on this subject and if he has to appeal cognizance is reserved to his Majesty's Council and forbidden to all the Courts, Chambers, *Chambres de Compensation* and other judges whatsoever.

6. In order to provide for the expenses which it will be necessary to make with all risks and hazards, as also the necessary advances for this enterprise the Sieur de Mons supplicates most humbly His Majesty to order and appoint as well to him as to those who will be retained with him, all the trade of peltry [=trade in furs and skins] in the Bay of St. Clair [Gulf of St. Lawrence?] and the River of Canada, during the time and space of ten years and all persons be forbidden to trade there under penalty of 30,000 livres.

[The King replies:] Agreed for the Sieur de Mons and his associates and express mention of this privilege will be made by the Lord Admiral's notification which he will deliver each year to make this same effective.

His Majesty wishes also and intends that at this first voyage which the said Sieur de Mons has promised to make, those of his subjects who will wish to associate with him, be received and admitted to contribute to the costs and expenses of the said enterprise and may continue there from year to year according to their offers and means to participate in the profits which will provide to each a sol for a livre of what they will have furnished and in default of being among the said subjects associated with the said Sieur de Mons in the first voyage they will not be from that time forward more acceptable.

7. And to provide the costs and expenses of the said voyage to accept the offers to make payments and contributions of such merchants, selected under the good pleasure of his Majesty, the city of Rouen to be the place to which will be brought back what will be gained, as well by trade as traffic in peltry to be there rendered rateably to each as appertains to him.

[The King replies:] Agreed.

Made at Fontainebleau, the 6th of November 1603.

690. November 8, 1603. Patent granting a monopoly of trade and settlement to Pierre du Gua, Sieur de Monts.

Translated in S. Purchas, Pilgrimes, IV (1625), IV, 1621–1622 (XVIII [1907], 226–228).

The Patent of the French King to Monsieur de Monts for the inhabiting of the Countries of La Cadia Canada, and other places in New France.

Henry by the grace of God King of France and Navarre. To our deare and well beloved the Lord of Monts, one of the ordinarie Gentlemen of our Chamber, greeting. As our greatest care and labour is, and hath alwayes beene, since our comming to this Crowne, to maintaine and conserve it in the ancient dignitie, greatnesse and splendour thereof, to extend and amplifie, as much as lawfully may bee done, the bounds and limits of the same. We being, of a long time, informed of the situation and condition of the Lands and Territories of La Cadia, moved above all things, with a singular zeale, and devout and constant resolution, which we have taken, with the helpe and assistance of God, Author, Distributour, and Protectour of all Kingdomes and Estates, to cause the people, which doe inhabit the Countrey, men (at this present time) Barbarous, Atheists, without Faith, or Religion, to be converted to Christianitie, and to the Beliefe and Profession of our Faith and Religion: and to draw them from the ignorance and unbeliefe wherein they are. Having also of a long time knowne by the Relation of the Sea Captaines, Pilots, Merchants and others, who of long time have haunted, frequented and trafficked with the people that are found in the said places, how fruitfull, commodious and profitable may be unto us, to our Estates and Subjects, the Dwelling, Possession, and Habitation of those Countries, for the great and apparent profit which may be drawne by the greater frequentation and habitude which may bee had with the people that are found there, and the Trafficke and Commerce which may be by that meanes safely treated and negotiated. We then for these causes fully trusting on your great wisdome, and in the knowledge and experience that you have of the qualitie, condition and situation of the said Countrie of La Cadia: for divers and sundry Navigations, Voyages and Frequentations that you have made into those parts, and others neere and bordering upon it: Assuring our selves that this our resolution and intention, being committed unto you, you will attentively, diligently, and no lesse couragiously and valorously execute and bring to such perfection as we desire: Have expresly appointed and established you, and by these Presents, signed with our owne hands, doe commit, ordaine, make, constitute and establish you, our Lieutenant Generall, for to represent our person, in the Countries, Territories, Coasts and Confines of La Cadia. To begin from the 40. degree unto the 46. And in the same distance, or part of it, as farre as may bee done, to establish, extend and make to be knowne our Name, Might and Authoritie. And under the same to subject, submit and bring to obedience all the people of the said Land and the Borderers thereof: And by the meanes thereof, and all lawfull wayes, to call, make, instruct, provoke and incite them to the knowledge of God, and to the light of the Faith and Christian Religion, to establish it there: And in the exercise and profession of the same, keepe and conserve the said people, and all other Inhabitants in the said places, and there to command in peace, rest and tranquillitie, as well by Sea as by Land: to ordaine, decide, and cause to bee executed all that which you shall judge fit and necessarie to be done, for to maintaine, keepe and conserve the said places under our Power and Authoritie, by the formes, wayes and meanes prescribed by our Lawes. And for to have there a care of the same with you, to appoint, establish, and constitute all Officers, as well in the affaires of Warre, as for Justice and Policie, for the first time, and from thence forward to name and present them unto us: for to be disposed by us, and to give Letters, Titles, and such Provisoes as shall be necessarie, &c.

Given at Fountain-Bleau the eight day of November: in the yeere of our Lord 1603. And of our Reigne the fifteenth. Signed Henry: and underneath by the King, Potier; And sealed upon single labell with yellow Waxe.

Chapter Eighty-seven
Champlain and the Acadia Voyages
of 1604 –1607

691. April to August, 1604. Voyage to Acadia and the establishment of the settlement on Ste Croix.

Champlain begins Les voyages *(Paris, 1613) with a historical retrospect (680) and proceeds at once to the first expedition made under the Sieur de Monts's patent, with two ships under François Gravé du Pont and the Sieur de Monts himself, Champlain being pilot and observer.*

S. de Champlain, Les Voyages *(1613), Bk. 1, Chap. 2–4, translated in H. P. Biggar (and others),* The Works of Samuel de Champlain, *I (1922), 233–280.*

2

The Sieur de Monts, having by virtue of his commission made known throughout all the ports and harbours of this Kingdom the injunction against fur-trading granted to him by his Majesty, collected about 120 workmen whom he embarked in two vessels: one of the burden of 120 tons wherein commanded the Sieur de Pont-Gravé, and the other, of 150 tons, wherein he himself took passage along with several noblemen.

We set out from Havre de Grace on the seventh of April, one thousand six hundred and four, and Pont-Gravé on the tenth, with a rendezvous at Canso, twenty leagues from Cape Breton. But when we were on the high sea, the Sieur de Monts changed his mind, and set his course towards Port Mouton, because it is farther to the south and also a more convenient place for making land than Canso.

On the first of May we sighted Sable island, where we ran the risk of being lost through the error of our pilots, who were wrong in their calculations, making us forty leagues farther on than we really were.

This island is distant some thirty leagues from Cape Breton island, north and south, and is about fifteen leagues in circumference. On it is a small lake. The island is very sandy, and contains no full-grown trees, but only underwood and grasses whereon pastured the bullocks and cows taken there over sixty years ago by the Portuguese. These cattle were of great service to the Marquis de La Roche's people, who, during the several years they remained there, captured a large number of very fine black foxes, the skins of which they carefully preserved. Seals are abundant, and in the skins of these the men clothed themselves after their own garments were quite worn out. By order of the Parliament of Rouen, a vessel was sent thither to bring them back, and her crew fished for cod at a place near this island, which island has shoals all about it.

On the eighth of the same month, we sighted cape La Have, to the eastward of which lies a bay containing a good many islands, covered with firs, and on the mainland are oaks, elms, and birches. This cape adjoins the coast of Acadia, and lies in latitude 44° 5′, with a magnetic variation of 16° 15′, distant 85 leagues, on an east-north-east line, from Cape Breton, of which place we shall speak further on.

On the twelfth of May we entered another port five leagues from cape La Have, where we seized a vessel that was carrying on the fur-trade in violation of the king's injunction. The master's name was Rossignol, and his name clung to this port, which lies in latitude 44° 15′.

On the thirteenth of May, we arrived at a very fine port, seven leagues from Port Rossignol, called Port Mouton, where there are two small rivers. The soil is very stony and covered with underwood and heaths. Here are great numbers of hares, and plenty of waterfowl in consequence of the ponds there.

As soon as we had landed, everybody began to

construct camps, each after his fancy, upon a point at the entrance of the port close to two ponds of fresh water. At the same time the Sieur de Monts despatched a shallop, wherein, with some Indians as guides, he sent one of our men carrying letters, to search along the coast of Acadia for Pont-Gravé, who had with him part of the supplies needed for our winter settlement. This man found him at the Bay of All Isles in a state of much anxiety concerning us; for he knew nothing of our change of plan: and to him the man delivered our letters. As soon as Pont-Gravé had read them, he returned towards his ship at Canso, where he seized some Basque vessels which were trading furs notwithstanding his Majesty's injunction, and sent their captains to the Sieur de Monts, who meanwhile had commissioned me to go and make an examination of the coast and of the ports suitable for the safe reception of our vessel.

Anxious to carry out his wishes, I set out from Port Mouton on 19 May in a pinnace of eight tons, accompanied by his secretary, the Sieur Ralleau, and ten men. Proceeding along the coast, we reached a very good port for vessels, at the head of which is a little river extending a good way inland. I named this the harbour of Cape Negro, on account of a rock which from a distance looks like one. It rises out of the water close to a cape which we passed the same day, and which is four leagues distant, and ten from Port Mouton. This cape is very dangerous because of the rocks which extend out to sea. The coast which I had thus far seen is very low, and covered with the same wood as cape La Have, while the islands are all full of waterfowl. Continuing our journey we passed the night at Sable Bay, where vessels can anchor without the least fear of danger.

The next day we reached Cape Sable, which is also very dangerous on account of certain rocks and shoals which project almost a league out to sea. It is two leagues from Sable Bay, where we had passed the preceding night. Thence we went to the Isle of Cormorants, a league beyond, and so named because of the infinite number of these birds, of whose eggs we took a barrel full. From this island we held to the westward some six leagues, crossing a bay which runs to the north two or three leagues: then we came upon several islands which project two or three leagues out to sea, and which may be in some cases two leagues

in circumference, in others three, and in others less, so far as I could judge. They are for the most part very dangerous of approach for large ships because of the strong tides, and of the rocks which lie on a level with the surface of the water. These islands are covered with pines, firs, birches, and poplars. A little farther on are four others. On one we saw so great a number of birds called *tangueux* that we killed them easily with a stick. On another we found the shore completely covered with seals, whereof we took as many as we wished. On the two others the abundance of birds of different kinds is so great that no one would believe it possible unless he had seen it—such as cormorants, ducks of three kinds, snow-geese, murres, wild geese, puffins, snipe, fish-hawks, and other birds of prey, sea-gulls, plover of two or three kinds, herons, herring-gulls, curlews, turnstones, divers, loons, eiders, ravens, cranes, and other kinds unknown to me which make their nests there. We named these islands the Seal Islands. They lie in latitude 43° 30′, distant from the mainland or Cape Sable about four to five leagues. After spending some time there in the pleasures of the chase (and not without taking many waterfowl), we reached a cape which we named Port Fourchu, because it has this [cleft] shape, distant from the Seal Islands five to six leagues. This port is a very good one for vessels at its entrance, but at its head it dries up almost entirely at low tide except for the channel of a small river completely bordered by meadows which make this place quite pleasant. The cod-fishing is good in the vicinity of this port. Setting out thence we held to the northward for ten or twelve leagues without discovering any harbour for vessels aside from a number of coves or very attractive places the soil of which seems suitable for cultivation. The woods there are very fine, though very few pines and firs occur. This coast is very clear, and without islands, rocks, or shoals, so that, in our opinion, vessels may go there in safety. A quarter of a league off shore we visited an island called Long Island, which lies north-north-east and south-south-west, and leaves a passage into the great French Bay, as it was named by the Sieur de Monts.

This island is six leagues in length and in some places nearly a league in breadth, though elsewhere only a quarter of a league. It is covered with quantities of trees, such as pines and birches. The whole shore is bordered with very dangerous rocks, and there is no place suitable for vessels except some little shelters for shallops at the end of the island, and three or four rocky islets where the Indians capture numbers of seals. Great tidal currents run there, and especially at Petit Passage of this island, which is very dangerous for ships should any take the risk of sailing through it.

From Long Island passage we made two leagues to the north-east, then found a cove, a quarter of a league or thereabouts in circumference, where vessels may anchor in safety. The bottom is only mud, and the shore round about wholly bordered with rocks of considerable height. In this place there is a very good silver mine, according to the report of the miner, Master Simon, who was with me. Some leagues farther on is also a little river, named Du Boulay, where the tide runs half a league into the land; and at its mouth vessels of a hundred tons can freely find shelter. A quarter of a league from this place there is a good harbour for vessels, and there we found an iron-mine which our miner estimated would yield fifty per cent. Sailing north-eastward three leagues farther we saw another rather good iron-mine, near which is a river bordered by fine and pleasant meadows. The soil round about is red like blood. Some leagues farther on is still another river which runs dry at low tide except its channel, which is very small; and this river flows from near Port Royal. At the extremity of this bay is a channel which likewise goes dry at low tide; and about it lie a number of meadows with tracts of land good for cultivation; the latter, moreover, filled with numbers of beautiful trees of all the kinds I have previously mentioned. This bay may be from Long Island to its extremity about six leagues in length. This entire coast of the mines consists of high land, cut up into capes which have a rounded aspect and project a little into the sea. On the other side of the bay, to the south-east, the land is low and fertile, with a very good port having at its entrance a bar which must be crossed, upon which there is at low tide a fathom and a half of water but beyond it three fathoms and good bottom. Between the two points of the port lies a gravelly islet covered at high tide. This port runs half a league inland. The tide falls three fathoms, and the place abounds in shellfish, such as mussels, clams, and sea-snails.

The soil is among the best I have seen. I named this harbour Port St. Margaret. This whole south-east coast is much lower than that where the mines occur, which are but a league and a half from the coast of Port St. Margaret, across the bay, though it is three leagues in width at its mouth. I took the altitude at this place, and found the latitude to be 45 degrees and a half and a little more, with 17 degrees 16 minutes of magnetic variation.

After having explored as minutely as I could these coasts, ports, and harbours, I returned to the passage of Long Island, without advancing any farther. Thence I went back outside all the islands in order to observe whether there were any dangers on the seaward side; but we found none at all, except some rocks which lie about half a league from Seal Islands and can easily be avoided inasmuch as the sea breaks over them. Continuing our voyage we were caught in a bad gale, which forced us to run our pinnace ashore on the coast, where we almost lost her, which would have placed us in dire distress. The storm over, we set sail again, and the next day arrived at Port Mouton, where the Sieur de Monts was expecting us from day to day, not knowing what to think of our delay except that some accident must have happened to us. I gave him an account of our whole trip, and told him where our vessels might proceed in safety. Meanwhile I made a particular study of this place, which lies in 44° of latitude.

On the following day the Sieur de Monts had the anchors weighed in order to proceed to St. Mary's Bay, which we had found suitable for our vessel, whilst we meanwhile sought out another locality better fitted for our residence. Coasting the shore, we passed close to Cape Sable and to the Seal Islands, at which point the Sieur de Monts decided to go in a shallop to view some islands whereof we had given him an account, as well as of the infinite number of birds there. He set off accordingly, accompanied by the Sieur de Poutrincourt and several other noblemen, with the intention of going to Gannet Island, where we had previously killed numbers of these birds by blows of a club. Having gone some distance from our ship, we were unable to reach the island, and still less to regain our vessel; for the tide was so strong that we were obliged to put in at a small islet in order to pass the night. Here were great numbers of waterfowl. I killed some river-birds, which stood us in good stead inasmuch as we had taken along only a few biscuits, expecting to return that same day. The next day we proceeded to Cape Fourchu, half a league distant. Keeping along the coast we discovered our vessel, which was in St. Mary's Bay. Our people were very anxious about us for two whole days, fearing lest some misfortune had befallen us; but when they saw we were quite safe, it greatly rejoiced them.

Two or three days after our arrival, one of our priests named Master Aubry, of the city of Paris, on going to fetch his sword which he had forgotten, lost his way in the woods so completely that he could not find the vessel again; and was seventeen days in this state without anything to live upon except some sour and bitter herbs resembling sorrel, and little fruits of small substance, as large as currants, which creep upon the ground. Being at his wits' end, without hope of ever seeing us again, feeble and weak, he found himself on the shore of French Bay, as it was named by the Sieur de Monts, near Long Island, where he was completely exhausted, when one of our shallops, going out to fish, caught sight of him. Unable to call to them, he signalled to them to come after him by means of a pole, on the end of which he had placed his hat. They did so immediately, and brought him away. The Sieur de Monts had had search made for him both by his own men and by the Indians of the country, who had scoured the woods everywhere but had brought back no news of him. Believing him dead, they see him, much to every one's satisfaction, return in the shallop, but it was a long time before he was restored to his original health.

3

Some days later the Sieur de Monts resolved to go and explore the coasts of French Bay, for which purpose he set off from the vessel on the sixteenth of May; and we passed through the strait of Long Island. Having found in St. Mary's Bay no place where we might fortify ourselves, except after a long delay, we determined to ascertain whether there might not be some more suitable place in the other bay. Standing to the north-east six leagues, we came to a cove where vessels can anchor in four, five, six, and seven fathoms, with sandy bottom. This place is only, as it were, a roadstead. Continuing two leagues on the same course, we entered one of the finest harbours I had seen on all these coasts, where a couple of thousand vessels

could lie in safety. The entrance is eight hundred paces wide, and leads into a port two leagues long and one league wide, which I named Port Royal. Into it fall three rivers, one of which tending towards the east is rather large and is called Equille river, which is the name of a little fish of the size of a smelt, caught there in plenty, as likewise are the herring and several other kinds of fish found there abundantly in their seasons. This river is about a quarter of a league wide at its mouth, where there is an island, some half a league in circumference, which, like the rest of the land, is covered with such trees as pines, firs, spruces, birches, aspens, and amongst the others some oaks in limited number. There are two entrances to the said river, one on the north and the other on the south side of the island. That on the north side is the better, and vessels can anchor there under the shelter of the island in five, six, seven, eight, and nine fathoms; but it is necessary to be on one's guard for some shoals which lie near the island and the mainland, and are very dangerous if one has not surveyed the channel.

We went up some fourteen or fifteen leagues as far as the tide reaches, and the river is not of sufficient size to carry boats much farther inland. At this place it is sixty paces wide and about a fathom and a half deep. The shores of this river are covered with numerous oaks, ashes, and other trees. From the mouth of the river to the point we reached are many meadows, but these are flooded at high tide, there being numbers of little creeks leading here and there, up which shallops and boats may pass at high tide. This place was the most suitable and pleasant for a settlement that we had seen. Within the port is a second island, distant from the first about two leagues, where there is another little river which runs some distance into the country; and this we named the River St. Anthony. Its mouth is distant from the head of St. Mary's Bay some four leagues through the woods. As for the remaining river, it is merely a brook full of rocks, which cannot be ascended at all on account of lack of water. It was named Rocky Brook. This place is in latitude 45°, and the magnetic variation is 17° 8′.

Having explored this port, we set out from it in order to go farther into French Bay and see if we could find the copper mine which had been discovered in the previous year. Steering north-east for eight or ten leagues along the coast of Port Royal, we crossed a portion of the bay for a distance of some five or six leagues, to a point which we have named the cape of the Two Bays. We passed an island a league from the latter, and the same distance in circumference. It is forty or forty-five fathoms in height, and wholly surrounded by great cliffs except in one place where there is a slope, at the foot of which lies a pond of salt water, that comes from beneath a gravelly point having the form of a spur. The summit of the island is flat, covered with trees, and has a very fine spring of water. In this place there is a copper mine. Thence we went to a port a league and a half distant, where we thought was the copper mine which a certain Prévert of St. Malo had discovered by means of the Indians of that country. This port lies in latitude 45° 40', and is dry at low tide. To enter one must lay down buoys, and mark a sandbar which lies at the entrance, and runs along a channel parallel with the opposite coast of the mainland. Then one enters a bay about a league in length and half a league in width. In some places the bottom is muddy and sandy, and vessels can there lie aground. The tide falls and rises from four to five fathoms. We landed to see whether we could discover the mines of which Prévert had told us. But after going about a quarter of a league along certain mountains, we found none of them, nor could we recognise any resemblance to the description of the port such as he had pictured it to us. He had, indeed, never been there, but two or three of his men, guided by some Indians, had gone thither, partly by land and partly along small rivers, whilst he awaited them in his shallop in the bay of St. Lawrence at the mouth of a little river. These men on their return brought him several small pieces of copper, which he showed us when he came back from his voyage. Nevertheless, in this port we found two copper mines, not in the native state, but apparently that metal, according to the miner, who considered them very good.

The head of French Bay which we crossed extends fifteen leagues inland. All the country we had seen in ranging the coast from Petit Passage of Long Island is nothing but rocks, without any place where vessels can lie in safety except Port Royal. The country is covered with numerous pines and birches, and in my opinion is none too good.

On the twentieth of May we set out from Port of Mines to seek without loss of time a place suitable for making a permanent settlement, in order afterwards to return and see whether we could discover the mine of pure copper which Prévert's men had found through the help of the Indians. We sailed westward two leagues as far as the cape of the Two Bays, then northward five or six leagues, and crossed the other bay in which we thought was this copper mine whereof we have already spoken, inasmuch as there are two rivers, one coming from the direction of Cape Breton, and the other from the coast of Gaspé or Tracadie, near the great river St. Lawrence. Sailing west some six leagues we came to a little river, at the mouth of which a rather low cape projects into the sea; and a little way inland there is a mountain having the shape of a cardinal's hat. At this place we found an iron-mine. There is anchorage only for shallops. Four leagues to the west-south-west lies a rocky point, which projects a little out to sea; and here run strong tidal currents which are very dangerous. Near this point we saw a cove about a half league in circumference, wherein we found another iron-mine which is also very good. Four leagues farther on there is a fine bay, running into the land, and at its head lie three islands and a rock. Two of these islands are a league distant from the cape toward the west, and the other is at the mouth of one of the largest and deepest rivers we had yet seen, which we named the river St. John, because it was on that day we arrived there. By the Indians it is called Ouygoudy. This river is dangerous if one does not take careful note of certain points and rocks lying on both sides. At its mouth it is narrow, but immediately expands. After rounding a point it narrows again and forms a waterfall between two lofty cliffs, where the water runs with such great swiftness that if a piece of wood be thrown in, it sinks and is never seen again. But by waiting for high tide one can pass this place very easily, and then the river broadens to as much as a league in certain places, and has three islands. We did not explore it farther. However, Ralleau, the Sieur de Monts' secretary, went there some time afterwards to find an Indian named Secoudon, chief of that river, and he reported that it was beautiful, large and wide, with quantities of meadows and fine trees, such as oaks, beeches, butternuts, and wild grape vines. The inhabitants of the country pass up this river as far as Tadoussac, which is on the great river St. Lawrence, and go overland only a short distance to reach that place. From the river St. John to Tadoussac the distance is sixty-five leagues. At its mouth, which is in latitude 45° 40′, there is an iron-mine.

From the river St. John we proceeded towards four islands, on one of which we landed, and found there great numbers of birds called margos; we captured many of their young, which are as good to eat as young pigeons. The Sieur de Poutrincourt was nearly lost here, but finally returned to our long-boat as we went about searching for him round the island, which is distant three leagues from the mainland. Farther west are other islands, and amongst them one six leagues in length called by the Indians Manthane, on the south side of which, among the islands, are several good ports for ships. From the Margos Islands we proceeded to a river on the mainland, called the river of the Etechemins, from a tribe of Indians so named in their own country. We passed such a great number of islands, fair enough in appearance, that it was not possible to count them. Some were two leagues in circumference, others three, and others more or less. All these islands lie in a bay, in my opinion more than fifteen leagues in circumference, with several good harbours for the reception of as many vessels as one might wish, which harbours abound with fish in their season, such as cod, salmon, bass, herring, halibut, and others in great numbers. Sailing west-north-west three leagues through the islands, we entered a river which is almost half a league wide at its mouth, wherein, after going a league or two, we found two islands—one very small and near the western shore, and the other in the middle of the river. The latter may be eight or nine hundred paces in circumference, rising on all sides in ledges of from three to four fathoms, excepting at one small spot, where there is a point of sand and clay which could be utilised for making bricks and other needful articles. There is another sheltered spot where vessels of eighty to one hundred tons can lie, but it goes dry at low water. The island is covered with firs, birches, maples, and oaks. It is naturally very well situated, with but one place where it is low, for about forty paces, and that easy to fortify. The shores of the mainland are distant on both sides some nine hundred to a thousand paces, so that vessels could only pass along the river at the mercy of the cannon on the island. This place we considered the best we had seen, both on account of its situation, and for the intercourse we were expecting with the Indians of these coasts and of the interior, since we should be in their midst. In course of time we hoped to pacify them, and to put an end to the wars which they wage against one another, in order that in the future we might derive service from them, and convert them to the Christian faith. This place was named by the Sieur de Monts the island of Ste Croix. Farther on one sees a great bay in which are two islands, one lofty and the other flat. There are also three rivers, two of which are of moderate size—one leading towards the east and the other to the north, while the third is large and leads towards the west. The latter is that of the Etechemins, which we have already mentioned. Two leagues up this river there is a waterfall, where the Indians carry their canoes overland some five hundred paces; then they re-enter the river, whence by traversing a short portage they pass into the rivers of Norumbega and St. John. Vessels cannot pass this waterfall, because it is nothing but rocks, with but four to five feet of water. In May and June, so great is the catch here of herring and bass that vessels could be loaded with them. The soil is of the very best, and on fifteen or twenty arpents of cleared land here, the Sieur de Monts had some wheat sown, which throve extremely well. The Indians resort thither sometimes five or six weeks during the fishing season. All the rest of the country is very thick forests. If the land were cleared, the seeds would flourish very well. This place lies in latitude 45° 20′, and the magnetic variation is 17° 32′.

4

Having found no place more suitable than this island, we began to erect a barricade on a small islet a little removed from it, and this served as a platform for mounting our cannon. Each worked so efficiently that in a very short time it was put in a state of defence, though the mosquitoes (which are little flies) gave us great annoyance while at work, and several of our men had their faces so swollen by their bites that they could scarcely see. The barricade being finished, the Sieur de Monts sent his long-boat to tell the rest of our people, who were aboard our vessel in St. Mary's Bay, to come to Ste Croix. This was quickly carried out; and while awaiting them, we passed our time pleasantly enough.

Several days afterwards, our vessels having arrived and anchored, everybody landed; then, without loss of time, the Sieur de Monts proceeded to set the workmen to build houses for our residence, and allowed me to draw up the plan of our settlement. After the Sieur de Monts had chosen the site for the storehouse, which was fifty-four feet long, eighteen broad, and twelve feet high, he settled the plan for his own house, which he had built quickly by good workmen. Then he assigned a place to each one, and immediately they began to collect in fives and sixes, according to their preferences. After that all set to work to clear the island, to fetch wood, to cut timber, to carry earth, and other things necessary for the construction of the buildings.

Whilst we were building our dwellings, the Sieur de Monts sent Captain Fouques in Rossignol's vessel to go and find Pont-Gravé at Canso in order to obtain what was left of the supplies for our settlement.

Some time after his departure there arrived a little eight-ton long-boat, on board of which was Du Glas, of Honfleur, the pilot of Pont-Gravé's ship, who brought with him the masters of the Basque vessels, who had been seized by the said Pont-Gravé whilst carrying on a barter in furs, as we have stated. The Sieur de Monts received them kindly, and sent them back by the said Du Glas to Pont-Gravé, with instructions to tell him to take the captured vessels to La Rochelle in order that the law might deal with them. Meanwhile work on the buildings went forward steadily and vigorously, the carpenters at the storehouse and dwelling of the Sieur de Monts, and all the others each at his own. I worked at mine, which I built with the aid of some servants of the Sieur d'Orville and myself. This was forthwith finished, and in it the Sieur de Monts then lodged until his own was ready. An oven was also built, and a hand-mill for grinding our wheat, which gave much trouble and labour to most of us, since it was a painful task. Afterwards some gardens were made, both on the mainland and on the island itself, wherein many kinds of grain were sown which came up very well, except on the island where the soil was nothing but sand in which everything was scorched when the sun shone, although great pains were taken to water the plants.

Several days later the Sieur de Monts decided to find out where the mine of pure copper lay for which we had made such diligent search. To this end he sent me with an Indian named Messamouet, who said he knew the site well. I set out in a small pinnace of five or six tons' burden, having with me nine sailors. Some eight leagues from the island, towards the river St. John, we found a mine of copper which was not pure; nevertheless it was good, according to the miner's report, who said that it would yield eighteen per cent. Farther on we found others, inferior to this. When we reached the spot where we hoped was the mine we were seeking, the Indian could not find it, so that we had to return, leaving this search for another occasion.

On my return from this voyage, the Sieur de Monts determined to send his ships back to France; and also the Sieur de Poutrincourt, who had come out only for pleasure and to explore the country and the places suitable for a settlement which he desired to found. Wherefore he asked the Sieur de Monts for Port Royal, and the latter gave it to him in conformity with his power and commission from the King. He also sent back Ralleau, his secretary, to attend to certain matters connected with the voyage. They set out from Ste Croix island on the last day of August in that same year, 1604.

692. September to October, 1604.
Champlain's first voyage
down the coast of Norumbega.

S. de Champlain, Les voyages (1613), Chap. 5, translated in H. P. Biggar (and others), The Works of Samuel de Champlain, I (1922), 280–300.

5

After the departure of the vessels, the Sieur de Monts decided, in order not to lose time, to send and explore along the coast of Norumbega, and entrusted to me this duty, which I found very agreeable.

For this purpose I set out from Ste. Croix on September 2 in a small vessel of seventeen to eighteen tons, with twelve sailors and two Indians to serve us as guides to the places with which they were acquainted. That day we met with the vessels having on board the Sieur de Poutrincourt, which lay at anchor at the mouth of the river Ste. Croix on account of the bad weather. From this place we could not set out until the fifth of the said month, and when we were two or three leagues at sea the fog came up so thick that we immediately lost sight of their vessels. Continuing our course along the coast we made this day some twenty-five leagues, and passed a great number of islands, sand-banks, shoals, and rocks, which in some places project more than four leagues out to sea. We named these islands the Ordered Islands. The greater part of them are covered with pines, firs, and other inferior woods. Among these islands are many ports which are attractive and safe, but unsuitable for settlement. That same day we also passed near an island about four or five leagues in length, off which we were almost lost on a little rock, level with the surface of the water, which made a hole in our pinnace close to the keel. The distance from this island to the mainland on the north is not a hundred paces. It is very high and cleft in places, giving it the appearance from the sea of seven or eight mountains one alongside the other. The tops of most of them are bare of trees, because there is nothing there but rocks. The woods consist only of pines, firs, and birches. I named it Mount Desert island. Its latitude is 44° 30′.

The next day, the sixth of the month, we made two leagues, and caught sight of smoke in a cove which was at the foot of the mountains above-mentioned; and we saw two canoes paddled by Indians, who came to observe us at a distance of a musket-shot. I sent our two Indians in a canoe to assure them of our friendship, but the fear they had of us made them turn back. The next morning they returned, and came alongside our pinnace, and held converse with our Indians. I had some biscuit, tobacco, and sundry other trifles given to them. These Indians had come to hunt beaver, and to catch fish, some of which they gave us. Having made friends with them, they guided us into their river Peimtegouet, as they call it, where they told us lived their chief named Bessabez, headman of that river. I believe that this river is the one which several pilots and historians call Norumbega, and which most of them have described as large and spacious, with a number of

islands, and with its entrance in latitude 43°, or 43° 30′, though others give 44°, more or less. As to the magnetic variation, I have never read nor heard any mention of it. They also described how there is a great town thickly peopled with skilled and clever Indians who use cotton thread. I am convinced that the majority of those who mention it never saw it, and speak of it only by hearsay from people who had no more knowledge of it than themselves. I can well believe that some may have seen its mouth, because in fact there are numerous islands there, and the latitude thereof is 44°, as they state; but there is no evidence whatever that any one ever entered it; for they would have described it differently in order to remove the doubts of many people on this score.

I shall accordingly relate exactly what I discovered and observed from its mouth as far as I went.

In the first place, at the mouth of it are many islands distant ten or twelve leagues from the mainland, and in latitude 44° with 18° 40′ of magnetic variation. The island of Mount Desert forms one of the points at its mouth, towards the east, while the other, on the west, is low land, called by the Indians Bedabedec, the distance between them being nine or ten leagues. Almost midway between them, out to sea, lies another very high and striking island which for this reason I named Isle Haute. Everywhere about it lie an infinite number of islands of diverse lengths and breadths, but the largest of all is Mount Desert.

The fishing for diverse sorts of fish is very good, as is also the hunting for waterfowl. Some two or three leagues from Bedabedec point, as one coasts the mainland towards the north leading into this river, are very lofty hills visible in fine weather from the sea twelve to fifteen leagues. On reaching the south of Isle Haute, and ranging it about a quarter of a league, to some shoals that are above the water, and then heading west until you open up all the mountains to the northward of this island, you can be sure, on catching sight of the eight or nine summits of the island of Mount Desert and the land of Bedabedec, that you are off Norumbega river. In order to enter this one must steer north, that is, towards the highest mountains of the said Bedabedec; and you will then find no islands ahead of you and can enter safely with plenty of water, although you will see a number of breakers, islands, and rocks both to east and west of you. For greater safety it is necessary to avoid them with the lead in hand. And I am of opinion, so far as I have been able to judge, that one cannot enter that river at any other place except with small craft or shallops; for as I have previously stated, the numerous islands, rocks, shoals, sand-banks, and breakers are here so scattered about as to form a remarkable sight.

Now to return to the continuation of our journey. Entering the river one sees fine islands, which are very pleasant on account of their beautiful meadows. We went as far as a place to which the Indians guided us, where the river is not over an eighth of a league in width; and here, some two hundred paces from the west shore and level with the surface of the water, is a rock which is dangerous. Thence to isle Haute it is fifteen leagues. After making some seven or eight leagues from this narrows (which is the narrowest spot we found), we came to a little river in the vicinity of which we had to anchor, for the reason that before us we saw a great many rocks which are exposed at low tide, and moreover, had we wished to go on, we could not have proceeded more than half a league on account of a waterfall which descends a slope of some seven to eight feet. This I saw when I went there in a canoe with the Indians we had with us, where we found only enough water for a canoe. But below the fall, which is some two hundred paces in width, the river is beautiful; and is unobstructed as far as the place where we had anchored. I landed to see the country; and going hunting, found the part I visited most pleasant and agreeable. One would think the oaks there had been planted designedly. I saw few firs, but on one side of the river were some pines, while on the other were all oaks, together with underwood which extends far inland. And I shall add that from the mouth of the river to the spot where we were, a distance of some twenty-five leagues, we saw neither town nor village, nor any traces that there ever had been any, but only one or two empty Indian wigwams which were constructed in the same manner as those of the Souriquois, that is, covered with tree-bark. So far as we could judge there are few Indians on this river, and these also are called Etechemins. They come there and to the islands only for a few months in summer during the fishing and hunting season, when game is plentiful. They are a people with no fixed abode, from what I have discovered and learned from themselves; for they pass the winter some-

times in one place and sometimes in another, wheresoever they perceive the hunting of wild animals is the best. Upon these they live when hunger presses, without putting anything aside for their support during the famines, which sometimes are severe.

Now this river must of necessity be that of Norumbega; for, after it, there is no other in the above-mentioned latitudes as far as 41°, to which we went, except the Kennebec, which is nearly in the same latitude, but of no great size. Moreover, there can be none here which extend far inland, because the great river St. Lawrence runs parallel to the coast of Acadia and of Norumbega, and the distance between them by land is not above forty-five leagues, or sixty at the widest part, as may be seen on my map.

I shall now leave this subject in order to return to the Indians, who had conducted me to the falls of Norumbega river, and who had gone to inform Bessabez their chief, and other Indians. They [in their turn] went to another little river to inform also their chief, whose name was Cabahis, and to notify him of our arrival.

On the sixteenth of the month, some thirty Indians came to us upon the assurance given to them by those who had acted as our guides. On the same day the above-mentioned Bessabez also came to see us with six canoes. As soon as the Indians on shore saw him arrive, they all began to sing, dance, and leap, until he had landed, after which they all seated themselves on the ground in a circle, according to their custom when they wish to make a speech or hold a festival. Cabahis, the other chief, also arrived a little later, with twenty or thirty of his companions, who kept by themselves; and they were much pleased to see us, inasmuch as it was the first time they had ever beheld Christians. Some time afterwards I landed with two of my companions and two of our Indians who acted as our interpreters. I ordered the crew of our pinnace to draw near the Indians, and to hold their weapons in readiness to do their duty in case they perceived any movement of these people against us. Bessabez, seeing us on shore, bade us sit down, and began with his companions to smoke, as they usually do before beginning their speeches. They made us a present of venison and waterfowl.

I directed our interpreter to tell our Indians that they were to make Bessabez, Cabahis, and their companions understand that the Sieur de

Monts had sent me to them to see them, and also their country; that he wished to remain friends with them, and reconcile them with their enemies, the Souriquois and Canadians; moreover, that he desired to settle in their country and show them how to cultivate it, in order that they might no longer lead so miserable an existence as they were doing; and several other remarks on the same subject. This our Indians made them understand, whereat they signified that they were well satisfied, declaring that no greater benefit could come to them than to have our friendship; and that they desired us to settle in their country, and wished to live in peace with their enemies, in order that in future they might hunt the beaver more than they had ever done, and barter these beaver with us in exchange for things necessary for their usage. When he had finished his speech, I made them presents of hatchets, rosaries, caps, knives, and other little knick-knacks; then we separated. The rest of this day and the following night they did nothing but dance, sing, and make merry, awaiting the dawn, when we bartered a certain number of beaverskins. Afterwards each returned, Bessabez with his companions in their direction and we in ours, well pleased to make acquaintance with these people.

On the seventeenth of the month I made an observation, and found the latitude to be 45° 25'. This done, we set out for another river called Kennebec, distant from this place thirty-five leagues, and from Bedabedec about twenty. The tribe of Indians at Kennebec is called Etechemins, like those of Norumbega.

On the eighteenth of the month we passed near a little river where lived Cabahis, who accompanied us in our pinnace some twelve leagues. Having asked him about the source of Norumbega river, he informed me that after passing the fall of which I have made mention above, and travelling some distance up the river, one entered a lake through which they go to the river of Ste. Croix, thence they go a short distance overland, and then enter the river of the Etechemins. Furthermore, into this lake falls another river, up which they travel several days, and afterwards enter another lake and pass through the midst of it; then, having reached the end of it, they travel again some distance overland and afterwards enter another little river that empties a league

from Quebec, which is on the great river St. Lawrence. All these peoples of Norumbega are very swarthy, and are clothed in beaverskins and other furs like the Canadian Indians and the Souriquois; and they have the same manner of life.

On the twentieth of the month, we coasted along the western shore and passed the mountains of Bedabedec, where we anchored. The same day we explored the entrance of the river into which large vessels can come; but inside are several shoals which must be avoided lead in hand. Our Indians left us here, because they were unwilling to come to Kennebec, inasmuch as the Indians of that place are their great enemies. We made some eight leagues to the westward along the coast as far as an island distant ten leagues from Kennebec, where we were obliged to put into harbour on account of the bad weather and head winds. In one portion of our route we passed a number of very dangerous islands and breakers which project several leagues out to sea. And seeing that the bad weather was so very unfavourable to us, we did not go more than three or four leagues farther. All these islands and shores are covered with quantities of the same trees mentioned before as occurring on the other coasts. In consideration of the scantiness of our provisions, we decided to return to our settlement and to wait until the following year, when we hoped to come back and explore more fully. Accordingly, on the twenty-third of September we turned back, and on the second of October following arrived at our settlement.

Such is a true statement of everything I observed both in regard to the coasts and peoples, as also to the river of Norumbega; but they are not the wonders described by some. I believe this region is as disagreeable in winter as is that of our settlement, in regard to which we were greatly deceived.

693. October, 1604 to June, 1605. The winter experiences of the settlers at Ste Croix.

S. de Champlain, Les voyages *(1613), Chap. 6, translated in H.P. Biggar (and others), The Works of Samuel de Champlain, I (1922), 301–311.*

6

When we arrived at Ste. Croix island, the dwellings had been completed. Winter came upon us sooner than we expected and prevented us from doing many things we had intended. Nevertheless, the Sieur de Monts did not fail for all that to have gardens made upon the island. Many commenced to clear the ground, each doing his own: and I also did mine, which was fairly big; and in it I sowed a quantity of seeds, as did the others who had any. These came up pretty well, but as the island was nothing but sand, everything was almost burnt when the sun shone; for we had no water with which to water them excepting from rain, and this did not fall often.

The Sieur de Monts also had clearings made on the mainland in order to form gardens there; and at the falls, three leagues from our settlement, he had the soil dug up and wheat sown, which came up very fine and ripened. About our settlement at low tide are plenty of shellfish, such as clams, mussels, sea-urchins, and sea-snails, which proved of great benefit to everybody.

Snow first fell on the sixth of October. On the third of December we saw ice passing, which came from some frozen river. The cold was severe and more extreme than in France, and lasted much longer; and it hardly rained at all that winter. I believe this is caused by the north and northwest winds, which pass over high mountains continually covered with snow. This we had to a depth of three or four feet up to the end of the month of April; and I believe also that it lasts much longer than it would if the land were under cultivation.

During the winter a certain malady attacked many of our people. It is called land-sickness, otherwise scurvy, according to what I have since heard stated by learned men. There was engendered in the mouths of those who had it large pieces of superfluous fungus flesh (which caused a great putrefaction); and this increased to such a degree that they could scarcely take anything except in very liquid form. Their teeth barely held in their places, and could be drawn out with the fingers without causing pain. This superfluous flesh was often cut away, which caused them to lose much blood from the mouth. Afterwards, they were taken with great pains in the arms and legs, which became swollen and very hard and

covered with spots like flea-bites; and they could not walk on account of the contraction of the nerves; consequently they had almost no strength, and suffered intolerable pains. They had also pains in the loins, stomach, and bowels, together with a very bad cough and shortness of breath. In brief, they were in such a state that the majority of the sick could neither get up nor move, nor could they even be held upright without fainting away; so that of seventy-nine of us, thirty-five died, and more than twenty were very near it. The majority of those who kept well complained of some minor pains and shortness of breath. We could find no remedy with which to cure these maladies. We opened several of them to determine the cause of their illness.

In many cases it was found that the interior parts were diseased; for example the lungs were so altered that no natural moisture could be seen; the spleen was watery and swollen; the liver very fibrous and mottled, with none of its natural color; the *vena cava*, both ascending and descending, full of thick, clotted and black blood; the gall tainted. Nevertheless many arteries, both in the mid and lower bowels, were in pretty good condition. In some cases incisions were made with a razor upon the thighs over the purple spots, whence there flowed a black clotted blood. This is what could be learned from the bodies infected with this disease.

Our surgeons were unable to treat themselves so as not to suffer the same fate as the others. Those who continued to be ill grew well in the spring, which in this country begins in May. This made us believe that the change of season restored them to health rather than the remedies which had been prescribed for them.

During this winter our beverages all froze except the Spanish wine. Cider was given out by the pound. This loss was due to the fact that the storehouse had no cellar, and that the air which entered through the cracks was more severe than that outside. We were obliged to make use of very bad water and to drink melted snow, since we had neither springs nor brooks; for it was not possible to go to the mainland on account of the great cakes of ice carried by the ebb and flow of the tide, which rises three fathoms between low and high water. The labour with the hand-mill was very painful, because most of us, having poor quarters and suffering from shortage of fuel which we could not procure on account of the ice, had almost no strength; and, again, we ate only salt meat and vegetables during the winter, which produced poor blood. Such in my opinion was in part the cause of these unfortunate maladies. All these circumstances made the Sieur de Monts and others dissatisfied with the settlement.

It was difficult to know this country without having wintered there; for on arriving in summer everything is very pleasant on account of the woods, the beautiful landscapes, and the fine fishing for the many kinds of fish we found there. There are six months of winter in that country.

The Indians who live there are few in number. During the winter, when the snow is deepest, they go hunting for moose and other animals, on which they live the greater part of the time. If the snow is not deep, they are scarcely rewarded for their pains, inasmuch as they cannot capture anything except with very great labour, whereby they endure and suffer much. When they do not go hunting, they live on a shellfish called the clam. In winter they clothe themselves with good furs of beaver and moose. The women make all the clothes, but not neatly enough to prevent one seeing the skin under the armpits; for they have not the skill to make them fit better. When they go hunting they make use of certain racquets, twice as large as those of our country, which they attach under their feet, and with these they travel over the snow without sinking, both the women and children as well as the men who hunt for the tracks of animals. Having found these they follow them until they catch sight of the beast, when they shoot at him with their bows, or else kill him with thrusts from swords set in the end of a half-pike. This can be done very easily, because these animals are unable to travel on the snow without sinking in. Then the women and children come up and camp there, and give themselves up to feasting. Afterwards they go back to see whether they can find other animals, and thus they pass the winter. In the month of March following, there arrived some Indians, who shared with us their game, for which we gave them in exchange bread and other articles. Such is the manner of life of these people in winter, and it seems to me very wretched.

We were expecting our vessels at the end of April, and after that date everybody began to have forebodings fearing lest some accident had befallen them. For this reason, on the fifteenth of May the Sieur de Monts decided to have a pinnace of fifteen tons' burden, and another of seven, fitted out so that at the end of June we might go to Gaspé to search for vessels in which to return to France, should our own meantime not arrive. But God helped us better than we hoped; for on the fifteenth of June, whilst I was on guard about eleven o'clock at night, there arrived in a shallop Pont-Gravé, captain of one of the Sieur de Monts' vessels, who informed us that his ship was at anchor six leagues from our settlement. He was welcomed to the joy of all.

The next day the vessel arrived, and came to anchor near our settlement. Pont-Gravé informed us that another vessel, the *St. Estienne* of St. Malo, was following him with provisions and supplies for our use.

On the seventeenth of the month the Sieur de Monts decided to go in search of a suitable site for a settlement, and one where the climate was milder than where we were. For this purpose he had fitted out the pinnace in which he had proposed going to Gaspé.

694. June 18 to August 3, 1605. The second voyage of Champlain and the Sieur de Monts along the New England coast.

S. de Champlain, Les voyages *(1613), Chaps. 7-9, translated in H. P. Biggar (and others), The Works of Samuel de Champlain, I (1922), 311-366.*

7

On the eighteenth of June, 1605, the Sieur de Monts set out from Ste. Croix island, accompanied by some gentlemen, twenty sailors, and an Indian named Panounias, with his wife, whom the Indian was unwilling to leave behind. We took along these Indians to serve as guides in the country of the Almouchiquois, in the hope of discovering and learning more exactly by their aid what kind of a country it was, inasmuch as she was a native thereof.

Coasting along inside Manan which is an island

three leagues from the mainland, we reached the Ordered Islands on the seaward side, and came to anchor at one of them. On this was a great multitude of crows, whereof our crew took a great number; and we named it the Isle of Crows. Thence we sailed to Mount Desert island, which lies at the mouth of the Norumbega river, as stated above. We made our way five or six leagues among some islands, and there three Indians came to us in a canoe from Bedabedec point, where was their chief. After some conversation they went back again the same day.

On Friday the first of July we set out from one of these islands which lies at the mouth of the river, where there is a pretty good harbour for vessels of one hundred and one hundred and fifty tons. That day we made some twenty-five leagues from Bedabedec point, past a number of islands and rocks which we explored as far as the Kennebec river. At the mouth of this is a rather lofty island, named by us the Tortoise, and between it and the mainland are some scattered rocks which are covered at high tide. Nevertheless one can observe the sea breaking over them. Tortoise Island and the [Kennebec] river lie south = south-east and north-north-west. On entering the river there are two moderate-sized islands which form the entrance, one on one side and the other on the other; and some three hundred paces farther in lie two rocks on which are no trees but only a little grass. We anchored three hundred paces from the entrance in five to six fathoms of water. Whilst lying here we were overtaken by fogs, which made us decide to go farther up in order to see the upper reaches of the river and the Indians who live there; and for this purpose we set off on the fifth of the month. Having gone some leagues our pinnace was almost lost upon a rock which we grazed as we passed. Farther on we met with two canoes which had come to hunt birds, the majority of which are moulting at this time and cannot fly. We accosted these Indians through our own, who went towards them with his wife, and she explained to them the reason of our coming. We made friends with them and with the Indians of that river who acted as our guides. And proceeding farther in order to see their chief, named Manthoumermer, when we had covered seven to eight leagues, we passed some islands, straits and streams which are spread along the course of the river, where we saw some fine meadows. Coasting an island some four leagues in length, they took us to the place where their chief then was in company with twenty-five or thirty Indians. As soon as we had anchored he came out to us in a canoe, separated a short distance from ten others in which were those who accompanied him. Drawing near our pinnace he made us a speech, in which he expressed his pleasure at seeing us, and said he desired an alliance with us, and through our mediation to make peace with their enemies. He added that the next day he would send word to two other Indian chiefs who were up country, one called Marchin, and the other Sasinou, chief of the Kennebec river. The Sieur de Monts had biscuits and peas given them, wherewith they were much pleased. The next day they guided us down the river by a different route than that by which we had come up, in order to reach a lake. Making our way through some islands, each left an arrow near a cape before which all the Indians pass. They believe that unless they do this, misfortune will befall them, for so the devil persuades them. Such superstitions and likewise many others do they practise. Beyond this cape we passed a very narrow waterfall, but not without a great deal of trouble, for although we had a fresh, favourable wind, of which we made our sails reap as much benefit as we possibly could, yet we were not able to pass it in that manner and were obliged to attach a hawser to some trees on shore and all to pull thereat. Thus we pulled so hard, in addition to the help of the wind which was favourable, that we passed it. The Indians who were with us portaged their canoes, being unable to pass it with the paddle. After clearing this fall, we saw some fine meadows. I was greatly astonished at this fall, since whilst we were descending, we found the tide in our favour, but at the fall itself, found it against us; but having passed the fall, the tide was running out as before, which gave us great satisfaction. Continuing our route we came to the lake, which is three to four leagues in length. It contains several islands, and into it fall two rivers, the Kennebec, which flows from the north-north-east, and another from the north-west, down which Marchin and Sasinou were to come. Having waited for them all that day, and seeing they did not arrive, we determined to improve our time. We therefore raised anchor and with our two Indians as guides left this lake, and came to anchor the same day at the mouth of the river, where we caught a great number of many kinds of fine fish. Meanwhile our Indians went hunting but did not return. The channel by which we descended the said river is very much safer and better than that by which we had gone up. Tortoise Island, which lies off the mouth of the said river, is in latitude 44°, and the magnetic variation is 19° 12'. One can go by this river across country some fifty leagues to Quebec without making a portage of more than two leagues; then one enters another little river which descends into the great river St. Lawrence. This river Kennebec, for half a league from its mouth, is very dangerous for vessels, because of the shallow water, great tides, rocks, and shoals found both outside and inside. There is, nevertheless, a good channel if it were well explored. The little of the country I saw along the banks is very bad; for it is nothing but rocks everywhere. There are quantities of small oaks but very little cultivable land. The place abounds in fish, as do the other rivers already described. The people live like those near our settlement; and they informed us that the Indians who cultivated Indian corn lived far inland, and had ceased to grow it on the coasts on account of the war they used to wage with others who came and seized it. That is what I was able to learn about this place, which I believe to be no better than the others.

On the eighth of the month we set out from the mouth of this river, having been unable to do so earlier on account of fogs. That day we made some four leagues, and passed a bay in which lie a great many islands: and from it one sees high mountains towards the west, where dwells an Indian chief named Aneda, who lives near the river Kennebec. From his name I am convinced it was one of this tribe who discovered the plant called Aneda, which was stated by Jacques Cartier to possess such potency against the disease called scurvy, of which we have already spoken—the same which tormented his men as well as our own when they wintered in Canada. The Indians are not acquainted with this plant, nor do they know what it is, although the said Indian bears the same name. The next day we made eight leagues. Continuing along the coast, we caught sight of two smokes which some Indians were making for us, and heading towards them we came to anchor behind a small island close to the mainland. Here we saw more than eighty Indians, who ran along the shore to observe us, dancing and showing by signs their pleasure thereat. The Sieur de Monts sent two men with our Indian to go and fetch them; and after these had spoken to them for some time and had assured them of our friendship, we left one of our men with them, and they delivered to us one of their companions as a hostage. Meantime the Sieur de Monts paid a visit to an island which is very beautiful on account of what it produces, having fine oaks and nut-trees, with cleared land and abundance of vines which in their season bear fine grapes. These were the first we had seen on any of these coasts from cape La Have. We named it the Island of Bacchus. As the tide was high, we weighed anchor and made our way into a small river, which we could not enter earlier because the harbour has a bar, on which at low tide there is not more than half a fathom of water, though at high tide there is a fathom and a half, and at spring tides two fathoms; inside there are three, four, five, and six. After we had cast anchor, a large number of Indians came towards us upon the bank of the river and began to dance. Their chief, whose name was Honemechin, was not then with them; but he arrived about two or three hours later with two canoes, and went circling round and round our pinnace. Our Indian could understand only certain words, inasmuch as the language of the Almouchiquois, for so that nation is called, differs entirely from that of the Souriquois and Etechemins. These people showed that they were much pleased. Their chief was good-looking, young and active. We sent some goods on shore to barter with them, but they possessed only their clothes; which they bartered; for they make no provision of furs except to clothe themselves. The Sieur de Monts had certain articles given to their chief, with which he was much pleased, and he came on board several times to visit us. These Indians shave off their hair fairly high up on the head, and wear the remainder very long, combing and twisting it very neatly behind in several ways, with feathers which they fasten on their heads. They paint their faces black and red, like the other Indians we have seen. They are an active people with well-formed bodies. Their weapons are spears, clubs, bows, and arrows. At the end of these latter some of them fasten the tail of a fish called signoc; others use bones, while others make them entirely of wood. They till and cultivate the land; a practice we had not seen previously. In place of ploughs they use an instrument of very hard wood made in the shape of a spade. This river is called by the inhabitants of the country Chouacoet.

The following day the Sieur de Monts went on shore to view their fields upon the bank of the river, and I with him. We saw their grain, which is Indian corn. This they grow in gardens, sowing three or four grains in one spot, after which, with the shells of the aforesaid signoc, they heap about it a quantity of earth. Then three feet away they sow as much again; and so on in order. Amongst this corn they plant in each hillock three or four Brazilian beans, which come up of different colours. When fully grown these plants twine around the aforementioned corn, which grows to a height of five to six feet; and they keep the ground very free from weeds. We saw there many squashes, pumpkins, and tobacco, which they likewise cultivate. The Indian corn we saw was then two feet in height, and there was also some three feet high. As for the beans, they were beginning to burst into flower, as were likewise the pumpkins and squashes. They plant their corn in May, and harvest it in September. We saw there a great many nuts, which are small and have several divisions. As yet there were none on the trees, but underneath we found plenty from the preceding year. We saw also many vines, on which were exceedingly fine berries, and from these we made some very good juice; we had not seen these previously except on the island of Bacchus, distant from this river about two leagues. The fixed abodes, the cultivated fields, and the fine trees led us to the conclusion that the climate here is more temperate and better than that where we wintered, and than at the other places on this coast. Not that I am of opinion that it is not cold here, although the place lies in latitude 43° 45′. The forests inland are very open, but nevertheless abound in oaks, beeches, ashes, and elms, and in wet places there are numbers of willows. The Indians remain permanently in this place, and have a large wigwam surrounded by palisades formed of rather large trees placed one against the other; and into this they retire when their enemies come to make war against them. They cover their wigwams with oak bark. This place is very pleasant, and as attractive a spot as one can see anywhere. The river; which is bordered with meadows; abounds

greatly in fish. At its mouth lies an islet adapted for the construction of a good fortress where one would be safe.

On Sunday; the twelfth of the month, we set out from the river called Saco, and, coasting along shore, made some six or seven leagues, when a contrary wind arose which obliged us to cast anchor. We landed, and saw two meadows, each of which contained about a league in length and a half league in breadth. We saw there two Indians, whom at first we mistook for those great birds called in that country bustards. As soon as they espied us they fled into the woods and did not reappear. Between Saco and this place we saw some little birds which have a note like blackbirds, and are black except the tips of the wings, which are orange. There are also numbers of grape-vines and nut-trees. This coast in most of the places on this side of Kennebec is sandy. That day we went back two or three leagues towards Saco, as far as a cape which we named Island harbour, with a harbour lying among three islands, and good for vessels of 100 tons. Heading north-east, a quarter north, one enters another harbour near this place, into which there is no entrance (although it is among islands) except that by which one enters. At the mouth of it are some breakers which are dangerous. Upon these islands grow so many red currants that one can hardly see anything else; and there are also countless numbers of pigeons, whereof we took a goodly quantity. This Island harbour lies in latitude 43° 25′.

On the fifteenth of this month we made twelve leagues. Coasting along the shore we perceived smoke upon the beach, whereupon we approached as close as we could, but did not see a single Indian, which made us believe they had fled. The sun was setting, and we were unable to find a place in which to pass the night, because the coast was low and sandy. Steering south to get away from the land that we might anchor, after sailing about two leagues we perceived a cape on the mainland to the south, one quarter south-east of us, at a distance of some six leagues. Two leagues to the east we saw three or four rather high islands, and to the westward a large bay. The coast of this bay, ranging around to the cape, extends inland from the place where we were about four leagues. It is some two leagues broad from north to south and three across its entrance.

Not discovering any suitable place to anchor, we determined to proceed to the above-mentioned cape under short sail for part of the night; and approached to sixteen fathoms of water, where we cast anchor to await daybreak.

The next day we made our way to the above-mentioned cape, where, close to the mainland, are three islands which are covered with trees of different sorts, like those at Saco and along this whole coast. There is another low island upon which the sea breaks, which extends a little farther out to sea than the others, and upon it are no trees. We named this place the Island Cape. Near it we caught sight of a canoe in which were five or six Indians, who came towards us, but after approaching our pinnace, went back to dance upon the beach. The Sieur de Monts sent me ashore to visit them, and to give to each a knife and some biscuit, which caused them to dance better than ever. When this was over, I made them understand as well as I could, that they should show me how the coast trended. After I had drawn for them with a charcoal the bay and the Island Cape, where we then were, they pictured for me with the same charcoal another bay which they represented as very large. Here they placed six pebbles at equal intervals, giving me thereby to understand that each one of these marks represented that number of chiefs and tribes. Next they represented within the said bay a river which we had passed, which is very long and has shoals. We found here quantities of vines on which the unripe grapes were a little larger than peas, and also many nut-trees, the nuts on which were no larger than musket-balls. These Indians informed us that all those who lived in this region cultivated the land and sowed seeds like the others we had previously seen. This place is in latitude 43° and some minutes. Having gone half a league we perceived upon a rocky point several Indians who ran dancing along the shore towards their companions to inform them of our coming. Having indicated to us the direction of their home, they made signal-smokes to show us the site of their settlement. We came to anchor close to a little island, to which we sent our canoe with some knives and biscuits for the Indians, and observed from their numbers that these places are more populous than the others we had seen. Having tarried some two hours to observe these people, whose canoes are built of birch-bark like

those of the Canadians, Souriquois, and Eteche-mins, we raised anchor and with promise of fine weather set sail. Continuing our course to the west-south-west, we saw several islands upon either hand. Having gone seven to eight leagues we anchored near an island, where we saw many columns of smoke along the coast and many Indians, who came running to see us. The Sieur de Monts sent two or three men to them in a canoe, giving these men knives and rosaries to present to the Indians, who were much pleased therewith, and danced several times in acknowledgment. We could not learn the name of their chief, because we did not understand their language. All along this coast there is much cleared land sown with Indian corn. The country is very pleasant and agreeable, with no lack also of many fine woods. Those who live here have canoes built of a single piece, and very liable to upset unless one is well skilled in managing them. We had heretofore not seen any of this kind. This is how they build them. After taking great trouble and spending much time in felling with hatchets of stone (for except a few who get them from the Indians of the Acadian coast, with whom they are bartered for furs, they possess no others) the thickest and tallest tree they can find, they remove the bark and round off the trunk, except upon one side, where they gradually apply fire throughout its whole length. Sometimes they also place glowing red-hot stones upon it. If the fire becomes too fierce, they extinguish it with a little water, not completely, but to prevent the edge of the canoe from burning. When it is hollow enough for their fancy, they scrape it all over with stones, which they use in place of knives. The stones from which they make their cutting tools are like our musket flints.

On the following day, the seventeenth of the same month, we weighed anchor to go towards a cape we had seen the day before, which appeared to lie to the south-south-west of us. That day we could only make five leagues, and passed several islands covered with trees. I recognised in this bay everything the Indians at Island Cape had drawn for me. On continuing our route, a great number of Indians came out to us in their canoes, both from the islands and the mainland. We proceeded to anchor a league from the cape, which we named St. Louis. At this place we perceived several smoke-signals, but on proceeding thither our pinnace grounded upon a rock, placing us in great danger; for if we had not promptly set matters right she would have upset, since the tide was running out and there was a depth of five to six fathoms of water. But God preserved us, and we came to anchor close to the said cape, where some fifteen or sixteen canoes of Indians visited us. In some of the canoes were fifteen or sixteen persons, who began to exhibit great signs of joy, and to make various kinds of harangues which we in no wise understood. The Sieur de Monts sent three or four men ashore in our canoe, both to obtain water and also to see their chief, named Honabetha, who was given several knives and other trifles which the Sieur de Monts sent him. This man came on board to see us, with a number of his companions, who were both along the shore and in their canoes. We received the chief very kindly, and gave him good cheer. After remaining with us some time, he went back. The men we had sent to them brought us little squashes as big as your fist, which we ate as a salad like cucumbers, and they were very good. They brought us also some purslane, which grows abundantly among the Indian corn, and of which they take no more account than if it were a weed. We saw in this place a great many little houses, which are situated in the fields where they sow their Indian corn.

Furthermore in this bay there is a very broad river which we named the River Du Gas. In my opinion it extends toward the Iroquois, a nation at open war with the Montagnais who live on the great river St. Lawrence.

8

The next day we doubled cape St. Louis, so named by the Sieur de Monts, a moderately low shore in latitude 42° 45′. That day we made two leagues along a sandy coast, and saw as we passed a number of wigwams and gardens. The wind coming ahead we entered a little bay to await suitable weather for continuing our route. Two or three canoes approached us on their way back from fishing for cod and other fish, which are plentiful thereabouts. These they catch with hooks made of a piece of wood, to which they attach a bone shaped like a harpoon, which they fasten very securely for fear lest it come out. The whole thing has the form of a little crook. The line which is attached to it is made of tree-bark. They gave me one of them, which I took as a curiosity.

In this the bone was attached with hemp, which in my opinion is like that of France. They informed me that they gathered this plant in their country without cultivating it, indicating its height as about four to five feet. The said canoe returned to shore to notify the people in the settlement, who made signal-smokes for us; and we perceived eighteen or twenty Indians who came down to the beach and began to dance. Our canoe went ashore to give them some trifles, with which they were much pleased. Some of them came out to beg us to enter their river. We raised anchor to do so, but were unable to get in because the tide was out and the water too shallow; and were obliged to anchor at the entrance. I went on shore, where I saw many more Indians, who received us very kindly. I went to explore the river, but saw only an arm of the sea which extends some little distance into the country, which is partially cleared. Here it becomes only a brook, which cannot float boats except at high tide. The bay is about a league in circumference. On one side of the entrance is a kind of island covered with trees, especially pines, and it adjoins some sand-dunes which are fairly extensive: on the other side the land is rather high. Within the said bay are two islets, which cannot be seen unless one is inside, and round about them the sea recedes almost completely at low tide. This place is very conspicuous from the sea, inasmuch as the coast is very low except the cape at the entrance to this bay, which we named Cape St. Louis harbour. It is distant from the said cape two leagues, and from Island Cape ten. It lies in approximately the same latitude as cape St. Louis.

On the nineteenth of the month we set out from this place. Coasting towards the south we made four to five leagues, and passed close to a rock which lies on a level with the surface of the water. Continuing our route, we caught sight of some land which we took to be islands, but when nearer perceived that it was mainland, which continued to the north-north-west of us, and that it was the cape of a large bay more than eighteen to nineteen leagues in circumference. We had run so far into this bay that we had to stand on the other tack to double the cape we had seen, which we named the White Cape, because there were sands and dunes which presented this appearance. The favourable wind was of great service here; for otherwise we should have been in danger of being driven upon the coast. This bay is very clear, provided one does not approach the shore nearer than a good league, there being no islands or rocks except the one I have mentioned, which is near a river that extends some distance inland and which we named Ste Suzanne of the White Cape. From here to cape St. Louis the distance is ten leagues. The White Cape is a point of sand which bends southward some six leagues. This coast has fairly high sand-banks which are very conspicuous from the sea, where soundings are found of thirty, forty and fifty fathoms nearly fifteen or eighteen leagues from land, until one comes to ten fathoms in approaching the shore, which is very clear. There is a great extent of open country along the shore before one enters the woods, which are very delightful and pleasant to the eye. We cast anchor off shore and saw some Indians, towards whom four of our party advanced. Making their way along the sandy beach, they perceived as it were a bay with wigwams bordering it all around. When they were about a league and a half from us an Indian came towards them dancing all over (as they reported to us). He had come down from the high shore, but returned shortly after to give notice of our arrival to those in his settlement.

The next day, the twentieth of the month, we went to the place which our men had discovered, and found it to be a very dangerous port on account of the shoals and sandbanks, where we saw breakers on every side. It was almost low tide when we entered, and there were only four feet of water in the north passage; at high tide there are two fathoms. When we were inside, we saw that this place was rather large, being about three to four leagues in circumference, with all around it little houses about which each owner had as much land as was necessary for his support. A little river enters it which is very pretty; at low tide it has some three and a half feet of water. There are also two or three brooks bordered with meadows. The place would be very fine if only the harbour were good. I took an observation, and found the latitude 42°; and the magnetic variation 18° 40′. There came to us from all sides, dancing, a number of Indians, both men and women. We named this place Mallebarre harbour.

On the next day, the twenty-first of the month, the Sieur de Monts resolved to go and inspect their settlement, and nine or ten of us accompanied him with our arms; the remainder stayed behind to guard the pinnace. We went about a league along shore. Before reaching their wigwams we entered a field planted with Indian corn in the manner I have already described. The corn was in flower, and some five and a half feet in height. There was some less advanced, which they sow later. We saw an abundance of Brazilian beans, many edible squashes of various sizes, tobacco, and roots which they cultivate, the latter having the taste of artichoke. The woods are full of oaks, nut-trees, and very fine cypresses, which are of reddish colour and have a very pleasant smell. There were also several fields not cultivated, for the reason that the Indians let them lie fallow. When they wish to plant them they set fire to the weeds and then dig up the field with their wooden spades. Their wigwams are round, and covered with heavy thatch made of reeds. In the middle of the roof is an opening, about a foot and a half wide, through which issues the smoke of their fire. We asked them if they had their permanent residence in this place, and whether there was much snow; but we could not find this out very well since we did not understand their language, although they attempted to explain by signs, taking up sand in their hand, then spreading it on the ground, and indicating that the snow was the same colour as our collars, and fell to the depth of a foot. Others indicated that it was less, giving us also to understand that the harbour never froze over; but we were unable to ascertain whether the snow lasted a long time. I consider, however, that this country is temperate and the winter not severe. During the time we were there it blew a gale from the north-east which lasted four days, with the sky so overcast that the sun was hardly visible at all. It was very cold, so that we were obliged to put on our greatcoats which we had entirely laid aside. However, I believe this was exceptional, just as often happens in other localities out of season.

On the twenty-third of the said month of July, four or five sailors having gone ashore with some large kettles to fetch fresh water from among the sand-hills at a distance from our pinnace, certain Indians, being desirous to possess some of these kettles, watched for the time when our men went there, and snatched one by force out of the hands of a sailor who had filled his the first and who had no weapons. One of his companions, starting to run after the Indian, quickly returned, being unable to catch him, inasmuch as the latter was a swifter runner than himself. The other Indians, when they saw our sailors running towards our pinnace and shouting to us to discharge some musket-shots at the Indians who were in considerable numbers, took to flight. At that time there were a few Indians on board our pinnace who threw themselves into the sea, and we were able to seize only one of them. Those on shore who had taken to flight, seeing the others swimming, turned back straight to the sailor from whom they had taken the kettle and shot several arrows at him from behind and brought him down. Perceiving his condition, they at once rushed upon him and despatched him with their knives. Meantime we made haste to go on shore, and fired muskets from our pinnace. Mine exploded in my hands and nearly killed me. The Indians, hearing this fusillade, again took to flight, and redoubled their speed when they saw that we had landed, being frightened on seeing us run after them. There was no likelihood of catching them; for they are as swift-footed as horses. The dead man was brought in, and some hours later was buried. Meanwhile we kept our prisoner bound hand and foot on board our pinnace, fearing lest he should escape. The Sieur de Monts determined to let him go, feeling persuaded he was not to blame and knew nothing of what had occurred, as was the case also with those who were at the time on board and alongside our pinnace. A few hours later some Indians came towards us, making excuses by signs and outward show that it was not they who had done this evil deed but others farther off in the interior. We were unwilling to do them harm, although it was in our power to avenge ourselves.

All these Indians from Island Cape onwards wear no skins nor furs, except very rarely; but their clothes are made from grasses and hemp, and barely cover their bodies, and come down only to the thighs. But the men have their privy parts concealed by a small skin. It is the same also with the women, who wear it a little lower behind than the men; all the rest of the body is naked. When the women came to see us they wore skins open in front. The men cut off the hair on top of their heads like those at Saco river. I saw, among other things, a girl with her hair quite neatly done up by means of a skin dyed red, and trimmed on the upper part with little shell beads. Some of her hair hung down behind, while the rest was braided in various ways. These people paint their faces red, black, and yellow. They have almost no beard, and pull it out as fast as it grows. Their bodies are well-proportioned. I do not know what government they have, but believe that in this they resemble their neighbours, who have none at all. They do not know what it is to worship or pray. They have indeed sundry superstitions, like the other Indians, and these I shall describe in their place. For weapons they have only spears, clubs, bows, and arrows. In appearance they seem to be of good disposition, and better than those to the northward; but the whole of them, to tell the truth, are not worth much. The slightest intercourse with them at once discloses their character. They are great thieves, and if they cannot lay hold of a thing with their hands, try to do so with their feet, as we have repeatedly learned by experience. I fancy that, had they anything to barter; they would not resort to thievery. They bartered their bows, arrows, and quivers for pins and buttons; and had they possessed anything better, would have done the same with it. One must be on one's guard against these people and mistrust them, yet without allowing them to perceive it. They gave us a quantity of tobacco, which they dry and then reduce to powder. When they eat Indian corn they boil it in earthen pots, which they make in a different way from ours. They crush it also in wooden mortars, and reduce it to flour, and then make cakes and biscuits of it as do the Indians of Peru.

In this place, and all along the coast from Kennebec, are a great many *siguenocs*[horseshoe crabs], which is a fish with a shell on its back like the tortoise, yet different; for it has along the median line a row of little prickles coloured like a dead leaf, as is the rest of this fish. At the end of this shell is another, which is smaller and bordered by very sharp points. The length of the tail varies according as the fish is large or small, and with the end of it these people tip their arrows. It has also a row of points like those on the large shell. In the latter are the eyes. It has eight small feet, like those of a crab, and at the back two more which are longer and flat, of which it makes use in swimming. It has also two more very small ones in front, with which it eats. When it walks, these are all hidden except the two hindermost, which show a little. Under the smaller shell are membranes which swell up and have a pulsation like the throat of a frog, and lie one over the other after the manner of the folds of a doublet. The largest I saw was a foot in breadth and a foot and a half long.

We saw also a sea-bird with a black beak somewhat aquiline at the top, and four inches long, shaped like a lancet, that is to say, with the lower part representing the handle and the upper the blade, which latter is thin, sharp on both sides, and shorter by a third than the other. This arrangement astonishes many people, who cannot understand how it is possible for this bird to eat with such a beak. It is as large as a pigeon, the wings being very long in proportion to the body, the tail short as are likewise the legs, which are red, the feet being small and flat. The plumage is grey-brown above, and very white underneath. They go always in flocks along the seashore, as do the pigeons on our side.

The Indians along all these coasts which we have visited, say that other birds, which are very large, come when their corn is ripe; and they imitated for us their cry, like that of the turkey. In several places they showed us their feathers, with which they feather their arrows, and which they place upon their heads as a decoration. They showed us also a kind of hair which these birds have under the throat, like those we have in France; and they declare that a red crest falls over upon their beak. They represented them to us as being as large as a bustard, which is a species of goose having the neck longer and twice as large as those we have. All these indications led us to conclude that they were turkeys. We should have liked very much to see some of these birds, as well as their feathers, for greater certainty. Before I had seen the feathers and the little tuft of hair they have under the throat, and before I had heard their cry imitated, I thought they were certain birds like turkeys which are found in some parts of Peru, where they live along the sea-coast, eating carrion and other dead things as do the ravens. But those are not so large, nor have they the tuft of hair so long nor a cry like the true turkeys; and they are not good to eat, as are these, which, the Indians say, come in flocks in the summer, and at the beginning of winter go off to warmer countries which are their natural dwelling-places.

9

We had taken more than five weeks to cover three degrees of latitude, and could not remain more than six weeks on our voyage, as we had carried provisions only for that length of time. And furthermore, being unable, on account of fogs and storms, to proceed beyond Mallebarre, where we remained for several days awaiting weather suitable for setting sail, and finding ourselves pressed by a scarcity of provisions, the Sieur de Monts decided to return to Ste. Croix island, in order to find another spot more suitable for our settlement; for we had been unable to find such a place on any of the coasts we had explored on this voyage.

And we set out from this port; to search elsewhere, on the twenty-fifth of the month of July. On going out we were nearly lost on the bar at the entrance through the fault of our pilots named Cramolet and Champdoré, masters of our pinnace, who had badly buoyed the entrance of the south channel through which we were to pass. Having escaped this danger we headed north-east six leagues as far as White Cape; thence fifteen leagues on the same tack to Island Cape. Then we sailed east-north-east sixteen leagues as far as Saco, where we saw the Indian chief Marchin whom we had hoped to see at Kennebec lake. He had the reputation of being one of the mighty men of his country, and he had indeed a fine appearance, all his gestures being dignified, savage though he was. The Sieur de Monts made him many presents, wherewith he was much pleased, and in return gave us a young Etechemin boy whom he had captured in war, and whom we took away with us. We set out from this place together in mutual good friendship. We sailed north-east a quarter east for fifteen leagues, as far as Kennebec, where we arrived on the twenty-ninth of the month. Here we expected to find an Indian named Sasinou, of whom I have previously spoken. Thinking he would come, we waited for him for some time, in order to get from him a young Etechemin man and girl whom he held prisoners. While we were waiting for him a chief named Anassou came to see us, and bartered a few furs; and we made friends with him. He told us that ten leagues from that port there was a ship engaged in the fishery, and that those on board, under cover of friendship, had killed five Indians from this river. From his description of the men on the ship we judged they were English. We named the island where they were, the Ship, because from a distance it had that appearance. Finding that the aforesaid Sasinou did not come, we sailed east-south-east twenty leagues, as far as Isle Haute, where we cast anchor to wait for daylight.

The next day, the first of August, we headed eastward some twenty leagues, as far as Crow Cape, where we passed the night. On the second of the month, sailing north-east seven leagues, we came to the western mouth of the Ste. Croix river. Having cast anchor between the two first islands, the Sieur de Monts embarked in a canoe to go up six leagues to the settlement of Ste. Croix, where we arrived the next day with our pinnace. We found there the Sieur des Antons of St. Malo, who had come out in one of the Sieur de Monts' vessels to bring provisions and other supplies for those who were to winter in this country.

695. June, 1605. The establishment of the settlement at Port Royal.

S. de Champlain, Les voyages (1613), Chaps. 10–12, translated in H. P. Biggar (and others), The Works of Samuel de Champlain, I (1922), 367–391.

10

The Sieur de Monts decided to remove elsewhere, and to build another settlement to escape the cold and the dreadful winter we had experienced at Ste Croix island. Having up to that time found no port that appeared to us suitable, and the time being short in which to build houses and to get settled, we fitted out two pinnaces which we loaded with the woodwork of the houses at Ste. Croix, to transport it to Port Royal twenty-five leagues distant, where we judged the climate to be much more agreeable and temperate. Pont-Gravé and I set out for this place, and on reaching it, searched for a suitable site for our residence, with shelter from the north-west wind, which we dreaded on account of having been greatly distressed thereby.

Having searched well in all directions, we found no place more suitable and better situated than a somewhat elevated spot, about which are some marshes and good springs. This place is opposite an island which is at the mouth of the Equille river. To the north of us, about a league distant, is a range of mountains, which extends nearly ten leagues north-east and south-west. The entire country is covered with very dense forests, as I have already mentioned, except a point a league and a half up the river, where there are some oaks which are very scattered, and numbers of wild vines. These could easily be cleared and the place brought under cultivation, notwithstanding it is sterile and sandy. We had almost resolved to build there, but considered that we should be too far within the harbour and river, and this made us change our minds.

Having seen that the site for our settlement was a good one, we began to clear the ground, which was full of trees, and to erect the houses as quickly as possible. Everybody was busy at this work. After everything had been set in order and the greater part of the dwellings built, the Sieur de Monts decided to return to France to obtain from His Majesty what was necessary for his enterprise. And as commander of the said place in his absence, he wished to leave the Sieur d'Orville; but the scurvy with which the latter was afflicted would not permit him to meet the wishes of the Sieur de Monts. For this reason the matter was mentioned to Pont-Gravé who was offered the position, which he accepted, and had the small unfinished part of the settlement completed. And I myself, at the same time, determined to remain there as well, in the hope of making new discoveries towards Florida; and of this the Sieur de Monts highly approved.

11

As soon as the said Sieur de Monts had departed, some of the forty or forty-five who stayed behind began to make gardens. I also, in order not to remain idle, made one which I surrounded with ditches full of water wherein I placed some very fine trout; and through it flowed three brooks of very clear running water from which the greater part of our settlement was supplied. I constructed in it near the seashore a little sluiceway, to draw off the water whenever I desired. This spot was completely surrounded by meadows, and there I arranged a summer-house with fine trees, in order that I might enjoy the fresh air. I constructed there likewise a small reservoir to hold salt-water fish, which we took out as we required them. I also sowed there some seeds which throve well; and I took therein a particular pleasure, although beforehand it had entailed a great deal of labour. We often resorted there to pass the time, and it seemed as if the little birds thereabouts received pleasure from this; for they gathered in great numbers and warbled and chirped so pleasantly that I do not think I ever heard the like.

The plan of the settlement was ten fathoms in length and eight in breadth, which makes thirty-six in circumference. On the eastern side is a storehouse of the full width, with a very fine cellar some five to six feet high. On the north side is the Sieur de Monts' dwelling, constructed of fairly good wood-work. Around the courtyard are the quarters of the workmen. At one corner on the western side is a platform whereon were placed four pieces of cannon; and at the other corner, towards the east, is a palisade fashioned like a platform, as can be seen from the following picture.

A few days after the completion of the buildings I went to the river St. John to find the Indian called Secoudon, who had conducted Prévert's men to the copper mine, for which I had already searched in company with the Sieur de Monts when we were at the Port of Mines but all to no purpose. Having found him I begged him to accompany us, to which he very readily agreed, and came with us to show it to us. We found there, embedded in greyish and red rocks, a few small bits of copper about as thick as a sou, and others thicker. The miner who was with us, named Master Jaques, a native of Sclavonia, a man well versed in the search for minerals, went all around the coasts to see if he could find any matrix, but saw none at all. He did find, however, a few paces from where we obtained the aforementioned pieces of copper, a kind of mine which somewhat resembled one. He stated that, from the appearance of the ground, it might prove good if it were worked, and that it was not likely there would be pure copper on the surface unless there was a quantity underneath. The truth is that if the sea did not cover these mines twice a day, and if they did not occur in rocks of such hardness, one might expect something therefrom.

After having examined it we returned to our settlement, where we found some of our men ill with scurvy, though not so seriously as at Ste Croix island. Yet, of the forty-five of us twelve died, of whom our miner was one, and five were ill who recovered on the approach of spring. Our surgeon, named Des Champs, of Honfleur, a man skilled in his profession, opened some of the bodies to see if he could discover the cause of this illness better than had those who had tried in the previous year. He found the same parts of the body affected as in those opened on Ste. Croix island, and could discover no remedy for curing them any more than had the others.

On the twentieth of December it began to snow, and some ice passed in front of our settlement. The winter was not so severe as it had been the year before, nor was the snow as deep or of such long duration. Among other occurrences, on the twentieth of February 1605 it blew so great a gale that a large number of trees were blown down, roots and all, and many broken off. It was a strange sight to behold. The rains were quite frequent, which was the cause of the mild winter in comparison with the preceding, although from Port Royal to Ste Croix the distance is only twenty-five leagues.

On the first of March, Pont-Gravé had a pinnace of some seventeen to eighteen tons' burden fitted out, which was ready on the fifteenth to proceed on a voyage of discovery along the coast of Florida.

For this purpose we set out on the sixteenth following, but were obliged to put in at an island to the south of Manan, having made that day eighteen leagues. We anchored in a sandy cove open to the sea, into which the south wind blew. During the night it increased to such force that the anchor could not hold, and we were driven towards the coast at the mercy of God and the waves, which were so furious and dangerous that when at anchor we were hoisting the lugsail in order afterwards to cut the cable at the hawse-hole, it did not give us time but straightway broke of itself. In the surf the wind and waves threw us upon a small rock, and we only awaited the moment when we should see our boat break up, to save ourselves if we could upon some wreckage. In this desperate situation, after we had withstood several other waves, there came one so huge and fortunate that it carried us over the rock and threw us upon a little sandy beach which preserved us for the nonce from shipwreck.

The pinnace being aground we immediately began to unload what was in her to see where was the damage, which was not so great as we imagined. She was speedily repaired by the diligence of Champdoré her master. When she was refitted, we reloaded her, and awaited fine weather and for the fury of the sea to abate. This did not happen for four days, that is to say on the twenty-first of March, when we left this place of misfortune, and proceeded to Shell harbour, seven or eight leagues distant, which is at the mouth of the Ste. Croix river, where lay a great quantity of snow. On account of fogs and head winds, which are usual at this season, we remained there until the twenty-ninth of this same month, when Pont-Gravé decided to put back to Port Royal to see in what state were our companions whom we had left there ill. On our arrival Pont-Gravé fell ill with an affection of the heart, which delayed us until the eighth of April.

On the ninth of the same month, although still indisposed, he embarked again, because of his desire to explore the coast of Florida, and in the belief that the change of air would restore him to health. That day we cast anchor and passed the night at the entrance of the port, two leagues from our settlement.

The next morning before daybreak Champdoré came and asked Pont-Gravé whether he wished to have the anchor up, and the latter answered that if Champdoré considered the weather favourable, he should get under way. Thereupon Champdoré at once had the anchor raised and the lugsail spread to the wind, which according to him was north-north-east. The weather was very thick, being rainy and very foggy, with more prospect of bad weather than of good. As he sought to pass through the entrance of the port, we were suddenly carried by the tide out of the passage, and were upon the rocks on the east-north-east side before we had seen them. Pont-Gravé and I, who were in bed, heard the sailors crying out and exclaiming, "We are lost," which soon brought me to my feet to see what had happened. Pont-Gravé was still ill, and this prevented him from getting up as quickly as he wished. I was no sooner on deck than the pinnace was thrown upon the coast, and the wind which was north drove us upon a point. We unfurled the mainsail, which we set and

hoisted as high as we could in order to drive ourselves still farther upon the rocks, for fear lest the ebb of the tide, which by good fortune was running out, should drag us where it would have been impossible to save ourselves. At the first bump of our boat upon the rocks the rudder was broken, part of the keel and three or four planks were stove in, and some ribs were broken. This astonished us, for our pinnace immediately filled, and all we could do was to wait until the tide ran out to get ashore; for otherwise we risked our lives in consequence of the swell, which was very great and furious all about us. The tide having at length ebbed, we went ashore amid the storm, and immediately unloaded the pinnace of her contents; and we saved a good part of the commodities in her, with the help of the Indian chief Secoudon and his companions, who came to us in their canoes to carry to our settlement what we had saved from our pinnace, which, being all battered, on the return of the tide, went to pieces. We were very happy to have saved our lives, and returned to our settlement with our poor Indians, who remained there the greater part of the winter. We praised God for saving us from this shipwreck, from which we did not expect to escape so easily.

The loss of our pinnace caused us great sorrow; for we saw ourselves through want of a vessel without hope of completing the voyage we had undertaken; and we were unable to construct another; for time was pressing, and although there was another pinnace on the stocks, it would have taken too long to get her ready, and we could not have made use of her before the return from France of the vessels we were expecting from day to day.

This was a great disaster and a lack of foresight on the part of the master, who was obstinate and little versed in seamanship, and would have his own way. He was a good carpenter, skilled in building vessels and careful in fitting them out with everything needful, but he was in no wise qualified to navigate them.

On reaching the settlement, Pont-Gravé held an inquiry against Champdoré, who was accused of having run our pinnace ashore with malicious intent, and after his examination he was imprisoned and handcuffed, in order to be taken to France and delivered into the custody of the Sieur de Monts, and justice demanded against him.

On the fifteenth of June Pont-Gravé, seeing that the vessels from France did not return, had Champdoré set free to finish the pinnace which was on the stocks; and this duty he discharged very well.

And on the sixteenth of July, which was the date when we were to leave in case the vessels had not returned, as was set out in the commission which the Sieur de Monts had given to Pont-Gravé, we departed from our settlement to go to Cape Breton or to Gaspé, to seek means of returning to France, since we were without any news from that quarter.

There were two of our men who of their own accord remained to take care of what was left of the goods in the settlement, to each of whom Pont-Gravé promised fifty silver crowns, and fifty more which he agreed to pay to their representatives, on coming to get them in the following year.

There was an Indian chief named Membertou, who promised to look after them, and that they should be no more unhappy than if they were his own children. We had found him a good Indian all the time we were there, although he had the reputation of being the worst and most treacherous man of his tribe.

12

On the seventeenth of the month, in accordance with the resolution we had formed, we set out from the entrance to Port Royal in two pinnaces, one of eighteen and the other of seven to eight tons' burden, to make the journey to Cape Breton or Canso. We came to anchor in Long Island strait, where during the night our cable broke, and we were in danger of being lost because of the great tidal currents which dash against numerous rocky points that lie within and at the outlet of this place: but by the efforts of all, this was avoided and we managed that time to escape.

On the twenty-first of the month, between Long Island and Cape Fourchu, there arose a heavy squall which broke our rudder-irons and placed us in such a predicament that we did not know what to do; for the fury of the sea did not permit us to land, since the breakers ran mountains high along the coast. Consequently we determined rather to die at sea than to land, in the hope that the wind and the tempest would abate so that with the wind astern we might afterwards run ashore on some sandy beach. As each was thinking for himself what should be done for our safety, a sailor suggested that a mass of rope attached to the stern of the pinnace and dragging in the water would serve to some extent to steer our vessel; but this had no effect at all, and we saw clearly that unless God aided us by other means, this one would not preserve us from shipwreck. As we were thinking what could be done for our safety, Champdoré, who had again been handcuffed, said to some of us that if Pont-Gravé were willing, he would find a means of steering our pinnace. We reported the matter to Pont-Gravé, who did not refuse this offer, and the others even less. Champdoré was accordingly set free for the second time; and thereupon, taking a rope and cutting it, he very cleverly mended the rudder, and made it act as well as ever it had done. In this way he makes amends for the mistakes he had committed on the first pinnace, which was lost; and through the entreaties we made for him to Pont-Gravé, who had some reluctance in coming to this decision, he was freed from the accusation against him.

The same day we came to anchor near the Bay of Currents, two leagues from Cape Fourchu, and there our pinnace was repaired.

On the twenty-third of July we were off Cape Sable.

On the twenty-fourth of the same month, at two o'clock in the afternoon, we caught sight, near the Isle of Cormorants, of a shallop coming from Cape Sable. Some of us thought it contained Indians who were leaving Cape Breton or the island of Canso: others said it might be one of the shallops they were sending from Canso to obtain news of us. Finally, on drawing nearer, we saw they were Frenchmen, which gave us great joy; and when the boat had almost reached us, we recognised Ralleau, the secretary of the Sieur de Monts, which redoubled our joy. He informed us that the Sieur de Monts was sending a vessel of one hundred and twenty tons, commanded by the Sieur de Poutrincourt, who as lieutenant-general had come to remain in the country with fifty men whom he had landed at Canso. Thence the vessel had taken the open sea to try and find us, whilst Ralleau in a shallop skirted the coast to meet us in case we should come that way, thinking we might have left Port Royal, as indeed was the case; and in so doing they acted very wisely. All this news made us turn back, and we arrived on the twenty-fifth of the month at Port Royal, where we found the said vessel, and the Sieur de Poutrincourt, which gave us great delight thus to see revived what had been beyond hope. He told us that the delay had been caused by an accident which had happened to the vessel on leaving the chain at La Rochelle, whence they had set out; and during the voyage they had been delayed by bad weather.

The next day the Sieur de Poutrincourt proceeded to explain what ought to be done, and with the approval of every one decided to remain at Port Royal for this year, inasmuch as nothing had been discovered since the Sieur de Monts' voyage, and the four months which remained before winter were not sufficient to seek a new site and make another settlement, especially with a large vessel, which is unlike a pinnace that draws little water, ferrets everywhere, and finds suitable places for settlements: but during this time we should merely discover some more commodious situation for our abode.

Upon this decision, the Sieur de Poutrincourt at once despatched some labourers to cultivate the land at a spot he considered suitable, which is up the river a league and a half from the settlement of Port Royal, where we had thought of making our abode. There he had wheat, rye, hemp, and several other seeds sown to ascertain how they would thrive.

On the 22nd of August, a small pinnace was seen approaching our settlement. It was Des Antons of St. Malo who came from Canso, where his vessel was fishing, to inform us that about Cape Breton were several vessels engaged in the fur trade, and that if we cared to send our ship, we might capture them on our way back to France. It was decided to do so when the ship had unloaded the goods which were on board.

When this had been done Pont-Gravé embarked with the remainder of his companions who had spent the winter with him at Port Royal, excepting one or two, who were Champdoré and Foulgeré of Vitré. I also remained with the Sieur de Poutrincourt, in order with God's help to complete the map I had begun of these coasts and countries. Everything having been put in order at the settlement, the Sieur de Poutrincourt had provisions placed on board for our voyage to the coast of Florida.

On the 29th of August we set out from Port Royal, along with Pont-Gravé and Des Antons, who were on their way to Cape Breton and Canso to seize the ships which were trading in furs, as I have already mentioned. Having reached the sea, we were obliged to put back to port on account of the bad weather we met. The large vessel held on her course, and was soon lost to view.

696. September to November, 1605. The third voyage along the New England coast.

S. de Champlain, Les voyages (1613), Chaps. 13–15, translated in H. P. Biggar (and others), The Works of Samuel de Champlain, I (1922), 392–437.

13

On the 5th of September we set out anew from Port Royal.

On the 7th we were off the mouth of the river Ste. Croix, where we found a number of Indians, among others Secoudon and Messamouet. We were like to have been lost there on a rocky islet through Champdoré's obstinacy, to which he was very subject.

The next day we went in a shallop to Ste Croix island, where the Sieur de Monts had wintered, to see if we could find any spikes of wheat and other seeds he had had sown there. We found some wheat which had fallen to the ground and had come up as fine as one could desire, and a quantity of garden vegetables which had grown up fair and large. It gave us the greatest pleasure to see that the soil there was good and fertile.

After visiting the island we returned to our pinnace, which was of eighteen tons' burden; and on the way caught a number of mackerel, which abound there at this season. It was decided to continue our voyage along the coast, which was not a wise decision, inasmuch as we lost much time in going over again the discoveries that the Sieur de Monts had made as far as Port Mallebarre. It would have been more to the purpose in my opinion, to cross from where we were to the aforementioned Mallebarre, the route to which we knew, and then to employ the time in exploring to the 40th degree or farther south, revisiting on our return the entire coast at our leisure.

Upon this decision we took with us Secoudon and Messamouet, who came in a boat as far as Saco, where they wished to go to make an alliance with those of that country by offering them sundry presents.

On the 12th of September we set out from the river Ste Croix.

On the 21st we reached Saco, where we saw Onemechin, chief of that river, and Marchin, who had finished harvesting their corn. At the island of Bacchus, we saw grapes which were ripe and fairly good, and others which were not; they had a fruit as fine as those of France, and I am convinced that if they were cultivated one could make good wine from them.

In this place the Sieur de Poutrincourt rescued a prisoner from Onemechin, to whom Messamouet made presents of kettles, axes, knives and other articles. Onemechin made return in Indian corn, squashes, and Brazilian beans; but these did not altogether satisfy Messamouet, who departed much displeased because he had not been suitably repaid for what he had given them, and with the intention of making war upon them before long; for these people give only with the idea of receiving something, except to persons who have done them some signal service, such as aiding them in their wars.

Continuing our route we went to Island Cape, where we were delayed a little by bad weather and fog, and where we did not see much probability of spending the night, inasmuch as the place was not suitable for this purpose. Whilst we were in this predicament I remembered that when following this coast with the Sieur de Monts, I had noted on my map at a league's distance a place which appeared suitable for vessels, into which we had not entered because, at the time we were passing, the wind was favourable for holding on our course. This place lay behind us, on which account I said to the Sieur de Poutrincourt that we must stand in for a point which was then visible, where was situated the place in question which seemed to me suitable for passing the night. We proceeded to anchor at the entrance, and the next day went inside.

The Sieur de Poutrincourt landed with eight or ten of our company. We saw some very fine grapes which were ripe, Brazilian peas, pumpkins, squashes, and some good roots with a flavour like that of chards, which the Indians cultivate. They presented us with a number of these in exchange for other little trifles which we gave them. They had already completed their harvest. We saw two hundred Indians in this place, which is pleasant enough; and here are many nut-trees, cypresses, sassafras, oaks, ashes, and beeches, which are very fine. The chief of this place, who is called Quiouhamenec, came to see us with another chief, a neighbour of his named Cohouepech, whom we entertained. Onemechin, chief of Saco, also came to see us there, and we gave him a coat, which he did not keep long, but presented to another because, being uncomfortable in it, he could not adapt himself to it. At this place we also saw an Indian who wounded himself so badly in the foot, and lost so much blood, that he fainted. A number of other Indians gathered about him, and sang for some time before touching him. Afterwards they made certain motions with their feet and hands, and shook his head; then while they breathed upon him, he came to. Our surgeon dressed his injuries, and afterwards he was able to go off in good spirits.

The next day, as we were caulking our shallop, the Sieur de Poutrincourt caught sight in the woods of a great many Indians, who with the intention of doing us some injury were on their way towards a little brook in the strait at the causeway leading to the mainland, where some of our men were washing their clothes. As I was walking along the causeway these Indians caught sight of me, and in order to put a good face upon the matter, since they saw clearly that I at the same time had discovered them, they began to shout and to dance; then they came towards me with their bows, arrows, quivers, and other arms. And inasmuch as there was a meadow between them and me, I made a sign to them to dance again, which they did in a circle, putting all their arms in the centre. They had hardly begun when they espied in the woods the Sieur de Poutrincourt with eight musketeers, which astonished them. Nevertheless they did not fail to complete their dance, but when it was finished, they withdrew in all directions, being apprehensive lest some bad turn should be done to them. However, we said nothing to them, and showed them only evidences of good will. Then we returned to our shallop to launch it and to take our departure. They begged us to remain a day longer, saying that more than two thousand men would come to see us; but as we could not afford to lose time we were unwilling to delay any longer. I believe that their plan was to surprise us. Some of the land is cleared, and they were constantly clearing more, in the following fashion. They cut down the trees at a height of three feet from the ground; then they burn the branches upon the trunk, and sow their corn between the fallen timber; and in course of time they take out the roots. There are also fine meadows for supporting numbers of cattle. This port is very beautiful and a good one, with water enough for vessels, and shelter behind the islands. It lies in latitude 43°, and we have named it the Beautiful Port.

On the last day of September we departed from the Beautiful Port and passed St. Louis; and we sailed all night to reach the White Cape. The next morning, an hour before daylight we found ourselves in the White Bay to leeward of White Cape, in eight feet of water, at a distance of a league from the land. Here we cast anchor in order not to approach closer before daylight, and in order to see how we stood regarding the tide. Meanwhile we sent our shallop to make soundings, and they did not find more than eight feet of water, so that it was necessary to determine, while awaiting daylight, what we should do. The water fell to five feet, and our pinnace sometimes touched upon the sand, without, however, being injured or doing herself any damage; for the sea was calm; and we had not more than three feet of water under us, when the tide began to come in, which gave us great encouragement.

When day dawned we descried to leeward a very low sandy coast off which we lay. We sent the boat to make soundings in the direction of a tract of upland which is somewhat elevated, and where we judged there was much water; and in fact we found there seven fathoms. We went there and cast anchor, and at once prepared the shallop with nine or ten men to go on shore and examine a place where we judged there was a good, safe harbour in which we might find safety should the wind become stronger. Having explored it, we entered with two, three, and four fathoms of water. When we were inside, we found

five and six. There were plenty of oysters, of very good quality, which we had not hitherto seen; and we named the port Oyster Harbour. It is in latitude 42°. There came to us three canoes of Indians. That day the wind was favourable, and for this reason we weighed anchor to go to White Cape, distant from this place five leagues north a quarter north-east, and we doubled it.

The following day, the second of October, we arrived off Mallebarre, where we remained some time on account of the bad weather we experienced. During this time the Sieur de Poutrincourt, accompanied by twelve to fifteen men, paid a visit to the port in the shallop. There came to meet him some 150 Indians, singing and dancing, in accordance with their custom. After having viewed this place we returned to our vessel, and, the wind coming fair, made sail along the coast, steering south.

14

When we were some six leagues from Mallebarre, we cast anchor near the shore because the wind was not favourable. Along this coast we observed smoke which the Indians were making; and this made us decide to go and visit them. For this purpose the shallop was got ready; but when we were near the shore, which is sandy, we were unable to land, as the swell was too great. The Indians, seeing this, launched a canoe; and eight or nine of them came out to us, singing and indicating by signs the joy it gave them to see us; and they showed us that lower down was a port where we could place our pinnace in safety.

Being unable to land, the shallop came back to the pinnace, and the Indians, who had been kindly treated, returned to the shore.

The next day, the wind being fair, we continued our course to the north five leagues, and we had no sooner gone this far than we found three and four fathoms of water at a distance of a league and a half from the shore. And going a little farther, the depth suddenly lessened to a fathom and a half and two fathoms, which made us apprehensive, since the sea was breaking everywhere, and we could perceive no passage along which we could return upon our course; for the wind was altogether against us.

So it came about that, being caught among the breakers and sand-banks, we had to run at haphazard where one judged there was water enough for our pinnace, which drew but at the most four feet. We kept on among these breakers until we found four feet and a half. Finally by God's favour we succeeded in passing over a sandy point which projects about three leagues into the sea to the south-south-east, making a very dangerous place. Doubling this cape, which we named Reef Cape, and which is twelve or thirteen leagues from Mallebarre, we anchored in two and a half fathoms of water, inasmuch as we found ourselves surrounded on all sides by breakers and shoals, save only in certain places where the sea was not breaking very much. We sent the shallop to seek out a channel in order that we might go to a place which we concluded was the one indicated to us by the Indians. We also believed there was a river there where we could lie in safety.

When our shallop reached the place, our men landed and inspected the locality, after which they came back with an Indian whom they brought with them. They informed us that at high tide we could enter, and it was resolved to do so. We at once weighed anchor and, under the guidance of the Indian, who acted as our pilot, proceeded to anchor in a road-stead in front of the port, in six fathoms of water and good bottom; for we could not go inside because night had overtaken us.

The next day men were sent to place buoys upon the extremity of a sand-bank which lies at the harbour's mouth; then at high tide we entered the place with two fathoms of water. Once inside we gave praise to God for bringing us to a place of safety. Our rudder had broken and been mended with ropes, and we feared lest in the midst of these shallows and strong tides it should break again, which would have resulted in our destruction. Inside this harbour there is but one fathom of water, and at high tide two fathoms. Towards the east lies a bay which doubles to the north some three leagues, and therein is an island and two other little covers, which give beauty to the landscape. Here there is much cleared land and many little hills, whereon the Indians cultivate corn and other grains on which they live. Here are likewise very fine vines, plenty of nut-trees, oaks, cypresses, and a few pines. All the inhabitants of this place are much given to agriculture, and lay up a store of Indian corn for the winter, which they preserve in the following manner.

In the sand on the slope of the hills they dig holes some five to six feet more or less, and place their corn and other grains in large grass sacks, which they throw into the said holes, and cover them with sand to a depth of three or four feet above the surface of the ground. They take away this grain according to their needs, and it is preserved as well as it would be in our granaries.

At this place we saw some five to six hundred Indians who were all naked except for their privy parts, which they cover with a little piece of deer or sealskin. The women are the same, and, like the men, cover their parts with skins or leaves. Both men and women wear their hair neatly combed and braided in various ways, after the fashion of the Indians at Saco, and are well-proportioned in body, with olive-coloured skins. They adorn themselves with feathers, wampum beads, and other knick-knacks, which they arrange very neatly after the manner of embroidery. Their arms consist of bows, arrows, and clubs. They are not so much great hunters as good fishermen and tillers of the soil.

Regarding their polity, government, and religious belief, we were unable to form a judgment, and I believe that in this they do not differ from our Souriquois and Canadians, who worship neither moon nor sun nor any other thing, and pray no more than the beasts. They have indeed among them certain persons who, they say, have communication with the devil, and in these they have great faith. These persons tell them all that is to happen, in which for the most part they lie. Sometimes they succeed in hitting it right, and in telling them things similar to what actually happens. This is why they have faith in these persons, as if they were prophets, although they are naught but scamps who inveigle them, as the Egyptians and gypsies do the simple village folk. They have chiefs whom they obey in regard to matters of warfare but not in anything else. These chiefs work, and assume no higher rank than their companions. Each possesses only sufficient land for his own support.

Their lodges are separated from one another according to the extent of land that each is able to occupy. They are lofty, circular, and covered with matting made of grass or husks of Indian corn. Their only furniture consists of a bed or two raised one foot from the floor, and made of a number of saplings laid one against the other, whereon they place a reed-mat, in the Spanish manner (which is a kind of thick mattress two or three fingers in depth), and upon this they sleep. They have a great many fleas in summer, even in the fields. One day when we were out walking, we attracted such a number of them that we were obliged to change our clothes.

All the harbours, bays, and coasts from Saco onward are filled with every kind of fish like those we have near our settlements, and in such abundance that I can guarantee there was never a day or a night during which we did not see and hear more than a thousand porpoises passing alongside our pinnace and chasing the smaller fry. Here are likewise plenty of shellfish of several kinds, and especially oysters. Game birds are very plentiful.

This would prove a very good site for laying and constructing the foundations of a state, if the harbour were a little deeper and the entrance safer than it is.

Before leaving port our rudder was repaired, and we made bread from flour we had brought for our subsistence when our biscuit gave out. Meanwhile we sent the shallop with five or six men and an Indian to see whether they could find a passage more suitable for leaving than that by which we had entered.

When they had gone five or six leagues, and were close inshore, the Indian took to flight. He gave those in the shallop to understand that he was afraid lest he should be carried off to other Indians farther south who are enemies of his tribe. Upon their return they reported that as far as they had gone, there were at least three fathoms of water, and that farther on there were neither shoals nor reefs.

We accordingly made haste to repair our pinnace and to provide bread for fifteen days. Meanwhile the Sieur de Poutrincourt, accompanied by ten or twelve musketeers, visited all the surrounding country, which is very fine, as I have already stated. Here and there we saw a good number of small lodges.

Some eight or nine days later, on the Sieur de Poutrincourt's going out walking as he had done before, we observed that the Indians were taking down their wigwams and were sending into the woods their wives, children and provisions, and other necessaries of life. This made us suspect some evil design, and that they wished to attack our people who were working on shore, where they remained every night to guard whatever could not be taken on board in the evening except with much labour. This proved to be quite true; for they had resolved among themselves that, when all their goods were in safety, they would surprise the men on shore as best they could, and would carry off everything these men had there. But if perchance they found them on their guard, they would come with signs of friendship, as they were accustomed to do, laying aside their bows and arrows.

Now in view of what the Sieur de Poutrincourt had seen, and of the mode of procedure he had been told they observed when they wished to do a bad turn, we passed among their wigwams where were a number of women, to whom we gave bracelets, and rings, in order to keep them quiet and from becoming afraid of us, while to the majority of the prominent and older men we gave axes, knives, and other articles of which they stood in need. This pleased them much, repaying for all by dances, gambols, and speeches, which latter we did not in the least understand. We went about everywhere without their having the boldness to say anything to us. It amused us greatly to see them look so innocent as they made themselves appear.

We came back very quietly to our pinnace, accompanied by a few Indians. On the way we met with several small troops who were gradually collecting together, fully armed, and were much surprised to see us so far inland, little thinking that we had just made a tour of from four to five leagues through their country. When passing near us they trembled for fear lest we should harm them, which it was in our power to do; but we did nothing, although we were aware of their evil intentions. On reaching the spot where our men were at work, the Sieur de Poutrincourt asked if all things were in readiness to oppose the designs of these rascals.

He gave orders for every one on shore to be taken on board: which was done, except that the man who was making the bread remained behind to finish a baking, and two other men with him. They were told that the Indians had some evil design, and that they should make haste in order to come on board in the evening, as it was known that the Indians only put their plans into execution at night or at daybreak, which is the hour for making surprises in most of their schemes.

The evening having come, the Sieur de Poutrincourt ordered the shallop to be sent ashore to fetch the men who were left. This was done as soon as the tide would permit, and those on shore were told that they must embark for the reason already given them. This they refused to do despite the remonstrances made to them on the risks they were running and the disobedience they were showing to their chief. To these they paid no attention, except a servant of the Sieur de Poutrincourt, who came aboard; but two others disembarked from the boat and went off to the three on shore, who remained to eat some biscuits made at the same time as the bread. Since these were unwilling to do what they were told, the shallop returned alongside, but without informing the Sieur de Poutrincourt who was asleep, and who believed they were all on board the vessel.

The next morning, the fifteenth of October, the Indians did not fail to come and see in what state were our men, whom they found asleep, except one who was before the fire. Seeing them in this condition, the Indians, to the number of four hundred, came quietly over a little hill, and shot such a salvo of arrows at them as to give them no chance of recovery before they were struck dead. Fleeing as fast as they could towards our pinnace, and crying out, "Help, help, they are killing us," some of them fell dead in the water, while the rest were all pierced with arrows, of whom one died a short time afterwards. These Indians made a desperate row, with war-whoops which it was terrible to hear.

At this noise, and that of our men, the sentinel on our vessel cried out, "To arms; they are killing our men." Thereupon each quickly seized his weapons, and at the same time some fifteen or sixteen of us embarked in the shallop to go ashore. But being unable to land on account of a sandbank which lay between us and the shore, we jumped into the water and waded from this bank to the mainland, a distance of a musket-shot. As soon as we reached it, the Indians, seeing us within bowshot, fled inland. To pursue them was useless, for they are wonderfully swift. All we could do was to carry off the dead bodies and bury them near a cross which had been set up the day before, and then to look about to see whether we could catch sight of any Indians; but in this we wasted our time. Realising this we returned. Three hours later they reappeared on the shore.

We discharged several shots at them from our little brass cannon; and whenever they heard the report, they threw themselves flat on the ground to avoid the charge. In derision of us they pulled down the cross, and dug up the bodies, which displeased us greatly, and made us go after them a second time; but they fled as they had done before. We again set up the cross, and reinterred the bodies, which they had scattered here and there among the heaths, where they had kindled a fire to burn them. We returned without having accomplished more than before, seeing clearly that there was hardly any chance of taking vengeance for this blow, and that we must postpone the matter until it should please God.

On the sixteenth of the month we set out from Misfortune harbour, so named by us on account of the misfortune which happened to us there. This place is in latitude 41° 20', and distant some twelve or thirteen leagues from Mallebarre.

15

After we had gone some six or seven leagues we caught sight of an island which we named the Dubious island, since from a distance we several times thought it was something else than an island. Then the wind came against us, which made us put back to the place whence we had come; and there we remained two or three days, during which time none of the Indians came to visit us.

On the twentieth we set out again, and coasting along to the south-west about twelve leagues, passed near a river which is small and difficult to approach on account of shoals and rocks which lie at its mouth. To this I gave my own name. What we saw of these shores were low and sandy islands. The wind again came ahead, and very strong, which made us steer towards the sea, being unable to advance either on one tack or the other. But finally it fell a little and was favourable to us, but only for putting again into Misfortune harbour. The coast here though low is fine and good, yet difficult of access, there being no shelters, with reefs everywhere, and little water at a distance of two leagues from land. The most we found was, in certain holes, seven to eight fathoms; but this did not last more than a cable's length, and suddenly one was back to two or three fathoms. No one should venture here without first surveying the coast lead in hand.

Some hours after we had put into the harbour,

Pont-Gravé's son named Robert lost a hand in firing off a musket, which burst into many pieces, but did not injure any of those near him.

Now as the wind was constantly against us, and we were unable to put to sea, we determined in the meantime to seize a few Indians of this place, in order to take them to our settlement and make then grind corn at a hand-mill as a punishment for the murderous assault committed upon five or six of our men. But to do this when we were armed was very difficult, since whenever we went to them prepared to fight, they ran away, and betook themselves to the woods where we could not catch them. It was necessary, therefore, to resort to stratagem, and this is what we decided: that when they should come to make friends with us again, we should coax them, by showing them beads and other trifles, and should reassure them repeatedly; then we should take the shallop well armed, and the stoutest and strongest men we had, each with a chain of beads and a fathom of match on his arm, and should set these men on shore, where, pretending to smoke with them (each with one end of his match alight, in order not to arouse suspicion, it being customary to carry light at the end of a cord for lighting the tobacco), we were to coax them with soft words in order to draw them into the shallop; and, should they be unwilling to enter, each of our men as he approached was to choose his man, and throwing the beads about his neck should at the same moment put a cord around the man to drag him on board by force; but should they raise too great a commotion, and our men be unable to master them, then, tightening the cord well, our men were to stab them; and if by chance any should escape, there were to be men on shore to charge against them with swords. Meanwhile on board our pinnace the small cannon were to be in readiness to fire upon their companions in case any should come to their assistance, under cover of which cannon the shallop would be able to withdraw in safety. This was very well carried out, as arranged.

Several days after these things had happened, some Indians came to the sea-shore by threes and fours, making signs to us to go to them. But we saw distinctly their main body, which was in ambush under a hillock behind some bushes; and I believe their only desire was to catch us in the shallop in order to discharge a number of arrows at us, and then to take to flight. Nevertheless, the Sieur de Pourtrincourt went ashore with ten of us who were well armed and resolved to fight them if occasion arose. We proceeded to land at a spot which we thought outside their ambush, where they could not surprise us. Three or four of us landed along with the Sieur de Poutrincourt; the rest did not leave the shallop, in order to defend it and hold it ready in case of emergency. We ascended a knoll and walked round the woods to see if we could discover more clearly the said ambush. When they saw us coming towards them so freely they raised the siege, and went to other places which we were unable to discover; and of the four Indians, we saw only two, who went away quite quietly. While departing they made signs to us to take our shallop elsewhere, judging it to be in the way of their plan. And we, seeing also that they did not wish to come to us, embarked again and went to the spot they indicated, which was the second ambush they had made in their endeavour to allure us in sign of friendship to come to them unarmed. For the nonce this was not allowed to happen to us; nevertheless we approached fairly close to them without seeing this ambush, which in our opinion was not far distant. As our shallop neared the shore, they took to flight, as did also those from the ambush, at whom we fired some musket-shots, seeing their intention was but to deceive us by cajolery. In this they failed, for we saw clearly their intention, which had only mischief in view. We withdrew to our pinnace, having accomplished what we could.

That same day the Sieur de Poutrincourt decided to return to our settlement on account of four or five sick and wounded, whose wounds were growing worse through lack of ointment; for our surgeon had brought but very little. This was a great mistake on his part, and a grief to the sick men as well as to us, inasmuch as the stench from their wounds in a small vessel like ours was so great that we could scarcely bear it; and we feared lest these should engender disorders. Furthermore, we had provisions for but eight or ten days more, whatever economy we might practise; and we knew not whether the return journey might not last as long as our coming hither, which took nearly two months.

Nevertheless, our decision having been taken, we did not depart without the satisfaction of feeling that God had not left unpunished the misdeeds of these barbarians. We had indeed only reached 41° 30', which was but half a degree further than the Sieur de Monts had gone on his discovery. Accordingly we set out from this harbour.

The next day we cast anchor near Mallebarre, where we remained until the twenty-eighth of the month, when we set sail. That day the air was quite cold and there fell a little snow. We took the direct route for Norumbega or Isle Haute. Setting a course east-north-east we were two days at sea without sighting land, being delayed by bad weather. The next night we sighted the islands that lie between Kennebec and Norumbega. The wind was so high that we were obliged to put to sea to await daybreak, and we made such headway off shore, although we carried very little sail, that we could not sight it again until the next day, when we found ourselves off Isle Haute.

That day, the last of October, between Mount Desert island and Crow Cape, our rudder broke into several pieces without our knowing the cause. Each expressed his opinion about it. Night coming on with a fresh breeze, we found ourselves among a number of islands and rocks whither the wind was driving us; and we made up our minds to save ourselves if possible on the first land we should meet.

For some time we were at the mercy of wind and sea with only the foresail set: but the worst of it was that the night was dark, and we knew not where we were going; for our pinnace would not steer at all, though we did everything in our power, sometimes holding the foresail sheets in our hands, which made her steer a little. The whole time we were sounding to try and find bottom, in order to anchor and prepare ourselves for whatever might happen; but we found none. Finally, as we were going faster than we wished, it was decided to rig an oar astern, with some men to steer us to an island of which we caught sight, in order to run under the lee of it. We also put out two other oars on the gunwales towards the stern of the pinnace to help those who were steering, in order to make the vessel bear up on each tack. This invention worked so well that we steered where we wished, and sailed behind the point of the island we had seen, and cast anchor in twenty-one fathoms, waiting for daybreak to know where we were, and to find a place for making another rudder. The wind abated. At daybreak we found ourselves close to the Ordered

Islands, with breakers all about; and praised God for having preserved us so miraculously amid so many dangers.

On the first of November we went to a place we thought suitable for beaching our vessel and repairing our helm. That day I went ashore, and there saw ice two inches thick which had been frozen some eight or ten days. I noticed clearly that the temperature here differed greatly from that at Mallebarre and Misfortune harbour; for the leaves of the trees were not yet dead, nor had any fallen when we left those places. Here they had all fallen and it was much colder than at Misfortune harbour.

The next day as we were about to beach the pinnace, there arrived a canoe in which were some Etechemin Indians, who told the Indian we had with us in our pinnace, namely Secoudon, that Iouaniscou and his companions had killed some other Indians and carried off some women as prisoners, and that near Mount Desert island they had put these to death.

On the ninth of the month we set out from near Crow Cape, and on the same day cast anchor in the Petit Passage of the river Ste. Croix.

The next morning we put our Indian ashore with some supplies which we had given to him. He was much pleased and well satisfied at having made this voyage with us, and carried off some scalps of the Indians who had been killed at Misfortune harbour. The same day we came to anchor in a very fine cove on the south side of Manan island.

On the twelfth of the month we set sail, and, while under way, the shallop we were towing behind our pinnace gave the latter such a heavy and severe blow that it broached and shattered all the upper works of the pinnace, and again on the rebound broke the rudder-irons. We thought at first that the earlier blow had stove in some of our bottom-planking, which would have sunk us; for the wind was so high that we could only carry our foresail; but after inspecting the damage, which was slight, and seeing there was no danger, we managed with ropes to repair the rudder as best we could, in order to last us for the rest of our voyage. This was only until the fourteenth of November, when, at the entrance to Port Royal, we were almost lost upon a point; but God delivered us from this peril as He had from many others to which we had been exposed.

697. 1605-1606. Notes on specimens and pictures of specimens brought by the Sieur de Monts from Acadia.

A number of manuscripts exist of these notes of Nicolas-Claude de Fabri, Seigneur de Peiresc, who encountered Pierre du Gua after his return to France late in 1605. Peiresc collected what information he could about the animals, specimens, and pictures the Sieur de Monts brought back. Although the text refers to some illustrations which should go with the notes, they are missing in the manuscripts. The drawings on playing cards to which he refers were most probably made by Champlain, and it is most regrettable that none has survived. His notes help to convey the interest that the Acadian voyages were beginning to generate in France.

The notes were first published by Francis W. Gravit, "Un document inédit sur de Canada," Revue de l'Université Laval, I (1946), 282-288. They were reprinted in R. Le Blant and R. Baudry, Nouveaux documents sur Champlain et son époque (1967), pp. 102-106; they are translated for the first time.

Peiresc's observations on the curiosities brought back from Acadia by Pierre du Gua, Sieur de Mons.

[a]   November 26, 1605. After returning in 31 days from the land of Acadia in New-France, Monsieur De Mons showed us a live female moose, at the most six months old and yet as high as a medium-sized horse, with legs, like those of the doe, very small in proportion to its body. The head was very long for its size, and the ears very broad, while the tail was so short as to be more or less invisible. The hair was three or four fingerbreadths in length and in colour a pinkish-brown (rose seiche), very burnt and blackish looking and intermingled with short white and russet hairs. In short, its shape was not so different from that of a doe, except that it was more heavily built.

We saw too a tiny bird no bigger, including all its feathers, than an almond in its shell. It flits about like a butterfly and lives only on flowers, just like the honey bees. Its plumage is greyish, most of it embellished with golden-green like a peacock's. The natives of the land call it in their language *nirido* (humming-bird). It has feet and claws like a sparrow's, but so fine they look like hairs. Its beak is black, half as long as one's thumb and very pointed.

It was, however, the horseshoe crab that seemed to me more wondrous than anything on account of the great shell that covers its head and entire body: it is more than a span in diameter and as thick as a finger. It is true that the space within the shell is filled with very delicate flesh. It is pinkish-brown in colour. A rudimentary tail is attached to the shell, becoming thinner and thinner to a length of one and a half spans.

There was also the head of a bird with white feathers underneath and black on top like a magpie. Its bill was fashioned exactly like a pair of shears or scissors, seven or eight fingerbreadths in length, and apart from the tip which was black, reddish-yellow in hue. The upper part was a good two fingerbreadths shorter than the lower.

He had moose antlers so enormous that it was all a man could do to carry one. Two sets were still attached to the animals' skulls, with the skin of most of the head still to be seen. Among other things there was a tail (covered with hair like a fox's) of one and a half spans in length, which according to Monsieur Du Mons, hangs beneath the lower jaw; it seemed to me though more likely that it would be on the animal's nose, just as one sees on the beaks of turkey-cocks. In short the hair was the same colour as that of the live animal, so that there is no doubt that the antlers (*here there appears a sketch of these moose antlers*) claimed to be those of the huge beast really are just that.

Last of all [*sic*] we saw several bows longer that a man is tall, and a mace as long as one's arm made of the wood of the *plantanus* (plane tree), which was fashioned very strangely and inlaid with little bits of bone and shells. (*here there appears a sketch of this mace*)

Finally we saw a little boat about thirty spans in length, four or five spans in width and as many in depth. It was constructed of interwoven ribs which were two fingerbreadths in width, as thick as a ducatoon and made of a wood similar to that used in Marseille for basket-making. The outside of the boat was then covered over with large pieces of bark sewn together very crudely; this bark, taken from the tree known as birch, is extremely smooth and supple and dappled like that of . . . (*there are dots thus in the manuscript*). The seams are spread with gum and the whole painted red; the paddles too are half-painted.

[b]   March 13th, 1606. Monsieur De Mons' *nerido* (humming-bird) has a beak twice the length of Clusius' (Charles de l'Écluse), and a much smaller body. Its tail is black with a white tip; the whole of the back and head are green touched with gold and mixed with greyish-brown. The beak is not much broader at its base than at its tip. Its plumage shows no trace of any red colouring, contrary to what Clusius claims.

Clusius has described the same horseshoe crab, but has only given an illustration of the underside. Monsieur De Mons brought back three specimens: the first, a huge one, he gave to the king; the second has a shell merely twice the size of an average tortoise's; the third is no bigger than an egg. This latter is newly hatched, since the shell is of a whitish colour and almost transparent; besides it is no thicker than a sheet of parchment. Furthermore, the creature's head is concealed either between its legs or underneath the membranes (or gills) which extend almost to the tail. There are five legs on each side, and they are in all respects like those of the *pagurus* (hermit-crab). The part which is attached to the tail and has pointed ends is likewise very similar to the casing of the *pagurus*. Each leg is split at the end, as in the case of two large specimens, or to more exact *chelas habet* (it has claws), as do the two large crabs.

Monsieur De Mons had also a little bird like a red-winged blackbird, black all over apart from the upper wings which were a golden-red colour, but only at the very top end, like the *phoenicopterus* (flamingo). Another bird he had resembled the jay, though only one wing and the tail remained. The plumage was blue mingled with black with a white patch at the tips of some of the wing feathers.

He showed me in addition some oil paintings executed on playing cards. One showed the head and bill of a bird that was all black apart from a white patch on the head, the bill itself being fairly large, yellow at the tip, red in the middle and the rest black spotted with white and red. Another card portrayed an aquatic bird with a grey beak the same shape as a heron's. The neck was white and the top of the head red with a little red-feathered crest. The rest of the bird was grey, lighter on the breast, darker over the wings; the legs are a little on the short side for an aquatic bird. The third card depicted a kind of goose, grey all over with a fairly long bill that was curved at the tip. Its head and neck were russet coloured and it had a considerable crest of the same shade. The fourth card showed another bird whose head and neck were covered in white feathers, and its body in black ones with a little white on the wings. The tail was extremely long and pointed and consisted of most beautiful black feathers that make plumes almost as lovely as those from the heron. The eye was very red, as was the beak, though the tip which was curved and the base were both black. The fifth depicted a bird rather like a blackbird, white on the breast and speckled in black and white over all the rest of the body.

On another piece of card was a painting of a naked savage with a deeply bronzed skin, who was wearing a *plivial* (cape?) on his shoulders and a fringed loin-cloth (*devantier*) embroidered with feathers; a mace was tucked through his belt. He was leaning on a shield made in the shape of an arched door, and carried in his right hand a bow and two arrows; he wore black and white bracelets; his hair hung down to his shoulders and he wore a red cap adorned with black feathers.

Monsieur Du Mons says there are rats in that land whose nipples give off an odour of musk. He showed me some dissicated specimens which smelt almost the same, though perhaps a little sweeter. They were a bit larger than a weasel.

Last year he sent to the king an animal called a caribou, which is of the size and proportions of a doe, but with a chest just slightly larger. It has a very small head and its feet are extremely broad and large for the size of the creature. The hair is greyish-reddish. It was left to die in the moat at Saint-Germain-en-Laye through lack of water or other necessities.

698. 1606–1607. The second winter at Port Royal and its abandonment in August, 1607.

The second winter at Port Royal proved quite reasonable and the settlement was considerably developed. The Bay of Fundy was reexplored. But the Sieur de Monts' patent was cancelled and the settlement recalled. They did not leave until August 11, and on September 30 put in at St. Malo.

S. de Champlain, Les voyages *(1613), Chaps. 16–17, translated in H. P. Biggar (and others),* The Works of Samuel de Champlain, *I (1922), 438–469.*

16

Upon our arrival, Lescarbot, who had remained at the settlement, along with the others who had stayed there, welcomed us with sundry jollities for our entertainment.

Having landed, and recovered breath, each began to make small gardens, and I myself began to take care of mine, in preparation for the spring, in order to sow several kinds of seed which we had brought from France and which throve extremely well in all the gardens.

The Sieur de Poutrincourt on the other hand had a water-mill built about a league and a half from our settlement, close to the point where wheat had been sown. The mill was built near a waterfall formed by a small river which is not navigable on account of the number of rocks in it, and which falls into a small lake. At this place is such abundance of herring in their season that one could fill shallops with them, if one would take the trouble and bring thither the requisite appliances. Indeed the Indians of these parts come there at times to fish. Here we also made a quantity of charcoal for our forge. During the winter, in order not to be idle, I undertook to construct a road along the edge of the woods leading to a little river, which is like a brook, and which we named the troutery, for the reason that there were in it many of these fish. I asked the Sieur de Poutrincourt for two or three men, whom he gave me to assist me in making this walk. I got on so well that in a short time I had cleared it. It extends as far as the troutery, and is nearly two thousand paces long; and served as our promenade under the shade of the trees I had left standing on both sides. This induced the Sieur de Poutrincourt to have another made through the woods as a direct route to the entrance of Port Royal, about three and a half leagues by land from

our settlement. He had a beginning made from the troutery for about half a league, but never finished it because the labour was too great, and he was busy with other things then more necessary.

Some time after our arrival, we caught sight of a shallop in which were some Indians, who informed us that at the place whence they came, which was Norumbega, an Indian, who was one of our friends, had been killed out of vengeance because another Indian, Iouaniscou, and his people had killed some Indians from Norumbega and Kennebec, as I have already related; and that the Etechemins had told this to Secoudon, the Indian who was at that time with us.

The Indian in command of the boat was called Ouagimou, who was on familiar terms with Bessabes, chief of Norumbega river, from whom he asked the body of Panonias who had been killed. Bessabes granted him this, begging him to say to his friends that he was very sorry for Panonias' death, assuring Ouagimou that it was without his knowledge that Panonias had been killed, and that, since it was not his fault, he begged him to say to them that he hoped they would remain friends as heretofore. This Ouagimou promised to do on his return home. He told us he was much worried until he got away from them, however much friendliness they showed him; for they were liable to change, and he feared lest they would treat him as they had him who was slain. Accordingly he did not tarry long after his dismissal. He brought the body in his shallop from Norumbega to our settlement, a distance of fifty leagues.

As soon as the body was brought on shore, the relatives and friends began to make outcries beside it, their faces being painted all over with black, which is their manner of mourning. After a great deal of weeping, they took a quantity of tobacco and two or three dogs and other things belonging to the deceased, and burnt them upon the shore some thousand paces from our settlement. Their cries continued until they had returned to their wigwams.

The next day they took the body and wrapped it in a red coverlet which Membertou, the chief of these parts, had much importuned me to give him, inasmuch as it was handsome and large. This he presented to the relatives of the dead man, who thanked me very much for it. Then after having bound up the body, they decorated it with many kinds of ornaments, such as beads and bracelets of several colours; painted his face, and upon his head stuck many feathers and other objects the fairest they had. Then they placed the body on its knees between two stakes, with another supporting it under the arms; and about to body were his mother, his wife, and other relatives and friends, both women and girls, who howled like dogs.

Whilst the women and girls were lamenting, the Indian named Membertou made a speech to his companions upon the death of the deceased, inciting each to take vengeance for the wickedness and treachery committed by the subjects of Bessabes, and to make war on them as soon as possible. All promised him to do so in the spring.

When the speech was finished and the cries over, they carried the body of the dead man into another wigwam. Having smoked, they again wrapped it in a moose-skin and tied it up very securely, and preserved it until there should be a larger number of Indians present, from each of whom the brother of the dead man expected to receive presents, since it is their custom to give such to those who have lost their fathers, mothers, wives, brothers, or sisters.

On the night of the twenty-sixth of December, a wind from the south-east blew down a number of trees.

The last day of December it began to snow, and continued to do so until the next morning.

On the sixteenth of January following, in the year 1607, the Sieur de Pourtrincourt, wishing to go to the head of Equille river, found it closed with ice some two leagues from our settlement, and had to return since he was unable to go farther.

On the eighth of February some ice-floes began to come down from the head of the river into the port, which only freezes along the shore.

On the tenth of May following it snowed the whole night, and towards the end of the month there were several heavy white frosts which lasted as late as the tenth and twelfth of June, when all the trees were covered with leaves, except the oaks which do not put out theirs until about the fifteenth.

The winter was not so long as in the preceding years, nor did the snow remain so late upon the ground. It rained pretty often, on which account the Indians suffered a severe famine, because of the scarcity of snow. The Sieur de Poutrincourt fed part of those who were with us, that is to say Membertou, his wife and his children, and some others.

We spent this winter very pleasantly, and had good fare by means of the Order of Good Cheer which I established, and which everybody found beneficial to his health, and more profitable than all sorts of medicine we might have used. This Order consisted of a chain which we used to place with certain little ceremonies about the neck of one of our people, commissioning him for that day to go hunting. The next day it was conferred upon another, and so on in order. All vied with each other to see who could do the best, and bring back the finest game. We did not come off badly, nor did the Indians who were with us.

There was scurvy among our men, but not so violent as it had been in the previous years. Nevertheless, seven of them died, as did another from an arrow-shot received from the Indians at Misfortune harbour.

Our surgeon, named Master Stephen, opened a few bodies, and, as had been done in the other cases in the previous years, found almost all the interior parts affected. Some eight or ten who were sick got well in the spring.

At the beginning of March and of April, each began to prepare the gardens for the sowing of the seeds in May, which is the proper season. These seeds came up just as well as they could have done in France, but a little later. I believe that in France the season is at the most a month and a half earlier. As I have said, the season for sowing is in May, although sometimes one can sow in April; but such sowings advance no faster than those made in May, when there are no longer any frosts that can injure the plants except the very tender ones; for there are many that cannot withstand the white frosts except after much care and labour.

On the twenty-fourth of May we caught sight of a small pinnace of six to seven tons' burden, which we sent men to examine. They found it was a young man of St. Malo, named Chevalier, who brought letters from the Sieur de Monts to the Sieur de Poutrincourt, by which he directed the latter to bring back his company to France. He told us of the birth of Monseigneur the Duke of Orleans, which rejoiced us, and in honour thereof we made bonfires and chanted the *Te Deum*.

Between the beginning and the twentieth of June some thirty or forty Indians assembled at this place in order to go upon the war-path against the Almouchiquois, and to avenge the death of Panonias, who was buried by the Indians according to their rites, after which they gave a quantity of furs to a brother of his. When these presents had been made, they all set out from this place on the twenty-ninth of June to go on the war-path at Saco, which is the country of the Almouchiquois.

Some days after the said Chevalier's arrival, the Sieur de Poutrincourt sent him to the rivers St. John and Ste Croix to trade for furs; but he did not allow him to go there without men to bring the long-boat back, since some persons had reported that Chevalier was desirous of returning to France with the vessel in which we had come out and of leaving us in our settlement. Lescarbot was among those who accompanied him, having not yet left Port Royal. This is the farthest he went, which is only fourteen to fifteen leagues beyond the said Port Royal.

While awaiting the return of the said Chevalier, the Sieur de Poutrincourt went in a shallop with seven or eight men to the head of French Bay [Bay of Fundy]. Leaving port and sailing north-east one quarter east along the coast for some twenty-five leagues, we came to a cape where the Sieur de Poutrincourt wished to climb a cliff more than thirty fathoms in height. Here he ran the risk of losing his life; for having reached the top of the rock, which is very narrow, and which he had ascended with considerable difficulty, the summit trembled beneath him. The cause of this was that in course of time moss had accumulated there to a thickness of four to five feet, and not being solid, trembled when trodden upon; and very often when one stepped upon a stone three or four others fell: so that, although he had got up with difficulty, he came down with much greater trouble, though some sailors, who are men fairly skilful in climbing, had passed him a hawser (which is a rope of medium size), by the aid of which he descended. This place was named Cape Poutrincourt, and is in latitude 45° 40'.

We went to the head of this bay, but saw nothing except certain white stones for making lime, which were few in number, and many sea-gulls, which are birds that were upon some islands. We captured as many of these as we wished. We made the circuit of the bay in order to visit the Port of Mines, where I had been already. I conducted thither the Sieur de Poutrincourt, who gathered some small pieces of copper which were obtained with very great difficulty. This whole bay is about twenty leagues in circumference, and at its head is a small stream which is very shoal and has little water. There are a number of other small streams and certain places where there are good harbours, but only at high tide, which here rises five fathoms. In one of these harbours, three to four leagues north of Poutrincourt Cape, we found a very old cross, all covered with moss, and almost wholly rotted away, an unmistakable sign that formerly Christians had been there. This whole country is covered with very dense forests, and the land is not very pleasant except in certain places.

From the Port of Mines we went back to our settlement. Inside that bay are great tidal currents which set to the south-west.

On the twelfth of July arrived Ralleau, secretary of the Sieur de Monts, with three others in a shallop which came from a place called Ingonish, distant from Port Royal some hundred and sixty or hundred and seventy leagues. He confirmed to the Sieur de Poutrincourt the report brought by Chevalier.

On the third of July, we made ready three long-boats to send the people and stores from our settlement to Canso, distant some hundred and fifteen leagues, and in latitude 45° 40'. Here, engaged in the fishery, was the ship which was to take us back to France.

The Sieur de Poutrincourt sent away all his companions, but remained with eight others at the settlement in order to take back to France certain grains which were not yet quite ripe.

On the tenth of August, Membertou returned from the war. He told us he had been to Saco and had killed twenty Indians and wounded ten or twelve others; and that Onemechin, chief of that locality, Marchin, and another, had been killed by Sasinou, chief of the Kennebec river, who was afterwards killed by the companions of Onemechin and Marchin. This whole war was solely on account of Panonias, one of our Indian friends, who, as I have already stated, had been killed at Norumbega by the said Onemechin's and Marchin's people.

The chiefs who have now replaced Onemechin, Marchin, and Sasinou are their sons—that is to say, for Sasinou, Pememen, Abriou for Marchin his father, and for Onemechin, Queconsicq. The two latter were wounded by Membertou's men, who ambushed them under pretence of friendship, as is their custom, against which it is necessary to be on one's guard as much with one party as the other.

17

On the eleventh of August we set out from our settlement in a shallop, and coasted the shore as far as Cape Fourchu, where I had been already.

Continuing our route along the coast as far as cape La Have (where we made our first landing with the Sieur de Monts on the eighth of May, 1604), we explored the coast from this place as far as Canso, a distance of nearly sixty leagues, which I had not yet done. I examined it very carefully, and made a map of it, along with the rest.

Leaving cape La Have, we went to Sesambre, which is an island so named by some men of St. Malo, and distant from La Have fifteen leagues. On the way are a large number of islands which we had named the Martyrs, because some Frenchmen had once been killed there by the Indians. These islands lie in several coves and bays, in one of which is a river called Ste. Marguerite. It is seven leagues from Sesambre, which is in latitude 44° 25′. The islands and coasts are covered with quantities of pines, firs, birches, and other woods of poor quality. The fishing is abundant, as are also the game-birds.

Beyond Sesambre we passed a bay very free from obstructions and seven to eight leagues in circumference, where there are no islands in the passage but only at its head, which forms the mouth of a small shallow river. We went to a harbour, distant from Sesambre some eight leagues on a course north-east one quarter east, which is fairly good for ships of the burden of one hundred to one hundred and twenty tons. In the entrance lies an island, from which at low water one can pass to the mainland. We named this place St. Helen's harbour. It lies in latitude 44° 40′, a little more or less.

From this place we went to a bay called bay of All Islands, which is some fourteen to fifteen leagues in circumference; a dangerous place on account of the reefs, shoals, and flats there. The land presents a most unattractive appearance, being covered with the same trees I have mentioned above. In this place we were delayed by bad weather.

Thence we passed close to a river distant from the preceding bay six leagues, and called the river of Isle Verte, because it has such an island at its mouth. This short distance we made is filled with numbers of rocks projecting about a league out to sea, which breaks over them strongly. The latitude is 45° 15′.

Then we went to a place where there is a cove with two or three islands and a rather fine harbour, distant from Isle Verte three leagues. We also passed many islands which lie in a row one after another, and named them the Ordered Islands, distant from Isle Verte some six to seven leagues. Afterwards we passed another bay, where there are many islands, and came to a place where we found a vessel that was fishing among the islands which lie some distance from the coast and four leagues from the Ordered Islands. This place we named Savalette harbour, after the master of the ship that was fishing there. He was a Basque, who received us well; and was very glad to see us, inasmuch as some Indians thereabouts wished to do him a bad turn, which we prevented.

Setting out from this place, we reached Canso, distant from Savalette harbour six leagues, on the twenty-seventh of the month. On the way we passed a number of islands extending as far as Canso, where we found the three long-boats safely in port. Champdoré and Lescarbot came out to meet us. We also found that the vessel, having completed her catch, was ready to set sail, and was only waiting for fair weather to return home. Meanwhile we enjoyed ourselves among the islands, on which was such an abundance of raspberries that it would be impossible to exaggerate their number.

All the coasts we had passed from Cape Sable to this place are of moderate height, and bordered with rocks, and, in the majority of places, have a fringe of numerous islands and reefs which at times extend out to sea nearly two leagues, making the approach very bad for vessels. Nevertheless there are not wanting good harbours and roadsteads along this coast and amid these islands, if only they were explored. As for the land, it is of worse quality and less attractive than in the other places we had seen, except up certain rivers or streams where the country is fairly pleasant.

There can be no question that in these places the winter is cold, and lasts from six to seven months.

This port of Canso is situated among islands, and is very difficult to approach except in fine weather, on account of the rocks and reefs which lie thereabouts. Fishing for both green and dry fish is carried on.

From this place to the island of Cape Breton, which lies in latitude 45° 45′ with 14° 50′ of magnetic variation, the distance is eight leagues. To Cape Breton itself it is twenty-five leagues. Between the two is a great bay which penetrates some nine or ten leagues into the country, and forms a passage between the island of Cape Breton and the mainland. This passage leads into the great bay of St. Lawrence, by which one goes to Gaspé and Isle Percée, where the fishery is carried on. This passage of the island of Cape Breton is very narrow. Large vessels do not go that way, although there is plenty of water, on account of the great currents and tidal movements which occur there. We named this place the Strait of Currents, lying in latitude 45° 45′.

This island of Cape Breton is triangular in shape and about eighty leagues in circumference. For the most part it is a mountainous country, though in certain places very pleasant. In the interior is a kind of lake into which the sea flows from the north a quarter north-west and from the south a quarter south-east. Therein lie many islands filled with large numbers of waterfowl, and shellfish of many kinds, including oysters which are not of good flavour. At this place are two harbours where the fishing is carried on, namely English harbour, some two or three leagues from Cape Breton, and Ingonish, eighteen or twenty leagues to the north a quarter north-west. The Portuguese formerly attempted to settle upon this island, and passed a winter there: but the rigour of the season and the cold made them abandon their settlement.

On the third of September we set sail from Canso.

On the fourth we were off Sable Island.

On the sixth we reached the Grand Bank, where the green fishing is carried, on, in latitude 45° 30′.

On the twenty-sixth we were on soundings near the coasts of Brittany and England, in sixty-five fathoms of water, and in latitude 49° 30′.

On the twenty-eighth we put in at Roscoff, in lower Brittany, where we were detained by bad weather until the last day of September, when the wind coming fair, we put to sea in order to complete our course to St. Malo. This was the end of these voyages, throughout which God guided us without shipwreck or peril.

699. August 22, 1606. Marc Lescarbot writes of his first impressions of Port Royal.

It is not known to whom the letter was written.
Ministère des Affaires Étrangères, Paris, Mémoires et documents, Amerique 4, fols. 49–50; printed and translated in Marc Lescarbot, Histoire de la Nouvelle France, edited by H. P. Biggar and W. L. Grant, 3 vols. (Toronto, Champlain Society, 1907–1912), II, 523–526.

From Port Royal, on the Riviere de l'Equille, in New France.
22nd August 1606.

You know well how for a long time I have had my mind and my desire turned toward this country. By the Grace of God I have reached it, after the trials of the ocean. These were greater on the French side of the Bank than on this side, by reason of the storms which are more frequent there, especially in the neighbourhood of the Azores. We had few favouring winds, being almost always driven northward or southward instead of westward, whereby we were kept at sea for a full two months and a half before setting foot on land, save at the harbour called Port Mouton, where we went in a long-boat in search of fresh water. The shores were sandy, and yet we found there great quantity of peas, gooseberries, musk-roses, walnuts, ferns, pines, cypresses, oaks, and raspberries, and also purples, angelica, scammony, and other simples, which we had no time to identify, since we remained there only two hours. Thence we rounded Cape Sable, which is not the same as Sable Island, which is three and a half degrees distant; and at last came to anchor off the entrance to Port Royal on the Riviere de l'Equille, where we are, the wind not being favourable to enter. This entrance is twelve, fifteen, and twenty fathoms deep, but sometimes it is difficult owing to its narrowness. I call it narrow, yet it is fairly wide, about the same as from the Cross of the Carmelites to the Strappado-gibbet of the Place Maubert, and with a mountain on either hand. There are eddies which sometimes make this entrance difficult if the wind is not from the right quarter.

This harbour is the most beautiful spot that can be imagined in all the world, being eight leagues in circumference, and surrounded on all sides with most delightful slopes. I have composed some verses about it which M. de Reguesson, or in his absence M. de Vaudin, will show you, with the letter which I have written him at greater length than this. The sea here on this side of the Bank so abounds in fish that one never casts a line in vain, which is one of the true perfections of life; for there we leave off meat for fish, so good is it, and one must give this sea the credit for part of the sustenance of the whole of Christendom, which is caught here everywhere where one can throw a line; for our sailors fished successfully in fifty and sixty fathoms, and at twenty, thirty, and forty fathoms one never fails to get a bite, though of course some spots yield more than others. After reaching the Bank, we had the feeling of being at home, as indeed we were: and all comers from the Old World must salute the King's ship.

M. de Poutrincourt has had a field dug over, wherein he has sown seeds of all sorts with the intention of doing the same in a fortnight and again in a month; in short, at every season to make trial of the soil. In a week the seeds have already sprouted well above the ground. Some time ago the savages left lying about some grains of wheat, oats, peas, and beans, which had been given them, and although these had fallen accidentally and on untilled soil, yet they have grown most successfully, and the grains are goodly and ready for grinding, as we saw for ourselves at the spot where the savages' encampment stood.

We intended going on farther without landing, but those who had been left here having lost their long-boat in their voyage of discovery along the coast, we were unable to proceed farther. Yet I think that we shall do so with the ship which brought us here; one on the one hand to France, and the other will make this exploration of the coast as far as 40° or 38°.

There are two reasons for changing our abode,

apart from reasons of state: first, the scurvy; secondly, the laziness of the savages in these parts, who are not accustomed to work, whereas those who live sixty and eighty leagues farther on till the soil, and dig it up lightly, so that they reap from it millet and Indian corn such as I have sometimes seen in France. The land is open; there are more meadows than here and also wild vines in abundance. I have been told that they are also found in some places about here. In any case, that country being on the forty-fifth parallel is full of fair slopes and very suitable for vines. There are also squashes and walnut trees, of which I have seen the fruit. They wish to make me believe that that country is a thousand times fairer than this; but I do not believe a word of it, for the Earthly Paradise could not be more delightful than these regions. As for the scurvy, the true and certain remedy in my opinion is to burn down the woods and thus to purify the soil, which is full of rotten wood which has fallen there since the beginning of time. The vapours from this are sucked up by the sun and make the air unhealthy. This would also cure another evil, which is the insatiability of certain small red flies, with long feet, which come out of the woods, from which it is hard to protect oneself when there is no wind, unless the heat is great, for this they cannot endure, nor wind or cold. Moreover, a special property which protects the country is that the sea in summer is almost always driven back from the land; and besides, the land is in itself difficult of approach by ships, by reason of the multitude of islands which fringe it; and once at least we had a narrow escape when we found ourselves almost among the breakers, and would have fallen among them had it not been for a sudden burst of sunlight which God sent us, which disappeared forthwith. But I become too prolix and fear to prejudice your clients by my interruptions.

700. 1606–1607. Marc Lescarbot's experiences at Port Royal.

Marc Lescarbot's Histoire de la Nouvelle France *(1609) contained a survey of French activity in America before 1606, but its main interest is for the period from July, 1606 to August, 1607 when he accompanied the Sieur de Poutrincourt to Port Royal. His narrative of this period and his long description of the Micmac Indians, based largely on personal observation, both added to slightly in later editions of his book (1612 and 1618), constitute its main documentary importance. The Indian sections are too long for inclusion, but the narrative from the time of his rounding Cape Sable on June 25, 1606, to his departure in August of the following year is given below.*

M. Lescarbot, Histoire de la Nouvelle France *(Paris, 1609), translated as* Nova Francia, *by Pierre Erondelle (London, 1609); Charles L. Levermore,* Forerunners and Competitors of the Pilgrims and Puritans, *2 vols. (Brooklyn, 1912), I, 250-296; H. P. Biggar and W. L. Grant, eds.,* Histoire de la Nouvelle France, *3 vols. (Toronto, Champlain Society, 1907-1914), I. The version which follows is taken from Levermore and incorporates the omissions of the 1609 English edition and Lescarbot's additions in 1618.*

Tuesday the five and twentieth day we were about the Cap de Sable, in faire weather, and made a good journey, for about the evening we came to sight of Long Ile, and the Bay of Sainte Marie, but because of the night we put back to Seaward. And the next day we cast Anchor at the mouth of Port Royall, where wee could not enter by reason it was ebbing water, but we gave two Canon shot from our ship to salute the said Port, and to advertize the Frenchmen that we were there.

Thursday the seven and twentieth of July, we came in with the floud, which was not without much difficultie, for that we had the wind contrarie, and gusts of wind from the Mountains, which made us almost to strike upon the Rockes. And in these troubles our ship bare still contrarie, the Poope before, and sometimes turned round, not being able to do any other thing else. Finally, being in the Port, it was unto us a thing marvellous to see the faire distance and largenesse of it, and the Mountaines and Hils that invironed it, and I wondered how so faire a place did remayne desert, being all filled with Woods, seeing that so many pine away in the World which might make good of this Land, if onely they had a chiefe Governour to conduct them thither. We knew not yet if Monsieur de Pont was gone or no, and therefore wee did expect that hee should send some men to meete us; but it was in vaine: for hee

was gone from thence twelve dayes before. And whilest we did hull in the middest of the Port, Membertou, the greatest Sagamos of the Souriquois (so are the people called with whom we were) came to the French Fort, to them that were left there, being only two, crying as a mad man, saying in his Language; "What! You stand here a dining (for it was about noone) and doe not see a great ship that commeth here; and we know not what men they are:" Suddenly these two men ranne upon the Bulwarke, and with diligence made readie the Canons, which they furnished with Pellets and touch-Powder. Membertou, without delay, came in a Canow made of barkes of trees, with a Daughter of his, to view us: And having found but friendship, and knowing us to be Frenchmen, made no alarme. Notwithstanding one of the two Frenchmen left there, called La Taille, cam to the shoare of the Port, his match on the cocke, to know what we were (though he knew it well enough, for we had the white Banner displayed at the top of the Mast) and on the sudden foure volley of Canons were shot off, which made innumerable echoes: And from our part, the Fort was saluted with three Canon shots, and many Musket shots, at which time our Trumpeter was not slacke of his dutie. Then we landed, viewed the house, and we passed that day in giving God thankes, in seeing the Savages Cabins, and walking thorow the Medowes. But I cannot but praise the gentle courage of these two men, one of them I have alreadie named, the other is called Miquelot: which deserve well to be mentioned here for having so freely exposed their lives in the conservation of the welfare of New France. For Monsieur de Pont having but one Barke and a Shallop, to seeke out towards Newfound-land for French shippes, could not charge himselfe with so much furniture, Corne, Meate, and Merchandises as were there; which he had bin forced to cast into the Sea (and which had bin greatly to our prejudice, and we did fear it very much) if these two men had not adventured themselves to tarrie there, for the preserving of those things, which they did with a willing and joyfull minde.

13

The Friday, next day after our arrivall, Monsieur de Poutrincourt affected to this Enterprize as for himselfe, put part of his people to worke in the tillage and manuring of the ground, whilest the others were employed in making cleane of the Chambers, and every one to make readie that which belonged to his Trade. My desire to know what we could hope from this land made me more eager than the others to set to work. In the meane time those people of ours that had left us at Campseau to come along the Coast, met (as it were miraculously) with Monsieur du Pont among Ilands that bee in great number in those parts. To tell how great was the joy on both sides is impossible. The said Monsieur du Pont, at this happie and fortunate meeting, returned backe to see us in the Port Royall, and to ship himselfe in the Jonas, to returne into France. As this chance was beneficiall unto him, so was it unto us, by the meanes of his ships that hee left with us. For without that wee had beene in such extremitie that we had not beene able to goe nor come any where, our ship being once returned into France. Hee arrived there on Monday the last of July, and tarried yet in Port Royall, untill the eight and twenty of August. All this moneth we made merry. Monsieur de Poutrincourt broached a cask of wine which had been given him for his own use, and announced permission for all comers to drink their fill as long as it lasted, so that it happened that a number became very like foolish children.

At the very beginning, we were desirous to see the Countrie up the River, where wee found Medowes almost continuall above twelve leagues of ground, among which brookes doe runne without number, which come from the Hills and Mountaines adjoyning. The Woods are very thicke on the water shoares, and so thicke that sometimes one cannot goe thorow them.

I will not, however, aver that they are equal to the forests of Peru described by Joseph Acosta. He says, "One of our brothers, a man worthy of all confidence, told us how, when he was once lost in the mountains, without knowing where he was or whither he should go, he found himself in a place so thickly covered with underbrush that he travelled over it for fifteen days without touching foot to the ground." I will leave it to each one to believe it if he chooses, but I will say that I myself have not yet attained sufficient credulity.

The woods are less dense farther from the rivers and damp places. The beauty of it is so great that in truth the country resembles the land promised by God to his chosen people by the mouth of Moses: "For the Lord thy God bringeth thee into a good land, a land of brooks and of water, of fountains and depths that spring out of valleys and hills. . . . A land wherein thou shalt eat bread without scarceness, thou shalt not lack anything in it; a land whose stones are iron, and out of whose hills thou mayest dig brass."

And in further confirmation of the goodness and of the wonderful situation of the land he promised to give them he says: "For the land, whither thou goest in to possess it, is not as the land of Egypt, from whence ye came out, where thou sowest thy seed, and wateredst it with thy foot, as a garden of herbs: But the land, whither ye go to possess it, is a land of hills and valleys, and drinketh water of the rain of heaven."

As we described Port Royal and its environs before in recounting the first voyage of Monsieur de Monts, and as we repeat here, the country abounds plentifully in small streams as is shown by the number of great rivers that water it. In this matter the land yields not one whit to the country of the Gauls (which is very fortunate in this respect). It will be famous for its felicity if it is ever inhabited by an industrious people who will know how to cultivate it. It is verily the promised land "whose stones are iron and out of whose hills thou mayest dig brass." We have already spoken of the mines of iron and brass and of the steel, and we will have more to say of them hereafter. Around about Port Royal the country is very diversified. In the mountains there are stretches of beautiful country; wherein I have seen lakes and streams no less than in the valleys.

In the passage to come forth from the same Port, for to goe to Sea, there is a Brooke, which falleth from the high Rockes downe, and in falling disperseth it selfe into a small raine, which is very delightfull in Summer, because that at the foote of the Rocke there are Caves, wherein one is covered, whilest that this raine falleth so pleasantly: And in the Cave (wherein the raine of this Brooke falleth) is made, as it were, a Rain-bowe when the Sunne shineth: which hath given me great cause of admiration.

Once when we went from our fort to the sea through the woods (a distance of three leagues) we met with a pleasant surprise upon the return trip. We thought ourselves on a flat stretch when we suddenly found ourselves on the summit of a high mountain. The descent was not so pleasant, however, as we had much difficulty on account of the snow. But the mountains in the country are never continuous or universal.

Within ten leagues of our dwelling, the Countrey, thorow which the River L'Equille passeth, is all plaine and even. I have seene in those parts many Countries, where the land is all even, and the fairest of the world. But the perfection thereof is, that it is well watered. And for witnesse whereof, not onely in Port Royall but also in all New France, the great River of Canada is proofe thereof, which at the end of foure hundred leagues is as broad as the greatest Rivers of the world, replenished with Iles and Rockes innumerable: taking her beginning from one of the Lakes which doe meete at the streame of her course (and so I thinke) so that it hath two course, the one from the East towards France: the other from the West towards the South Sea: which is admirable, but not without the like example found in our Europe. For I understand that the River which commeth downe to Trent and to Verone proceedeth from a Lake which produceth another River, whose course is bent opposite to the River of Lins which falleth into the River Danube. So our Geographies show that the Nile issueth from a Lake that bringeth forth other Rivers, which discharge themselves into the great Ocean.

Let us returne to our tillage: for to that must wee apply our selves: it is the first mine that must bee sought for, which is more worth than the treasures of Atabalipa: And hee that hath Corne, Wine, Cattell, Woollen and Linnen, Leather, Iron, and afterward Cod-fish, he needeth no other treasures, for the necessaries of life. Now all this is (or may be) in the Land by us described: upon which Monsieur de Poutrincourt having caused a second tillage to be made, in fifteene dayes after his arrivall thither, he sowed it with our French Corne, as well Wheat and Rie, as with Hempe, Flaxe, Turnep seed, Radice, Cabages, and other seeds: And the eight day following, he saw that his labour had not beene in vaine, but rather a faire hope, by the production that the ground had already made of the seedes which shee had received. Which being shewed to Monsieur du Pont was unto him a faire subject to make his relation in France, as a thing altogether new there. The twentieth day of August was already come, when these faire shewes were made, and the time did admonish them that were to goe in the Voyage, to

make ready. Whereunto they beganne to give order, so that the five and twentieth day of the same moneth, after many peales of Ordnance, they weighed anchor to come to the mouth of the Port, which is commonly the first dayes journey.

Monsieur de Monts being desirous to reach as farre into the South as he could, and seeke out a place very fit to inhabit beyond Malebarre, had requested Monsieur de Poutrincourt to passe farther than yet he had done, and to seeke a convenient Port in good temperature of aire, making no greater account of Port Royall than of Sainte Croix, in that which concerneth health. Whereunto the said Monsieur de Poutrincourt being willing to condescend, would not tarrie for the Spring time, knowing he should have other employments to exercise himselfe withall. But seeing his sowings ended, and his field greene, resolved himselfe to make this Voyage and Discoverie before Winter. So then hee disposed all things to that end, and with his Barke anchored neere to the Jonas, to the end to get out in companie.

During the three days that he was obliged to wait for a favorable wind a whale (which the natives call Maria) came each morning into the Port with the high tide, and there wallowed at her ease, going out with the ebb.

Moreover taking advantage of a little leisure I composed in French verse an "Adieu to the Sieur du Pont and his company," which is published among the poems called "The Muses of New France."

The eight and twentieth day of the said moneth each of us tooke his course, one one way, and the other another, diversely to Gods keeping. As for Monsieur du Pont he purposed by the way to set upon a Merchant of Rouen, named Boyer, who (contrary to the Kings inhibitions) was in those parts to trucke with the Savages, notwithstanding hee had beene delivered out of prison in Rochell, by the consent of Monsieur de Poutrincourt, under promise hee should not goe thither; but the said Boyer was already gone. And as for Monsieur de Poutrincourt, hee tooke his course for the Ile of Sainte Croix, the Frenchmens first abode, having Monsieur de Champdoré for Master and Guide of his Barque: but beeing hindered by the winde, and because his Barque did leake, hee was forced twice to put backe againe. In the end hee quite passed the Bay Françoise, and viewed the said Ile, where hee found ripe Corne, of that which two yeeres before was sowed by Monsieur de Monts, which was faire, bigge, weighty, and well filled. Hee sent some of that Corne to Port Royall, where I was requested to stay, to looke to the house, and to keepe the rest of the companie there in concord. Whereunto I did agree (though it was referred to my will) for the assurance that wee had among our selves, that the yeere following wee should make our habitation in a warmer Countrie beyond Malebarre, and that wee should all goe in companie with them that should bee sent to us out of France. In the meane while I employed my selfe in dressing the ground, to make inclosures and partitions of Gardens, for to sowe Corne and Kitchin herbes. Wee caused also a Ditch to bee made all about the Fort, which was very needfull to receive the waters and moistnesse, that before did runne underneath among the rootes of trees, that had beene fallen downe: which peradventure did make the place unhealthfull. I will not stand in describing heere, what each of our other workmen and labourers did particularly make. It sufficeth, that wee had store of Joyners, Carpenters, Masons, Stone-Carvers, Lock-Smithes, Taylors, Boord-sawyers, Mariners, &c. who did exercise their Trades, which (in doing their duties) were very kindly used, for they were at their owne libertie for three houres labour a day. The overplus of the time they bestowed in going to gather Mussels, which are at low water in great quantitie before the Fort, or Lobsters, or Crabbes, which are in Port Royall, under the Rockes in great abundance, or Cockles, which are in every part of the ooze, about the shoares of the said Port: All that kinde of fish is taken without Net or Boat. Some there were that sometimes tooke wilde-fowle, but not being skillfull, they spoyled the game. And as for us, our Table was furnished by one of Monsieur de Monts men, who provided for us in such sort that wee wanted no fowle, bringing unto us, sometimes halfe a dozen of birds, called by Frenchmen, Outards (a kind of wilde Geese) sometimes as many Mallards, or wilde Geese, white and gray, very often two or three dozen of Larkes, and other kindes of birds. As for Bread, no body felt want thereof. Every one had three quarts of pure and good Wine a day, which hath continued with us as long as we have been there, saving that when they who came to fetch us,

instead of bringing commodities unto us, helped us to spend our owne, and when it was necessary to reduce the allowance to one pint. Nevertheless as a rule we had an unusual abundance of it.

This voyage was in this respect the best of all, for which much praise is due to Monsieur de Monts and his associates, Messieurs Georges and Macquin of Rochelle, who fitted us out in the beginning so handsomely. For indeed I found that the September wine with which they furnished us was, with various uses, a sovereign preventive of the scurvy. I believe that the use of spices does certainly, in a measure at least, correct the noxiousness of the air of the country, which air, however, I myself have always found bracing and pure, notwithstanding all the considerations touching this malady that I have already discussed. For our allowance, wee had Pease, Beanes, Rice, Prunes, Raisins, drie Codde, and salt Fleshe, besides Oyle and Butter. But whensoever the Savages, dwelling neere us, had taken any quantitie of Sturgions, Salmons, or small fishes; Item, any Bevers, Ellans, Carabous (or fallow Deere), or other animals mentioned in my "Adieu to New France," they brought unto us halfe of it: and that which remained they exposed it sometimes to sale publikely, and they that would have any thereof would trucke Bread for it.

Such was in part our means of living. Although each one of our workmen had his own trade, yet each one gave himself to whatever work was necessary. Several masons and stone cutters turned bakers and made us as good bread as can be bought in Paris. Also one of our wood-sawyers several times made a good quantity of coal.

Wherein is to be noted a thing that now I remember. It is, that being necessary to cut turfes to cover the piles of wood, heaped to make the said Coales, there was found in the Medowes three foote deepe of earth, not earth, but grasse or herbes mingled with mudde, which have heaped themselves yeerely one upon another from the beginning of the world, not having been mooved. Neverthelesse the greene thereof serveth for pasture to the Ellans, which wee have many times seene in our Medowes of those parts, in herds of three or foure, great and small, suffering themselves sometimes to bee approached, then they ranne to the Woods: But I may say moreover, that I have seene, in crossing two leagues of our said Medowes, the same to be all trodden with trackes of Ellans, for I knowe not there any other cloven footed beasts. There was killed one of those beasts, not farre off from our Fort at a place where Monsieur de Monts having caused the grasse to bee mowed two yeeres before, it was growne again the fairest of the world. Some might marvell how these Medowes are made, seeing that all the ground in those places is covered with Woods. For satisfaction whereof, let the curious Reader knowe, that in high Spring tides, especially on March and September, the floud covereth those shoares, which hindereth the trees there to take roote. But everywhere, where the water overfloweth not, if there bee any ground, there are Woods.

14

Let us return to Monsieur de Poutrincourt, whom we have left in the Ile Sainte Croix. Having made there a review, and cherished the Savages that were there, hee went in the space of foure dayes to Pemptegoet, which is that place so famous under the name of Norombega. There needeth not so long a time in coming thither, but he tarried on the way to mend his Barke: for to that end he had brought with him a Smith and a Carpenter, and quantitie of boords. Hee crossed the Iles, which bee at the mouth of the River, and came to Kinibeki, where his Barke was in danger, by reason of the great streames that the nature of the place procureth there. This was the cause why hee made there no stay, but passed further to the Bay of Marchin, which is the name of a Captaine of the Savages, who at the arrivall of the said Monsieur de Poutrincourt, beganne to crie out aloud He He: whereunto the like answere was made unto him. Hee replied, asking in his Language, What are yee? They answered him, Friends: And thereupon Monsieur de Poutrincourt approaching, treated amitie with him, and presented him with Knives, Hatchets, and Matachiaz, that is to say, Scarfes, Karkenets and Bracelets made of Beades, or Quills made of white and blue Glasse; whereof hee was very glad, as also for the confederacy that the said Monsieur de Poutrincourt made with him, knowing very well that the same would bee a great aide and support unto him. Hee distributed to some men that were about him, among a great number of people, the Presents that the said Monsieur de Poutrincourt gave him, to whom hee brought store of Orignac,

or Ellans flesh (for the Baskes doe call a Stagge, or Ellan, Orignac) to refresh the companie with victuals. That done, they set sayles towards Chouakoet, where the River of Captaine Olmechin is, and where the yeere following was made the warre of the Souriquois and Etechemins, under the conduct of the Sagamos Membertou, which I have described in Verses, which Verses I have inserted among the Muses of New France. At the entry of the Bay of the said place of Chouakoet there is a great Iland, about halfe a league compasse, wherein our men did first discover any Vines (for, although there bee some in the Lands neerer to Port Royall, notwithstanding there was yet no knowledge had of them) which they found in great quantitie, having the trunke three and foure foote high, and as bigge as ones fist in the lower part, the Grapes faire and great, and some as big as Plummes, or lesser: but as blacke, that they left a staine where their liquor was spilled: Those Grapes, I say, lying over bushes and brambles that growe in the same Iland, where the trees are not so thicke as in other where, but are six or seven rods distant asunder, which causeth the Grapes to be ripe the sooner; having besides a ground very fit for the same, gravelly and sandy. They tarried there but two houres: but they noted, that there were no Vines on the North side, even as in the Ile Sainte Croix are no Cedar trees, but on the West side.

From this Iland they went to the River of Olmechin, a Port of Chouakoet, where Marchin and the said Olmechin brought to Monsieur de Poutrincourt a prisoner of the Souriquois (and therefore their enemy) which they gave unto him freely. Two houres after, there arrived two Savages, the one an Etechemin, named Chkoudun, Captaine of the River Saint John, called by the Savages Oigoudi: The other a Souriquois, named Messamoet, Captaine or Sagamos of the River of the Port De la Heve, where this prisoner was taken. They had great store of Merchandises trucked with Frenchmen, which they were comming to utter, that is to say, great, meane, and small Kettles, Hatchets, Knives, Gownes, short Clokes, red Waste-coates, Bisket, and other things: whereupon there arrived twelve or fifteene Boats, full of Savages of Olmechins subjection, being in very good order, all their faces painted, according to their wonted custome, when they will seeme faire, having their Bow and

Arrow in hand, and the quiver, which they layed downe aboord. At that houre Messamoet beganne his Oration before the Savages: shewing them, how that in times past, they often had friendship together: and that they might easily overcome their enemies, if they would have intelligence and serve themselves with the amitie of the Frenchmen, whom they saw there present to knowe their Countrey, to the end to bring commodities unto them hereafter, and to succour them with their forces, which forces he knew, and hee was the better able to make a demonstration thereof unto them, by so much that hee which spake, had before time beene in France, and dwelt there with Monsieur de Grandmont, Governour of Bayonne. Finally, his speech continued almost an houre with much vehemency and affection, with a gesture of body and armes, as is requisite in a good Oratour. And in the end he did cast all his merchandises (which were worth above three hundred crownes, brought into that Countrie) into Olmechin his Boat, as making him a present of that, in assurance of the love hee would witnesse unto him. That done the night hasted on, and every one retired himselfe. But Messamoet was not pleased, for that Olmechin made not the like Oration unto him, nor requited his present: For the Savages have that noble qualitie, that they give liberally, casting at the feet of him whom they will honour, the Present that they give him: But it is in hope to receive some reciprocall kindnesse, which is a kinde of contract, which wee call without name, I give thee, to the end thou shouldest give mee. And that is done thorow all the world. Therefore Messamoet from that day had in minde to make warre to Olmechin. Notwithstanding, the next day in the morning he and his people did returne with a Boate laden with that which they had, to wit, Corne, Tabacco, Beanes, and Pumpions, which they distributed here and there. Those two Captaines Olmechin and Marchin have since beene killed in the warres. In whose stead was chosen by the Savages, one named Bessabes, which since our returne hath beene killed by Englishmen: and in stead of him they have made a Captaine to come from within the Lands, named Asticou, a grave man, valiant and redoubted, which, in the twinkling of an eye, will gather up a thousand Savages together, which thing Olmechin and Marchin might also doe. For our Barkes being there, presently

the Sea was seene all covered over with their Boates, laden with nimble and lusty men, holding themselves up straight in them: which wee cannot do without danger, those Boates being nothing else but trees hollowed. From thence Monsieur de Poutrincourt following on his course, found a certain Port very delightfull, which had not beene seene by Monsieur de Monts: And during the Voyage they saw store of smoke, and people on the shoare, which invited us to come aland: And seeing that no account was made of it, they followed the Barke along the sand, yea most often they did outgoe her, so swift are they, having their Bowes in hand, and their Quivers upon their backes, alwaies singing and dancing, not taking care with what they should live by the way. Happy people! A thousand times happier than those across the sea. If they but knew of God and his salvation!

Monsieur de Poutrincourt having landed in this Port, behold among a multitude of Savages a good number of Fifes, which did play with certaine long Pipes, made as it were with Canes of Reedes, painted over, but not with such an harmonie as our Shepheards might doe; And to shew the excellency of their arte, they whistled with their noses in gambolling, according to their fashion.

And as this people did runne headlong, to come to the Barke, there was a Savage which hurt himselfe grievously in the heele against the edge of a Rocke, whereby hee was enforced to remayne in the place. Monsieur de Poutrincourt his Chirurgion, at that instant would apply to this hurt that which was of his Arte, but they would not permit it, untill they had first made their mouthes and mops about the wounded man. They then layed him downe on the ground, one of them holding his head on his lappe, and made many bawlings and singings, whereunto the wounded man answered but with a Ho, with a complayning voice, which having done they yeelded him to the cure of the said Chirurgion, and went their way, and the Patient also after hee had beene dressed; but two houres after he came againe, the most jocund in the world, having put about his head the binding cloth wherewith his heele was wrapped, for to seeme the more gallant.

The day following, our people entred farther into the Port, where being gone to see the Cabins of the Savages, an old woman of an hundred or sixscore yeeres of age came to cast at the feete of

Monsieur de Poutrincourt a loafe of bread, made with the Wheat called Mahis, then very faire Hempe of a long growth: Item, Beanes, and Grapes newly gathered, because they had seene Frenchmen eate of them at Chouakoet. Which the other Savages seeing, that knew it not, they brought more of them than one could wish, emulating one another; and for recompence of this their kindnesse, there was set on their foreheads a Fillet or Band, of paper, wet with spittle, of which they were very proud. It was shewed them, in pressing the Grape into a Glasse, that of that we did make the Wine which wee did drinke. Wee would have made them to eate of the Grape, but having taken it into their mouthes, they spitted it out, just as did our Gallic forefathers (as Ammion Marcellin relates), thinking it poisonous so ignorant is this people of the best thing that God hath given to Man, next to Bread. Yet notwithstanding they have no want of wit, and might be brought to doe some good things, if they were civilized, and had the use of Handy-crafts. But they are subtile, theevish, traiterous, and though they be naked, yet one cannot take heed of their fingers: for if one turne never so little his eyes aside, and that they spie the opportunitie to steale any Knife, Hatchet, or any thing else, they will not misse nor fayle of it; and will put the theft betweene their buttockes, or will hide it within the sand with their foot so cunningly, that one shall not perceive it. I have read that in Florida the natives have the same instincts and the same cleverness in the art of thievery. Indeed I doe not wonder if a people poore and naked be theevish; but when the heart is malicious, it is unexcusable. This people is such, that they must be handled with terrour: for if through love and gentlenesse one give them too free accesse, they will practise some surprize, as it hath beene knowne in divers occasions heretofore, and will yet hereafter be seene. And without deferring any longer, the second day after our comming thither, as they saw our people busie awashing Linnen, they came some fifty, one following another, with Bowes, Arrowes and Quivers, intending to play some bad part, as it was conjectured upon their manner of proceeding; but they were prevented, some of our men going to meet them, with their Muskets and Matches at the cocke, which made some of them runne away, and the others being compassed in, having put downe their weapons, came to a

Peninsula, or small head of an Iland, where our men were, and making a friendly shew, demanded to trucke the Tabacco they had for our merchandises.

The next day the Captaine of the said place and Port, came into Monsieur de Poutrincourts Barke to see him; wee did marvell to see him accompanied with Olmechin, seeing the way was marvellous long to come thither by Land, and much shorter by Sea. That gave cause of bad suspicion, albeit hee had promised his love to the Frenchmen. Notwithstanding they were gently received. And Monsieur de Poutrincourt gave to the said Olmechin a complete garment, wherewith being clothed, hee viewed himselfe in a Glasse, and did laugh to see himselfe in that order. But a little while after, feeling that the same hindred him, although it was in October, when hee was returned unto his Cabins, he distributed it to sundry of his men, to the end that one alone should not be over-pestered with it.

This might serve as a lesson to our dandies of either sex (*mignons & mignonnes*) across the sea with their superabundance of clothing and their corsets hard as wood in which they suffer such a veritable hell that they are scarcely good for anything when wrapped up in their trappings. If the weather is hot they endure insufferable torments of heat in their thick plaited breeches— suffering equal to the tortures inflicted upon criminals.

Now during the time that the said Monsieur de Poutrincourt was there, being in doubt whether Monsieur de Monts would come to make an habitation on that Coast, as hee wished it, hee made there a piece of ground to be tilled, for to sowe Corne and to plant Vines, [aided by our apothecary Monsieur Louis Hebert, a man who, aside from his work in his profession, took extreme pleasure in tilling the land. We may compare Monsieur de Poutrincourt with our good father Noah who made necessary provision for a wheat crop and then planted the vine of which he perceived the full effect later.]

As they were deliberating to passe farther, Olmechin came to the Barke to see Monsieur de Poutrincourt, where having tarried certaine houres, either in talking or eating, hee said, that the next day an hundred Boates should come, contayning every one six men: but the coming of such a number of men being only troublesome,

Monsieur de Poutrincourt would not tarrie for them; but went away the same day to Malebarre, not without much difficultie, by reason of the great streames and shoalds that are there. So that the Barke having touched at three foot of water onely, we thought to be cast away, and we beganne to unlade her, and put victuals into the Shalop, which was behind, for to save us on land: but being no full Sea, the Barke came aflote within an houre. All this Sea is a Land overflowed, as that of Mount Saint Michaels, a sandy ground in which all that resteth is a plaine flat Countrey as farre as the Mountaines, which are seene fifteene leagues off from that place. And I am of opinion that as farre as Virginia it is all alike. Moreover, there is here great quantity of Grapes, as before, and a Countrey very full of people. Monsieur de Monts, being come to Malebarre in an other season of the yeare, gathered onely greene Grapes; which he made to be preserved, and brought some to the King. But it was our good hap to come thither in October, for to see the maturity thereof. I have here before shewed the difficulty that is found in entering into Malebarre. This is the cause why Monsieur de Poutrincourt came not in with his Barke, but went thither with a Shallop onely, which thirty or forty Savages did helpe to draw in; and when it was full tide (but the tide doth not mount here but two fathams high, which is seldome seene) he went out, and retired himselfe into his said Barke, to passe further in the morning, as soone as he should ordaine it.

15

The night beginning to give place to the dawning of the day, the sailes are hoised up, but it was a very perilous navigation. For with this small Vessell of only 18 tons they were forced to coast the land, where they found no depth: going backe to Sea it was yet worse; in such wise that they did strike twice or thrice, being lifted off againe onely by the waves, and the rudder was broken, which was a dreadfull thing. In this extremity they were constrained to cast anker in the Sea, at two fathams deepe, and three leagues off from the land. Which being done, Daniel Hay (a man which taketh pleasure in shewing forth his vertue in the perils of the Sea) was sent by Sieur de Poutrincourt towards the Coast to view it, and see if there were any Port. And as he was neere land he

saw a Savage, which did dance, singing, yo, yo, yo; he called to him to come neerer, and by signes asked him if there was any place to retire Ships in, and where any fresh water was. The Savage having made signe there was, hee tooke him into his Shallop, and brought him to the Barke, wherein was Chkoudun, Captaine of the River of Oigoudi, otherwise Saint Johns River; who being brought before this Savage, he understood him no more than did our owne people: true it is, that by signs he comprehended better than they what he would say. This Savage shewed the places where no depth was, and where was any, and did so well indenting and winding here and there, alway the land in hand, that in the end they came to the Port shewed by him, where small depth is; wherein the Barke being arrived, diligence was used to make a forge for to mend her with her rudder, and an Oven to bake Bread, because there was no more Bisket left.

Fifteene dayes were imployed in this worke, during the which Monsieur de Poutrincourt, according to the laudable custome of Christians, made a Crosse to be framed and set up on a greene Banke, as Monsieur du Monts had done two yeeres before at Kinibeki and Malebarre. Now among these exhausting labors they gave not over making good cheere, with that which both the Sea and Land might furnish in that region. For in this Port is plenty of Fowle, in taking of which many of our men applied themselves: especially the Sea Larkes are there in so great flights that Monsieur de Poutrincourt killed eight and twenty of them with one Caliver shot. As for fishes, there be such abundance of Porpeses, and another kinde of fish, called by Frenchmen Souffleurs (*that is to say, Blowers*), that the Sea seemes to be covered all over with them. But they had not the things necessary for this kinde of fishing. They contented themselves then with shel-fish, as of Oysters, Skalops, Periwincles, whereof there was enough. The Savages on the other hand did bring fish, and Grapes within baskets made of rushes, for exchange with some of our wares.

Monsieur de Poutrincourt, admiring the splendid grapes, commanded his servant to load into his boat a bundle of the vines that produced them. Master Louis Hebert, our apothecary, wishing to live in that country, had also uprooted a great quantity of them intending to plant them at Port

Royal, where no grapes are found although the soil there is well adapted to vine growing. Nevertheless (by a stupid oversight) these orders were not performed, to the great displeasure of the Sieur and of us all.

After certaine dayes, the said Monsieur de Poutrincourt, seeing there great assembly of Savages, came ashoare, and to give them some terrour, made to march before him one of his men, flourishing with two naked swords and making a great sword-play. Whereat they much wondred, but yet much more when they saw that our Muskets did pierce thicke peeces of wood, where their Arrows could not so much as scratch. And therefore they never assailed our men, as long as they kept watch. And it had been good to sound the Trumpet at every houres end, as Captaine James Quartier did. For (as Monsieur de Poutrincourt doth often say) one must never lay bait for theeves; meaning, that one must never give cause to any enemy to thinke that he may surprise you: But one must alwayes shew that he is mistrusted, and that you are not asleepe, chiefly when one hath to doe with Savages, which will never set upon him that resolutely expects them.

Those who did not heed these instructions paid dearly for thier rashness, as we shall recount.

At the end of fifteen days Monsieur de Poutrincourt, having completed the repairing of his boat and seeing that there remained but one ovenful of bread to finish, started out to reconnoiter the country for a distance of about three leagues to see whether he could discover anything unusual. Upon his return he and his companions observed natives fleeing among the trees in groups of twenty, thirty or more—some crouching as they ran like people who wish to be concealed; others squatting in the bushes, so as not to be seen; some bearing their belongings and their canoes full of wheat, as if about to emigrate, the women carrying their children and as much of their possessions as they could. Monsieur de Poutrincourt knew at once that some deviltry was on foot. As soon as he reached the landing-place, he commanded the men engaged in baking the bread to withdraw to the boat. But as young folks are often heedless of their duty, so these preferred providing for their appetites rather than to obey commands. They let themselves be tempted by the prospect of their cakes and tarts, and when night fell they had not come on the boat.

At midnight Monsieur de Poutrincourt, thinking of what had happened during the day, called out to know if they were all aboard. Hearing that they were not, he sent out the shallop to bring them. But they were unwilling to hearken, save only his valet, who was afraid of being beaten. They were five men and were armed with swords and muskets which they had been warned to keep always ready. Nevertheless, so devoted to their own pleasure were they that they kept no watch whatever. It was said that some time before they had twice shot at the natives because one of them had stolen an axe. At all events the savages, whether angered by that deed or simply out of pure deviltry, at dawn stole up silently (which is an easy matter for them, having no horses, vehicles, or sabots) to the place where our men lay sleeping and, seeing the opportunity was good for an attack, fell upon them with arrows and clubs. Two of our men were killed, and the rest, wounded, fled to the shore shouting for help. The sentinel in the boat cried out in terror, "To arms! They kill our men!" At this call every one jumped out of bed and flew to the shallop without waiting to dress or light tinder. Ten men jumped into the shallop, among whom I now recall Monsieur Champlain, Robert Gravé, son of Monsieur du Pont, Daniel Hay, the ship's surgeon, the apothecary, and the trumpeter. All of these followed Monsieur de Poutrincourt, who had with him his son, and all, naked as they were, leaped on land. But the natives fled at full speed, more than three hundred of them, not including those hidden in the bushes (as is their manner of warfare), who did not show themselves at all. It was an instance of the terror God's people can inspire in the breasts of infidels according to his word to his chosen people: "There shall no man be able to stand before you; for the Lord your God shall lay the fear of you and the dread of you upon all the land that ye shall tread upon, as he hath said unto you." And we know that a hundred and thirty-five thousand Midianites fell upon each other and then fled before Gideon and his three hundred men.

It was useless to think of pursuing these light footed natives. With horses they would be an easy prey, for there are many by-paths leading from one place to another (such as we do not have at Port Royal) and there are open woods and level stretches of country where they have their cabins in the midst of their fields.

While Monsieur de Poutrincourt was landing, the men in the boat fired with the small cannon on some savages who showed themselves on a knoll, and several were seen to fall. But they are so skillful in carrying off their dead that it is only possible to guess about it. Monsieur de Poutrincourt, perceiving that pursuit would be fruitless, ordered coffins to be made for the interment of those who were killed, who were, as I said, two in number; but a third died on the shore while attempting to save himself, and a fourth later at Port Royal died from his arrow wounds. A fifth who was pierced in the breast with an arrow was saved, but it would have been better for all concerned had he died also, for we have recently heard that he has been hung as the ringleader of a conspiracy against Champlain at the settlement which the Sieur de Monts founded at Quebec, upon the great river of Canada.

This disaster was due to the folly and disobedience of one man (whom I will not name, since he died on account of it). This fellow played the braggart (*faisoit le coq*) among the younger people of the company, who confided in him too much. Otherwise he was a fairly good fellow. Because an attempt was made to prevent him from getting tipsy he had sworn (according to his custom) that he would not return to the boat at all; which in fact he did not do, for he was found dead, face downward on the ground, a little dog on his back, both stitched together and pierced by the same arrow.

By this prophecy I am reminded of two others of the same sort that contributed to the safety of France on Saint Mark's Eve in the year 1617. They concern the Marquis d'Ancre and seem to have been overlooked by those who have written about his death.

The first relates to Barbin, who was made Controller-General of Finance in place of Monsieur le President Jeannin, who was too good a Frenchman to keep the place. Monsieur Barbin, who saw three or four Princes and certain Lords, solitary and feeble, stand out against the tyranny that the Marquis d'Ancre imposed in the name of the King, prophesied that they could not hold out later than the end of May, and that then these Princes and Lords (who were sacrificing themselves for their fatherland) would be obliged to abandon the struggle. His prediction had every appearance of coming true. But God in His justice

intervened, and beyond all expectation strengthened the courage and will of that young Royal Prince so that as by a whirlwind this haughty power, which seemed to show how high Fortune can lift a man, was prostrated in the dust and completely wrecked by the death of that ambitious man too drunk with the favors that he merited not.

The other prophecy concerns this same Marquis d'Ancre. On his last journey to Paris he stopped at Ecouï, seven leagues distant from Rouen. There a woman servant of "L'Epée Royale," the inn where he was lodged, complained to him that the war cost them dear and sent them no lodgers. As he left, he said to her, "My good woman, I am going to Paris. If I return we will have war, if I do not we will have peace"; which happened, but not in the way he intended; for surely he did not expect to die so soon. His greatly desired and most necessary death brought to us peace at once, rescued the good and patriotic Princes from utter ruin, and saved the King and all the Royal House, whose power and existence were hanging by a thread which seemed destined to be speedily cut by that accursed foreigner.

Therefore many make prophecies ofttimes against their own idea and intention. A notorious instance of which, in sacred history, is the story of Baalam.

But to return to our Armouchiquois.

In this unfortunate affair Monsieur de Poutrincourt's son had three fingers torn off by a musket that burst from having been too fully charged. This added another grief to the already afflicted company. Nevertheless they did their duty by their dead, burying them at the foot of the cross that I have before mentioned. But the barbarians showed great insolence after the murders that they had committed, for as our people chanted above their dead the funeral prayers and hymns prescribed by the church, those rascals danced and howled in the distance exulting over their treachery. Though they were in great number, they dared not attack our men. These rites ended, and the sea being at low-tide, our men went again aboard the boat where Monsieur Champ-doré had remained on guard. Now these evil savages waited until the tide was too low for our men to come to land again and then returned to the scene of their murders. They tore down the cross, unearthed one of our dead, and taking off his shirt dressed one of their number in it and displayed the booty which they had carried off. Meantime some turned their backs upon our ship and, mocking, scooped up sand and threw it at our boat from between their buttocks, howling all the while like wolves. Our men were in a fine fury and fired upon them from the cannon; but the distance was great, and, too, they employ always their ruse of throwing themselves on the ground when we fire so we never know whether or not they are wounded.

There was nothing to do but drink this bitter cup and await full tide. When it came and the savages saw our men getting into the shallop they fled like hares, relying upon their nimbleness. A Sagamos named Chkoudun, of whom I have before spoken, was among our men all this while. He was greatly angered and wished to go out alone and fight the whole multitude, but of course was not permitted to do so. Our men raised up the cross with reverence, and buried again the dead body which had been disinterred.

And this was the port named "Port Fortuné."

The next day Monsieur de Poutrincourt hoisted sail intending to start out to seek new lands; but contrary winds forced him to put back. The following day he had no better success, and it was necessary to remain quiet until the wind was favorable.

During this delay the natives (thinking, I suppose, that what had happened was only sport) came back attempting this time to be friendly and offering to trade, pretending it was not they, but others, who had attacked our men. They evidently knew not the wise fable of the stork who found herself among the cranes caught in the act of crime, and who therefore was punished with them in spite of all her arguments to prove that instead of doing evil she wrought good by purging the earth of the serpents she ate.

Monsieur de Poutrincourt allowed the savages to approach as if he was willing to trade. They brought tobacco, chains, collars and bracelets made of periwinkle shells (called "Esurgni" in the narrative of Jacques Quartier's second voyage) highly esteemed among them; wheat, beans, bows, arrows, quivers and trifling trinkets. And as the acquaintance was renewed, Monsieur de Poutrincourt ordered nine or ten men to arrange the laces or straps of their muskets in the form of a

lasso, and when he should give the signal throw each man his cord over the head of the savage with whom he was speaking, and to grip it as the executioner holds his victim. He ordered half the company to land, the others to engage the natives in trading about the shallop. This plan was carried out, but, unfortunately, too precipitately and with no great success. Monsieur de Poutrincourt hoped to take them prisoners so as to be able to employ them to turn the hand mills and to cut wood. Nevertheless six or seven who could not run in water as well as on land were cut down and hacked to pieces, escape being impossible because of those of the company waiting for them on land. The forementioned native, Chkoudun, was bringing one of the heads of these people, but chanced to lose it in the water. He grieved so sorely over this that he wept hot tears.

The next day an attempt was made to depart notwithstanding a contrary wind. Little progress was made. An island six or seven leagues in length was seen and an unsuccessful attempt made to reach it. They called it "l' Isle Douteuse."

Considering all this, and also the fear that provisions would fail, that approaching winter would hinder travel, and, besides, that there were two sick men whose recovery was despaired of.

Counsell being taken, it was resolved to returne into Port Royall: Monsieur de Poutrincourt besides all this, being yet in care of them whom he had left there, so they came againe for the third time into Port Fortuné, where no Savage was seene. Upon the first winde, the said Monsieur de Poutrincourt weighed anker for the returne, and being mindfull of the dangers passed he sailed in open Sea: which shortned his course, but not without a great mischiefe of the rudder, which was againe broken; in such sort, that being at the mercy of the waves, they arrived in the end, as well as they could amongst the Ilands of Norombega, where they mended it.

Leaving this place they came to Menane, an island about six leagues long between Sainte Croix and Port Royal, where they again waited for wind. New disasters followed their departure from this point. The shallop, which was attached to the boat, was dashed by a wave against the boat with such force that its prow smashed into the rear of the vessel where were Monsieur de Poutrincourt and several others. Meantime, having scarcely made the entrance of the passage into Port Royal, the tide, which is very strong in that place, was carrying them towards the end of the French Bay from whence it would not be easy to emerge. Thus they found themselves in the greatest danger they had yet known. Attempting to turn about in their course they were carried by the tide and the wind toward the coast which here has high rocks and precipices. In doubling one menacing point they thought their end had come. But in these noble enterprises God often thus proves the courage of those who fight for his name to see if their faith cannot be shaken. He leads them ofttimes to the very gates of hell, i.e., to the very doors of their sepulchres, yet all the while holds them by the hand that they fall not into the grave, as is written:

"See now that I, even I, am he, and there is no God besides me! I kill, and I make alive; I wound, and I heal: neither is there any that can deliver out of my hand."

We have often spoken of the many and great dangers encountered on this voyage, yet never was a single man lost at sea, as so often happens among those who fish for cod or trade for furs. Just as we were on the point of returning to France four fishermen from St. Malo were engulfed in the waters.

God wished us to recognize that our blessings come from Him, so he manifested His glory to us in these ways to the end that we might know Him as Author of these pious expeditions that are not undertaken for gain, (nor carried on by the unjust shedding of blood) but in a holy zeal to establish His name and His greatness among the peoples who know Him not. After so many favors from heaven those who received them can say with the Psalmist-King beloved of God: "Nevertheless I am continually with thee; Thou hast holden me by my right hand. Thou shalt guide me with thy counsel, and afterward receive me to glory.

After many perils (I will not compare them to those of Ulysses and Æneas, for I wish not to stain our missionary voyages with such pagan associations) Monsieur de Poutrincourt arrived at Port Royal on the fourteenth day of November, where we received him joyfully and with unusual solemnity. For because we had awaited him with exceeding great desire (the more because if any evil had befallen him we should have found ourselves in great trouble), I ventured to express the feel-

ing of the moment in a bit of literary mirthfulness. And inasmuch as this was done in French verse made in a hurry I have put it with "Les Muses de la Nouvelle France," under the title "Théâtre de Neptune," to which I refer my reader.

In order to signalize still further this turning point in our enterprise, we placed over the door of the fort the arms of France crowned with laurel (which grows in quantity along the edges of the woods here) and the device of our King, *Duo protegit unus.* Beneath them we put the arms of Monsieur de Monts with this inscription, *Dabit Deus his quoque finem;* and those of Monsieur de Poutrincourt with *Invia virtuti nulla est via;* both of these also wreathed with chaplets of laurel.

16

The publike rejoicing being finished, Monsieur de Poutrincourt had a care to see his corne, the greatest part whereof he had sowed two leagues off from our Port, by the River L'Esquelle; and the other part about our said Port: and found that which was first sowen very forward, but not the last that had beene sowed the sixth and tenth days of November, which notwithstanding did grow under the Snow during Winter, as I have noted it in my sowings. It would be a tedious thing to particularise all that was done amongst us during Winter: as to tell how the said Monsieur de Poutrincourt caused many times coales to be made, the forge-coale being spent: That he caused waies to be made thorow the woods: That he went thorow the Forrests by the guide of the Compasse, and other things of such nature. But I will relate that, for to keepe us merry and clenly concerning victuals, there was an order established at the Table of the said Monsieur de Poutrincourt, which was named "L'ordre de bon temps," the order of good time (or the order of mirth) at first invented by Monsieur Champlein, wherein they (who were of the same table) were every one at his turne and day (which was in fifteene dayes once) Steward and Caterer. Now his care was that he should have good and wirshipfull fare, which was so well observed, that (although the Belly-gods of these parts doe often reproach unto us that we had not *La Rue aux Ours* of Paris with us) we have ordinarily had there as good cheere as we could have at *La Rue aux Ours*, and at farre lesser charges. For there was none, but (two dayes before his turne came) was carefull to goe ahunting or fishing, and brought some daintie thing, besides that which was of our ordinary allowance. So well, that at breakfast we never wanted some modicum or other, of fish or flesh: and at the repast of dinners or suppers, yet lesse; for it was the great banquet, where the Architriclin, or Governour of the feast, or Steward (whom the Savages doe call Atoctegis), having made the Cooke to make all things ready, did march with his Napkin on his shoulder, and his staffe of office in his hand, with the colour of the order about his necke, which was worth above foure crownes, and all of them of the order following him, bearing every one a dish. The like also was at the bringing in of the Fruit, but not with so great a traine. And at night after grace was said, he resigned the Collar of the Order, with a cup of wine, to his successor in that charge, and they dranke one to another. I have heretofore said that we had abundance of Fowle, as Mallards, Outards, Geese gray and white, Partridges and other Birds: Item, of Elans, or Stag-flesh, of Caribous or Deere, Bevers, Otters, Beares, Rabbets, Wilde-cats or Leopards, Nibaches, and such like, which the Savages did take, wherewith we made as good dishes of meate, as in the Cookes shops that be in *La rue aux Ours*, Beare Streete, and greater store: for of all meates none is so tender as Ellans flesh (whereof we made good pasties) nor so delicate as the Beavers-taile. Yea, we have had sometimes halfe a dosen Sturgions at one clap, which the Savages did bring to us, part whereof we did take, paying for it, and the rest was permitted them to sell publikely, and to trucke it for Bread, whereof our people had abundantly. And as for the ordinary meate brought out of France, that was distributed equally, as much to the least as to the biggest. And the like with Wine, as we have said. In such actions we had alwayes twenty or thirty Savages, men, women, girls, and Boies who beheld us doing our offices. Bread was given them gratis, as we doe here to the poore. But as for the Sagamos Membertou, and other Sagamos (when they came to us) they sat at table eating and drinking as we did; and wee tooke pleasure in seeing them, as contrariwise their absence was irksome unto us; as it came to passe three or foure times that all went away to the places where they knew that game and Venison was, and brought one of our men with them, who lived some six weekes as they did without

Salt, without Bread, and without Wine, lying on the ground upon skins, and that in snowie weather. Moreover they had greater care of him (as also of others that have often gone with them) than of themselves, saying, that if they should chance to dye, it would be laid to their charges to have killed them.

All of which shows that we were not imprisoned on an island as, for example, was Monsieur de Villegagnon in Brazil. These savage people love the Frenchmen and upon necessity will all fly to arms to protect them.

Such government as we have spoken of, did serve us for preservatives against the Country disease. And yet foure of ours died in February and March, of them who were of a fretfull condition or sluggish. And I remember I observed that all had their lodgings on the West side, and looking towards the wide open Port, which is almost foure leagues long, shaped ovalewise, besides they had all of them ill bedding. Because of the foregoing sicknesses and of the departure of Monsieur du Pont as was described above, we had to throw away the rotten mattresses; and those who left with Monsieur du Pont took most of the sheets with them, claiming them as their own. So several of our number fell ill with sore mouths and swollen legs, like those afflicted with phthisic, the illness God sent upon those of his people in the desert who fattened themselves gluttonously on flesh, not being content with that food which the desert furnished them by the command of the Divine Benevolence.

We had faire weather during almost all the Winter: for neither raines nor fogges are so frequent there as here, whether it be at Sea or on the land: The reason is, because the Sunbeames, by the long distance, have not the force to raise up vapours from the ground here chiefly in a Countrey all wooddy. But in Summer it doth, both from the Sea and the Land, when as their force is augmented, and those vapors are dissolved suddenly or slowly, according as one approacheth to the Equinoctiall line.

In the tropics the rain is always abundant both on land and on sea. Especially is this true in Peru and in Mexico (more so than in Africa) because of the amount of moisture which the sun draws up in crossing the great expanse of the ocean. It resolves these vapors in a moment by the great power of its heat. Near Newfoundland these vapors remain in the air a long time before falling as rain or before being scattered. In summer there is more rain than in winter, and on the sea more than on land. On land the morning fogs disappear at about eight o'clock, on the sea they last two and three and even eight days, as we have often experienced.

While we are talking about the winter, let us say that Raines are in that season rare. The Sunne likewise shineth there very faire after the fall of Snowes, which we have had seven or eight times, but it is easily melted in open places, and the longest abiding have beene in February. Howsoever it be, the Snow is very profitable for the fruits of the earth, to preserve them against the frost, and to serve them as a fur-gowne.

In this we see an admirable Providence protecting the labor of man from ruin. As the Psalmist says: "He giveth snow like wool; he scattereth the hoar frost like ashes. He casteth forth his ice like morsels; who can stand before his cold."

And as the skie is seldome covered with clouds towards New-found-land in Winter time, so are there morning frosts, which doe increase in the end of January, February, and in the beginning of March, for untill the very time of January, we kept us still in our doublets: And I remember that on a Sunday, the fourteenth day of the moneth, in the afternoone, wee sported our selves singing in Musicke upon the River L'Esquelle, and in the same moneth wee went to see Corne two leagues off from our Fort, and did dine merrily in the Sunshine: I would not for all that say that all other yeares were like unto this. For as that Winter was as milde in these parts, these last Winters of the yeares 1607, 1608, have beene the hardest that ever was seene. It hath also beene alike in those Countries, in such sort that many Savages died through the rigour of the weather, as in these our parts many poore people and travellers have beene killed through the same hardnesse of Winter weather. But I will say, that the yeare before we were in New France, the Winter had not beene so hard, as they which dwelt there before us have testified unto me. Let this suffice for that which concerneth the Winter season. But I am not yet fully satisfied in searching the cause, why in one and the selfesame parallel the season is in those parts of New France more slow by a moneth than in these parts, and the leaves appeare not upon the trees but towards the end of

the moneth of May: unlesse wee say that the thicknesse of the wood and greatnesse of Forrests doe hinder the Sunne from warming of the ground: Item, that the Country where we were is joyning to the Sea, and thereby more subject to cold. Peru for the same reason is colder than parts of Africa. And besides that, the land having never beene tilled is the more dampish, the trees and plants not being able easily to draw sap from their mother the earth. In recompence whereof the Winter there is also more slow, as we have heretofore spoken.

The cold being passed, about the end of March the best disposed amongst us strived who should best till the ground, and make Gardens, to sowe in them, and gather fruits thereof. Which was to very good purpose, for wee found great discommodity in the Winter for want of Garden hearbes. When every one had done his sowing, it was a marveilous pleasure in seeing them daily grow and spring up, and yet greater contentment to use thereof so abundantly as wee did: so that this beginning of good hope made us almost forget our native Countrie, and especially when the fish began to haunt fresh-water, and came abundantly into our brookes, in such innumerable quantity that we knew not what to doe with it. Seeing this I am the more and more astonished that in Florida, where they are practically without winter, the colonists ever suffer from famine, and above all that they should have famine in April, May and June, the months when fish cannot be lacking there.

Whilest some laboured on the ground, Monsieur de Poutrincourt made some buildings to be prepared, for to lodge them which he hoped should succeede us. And considering how troublesome the Hand-mill was, he caused a Water-mill to be made, which caused the Savages to admire much at it. For indeede it is an invention which came not into the spirit of men from the first ages. After that, our workmen had much rest, for the most part of them did almost nothing. But I may say that this Mill, by the diligence of our Millers, did furnish us with three times more Herrings than was needefull unto us for our sustenance. At high tide the sea came up to the mill, and the herrings came also, to sport a couple of hours in fresh water. When the tide went out they went with it and were then prey for our men. Monsieur de Poutrincourt made two Hogsheads full of them to be salted, and one hogshead of Sardines, or Pilchers to bring into France for a shew, which were left in our returne at Saint Maloes, to some Merchants.

Among all these things the said Monsieur de Poutrincourt did not neglect to thinke on his returne. Which was the part of a wise man, for one must never put so much trust in mens promises, but one must consider that very often many disasters doe happen to them in a small moment of time. And therefore, even in the Moneth of Aprill, he made two Barkes to be prepared, a great one and a small one, to come to seeke out French-ships towards Campseau, or New-found-land, if it should happen that no supply should come unto us. But the Carpentry-worke being finished, one onely inconvenience might hinder us, that is, we had no Pitch to calke our Vessels. This (which was the chiefest thing) was forgotten at our departure from Rochel. In this important necessitie, the said Monsieur de Poutrincourt advised himselfe to gather in the woods quantity of the gumme issuing from Firre-trees. Which he did with much labour, going thither himselfe most often with a boy or two: so that in the end hee got some hundred pounds weight of it. Now after these labours, it was not yet all, for it was needefull to melt and purifie the same, which was a necessary point and unknowne to our ship-Master Monsieur de Champdoré, and to his Marriners, for as much as that the Pitch we have, commeth from Norwege, Suedland, and Danzick. Neverthelesse the said Monsieur de Poutrincourt found the meanes to draw out the quintessence of these Gummes and Firre-tree barkes: and caused quantity of Brickes to be made, with the which he made an open furnace, wherein he put a limbecke made with many kettles, joyned one in the other, which hee filled with those gummes and barkes: Then being well covered, fire was put round about it, by whose violence the gumme enclosed within the lembecke melted, and dropped downe into a bason; but it was needefull to be very watchfull at it, by reason that if the fire had taken hold of the Gumme, all had beene lost. That was admirable, especially in a man that never saw any made. Whereof the Savages being astonied, did say in words borrowed from the Basques, Endia chavé Normandia, that is to say, that the Normans know many things. Now they call all Frenchmen Normands, except the Basques, because the most

part of fishermen that goe afishing there, be of that Nation. This remedie came very fitly unto us, for those which came to seeke us were fallen into the same want that we were.

One who waits and expects has no rest nor peace until the object desired arrives. So our men had their eyes ever fixed on the horizon to discover an approaching vessel. Many times they were deceived, thinking that they heard a cannon-shot or saw the sails of a vessel. Often they mistook the numerous native boats for the shallops of Frenchmen. The natives passed in great numbers these days on their way to the Armouchiquois war, about which we shall speak in the following book. At last our hopes were fulfilled and in the morning of Ascension Day we had news from France.

17

The Sunne did but beginne to cheere the earth, and to behold his Mistris with an amorous aspect, when the Sagamos Membertou (after our Prayers solemnely made to God, and the break-fast distributed to the people, according to the custome) came to give us advertisement that he had seene a sayle upon the Lake, which came towards our Fort. At this joyfull newes every one went out to see, but yet none was found that had so good a sight as he, though he be above a 100. yeeres old; neverthelesse we spied very soone what it was. Monsieur de Poutrincourt in all haste made ready the small boat to go out to meet the approaching sail. Monsieur Champ-doré and Daniel Hay set forth in it. From their signals we knew it was a friendly vessel and at once we saluted our visitors with four cannon and a dozen small guns. They also failed not to begin rejoicing; they discharged their artillery, to which payment was returned with interest. It was only a small Bark under the charge of a young man of Saint Maloes, named Chevalier, who beeing arrived at the Fort, delivered his Letters to Monsieur de Poutrincourt, which were read publikely. They did write unto him, that for to helpe to save the charges of the Voyage, the ship (being yet the Jonas) should stay at Campseau Port, there to fish for Cods, by reason that the Merchants associate with Monsieur de Monts knew not that there was any fishing farther than that place: Notwithstanding if it were necessary he should cause the ship to come to Port Royall. Moreover, that the grant was revoked, because that contrary to the King his Edict, the Hollanders, (who owe so much to France) conducted by a traiterous Frenchman, called La Jeunesse, had the yeere before taken up the Bevers and other Furres, of the great River of Canada. This dishonest act had turned to the detriment of the Society and they feared they would be unable to furnish further funds for the expedition. The privilege to trade for beaver furs, given to Monsieur de Monts for ten years, was now withdrawn, a disaster never dreampt of. For this reason no more men were to be sent out to replace us. Our joy at receiving assurance of succor was dampened by our grief at the thought of the ruin of this beautiful and pious enterprise. So many hardships endured, so many perils met,—for nothing. All our hopes of here planting the name of God and the Catholic faith vanished. Notwithstanding, after that Monsieur de Poutrincourt had a long while mused hereupon, he said that although he should have no bodie to come with him but onely his family, hee would not forsake the enterprize. It was great griefe unto us to abandon (without hope of returne) a Land that had produced unto us so faire Corne, and so many faire adorned Gardens. All that could be done untill that time, was to find out a place fit to make a setled dwelling, and a Land of good fertilitie. And that being done, it was great want of courage to give over the enterprise, for another yeare being passed, the necessitie of maintayning an habitation there should be taken away, for the Land was sufficient to yeeld things necessarie for life. This was the cause of that griefe which pierced the hearts of them which were desirous to see the Christian Religion established in that Countrey. But on the contrary, Monsieur de Monts, and his associates, reaping no benefit, but losse, and having no helpe from the King, it was a thing which they could not doe but with much difficultie to maintayne an habitation in those parts.

Now this envie for the Trade of Beavers with the Savages, found not onely place in the Hollanders hearts, but also in French Merchants, in such sort that the priviledge which had beene given to the said Monsieur de Monts for ten yeeres was revoked. The unsatiable avarice of men is a strange thing, which have no regard to that which is honest, so that they may rifle and catch by what meanes soever. And thereupon I will say more-

over, that there have beene some of them that came to that Countrey to fetch us home, that wickedly have presumed so much as to strip the dead, and steale away the Beavers, which those poore people doe put for their last benefit upon them whom they bury, as we will declare more at large in the Booke following. A thing that maketh the French name to be odious, and worthy disdaine among them which have no such sordid qualitie at all, but rather hearts noble and generous. It is their custom to hold all in common, no man having any thing solely his own. To those they love and honor they make liberal presents, as far as lies in their means.

Besides this evil, it happened, while we were at Campseau, that the savages killed him who had made known to our men the graves of their dead. I am reminded here of Herodotus' account of King Darius' villainy and of how when he thought to find the mother on the nest (as the saying is), that is to say: grand treasure in the tomb of Semiramis, Queen of the Babylonians, he found there only a writing which rebuked him sharply for his greed and wickedness.

To return to our sad news and to our regrets for it. Monsieur de Poutrincourt asked of the company who among them would be willing to remain there one year. Eight good companions presented themselves. They were each promised a cask of wine (of that which remained to us) and wheat in sufficient quantity, but they asked besides this such high wages that no agreement could be reached. Nothing remained but to face the return to France.

Nevertheless in the evening we built bonfires in honor of the birth of Monseigneur the Duke of Orleans and fired off our cannon and small pieces and volleys of musketry, after having first solemnly chanted the Te Deum. The messenger, Chevalier, had been captain of the vessel now at Campseau, so they had intrusted him with a great stock of provisions for us, viz.: six sheep, twenty-four hens, one pound pepper, twenty pounds rice, the same number pounds raisins and prunes, one thousand pounds of almonds, one pound nutmeg, a quarter pound cinnamon, a half pound cloves, two pounds lemon peel, two dozen lemons and as many oranges, a ham from Mayence, six other hams, a cask of Gascon wine, one of Spanish wine, a barrel of salt beef, four and a half pots olive oil, one jar olives, one barrel vinegar and two loaves of sugar—and the whole lost en route (down the throats of those intrusted to bring it). I mention the list of things sent, however, thinking it may serve as a guide to the provisionment of some future expedition.

The chickens and sheep died during the voyage (he said), which we can easily believe. We wished, however, that he had brought us the bones. He added further that he had felt sure in any event we were all dead. Behold the foundation of the gluttonous feasting! Nevertheless we made good cheer for Chevalier and his men, who were not few in number, and not so temperate in drinking as the late M. le Marquis Pisani. They were well pleased to stay with us. On their boat they had had for some time only well watered cider to drink.

But from the first day Chevalier talked of departing at once. However Monsieur de Poutrincourt kept him in hope for eight days, then seeing he was quite determined upon leaving, Monsieur de Poutrincourt helped him and his men into their boat. He had detained him on account of a report that Chevalier had declared at Campseau that he would hoist sail on his ship and leave us in the lurch.

Fifteene dayes after, the said Monsieur de Poutrincourt sent a Barke to Campseau, with part of our Workmen, for to beginne to pull downe the house. In the beginning of June the Savages, about foure hundred in number, went away from the dwelling that the Sagamos Membertou had newly made, in forme of a Towne, compassed about with high pales, for to go to warres against the Armouchiquois, which was at Chouakoet some eightie leagues distant from Port Royall; from whence they returned victorious, by the stratagems that I have described in my French poem about this war.

The savages were nearly two months gathering together. Membertou, the great Sagamos, had sent messengers (his two sons Actandin and Actandinech) to them during and before the winter giving them rendezvous here.

This Sagamos is already a very old man. He saw Jacques Quartier in this country, was even married and had children at that time, yet now he looks not more than fifty years old. He was a fierce and bloody warrior in his young days and has now many enemies. They say it is for that reason that he is very pleased to be friendly with

the French, that he may live in more security. During this assembly it was necessary to make him many presents—gifts of wheat and beans, and even a barrel of wine with which to feast his friends. For he explained to Monsieur de Poutrincourt, "I am the Sagamos of this country. It is known that I am friendly to you and to all the Normans and that you think much of me, and it would be a reproach to me if I had nothing to show for this friendship." Meantime another chief named Chkoudun, incited by envy or some other feeling, also a friend of the French, brought us word that Membertou was secretly plotting against us and had made a speech to that effect. Monsieur de Poutrincourt sent at once for Membertou, thinking to frighten him and to see if he would obey. At the first order, he came immediately among us and alone, without the least reluctance. So he was given some of the wine he liked so much (for he said he could sleep so well after drinking it, and had then no cares or fears), and he was allowed to return to his friends in peace.

This Membertou told us that he wished to present his mine of copper to our King, when he saw that we prized metals highly. He said moreover that chiefs must always be honest and liberal with one another. For he considered himself the equal of our King and of all his lieutenants, and often styled himself great friend and brother companion of Monsieur de Poutrincourt. This equality he showed by joining his two index fingers. Although his offering to the King was not of great value yet it showed his good feeling and it must be prized as if it were most precious. The King of Persia once accepted from a poor peasant a handful of water as if it were the richest of his presents. If Membertou had had more he would have generously offered more.

Monsieur de Poutrincourt being not willing to depart thence, untill hee had seene the issue of his expectation, that is to say, the ripenesse of his Corne, hee deliberated, after that the Savages were gone to warres, to make Voyages along the Coast. And because Chevalier was desirous to gather some Bevers, he sent him in a small Barke to the River of Saint John, called by the Savages, Oüigoudi, and to the Ile Saint Croix: And he, the said Monsieur de Poutrincourt, went in a shallop to the Copper Myne. I was of the said Chevalier his Voyage: we crossed the French Bay to goe to the said River, where, as soone as wee arrived, halfe a doozen Salmons newly taken, were brought to us: we sojourned there foure dayes, during which we went into the Cabins of Sagamos Chkoudun, where we saw some eightie, or a hundred Savages, all naked except their privie members, which were a making Tabagy (that is to say, a banquetting) with the meale that the said Chevalier had trucked with them for their old skinnes full of Lice, for they would sell only the skins they did not want themselves. I cannot praise this sordid trafficking. But the odor of gain is to some soft and sweet no matter what its source, as it must have been to the Emperor Vespasian when he accepted in his hand the tribute from the public urinals of Rome.

The Sagamos Chkoudun wished to give us, while we were among them, the pleasure of seeing his men in battle array, so he made them to pass before us as they would go to the war, which display I will describe in another book.

The Towne of Oüigoudi (so I call the dwelling of the said Chkoudun) was a great inclosure upon an Hill, compassed about with high and small Trees, tied one against another, and within it many Cabins, great and small, one of which was as great as a Market Hall, wherein many households retired themselves: And as for the same where they made their Tabagie it was somewhat lesse. A good part of the said Savages were of Gachepe, which is the beginning of the great River of Canada; and they told us, that they came from their dwelling thither in six dayes, which made me much to marvell, seeing the distance that there is by Sea, but they shorten very much their wayes, and make great Voyages by the meanes of Lakes and Rivers, at the end of which being come, in carrying their Canowes three or foure leagues, they get to other Rivers that have a contrary course. All these Savages were come thither to goe to the warres with Membertou against the Armouchiquois. I have already spoken of this river Ouigoudi in my account of Monsieur de Monts' voyage.

When we returned to our Barke, which was at the comming in of the Port, halfe a league off from thence, sheltered by a causie that the Sea hath made there, our men were in doubt, lest some mischance should happen unto us, and having seene the Savages in armes, thought it had beene to doe us some mischiefe, which had beene very

easie for we were but two, and therefore they were very glad of our returne. After which, the next day came the Wizard or Sooth-sayer of that quarter, crying as a made man towards our Barke. Not knowing what he meant, hee was sent for in a Cock-boat and came to parley with us, telling us that the Armouchiquois were within the Woods, which came to assaile them, and that they had killed some of their folkes that were a hunting: And therefore that we should come a-land to assist them. Having heard this discourse, which according to our judgement tended to no good, we told him that our journies were limited, and our victuals also, and that it was behoovefull for us to be gone. Seeing himselfe denied, he said that before two yeeres were come about, they would either kill all the Normans, or that the Normans should kill them. We mocked him and told him that we would bring our Barke before their Fort to ransack them all: but we did it not, for we went away that day: And having the wind contrarie, we sheltred ourselves under a small Iland, where we were two dayes: during which, some went a shooting at Mallard for provision; others attended on the Cookerie: And Captaine Champdoré and my selfe, went along the Rockes with Hammers and Chissels, seeking if there were any Mynes. In doing whereof we found quantitie of Steele among the Rockes, which was since molten by Monsieur de Poutrincourt, who made wedges of it, and it was found very fine Steele, whereof he caused a Knife to be made, that did cut as a Razor, which at our returne he shewed to the King.

From thence we went in three dayes to the Ile Saint Croix, being often contraried with the winds. And because we had a bad conjecture of the Savages, which we did see in great number at the River of Saint John, and that the troupe that was departed from Port Royall was yet at Menane, (an Ile betweene the said Port Royall and Saint Crois) which we would not trust, we kept good watch in the night time: At which time wee did often heare Seales voyces, which were very like to the voice of Owles: A thing contrarie to the opinion of them that have said and written that fishes have no voice.

Being arrived at the Ile Saint Crois, we found there the buildings left there all whole, saving that the Store-house was uncovered of one side. Wee found there yet Sacke in the bottome of a Pipe, whereof we dranke, and it was not much the worse. As for Gardens, wee found there Coale-worts, Sorrell, Lettuces, which we used for the Kitchin. Wee made there also good Pasties of Turtle Doves, which are very plentifull in the Woods, but the grasse is there so high that one could not find them when they were killed and fallen in the ground. The Court was there, full of whole Caskes, which some ill disposed Mariners did burne for their pleasures, which thing when I saw I did abhorre, and I did judge better than before that the Savages were (being lesse civilized) more humane and honester men then many that beare the Name of Christians, having during three yeeres spared that place, wherein they had not taken so much as a piece of Wood, nor Salt, which was there in great quantitie, as hard as a Rocke.

I do not know for what reason Monsieur Champlain, in his narrative printed in 1613, says that I went no farther than Sainte Croix, inasmuch as I have never said the contrary. He seems to have a poor memory of where he himself went, for in one place he says that Sainte Croix is distant from Port Royal but fourteen leagues, while he has already said that the distance is twenty-five leagues, and if you consult his map you will find that he has estimated it as at least forty.

Going from thence, we cast Anchor among a great number of confused Iles, where wee heard some Savages, and wee did call to make them come to us. They answered us with the like call. Whereunto one of ours replied, Ouen Kirau? that is to say, What are yee? they would not discover themselves. But the next day Oagimont, the Sagamos of this River, came to us, and wee knew it was he whom we heard. Hee did prepare to follow Membertou and his troupe to the warres, where he was grievously wounded, as I have said in my Verses upon this matter. This Oagimont hath a Daughter about eleven yeeres old, who is very comely, which Monsieur de Poutrincourt desired to have, and hath oftentimes demanded her of him to give her to the Queene, promising him that he should never want Corne, nor any things else, but he would never condiscend thereto.

Being entred into our Barke he accompanied us, untill wee came to the broad Sea, where hee put himselfe in his shallop to returne backe; and for us we bent our course for Port Royall where we arrived before day, but we were before our Fort just at the very time when faire Aurora began to shew her reddie cheekes upon the top of our woodie Hils; every bodie was yet asleepe, and there was but one that rose up by the continuall barking of Dogges; but wee made the rest soone to awake, by Peales of Musket-shots and Trumpets sound. Monsieur de Poutrincourt was but the day before arrived from his Voyage to the Mynes, whither we have said that hee was to goe, and the day before that, was the Barke arrived that had carried part of our Workmen to Campseau. So that all being assembled, there rested nothing more then to prepare things necessary for our shipping. And in this businesse our Water-Mill did us very good service, for otherwise there had beene no meanes to prepare Meale enough for the Voyage, but in the end wee had more then wee had need of, which was given to the Savages, to the end to have us in remembrance.

18

Upon the point that we should take our leave of Port Royall, Monsieur de Poutrincourt sent his men, one after another, to find out the ship at Campseau, which is a Port being betweene seven or eight Ilands where ships may be sheltered from windes: and there is a Bay of above fifteene leagues depth, and six or seven leagues broad, the said place being distant from Port Royall above one hundred and fiftie leagues.

We had one large boat, two small ones and the shallop. One of the small boats went ahead. On the thirtieth day of July the two others followed. I was in the large boat commanded by Champ-doré. Monsieur de Poutrincourt wished so to see the result of the wheat we had sown that he would wait for its maturity, and did not sail until eleven days later. . . .

Chapter Eighty-eight
The Revival of Port Royal as a Missionary Center

IN 1608 the Sieur de Monts turned over Port Royal and its immediate surroundings to the Sieur de Poutrincourt, who did not occupy it during 1608 and 1609. In 1611 he and his son, Charles de Biencourt, brought out a party to reestablish the *habitacion* on its old footing. Missionary enterprise seemed to be the only device to raise money. In France in 1610–1611, Charles de Biencourt made terms with the Jesuit Order. They would put up money (and share profits) for development. Fathers Pierre Biard and Enemond Massé came to Port Royal with him in 1611. Poutrincourt did not care for the arrangement of sharing control with the Jesuits, but in 1612 was bested when the Sieur de Monts' residual "rights," from Cape Breton down to 40°, as covered by his monopoly patent of 1603, were acquired by Madame de Guercheville for the Order, leaving Poutrincourt only the Port Royal estate. Relations gradually worsened until in 1613 the Jesuits left Port Royal to make a new, separate mission, under the protection of the fort, on Frenchman Bay farther down the coast of the mainland, from which they were promptly removed by Samuel Argall acting for the Virginia Company.

Materials on missionary activity include the following:

1. "Raisons pour lesquelles il semble que le mission de Canada se doibt encore différer" [13 Mars 1605 ?]
The original is in Archivum Historicum Societas Iesu, Rome. Gal. I, fols. 5–6.
It was printed by Lucien Campeau, in *Lettres du Bas-Canada*, VIII (Montreal, 1954), 133–136, and in Lucien Campeau, ed., *Monumentia Novae Franciae. I. La première mission d'Acadie, (1602–1616)* (Rome and Québec, Monumenta Historica Societatis Iesu, XCVI, 1967), document no. 8, pp. 11–13.

2. Marc Lescarbot, *La conversion des sauvages qui ont esté baptizés en la Nouvelle-France, cette année 1610, avec un bref récit de voyage du sieur de Poutrincourt* (Paris, 1610).
The first part was written after September 9, 1610, and printed before October 1, 1610. It was reprinted in L. Campeau, *La première mission d'Acadie*, document no. 47, pp. 62–93, using the original in the John Carter Brown Library. The work was translated by Reuben G. Thwaites, using the originals in the Lenox Library, New York, and in the John Carter Brown Library, and was published in *Jesuit Relations*, I (Cleveland, 1896), 49–113. Pages 109–113 are used here.

3. Marc Lescarbot, *Relation dernière de ce qui s'est passé au voyage de sieur de Poutrincourt en la Nouvelle France depuis 20 mois ença, par Marc Lescarbot advocat en Parlement* (Paris, 1612).
This work continues the story of Acadia from where Lescarbot left off in the previous work. It was reprinted in L. Campeau, *La première mission d'Acadie*, document no. 76, pp. 169–202, from the original in the Bibliothèque Nationale. It was translated by R. G. Thwaites in *Jesuit*

Relations, II, *Acadia, 1612–1614* (Cleveland, 1896), 123–187, using the copy in Harvard University Library.

4. Père Pierre Biard au Père Christophe Baltazar, Paris. Port Royal, June 10, 1611. A contemporary copy of the letter can be found in the Archives de la Province de Paris, Chantilly, Fonds Brotier 200, document no. 170, and another in Archivum Historicum Societatis Iesu, Gal. 109, I, fols. 18–23. It was printed in Auguste Carayon, *Première Mission des Jésuites au Canada* (Paris, 1864), no. II, 9–38, and was reprinted from one of the contemporary copies in L. Campeau, *La première mission d'Acadie,* document no. 63, pp. 126–151. A translation from the Carayon text was made by R. G. Thwaites in *Jesuit Relations*, I, 138–183. This is reprinted as (702).

701. February 29, 1608. Pierre de Gua, Sieur de Monts, grants Port Royal to the Sieur de Poutrincourt.

The Sieur de Monts, though he lost his ten-year monopoly of the trade of Acadia in 1607, retained the office of lieutenant-general of New France and was still, in 1608, entitled to make grants of lands in that area. He therefore conveyed the site of Port Royal and the lands immediately pertaining to it to Poutrincourt, which his family was to retain.

Archives Nationales, Paris, Minutier, XXIV, 2, 32 (minutes de Des Quatrevaulx), printed in R. Le Blant and R. Baudry, eds., Nouveaux documents sur Champlain et son époque (1967), pp. 90–91, translated.

Declaration of Pierre du Gua according to the Sieur de Poutrincourt the enjoyment of the buildings situated in Acadia, with the responsibility of transporting French households there and settling them within the term of three years.

Before the notaries of our lord the king in the Chatelet of Paris, undersigned, there was present in person Master Pierre du Gua, knight, Sieur de Monts, gentlemen in ordinary of the King's Chamber, and his lieutenant general in New France and the country of Acadia, dwelling in the Rue de Prouvaires, parish of Saint-Eustache in this city of Paris, who, as he may do by virtue of the powers given to him by his Majesty by his letters patents of the month of November 1603, has ceded, acquitted, transferred and released to the Sieur de Poutrincourt, for him and his heirs, and those to come after, the land, rivers, lakes, woods, forests and other things, and terrestrial substances, which are on and within the coast of the River of Esguille, situated in the said country of Acadia, under the latitude of 48° 45′ or thereabouts, and under the conditions and reservations accordingly thus more amply set out by the letters of provision for this by him granted to the said Sieur de Poutrincourt at the Island of Sainct-Croix on the last day of August 1604, and that to facilitate the settlement and having had certain buildings made for the refuge of the Frenchmen, the said Sieur de Mont declared and declares, that by these presents he consents and accords to the said Sieur de Poutrincourt, also at this present and acceptable by him, his heirs and those to come after, that the said buildings should be his and remain to be disposed of by him as his own property, true conquest and loyal acquisition of the same so far as is or may be, making cession and transfer of all his rights, names, reasons, and actions, and making him his surrogate in his position or place, without, in regard to them or the above said things by him before ceded and transferred, the said Sieur de Poutrincourt, his heirs and those to come after, being troubled in any manner and for any causes that may be, on condition that the said Sieur de Poutrincourt will transport himself to the said country with as many households as he can and dwell there so that the buildings and houses ceded above need not waste away, and that within the limit of three years for all time and delay [the last phrase being struck through].

For thus etc., promising etc., obliging etc. renouncing etc.

Made and passed the scrutiny of the said notaries 1608, the last day of February, the current Leap Year, and the said Sieurs de Monts and de Poutrincourt signed these presents with the said notaries.

[Signed:] Pierre du Gua
Mancheville (notary)
[Signed:] De Biencourt
Des Quatreveaulx (notary)

702. June 10, 1611. Father Pierre Biard, S. J., to Father Christophe Baltazar, Jesuit provincial in France.

Biard records the initial optimistic reactions of a newcomer to a potentially attractive mission field.

The original is in the records of the Jesuit Order in Rome. Printed and translated in Reuben G. Thwaites, ed., Jesuit Relations and Allied Documents, 73 vols. (Cleveland, 1896–1901), I (1896), 138–183.

My Reverend Father, The peace of Christ be with you.

At last by the grace and favor of God, here we are at Port Royal, the place so greatly desired, after having suffered and overcome, during the space of seven months, a multitude of trials and difficulties raised up against us at Dieppe by those belonging to the pretended religion; and after having survived at sea the fatigues, storms, and discomforts of winter, winds, and tempests. By the mercy of God, and through the prayers of Your Reverence and of our good Fathers and Brothers, here we are at the end of our journey and in the long-wished-for place. And I am now taking the first opportunity which presents itself to write to Your Reverence, and to communicate to you news of ourselves and of our present situation. I am sorry that the short time we have been in this country does not permit me to write about

it at length, as I was desirous of doing, and about the condition of these poor people; however, I will try to describe to you not only what happened in our voyage, but also all that we have been able to learn of these peoples since our arrival, as I believe all our good noblemen and friends, as well as Your Reverence, expect and desire me to do.

So, to begin with the preparations for our voyage, Your Reverence must know about the effort put forth by two Dieppe merchants of the pretended religion, who were charged with freighting the ship, to prevent our being received upon it. For a number of years past, those who began and continued to make voyages to Canada have wished some of our Society to be employed for the conversion of the people of that country; and Henry the Great, the late King, of happy memory, had set aside five hundred écus for the voyage of the first ones who should be sent there: at this time Reverend Father Enmond Masse and I, chosen for this mission, after having saluted the Queen Regent and learned from her own utterances the holy zeal which she felt for the conversion of this barbarous people, and having received the above-mentioned five hundred écus for our viaticum, aided also by the pious liberality of the Marchionesses de Guercheville, Verneuil, and de Sourdis, left Paris and arrived at Dieppe upon the day which Monsieur de Biancourt, [Charles] son of Monsieur de Potrincourt, had designated for our departure, the 27th of October, 1610.

The two above-mentioned merchants, as soon as they heard that two Jesuits were going to Canada, addressed themselves to Monsieur de Biancourt and warned him that, if the said Jesuits intended to embark upon the ship, they would have nothing to do with it: they were told that the presence of the Jesuits would in no wise interfere with them; that, thanks to God and the Queen, they had the money to pay their passage without in the least disturbing their cargo. They still persisted, however, in their refusal; and although Monsieur de Sicoine, governor of the city, a very zealous catholic, kindly interposed, he could gain nothing from them. For this reason, Monsieur Robbin, his son, otherwise called de Cologne, a partner of Monsieur de Biancourt in this voyage, thought he would go to Court and make known this difficulty to the Queen; he did so. The Queen, thereupon, sent letters addressed to Monsieur de Sicoigne, telling him to announce that the will of the present King, as well as that of the late King of eternal memory, was that these Jesuits should go to Canada; and that those who were opposing their departure were doing so against the will of their Prince. The letters were very kind: and Monsieur de Sicoigne was pleased to assemble the consistory, and read them to that body. Notwithstanding all this, the merchants would not yield in the least; it was merely granted that, leaving the Jesuits out of the question, they should promptly load their ship, lest these perplexities and disputes should cause some delay in bringing the succor to Monsieur de Potrincourt, which must be given promptly. Then I almost made up my mind that all our hopes were doomed to disappointment, for I did not see how we were to be extricated from these difficulties. Monsieur de Coloigne did not despair; but, showing himself in his kindness always more eager to pursue the case for us, by a second journey he convinced the Court of an excellent plan for thwarting the merchants: namely, by paying them for their cargo, and thus indemnifying them. Madame de la Guercheville, a lady of great virtue, recognizing the expediency of this plan, and deeming it inconsistent with real piety to allow a godly work to be checked for such a trifle, and thus that satan should be permitted to triumph, determined to try and raise the sum of money required; and she did so with such diligence and success, through the pious generosity of several Noblemen and Ladies of the court, that she soon collected four thousand livres and sent them to Dieppe. Thus the merchants were deprived of all the rights which they might have had in the vessel, without losing anything, and we were admitted into it.

This, and other incidents interfering with the preparations for our voyage, were the reasons why we could not leave Dieppe before the 26th of January, 1611. Monsieur de Biancourt, a very accomplished young gentleman, and well versed in matters pertaining to the sea, was our leader and commander. There were thirty-six of us in the ship, which was called *la Grace de Dieu*, of about sixty tons burden. We had only two days of favorable winds; on the third day we suddenly found ourselves carried, by contrary winds and tides, to within a hundred or two hundred paces of

the breakers of the isle of Wight, in England; and it was fortunate for us that we found good anchorage there, for otherwise we certainly should have been lost.

Leaving this place we put into port at Hyrmice, and then at Newport; by which we lost eighteen days. The 16th of February, first day of lent, a good northwester arising allowed us to depart, and accompanied us out of the English Channel. Now mariners, in coming to Port Royal, are not accustomed to take the direct route from the Ouessant islands to Cape Sable, which would lessen the distance, for in this way, from Dieppe to Port Royal, there would only be about one thousand leagues; but they are in the habit of going South as far as the Azores, and from there to the great bank, thence, according to the winds, to strike for Cape Sable, or Campseaux, or elsewhere. They have told me that they go by way of the Azores for three reasons: first, in order to avoid the north sea, which is very stormy, they say; second, to make use of the south winds, which usually prevail there; third, to be sure of their reckonings; for otherwise it is difficult to take their bearings and arrange their route without error. But none of these causes affected us, although we followed this custom. Not the first, for we were so tossed about by tempests and high seas, that I do not think we gained much by going north or south, south or north; nor the second, because often when we wanted the South, the North wind blew, and vice versa; and certainly not the third, inasmuch as we could not even see the Azores, although we went down as far as 39° 30'. Thus all the calculations of our leaders were confounded, and we had not yet reached the Azores of the great bank when some of them thought we had passed it.

The great codfish bank is not, as I thought in France, a kind of sand or mud-bank, appearing above the surface of the sea; but is a great submarine plateau 35, 40 and 45 fathoms deep, and in some places twenty-five leagues in extent. They call it bank, because, in coming from the deep sea, it is the first place where bottom is found with the sounding lead. Now upon the border of this great bank, for the space of three or four leagues, the waves are generally very high, and these three or four leagues are called the Azores.

We were near these Azores on Tuesday of

Easter week, when suddenly we became a prey to our sworn foe, the West wind, which was so violent and obstinate that we very nearly perished. For eight entire days it gave us no quarter, its vindictiveness being augmented by cold and sometimes rain or snow.

In taking this route to New France, so rough and dangerous, especially in small and badly-equipped boats, one experiences the sum total of all the miseries of life. We could rest neither day nor night. When we wished to eat, a dish suddenly slipped from us and struck somebody's head. We fell over each other and against the baggage, and thus found ourselves mixed up with others who had been upset in the same way; cups were spilled over our beds, and bowls in our laps, or a big wave demanded our plates.

I was so highly honored by Monsieur de Biancourt as to share his cabin. One fine night, as we were lying in bed, trying to get a little rest, a neat and impudent wave bent our window fastenings, broke the window, and covered us over completely; we had the same experience again, during the day. Furthermore, the cold was so severe, and continued to be for more than six weeks, that we lost nearly all sensation from numbness and exposure. Good Father Masse suffered a great deal. He was ill about forty days, eating very little and seldom leaving his bed; yet, notwithstanding all that, he wanted to fast. After Easter he continued to improve, thank God, more and more. As for me, I was gay and happy, and, by the grace of God, was never ill enough to stay in bed even when several of the sailors had to give up.

After escaping from these trials, we entered the ice at the Azores of the bank, 46 degrees north latitude. Some of these masses of ice seemed like islands, others little villages, others grand churches or lofty domes, or magnificent castles: all were floating. To avoid them we steered towards the south; but this was falling, as they say, from Charybdis into Scylla, for from these high rocks we fell into a level field of low ice, with which the sea was entirely covered, as far as the eye could reach. We did not know how to steer through it; and had it not been for the fearlessness of Monsieur de Biancourt, our sailors would have been helpless; but he guided us out, notwithstanding the protests of many of them, through a place where the ice was more scattered, and God, in his goodness, assisted us.

On the 5th of May, we disembarked at Campceau, and there had the opportunity of celebrating holy mass after so long a time, and of strengthening ourselves with that bread which never fails to nourish and console. Then we coasted along until we reached Port Royal, where we arrived under good and happy auspices early in the morning of the holy day of Pentecost, the 22nd of May, the day upon which the sun enters the constellation Gemini. Our voyage had lasted four months.

The joy of Monsieur de Potrincourt and his followers, at our arrival, is indescribable. They had been, during the entire winter, reduced to sore straits, as I am going to explain to you.

Monsieur de Potrincourt had accompanied his son a part of the way upon the latter's return to France the last of July, 1610, and had gone as far as port Saint John, otherwise called Chachippé, 70 leagues east and south of Port Royal. When he was returning, as he veered around Cape Sable, he found himself in a strong current; weakened by hardships, he was obliged to yield the helm, in order to take a little rest, commanding his successor to always keep near the shore, even in the deepest part of the Bay. This pilot, I know not why, did not follow his orders, but soon afterward changed his course and left the shore.

The Savage, Membertou, who was following in his boat, was astonished that Potrincourt should take this route; but, not knowing why he did so, neither followed him nor said anything about it. So he soon arrived at Port Royal, while Monsieur de Potrincourt drifted about for six weeks, in danger of being hopelessly lost; for this worthy gentleman, when he awoke, was very much surprised at seeing himself in a small boat in the open sea, out of sight of land. He looked at his dial in vain, for not knowing what route his amiable pilot had taken, he could not guess where he was, nor in what direction to turn. Another misfortune was that his boat would not sail on a bowline, having been somehow damaged in the sides. So, whether he wished to do so or not, he was always obliged to sail before the wind.

A third inconvenience and misfortune was a lack of food. However, he is a man who does not easily give up, and good luck follows him. Now in this perplexity about the route, he fortunately decided to turn to the north, and God sent him what he desired, a favorable South wind. His thrift served him against the misfortune of hunger, for he had hunted and kept a certain number of cormorants. But how could they be roasted in a small boat, so as to be eaten and kept? Fortunately he found he had a few planks, upon which he built a fire-place, and thus roasted the game; by the aid of which he arrived at Pentegouët, formerly Norembegue, and from there to the Etechemins, thence to the harbor of Port Royal, where by a piece of ill luck, he was nearly shipwrecked.

It was dark when he entered this harbor, and his crew began to oppose him, stoutly denying that they were in the harbor of Port Royal. He was willing to listen to their objections, and unfortunately even yielded to them; and so turning to the lower part of French Bay, he went wandering away off at the mercy of the winds and waves. Meanwhile the colonists of Port Royal were in great anxiety, and had already nearly made up their minds that he was lost; the savage, Membertou, strengthened this fear by asserting that he had seen him sail out of sight upon the sea; whence it was inferred, since people believe as easily what they fear as what they favor, that as such and such a wind had prevailed, it was impossible for them to escape in such a boat. And they were already planning their return to France. Now they were greatly astonished, and at the same time exceedingly happy when they saw their Theseus return from another world; this was six weeks after his departure, just when Monsieur de Biancourt arrived in France, whose return was expected at Port Royal during the whole month of November of the same year, 1610. But they were very much surprised when they did not see him at Christmas; then they lost all hope, on account of the winter weather, of seeing him again before the end of the following April.

For this reason they cut down their rations; but such economy was of little avail, since Sieur de Potrincourt did not lessen his liberality toward the Savages, fearing to alienate them from the christian faith. He is truly a liberal and magnamimous gentleman, refusing all recompense for the good he does them; so when they are occasionally asked why they do not give him something in return for so many favors, they are accustomed to answer, cunningly: *Endries ninan metaij Sagamo*, that is to say, "Monsieur does not care for our beaver skins." Nevertheless, they have

now and then sent him some pieces of elkmeat, which have helped him to gain time [i.e., to save his own provisions]. But they, the French, had a good chance of economizing when winter came, for their mill froze up, and they had no way of making flour. Happily for them they found a store of peas and beans, which proved to be their manna and ambrosia for seven weeks.

Then April came, but not the ship; now it was just as well that the mill was frozen up, for they had nothing to put in the hopper. What were they to do? Hunger is a bad complaint. Some began to fish, others to dig. From their fishing they obtained some smelts and herrings: from their digging some very good roots, called *chiqueli*, which are very abundant in certain places.

Thus this importunate creditor was somewhat satisfied; I say somewhat, because, when there was no bread, everything else was of little account; and they had already made up their minds that, if the ship did not come during the month of May, they would resort to the coast, in search of ships to take them back to the sweet land of wheat and vines. It was Monsieur de Potrincourt's followers who talked this way; as for him, he was full of courage and knew well how he could manage to hold out until saint John's day [midsummer]. Thank God, there was no need of this, for, as has been said, we arrived the 22nd of May. Those who know what hunger, despair, fear and suffering are, what it is to be a leader and see all one's enterprises and hard work come to nought, can imagine what must have been the joy of Monsieur de Potrincourt and his colony upon seeing us arrive.

We all wept at this meeting, which seemed almost like a dream; then when we had recovered ourselves a little and had begun to talk, this question (mine, in fact) was proposed, to wit: Which was the happier of the two, Monsieur de Potrincourt and his people, or Monsieur de Biancourt and his? Truly, our hearts swelled within us, and God, in his mercy, showed that he took pleasure in our joy; for, after mass and dinner, there was nothing but going and coming from the ship to the settlement, and from the settlement to the ship, each one wanting to embrace and be embraced by his friends, just as, after the winter, we rejoice in the beautiful spring, and after a siege, in our freedom. It happened that two persons from the settlement took one of the canoes of the savages to go to the ship. These canoes are so made that, if you do not sit very straight and steady, they immediately tip over; now it chanced that, wishing to come back in the same canoe from the ship to the settlement, somehow they did not properly balance it, and both fell into the water.

Fortunately, it occurred at a time when I happened to be walking upon the shore with Monsieur de Potrincourt. Seeing the accident, we made signs with our hats as best we could to those upon the ship to come to their aid; for it would have been useless to call out, so far away was the ship, and so loud the noise of the wind. At first no one paid any attention to us, so we had recourse to prayer, and fell upon our knees, this being our only alternative; and God had pity upon us. One of the two caught hold of the canoe, which was turned upside down, and threw himself upon it: the other was finally saved by a boat, and thus both were rescued; so our cup of joy was full in seeing how God in his all paternal love and gentleness, would not permit the evil one to trouble us and to destroy our happiness upon this good day. To him be the glory forever. Amen!

But now that we have arrived in good health, by the grace of God, it is time we were casting our eyes over the country, and were giving some consideration to the condition in which we find christianity here. Its whole foundation consists, after God, in this little settlement of a family of about twenty persons. Messire Jessé Flesche, commonly called the Patriarch, has had charge of it; and, in the year that he has lived here, has baptized about one hundred Savages. The trouble is, he has not been able to instruct them as he would have wished, because he did not know the language, and had nothing with which to support them: for he who would minister to their souls, must at the same time resolve to nourish their bodies. This worthy man has shown great friendliness toward us, and thanked God for our coming; for he had made up his mind some time ago to return to France at the first opportunity, which he is now quite free to do without regret at leaving a vine which he has planted.

They have not yet succeeded in translating into the native language the common creed or symbol, the Lord's prayer, the commandments of God, the Sacraments, and other principles quite necessary to the making of a christian.

Recently, when I was at port Saint John, I was informed that among the other Savages there were five who were already christians. Thereupon I took occasion to give them some pictures, and to erect a cross before their wigwams, singing a *Salve Regina.* I had them make the sign of the cross; but I was very much astonished, for the unbaptized understood almost as much about it as the christians. I asked each one his baptismal name; some did not know theirs, so they called themselves *Patriarchs,* because it is the Patriarch who gives them their names, and thus they conclude that, when they have forgotten their own names, they ought to be called *Patriarchs.*

It was also rather amusing that, when I asked them if they were christians, they did not know what I meant; when I asked them if they had been baptized, they answered: *Hetaion enderquir Vortmandia Patriarché,* that is to say, "Yes, the Patriarch has made us like the Normans." Now they call all the French "Normans," except the Malouins, whom they call Samaricois, and the Basques, Bascua.

The name of the *sagamore,* that is, the lord of port Saint John, is Cacagous, a man who is shrewd and cunning as are no others upon the coast; that is all that he brought back from France (for he has been in France); he told me he had been baptized in Bayonne, relating his story to me as one tells about going to a ball out of friendship. Whereupon, seeing how wicked he was, and wishing to try and arouse his conscience, I asked him how many wives he had. He answered that he had eight; and in fact he counted off seven to me who were there present, pointing them out with as much pride, instead of an equal degree of shame, as if I had asked him the number of his legitimate children.

Another, who was looking out for a number of wives, made the following answer to my objections on the ground that he was a christian: *Reroure quiro Nortmandia:* which means, "That is all well enough for you Normans." So there is scarcely any change in them after their baptism. The same savagery and the same manners, or but little different, the same customs, ceremonies, usages, fashions, and vices remain, at least as far as can be learned; no attention being paid to any distinction of time, days, offices, exercises, prayers, duties, virtues, or spiritual remedies.

Membertou, as the one who has most associated with Monsieur de Potrincourt for a long time, is also the most zealous and shows the greatest faith, but even he complains of not understanding us well enough; he would like to become a preacher, he says, if he were properly taught. He gave me a witty answer the other day, as I was teaching him his *Pater*, according to the translation made of it by M. de Biancourt, when I had him say: *Nui en caraco nac agorm csmoi ciscou;* that is, "Give us this day our daily bread." "But," said he, "if I did not ask him for anything but bread, I would be without moose-meat or fish."

The good old man told us, with a great deal of feeling, how God is helping him since he has become a christian, saying that this spring it happened that he and his family were suffering much from hunger; then he remembered that he was a christian, and therefore prayed to God. After his prayer, he went to the river and found all the smelts he wanted. And while I am speaking of this old sagamore, the first fruit of this heathen nation, I will tell you also what happened this winter.

He was sick, and what is more, had been given up to die by the native *aoutmoins*, or sorcerers. Now it is the custom, when the Aoutmoins have pronounced the malady or wound to be mortal, for the sick man to cease eating from that time on, nor do they give him anything more. But, donning his beautiful robe, he begins chanting his own death-song; after this, if he lingers too long, a great many pails of water are thrown over him to hasten his death, and sometimes he is buried half alive. Now the children of Membertou, though christians, were prepared to exercise this noble and pious duty toward their father; already they had ceased giving him anything to eat and had taken away his beautiful otter robe, and he had, like the swan, finished his Nænie, or funeral chant. One thing still troubled him, that he did not know how to die like a christian, and he had not taken farewell of Monsieur de Potrincourt. When M. de Potrincourt heard these things, he went to see him, remonstrated with him, and assured him that, in spite of all the Aoutmoins and Pilotois, he would live and recover his health if he would eat something, which he was bound to do, being a christian. The good man believed and was saved;

to-day he tells this story with great satisfaction, and very aptly points out how God has thereby mercifully exposed the malice and deceit of their aoutmoins.

I shall here relate another act of the same Sieur de Potrincourt, which has been of great benefit to all these heathen. A christian savage had died, and (as a mark of his constancy) he had sent word here to the settlement during his sickness, that he desired our prayers. After his death the other Savages prepared to bury him in their way; they are accustomed to take everything that belongs to the deceased, skins, bows, utensils, wigwams, etc., and burn them all, howling and shouting certain cries, sorceries, and invocations to the evil spirit. M. de Potrincourt firmly resolved to oppose these ceremonies. So he armed all his men, and going to the Savages in force, by this means obtained what he asked, namely, that the body should be given to the Patriarch, and so the burial took place according to christian customs. This act, inasmuch as it could not be prevented by the Savages, was and still is, greatly praised by them.

The chapel they have been using until now is very small, badly arranged, and in every way unsuited for religious services. To remedy this, M. de Poutrincourt has given us an entire quarter of his habitation, if we can roof it over and adapt it to our needs. But I shall add one more word which will be pleasant and edifying news to many.

After my arrival here at Port Royal, I went with M. de Potrincourt as far as the Etechemins. There God willed that I should meet young du Pont, of Sainct Malo, who, having been for some reason frightened away [from the settlement], had passed the entire year with the Savages, living just as they did. He is a young man of great physical and mental strength, excelled by none of the savages in the chase, in alertness and endurance, and in his ability to speak their language. He was very much afraid of M. de Potrincourt: but God inspired me with so much faith in him that, relying upon my word, Du Pont came with me to our ship; and after making some apologies and promises, peace was declared, to the great satisfaction of all. When he departed, as the cannon were sounding, he begged me to appoint an hour to receive his confession. The next morning, in his great eagerness, he anticipated the hour, and made his confession upon the shores of the sea in the presence of all the Savages, who were greatly astonished at thus seeing him upon his knees so long before me. Then he took communion in a most exemplary manner, at which I can say tears came into my eyes, and not into mine alone. The devil was confounded at this act; so he straightway planned trouble for us that very afternoon; but thank God, through the justice and goodness of M. de Potrincourt, harmony was everywhere restored.

And now you have had, my Reverend Father, an account of our voyage, of what happened in it, and before it, and since our arrival at this settlement. It now remains to tell you that the conversion of this country, to the Gospel, and of these people to civilization, is not a small undertaking nor free from great difficulties; for, in the first place, if we consider the country, it is only a forest, without other conveniences of life than those which will be brought from France, and what in time may be obtained from the soil after it has been cultivated. The nation is savage, wandering and full of bad habits; the people few and isolated. They are, I say, savage, haunting the woods, ignorant, lawless and rude: they are wanderers, with nothing to attach them to a place, neither homes nor relationship, neither possessions nor love of country; as a people they have bad habits, are extremely lazy, gluttonous, profane, treacherous, cruel in their revenge, and given up to all kinds of lewdness, men and women alike, the men having several wives and abandoning them to others, and the women only serving them as slaves, whom they strike and beat unmercifully, and who dare not complain; and after being half killed, if it so please the murderer, they must laugh and caress him.

With all these vices, they are exceedingly vainglorious: they think they are better, more valiant and more ingenious than the French; and, what is difficult to believe, richer than we are. They consider themselves, I say, braver than we are, boasting that they have killed Basques and Malouins, and that they do a great deal of harm to the ships, and that no one has ever resented it, insinuating that it was from a lack of courage. They consider themselves better than the French; "For," they say, "you are always fighting and quarreling among yourselves; we live peaceably. You are envious and are all the time slandering each other; you are thieves and deceivers: you

are covetous, and are neither generous nor kind; as for us, if we have a morsel of bread we share it with our neighbor."

They are saying these and like things continually, seeing the above-mentioned imperfections in some of us, and flattering themselves that some of their own people do not have them so conspicuously, not realizing that they all have much greater vices, and that the better part of our people do not have even these defects, they conclude generally that they are superior to all christians. It is self-love that blinds them, and the evil one who leads them on, no more nor less than in our France, we see those who have deviated from the faith holding themselves higher and boasting of being better than the catholics, because in some of them they see many faults; considering neither the virtues of the other catholics, nor their own still greater imperfections; wishing to have, like Cyclops, only a single eye, and to fix that one upon the vices of a few catholics, never upon the virtues of the others, nor upon themselves, unless it be for the purpose of self-deception.

Also they [the savages] consider themselves more ingenious, inasmuch as they see us admire some of their productions as the work of people so rude and ignorant; lacking intelligence, they bestow very little admiration upon what we show them, although much more worthy of being admired. Hence they regard themselves as much richer than we are, although they are poor and wretched in the extreme.

Cacagous, of whom I have already spoken, is quite gracious when he is a little elated about something; to show his kindly feelings toward the French he boasts of his willingness to go and see the King, and to take him a present of a hundred beaver skins, proudly suggesting that in so doing he will make him richer than all his predecessors. They get this idea from the extreme covetousness and eagerness which our people display to obtain their beaver skins.

Not less amusing is the remark of a certain Sagamore, who, having heard M. de Potrincourt say that the King was young and unmarried: "Perhaps," said he, "I may let him marry my daughter; but according to the usages and customs of the country, the King must make me some handsome presents; namely, four or five barrels of bread, three of peas or beans, one of tobacco, four or five cloaks worth one hundred sous apiece, bows, arrows, harpoons, and other similar articles."

Such are the marks of intelligence in the people of these countries, which are very sparsely populated, especially those of the Soriquois and Etechemins, which are near the sea; although Membertou assures us that in his youth he has seen *chimonutz*, that is to say, Savages, as thickly planted there as the hairs upon his head. It is maintained that they have thus diminished since the French have begun to frequent their country; for, since then they do nothing all summer but eat; and the result is that, adopting an entirely different custom and thus breeding new diseases, they pay for their indulgence during the autumn and winter by pleurisy, quinsy and dysentery, which kill them off. During this year alone sixty have died at Cape de la Hève, which is the greater part of those who lived there; yet not one of all M. de Potrincourt's little colony has even been sick, notwithstanding all the privations they have suffered: which has caused the Savages to apprehend that God protects and defends us as his favorite and well-beloved people.

What I say about the sparseness of the population of these countries must be understood as referring to the people who live upon the coast; for farther inland, principally among the Etechemins, there are, it is said, a great many people. All these things, added to the difficulty of acquiring the language, the time that must be consumed, the expenses that must be incurred, the great distress, toil and poverty that must be endured, fully proclaim the greatness of this enterprise and the difficulties which beset it. Yet many things encourage me to continue in it.

First, my trust in the goodness and providence of God. Isaiah assures us that the kingdom of our Redeemer shall be recognized throughout the earth; and that there shall be neither caves of dragons nor dens of cockatrices, nor inaccessible rocks, nor abysses so deep, that his grace will not soften and his salvation cure, his abundance fertilize, his humility raise up, and over which his cross will not at last victoriously triumph. And why shall I not hope that the time has come when this prophecy is to be fulfilled in these lands? If that be so, what can there be so difficult that our Lord cannot make it easy?

In the second place, I rely upon the King, our Sire. He is a Sovereign who promises us nothing less than the late King, his father, the incomparable Henry the Great. This work began in the latter's reign, and it may be said that in the century since France has appropriated this country, or has so completely taken possession of it, there has not been so much accomplished at any time as since our present king became sovereign; may God fill his reign with all blessings. He will not permit his name and arms to stand in these regions side by side with paganism, his authority with barbarism, his renown with savagery, his power with poverty, his faith with lack of works, nor leave his subjects without aid or succor. His mother also, another Queen Blanche, looking to the glory of God, will contemplate these lately-acquired wildernesses, where in the beginning of her Regency the Gospel plough has, through her instrumentality, created some hope of a harvest; and will recall what the late King, great in wisdom as well as in courage, said to Sieur de Potrincourt when he came to this country: "Go," said he. "I plan the edifice; my son will build it." We beg your Reverence to lay this matter before him, together with the work which might be done by their Majesties in these lands, if it were their good pleasure to endow and to give a fair revenue to this mission, from which all those who would be educated and maintained here might go forth through the whole country.

That is the second resource upon which our hopes are founded; to which I will add the piety and liberality which we experienced upon our departure from the lords and ladies of this most noble and most christian court, who promised me that they would not fail to assist this enterprise with their means, in order not to lose what they have already invested in it, which serves them as monuments of glory and of eternal happiness before God.

M. de Potrincourt, a mild and upright Gentleman, brave, beloved and well-known in these parts, and M. de Biancourt, his son, who reflects the virtues and good qualities of his father, both zealous in serving God, and who honor and cherish us more than we deserve, also encourage us in devoting all our energy to this work.

Finally, we are encouraged by the situation and condition of this place, which, if it is cultivated, promises to furnish a great deal for the needs of human life; and its beauty causes me to wonder that it has been so little sought up to the present time. From this port where we now are, it is very convenient for us to spread out to the Armouchiquois, Iroquois, and Montagnais, our neighbors, which are populous nations and till the soil as we do; this situation, I say, makes us hope something for the future. For, if our Souriquois are few, they may become numerous; if they are savages, it is to domesticate and civilize them that we have come here; if they are rude, that is no reason that we should be idle; if they have until now profited little, it is no wonder, for it would be too much to expect fruit from this grafting, and to demand reason and maturity from a child.

In conclusion, we hope in time to make them susceptible of receiving the doctrines of the faith and of the christian and catholic religion, and later, to penetrate farther into the regions beyond, which they say are more populous and better cultivated. We base this hope upon Divine goodness and mercy, upon the zeal and fervent charity of all good people who earnestly desire the kingdom of God, particularly upon the holy prayers of Your Reverence and of our Reverend Fathers and very dear Brothers, to whom we most affectionately commend ourselves.

From Port Royal, New France, this tenth day of June, one thousand six hundred and eleven.

[Signed:] Pierre Biard

Chapter Eighty-nine
Champlain in the St. Lawrence

703. March to September, 1603. The expedition of François Gravé du Pont and Samuel de Champlain to the St. Lawrence.

Pierre Chauvin's monopoly had passed (informally) to Aymar de Chaste and François Gravé in 1603 and they set to work to find out what, in fact, the St. Lawrence situation was. La Bonne Renommée, *under Gravé, had with her a close associate of the captain, Samuel Champlain, and it was his expert eye and facile pen which effectively made the expedition one of note. It is the first clear view we have of the St. Lawrence since the time of Cartier. The report did little to convince those like the Sieur de Monts, who were watching from the sidelines for favorable prospects for settlement. Without settlement perhaps there could not be a monopoly. Champlain's book,* Des Sauvages, *published in Paris, focused the attention not merely of merchants but of Court and church on North America to a degree not hitherto possible.*

Des Sauvages, ou voyage de Samuel Champlain, de Brouage, faict en la France l'an mil six cents trois *(Paris, 1603), edited and translated by H. P. Biggar (and others),* The Works of Samuel de Champlain, *I (Toronto, Champlain Society, 1922), 91–189, and reprinted here.*

1

We set out from Honfleur, the fifteenth day of March 1603. This same day we put into the roadstead of Havre de Grace, because the wind was contrary. On Sunday following, the sixteenth day of the said month, we set sail to proceed on our voyage. On the next day, the seventeenth, we sighted Alderney and Guernsey which are islands between the coasts of Normandy and England.

On the eighteenth of the said month, we sighted the coast of Brittany. On the nineteenth, at seven o'clock in the evening, we reckoned that we were off Ushant. On the twenty-first, at seven o'clock in the morning, we met with seven Flemish ships, which, as we judged, were coming from the Indies. On Easter Sunday, the thirtieth of the said month, we were impeded by a great storm, which seemed to be rather thunder than wind, and lasted the space of seventeen days, but was not so severe as it had been the first two days. During that time we rather lost than gained ground. On the sixteenth day of April the weather began to moderate, and the sea became calmer than before, to the contentment of all; so that we continued our said course until the twenty-eighth of the said month, when we met with a very high iceberg. The next day, we sighted an ice-floe more than eight leagues in length, with an infinite number of other smaller pieces of ice, which hindered our passage. And, by the reckoning of the pilot, this ice was some hundred or hundred and twenty leagues from the coast of Canada. We were in latitude 45° 40', and found passage in latitude 44°. On May 2, at eleven o'clock in the morning, we came upon the Bank in latitude 44° 20'. On the sixth of the said month, we came so near land that we heard the sea beat against the shore, but could not see it for the thickness of the fog, to which these coasts are subject; and on this account we again put out to sea some leagues, until the next morning, when, the weather being very clear, we sighted land, which was Cape St. Mary. On the next day, the twelfth, we were overtaken by a great gale of wind, which lasted two days. On the fifteenth of the same month, we sighted the islands of St. Pierre. On the seventeenth, we met with an ice-floe near cape Ray, six leagues in length, which caused us to strike sail for the whole night, to avoid the danger we might incur. The next day we set sail, and sighted cape

Ray, and the St. Paul islands, and cape St. Law-rence, which is the mainland on the south side. And from cape St. Lawrence to cape Ray is eighteen leagues, which is the breadth of the entrance to the great Gulf of Canada. The same day, about ten o'clock in the morning, we met with another ice-floe, more than eight leagues long. On the twentieth of the said month, we came in sight of an island, some twenty-five or thirty leagues in length, called Anticosti, which is the entrance to the river of Canada. The next day we sighted Gaspé, a very high land, and began to enter the said river of Canada, skirting the south coast as far as Mantanne, distant from Gaspé sixty-five leagues; from the said Mantanne we came to within sight of Bic, a distance of twenty leagues, which is on the south side also; from the said Bic we crossed the river to Tadoussac, a distance of fifteen leagues. All these places are very high, and barren, producing nothing.

On the twenty-fourth of the said month, we cast anchor before Tadoussac, and on the twenty-sixth entered the said harbour, which is like a cove at the mouth of the Saguenay river. Here there is a current and tide, very unusual for its swiftness and depth, where sometimes boisterous winds blow because of the cold they bring with them. It is supposed that the distance up the said river is some forty-five or fifty leagues to the first fall, and that it comes from the north-north-west. The said harbour of Tadoussac is small; and could not hold above ten or twelve ships: but there is water enough towards the east, with shelter from the river Saguenay along a little hill, which is almost cut off by the sea. The rest consists of high mountains, whereon is little soil, but only rocks and sands overgrown with pine, cypress, firs, birch, and other varieties of trees of small value. There is a little lake near the said harbour, en-closed by well-wooded mountains. At the en-trance of the said harbour are two points, one on the west called St. Matthew's point, running a league out into the sea, and the other on the south-east side called All Devils' point, running out a quarter of a league. The south, south-south-east and south-south-west winds strike into the harbour. But from St. Matthew's point to the said All Devils' point is nearly a league: both these points are dry at low water.

2

On the twenty-seventh, accompanied by the two savages whom Monsieur du Pont brought to make report of what they had seen in France, and of the good reception the King had given them, we sought the savages at St. Matthew's point, which is a league from Tadoussac. As soon as we had landed we went to the lodge of their grand Saga-more, named Anadabijou, where we found him and some eighty or a hundred of his companions, making *Tabagie* (that is to say, a feast). He re-ceived us very well, after the fashion of the coun-try, and made us sit down beside him, while all the savages ranged themselves one next the other on both sides of the lodge. One of the savages whom we had brought began to make his oration, of the good reception that the king had given them, and of the good entertainment they had received in France, and that they might feel assured His Majesty wished them well, and desired to people their country, and to make peace with their enemies (who are the Iroquois) or send forces to vanquish them. He also told of the fine castles, palaces, houses, and peoples they had seen, and of our manner of living. He was heard with the greatest possible silence. Now when he had ended his oration, the said grand Sagamore Anadabijou, who had listened to him attentively, began to smoke tobacco, and to pass on his pipe to Monsieur du Pont-Gravé of St. Malo, and to me, and to certain other Sagamores who were near him. After smoking some time, he began to ad-dress the whole gathering, speaking with gravity, pausing sometimes a little, and then resuming his speech, saying to them, that in truth they ought to be very glad to have His Majesty for their great friend. They answered all with one voice, *Ho, ho, ho,* which is to say, *yes, yes.* Continuing his speech, he said that he was well content that His said Majesty should people their country, and make war on their enemies, and that there was no nation in the world to which they wished more good than to the French. Finally, he gave them all to understand the advantage and profit they might receive from His said Majesty. When he had ended his speech, we went out of his lodge, and they began to hold their *Tabagie* or feast, which they make with the flesh of moose, which is like beef, with that of bear, seal, and beaver, which are their most ordinary meats, and with great quantities of wild fowl. They had eight or ten kettles full of meats in the midst of the said lodge, and these were set some six paces apart, and each on its own fire. The men sat on both sides (as I said before), each with his porringer made of the bark of a tree; and when the meat is cooked, one of them apportions to every man his part, into these dishes, out of which they feed very filthily, for when their hands are greasy they rub them on their hair, or else on the hair of their dogs, of which they have many for hunting. Before their meat was cooked, one of them rose up, and took a dog, and went leaping about the said kettles from one end of the lodge to the other. When he came in front of the grand Sagamore, he threw his dog violently upon the ground, and then all with one voice cried, *Ho, ho, ho;* having done this, he went and sat down in his place. Immediately another rose up and did the like, and so they continued until the meat was cooked. Then when they had ended their feast, they began to dance, taking in their hands as a mark of rejoicing the scalps of their enemies, which hung behind them. There were one or two who sang, keeping time by the beat of their hands, which they strike upon their knees; then they stop sometimes, and cry, *Ho, ho, ho*, and begin again to dance, panting like a man out of breath. They were celebrating this triumph for a victory they had won over the Iroquois, of whom they had slain about a hundred, whose scalps they cut off, and had with them for the ceremony. Three nations had taken part in the war, the Etechemins, Algonquins, and Montagnais, to the number of a thousand, and these went on the war-path against the Iroquois, whom they encountered at the mouth of the river of the Iroquois and slew a hundred of them. The mode of warfare which they practise is altogether by surprises; for otherwise they would be afraid, and too much in dread of the said Iroquois, who are in greater number than the said Montagnais, Etechemins, and Algonquins.

On the twenty-eighth day of this month, they came and encamped at the aforesaid harbour of Tadoussac, where lay our ship. At daybreak their grand Sagamore came out of his lodge, going round about all the other lodges, and crying with a loud voice that they should break camp to go to Tadoussac, where their good friends were. Immediately every man in a trice took down his lodge, and the said grand Captain was the first to begin to take his canoe and carry it to the water, wherein he embarked his wife and children, and a quantity of furs; and in like manner were launched well nigh two hundred canoes, which go extraordinarily well; for though our shallop was well manned, yet they went more swiftly than we. There are but two that paddle, the man and the wife. Their canoes are some eight or nine paces long, and a pace or a pace and a half broad amidships, and grow sharper and sharper toward both ends. They are very liable to overturn, if one know not how to manage them rightly; for they are made of a bark of trees called birch-bark, strengthened within by little circles of wood strongly and neatly fashioned, and are so light that a man can carry one of them easily; and every canoe can carry the weight of a pipe. When they wish to go overland to get to some river where they have business, they carry them with them.

Their lodges are low, made like tents, covered with the aforesaid tree-bark; they leave all the top uncovered about a foot space, through which the light comes in; and make many fires right in the midst of their lodge, where there are sometimes ten households together. They sleep upon skins one beside another, and their dogs with them.

They were in number about a thousand persons, men as well as women and children. The spot at St. Matthew's point, where they were first encamped, is very pretty. They were at the bottom of a little hill, covered with fir and cypress trees. Upon this point there is a little level plot, which is visible from afar off, and upon the top of the hill is a level plain, a league long, and half a league broad, covered with trees; the soil is very sandy, and there is good pasture there. All the rest is nothing but mountains of very barren rocks. The sea beats round about the said hill, which is dry almost for a full half league at low water.

3

On the ninth day of June the savages all began to make merry together, and to hold their feast, as I have described before, and to dance, in honour of the aforesaid victory which they had obtained over their enemies. Now after they had made good cheer, the Algonquins, one of the three nations, went out of their lodges, and withdrew by themselves into an open place. Here they arranged all their women and girls side by side, and themselves stood behind, singing all in unison in the manner I have already described. Suddenly all the women and girls proceeded to cast off their mantles of skins, and stripped themselves stark naked, showing their privities, but retaining their ornaments of matachias, which are beads and braided cords made of porcupine quills, dyed of various colours. After they had made an end of their songs, they cried all with one voice, *Ho, ho, ho;* at the same instant all the women and girls covered themselves with their mantles, which were at their feet, and they had a short rest; then all at once beginning again to sing, they let fall their mantles as before. They do not stir from one spot when they dance, but make certain gestures and motions of the body, first lifting up one foot and then the other, and stamping upon the ground. While they were performing this dance, the Sagamore of the Algonquins, whose name was Besouat, was seated before the said women and girls, between two poles, on which hung the scalps of their enemies. Sometimes he arose and moved away to address the Montagnais and Etechemins, saying to them: "See how we rejoice for the victory which we have obtained over our enemies; ye must do the like, that we may be satisfied." Then all cried together, *Ho, ho, ho.* As soon as he had returned to his place, the grand Sagamore and all his companions cast off their mantles, being stark naked save their privities, which were covered with a small piece of skin, and each of them took what seemed proper to him, such as matachias, tomahawks, swords, kettles, pieces of fat, moose flesh, seal; in a word, every one had a present, which they proceeded to give to the Algonquins. After all these ceremonies the dance came to an end, and the Algonquins, both men and women, carried away their presents to their lodges. They also matched two of the fittest men of each nation, whom they caused to run, and he who was swiftest in the race had a present.

All these people are to a man of a very cheerful disposition, and laugh frequently; yet they are somewhat phlegmatic. They speak very deliberately, as though they would make themselves well understood, and, stopping suddenly, reflect for a good while, and then begin to speak again. They often conduct themselves in this fashion in the midst of their harangues in council, where there are none but the chief men, who are the elders: the women and children are never present.

All these people sometimes suffer so great extremity, on account of the great cold and snow, that they are almost constrained to eat one another; for the animals and fowl on which they live migrate to warmer countries. I think that if

any one would show them how to live, and teach them to till the ground, and other matters, they would learn very well; for I assure you that plenty of them have good judgment, and answer very properly any question put to them. They have one evil quality in them, which is, that they are given to revenge, and are great liars, a people in whom it is not well to put confidence, except for good reason, and standing on your guard. They promise much and perform little.

They are for the most part a people that has no law, as far as I could see and learn from the said grand Sagamore, who told me that in truth they believe there is a God, who has made all things. Then I said to him, "Since they believe in one God only, how had He brought them into the world, and whence had they come?" He answered me, that after God had made all things, He took a number of arrows, and stuck them in the ground, whence He drew men and women, which have multiplied in the world up to the present, and had their origin in this fashion. I replied to him, that what he said was false; but that in truth there was but one God, who had created all things on earth, and in the heavens. Seeing all these things so perfect, without anybody to govern this world beneath, He took the slime of the earth, and of it created Adam, our first father. While Adam slept, God took a rib of the said Adam, and out of it formed Eve, whom He gave him for his companion; and that it was the truth that they and we had our origin after this manner, and not from arrows as was their belief. He replied nothing, save that he approved rather what I said, than that which he told me. I asked him also, whether he did not believe there was more than one God. He replied that their belief was, that there was one God, one Son, one Mother, and the Sun, which were four; yet that God was above them all; but that the Son and the Sun were good, because of the benefit they received of them, but that the Mother was of no value, and ate them up, and that the Father was not very good. I showed him his error according to our faith, in which he manifested some small belief. I asked him whether they had not seen, or heard their ancestors tell that God had come into the world. He told me that he had not seen Him; but that in old time there were five men who went toward the setting sun and met God, who asked them, "Whither go ye?" They said, "We go in search of a living." God answered them,

"You shall find it here." They went on without regard to what God had said to them: who took a stone, and touched two of them with it, and they were turned into stones. And He said again to the other three, "Whither go ye?" And they answered as at first: and God said to them again, "Go no further, you shall find it here." And seeing that nothing came to them, they went on: and God took two sticks, and touched the two first with them, and they were turned into sticks; and the fifth halted and would go no further. And God asked him again, "Whither goest thou?" "I go in search of my living." "Stay, and thou shalt find it." He stayed without going any further, and God gave him meat, and he ate it; after he had made good cheer, he returned among other savages, and told them all the above story.

He told me also, that once upon a time there was a man who had a good supply of tobacco (which is a herb, of which they take the smoke), and that God came to this man, and asked him where was his tobacco-pipe. The man took his tobacco-pipe and gave it to God, who smoked tobacco a great while: after He had smoked enough, God broke the said pipe into many pieces: and the man asked Him, "Why hast Thou broken my pipe? Surely Thou seest that I have no other." And God took one of His own, and gave it to him, saying to him: "Here is one that I give thee, carry it to thy grand Sagamore; charge him to keep it, and if he keep it well, he shall never want for anything whatever, nor any of his companions." The man took the pipe, and gave it to his grand Sagamore, and as long as he kept it the savages wanted for nothing in the world; but afterwards the said Sagamore lost this pipe, and this is the reason of the great famine which sometimes comes among them. I asked him whether he believed all this; and he said yes, and that it was true. Now I believe this is the reason why they say that God is not very good. But I replied and told him, that God was wholly good; and that without doubt it was the Devil who had appeared to those men, and that if they believed in God as we do, they should lack nothing of which they stood in need; that the sun which they beheld, the moon and the stars, had been created by this great God, who made heaven and earth; and that these have no power but that which God has given them; that we believe in this great God, who of His goodness had sent us His dear Son, who,

being conceived by the Holy Ghost, became human flesh in the virginal womb of the Virgin Mary, lived thirty-three years on earth, working infinite miracles, raising up the dead, healing the sick, casting out devils, giving sight to the blind, teaching men the will of God His Father, in order to serve, honour, and worship Him; shed His blood, and suffered death and passion for us and for our sins, and redeemed mankind, and being buried rose again, descended into hell and ascended into heaven, where He sat on the right hand of God His Father. I told him this was the belief of all Christians, who believe in the Father, the Son, and the Holy Ghost, which nevertheless are not three Gods, but one same and one sole God, and a Trinity, in which is no before or after, no greater or less; that the Virgin Mary, the Mother of the Son of God, and all men and women who have lived in this world doing the commandments of God, and have suffered martyrdom for His name's sake, and who by God's permission have wrought miracles, and are saints in heaven in His Paradise, do all pray this great divine Majesty for us, to pardon us our faults and sins which we commit against His law and commandments. And so, by the prayers of the saints in heaven, and by our prayers which we offer to His divine Majesty, He gives us that which we need, and the Devil has no power over us, and can do us no harm; that if they had this belief, they should be as we, and the Devil would be unable to do them more harm, and they should lack nothing they required.

Thereupon the said Sagamore told me that he approved what I said. I asked him what ceremony they used in praying to their God. He told me, that they did not make much use of ceremonies, but that every one prayed in his heart as he thought good. This is why I believe they have no law among them, nor know what it is to worship and pray to God, and that most of them live like brute beasts; and I think they would speedily be brought to be good Christians, if their country were colonised, which most of them would like.

They have among them certain savages whom they call *Pilotoua*, who speak to the Devil face to face and he tells them what they must do, both in war and in other affairs; and if he should command them to put into execution any enterprise, either to kill a Frenchman or one of their own nation, they would immediately obey his command.

Moreover they believe that all the dreams they dream are true; and indeed there are many of them who say that they have seen in dreams things which happen or will happen. But to speak the truth about them, these are visions of the Devil, who deceives and misleads them. This is all their beliefs that I could learn from them, and they are brutish.

All these peoples are well proportioned in body, without any deformity; they are agile, and the women are well shapen, filled out and plump, of a swarthy colour on account of the profusion of a certain pigment with which they rub themselves, and which gives them an olive hue. They are clad in skins, one part of their bodies is covered, and the other part uncovered. But in winter they provide for the whole body; for they are clad with good furs, such as the skins of moose, otter, beavers, bears, seals, stags, and deer, which they have in abundance. In the winter when the snows are heavy they make a kind of racket twice or thrice as big as ours in France, which they fasten to their feet, and so walk on the snow without sinking; for otherwise they could not hunt nor make their way in many places.

They have also a kind of marriage, which is, that when a girl is fourteen or fifteen years old, she may have several suitors and friends, and keep company with all whom she likes: then at the end of some five or six years, she will take which of them she pleases for her husband, and they will live together thus to the end of their lives, unless after they have lived some time together they have no children, when the man may get a divorce and take another wife, saying that his own is worth nothing. Thus the girls are more free than the married women; but after they are married they are chaste, and their husbands for the most part are jealous, and these give presents to the father or kindred of the girl whom they have married. This is the ceremony and manner of their conduct in their marriages.

Touching their burials, when a man or woman dies, they make a pit, in which they put all the goods they have, such as kettles, furs, hatchets, bows and arrows, robes and other things, and then they place the body in the pit, and cover it with earth, and lay on top a great many large pieces of wood, and one stake they set up on end and paint it red on the upper part. They believe in the immortality of the soul, and say that when they die they go into other lands to make merry with their kindred and friends.

4

On the eleventh day of June, I went some twelve or fifteen leagues up the Saguenay, which is a fine river, and of incredible depth; for, according to what I have heard related of its source, I think that it comes from a very high place whence a torrent of water descends with great violence: but the water from that source is not sufficient to make such a river as this; which nevertheless extends only from this torrent of water (where is the first fall) to the harbour of Tadoussac, which is the mouth of the said Saguenay river, a distance of some forty-five or fifty leagues, and it is a good league and a half broad at the most, and a quarter of a league where it is narrowest, which makes a great flow of water. The whole region so far as I saw was nothing but rocky mountains, the most part covered with fir, cypress, and birch, a most unpleasant land, where, neither on the one side nor on the other, did I find a league of meadow-land. There are certain sandy hills and islands in the said river, which stand high above the water. In short, these are very deserts, unfit for animals or birds; for I assure you, as I went hunting through places which seemed to me the most attractive, I found nothing at all but small birds, like nightingales and swallows, which come in the summer; for at other times I think there are none, because of the excessive cold there, this river coming from the north-west.

They reported to me, that having passed the first fall, whence comes this torrent of water, they pass eight others and then they travel one day's journey without finding any; then they pass ten other rapids, and enter a lake, which they take two days to cross; each day they can make easily twelve or fifteen leagues. At the end of the lake are people encamped; then they enter three other rivers, [making] three or four days' journey in each; where at the end of these rivers are two or three bodies of water, like lakes, whence the Saguenay takes its rise: from which headwaters to the said harbour of Tadoussac is a journey of ten days in their canoes. On the banks of the said rivers are many lodges, where other tribes come from the north, to barter beaver and marten skins with the Montagnais for other merchandise, which the French ships bring to the said

Montagnais. These said savages from the north say that they are in sight of a sea which is salt. I hold that, if this be so, it is some gulf of this our sea, which overflows in the north into the midst of the continent; and indeed it can be nothing else. This is what I have learned of the river Saguenay.

5

On Wednesday the eighteenth day of June, we set out from Tadoussac, to go to the Rapid. We passed near an island, called Hare island, which may be about two leagues from the mainland on the north side, and some seven leagues from Tadoussac, and five leagues from the south shore.

From Hare island we followed the north shore about half a league, as far as a point which runs out into the river, where one must keep farther off. The said point is a league from the island called Coudres island, which may be about two leagues in width; and from this said island to the north shore is a league. The said [Coudres] island is somewhat flat, and comes to a point at either end; at the west end are meadows and rocky points which stretch out somewhat into the river. This island is somewhat pleasant, because of the woods which surround it. There is much slate, and the soil is somewhat gravelly: at the extremity is a rock which extends into the sea about half a league. We passed to the north of this island, distant from Hare island twelve leagues.

The Thursday following we set out from there, and came to anchor at a dangerous cove on the north shore, where are some meadows, and a little river alongside which the savages sometimes encamp. That day we continued to skirt the north shore, as far as a place where we put in on account of the winds which were contrary, where were many rocks and very dangerous places: here we stayed three days waiting for fair weather. All this coast is nothing but mountains both on the south side and on the north, most of it like the Saguenay coast.

On Sunday, the twenty-second day of the month, we set out to go to the island of Orleans. On the way there are many islands along the south shore, which are low and covered with trees, very pretty in appearance, and in circumference (as well as I was able to judge) some two leagues, some one league, and others half a league. About these islands is nothing but rocks and shallows, very dangerous to pass; and they

are distant some two leagues from the mainland on the south. And from there we skirted the island of Orleans on the south side. It is a league from the north shore, very pretty and level, extending eight leagues in length. The shore of the land on the south is low for some two leagues inland: the country begins to be low at this island, which may be two leagues from the mainland on the south. It is very dangerous to pass on the north side on account of the sandbanks and rocks, which lie between this island and the mainland, and it is almost all dry at low water.

At the end of the said island I saw a torrent of water, falling from the top of a great mountain along the said river of Canada, and on the top of the mountain the ground is level and pleasant to look at, although in the interior of the country one sees high mountains which may be distant some twenty or twenty-five leagues towards the interior, and are near the first fall of the Saguenay.

We came to anchor at Quebec, which is a narrow part of the said river of Canada, some three hundred paces broad. At these narrows on the north side is a very high mountain, which slopes down on both sides: all the rest is a level and beautiful country, where there is good land covered with trees, such as oaks, cypresses, birches, fir-trees and aspens, and also wild fruit-bearing trees, and vines; so that in my opinion, if this soil were tilled, it would be as good as ours. Along the shore of the said Quebec are diamonds in the slate rocks which are better than those of Alençon. From Quebec to Coudres island is twenty-nine leagues.

6

On Monday, the twenty-third of the month, we set out from Quebec, where the river begins to broaden, sometimes to one league, then again to a league and a half or two leagues at most. The country grows finer and finer; it is all low ground, without rocks, or with very few. The north shore abounds in rocks and sand-banks: you must take the south side, about half a league from the shore. There are some small rivers, not navigable except for the canoes of the savages, and in which are many rapids. We came to anchor at Ste. Croix, distant from Quebec fifteen leagues; it is a low point, rising up on both sides. The country is fine and level, and the soil better than in any place I had seen, with extensive woods, but very few fir-trees and cypresses. In these parts are found quantities of grapes, pears, hazel-nuts, cherries, red and green currants, and certain small roots, the size of a small nut, tasting like truffles, which are very good roasted or boiled. It is all black soil, without any rocks, except that there is a good deal of slate: the soil is very soft, and if it were well tilled would yield great increase.

On the north side is a river called Batiscan, which extends far into the interior, down which the Algonquins sometimes come: and there is another on the same side three leagues from the said Ste. Croix, on the way from Quebec, which is that which Jacques Cartier reached in the beginning of his explorations, and he ascended no farther. The said river is pleasant, and goes far up into the interior, All this north shore is very level and pretty.

On Wednesday, the twenty-fourth day of the month, we set out from the said Ste. Croix, where we had stayed a tide and a half, that we might be able the following day to pass on by daylight, because of the great number of rocks in the channel of the river which, a peculiar sight, are left almost dry at low water. But at half flood, one may begin to pass freely; yet with great heed, and lead in hand. The tide rises here almost three fathoms and a half.

The farther we went, the finer was the country. We proceeded some five leagues and a half, and anchored on the north shore. On Wednesday following we set out from this place, which is a flatter country than that lower down, and as heavily wooded as at Ste. Croix. We passed close to a small island, covered with vines, and came to anchor on the south side near a little hill: but on ascending it found the country level. There is another small island three leagues from Ste. Croix, near the south shore. On the following Thursday we set out from this highland, and passed close to a small island, near the north shore, where I landed, in the neighbourhood of some six small rivers, two of which are navigable for boats far up-stream, and another is some three hundred paces broad; at its mouth are some islands; it extends very far into the interior, and is deeper than all the rest. These rivers are very pleasing in appearance, the landscape being covered with trees resembling walnut-trees, and having the same smell: but I saw no fruit, which makes me doubtful. The savages told me they bear fruit like ours.

Passing on we came to an island, called St. Eloi, and another small island, which is quite close to the north shore. We passed between this island and the said north shore, where the distance from one to the other is some hundred and fifty paces. From this island to the south shore is a league and a half. We passed near a river, up which canoes may proceed. All this north shore is very good; one may pass freely there, yet with the lead in hand, to avoid certain points. All this shore which we followed is shifting sand; but after penetrating a little way into the woods, the soil is good.

On Friday following we set out from this island, still coasting the north shore quite near the land, which is low and covered with all sorts of good trees, and in great number, as far as Three Rivers, where the climate begins to be somewhat different from that at Ste. Croix: inasmuch as the trees are more forward there than in any place I had hitherto seen. From Three Rivers to Ste. Croix is fifteen leagues. In this river are six islands, three of which are very small, and the others some five to six hundred paces long, very pleasant and fertile considering their small extent. There is one in the middle of the said river, opposite the channel of the river of Canada, and commanding the others which lie four or five hundred paces distant from the shore on either side. It is high on the south side, and falls somewhat toward the north side. In my judgment this would be a place suitable for settlement, and might be quickly fortified; for the situation is strong of itself, and near a large lake, not more than some four leagues distant. It almost connects with the Saguenay river, according to the report of the Indians, who travel nearly a hundred leagues northward, and pass many rapids, then go by land some five or six leagues, and enter a lake, whence the said Saguenay takes the best part of its source; and from the said lake the said Indians come to Tadoussac. Moreover, a settlement at Three Rivers would be a boon for the freedom of some tribes who dare not come that way for fear of their enemies, the said Iroquois, who infest the banks all along the said river of Canada; but if this river were inhabited we might make friends with the Iroquois and with the other savages, or at the very least under protection of the said settlement the said savages might come freely without fear or danger, inasmuch as the said Three Rivers is a place of passage. All the soil that I saw on the north shore is sandy. We went up the said river about a league, and could proceed no farther, on account of the strong current. With a skiff we went to explore higher up, but had not gone more than a league before we encountered a very narrow rapid, about twelve paces wide, on account of which we could proceed no farther. All the land I saw on the banks of the said river rises more and more, and is covered with numbers of fir and cypress-trees, and very few other trees.

7

On the Saturday following, we set out from Three Rivers, and anchored at a lake four leagues distant. All this region from Three Rivers to the entrance of the said lake is low ground, level with the water, but on the south side somewhat higher. The land is very good, and the most pleasant we had yet seen; the woods are very open, so that a man may easily go through them.

The next day, the twenty-ninth of June, we entered the lake, which is some fifteen leagues in length, and seven or eight leagues broad. About a league from the entrance on the south side there is a fairly large river which extends into the interior some sixty or eighty leagues; and further along, on the same side, is another small river, which extends inland about two leagues and issues from another small lake, some three or four leagues in length. On the north side, where the land appears very high, one sees for a distance of some twenty leagues; but little by little the mountains fall away toward the west, as if the country were flat. The savages say, that these mountains for the most part are poor soil. The said lake is some three fathoms deep where we passed, which was nearly in the middle. The length lies east and west, and the breadth from north to south. I think it will not be found wanting in good fish, of such kinds as we have in our own country. We passed through it the very same day, and came to anchor about two leagues farther on in the river which leads into the interior, at the mouth of which are thirty small islands. As far as I could discern, some are two leagues in circumference, others a league and a half, and others less; and they are full of quantities of walnut-trees, which are not very different from ours; and I think their nuts are good in season: under the trees I saw quantities of them, of two sorts, some small, others an inch long, but they were decayed. There are also a great many vines on the shores of the said islands; but when the waters are high, the most part of them are covered with water. This region is still better than any I had seen.

The last day of June we departed thence, and passed along to the mouth of the river of the Iroquois, where the savages who were about to make war against these were lodged and fortified. Their fortress is constructed of a number of stakes set very close together, and on the one side comes down to the bank of the great river, and on the other to the bank of the river of the Iroquois: and their canoes were drawn up side by side on the bank, so that they may quickly take to flight, if peradventure they be surprised by the Iroquois; for their fort is covered with oak bark, and serves only to give them time to embark.

We went up the river of the Iroquois some five or six leagues, and could pass no farther with our long-boat, by reason of the strong current flowing down, and we could also not go by land, and drag the long-boat, for the quantity of trees on the banks. Seeing we could pass no farther, we took our skiff, to see if the current slackened; but after going some two leagues, it became still stronger, and we could advance no higher up. Being unable to do anything else, we came back to our long-boat. The whole of this river is some three to four hundred paces broad, and very free from shoals. We saw five islands in it, distant one from the other a quarter or half a league, or a league at most, one of which, the nearest, is a league long; the others are very small. All this country is covered with trees and the land is low, like that I had seen before; but there are more firs and cypresses than in other places. Nevertheless, the soil is good, although somewhat sandy. This river runs about south-west.

The savages say, that some fifteen leagues from where we had been, there is a rapid which descends from a much higher level, to pass which they carry their canoes about a quarter of a league, and then enter a lake, at the entrance of which are three islands, and in the lake they meet with yet more islands. This lake is some forty or fifty leagues in length, and some twenty-five leagues in breadth, and into it fall a number of rivers, as many as ten, which are navigable for canoes a long way. Then when they come to the end of this lake, there is another rapid, and they enter another lake, which is as large as the former, and at the extremity of this are lodged the Iroquois. They say, moreover, that there is a river, which leads down to the coast of Florida, whence from the lake last mentioned the distance is some hundred or hundred and forty leagues. All the country of the Iroquois is somewhat hilly, nevertheless a very good country, temperate, without much winter, nay, very little.

8

Setting out from the river of the Iroquois, we came to anchor three leagues from there on the north shore. This whole region is low land, covered with all the various sorts of trees I have mentioned above.

On the first day of July we coasted along the north shore, where the woods are very open, more so than in any place we had seen before, and all good land for tillage. I went in a canoe to the south shore, where I saw a number of islands, very productive of fruits, such as grapes, walnuts, hazel-nuts, and a kind of fruit like chestnuts, cherries, oaks, aspens, poplars, hops, ash, maple, beech, cypress, very few pines and fir-trees. There are also other trees with which I am not acquainted, but which are very fine-looking. One finds there quantities of strawberries, raspberries, red, green, and blue currants, together with many small fruits which grow there in the thick grass. There are also many wild beasts, such as moose, stags, hinds, deer, bears, porcupines, hares, foxes, beavers, otters, muskrats and certain other kinds of animals that I am unacquainted with, which are good to eat, and on which the savages subsist.

We passed close to a very pretty island, which is some four leagues long and half a league wide. I saw on the south side two high mountains, which appeared to be some twenty leagues inland; the savages informed me, that there was the first rapid of the river of the Iroquois.

On Wednesday following we set out from this place, and made some five or six leagues. We saw many islands; the land there is very low, and these islands are covered with trees, like those along the river of the Iroquois. The following day we made some leagues, and passed many other islands also, which are very good and pleasant from the many meadows thereabouts, both on the mainland and also on the islands: and the woods there are all of very small growth, in comparison with those we had passed.

At length we arrived this same day at the entrance of the rapid, with the wind behind us;

and came to an island, almost in the midst of the said entrance, a quarter of a league long, and passed on the south side of it, where there was only from three to four or five feet of water; sometimes there was a fathom or two, but then suddenly we found again not more than three or four feet. There are many rocks, and little islands, with no trees at all on them, and level with the water. From the beginning of the above-mentioned island, which is in the midst of the said entrance, the water begins to come with great force. Although we had the wind very favourable, yet we could not with all our might make any great way: nevertheless we passed the said island which is at the entrance of the rapid. When we perceived that we could go no farther, we came to anchor on the north shore over against a small island, abounding in most of those fruits I have spoken of before. We at once made ready our skiff, which had been constructed on purpose for passing the said rapid, and into it entered the Sieur du Pont and myself, besides certain savages, whom we had brought to show us the way. Leaving our long-boat, we had scarce gone three hundred paces, when we were forced to get out, and some sailors had to get into the water to free our skiff. The savages' canoe passed easily. We met with an infinite number of small rocks, level with the surface of the water, whereon we frequently touched.

There are two large islands; one on the north side, some fifteen leagues long, and almost as many broad, begins some twelve leagues down the river of Canada, as you go toward the river of the Iroquois, and extends beyond the rapid; the island on the south side is some four leagues long, and half a league broad. There is also another island, near that on the north side, which may be half a league long, and a quarter broad: and another little island lying between that on the north side, and the other nearer to the south shore, where we passed the entrance to the rapid. Past this entrance, there is a kind of lake, wherein lie all these islands, which may be some five leagues long and almost as many broad, and where are many small rocky islands. Near the said rapid is a mountain, visible from very far in the interior, and a little river that flows from the said mountain into the lake. One sees on the south side three or four mountains, which seem to be about fifteen or sixteen leagues in the interior. There are also two rivers; one leading to the first lake of the river of the Iroquois, up which some-times the Algonquins make war on them; and the other which is near the rapid, and extends a little way inland.

As we began to approach the said rapid with our little skiff and the canoe, I assure you I never saw any torrent of water pour over with such force as this does, although it is not very high, being in some places only one or two fathoms, and at the most three. It descends as it were step by step: and wherever it falls from some small height, it boils up extraordinarily, owing to the force and speed of the water as it passes through the said rapid, which may be a league in length. There are many rocks out in the stream, and about the middle are very long narrow islands, where the current runs both beside the islands that are toward the south, and also to the north: and it is so dangerous, that it is beyond the power of man to pass with any boat, however small it be. We went by land through the woods, to see the end of the rapid, which is a league away, and there we saw no more rocks or falls, but the water runs with the utmost possible swiftness; and this cur-rent extends for three or four leagues, so that it is vain to imagine that any boats could be conveyed past the same rapids. But he who would pass them must provide himself with the canoes of the savages, which a man can easily carry; for to transport a boat is a thing that cannot be done in the short time necessary to enable one to return to France to winter. And besides this first rapid, there are ten more, for the most part difficult to pass; so that it would be a matter of great toil and labour to be able to see and do by boat what a man might propose, except at great cost and expense, besides the risk of labouring in vain. But with the canoes of the savages one may travel freely and quickly throughout the country, as well up the little rivers as up the large ones. So that by directing one's course with the help of the savages and their canoes, a man may see all that is to be seen, good and bad, within the space of a year or two.

The whole of that small extent of country we passed through by land alongside the said rapid is very open woods, and one may easily carry one's weapons, without much toil; the climate there is milder and more equable, and the soil better, than in any place I had seen, with trees and fruit in great quantity, as in all the other places above-mentioned; and it is in 45° and some minutes.

When we saw we could do no more, we re-turned to our long-boat, where we questioned the savages we had with us about the end of the river, which I made them draw by hand, and [show] whence was its source. They told us, that beyond the first rapid we had seen, they go up the river in their canoes some ten or fifteen leagues to a river which extends to the dwelling-place of the Algon-quins, who dwell some sixty leagues distant from the great river; and then they pass five rapids, which from the first to the last may extend eight leagues, and at two of them they carry their canoes to get past them. Each rapid may extend an eighth of a league or a quarter at the most. Then they come to a lake, which may be fifteen or sixteen leagues long. Beyond it they again enter a river, which may be a league broad, and travel some two leagues up it; and then enter another lake some four or five leagues in length; at the end of which they pass five other rapids, the distance from the first to the last being some twenty-five or thirty leagues: past three of these they carry their canoes, and at the other two they do but track them in the water, because the current is not so strong there nor so difficult as in the others. None of all these rapids is so hard to pass as that we had seen. Then they come into a lake, which may be some eighty leagues in length, and in which are many islands, and at the extremity of it the water is brackish and the winter mild. At the end of the said lake they pass a fall which is somewhat high, and where little water flows over: there they carry their canoes by land about a quarter of a league in order to pass this fall. From here they enter another lake, which may be some sixty leagues long, and its water is very brackish. Having reached the end of it they come to a strait two leagues broad, which leads far into the interior. They told us that they themselves had passed no farther, and had not seen the extremity of a lake, which is some fifteen or sixteen leagues beyond where they themselves had been, nor had they who told them of it known any man that had seen it, because it is so vast that they will not venture to put out into the same, for fear lest some storm or gale should surprise them. They say that in summer the sun sets to the north of this lake, and in winter it sets as it were in the middle of it; and that the water there is very salt, like that of our sea.

I asked them whether from this said last lake which they had seen the water still flowed down the river towards Gaspé. They said no; that it was from the third lake only that it flowed towards Gaspé, but that beyond the last fall, which is somewhat high, as I have said, the water was almost still, and that the said lake might find an outlet by other rivers, which flow into the interior, either to the south, or to the north, of which there are many, and of these they know not the extremity. Now, in my judgment, if so many rivers fall into this lake, which has so small a discharge at the said fall, it must of necessity have an outflow by some very large river. But what makes me believe there is no river by which this lake has its outflow (considering the number of all the rivers which fall into it) is that the savages have not seen any river taking its course into the interior, save in the place where they were; which makes me believe that this is the South Sea, being salt as they say. Nevertheless we must not give too much credence to this view, except it be with manifest reason, even though there be some small grounds. This is all I have seen in the matter or heard for certain from the savages, in reply to what we asked of them.

9

We set out from the said rapid on Friday the fourth day of June, and returned the same day to the river of the Iroquois. On Sunday the sixth of June we set out thence, and came to anchor at the lake. On Monday following we cast anchor at Three Rivers. The same day we made some four leagues beyond the said Three Rivers. On Tuesday following we came to Quebec; and the next day reached the end of the island of Orleans, where the savages came to us, who were encamped on the mainland to the north. We questioned two or three Algonquins to find out whether they would agree with those whom we had examined about the end and source of the said river of Canada.

They said, according to the sketch they gave of it, that, some two or three leagues past the rapid we had seen, a river leads towards their territory, which is on the north side. Continuing the course up the said great river, they pass a rapid where they carry their canoes, and then pass five other rapids, which may occupy from the first to last some nine or ten leagues; that these rapids are not hard to pass, and that they do but track their canoes in most of them, except at two, where they

carry them. Thence they enter a river, which is a kind of lake, and may extend some six or seven leagues: and then they pass five other rapids, where they track their canoes as in the first-mentioned, except at two, where they carry them as at the first; and from the first to the last is a distance of some twenty or twenty-five leagues. Then they come into a lake which is some hundred and fifty leagues in length; and about four or five leagues from the entrance of that lake there is a river leading northward to the Algonquins, and another leading to the Iroquois, by way of which the said Algonquins and Iroquois make war upon one another. And a little higher up on the south side of the lake is another river leading to the Iroquois. Then when they come to the end of the said lake, they meet with another fall, where they carry their canoes. Thence they enter another very large lake, which may be as big as the former. They have been but very little in this last lake and have heard tell that at the extremity thereof is a sea, the end of which they have not seen, nor have they heard of any one who has seen it; but where they have been, the water is not salt, inasmuch as they have not advanced far into it; and the course of the waters is from the direction of the setting sun toward the east; and they know not whether beyond the lakes they have seen there be another watercourse flowing westward. They say that the sun sets to the right hand of this lake; which, in my judgment, is more or less to the north-west; and that in the first lake the water does not freeze, which makes me think the climate there is temperate. All the territory of the Algonquins is low land, thinly wooded: while the Iroquois country is hilly, but nevertheless very good and fertile, and better than any region they had seen. The said Iroquois dwell some fifty or sixty leagues from the said great lake. This is an exact report of what they told me they had seen; and differs but very little from the account of the first savages.

This day we made our way nearly to Coudres island, somewhere about three leagues. On Thursday, the tenth of the said month, we came within about a league and a half of Hare island, on the north side, where other savages came to our long-boat, among whom was a young Algonquin, who had travelled much in the said great lake. We questioned him very particularly, as we had done the other savages. He told us, that past the said rapid which we had seen, within some two or three leagues, is a river which leads to where the Algonquins dwell, and that, passing up the great river, there are five rapids, which from first to last may cover some eight or nine leagues, at three of which they carry their canoes, and at two others they track them: each of these rapids may be a quarter of a league long: then they come into a lake, which may extend some fifteen leagues. Then they pass five other rapids, which may cover from first to last some twenty to twenty-five leagues; and only two of the rapids do they pass in their canoes; at the other three they track them. Thence they enter a very large lake, which may have a length of some three hundred leagues. Proceeding some hundred leagues into the said lake, they come to a very large island, and beyond this island the water is brackish; but when they have passed some hundred leagues farther, the water becomes more brackish; and when they get to the end of the said lake, the water is wholly salt. There is a fall that may be a league broad, over which an exceeding great current of water descends into the said lake. Past this fall, no more land is seen either on the one side or on the other, but a sea so great that they never have seen the end of it, nor heard of any one that has. The sun sets to the right hand of the said lake, and at the entrance of it is a river leading to the territory of the Algonquins, and another to that of the Iroquois, by way of which they make war on one another. The country of the Iroquois is somewhat hilly, yet very fertile, and in it is grown a quantity of Indian corn, and other products which they have not in their own country: the country of the Algonquins is low land and fertile.

I inquired of them, whether they had knowledge of any mines? They told us, that there is a tribe called the good Iroquois, who come to barter for the merchandise which the French ships furnish to the Algonquins, and that these say there is toward the north a mine of pure copper, of which they showed us some bracelets obtained from the good Iroquois. They said that if any desired to go thither, they would guide there those who should be appointed for that purpose. This is all I could learn from both parties, who differed but very little; except that the second who were questioned said they had not tasted the salt water; moreover they have not been so far up the said lake as the others, and they differ in some small

extent in the length of the journey, the one party making it shorter, the other longer; so that, according to their account, from the rapid where we had been, to the salt sea, which may be the South Sea, is some four hundred leagues. Without doubt, from their account, this can be nothing else than the South Sea, the sun setting where they say it does. On Friday the tenth of the said month we were back at Tadoussac, where lay our ship.

10

As soon as we were come to Tadoussac, we re-embarked to go to Gaspé, which is distant from Tadoussac about a hundred leagues. On the thirteenth day of the said month we met with a troop of savages, who were encamped on the south shore, almost midway from Tadoussac to Gaspé. Their Sagamore who led them is named Armouchides, and is held to be one of the wisest and boldest of the savages. He was on his way to Tadoussac to barter arrows and moose-flesh for the beaver and marten of the other Montagnais, Etechemin, and Algonquin Indians.

On the fifteenth of the said month we reached Gaspé, which is in a bay, about a league and a half from the north side of it; and this bay is some seven or eight leagues in length, and at its mouth is four leagues broad. There is a river which leads some thirty leagues inland. Then we saw another bay, called Codfish bay, which may be some three leagues long, and as much in breadth at the entrance. Thence one comes to isle Percée, which is a sort of very high rock, steep on both sides, with a hole in it, through which shallops and boats can pass at high water: and at low water one can walk from the mainland to the said island, which is only some four or five hundred paces off. Then there is another island, about a league from isle Percée towards the south-east, called Bonaventure island, which may be half a league long. All these places, Gaspé, Codfish bay, and isle Percée, are places where fishing is carried on, both dry and green.

After passing isle Percée, there is a bay called Chaleur bay, which runs inland about west-south-west some eighty leagues, having a breadth at its entrance of about fifteen leagues. The savages of Canada say that up the great river of Canada about sixty leagues, along the south shore, is a little river called Mantanne, which extends inland some eighteen leagues, and when they get to the head of it they carry their canoes inland about a league, and reach the said Chaleur bay, down which they sometimes proceed as far as isle Percée. Also they go from the said bay to Tracadie and Misamichy.

Proceeding along this coast you pass many rivers, and come to a place where there is a river called Souricoua, where Monsieur Prévert went in search of a copper mine. They go with their canoes up this river for two or three days, then they go across country for two or three leagues to the said mine, which is hard upon the seashore to the south. At the mouth of the said river, there is an island about a league out to sea; from this island to isle Percée is some sixty or seventy leagues. Then still following the said coast, which trends toward the east, you meet with a strait, which may be two leagues broad, and five and twenty long. On the east side is an island called St. Lawrence, where lies Cape Breton; and where a tribe of savages, called the Souriquois, winter. Passing the strait of the island of St. Lawrence, and ranging the coast of Acadia, one enters a bay which comes as far as the said copper mine. Passing farther on one finds a river, which extends some sixty or eighty leagues inland and reaches near to the lake of the Iroquois, along which the said savages of the coast of Acadia go to make war upon them. It would be a great boon if there might be found on the coast of Florida a passage which should lead near to the great lake before-mentioned, where the water is salt; as well for the navigation of ships, which would not be subject to so many perils as they are in Canada, as for the shortening of the way more than three hundred leagues. And it is most certain that on the coast of Florida there are rivers not yet discovered, which reach the interior, where the soil is very good and fertile, and very good harbours. The country and coast of Florida may have a different climate, and be more abundantly productive of fruits and other things than that which I have seen; but there cannot be lands more level nor of better quality than those which we have seen.

The savages say, that in the said great Chaleur bay is a river, extending some twenty leagues inland, at the head of which there is a lake, which may be some twenty leagues long and in which there is very little water; and that in summer it dries up, when they find in it, about a foot or a foot

and a half under the ground, a kind of metal resembling the silver which I showed them; and that in another place near the said lake there is a copper mine. And this is what I learned from these savages.

11

We set out from isle Percée on the nineteenth of the said month to return to Tadoussac. When we were some three leagues from cape Bishop, we encountered a storm which lasted two days; and this forced us to put into a great creek, and wait for fair weather. The day following we set out from there, and again encountered another storm. Being loath to put into port, and thinking to make headway, we proceeded to the north shore on the twenty-eighth day of July, and cast anchor in a cove which is a very bad place, because of the rocky reefs there. This cove is in latitude 51° and some minutes.

The next day we anchored near a river, called St. Margaret river, where at high tide there is some three fathoms of water, and a fathom and a half at low tide; this river goes pretty far into the interior. By what I saw inland on the east shore, there is a fall of water which enters the said river, descending from a height of some fifty or sixty fathoms, whence comes the greater part of the water which forms its current. At its mouth there is a sand-bank, on which at the ebb there may be half a fathom of water. All the coast toward the east is shifting sand; there is a point some half a league from the said river, projecting half a league out into the sea; and toward the west there is a small island. This place is in latitude 50°. All this region is very poor soil, and covered with fir-trees. The land there is somewhat high, but not so high as that on the south side.

Some three leagues beyond we passed near another river, which seemed to be very large, yet barred at the mouth for the most part with rocks. Some eight leagues farther there is a point projecting a league and a half into the sea, where there is only a fathom and a half of water. Past this point there is another about four leagues off, where there is water enough. All this coast is low and sandy. Some four leagues farther on there is a creek where a river enters. On the west side there is room for many ships. There is a low point, running out about a league into the sea. One must skirt the eastern shore for about three hundred paces to be able to make an entrance. This is the best harbour along the whole of the north shore; but it is very dangerous to approach, because of the shoals and sand-banks, which lie all along the greater part of the coast, almost two leagues out to sea. About six leagues from here is a bay where there is a sandy island. All this bay is very shoal, except on the east side, where there may be about four fathoms of water. Within the channel which enters the bay, some four leagues up, there is a fine cove into which a river empties. All this coast is low and sandy. A large fall of water comes down there. About five leagues farther is a point projecting about half a league into the sea, where there is a cove, and from the one point to the other is three leagues, but it is nothing but shoals, with little water. About two leagues off, there is a beach where there is a good harbour, and a small river, and in it are three islands, and ships may take shelter there.

Some three leagues beyond there is a sandy point running out about a league, at the end of which there is a little islet. Then going forward towards Escoumains you come to two small low islands and a little rock in shore. These islands are about half a league from Escoumains, which is a very bad harbour, surrounded by rocks, and dry at low tide; and in order to make an entrance one must go about behind a little rocky point, where there is room for only one ship at a time. A little higher up there is a river, which extends a little way inland; this is the place where the Basques fish for whales. To tell the truth, the harbour is of no value at all.

We came thence to the aforesaid harbour of Tadoussac, on the third of August. All this region above-mentioned is low along the shore, and in the interior very high. It is neither so pretty nor so fertile as that on the south, although it is lower ground. And this is an exact report of all I have seen of this northern coast.

12

On our arrival at Tadoussac, we found the savages whom we had met in the river of the Iroquois; they had had an encounter at the first lake with three canoes of Iroquois who fought against ten of the Montagnais; and they brought the heads of the Iroquois to Tadoussac. There was but one Montagnais wounded in the arm by an arrow; and when he had a dream, all the rest of the ten had to carry it into effect to satisfy him, thinking moreover that his wound would thereby get better. If this savage should die, his kinsmen will revenge his death, either upon their own tribe or upon others, or else the captains must give presents to the kinsmen of the dead, in order to content them; otherwise, as I have said, they would take revenge, which is a great fault among them.

Before these Montagnais set out on the warpath, they all collected, with their richest fur garments of beaver and other skins, adorned with beads and cords of various colours, and assembled in a large public square, where at their head was a Sagamore named Begourat, who used to lead them to war; and they marched one behind the other, with their bows and arrows, clubs and round shields, with which they equip themselves for fighting. And they went leaping one after the other, striking attitudes with their bodies, and executed many turns and twists like soldiers casting themselves into a ring. Afterwards they began to dance in their accustomed manner, as I have described above; then they held their *tabagie*, and after they had finished, the women stripped themselves stark naked, being decked with their finest matachias, and thus naked and dancing got into their canoes, and then they put out upon the water, and struck at one another with their paddles, splashing a quantity of water over one another. Yet they did themselves no harm, for they warded off the blows which they struck at one another. Having ended all these ceremonies, they withdrew into their lodges, and the savages went off to war against the Iroquois.

On the sixteenth day of August we set out from Tadoussac, and on the eighteenth of the said month arrived at isle Percée, where we found the Sieur Prévert of St. Malo, who was on his way from the mine, where he had gone with much trouble, for the fear which the savages had of meeting their enemies, the Armouchiquois, who are savages of quite monstrous shape: for their head is small and their body short, their arms and likewise their thighs slender like those of a skeleton, their legs thick and long, and of the same size all the way down; and when they sit upon their heels, their knees are higher by half a foot than their head, which is a strange thing, and they seem to be out of the course of nature. Nevertheless, they are very agile and resolute, and are settled in the best land of all the coast of Acadia; hence the Souriquois fear them greatly. But with the confidence which the said Sieur de Prévert gave them, he brought them as far as the said mine, to which the savages guided him. It is a very high mountain, jutting out somewhat into the sea, and glitters brightly in the sunlight; it contains a large quantity of verdigris which issues out of the said copper mine. He said that at the foot of this mountain at low water there were quantities of pieces of copper, such as he showed us, which fall from the top of the mountain. Some three or four leagues farther along the coast of Acadia, there is another mine, and a small river which extends some little way inland, towards the south, where there is a mountain of a black pigment, with which the savages paint themselves. Then some six leagues from the second mine toward the sea, about a league off the coast of Acadia, lies an island on which is found a kind of metal, of a dark brown colour, but white when cut, which formerly they used for their arrows and knives, and beat out with stones. This makes me think that it is not tin, nor lead, being so hard as it is; and when I showed them silver, they said that the metal from the said island was similar, and they find it in the earth about a foot or two deep. The said Sieur Prévert gave the savages wedges and chisels and other things necessary to extract ore from the said mine; which they have promised to do, and next year to bring some of it and give it to the said Sieur Prévert.

They say also that at some hundred or hundred and twenty leagues are other mines, but that they dare not go thither unless they have Frenchmen with them to make war upon their enemies, who have the mine in their possession.

This place where the mine is, which is in latitude 44° and some few minutes, about five or six leagues from the coast of Acadia, is a kind of bay, several leagues broad at its mouth, and somewhat more in length, where there are three rivers which fall into the Great bay, near the island of Saint John, which is thirty or thirty-five leagues long, and some six leagues distant from the land to the south. There is also another small river, which empties about half-way from that by which the Sieur Prévert returned, and there are two lake-like expanses in the said river. Furthermore, there is yet another small river which extends toward the mountain of pigment. All

these rivers fall into the said bay about southeast of the island, where the savages say there is this mine of white metal. On the north side of the said bay are the copper mines, where there is a good harbour for ships, and a small island at the mouth of the harbour; the bottom is ooze and sand, where a ship may be run ashore.

From this mine to the beginning of the mouth of the said rivers, it is some sixty or eighty leagues over land. But along the sea coast, according to my judgment, from the passage between the island of Saint Lawrence and the mainland, it may be upwards of fifty or sixty leagues to the said mine.

All this country is very beautiful and flat, and in it are all the kinds of trees, which we saw as we went to the first rapid of the great river of Canada, but very few fir-trees and cypresses.

This is an exact statement of what I learned and heard from the said Sieur Prévert.

13

There is another strange thing worthy of narration, which many savages have assured me was true; this is, that near Chaleur bay, towards the south, lies an island where makes his abode a dreadful monster, which the savages call *Gougou*. They told me it had the form of a woman, but most hideous, and of such a size that according to them the tops of the masts of our vessel would not reach his waist, so big do they represent him; and they say that he has often devoured and still devours many savages; these he puts, when he can catch them, into a great pocket, and afterwards eats them; and those who had escaped the danger of this ill-omened beast said that his pocket was so large that he could have put our vessel into it. This monster, which the savages call the Gougou, makes horrible noises in that island, and when they speak of him it is with unutterably strange terror, and many have assured me that they have seen him. Even the above-mentioned Sieur Prévert from St. Malo told me that, while going in search of mines, as we have mentioned in the preceding chapter, he passed so near the haunt of this frightful beast, that he and all those on board his vessel heard strange hissings from the noise it made, and that the savages he had with him told him it was the same creature, and were so afraid that they hid themselves wherever they could, for fear it should come to carry them off. And what makes me believe what they say, is the fact that all the savages in general fear it, and tell such strange stories of it that, if I were to record all they say, it would be considered untrue; but I hold that this is the dwelling-place of some devil that torments them in the manner described. This is what I have learned about this Gougou.

Before we set out from Tadoussac to return to France, one of the Sagamores of the Montagnais, named Bechourat, gave to the Sieur du Pont his son to take with him to France, being well recommended to him by the great Sagamore Anadabijou, who prayed him to use him well, and to let him see what the other two savages had seen whom we had brought back. We asked them for an Iroquois woman, whom they were intending to eat; and they gave her to us, and we brought her also home with the aforesaid savage. The Sieur de Prévert in like manner brought along four savages, a man from the coast of Acadia, a woman and two children from the Canadians.

On the twenty-fourth day of August, we set out from Gaspé, the said Sieur Prévert's ship and ours. The second day of September we reckoned we were as far as cape Race. On the fifth day of the same month we entered upon the Bank, where the fishing is carried on. On the sixteenth we were on soundings, which may be some fifty leagues from Ushant. On the twentieth of the said month we arrived, by God's grace and to the joy of all, and with a constantly favourable wind, at the port of Havre de Grace.

Chapter Ninety
Champlain in Québec

704. 1608. Champlain's voyage to Canada and his establishment of Québec.

S. de Champlain, Les voyages (1613), Bk. 2, Chaps. 1–3, translated in H. P. Biggar (and others), The Works of Samuel de Champlain, II, 3–34.

1

Having returned to France after a stay of three years in the country of New France, I went to see the Sieur de Monts, to whom I related the most striking things I had observed there since his departure, and I gave him the map and drawings of the more remarkable coasts and harbours in those parts.

Some time afterwards, the Sieur de Monts determined to continue his plans and to complete the exploration of the interior along the great river St. Lawrence, where in the year 1603 by the command of the late King Henry the Great, I had travelled some 180 leagues, beginning in the latitude 48° 40′ which is Gaspé, the entrance to the said river, as far as the great fall in latitude 45° and some minutes, where our exploration ended and where in our then opinion no boats could pass farther; for we had not yet thoroughly reconnoitred it as we have done since.

When the Sieur de Monts had conversed with me several times regarding his intention on the subject of the explorations, he decided to continue such a noble and worthy enterprise, notwithstanding the difficulties and labours it had cost him in the past. He honoured me by choosing me as his lieutenant for the expedition; and for this purpose had two vessels equipped, one of which was commanded by Pont-Gravé, who was deputed to carry on negotiations with the natives of the region and to bring back the vessels with

him, whilst I was to spend the winter in those parts.

The Sieur de Monts, in order to bear the expense, obtained from His Majesty letters for one year, wherein all persons were forbidden to trade in peltries with the natives, under the penalties set forth in the following Commission:

Henry, by the Grace of God, King of France and of Navarre, to our well-beloved and faithful councillors, the officers of our Admiralty of Normandy, Brittany, and Guyenne, magistrates, marshals, provosts, judges or their deputies, and to each of them for his own part, to the extent of their powers, jurisdictions and authority, Greeting: Upon the information which has been given to us by those who have come from New France regarding the good quality and fertility of the lands in that country, and that the inhabitants thereof are disposed to receive the knowledge of God, we have resolved to continue the settlement which had already been begun in those parts, in order that our subjects may go there and trade freely. And by virtue of the offer made to us by the Sieur de Monts, Gentleman-in-Ordinary of our chamber, and our Lieutenant-General in that country, to undertake the said settlement if we grant him the means and possiblity of bearing the expense thereof, it has pleased us to promise and assure him that none of our subjects but himself shall be permitted to barter in furs or other merchandise for the period of one year only, in the lands, regions, harbours, rivers and points of access throughout his jurisdiction. This we desire to be done. We, for these causes and other considerations thereto us moving, command and order that each of you, to the extent of your powers, jurisdictions and authority, shall on our behalf, as we ourselves do, very expressly prohibit and forbid all merchants, masters and captains of vessels, sailors, and others of our subjects of whatever rank and condition they may be, to equip any ships, in which to carry on themselves, or to send others to carry on, trade or barter in furs or in any other things with the natives of New France or to visit, trade and communicate with them for the said period of one year throughout the extent of the jurisdiction of the Sieur de Monts, on pain of disobedience and of complete confiscation of their ships, provisions, arms and merchandise to the profit of the said Sieur de Monts, and to ensure the punishment of their disobedience you will permit, as we have permitted and do permit, the said Sieur de Monts or his lieutenants to seize, apprehend, and arrest all those violating our present injunction and ordinance as well as their vessels, merchandise, arms, provisions, and victuals, in order to bring and deliver them into the hands of the officers of the law, and to take action, as well against the persons as against the property of the delinquents as the case may require. This is our will, which we order you immediately to have read and published in all parts and public places of your authority and jurisdiction, where you shall judge this to be necessary, by the first of our bailiffs or sergeants so asked to do, by virtue of these presents, or a copy of the same duly collated once only by one of our well-beloved and faithful councillors, notaries, and secretaries, to which it is our will that authority should be accorded as to this present original, so that none of our subjects may urge the plea of ignorance, but that every one may obey and conform in this matter to our will. We order, moreover, all captains of ships, masters, mates, sailors and others on board vessels or ships in the ports and harbours of that country to allow, as we have allowed the said Sieur de Monts and others holding power and authority from him, to make search in their said vessels which have engaged in the fur-trade after they have received notice of this present prohibitory order. It is our will that, on the request of the said Sieur de Monts, his deputies or others in authority, you should proceed against those disobeying and contravening this order as the case may require: to do this we grant you power, authority, warrant, and special mandate, notwithstanding the decision of our council of the seventeenth day of July last, of protest, of privilege granted by letters patent, accusation of one's judge, opposition, or appeals of whatsoever kind; on account of which and with-

out renouncing them, it is our will that there should be no delay, and if any such should occur, we have retained and reserved cognisance thereof for ourselves and our Council, exclusive of all other judges, and have prohibited and forbidden them to all our Courts and judges: for such is our pleasure. Given at Paris on the seventh day of January in the year of Grace, one thousand six hundred and eight and of our reign the nineteenth. [Signed:] Henry. And lower down, By the King Delomenie. And sealed with a single label of the great seal of yellow wax.

Collated with the original by me, councillor, notary and secretary of the King.

For the purpose of embarking I went to Honfleur where I found Pont-Gravé's vessel ready, who sailed from that port on the fifth of April. I sailed on the thirteenth and arrived on the Grand Bank on the fifteenth of May in latitude 45° 15', and on the twenty-sixth, in latitude 46° 45', we sighted cape St. Mary, being part of the island of Newfoundland. On the twenty-seventh of the month we sighted cape St. Lawrence, forming part of Cape Breton island; and the island of St. Paul, eighty-three leagues distant from cape St. Mary. On the thirtieth of the month we sighted isle Percée and Gaspé which is in latitude 48° 40', and distant from cape St. Lawrence from seventy to seventy-five leagues.

On the third of June we arrived off Tadoussac, eighty or ninety leagues from Gaspé, and cast anchor in the roadstead of Tadoussac, a league from the harbour, which is a sort of cove at the mouth of the river Saguenay, where there is a tide quite remarkable for its swiftness, and where sometimes there come impetuous winds bringing with them intense cold. It is said that from the harbour of Tadoussac there are forty-five or fifty leagues to the first fall in this river which comes from the north-north-west. This harbour is small and can hold only some twenty vessels. There is water enough, and it is sheltered by the river Saguenay and by a small rocky island which is almost cut off by the sea. The rest of the shore is high mountains, where there is little soil and only rocks and sand covered with trees such as fir and birch. There is a small pond near the harbour enclosed with mountains covered with trees. There are two points at the mouth of the river, one on the south-west side, stretching nearly a league into the river [St. Lawrence], which is called point St. Matthew, or otherwise Lark point, and the other on the north-west, stretching out an eighth of a league, and called All Devils' point, because of the great danger there. The winds from the south-south-east strike into the harbour, but are not dangerous. That from the Saguenay, however, is so. The two above-mentioned points are dry at low tide, and our vessel could not enter the harbour, because wind and tide were unfavourable. I at once had our long-boat lowered to row to the harbour to see whether Pont-Gravé had arrived. On the way I met a shallop with Pont-Gravé's pilot and a Basque, who were coming to tell me what had happened to them because they had tried to prevent the Basque vessels from trading, in accordance with the commission which the Sieur de Monts had obtained from His Majesty, viz., that no vessels should be allowed to trade without the Sieur de Monts' permission, as set forth in the said commission.

He told me that notwithstanding all the notifications which Pont-Gravé could make in His Majesty's name, they ceased not from forcibly carrying on barter, and that they had taken arms and defended themselves so well in their vessel, by bringing all their cannon to play upon Pont-Gravé's vessel, and by firing many musket shots, that he was severely wounded, as well as three of his men, one of whom had died. He had made no resistance; for, at the first round of musketry which they fired, he was struck down. The Basques came aboard his ship and took away all his cannon and arms, saying that they would barter in spite of the king's orders and that when they were ready to sail for France they would give him back his cannon and ammunition, and that this action of theirs was for safety's sake. On hearing all this I was much annoyed at the brewing of a quarrel we could well have dispensed with.

Whereupon having listened to all these things from the pilot, I asked him what the Basque had come to do on board our ship. He told me that he came to me on behalf of their master, called Darache, and of his crew, to obtain assurance from me that I should do them no harm when our ship came into harbour.

I replied that I could do nothing until I had seen Pont-Gravé. The Basque said that if I had need of anything that depended upon them, they would help me. What made him speak thus was merely the conviction of having done wrong, as they confessed, and the fear lest they should not be allowed to fish for whale.

After a good deal of talk, I went ashore to see Pont-Gravé in order to deliberate as to what we should do, and found him in a serious condition. He related to me in detail all that had happened. We concluded that only by force could I enter the harbour, and to avoid the loss to the settlement for this year, we thought it best (so that a good cause should not become a poor one and thus all be ruined) to reassure them on my behalf so long as I was there, and that Pont-Gravé should undertake nothing against them, but that in France justice should be done and the differences between them settled.

Darache, master of this ship, invited me to go aboard, where he received me well. After a good deal of discussion, I made peace between Pont-Gravé and him, and made him promise that he would undertake nothing against Pont-Gravé, nor against the king's interest nor that of the Sieur de Monts. That should they do the contrary, I would regard my promise as null and void. All this was agreed to and signed by each of us.

In this place were many Indians, who had come there for the fur-trade, several of whom came to our ship with their canoes, which are eight or nine yards long and about a yard or a yard and a half wide in the middle, tapering off at the two ends. They are very liable to upset if one does not know how to handle them, and are made of birch bark, strengthened inside with little hoops of white cedar, very nicely arranged, and are so light that a man can easily carry one of them. Each of them can hold the weight of a hogshead. When they wish to cross land to go into some river where they have business, they carry them with them. From Saco along the whole coast as far as Tadoussac they are all alike.

2

When this truce had been arranged, I set the carpenters to fit out a small pinnace of from twelve to fourteen tons, to transport all that would be necessary for our settlement, but it could not be got ready before the end of June.

Meanwhile I was able to visit certain parts of the river Saguenay, which is a fine river, and of an incredible depth, as much as 150 and 200 fathoms.

Some fifty leagues from the mouth of the harbour, as already stated, there is a great waterfall, which descends from a considerable height and with great impetuosity. There are some islands in this river which are very barren, being nothing but rocks, covered with small spruce and heath. It is half a league wide in places, and a quarter of a league at its mouth, where there is such a strong current that at three-quarter tide running into the river, it is still running out. All the land I saw there was nothing but mountains and rocky promontories, for the most part covered with spruce and birch, a very disagreeable country on both sides of the river; in short a real wilderness uninhabited by animals and birds; for on going hunting in the places which seemed to me the most agreeable, I found only quite small birds, such as swallows, and some river birds, which come there in summer. Beyond these there are none, by reason of the excessive cold which prevails. This river comes from the north-west.

The natives reported to me that, after passing the first fall, they come to eight others, then travel for a whole day without finding any, and again pass ten others and enter a lake, which takes three days to traverse, and each day they can easily make ten leagues going up stream. At the end of the lake there are tribes who live in a nomad state, and three rivers which flow into this lake, one coming from the north, very near the sea, which they hold to be much colder than their country, and the other two from other directions in the interior, where there are migratory tribes of savages who also live entirely by hunting. This is the region to which our savages go with the merchandise we give them in exchange for their furs, such as beaver, marten, lynx and otter which are found there in large numbers and which they then bring to our ships. These northern tribes tell our Indians that they see the salt sea, and if this be true, as I consider certain, it can only be a gulf which penetrates into these northern parts. The natives say that from the northern sea to Tadoussac harbour there may be from forty to fifty days' journey, on account of the difficulty of the trails, rivers and very hilly country in which there is snow for the greater part of the year. That is what I have learned with certainty about that river. I have often desired to explore it, but have been unable to do so without the natives, who have been unwilling that I or any of our

people should go with them. However, they have promised me to do so. This exploration would not be a bad thing for removing the doubts of many people regarding that northern sea, where it is claimed the English have gone during these last few years to find a route to China.

I set out from Tadoussac on the last day of the month to go to Quebec, and we passed near an island, called Hare island, distant six leagues from the above-mentioned harbour. It is two leagues from the north shore and about four leagues from the south shore. From Hare island we went to a small river, dry at low tide, up which some 700 or 800 yards there are two waterfalls. We called it Salmon river, because we caught some of these fish there. Coasting along the north shore, we came to a point which projects into the river, which we named cape Dauphin, distant from Salmon river three leagues. Thence we went to another cape which we named Eagle cape, distant from cape Dauphin eight leagues. Between the two there is a large cove, at the extremity of which is a small river which is dry at low tide. From Eagle cape we went on to Coudres island, which is a good league distant, and may be a league and a half in circumference. It is rather level and tapers off towards the two extremities; at the west end there are meadows and rocky points which project some distance into the river, and on the south-west side there are many shoals; still it is quite agreeable on account of the woods which surround it. It is about half a league from the north shore, where there is a small river, extending some distance into the interior. This we named Whirlpool river, because the tide runs against it strongly, and although the weather may be calm, the river is always agitated, being very deep there; but the shore of the river is flat, with many rocks at its mouth and round about. From Courdres island coasting the shore, we came to a cape, which we named cape Tourmente, which is five leagues distant, and we named it thus, because, however little wind there may be, the water rises as at full tide. At this point the water begins to be fresh. Thence we went on to the island of Orleans, two leagues off, where on the south side there are a number of islands, which are low, covered with trees, and very pleasant, filled with large meadows and much game. Some of them are, as nearly as I could judge, two leagues in circumference, and the others a little more or less. Round about these islands are many rocks and shoals, very dangerous to sail through, lying some two leagues from the south shore. All this coast, both on the north and south sides, from Tadoussac to the island of Orleans, is hilly country, and very poor, with nothing but pine, spruce and birch, and very ugly rocks, amongst which, in most places, one cannot penetrate.

We sailed along the south side of the island of Orleans, distant from the mainland a league and a half, and from the north shore half a league. It has a length of six leagues, and a breadth of a league or in places a league and a half. On the north side it is very pleasant, by reason of the great extent of woods and meadows which are there. But this passage is very dangerous on account of the large number of points and rocks lying between the mainland and the island, on which are many fine oaks and in some places nut-bearing trees, and at the [western] extremity there are vines and other trees such as we have in France. Here begins the fine, good country of the great river, distant one hundred and twenty leagues from its mouth. At the end of the island, on the north shore, there is a torrent of water which comes from a lake, some ten leagues in the interior, and falls from an elevation nearly twenty-five fathoms high, above which the land is level and pleasant to see, although in the interior one can see high mountains which seem to be fifteen or twenty leagues away.

3

From the island of Orleans to Quebec is one league, and I arrived there on July the third. On arrival I looked for a place suitable for our settlement, but I could not find any more suitable or better situated than the point of Quebec, so called by the natives, which was covered with nut-trees. I at once employed a part of our workmen in cutting them down to make a site for our settlement, another part in sawing planks, another in digging the cellar and making ditches, and another in going to Tadoussac with the pinnace to fetch our effects. The first thing we made was the storehouse, to put our supplies under cover, and it was promptly finished by the diligence of everyone and the care I took in the matter.

Some days after my arrival at Quebec, there was a locksmith who conspired against the king's service, and his plan was to put me to death, and having made himself master of our fort, to hand it over to the Basques or Spaniards who were then at Tadoussac; for vessels cannot pass farther up on account of ignorance of the channel and of the sandbanks and rocks on the way.

In order to carry out his wicked plan, hoping thereby to make his fortune, he corrupted four of those whom he considered the worst characters, by telling them a host of falsehoods and leading them to hope for gain.

After these four men had been won over, they all promised to act in such a way as to attract the rest to their side, so that I should have nobody with me in whom I could place confidence, which gave them still greater hopes of carrying out their plan, particularly since four or five of my companions in whom they knew I had confidence were on board the pinnace for the purpose of taking care of the provisions and other articles which were necessary for our settlement.

In short so successful were they in their intrigues with those who remained that they would have attracted all to their side, and even my lackey, making them many promises which they could not have fulfilled.

Being thus all agreed, they made different plans from day to day as to how to kill me in order not to be accused thereof, but this they considered difficult. However, the devil blinding all their eyes, and taking away their reason and any scruples they might have had, they resolved to seize me unarmed and to strangle me, or to give a false alarm at night and to shoot me as I came out, and they would rather have accomplished their purpose in this way than otherwise. All promised mutually to make no disclosure, on penalty that the first who should open his mouth should be stabbed to death. In four days they were to execute their plan, before our pinnaces arrived: otherwise they would have been unable to accomplish their design.

On that same day arrived one of our pinnaces, in which was our pilot, whose name was Captain Testu, a very discreet man. After the pinnace had been unloaded, and was ready to go back to Tadoussac, there came to him a locksmith named Natel, a comrade of Jean Duval's, the head of the conspiracy, who told him that he had promised the others to do just the same as they did, but that in reality he did not desire the execution of the plot; but he did not dare to divulge anything, and that what had hindered him was the fear that they would kill him.

Then Antoine Natel made the pilot promise that he would disclose nothing of what he should tell him; for if his companions should find it out, they would put him to death. The pilot reassured him on all points and demanded of him that he should disclose the whole enterprise which they wished to carry out. This Natel did quite fully. The pilot then said to him, "My good man, you have done well to divulge such a wicked scheme, and you show that you are an honest man and are guided by the Holy Spirit. But these things must not go on without the Sieur de Champlain being told, in order that he may take measures against them, and I promise you to use such influence with him that he will forgive you and some of the others." "And," said the pilot, "I shall go to him quietly at once, and do you go about your work, and keep your ears open to hear what they say, and do not worry about the rest."

The pilot came at once to me in a garden which I was having made, and said that he desired to speak to me privately, where there should be only the two of us. I said to him that I was quite willing. We went into the wood, where he related to me the whole affair. I asked him who had told him? He begged me to pardon the man who had told him, to which I consented, although he ought to have come to me. This man feared, said he, lest I should be angry and do him harm. I told him that I was better able to control myself in such affairs and that he was to bring the man so that I might hear his tale. He went, and brought him all trembling with fear lest I should do him some harm. I reassured him and told him not to be afraid; that he was in a place of safety and that I forgave him all that he had done with the others, provided he told the whole truth on every point, and the reason which had moved them to this. He said there was no reason, save that they had imagined that, in handing over the place to the Basques or Spaniards they would become very rich, and that they did not wish to go back to France. He also related to me the remaining details of their project.

After hearing him and questioning him, I told him to go about his work. Meanwhile, I ordered the pilot to bring in his shallop and he did so. Then

I gave two bottles of wine to a young fellow, and directed him to tell these four worthy ringleaders of the undertaking that it was wine which his friends at Tadoussac had given him as a present, and that he wanted to share it with them. They did not decline the invitation, and towards evening went on board the pinnace where he was to offer them the refreshment. I was not long in following them, and ordered them to be seized and held until the following day.

There then were my gentry properly astonished. I at once made everyone get up, though it was nearly ten o'clock in the evening, and forgave them all, on condition they should tell the truth about everything that had happened. This they did and I then ordered them to retire.

On the following day I received all their depositions, one after the other, in presence of the pilot and of the sailors of the ship, and had them committed to writing. And they were very glad, according to their statements; for they were living in constant fear of one another and particularly of the four scoundrels who had misled them. Since then they have lived in peace, satisfied, according to their deposition, with the treatment they here received.

The same day I had six pairs of handcuffs made for the authors of the plot, one for our surgeon, named Bonnerme, one for another man named La Taille whom the four conspirators had accused, which charge however turned out to be false, and this was the justification for giving them their liberty.

When this had been done, I took my fine fellows off to Tadoussac, and begged Pont-Gravé to do me the favour of guarding them, particularly as I had not yet any safe place to put them in, and we were much occupied with the construction of our houses. I wished also to consult with him and others of the ship as to what we should do in the matter. We decided that after he had completed his business at Tadoussac, he should come up to Quebec with the prisoners, where we should have them confronted with their witnesses. Then after hearing them we should order justice to be done according to the offence they had committed.

On the following day I went back to Quebec to hasten the completion of our storehouse, in order to gather in our provisions which had been left unprotected by all these scoundrels, who husbanded nothing, never considering where they were to find more when these failed; for I could not mend matters until the storehouse had been built and covered in.

Some time after this arrived Pont-Gravé with the prisoners, which stirred up discontent amongst the other workmen who feared lest I had forgiven the wrongdoers and lest these should wreak vengeance upon them for having disclosed their wicked plot.

We had them confronted and all that had been stated in the depositions was reaffirmed, without any denial on the part of the prisoners, who confessed that they had acted wickedly, and deserved punishment, unless mercy should be shown them; and they cursed Jean Duval for being the first who led them into this conspiracy as soon as they sailed from France. The said Duval was unable to say anything, except that he deserved death; and that everything contained in the depositions was true, begging for pity for himself and for the others who had sided with him in his wicked intentions.

After Pont-Gravé and I, along with the Captain of the ship, the surgeon, master, mate, and other seamen, had heard their depositions and cross-examinations, we decided that it would be sufficient to put to death Duval as the first mover in the conspiracy, and also to serve as an example to those who remained, to behave properly in future in doing their duty, and in order that the Spaniards and Basques who were numerous in the region might not rejoice over the affair. We decided that the three others should be condemned to be hanged, but meanwhile should be taken back to France and handed over to the Sieur de Monts, to receive fuller justice, according as he might decide, with all the papers and the sentence upon Jean Duval before him, by virtue of which sentence Duval was hanged and strangled at Quebec, and his head placed on the end of a pike and set up in the highest spot in our fort, and the other three were sent back to France.

705. September, 1608 to June, 1609. The first winter at Québec.

S. de Champlain, Les voyages (1613), Bk. 2,

Chaps. 4–8, translated in H. P. Biggar (and others), The Works of Samuel de Champlain, II (1922), 35–81.

4

When all this was over, Pont-Gravé sailed from Quebec on September 18, to return to France with the three prisoners. After their departure the others all conducted themselves properly in their duty.

I continued the construction of our quarters, which contained three main buildings of two stories. Each one was three fathoms long and two and a half wide. The storehouse was six long and three wide, with a fine cellar six feet high. All the way round our buildings I had a gallery made, outside the second story, which was a very convenient thing. There were also ditches fifteen feet wide and six deep, and outside these I made several salients which enclosed a part of the buildings, and there we put our cannon. In front of the building there is an open space four fathoms wide and six or seven long, which abuts upon the river's bank. Round about the buildings are very good gardens, and an open place on the north side of a hundred, or a hundred and twenty, yards long and fifty or sixty wide. Nearer Quebec there is a little river, which comes from a lake in the interior, distant six or seven leagues from our settlement. I consider that in this river, which is north a quarter north-west of our settlement, was the place where Jacques Cartier passed the winter; since at a league's distance up this river are still the remains as of a chimney, whose foundation we discovered, and to all appearance what seem to have been ditches about his house, which was small. We found also large, squared, worm-eaten pieces of wood, and some three or four cannon-balls. All these things show clearly that this was a settlement which was founded by Christians. And what makes me say and think that it was Jacques Cartier, is the fact that there is no evidence that anyone wintered or put up buildings there, except Jacques Cartier at the time of his explorations. And in my opinion it must have been this place that was named Ste Croix, as he called it, which name was afterwards transferred to another place, fifteen leagues to the west of our settlement; and there is no sign that he wintered in the place now called Ste Croix, nor in any others near there. For on the way thither there is no river or any other place where there is room for ships, except in the great river or in the one of which I have spoken above, where at low tide there is half a fathom of water, with many rocks and a shoal at its mouth: for to keep ships in the great river, where there are strong currents, tides, and ice floating about in winter, would be to run the risk of losing them, particularly since there is a sandy point jutting out into the river, covered with boulders, amongst which we found during the last three years a passage, which had not been discovered before. But in order to get through it, one must choose the right moment, on account of the points and other dangers there. This place is open to north-west winds, and there the river runs as if it were a rapid, and at low tide falls two and a half fathoms. There is no sign whatsoever of buildings there, nor anything to show that a man of judgment would have tried to make a settlement at that spot, there being many other better places, if one were forced to stay there. I very much desired to discuss this point, particularly since there are many who think that this spot was the residence of Jacques Cartier, which view I do not accept for the reasons given above; for the said Cartier would moreover have left an account of it for posterity, just as he did of all that he saw and explored. And I maintain that what I say is true, and that it can be proved from the account which he wrote.

And to show still further that the place now called Ste Croix is not the place where Jacques Cartier wintered, as the majority suppose, here is what he says about it in his explorations, taken from his voyages, that is to say: that he arrived at Coudres island on December 5 in the year 1535; that he called it by this name, because there were hazelnuts on it; that at this place there is a strong tidal current, and that the island is three leagues long; but really if you reckon it at a league and a half it is a good deal.

And on the seventh of the month, being Our Lady's Day, he sailed from this island to go up the river, and discovered fourteen islands, seven or eight leagues to the south of Coudres island. In this reckoning he is a little astray; for these islands are not more than three leagues away. And he says that the place where the above islands lie is the beginning of the land or province of Canada, and that he came to an island ten leagues long and five wide where much fishing is carried on, as indeed they do greatly abound there, especially sturgeon. But regarding the length of the island, it is well known now that it is not more than six leagues long and two wide. He states also that he cast anchor between this island and the north shore, which is the narrowest passage and a dangerous one, and that there he put on shore two natives whom he had taken to France and that, after having stayed in this place for some time with the tribes of the region, he had his longboats brought up, and went farther up the river with the tide, to seek harbour and a place of safety for the ships. And he says that he went on up the river coasting this island, which he makes ten leagues long, and that at the end of it they found a very fine and agreeable forking of the waters, where there was a small river and a shallow harbour, which they considered very suitable for sheltering their vessels. And this they called Ste Croix because they arrived there on that day, but at the time of Cartier's expedition it was called Stadaca. We now call it Quebec. After having reconnoitred the place he sent back to bring up his ships in order to winter there.

Now from Coudres island to the island of Orleans there are only five leagues, and at the western end of this latter the river is very wide, and at this forking, as Cartier calls it, there is no river but the one which he named Ste Croix, distant a full league from the island of Orleans. Here at low water there is only half a fathom, and the entrance is very dangerous for ships, there being many spurs, composed of boulders lying here and there. In order to get inside, buoys are needed where at high tide, as I have said, there are three fathoms of water, and at spring tides four, and at high tides ordinarily four and a half. It is only fifteen hundred yards from our settlement, which is higher up the said river, and as I have stated, after leaving the place which is now called Ste Croix, there is no other river in which ships can be laid up: there are nothing but small brooks. The shores are flat and dangerous, a fact of which Cartier only makes mention at the time he left the place, Ste Croix, now called Quebec, where he laid up his ships. Here he built his house as may be seen from what follows:

On September the nineteenth he departed from Ste Croix, where lay his ships, and set sail in order with the tide to proceed up the river, which he and his men found very pleasant, both on account of the woods, vines and habitations, which were there in his times, as for other reasons. And they cast anchor twenty-five leagues from the entrance to the land of Canada, which is at the eastern extremity of the island of Orleans as it was named by Cartier. What is to-day called Ste Croix was then called Achelacy, a narrow part of the river, swift and dangerous, both on account of the rocks as for other reasons, where one can only pass up at high tide. It is distant from Quebec and from the river where Cartier spent the winter fifteen leagues.

Now, in all this river there are no narrows, from Quebec as far as the Great Rapid, except in the place now called Ste Croix, to which this name has been transferred from another place, which former place is a very dangerous spot as I have already described. And it appears quite clear from what he states that this was not the place where he abode, as has been said, but that it was near Quebec, and that no one has ever investigated this matter, except what I have done in my travels. For the very first time I was told that he had lived in this place I was much surprised since there was no sign of a river in which to shelter ships as he describes. This was what caused me to make a careful examination in order to remove uncertainty and doubt from many minds.

Whilst the carpenters, sawyers, and other workmen were busy at our quarters, I set all the rest to work clearing the land about our settlement in order to make gardens in which to sow grains and seed, for the purpose of seeing how the whole thing would succeed, particularly since the soil seemed to be very good.

Meanwhile many of the natives had encamped near us, who used to fish for eels, which began to come up about September 15 and finish on October 15. During this time the natives all live upon this manna and dry some for the winter to last till the month of February, when the snow is two and a half or even three feet deep at the most. At that time when their eels and the other things which they dry are prepared, they go off beaver-hunting and remain away until the beginning of January. When they were engaged on this, they left in our keeping all their eels and other things till their return, which took place on December 15. And they told us that they did not take many beavers

because the waters were too high, on account of the rivers overflowing. I gave them back all their provisions which only lasted them till January 20. When their eels give out they resort to hunting the moose and any other wild beasts they may find, until springtime, at which season I was able to furnish them with various supplies. I studied their customs very particularly.

All these tribes suffer so much from hunger that sometimes they are obliged to live on certain shell-fish, and to eat their dogs and the skins with which they clothe themselves against the cold. I consider that, if anyone were to show them how to live, and how to till the soil, and other things, they would learn very well; for there are many of them who have good judgment, and reply pointedly to the questions put to them. But they have bad points: they are revengeful and awful liars, people whom one must not trust too far, but rather judiciously, and with force in one's hand. They promise readily, but perform badly. They are people, the majority of whom, so far as I have been able to see, respect no law, but have plenty of false beliefs. I asked them what sort of ceremonies they used in praying to their God. They told me that they had no other than this, that each one prayed to God in his heart, just as it suited him. That is why there is no law amongst them, and that they do not know what it is to pray to and worship God, living as they do like brute beasts. I believe they would soon be brought to be good Christians, if one were to live in their country, as the majority of them desire. They have amongst them some natives whom they call *Pillotois*, who, they believe, speak to the devil face to face, and he tells them what they must do in war as well as in other matters, and if he were to order them to put any enterprise into execution, they would at once obey his command. So, also, they believe that all their dreams are true, and indeed there are many of them who say they have had visions and dreamed things which came to pass, or will come to pass. But to tell the truth about these things, they are visions from the devil who deceives them and leads them astray. That is all I have been able to learn about their brutish beliefs. All these people are well-proportioned in body, without deformity, and are agile. The women are also well-formed, plump, and of a dusky hue, on account of certain colouring materials with which they rub themselves, which render them permanently olive-coloured. They are clothed in skins; a part of their bodies is covered, and the other part is bare. But in winter they are completely covered, for they are clad in good furs, such as the skins of moose, otter, beaver, bear, seal, deer (male and female), which are very numerous. In the winter when the snow is deep, they make a kind of racket, two or three times as large as those in France, and attach them to their feet, and with these they walk over the snow without sinking. Otherwise they could not hunt nor travel in many places.

They have also a sort of marriage, which is after this fashion. When a girl is fourteen or fifteen years of age and has several suitors, she keeps company with as many as she wishes. Then after five or six years she chooses the one she likes best for her husband, and they live together to the end of their lives, unless, after they have lived together for some time, the woman has no children, when the husband may divorce her and take another wife, alleging that his own is no good. In this way the girls have greater freedom than the women. After they are married they are chaste and their husbands are generally jealous, and they give presents to the fathers or relatives of the girls they have married. Such are the ceremonies and customs followed in their marriages.

As regards their burials, when a man or a woman dies, they make a grave, into which they put everything they own, such as kettles, furs, hatchets, bows, arrows, skins and other things. Then they put the body into the grave, and cover it with earth, and put many big pieces of wood on top, and set one piece on end and paint it red in the upper part. They believe in the immortality of souls, and say that the dead enjoy happiness in other lands with their relatives and friends who have died. In the case of chiefs, or others having influence, they hold a banquet after their death three times a year and sing and dance upon their grave.

The whole time they were with us, which was the safest place for them, they were in such constant dread of their enemies, that they often took fright at night in their dreams, and would send their wives and children to our fort, the gates of which I used to have opened for them, but let the men remain about the fort, not permitting them to enter; for they were as safe there as to their persons as if they had been inside. And I used to send out five or six of our men to give them courage, and to go and search the woods whether they could see anything, which used to satisfy them. They are very timid and fear their enemies greatly, and hardly ever sleep quietly wherever they are, although I reassured them every day as much as I could, by admonishing them to do as we did, that is to say that some of them should watch, whilst the others slept, and that each should have his arms ready like a sentinel on duty, and that they should not take dreams as truth upon which to rely, since most of them are only fables, with other considerations on the same subject. But these admonitions were of small avail, and they used to say that we knew better than they did how to protect ourselves in every way, and that in time if we were to come and live in their country they would be able to learn these.

5

On the first of October I had some wheat sown and on the fifteenth some rye. On the third of the month there was a white frost and on the fifteenth the leaves of the trees began to fall. On the twenty-fourth of the month I had some native vines planted and they prospered extremely well, but after I left the settlement to come back to France, they were all ruined, for want of care, which distressed me very much.

On the eighteenth of November there was a heavy fall of snow. It lay on the ground only two days, but during that time there was a great gale. During that month there died of dysentery a sailor and our locksmith, as well as several natives, on account, in my opinion, of having eaten badly-cooked eels.

On the fifth of February it snowed hard and there was a high wind which lasted for two days.

On the twentieth of the month some Indians made their appearance on the other side of the river, and shouted to us to go to their aid, but this was out of our power, on account of the large amount of ice which was floating down the river. So hungry were these poor wretches, that being at their wits' end, they, men, women and children, resolved to die or to cross the river, in the hope that I would succour them in their dire need. Accordingly having taken this resolution, the men and women seized their children and got into their canoes, thinking they would reach our shore by an opening in the ice which the wind had made;

but no sooner were they in the middle of the river, than their canoes were caught between the ice floes and broken into a thousand pieces. They manœuvred so well that they jumped with their children, whom the women were carrying on their backs, upon a large block of ice. While they were upon it, we could hear them screaming so much that it was pitiful; for they expected nothing less than death. But fortune favoured these poor wretches so much that a large ice floe struck the side of the one upon which they stood with such force that it threw them upon the land. They, seeing such a favourable turn of events, went ashore with as great joy as they ever experienced in spite of the famine they had endured. They came to our settlement so thin and emaciated that they looked like skeletons, most of them being unable to stand. I was astonished at their appearance, and at the way they had crossed the river, seeing them so weak and faint. I ordered bread and beans to be given to them. They could not wait for these to be cooked before eating them. To cover their wigwams I lent them also some bark, which other Indians had given me. As they were making their wigwams they noticed some carrion which about two months previously I had thrown out to attract foxes, of which we had caught both black and red ones, like those in France, but with heavier fur. This carrion was a sow and a dog which had lain there through the hot and cold weather. When the weather was mild it stank so strongly that one could not stay near it. Nevertheless they took it and carried it off to their wigwam, where they quickly devoured it half-cooked, and never did meat seem to them to have a better taste. I sent two or three men to warn them not to eat any of it, if they did not wish to die. As these men came near to the Indians' wigwam, they smelt such a stench from this half-cooked carrion, of which each of them had a piece in his hand, that they almost vomited, so that they did not stay there long. These poor wretches finished their banquet. I did the best I could to furnish them with supplies, but it was little in comparison with their large numbers. In a month they would have eaten up all our provisions, such hearty eaters are they. For when they have food, they lay nothing by, but eat their fill day and night and then starve. And they did another thing as disagreeable as the first. I had had a bitch hung in a tree-top to serve as bait for martens and birds of prey; and the thing interested me, inasmuch as the carcass was often attacked by them. These savages went to the tree, and not being able to climb up it on account of their weakness, they felled it, and at once carried off the dog, which was now only skin and bones, with the head stinking and rotten, and immediately devoured it.

This is their most usual pleasure in winter: for in summer they have enough to keep themselves, and also to lay up provisions, so as not to be attacked by such extreme famine, the rivers abounding in fish, and there being birds and other wild beasts to hunt. The soil is very good and suitable for cultivation, if they were willing to take the trouble to sow Indian corn, as do all their neighbours, the Algonquins, Ochastaiguins, and Iroquois, who are free from such cruel attacks of famine because they know how to ward them off by the care and foresight they show, the result of which is that they live prosperously in comparison with these Montagnais, Canadians, and Souriquois, who inhabit the sea coast. That is the kind of miserable existence they lead for the most part. Snow and ice remain on the ground for three months, that is from the month of January until about the eighth of April, by which time it is nearly all melted. And moreover towards the end of this month only rarely is any seen about our settlement. It is a remarkable thing that two or three fathoms of snow and ice on the river should all be melted in less than twelve days. From Tadoussac to Gaspé, cape Breton, Newfoundland, and the Grand Bay, one still finds ice and snow in most places up to the end of May, at which time the whole mouth of the great river is blocked with ice, whilst at Quebec there is none. This shows a remarkable difference for a hundred and twenty leagues of distance in longitude; for the mouth of the river lies in 49° 50° and 51° degrees of latitude and our settlement in 46° 40'.

6

The scurvy began very late, that is in February, and lasted till the middle of April. Eighteen were struck down with it and of these ten died: and five others died of dysentery. I had some of them opened to see if they were affected like those I had seen in the other settlements. The same conditions were found. Some time after our surgeon died. All this gave us much trouble, on account of the difficulty we had in nursing the sick. I have already described the form of this sickness.

Now it is my view that it comes altogether from eating too much salt food and vegetables which heat the blood and corrupt the inward parts. The winter too is partly the cause; for it checks the natural heat and causes greater corruption of the blood. And from the earth, when it is opened, there come forth certain vapours enclosed therein and these infect the air. This has been seen by experience in those people who have been in other settlements after the first year that the sun had shone on what had been cleared. This was true of our own settlement as well as of other places, and the air was much better there and the sickness less severe than before. As for the country itself, it is beautiful and agreeable, and it brings all sorts of grain and seed to maturity. There are in it all the varieties of trees we have in our forests on this side of the ocean and many fruits, although they are wild for lack of cultivation: such as butternut trees, cherry-trees, plum-trees, vines, raspberries, strawberries, gooseberries and red currants, and several other small fruits, which are quite good. There are also several sorts of useful herbs and roots. Fish are plentiful in the rivers, along which are meadows and game in vast quantity. From the month of April until the fifteenth of December the air is so healthy and good, that one feels in oneself no tendency to sickness: but January, February and March are dangerous for the maladies which prevail rather in that season than in summer for the reasons given above. As to the treatment, all those who were with me were well clad, slept in good beds, and were kept warm and well fed, that is on the salted meats which we had, which in my opinion, did them much harm, as I have already stated. And as far as I have seen, this sickness attacks quite as much the man who lives in a nice way, and takes great care of himself, as it does the man who is very wretched. At first we thought that it was only the workmen who were struck down by this sickness: but we have seen that this is not true. Those who sail to the East Indies and various other regions, such as Germany and England, are stricken by it, just as much as those in New France. Some time ago, the Dutch, being attacked by it in their expeditions to the Indies, found a very remarkable remedy for

this sickness, which might be of use to us, but not having looked for it, we have no knowledge of it. However I hold it to be true that with good bread and fresh meat, one would not be subject to it.

On the eighth of April the snow was all melted and yet the air was still rather cold until April, when the trees began to break into leaf.

Some of those who were ill with the scurvy got better as spring came on, which is the time for recovery. I had a native of the region who spent the winter with me and was attacked by this malady because he had changed his diet to salt meat, and he died of it, which clearly shows that salted food is not good, and indeed quite the contrary as regards this disease.

On the fifth of June there arrived at our settlement a shallop, in which was the Sieur des Marais, Pont-Gravé's son-in-law, who brought us news of the arrival of his father-in-law at Tadoussac on the twenty-eighth of May. This gave me much satisfaction; for we hoped to have relief from him. Of our company now only eight of the twenty-eight remained and half of these were ailing.

On the seventh of June I left Quebec for Tadoussac to attend to some business and invited the Sieur des Marais to stay in my place until my return, and he did so.

As soon as I had arrived there, Pont-Gravé and I had some talk together on the subject of certain explorations which I was to make into the interior, whither the Indians had promised to conduct us. We decided that I should go there in a shallop with twenty men and that Pont-Gravé should stay at Tadoussac to direct the business of our settlement. And as had been decided, so it was carried out; and he passed the winter there. For, according to the orders of the Sieur de Monts in a letter he had written to me, I was to return to France, to inform him of what I had done and of the explorations made in that country. When this decision had been reached, I left Tadoussac at once and went back to Quebec, where I had a shallop fitted out with everything necessary to carry out explorations in the country of the Iroquois, to which I was to go with our allies, the Montagnais.

7

And for this purpose I set out on the eighteenth of the month. Here the river begins to widen in some places to a league or to a league and a half. The country becomes more and more beautiful as you advance. Along the river there are some hills and in other parts level land without rocks, but not much. As for the river it is dangerous in many places, on account of the shoals and rocks which lie in it, and it is not safe sailing except with the sounding-lead in hand. The river is very rich in many varieties of fish, both of those we have in France, and of others which we do not have. The country everywhere is covered with great, high forests of the same kinds of trees as those near our settlement. There are also several sorts of vines and nut-bearing trees on the banks of the river, and many brooks and small rivers, which are navigable only in canoes. We passed near point Ste Croix which, as I have stated elsewhere, many hold to be the place where Jacques Cartier wintered. It is a sandy point which projects some little distance into the river, and it is open to the north-west wind which beats upon it. There are some meadows, which are flooded whenever there are high tides, which rise and fall nearly two fathoms and a half. This is a very dangerous place to go through on account of the many rocks lying across the river, although there is a good, but very crooked, channel, through which the river runs very swiftly; and you must seize the right moment to get through. This place has deceived a good many who thought they could pass through only at high tide, because there was no channel: now we have found the opposite to be the case; for one can go downward when the tide is low, but as to going up, it would be difficult, except with a high wind, on account of the strong current. And so to pass up one is obliged to wait for a third of high tide, when there are in the channel six, eight, ten, twelve and fifteen fathoms of water.

Continuing our course we came to a very beautiful river nine leagues from the place called Ste Croix, and twenty-four from Quebec, and we named it St. Mary's river. The whole river from Ste Croix upward is delightfully beautiful.

Still continuing our journey I met with some two or three hundred Indians who were encamped near a small island called St. Eloi, a league and a half from St. Mary. We approached to investigate and found that they were tribes of Indians called Ochateguins and Algonquins, who were on their way to Quebec to help us to explore the country of the Iroquois, with whom they are in mortal conflict, and they spare nothing belonging to these enemies.

Having recognized them I went ashore to see them and enquired who was their chief. They told me there were two, one called Iroquet, and the other Ochasteguin, whom they pointed out to me. I went into their wigwams where they received me well, according to their custom.

I began to give them some idea of the object of my expedition, at which they were much pleased, and after some talk, I withdrew. A little time after they came to my shallop and made me a present of some furs, showing many signs of pleasure. Then they returned on shore.

On the following day the two chiefs came to see me and for some time remained silent, meditating and smoking all the while. After much reflection they began in a loud voice to harangue their companions who stood on the shore with their weapons in their hands, listening very attentively to what their chiefs said to them, which ran thus:—

That some ten moons ago, which is their way of counting, Iroquet's son had come to see me, when I had given him a kind reception, and had told him that Pont-Gravé and I wished to help them against their enemies. With these they had long been at war, on account of many cruelties practised against their tribe under colour of friendship. They said that, having ever since desired vengeance, they had asked all the Indians I saw on the river's bank to come to meet us for the purpose of making an alliance with us. Since these had never seen Christians, this fact also moved them to come and see us; that I might do with them and their companions whatever I liked; that they had no children with them, but only men skilled in war and full of courage, who knew the country and the rivers in the land of the Iroquois. And that they now besought me to return to our settlement, for them to see our houses, and that three days later we should all set off on the war-path together. They also asked me as a token of great friendship and rejoicing to have muskets and arquebuses fired off, whereat they would be much pleased. I did so and they uttered loud shouts of astonishment, especially those who had never heard or seen the like.

After listening to their speech, I made answer, that to please them I was glad to go back to our settlement for their greater satisfaction, and that they could see that I had no other intention than to make war; for we had with us only arms and not merchandise for barter, as they had been led to understand, and that my only desire was to perform what I had promised them. I told them that, had I known what evil reports would be made to them, I should have held those making such reports for greater enemies than their own enemies. They told me they did not believe such stories, and that indeed they had never listened to them. Yet the contrary was the case; for certain Indians had told it to our Indians. I said no more, awaiting an opportunity of showing them by results more than they could expect from me.

8

On the following day we all set out together for our settlement, where they enjoyed themselves for about five or six days, which time was spent in dancing and feasting, on account of their desire that we should go on the war-path.

Pont-Gravé soon came from Tadoussac with two small pinnaces filled with men, in response to a letter in which I begged him to come as promptly as he could.

The Indians seeing him arrive rejoiced even more than before; for I told them that he was giving me some of his men to assist them; and that we might perhaps all go together.

On the twenty-eighth of the month we fitted out the shallops for the purpose of assisting these natives. Pont-Gravé got into one, and I into another, and we all set off together. On the first of June we arrived at Ste Croix, distant from Quebec fifteen leagues. There we decided, Pont-Gravé and I, that for certain reasons, I should go along with the Indians and that he should return to our settlement and to Tadoussac. This decision having been reached, I put aboard my shallop all that was needed, with nine men in addition to Des Marais, La Routte, our pilot, and myself.

On the third of June, in company with all the Indians, I left Ste. Croix and we passed the Three Rivers, which is a very beautiful country, covered with large numbers of fine trees. From this place to Ste Croix there are fifteen leagues. At the mouth of that river there are six islands, three of which are very small, and the others about 1500 to 1600 yards long, and in appearance they are very pretty. Near lake St. Peter, about two leagues up the river there is a small rapid which is not very difficult to pass. This place is latitude 46°, less a few minutes. The savages of the region gave us to understand that some days' journey [up this river], there is a lake of ten days' journey through which flows the river. And then they pass some rapids, and then three or four other lakes of five or six days' journey. And having arrived at the end of these, they go by land four or five leagues and again enter another lake whence the Saguenay receives most of its waters. The Indians come from this lake to Tadoussac. The Three Rivers extend inland forty days' journey from the Northern Sea. The small extent of country I have seen is sandy, rather hilly, and thickly covered with pine and spruce on the river banks: but inland, a quarter of a league or so, the forest is very beautiful and open, and the land level.

We continued our journey through a very beautiful and level region, as far as the entrance to lake St. Peter, which is some eight leagues long and four wide, and sailing through it, we found two, three and four fathoms of water. On the north side we saw a very beautiful river which extends inland some twenty leagues and I named it Ste Suzanne. On the south side are two rivers, one called Du Pont and the other Gennes. These are very beautiful and in a fine, rich region. The water of the lake is almost still and it is full of fish. On the north side, some twelve or fifteen leagues from the lake, there seems to be a somewhat hilly region. Having passed through the lake we made our way among a large number of islands of various sizes where there are many butternut trees and vines and beautiful meadows with much game—birds and beasts—which go from the mainland to these islands. More fish are caught there than in any other part of the river we had visited. From these islands we went to the mouth of the river of the Iroquois, where we stayed two days and refreshed ourselves with choice game, birds, and fish which the Indians gave us. Here there broke out amongst them some difference of opinion regarding the war, the result of which was that only a part of them decided to come with me, whilst the rest went back to their own country with their wives and the goods they had bartered.

Setting out from the mouth of that river, which is some four or five hundred yards wide and very beautiful, and proceeding southward we reached a place in latitude 45°, twenty-two or twenty-three leagues from the Three Rivers. The whole of this river from its mouth to the first rapid, a distance of fifteen leagues, is very level and bordered with woods, as are all the other places mentioned above, and with the same varieties of wood. There are nine or ten beautiful islands as far as the first rapid of the river of the Iroquois, and these are about a league or a league and a half long and covered with oaks and butternuts. The river is in places nearly half a league wide and full of fish. We did not find anywhere less than four feet of water. The approach to the rapid is a sort of lake into which the water flows down, and it is about three leagues in circumference. Near by are meadows where no Indians live, by reason of the wars. At the rapids there is very little water, but it flows with great swiftness, and there are many rocks and boulders, so that the Indians cannot go up by water; but on the way back they run them very nicely. All this region is very level and full of forests, vines and butternut trees. No Christians but ourselves had ever penetrated to this place; and we had difficulty enough in getting up the river by rowing.

As soon as we reached the rapids, Des Marais, La Routte and myself, with five men, went ashore to see whether we could pass this spot, and walked about a league and a half without seeing how this could be done. There was only the river running with great swiftness, and on either side many very dangerous stones, and little water. The rapid is perhaps six hundred yards wide. Seeing that it was impossible to cut down the trees and make a road with the few men I had, I resolved, by common consent, to do something different from what we had originally intended when we trusted to the assurances of the Indians that the way was easy, for, as I have stated, we found the contrary to be true, and this was the reason of our return to our shallop, where I had left some men to guard it, and to inform the Indians, when they arrived, that we had gone to explore the banks alongside the rapid.

Having seen what we wished of this place we met on our way back with some Indians who were coming to examine it as we had done, and they told us that all their companions had arrived at our shallop. There we found them quite pleased and satisfied because we had gone in this way without a guide, trusting only to the reports which they had several times made to us.

Having returned and realizing the small prospect there was of getting our shallop past the rapid, I was distressed, and I was particularly sorry to return without seeing a very large lake, filled with beautiful islands, and a large, beautiful region near the lake, where they had represented to me their enemies lived. Having thought it over well, I decided to proceed thither in order to carry out my promise and also to fulfil my desire. And I embarked with the Indians in their canoes and took with me two men who were eager to go. Having laid my plan before Des Marais and the other men in the shallop, I requested Des Marais to return to our settlement with the rest of our men, in the hope that shortly, by God's grace, I should see them again.

Thereupon, I went and conferred with the Indian chiefs and made them understand how they had told us the contrary of what I had seen at the rapids, that is to say, that it was impossible to pass them with the shallop: yet that this would not prevent me from assisting them as I had promised. This information troubled them greatly, and they wished to change their plan, but I told them and urged upon them to persist in their first design, and that with two others I would go on the war-path with them in their canoes; for I wished to show them that for myself I would not fail to keep my word to them, even if I went alone. And I told them that this time I should not force any of my companions to embark, and should take with me only two whom I had found eager to go.

They were quite satisfied with what I told them, and were glad to learn the resolution I had taken, persisting in their promise to show me fine things.

706. July to October, 1609. Champlain's voyage up the St. Lawrence and Richelieu rivers, and his return to France.

S. de Champlain, Les voyages, *Bk. 2, Chaps. 9–11, translated in H. P. Biggar (and others), The Works of Samuel de Champlain, II (1922), 82–112.*

9

I set out then from the rapid of the river of the Iroquois on the second of July. All the Indians began to carry their canoes, arms and baggage about half a league by land, to avoid the swiftness and force of the rapid. This they soon accomplished.

Then they put all the canoes into the water and two men with their baggage into each; but they made one of the men of each canoe go by land some three leagues which is about the length of the rapids, but the water is here less impetuous than at the entrance, except in certain places where rocks block the river, which is only some three or four hundred yards wide. After we had passed the rapids, which was not without difficulty, all the Indians who had gone overland, by a rather pleasant path through level country, although there were many trees, again got into their canoes. The men whom I had with me also went by land, but I went by water in a canoe. The Indians held a review of all their people and there were sixty men in twenty-four canoes. After holding the review we kept on our way as far as an island, three leagues long, which was covered with the most beautiful pines I had ever seen. There the Indians hunted and took some game. Continuing some three leagues farther, we encamped to take rest during the following night.

Immediately each began, some to cut down trees, others to strip bark from the trees to cover their wigwams in which to take shelter, others to fell big trees for a barricade on the bank of the river round their wigwams. They know how to do this so quickly that after less than two hours' work, five hundred of their enemies would have had difficulty in driving them out, without losing many men. They do not barricade the river bank where their boats are drawn up, in order to embark in case of need. After their wigwams had been set up, according to their custom each time they camp, they sent three canoes with nine good men, to reconnoitre two or three leagues ahead, whether they could perceive anything; and afterwards these retired. All night long they rely upon the explorations of these scouts, and it is a very bad custom; for sometimes they are surprised in their sleep by their enemies, who club them before they have time to rise and defend themselves. Realizing this, I pointed out to them the

mistake they were making and said that they ought to keep watch as they had seen us do every night, and have men posted to listen and see whether they might perceive anything, and not live as they were doing like silly creatures. They told me that they could not stay awake, and that they worked enough during the day when hunting. Besides when they go to war they divide their men into three troops, that is, one troop for hunting, scattered in various directions, another troop which forms the bulk of their men is always under arms, and the other troop of scouts to reconnoitre along the rivers and see whether there is any mark or sign to show where their enemies or their friends have gone. This they know by certain marks by which the chiefs of one nation designate those of another, notifying one another from time to time of any variations of these. In this way they recognise whether enemies or friends have passed that way. The hunters never hunt in advance of the main body, nor of the scouts, in order not to give alarm or to cause confusion, but only when these have retired and in a direction from which they do not expect the enemy. They go on in this way until they are within two or three days' march of their enemy, when they proceed stealthily by night, all in a body, except the scouts. In the day time they retire into the thick of the woods, where they rest without any straggling, or making a noise, or making a fire even for the purpose of cooking. And this they do so as not to be noticed, if by chance their enemy should pass that way. The only light they make is for the purpose of smoking which is almost nothing. They eat baked Indian meal, steeped in water, which becomes like porridge. They keep these meal cakes for their needs, when they are near the enemy or when they are retiring after an attack; for then they do not waste time in hunting but retire quickly.

Each time they encamp they have their *Pilotois* or *Ostemoy* who are people who play the part of wizards, in whom these tribes have confidence. One of these wizards will set up a tent, surround it with small trees, and cover it with his beaver-skin. When it is made, he gets inside so that he is completely hidden; then he seizes one of the poles of his tent and shakes it whilst he mumbles between his teeth certain words, with which he declares he is invoking the devil, who appears to him in the form of a stone and tells him whether his friends will come upon their enemies and kill many of them. This *Pilotois* will lie flat on the ground, without moving, merely speaking to the devil, and suddenly he will rise to his feet, speaking and writhing so that he is all in a perspiration, although stark naked. The whole tribe will be about the tent sitting on their buttocks like monkeys. They often told me that the shaking of the tent which I saw, was caused by the devil and not by the man inside, although I saw the contrary; for, as I have said above, it was the *Pilotois* who would seize one of the poles of the tent, and make it move in this way. They told me also that I should see fire coming out of the top, but I never saw any. These scamps also counterfeit a loud, distinct voice, and speak a language unknown to the other Indians. And when they speak in an old man's voice, the rest think that the devil is speaking, and is telling them what is going to happen in their war, and what they must do.

Yet out of a hundred words all these scoundrels, who pretend to be wizards, do not speak two that are true, and go on deceiving these poor people to get things from them, as do many others in this world who resemble these gentry. I often pointed out to them that what they did was pure folly, and that they ought not to believe in such things.

Having learned from their wizards what is to happen to them, the chiefs take sticks a foot long, one for each man, and indicate by others somewhat longer, their leaders. Then they go into the wood, and level off a place five or six feet square, where the headman, as sergeant-major, arranges all these sticks as to him seems best. Then he calls all his companions, who approach fully armed, and he shows them the rank and order which they are to observe when they fight with the enemy. This all these Indians regard attentively, and notice the figure made with these sticks by their chief. And afterwards they retire from that place and begin to arrange themselves in the order in which they have seen these sticks. Then they mix themselves up and again put themselves in proper order, repeating this two or three times, and go back to their camp, without any need of a sergeant to make them keep their ranks, which they are quite able to maintain without getting into confusion. Such is the method they observe on the war-path.

We departed on the following day, pursuing our way up the river as far as the entrance to the lake. In it are many beautiful low islands covered with very fine woods and meadows with much wild fowl and animals to hunt, such as stags, fallow deer, fawns, roebucks, bears, and other kinds of animals which come from the mainland to these islands. We caught there a great many of them. There are also many beavers, both in that river and in several small streams which fall into it. This region although pleasant is not inhabited by Indians, on account of their wars; for they withdraw from the rivers as far as they can into the interior, in order not to be easily surprised.

On the following day we entered the lake which is some 80 or 100 leagues in length, in which I saw four beautiful islands about ten, twelve and fifteen leagues in length, which, like the Iroquois river, were formerly inhabited by Indians: but have been abandoned, since they have been at war with one another. There are also several rivers flowing into the lake, on whose banks are many fine trees of the same varieties we have in France, with many of the finest vines I had seen anywhere. There are many chestnut trees which I had only seen on the shore of this lake, in which there is also a great abundance of many species of fish. Amongst others there is one called by the natives *Chaousarou*, which is of various lengths; but the largest of them, as these tribes have told me, are from eight to ten feet long. I have seen some five feet long, which were as big as my thigh, and had a head as large as my two fists, with a snout two feet and a half long, and a double row of very sharp, dangerous teeth. Its body has a good deal the shape of the pike; but it is protected by scales of a silvery gray colour and so strong that a dagger could not pierce them. The end of its snout is like a pig's. This fish makes war on all the other fish which are in these lakes and rivers. And, according to what these tribes have told me, it shows marvellous ingenuity in that, when it wishes to catch birds, it goes in amongst the rushes or reeds which lie along the shores of the lake in several places, and puts its snout out of the water without moving. The result is that when the birds come and light on its snout, mistaking it for a stump of wood, the fish is so cunning that, shutting its half-open mouth, it pulls them by their feet under the water. The natives gave me the head of one of them, a thing they prize highly, saying that when they have a headache, they bleed themselves with the teeth of this fish at the spot where the pain is and it eases them at once.

Continuing our way along this lake in a westerly direction and viewing the country, I saw towards the east very high mountains on the tops of which there was snow. I enquired of the natives whether these parts were inhabited. They said they were, and by the Iroquois, and that in those parts there were beautiful valleys and fields rich in corn such as I have eaten in that country, along with other products in abundance. And they said that the lake went close to the mountains, which, as I judged, might be some twenty-five leagues away from us. Towards the south I saw others which were not less lofty than the first-mentioned, but there was no snow on these. The Indians told me that it was there that we were to meet their enemies, that the mountains were thickly populated, and that we had to pass a rapid which I saw afterwards. Thence they said we had to enter another lake which is some nine or ten leagues in length, and that on reaching the end of it we had to go by land some two leagues and cross a river which descends to the coast of Norumbega, adjoining that of Florida. They could go there in their canoes in two days, as I learned afterwards from some prisoners we took, who conversed with me very particularly regarding all they knew, with the help of some Algonquin interpreters who knew the Iroquois language.

Now as we began to get within two or three days' journey of the home of their enemy, we proceeded only by night, and during the day we rested. Nevertheless, they kept up their usual superstitious ceremonies in order to know what was to happen to them in their undertakings, and often would come and ask me whether I had had dreams and had seen their enemies. I would tell them that I had not, but nevertheless continued to inspire them with courage and good hope. When night came on, we set off on our way until the next morning. Then we retired into the thick woods where we spent the rest of the day. Towards ten or eleven o'clock, after walking around our camp, I went to take a rest, and while asleep I dreamed that I saw in the lake near a mountain our enemies, the Iroquois, drowning before our

eyes. I wanted to succour them, but our Indian allies said to me that we should let them all perish; for they were bad men. When I awoke they did not fail to ask me as usual whether I had dreamed anything. I told them what I had seen in my dream. This gave them such confidence that they no longer had any doubt as to the good fortune awaiting them.

Evening having come, we embarked in our canoes in order to proceed on our way, and as we were paddling along very quietly, and without making any noise, about ten o'clock at night on the twenty-ninth of the month, at the extremity of a cape which projects into the lake on the west side, we met the Iroquois on the war-path. Both they and we began to utter loud shouts and each got his arms ready. We drew out into the lake and the Iroquois landed and arranged all their canoes near one another. Then they began to fell trees with the poor axes which they sometimes win in war, or with stone axes; and they barricaded themselves well.

Our Indians all night long also kept their canoes close to one another and tied to poles in order not to get separated, but to fight all together in case of need. We were on the water within bowshot of their barricades. And when they were armed, and everything in order, they sent two canoes which they had separated from the rest, to learn from their enemies whether they wished to fight, and these replied that they had no other desire, but that for the moment nothing could be seen and that it was necessary to wait for daylight in order to distinguish one another. They said that as soon as the sun should rise, they would attack us, and to this our Indians agreed. Meanwhile the whole night was spent in dances and songs on both sides, with many insults and other remarks, such as the lack of courage of our side, how little we could resist or do against them, and that when daylight came our people would learn all this to their ruin. Our side too was not lacking in retort, telling the enemy that they would see such deeds of arms as they had never seen, and a great deal of other talk, such as is usual at the siege of a city. Having sung, danced, and flung words at one another for some time, when daylight came, my companions and I were still hidden, lest the enemy should see us, getting our fire-arms ready as best we could, being however still separated, each in a canoe of the Montagnais Indians. After we were armed with light weapons, we took, each of us, an arquebus and went ashore. I saw the enemy come out of their barricade to the number of two hundred, in appearance strong, robust men. They came slowly to meet us with a gravity and calm which I admired; and at their head were three chiefs. Our Indians likewise advanced in similar order, and told me that those who had the three big plumes were the chiefs, and that there were only these three, whom you could recognize by these plumes, which were larger than those of their companions; and I was to do what I could to kill them. I promised them to do all in my power, and told them that I was very sorry they could not understand me, so that I might direct their method of attacking the enemy, all of whom undoubtedly we should thus defeat; but that there was no help for it, and that I was very glad to show them, as soon as the engagement began, the courage and readiness which were in me.

As soon as we landed, our Indians began to run some two hundred yards towards their enemies, who stood firm and had not yet noticed my white companions who went off into the woods with some Indians. Our Indians began to call to me with loud cries; and to make way for me they divided into two groups, and put me ahead some twenty yards, and I marched on until I was within some thirty yards of the enemy, who as soon as they caught sight of me halted and gazed at me and I at them. When I saw them make a move to draw their bows upon us, I took aim with my arquebus and shot straight at one of the three chiefs, and with this shot two fell to the ground and one of their companions was wounded who died thereof a little later. I had put four bullets into my arquebus. As soon as our people saw this shot so favourable for them, they began to shout so loudly that one could not have heard it thunder, and meanwhile the arrows flew thick on both sides. The Iroquois were much astonished that two men should have been killed so quickly, although they were provided with shields made of cotton thread woven together and wood, which were proof against their arrows. This frightened them greatly. As I was reloading my arquebus, one of my companions fired a shot from within the woods, which astonished them again so much that, seeing their chiefs dead, they lost courage and took to flight, abandoning the field and their

fort, and fleeing into the depth of the forest, whither I pursued them and laid low still more of them. Our Indians also killed several and took ten or twelve prisoners. The remainder fled with the wounded. Of our Indians fifteen or sixteen were wounded with arrows, but these were quickly healed.

After we had gained the victory, our Indians wasted time in taking a large quantity of Indian corn and meal belonging to the enemy, as well as their shields, which they had left behind, the better to run. Having feasted, danced, and sung, we three hours later set off for home with the prisoners. The place where this attack took place is in 43° and some minutes of latitude, and was named Lake Champlain.

10

Having gone about eight leagues, the Indians, towards evening, took one of the prisoners to whom they made a harangue on the cruelties which he and his friends without any restraint had practised upon them, and that similarly he should resign himself to receive as much, and they ordered him to sing, if he had the heart. He did so, but it was a very sad song to hear.

Meanwhile our Indians kindled a fire, and when it was well lighted, each took a brand and burned this poor wretch a little at a time in order to make him suffer the greater torment. Sometimes they would leave off, throwing water on his back. Then they tore out his nails and applied fire to the ends of his fingers and to his *membrum virile*. Afterwards they scalped him and caused a certain kind of gum to drip very hot upon the crown of his head. Then they pierced his arms near the wrists and with sticks pulled and tore out his sinews by main force, and when they saw they could not get them out, they cut them off. This poor wretch uttered strange cries, and I felt pity at seeing him treated in this way. Still he bore it so firmly that sometimes one would have said he felt scarcely any pain. They begged me repeatedly to take fire and do like them. I pointed out to them that we did not commit such cruelties, but that we killed people outright, and that if they wished me to shoot him with the arquebus, I should be glad to do so. They said no; for he would not feel any pain. I went away from them as if angry at seeing them practise so much cruelty on his body. When they saw that I was not pleased, they called me back and told me to give him a shot with the arquebus. I did so, without his perceiving anything, and with one shot caused him to escape all the tortures he would have suffered rather than see him brutally treated. When he was dead, they were not satisfied; they opened his body and threw his bowels into the lake. Afterwards they cut off his head, arms and legs, which they scattered about; but they kept the scalp, which they had dried, as they did with those of all the others whom they had killed in their attack. They did another awful thing, which was to cut his heart into several pieces and to give it to a brother of the dead man to eat and to others of his companions who were prisoners. These took it and put it into their mouths, but would not swallow it. Some of the Algonquin Indians who were guarding the prisoners made them spit it out and threw it into the water. That is how these people act with regard to those whom they capture in war. And it would be better for them to die fighting, and be killed at once, as many do, rather than to fall into the hands of their enemies. When this execution was over, we set out upon our return with the rest of the prisoners, who went along continually singing, without other expectation than to be tortured like him of whom we have spoken. When we arrived at the rapids of the river of the Iroquois, the Algonquins returned into their own country and the Ochateguins also with some of the prisoners, all much pleased at what had taken place in the war, and because I had gone with them willingly. So we all separated with great protestations of mutual friendship, and they asked me if I would not go to their country, and aid them continually like a brother. I promised them I would.

I came back with the Montagnais. After I had questioned the prisoners regarding their country and its characteristics, we packed our baggage for our return. This we accomplished with such speed that every day we made twenty-five or thirty leagues in their canoes, which was their usual rate. When we reached the mouth of the river of the Iroquois there were some of the Indians who dreamed that their enemies were pursuing them. This dream made them at once shift their camp, although the weather that night was bad on account of wind and rain; and they went and spent the whole night in the high bulrushes which are in lake St. Peter, for fear of their enemies. Two days

later we arrived at our settlement, where I ordered bread and peas to be given to them; and also some beads for which they asked me, to decorate the scalps of their enemies, which they carry in their festivities on returning home. On the following day I went with them in their canoes to Tadoussac to see their ceremonies. Approaching the shore each took a stick, on the end of which they hung the scalps of their slain enemies with some beads, singing meanwhile all together. And when all were ready, the women stripped themselves quite naked, and jumped into the water, swimming to the canoes to receive the scalps of their enemies which were at the end of long sticks in the bow of their canoes, in order later to hang them round their necks, as if they had been precious chains. And then they sang and danced. Some days afterwards they made me a present of one of these scalps as if it had been some very valuable thing, and of a pair of shields belonging to their enemies, for me to keep to show to the king. And to please them I promised to do so.

Some days later I went to Quebec, whither came some Algonquins who expressed to me their regret at having missed the defeat of their enemies; and they presented me with some furs in consideration of the fact that I had been there and had helped their friends.

Some days after their departure for their own country, which was 120 leagues distant from our settlement, I went to Tadoussac to see whether Pont-Gravé had returned from Gaspé where he had gone. He arrived only on the following day, and told me he had decided to return to France. We determined to leave as commander at Quebec, a gentleman called Captain Pierre Chavin, of Dieppe, who was to remain there until the Sieur de Monts should give orders on this subject.

11

This decision having been taken, we went to Quebec to install him and to furnish him with everything required and necessary for a settlement, along with fifteen men. When everything was in order we left there on the first day of September to go to Tadoussac to get our vessel ready, so that we might return to France.

We departed accordingly from that place on the fifth of the month and on the eighth we cast anchor at isle Percée.

On Thursday the tenth we set sail from this

place and on the Tuesday following, the eighteenth of the month, we arrived on the Grand Bank.

On the second of October we were on soundings. On the eighth we cast anchor at Le Conquet in Lower Brittany. On Saturday the tenth of the month we sailed from that place and arrived at Honfleur on the thirteenth.

Having disembarked, I did not stay there long before I took post to go to see the Sieur de Monts, who was then at Fontainebleau, where His Majesty was living. And I informed him [Monts] in detail of all that had taken place both in my winter quarters and also in my new explorations. And I spoke of our prospects for the future in view of the promises of the natives called Ochateguins, who are good Iroquois. The other Iroquois, who are their enemies, are farther south. The former understand and do not differ much in language from the tribes recently discovered, and who hitherto had been unknown to us.

I at once waited upon His Majesty, to whom I told the story of my expedition wherein he took pleasure and satisfaction.

I had a belt of porcupine quills, very well woven, according to the fashion of the country, which His Majesty deigned to accept, along with two small birds of the size of blackbirds and of a scarlet colour. I had also the head of a certain fish which was caught in the great Iroquois lake, having a very long snout with two or three rows of very sharp teeth. The picture of this fish is in the great lake on my map.

After the interview with His Majesty, the Sieur de Monts decided to go to Rouen to see his partners, the Sieurs Collier and Le Gendre, merchants of Rouen, in order to consider what they were to do in the following year. They decided to continue the settlement, and in accordance with the promises of the Ochateguins to complete the exploration of the region of the great river St. Lawrence, on condition we carried out the promise to assist them in their wars.

Pont-Gravé was chosen to go to Tadoussac as well for barter as for anything else which might provide the means of meeting the outlay.

And the Sieur Lucas Le Gendre of Rouen, one of the partners, was appointed to take charge of the purchase of goods and provisions, and of the hiring of ships, men, and other things necessary for the expedition.

When these things were settled, the Sieur de Monts went back to Paris, and I with him, where I remained until the end of February. And during this time the Sieur de Monts endeavoured to obtain a new commission for the fur-trade in the parts newly-discovered by us, in which previously no one had traded. This he could not obtain although his requests and proposals were just and reasonable.

And although he saw that it was hopeless to obtain this commission, he did not cease to pursue his project, from his desire that everything should turn out for the good and honour of France.

During this time the Sieur de Monts had not yet informed me of his wishes respecting myself, until I told him that it had been reported to me that he did not wish me to winter in Canada. This was not true; for he left the whole matter to my good pleasure.

I equipped myself with the things suitable and necessary for wintering at our settlement at Quebec, and for that purpose set out from Paris on the last day of February following, and went to Honfleur, where the embarkation was to take place. I went by way of Rouen, where I spent two days, and from there to Honfleur, where I found Pont-Gravé and Le Gendre, who told me they had put on board the things necessary for the settlement. I was very glad to find we were ready to set sail, although uncertain whether the provisions were of good quality and sufficient to sustain us throughout the winter.

707. March 7 to September 25, 1610. Return of Champlain to Canada and his St. Lawrence River expedition.

S. de Champlain, Les voyages (1613), Bk. 3, Chaps. 1-3, translated in H. P. Biggar (and others), The Works of Samuel de Champlain, II (1922), 115-154.

1

The weather becoming favourable, I embarked at Honfleur with a certain number of artisans on the seventh of March. We were delayed by bad weather in the Channel and were forced to put into harbour in England at a place called Portland, where we stayed for several days. But since we found the roadstead at Portland very bad, we weighed anchor for the Isle of Wight, which is near the coast of England. When we were off that island the fog became so thick that we were forced to put in at the Hogue.

Ever since leaving Honfleur, I had been attacked by a very serious illness, which gave me no hope of making the voyage, and I had embarked in a boat to take me back to Havre in France, to receive treatment there, being very ill in the ship. And I purposed when I should recover my health to take passage in another ship, which had not yet left Honfleur, on which Des Marais, Pont-Gravé's son-in-law, was to embark. But I had them take me, still quite ill, to Honfleur, where on the fifteenth of March the ship which I had left put in to take on board ballast which she needed to keep her trim. She remained here until the eighth of April. During this time I recovered my health fairly well, and although somewhat weak and debilitated, I nevertheless re-embarked.

We departed again on April 18, and arrived on the Grand Bank on the nineteenth of the month, sighting the islands of St. Pierre on the twenty-second. When we were off Menthane we met a vessel from St. Malo, on which was a young man, who, while drinking Pont-Gravé's health, lost his footing by reason of the motion of the ship and fell overboard. On account of the strong wind we were unable to rescue him and he was drowned.

On the twenty-sixth of the month we arrived at Tadoussac, where there were ships which had arrived as early as the eighteenth. Such a thing had not been seen for sixty years, according to the reports of old seamen who sail regularly to these parts. It was the mild winter and the small quantity of ice which had permitted these ships to enter. We learned from a young nobleman named the Sieur du Parc, who had spent the winter at our settlement, that all his companions were well and that only a very few of them had been slightly ill; and he informed us that there had been scarcely any winter and that they had generally had fresh meat all winter long. Their greatest trouble had been to amuse themselves.

This winter shows how in future those who undertake such enterprises ought to act, since it is difficult to make a new settlement without labour, and without incurring ill fortune the first year, as has been the case in all our first settlements. And in truth by doing without salt provisions, and having fresh meat, one's health is as good there as in France.

The Indians were daily expecting us, to go with them on the war-path. When they learned that Pont-Gravé and I had arrived together, they rejoiced greatly and came to confer with us.

I went ashore to assure them that we should go with them, in accordance with the promises they had made to me, that after we returned from their war, they would take me to explore the Three Rivers as far as a place where there is such a large sea, that they have not seen the end of it, and that we should then come back by way of the Saguenay to Tadoussac. I asked them whether they were still willing to do this. They said they were, but that it could only be done next year. This answer pleased me, but I had also promised the Algonquins and Ochateguins to assist them in their wars, and they had promised to show me their country and the great lake, and some copper mines and other things which they had mentioned to me. Hence I had two strings to my bow, and if one failed the other might stay taut.

On the twenty-eighth of the month I set out from Tadoussac for Quebec, where I found Captain Pierre, the commander, and all his comrades, hale and hearty. And with them was a native chief named Batiscan and some of his companions who were waiting for us. These rejoiced greatly at my arrival and sang and danced all the evening. I made a feast for them which pleased them much. They ate heartily and were not ungrateful for it. They invited me and seven others to a feast, which is no small favour amongst them. Each of us, as is the custom, carried his dish with him, and brought it back full of meat, and gave it to whomsoever we pleased.

Some days after I had left Tadoussac, the Montagnais, to the number of sixty valiant men, on their way to the war, arrived at Quebec. They stayed there some days, enjoying themselves, and not seldom they importuned me with questions as to whether I should fail in what I had promised them. I reassured them and made them fresh promises, asking them whether they had found me false in the past. They rejoiced greatly when I repeated my promises to them.

And they used to say to me: 'There are many Basques and Mistigoches (for so they call the Normans and the people of St. Malo) who say that they will accompany us on the war-path. What do you think of it? Do they speak the truth?' I replied that they did not, and that I knew well what they had in mind, and that what they said was merely in order to obtain possession of the Indians' goods. These said to me: 'You have spoken truly, they are women, who wish to make war only upon our beavers.' There were other facetious remarks, and discussion of the equipment and method of going on the war-path.

They decided to set out and to wait for me at Three Rivers, thirty leagues above Quebec, where I had promised to join them with four pinnaces loaded with merchandise, for bartering furs with among others the Ochateguins, who were to come and wait for me at the mouth of the river of the Iroquois. This they had promised me the previous year, and also to bring along as many as 400 men to go on the war-path.

2

I departed from Quebec on June 14, to go and meet the Montagnais, Algonquins, and Ochateguins who were to be at the mouth of the river of the Iroquois. When I was eight leagues from Quebec, I met a canoe in which were two Indians, one an Algonquin and the other a Montagnais, who were coming to ask me to push on as fast as possible. They said that in two days Algonquins and Ochateguins to the number of 200 would be at the rendez-vous, and that 200 more would come a little later with Iroquet, one of their chiefs. They asked me if I was pleased with the arrival of these Indians, and I said that I could not be displeased with it, since they had kept their promise. They got into my pinnace, where I entertained them well. After conversing with them a short time about a number of things touching their wars, the Algonquin Indian, who was one of their chiefs, drew out of a sack a piece of copper a foot long, which he presented to me. It was very fine and pure. He gave me to understand that the metal was abundant where he had obtained it, which was on the bank of a river near a large lake. He said that it was taken out in pieces, and when melted was made into sheets and smoothed out with stones. I was much pleased with this gift although it was of small value.

On our arrival at Three Rivers, I found all the Montagnais waiting for me, and four pinnaces which had gone there to barter, as I have already stated.

The Indians were very glad to see me. I went ashore to confer with them. They requested me when going on the war-path not to get into, nor to allow my companions to get into, any other canoes than theirs; for they were our old friends. This I promised and told them I was willing to start at once, since the wind was favourable and my pinnace was not so fast as their canoes, on which account I wanted to go on ahead. They besought me to wait until the next morning, when we should all go together, saying that they would not go faster than I. Finally, to please them, I consented, at which they were much gratified.

On the following day we set out all together, and sailed till the following morning, the nineteenth of the said month, when we arrived at an island at the mouth of the river of the Iroquois, and waited for the Algonquins who were to arrive that same day. While the Montagnais were cutting down trees to make a space for dancing and for preparing themselves for the arrival of the Algonquins, an Algonquin canoe was seen coming swiftly to warn us that the Algonquins had encountered the Iroquois to the number of a hundred, who had barricaded themselves well, and that it would be difficult to get the better of them if their friends did not come quickly and along with them the Matigoches, as they call us.

At once the alarm was given and each got into his canoe with his arms. They were quickly ready, but with some confusion; for they made such haste that instead of getting ahead they kept things back. They came to our pinnace and to the others, begging me and my companions to accompany them in their canoes, and they urged me so strongly that with four others I embarked with them. I asked our pilot, La Routte, to stay in the pinnace, and to send me four or five more of my companions, should the other pinnaces send shallops and men to our assistance; for none of the pinnaces would go with the Indians except that of Captain Thibaut who came with me. The Indians shouted to those who stayed behind that they were woman-hearted, and knew no other kind of fighting but the war on peltry.

Meanwhile all the Indians, after going about half a league and crossing the river, landed, and leaving their canoes, took their shields, bows, arrows, clubs, and swords, which were fixed to the ends of long sticks, and began to make their way through the woods so fast that we soon lost sight of them, and they left the five of us without guides. This displeased us; nevertheless as we could see their tracks we followed them, although we often went astray. When we had gone about half a league through the thick woods, among swamp and marsh, with water up to our knees, each loaded down with a pikeman's corselet, which bothered us greatly, as did the hosts of mosquitoes, a strange sight, which were so thick that they hardly allowed us to draw our breath, so greatly and severely did they persecute us, we should not have known where we were, had it not been for two Indians of whom we caught sight, moving through the bush, to whom we called. I said to them that they must stay with us to guide and conduct us to where the Iroquois were, and that if they did not, we should not reach there, but should get lost in the woods. They stayed to be our guides.

Having gone a short distance, we perceived an Indian coming in haste to look for us, to urge us on as quickly as possible. He gave me to understand that the Algonquins and Montagnais had tried to force the Iroquois barricade and had been repulsed, and that some of the best men among the Montagnais had been killed, and several more wounded, and that they had retreated to wait for us, and that their one hope was in us. Hardly had we gone an eighth of a league with this Indian, who was an Algonquin Chief, before we heard the howls and shouts of both parties, flinging insults at one another, and continually skirmishing whilst waiting for us. As soon as the Indians saw us they began to shout so loud that one could not have heard thunder.

I directed my companions to keep behind me and not to leave me. I approached the enemy's barricade to reconnoitre it. It was made of strong trees, placed one upon the other, in a circle, which is the ordinary form of their forts. All the Montagnais and Algonquins also approached the barricade. Then we began firing many arquebus-shots through the branches; for we could not see them as they could see us. As I was firing my first shot close to their barricade, I was wounded with an arrow which split the tip of my ear and pierced my neck. I seized the arrow which was still in my

neck and pulled it out. The point was tipped with a very sharp bit of stone. At the same time one of my companions was also wounded in the arm by another arrow, which I pulled out for him.

My wound did not hinder me, however, from doing my duty, and our Indian allies also did theirs, and the enemy too fought well; so much so that one could see the arrows flying on all sides as thick as hail. The Iroquois were astonished at the reports of our arquebuses, but most of all because the bullets pierced better than their arrows. And they were so frightened at the execution done by the bullets, having seen several of their companions fall dead and wounded, that out of fear, thinking these shots to be irresistible, they would throw themselves upon the ground when they heard the report. Besides, we hardly missed a shot, and fired two or three bullets each time, and for the most part had our arquebuses resting on the side of their barricade. When I saw that our ammunition was beginning to fail, I said to the Indians that they must carry the place by storm, by breaking down the barricades. To do this they must take their shields, and covering themselves therewith, must come near enough to be able to fasten strong ropes to the posts which supported the barricade and by main strength pull them down and so make an opening wide enough to let us into the fort, and that meanwhile by means of our arquebuses we should keep the enemy back, should he attempt to hinder them. I said also that a number of them should attack certain large trees which were near the barricade, in order to make them fall upon the enemy and crush him, and that others with their shields should keep the enemy from hurting these. All of which they carried out very promptly.

As we were on the point of completing this, the pinnaces, which were a league and a half away, heard the sound of our fighting, the echo of the firing being carried to them, with the result that a courageous young man of St. Malo named Des Prairies, who, like the others, had brought his pinnace for the purpose of bartering furs, said to those who had stayed behind, that it was disgraceful of them, to see me fighting in this way with savages without going to my help, and that for himself he held his honour too high for anyone to reproach him with such a thing. Thereupon he decided to come and join me in a shallop with some of his men, and some of mine whom he brought with him. As soon as he arrived, he went towards the Iroquois fort, which was on the bank of the river. Here he landed and came to look for me. When I saw him, I made our Indians cease breaking down the fort, so that the new-comers might have their share of this pleasure. I requested the Sieur des Prairies and his companions to fire some arquebus volleys before our Indians stormed the place, as they had decided to do. They did so, and fired several shots wherein each conducted himself very properly. And after sufficient firing had been done, I spoke to our Indians, inciting them to finish their work. At once they approached the barricade as they had done before, having us on their flanks to shoot at those who should try to prevent them from pulling it down. They behaved so well and so bravely, that, thanks to our volleys, they made an opening, which nevertheless was difficult to get through; for there still remained a part as high as a man, as well as branches of felled trees which impeded us greatly. Still, when I saw that there was a pretty fair opening, I gave orders for the firing to cease, which was obeyed. At the same moment, some twenty or thirty, both Indians and whites, went in, sword in hand, without meeting much resistance. Immediately all who were able began to flee, but they did not get far; for they were laid low by those about the barricade, and any who escaped were drowned in the river. We took some fifteen prisoners, the rest having been killed by arquebuses, arrows, and swords. When all was over there arrived another shallop with some of our companions, but it was too late, although in time to carry off the booty, which was small. There were merely some beaver-skins, and dead bodies covered with blood, which the Indians would not take the trouble to strip, and made sport of those who did so, who were the people in the last shallop. The others refused such a nasty occupation. In this way, by God's grace, was victory won, and the Indians gave us much praise on that account.

The Indians as is their custom scalped those who had been killed and carried these off as trophies of victory. With their prisoners, they went home singing, having fifty of their men wounded, and three of the Montagnais and Algonquins killed. They hung the scalps to sticks in front of their canoes with a dead body cut into quarters, to be eaten, as they said, out of vengeance, and thus furnished they came to the place where lay our pinnaces at the mouth of the river of the Iroquois.

My companions and I embarked in a shallop, where I had my wound dressed by the surgeon de Boyer, of Rouen, who had also come for the barter. The whole of that day was spent by the Indians in dancing and singing.

On the following day the Sieur de Pont-Gravé arrived in another shallop laden with some goods. He had left behind another in which was Captain Pierre who could only advance with difficulty, since that pinnace was rather heavy and not easy to navigate.

That day there was some trading in furs, but the other pinnaces carried off the better part of the goods. It was doing them a great favour to search out for them strange tribes, in order that they might later on carry off the whole profit without running any risk or hazard.

On that day I asked our Indians for an Iroquois prisoner of theirs, and they gave him to me. It was no small service I did him; for I saved him from numerous tortures, which he would have been forced to undergo, along with his fellow prisoners, whose nails were torn out, fingers cut off, and bodies burnt in several places. Two or three were put to death that day, and to make them suffer greater tortures their captors proceeded as follows:

Seizing their prisoners they took them to the water's edge and tied them upright to a stake. Then each came along with a birch-bark torch, burning them now in one part, now in another; and the poor wretches, feeling the fire, would utter such loud cries, that it was awful to hear, and indeed the cruelties which these barbarians practise upon one another are terrible. Having made them suffer in this way for some time, especially by burning them with this bark, they took water and threw it over their bodies to make them suffer still more. Then they would again apply the fire in such a way that the skin would fall from their bodies, and the captors would continue with loud shouts and whoops, dancing about, until these poor wretches fell dead on the spot.

As soon as one would fall to the ground, they would pound the body violently with clubs; then they would cut off arms, legs and other parts of the body, and amongst them no one was esteemed worthy who did not cut off a piece of flesh and give it to the dogs. Such is the courtesy which prisoners receive. Nevertheless, they endure all the tortures inflicted on them with such constancy that those who see them are struck with astonishment.

As to the other prisoners who were left, both with the Algonquins and the Montagnais, they were reserved to be put to death at the hands of the wives and daughters of these, who in this matter show themselves no less inhuman than the men; in fact they greatly surpass the men in cruelty; for by their cunning they invent more cruel torments, and take delight in them. Thus they cause the prisoners to end their lives in the deepest suffering.

On the following day arrived chief Iroquet and another Ochataguin who had with them some eighty men, and they were very sorry that they had not been present at the victory. Among these tribes were nearly two hundred men who had never before seen Christians, for whom they expressed great admiration.

For some three days we were together on an island at the mouth of the river of the Iroquois, and then each tribe went off to its own country.

I had with me a youth who had already spent two winters at Quebec who wished to go with the Algonquins to learn the language. Pont-Gravé and I decided that if he were so disposed, it would be better to send him there than elsewhere, to learn what their country was like, see the great lake, observe the rivers and what tribes lived in that region, while at the same time he might explore the mines and the rarest things amongst the tribes in those parts, so that on his return we might be informed of the truth thereof. We asked him if this would be agreeable to him; for it was not my wish to force him, but so soon as the request was made, he accepted the journey with great willingness.

I went to see chief Iroquet, who was very friendly to me, and asked him if he would take this lad home with him to spend the winter in his country, and to bring him back in the spring. He promised me to do so, and to treat him like his own son, saying that he was much pleased thereat. When he reported this to the rest of the Algonquins they were not too well satisfied; for they feared lest some accident might happen to the boy, on which account we might make war upon them. Their reluctance cooled Iroquet's readiness, and he came and told me that all his companions disapproved. Meanwhile the pinnaces had left, except Pont-Gravé's, and he having, as he said, some very pressing business, also took his departure. I remained with mine, to see what would come of this lad's journey, which I was anxious he should undertake. So I went ashore and demanded a pow-wow with the chiefs, who came to me; and we sat down with many other Indians, leaders of their bands. I asked them why chief Iroquet, whom I considered to be my friend, had refused to take the youth with him. I said that it was not like a brother or a friend to deny me a thing which he had promised me, and which could bring only good to them all. If I wished them to take this youth, it was for the purpose of increasing our friendship with them and their neighbours, beyond what it had been: but their hesitation gave me a bad opinion of them, and if they would not take this lad with them, as chief Iroquet had promised me, I should never have any friendship with them; for they were not children, that they should break this promise. Then they told me that they were quite satisfied to take the youth, but they were afraid that, if he changed his diet, and were fed less well than he had been accustomed to, some harm might befall him, at which I might be angry, and this, they said, was the sole cause of their refusal.

I answered them that as to the life they led and the food they ate, the lad could well adapt himself to these, and that if from sickness or the fortune of war, any harm should happen to him, this would not prevent me from being kindly disposed to them; for we were all liable to accidents which we ought to bear patiently. But I said that if they should illtreat him, and any misfortune happened to him through their fault, I should indeed be displeased. However, I did not look for such from them, but for the contrary.

They said to me: 'Since, then, you have this desire, we will take him along, and will treat him like one of ourselves. But you must take a young man in his place, who will go to France. We shall be very glad to have him report to us all the fine things he has seen.' I gladly accepted the proposal, and took the young man. He was of the tribe of the Ochateguins, and was also very glad to come with me. This gave an additional reason for the better treatment of my lad, whom I furnished with everything necessary. Then we promised one another to meet again at the end of June.

We separated with many protestations of friendship. They went off in the direction of the great rapid of the river of Canada, and I went back to Quebec. On my way I met with Pont-Gravé on lake St. Peter, who was waiting for me with a large patache with which he had fallen in on that lake. This boat, being a heavy sailer, had been unable to make speed to the place where were the Indians.

We all returned to Quebec together. Then Pont-Gravé went on to Tadoussac, to arrange certain matters of ours in those parts, and I remained at Quebec to attend to some repairs to the palissades about our settlement, awaiting Pont-Gravé's return, in order to consult together as to what was necessary to be done.

On June 4 Des Marais arrived at Quebec, which pleased us greatly; for we were afraid that some accident had happened to him at sea.

Some days later, an Iroquois prisoner whom I kept there under guard, but to whom I allowed too great liberty, fled and escaped, out of sheer fear and terror and in spite of the assurances given him by a woman of his tribe whom we had in our settlement.

A few days afterwards Pont-Gravé wrote to me that he was thinking of wintering in the settlement, being moved thereto by many considerations. I replied to him that if he thought he could do better than in the past I had done, he would do well.

He then hastened to have the supplies necessary for the settlement brought to us.

When I had completed the palisade about our settlement and had put everything in order again, Captain Pierre [Chavin], who had gone to Tadoussac to see some friends, returned in a pinnace. I went there also to see how the second barter would turn out, as well as for certain other private business I had at that place. Upon my arrival I saw Pont-Gravé, who informed me very particularly regarding his plan, and his reasons for wintering at the settlement. I told him plainly how the thing struck me, namely that I thought

he would get little advantage from it, according to all certain and clear appearances.

He thereupon decided to change his mind, and sent a pinnace with orders to Captain Pierre to come back from Quebec for some business he had with him; and he also sent word that some ships from Brouage had brought news that M. de Saint Luc having come by post from Paris, had driven the Protestants out of Brouage, had reinforced the garrison with soldiers, and had then returned to Court. Report said that the king had been killed, and two or three days later, the Duke de Sully and two other noblemen whose names were not known.

All these reports brought great sorrow to the true Frenchmen who were then in those parts. As for myself, it was very difficult to believe them, on account of the different versions which were told, and which had small appearance of truth. And yet I was much pained to hear such bad news.

Now having stayed three or four days at Tadoussac I saw the loss incurred by many merchants who had loaded much merchandise and equipped many ships, hoping to do well in the fur-trade. This was so poor, for the number of vessels employed, that many will long remember the loss they sustained that year.

The Sieur Pont-Gravé and I each embarked in a pinnace and left Captain Pierre with the ship. We took Du Parc with us to Quebec, where we finished our repairs to the settlement. When everything was in good order, we decided that Du Parc, who had wintered with Captain Pierre, should stay there again, and that Captain Pierre should also return to France, on account of business affairs which called him there.

Accordingly we left Du Parc in command with sixteen men, whom we admonished to live together discreetly in the fear of God, and to give to Du Parc, who was to be their chief and leader, all due obedience, the same as if one of us had remained behind. They all promised to do this and to live in peace with one another.

As for the gardens, we left these well provided with kitchen vegetables of all sorts, as also with very fine Indian corn, with wheat, rye and barley, which had been sown, and with vines which I had had planted there during my winter's stay. These they took no care to preserve; for on my return I found them all broken down, and was much displeased at the small amount of care they had taken in the preservation of a good and fine plot, out of which I had hoped to get something worth while.

Having seen that everything was in good order, we left Quebec on the eighth of the month of August and went to Tadoussac in order to prepare our ship for sea, and this was promptly done.

3

On the thirteenth of the month we set sail from Tadoussac and arrived on the following day at isle Percée, where we found a number of vessels, catching fish and curing them.

On the eighteenth of the month we left isle Percée and made our way as far as latitude 42° without having any knowledge of the Grand Bank where the green fishery is carried on, because it is too narrow at this latitude.

When we were about half-way across, we met with a whale which was asleep. The vessel passing over it, cut a very large opening near its tail, awakening it very quickly, and causing it to shed a great quantity of blood. Our vessel received no damage whatever.

It has seemed to me not inappropriate to describe here briefly the capture of whales which many have not seen. Some think that they are taken by cannon-shot; for there are liars so impudent as to assert this to those who have no knowledge thereof. Many have stoutly maintained to me the truth of this on the strength of these false reports.

The cleverest men at this fishing are the Basques, who, in order to carry it on, place their vessels in a safe port, or near the spot where they judge there are many whales, and then they man with stout sailors a number of shallops, and equip them with lines. These are small ropes made of the best hemp that can be found, having a length of at least one hundred and fifty fathoms. They have also many halberds, half a pike long, armed with an iron blade, six inches wide, and others a foot and a half or two feet long and very sharp. In each shallop there is a harpooner, who is one of the most nimble and wide-awake among them; and since his part is the most dangerous, he, after the masters, draws the highest pay.

When the shallop has come outside the harbour, the men look in all directions to catch sight of a whale, whilst they tack from side to side. If they see nothing, they land and place themselves upon the highest point they can find in order to have as wide a view as possible. Here they station a look-out for the whale. They are able to discover it both from its size and by the water which it spouts from its blow-holes, which amounts each time to a hogshead, and is blown as high as the length of two lances. From the quantity of water thrown up one estimates the amount of oil which the whale will produce. There are some from which you can get as much as six score hogsheads, but others give less.

Now when they see this enormous fish, they quickly get into their shallop and by dint of rowing or by help of the wind, reach the spot where they are over the whale. When it is seen near the surface, instantly the harpooner is in the bow of the boat with a harpoon, which is an iron weapon two feet long and half a foot wide at the lower part, set in a shaft half a pike in length. At mid-length there is a hole, where the line is fastened. As soon as the harpooner sees his chance, he throws his harpoon, which penetrates very deeply into the whale. Directly the whale feels itself wounded, it goes to the bottom, and if by chance in turning it strikes with its tail the shallop or the men, it crushes them as easily as a tumbler. This is the only risk they run of being killed, whilst harpooning; but as soon as they have thrown the harpoon, they let their line run out, until the whale reaches the bottom. And since it does not go straight down, it sometimes drags the shallop some eight or nine leagues, travelling as fast as a horse. And very often the men are forced to cut the line, for fear lest the whale should drag them under the water. But when the creature goes straight to the bottom, it stays there for a while, and then it slowly comes up to the surface. As it rises they haul in their line little by little. And when the whale comes up, two or three shallops surround it, and the men with their halberds give it many thrusts. Feeling itself struck it goes down again under the water, losing blood, and growing so weak that it has no more strength or vigour. When it comes again to the surface, they finally kill it. When dead it no longer sinks to the bottom, and they tie strong ropes to it and tow it ashore to the place where they do their curing, that is to say where they melt the fat of the whale, in order to obtain the oil. That is the way in which whales are caught, and they are not shot with cannon, which is what many think, as I have stated above.

But to resume. After wounding the whale as mentioned above, we took many porpoises which our mate harpooned, and from this we had pleasure and satisfaction. We caught also many tunnies with hook and line, to which we fastened a small fish resembling a herring, and which we allowed to trail behind the vessel. And the tunny, thinking it was really a live fish, would come to swallow it, and would soon be caught on the hook which had gone into the body of the little fish. The tunny is very good and has certain tufts which are very handsome and pleasant, resembling those which people wear in plumes.

On September 22 we came into soundings, and sighted twenty vessels some four leagues to the west of us, which we took to be Flemish; for such they appeared from our ship. On the twenty-fifth of the month we sighted the island of Guernsey, after a stiff blow which lasted till noon. On the twenty-seventh of the month we arrived at Honfleur.

708. March to September, 1611. Champlain trades with the Indians of the interior in the vicinity of Montreal.

S. de Champlain, Les voyages (1613), Bk. 4, Chaps. 1–3, translated in H. P. Biggar (and others), The Works of Samuel de Champlain, II (1922), 157–214.

1

We set sail from Honfleur on the first day of March with favourable winds till the eighth of the month. After that we were delayed by contrary winds from the S.S.W. and W.N.W., which drove us as far as latitude 42°, without our being able to make a southing, in order to take our direct course. Having in this way experienced several storms and been retarded by the bad weather, we still, with much difficulty and labour, by dint of going on one tack and then on the other, suc-

ceeded in reaching a point some eighty leagues from the Grand Bank, where the green fishing is carried on. Here we met with icebergs more than thirty, or even forty, fathoms high, which made us consider what we were to do; for we feared lest we might meet with them during the night and lest the wind, veering about, should drive us against them, suspecting indeed that these would not be the last, inasmuch as we had set out from France very early in the season. We sailed that day then with little sail and as near the wind as we could, and when night came on there arose such a thick, heavy mist that we could hardly see the length of the ship. About eleven o'clock at night the sailors noticed more icebergs, which frightened us, but in the end we made such efforts, joined to the diligence of the sailors, that we avoided them. When we thought we had passed all danger, we came upon one directly ahead of our ship, which the sailors sighted only just in time not to run into it. And as each one committed himself to God, thinking we should never escape the danger of that iceberg which was already under our bowsprit, we shouted to the helmsman to bear off. The great mass of ice was driving before the wind so fast that it passed close to our vessel, without striking it, but the ship stopped as if to let it go by. Although we were out of danger, yet each one's blood cooled down slowly from the fright we had had; and we praised God for having delivered us from this peril. After passing that one, the same night we escaped two or three others not less dangerous than the first, in the midst of a fog so wet and cold that we could scarcely keep warm. On the following day as we continued on our course we met with several other large and very high icebergs, which, from a distance, seemed to be islands. All these we avoided and arrived on the Grand Bank where we were delayed by bad weather for the space of six days. The wind having fallen a little and being rather favourable, we left the banks in latitude 44° 30', which was the farthest south that we could get. Having sailed some sixty leagues to W.N.W., we sighted a vessel, which drew near to see who we were, and then bore away to the E.N.E. to avoid a great bank of ice which extended as far as we could see. Thinking there might be a passage through the middle of this great bank, which was separated in two, and in order to finish our journey, we entered this opening, and sailed some ten leagues, without seeing anything but a free passage until evening, when we found the passage closed. This gave us much anxiety as to what we should do, with night coming on and no moon. There seemed no possible way for us to return whence we had come. Still, after due reflection, we decided to make an effort to find the opening by which we had entered, and this we set about to do; but with night, came on fog, rain, snow and such a high wind that we could hardly carry our mainsail, and we lost all bearings of our route. For, when we thought we could avoid the ice and pass through, the wind had already closed the passage. Hence we were forced to return on the other tack, and we could not remain longer than a quarter of an hour on one tack, before making the other tack, in order to avoid thousands of floes on all sides. More than a score of times we thought we should not come off alive. The whole night was spent amid difficulties and labours. Never was the watch better kept; for nobody had any desire to sleep, but rather to struggle to get out of the dangerous ice. The cold was so great that all the ship's running rigging was so frozen and covered with big icicles that we could not work it nor stand upon the vessel's deck. Having manœuvred then from side to side, we waited for daylight to give us hope. But when day came, bringing fog, we saw that labour and fatigue would be of no service to us, and decided to lie alongside a bank of ice where we should be sheltered from the high wind that was blowing, and to lower all sails and let ourselves drift like the ice, in order that, when we had got some distance away from the ice, we might hoist sail again, and go back to the bank of ice and do as we did before, waiting for the fog to lift, when we should come out of the ice as quickly as possible. We lay thus all day until the following morning, when we set sail, tacking from side to side, and nowhere did we go that we did not find ourselves shut in by great banks of ice, as if we were in ponds on land. In the evening we sighted a vessel which was on the other side of one of the banks of ice, and it was in no less anxiety, I am sure, than were we. We remained four or five days in this extreme danger, until one morning as we looked about us in all directions, we saw indeed no passage, but a place where we judged the ice not to be thick, and where we could easily pass through. We made for this spot and passed many *bour-*

guignons, which are pieces of ice separated from the great masses by the violence of the winds. On reaching the bank of ice, the sailors armed themselves with great bars and other pieces of wood to ward off the *bourguignons* we might meet, and in this way we cleared the bank, but not without striking smaller pieces, which did no good to our vessel, although no very great harm was done to us. Being outside, we praised God for our deliverance. On the following day we kept on our way, and met with other ice-fields in which we became entangled, so that we found ourselves surrounded on all sides except at the place where we had come in. Hence we were obliged to retrace our steps, and try to double the southern point. This we were not able to do until the second day, when in latitude 44° 30′, we passed several small blocks of ice, which had been separated from the great bank, and sailed towards the N.W. and N.N.W. until the following morning, when we met with another great bank of ice extending from east to west as far as the eye could reach; and when you saw it, you thought it was land; for it was so level that you would have really said it had been made so on purpose. It was more than eighteen feet high, with twice as much under the water. And on the twenty-sixth day of the month we estimated that we were only some fifteen leagues from cape Breton. These frequent encounters with ice annoyed us much. We thought also that the passage between cape Breton and cape Ray would be closed, and that we should have to keep out to sea a long time before finding an opening. Hence, being unable to make headway, we were forced to put to sea again for a distance of some four or five leagues in order to double another point of the same great ice-bank, which lay to the W.S.W. of us; and then we went back on the other tack to the north-west, in order to double this point, and sailed some seven leagues and then headed N.N.W. some three leagues, where we sighted another ice-bank. Night was approaching and a fog was coming up which made us head out to sea to spend the rest of the night waiting for daylight so that we might return and reconnoitre these ice-banks. On the twenty-seventh of the month we sighted land to the W.N.W. of us, and saw no ice lying to the N.N.E. We came closer in to examine the land better, and found that it was Canso, and accordingly headed north to make Cape Breton island, but we had not gone more than two leagues when we met with an ice-bank which stretched to the north-east. Night coming on, we were obliged to put to sea until the following day, when we headed north-east and met with another ice-bank, which lay to the east and E.S.E., along which we coasted, steering north and north-east for more than fifteen leagues. Finally we were forced to head again to the west, which vexed us greatly, seeing that we were unable to find an opening and were forced to draw back and to retrace our steps. And unfortunately for us, a calm fell upon us in such a way that the swell very nearly cast us against the ice-bank, and we were on the point of launching our boat, to use in case of need. Even had we escaped on this ice the only result would have been that we should all have starved miserably to death. As we were deliberating whether we should launch our boat, a light breeze sprang up, which pleased us greatly, and by it we escaped from the said ice.

After we had gone two leagues, night came on with a very thick fog, which made us strike sail; for we could not see, and besides there were several large fields of ice in our way into which we feared we might run. And thus we remained all night, until the following day, which was the twenty-ninth of the month, when the fog thickened so much that one could scarcely see the length of the ship, and there was very little wind. Yet we failed not to attempt to set sail in order to get out of the ice. But though we thought to free ourselves, we found ourselves so hemmed in that we did not know which way to tack. And once again we were forced to lower sail and to let ourselves drift until the ice made us hoist sail, and we tacked a hundred times from side to side and several times just escaped destruction. Here the coolest would quite lose his head, as well indeed as the greatest astrologer alive. What worried us still more was the short distance we could see, and the approach of night, nor could we do a leg of a quarter of a league without meeting icebergs, great or small, and also much floating ice, the smallest piece of which would have been sufficient to sink any vessel afloat.

Now, as we were still coasting about among these icebergs, such a strong wind arose that it very quickly dispersed the fog, opened up the view, and in no time gave us a clear sky and a bright sun. When we looked about us, we saw that we were enclosed within a small pond, less than a

league and a half in circumference, and we caught sight of Cape Breton island, lying almost four leagues to the north of us, and we supposed that the passage to Cape Breton was still closed. We saw also a small bank of ice astern of us and beyond it the open sea which made us decide to pass through the ice-bank which was loose. We accomplished this quite dexterously without injuring our vessel, and put out to sea for the night, heading to the south-east of the icebergs. And when we judged that we could double the bank of ice, we sailed E.N.E. some fifteen leagues, and saw only one small berg. At night we lowered sail till the following morning, when we saw another ice-bank to the north of us, stretching as far as the eye could reach. Having drifted to within about half a league of it we hoisted sail, and ran along the ice-bank to find the end of it.

As we were sailing along, we sighted, on the first of May, amongst the ice, a vessel, which, like us, had had difficulty in getting out of it. We ran up into the wind to wait for this vessel, which was bearing down upon us; for we wanted to know whether she had not seen other ice-fields. When she drew near, we saw that it was the Sieur de Poutrincourt's son, who was on his way to visit his father at the settlement at Port Royal, and he had left France three months previously (not without much difficulty, I imagine), and yet he and his crew were nearly a hundred and forty leagues from Port Royal, a long way out of their proper course. We told them that we had sighted the islands of Canso, which I think reassured them greatly, inasmuch as they had not yet sighted any land, and were heading straight between cape St. Lawrence and cape Ray, in which direction they would not have found Port Royal except by going overland. After some little conversation together, we separated, each one taking his own course.

On the following day we sighted the islands of St. Pierre without meeting any ice, and continuing on our course on the next day, being the third of the month, we sighted cape Ray, also without meeting ice. On the fourth day of the month we sighted St. Paul island and cape St. Lawrence, and were some eight leagues north of cape St. Lawrence. The next day we sighted Gaspé. On the seventh of the month we were held up by a north-west wind which drove us out of our course some thirty-five leagues. Then the wind dropped and it was fine and favourable until we reached Tadoussac on the thirteenth of May. Here we fired a cannon to warn the Indians so that we might have news of the people at our settlement at Quebec. The whole country was still almost covered with snow. Some canoes came out to us, and we learned that one of our pataches had been in port for a month and that three vessels had arrived a week before. We lowered our boat and went to see these Indians, who were in a rather miserable condition and had only a few articles which they wished to barter merely in order to get food. Furthermore, they wanted to wait until several ships had arrived in order to get our wares more cheaply. Thus those people are mistaken who think that by coming first they can do better business; for these Indians are now too sharp and crafty.

On the seventeenth of the month I set out from Tadoussac for the Great Rapid to meet the Algonquins and other tribes who had promised me the year before to be there with the youth whom I had given them, so that I might learn from him what he had seen while wintering in the interior. Those who were in this harbour, who suspected where I was going in accordance with the promises I had made to the Indians, as related above, began to build several small pinnaces for the purpose of following me as promptly as they could. And several, as I learned before leaving France, had ships and pataches equipped on the strength of our undertaking, hoping to come back as rich as if they had gone to the Indies.

Pont-Gravé remained at Tadoussac, intending, if he did no barter there, to take a patache and come and join me at the said rapids. Between Tadoussac and Quebec our pinnace leaked a good deal, which forced me to stay at Quebec to stop the leak. This was on the twenty-first of May.

2

On landing I found the Sieur du Parc who with his companions had spent the winter at the settlement. They were all very well, and had had no sickness. They told me there had been plenty of hunting—animals and birds—during the whole winter. I found the Indian chief Batiscan and some Algonquins who said they were waiting for me, not wishing to go back to Tadoussac until they had seen me. I made a proposal to them to take one of our men to Three Rivers to explore that region, but I could not obtain anything from them for that year, and so I postponed it for another year. However, I did not fail to question them particularly regarding the tribes who live there and their origin, which information they gave me accurately. I asked them for one of their canoes, but they would not part with it on any account whatever, because of the need they had of it: for I had intended to send two or three men to explore up the Three Rivers, to see what was there. But to my great regret I was unable to do this, and I put the thing off till the first opportunity that should present itself.

Meanwhile I pushed forward the repairs of our pinnace. And when it was ready, a young man of La Rochelle, called Tresart, begged me to allow him to accompany me to the rapid, but I declined, saying that I had private plans, and was not willing to lead anyone there to my own detriment; that there were other companies in existence than mine; that I did not wish to open the way and act as guide, but that he would find the place easily enough without me.

That same day I left Quebec and arrived on the twenty-eighth of May at the Great Rapid, where I found none of the Indians who had promised me to be there by the twentieth of the month. I at once got into a poor canoe with the Indian whom I had taken to France and one of our men. Having examined both shores, in the woods as well as along the river banks, in order to find a suitable place for the site of a settlement, and also to prepare the ground for building, I went some eight leagues by land, skirting the Great Rapid, through rather thin woods, until I came to a lake, to which our Indian led me. Here I examined the country very carefully, but after looking everywhere found no spot more suitable than a little place to which pinnaces and shallops can ascend, only however with a strong wind, or by going a roundabout way, on account of the strong current. For higher up than this place (which we named Place Royale) at a league's distance from Mount Royal, there are many small rocks and very dangerous shoals. And near this Place Royale there is a small river, which leads some distance into the interior, alongside which are more than sixty arpents of land, which have been cleared and are now like meadows, where one might sow grain and do gardening. Formerly Indians cultivated these lands, but they have abandoned them on account of the frequent wars which they carried on there. And there are many other fine meadows which would feed as many cattle as one could wish, and there are all the varieties of wood which we have in our forests in France, with many vines, butternuts, plums, cherries, strawberries, and other kinds of fruits which are very good to eat. Amongst others there is a very fine one with a sweetish taste, like that of the plantains (a fruit of the Indies) as white as snow, with leaves like those of the nettle, and it creeps up the trees and along the ground like ivy. An abundance of fish can be caught, of all the varieties we have in France, and of many other very good kinds which we do not have. Game birds too of different varieties are abundant, and animals are also numerous, such as stags, fallow deer, roebucks, caribous, rabbits, lynxes, bears, beavers, and many small animals; all of these are so abundant that during the time we were at the rapid, we lacked for none of them.

So, having examined very carefully and found this spot to be one of the finest on this river, I ordered the trees of the Place Royale to be cut down and cleared off, in order to level the ground and make it ready for building. Water can be made to encircle the place very easily, and a little island formed of it, on which to erect such an establishment as one may wish.

Some yards from the Place Royale lies a small island, about a hundred yards long, where a good strong dwelling might be built. There are also many level stretches of very good rich potter's clay suitable for brickmaking and building, which is a great convenience. I had a portion of it prepared, and built there a wall, four feet thick, three or four feet high and ten yards long, to see how it would last during the winter when the waters came down. I did not think the water would reach the wall; for the land was quite high, being twelve feet above the river. In the middle of the river is an island which we named St. Helen's island, three-quarters of a league in circumference, where there is room to build a good strong town. The river at the foot of this rapid is like a lake, where there are two or three islands, and fine meadows.

On the first day of June Pont-Gravé arrived at the rapid, having been unable to do any trade at Tadoussac. And a large company followed him, coming after him for the sake of the booty; for, without this hope they would be very backward.

Now, whilst waiting for the Indians, I had two gardens made, one in the meadows and the other in the woods, which I caused to be cleared. And on the second day of June I sowed some seeds there which all came up quickly and in perfect condition, which shows the good quality of the soil.

We decided to send our Indian, Savignon, along with another, to meet those of his tribe, to quicken their coming. They decided, after deliberation, to go in our canoe, of which they had doubts, since it was not a very good one.

They set out on the fifth day of the month. On the following day arrived four or five pinnaces to act as our escort, since they could do no trade at Tadoussac.

On the seventh I went to explore a little river by which the natives sometimes go on the warpath; for it leads away to the rapid of the river of the Iroquois. It is very pleasant and skirts more than three leagues of meadows and much arable land. It is situated one league from the Great Rapid and a league and a half from the Place Royale.

On the ninth day our Indian arrived. He had gone a little beyond the lake, which is about ten leagues long, and which I had seen before. He had not met with anything, and they could not go any farther on account of their canoe, which failed them, and so were obliged to come back. They reported to us that, when passing the rapid, they had seen an island where there were so many herons that the air was full of them. There was a young man called Louis, in the service of the Sieur de Monts, who was a great lover of hunting. On hearing this he wanted to go to the place and satisfy his curiosity, and urgently begged our Indian to take him there. The Indian consented and also took along a Montagnais chief, named Outetoucos, who was a very agreeable person. On the following morning Louis went and called the two Indians to go to the Herons' island. They got into a canoe and went there. This island is in the middle of the rapid. Here they caught as many young herons and other birds as they wished, and got into their canoe again. Outetoucos, against the wish of the other Indian and in spite of his earnest solicitation, was determined to go down a very dangerous place, where the water fell nearly three feet, saying that he had gone that way before, which was not true. For a long time he disputed with our Indian, who wanted to take him on the south side, along the main shore, which is the way they are more accustomed to go. This, Outetoucos did not wish, declaring that there was no danger. When our Indian saw that he was obstinate, he yielded to his desire, but said that at least the canoe should be lightened of some of the birds in it, as it was overloaded, or that otherwise they would certainly be swamped and lost. But Outetoucos would not do so, saying it would be time enough when they saw that they were in danger. So they let themselves drift with the current; but when they were on the brink of the rapid, they tried to get out of it by throwing overboard their load. It was now, however, too late, for the swift water had them completely in its power. And their canoe filled quickly in the whirling waters of the rapid, which tossed them up and down in all sorts of ways. They clung to it for a long time. At length the strength of the current wore them out, so that this poor Louis, who was quite unable to swim, lost his head completely, and the canoe going under, he was forced to abandon it. The other two continued to cling to it, and came to the surface, but saw nothing more of our Louis. In this miserable manner did the poor fellow die. The other two still clung to the canoe; but when they got clear of the rapid, Outetoucos, who was naked, and trusted to his ability to swim, abandoned it, thinking he could reach the shore, although the water was still running very swiftly. But he was drowned; for he was so exceedingly worn out by his exertions, and having abandoned the canoe, it was impossible to save himself. Our Indian Savignon, being more prudent, continued to hold firmly to the canoe, until it reached an eddy, to which the current carried it. Here he managed, in spite of the labour and fatigue he had undergone, to reach shore easily. He then emptied the water out of the canoe, and returned in great fear, lest vengeance should be visited upon him, as is usual amongst the Indians. He told us this sad story, which filled us with sorrow.

On the following day I went in another canoe to the rapid, along with this Indian, and one other of our men, to see the place where the two had perished, and whether we could find their bodies. And I assure you that when he showed me the spot my hair stood on end to see such an awful place, and I was astonished that the victims had been so lacking in judgment as to go through such a frightful place, when they might have gone another way; for it was impossible to go through

there, on account of seven or eight waterfalls which tumble from ledge to ledge, the lowest of which is three feet high. All this made a remarkable noise and whirl, and part of the rapid was completely white with foam, which indicated the worst spot. There was a noise so loud that one would have said it was thunder, as the air rang from the sound of these cataracts. Having viewed and carefully considered this place, and searched along the bank for the dead bodies, at the same time that a rather light shallop had gone in another direction, we came back without finding anything.

3

On the thirteenth of the aforesaid month, two hundred Charioquois Indians with the chiefs Ochateguin, Iroquet and Tregouaroti, brother of our Indian, brought back my youth. We were very glad to see them, and I went to meet them with a canoe and our Indian, and whilst they were approaching slowly and in order, our men got ready to receive them with a salute of arquebuses, muskets, and small pieces. As they drew near, they began to shout all together, and one of their chiefs ordered their harangue to be made, wherein they praised us greatly, regarding us as trustworthy, because I had kept my promise to come and meet them at the rapid. After three more shouts, two salutes were fired from thirteen pinnaces or patches which were there. This astonished them so much that they begged me to ask that there should be no more firing; for, said they, the greater number of these Indians had never seen Christians nor heard thunder of that sort, and were afraid it might hurt them. They were very glad to see our Indian in good health; for they thought he was dead, according to reports made to them by some Algonquins, who had heard the story from some Montagnais Indians. This Indian spoke well of the treatment I had given him in France and of the strange things he had seen, whereat they all wondered and went and set up a temporary encampment in the wood, waiting for the following day when I was to show them where I wished them to set up their lodges. I also saw my French boy who came dressed like an Indian. He was well pleased with the treatment received from the Indians, according to the customs of their country, and explained to me all that he had seen during the winter, and what he had learned from the Indians.

When the next day came, I showed them a place where they might encamp, and there the chief old men held a long deliberation together. After being thus engaged for some time they sent for me to come alone with my lad, who had learned their language very well. They told him they desired to form a close alliance with me and that they were sorry to see all these shallops here; for our Indian had told them that he neither knew these people nor what was in their minds; that they saw clearly, that it was only love of gain and avarice which brought these people thither, and that when the Indians should need their help they would give none; and would not do as I had done, who used to offer to go with my companions into their country and to help them, of which I had given them proofs in the past. They expressed satisfaction at the kind treatment I had shown to our Indian, as if he had been my brother, which placed them under such obligations to be kind to me that in anything I might desire of them, they would try to satisfy me; but they feared lest the other patches would do them harm. I assured them that the others would not do so and that we all served one king, whom our Indian had seen, and that we were all of the same nation, but that business was a private affair. And I said that they ought not to be afraid; for they were as safe as if they were in their own country. After several harangues, they made me a gift of a hundred beaver-skins, and I gave them in exchange other sorts of merchandise. They told me that more than four hundred Indians had intended to come down from their country, but what had kept them back was one of my Iroquois prisoners, who had escaped and gone back to his own country. He had spread the report that I had given him his liberty and certain goods, and that I was to go to the rapid with six hundred Iroquois to await the Algonquins and kill them all. They said that the fear aroused by this news had kept them back and that but for this they would have come down.

I replied that the prisoner had escaped without my giving him leave; that our Indian knew quite well how he had got away, and that there was no likelihood of my renouncing their friendship, as they had heard, after going with them on the war-path, and sending my young lad into their country in order to keep their friendship. Moreover, the promise I had so faithfully kept was a further confirmation of this. They said in reply that, as far as they were concerned, they had never believed such things; that they quite recognized that all this talk was far from the truth; that had they thought otherwise they would not have come and that it was the others who were afraid, because they had never seen any Frenchmen except my young lad. They told me also that in five or six days would arrive three hundred Algonquins, if we would wait for them, for the purpose of going on the war-path with them against the Iroquois, but that if I did not go, they would return without doing anything.

I had much conversation with them regarding the source of the great river and regarding their country, about which they told me many things, both of the rivers, falls, lakes, and lands, and of the tribes living there, and whatever is found in those parts. Four of them assured me that they had seen a sea, far from their country, but that the way to it was difficult, both on account of enemies, and of the wild stretches to be crossed in order to reach it. They told me also that during the preceding winter some Indians had come from the direction of Florida, beyond the country of the Iroquois, who were familiar with our ocean, and friendly with these latter Indians. In short they spoke to me of these things in great detail, showing me by drawings all the places they had visited, taking pleasure in telling me about them. And as for myself, I was not weary of listening to them, because some things were cleared up about which I had been in doubt until they enlightened me about them. When all this conversation was over, I told them they should barter the few articles they had, and they did so on the following day. Each pinnace carried off its share. We had had all the trouble and risk; others, who did not worry about discoveries, had the profit, which is the only motive that moves them since they invest nothing and risk nothing.

On the following day after bartering all they had, which was very little, they made a barricade about their camp on the side of the woods and partly on the side of our patches, saying that it was for greater security in case they were surprised by their enemies, which we believed to be the truth. When night came they called our Indian, who was sleeping in my patache, and my young lad, and the two went to them. After a good deal of talk, they sent also about midnight for me. When I arrived at their lodges, I found them all sitting in council, and they made me sit down beside them, saying that their custom was, when they wished to meet to discuss some matter, to do so at night, in order not to have their attention diverted by any objects; for at night one thought only of listening, whilst daylight distracted the mind by the objects seen. But it seemed to me that, having confidence in me, they wished to tell me their desire in secret. Moreover, they were afraid of the other pataches, as they gave me afterwards to understand; for they told me that they were displeased at seeing so many Frenchmen, who were not very friendly towards one another, and that they would have much liked to see me alone. They also said that some of their people had been beaten; that they were as kindly disposed to me as to their own children, and had such confidence in me that they would do whatever I told them, but that they much mistrusted the others. Furthermore, that should I return, I was to bring as many people as I liked, provided they were under the leadership of one chief; that they had sent for me to assure me again of their friendship, which would never be broken, and that they hoped I should not be angry with them. They said, moreover, that knowing I had resolved to visit their country, they would show it to me, at the risk of their lives, assisting me with a good number of men who could go anywhere, and that in future we should have the same confidence in them as they had in us.

Thereupon they sent for fifty beaver-skins and four wampum belts (which they value as we do gold chains) saying I was to share these with my brother (meaning Pont-Gravé, since we were together): and that these were gifts from other chiefs, who, though they had never seen me, sent them to me; and that they were desirous always to be my friends; and that if there were any Frenchmen who wished to go with them, they would be more pleased than ever in order to maintain a firm friendship between us. After much conversation I proposed to them that, since they were willing to show me their country, I should humbly request His Majesty to assist us, to the extent of forty or fifty men, equipped with arms and implements necessary for the expedition, and that I should embark with these men on condition that they, the natives, should provide us with provisions during our journey, but that I should bring them what was required to make presents to the chiefs of the regions through which we should pass, and that we should then return and spend the winter at our settlement. Furthermore, if I discovered

the country to be good and fertile, I promised to establish several settlements there whereby we should have communication with one another, and live happily in the future in the fear of God, whom we should make known to them. They were much pleased with this proposal, and urged me to see to it, saying that they on their part would do their utmost to bring it about, and that, as regards provisions, we should no more lack these than would they themselves, assuring me anew that they would show me what I desired to see. Thereupon, I took leave of them at daybreak, thanking them for their willingness to favour my wishes, and begging them to continue to do so.

On the following day, being the seventeenth of the month, they said they were going off to hunt beavers, but that they would all come back. When morning came they finished bartering the few things they still had left, and then got into their canoes, requesting us not to touch their lodges for the purpose of taking them down; and we promised not to do so. And so they separated, pretending to go hunting in several directions, but they left our Indian with me, so that we should have less suspicion of them. Nevertheless they had arranged a rendezvous above the rapid where they well knew we should be unable to take our pinnaces. Meanwhile we waited for them, relying upon what they had said.

On the following day came two Indians, Iroquet and the brother of our Indian Savignon. They came to get the latter and asked me, on behalf of all their companions, to go alone with my lad to their encampment; for they had something important to tell me which they did not wish to communicate in the presence of any Frenchmen. I promised them to go.

When day came, I gave some trinkets to Savignon who went off very happy, letting me know that he was going to lead a very hard life compared with the life he had lived in France. And so he went away regretfully, but I was glad to be relieved of the responsibility of him. The two chiefs told me that early on the following day they would send for me, and they did so. My lad and I embarked with those who came. On reaching the rapid, we went into the woods, about eight leagues to their encampment, on the bank of a lake, where I had been before.

When they saw me they rejoiced greatly, and began to shout as is their custom, and our Indian came out to meet me, inviting me to go to his brother's tent, where immediately meat and fish were put on the fire for my entertainment. Whilst I was there a feast was given, to which all the chief men were invited. I was not left out, and, although I had already had a good meal, I went to the feast, in order not to interrupt the custom of the country. After the banquet they went into the woods to hold their council, and meanwhile I amused myself by looking at the scenery of the place, which is very pleasant.

Some time afterwards they sent for me to communicate to me what had been decided. I went to them with my young lad. After taking my seat among them, they told me they were very glad to see me, and to know that I had not failed to keep my promise. They recognized more and more my affection and desire to continue our friendship, and said that before departing they wanted to take leave of me, and would have been quite hurt if they had gone away without seeing me; for otherwise they would have thought that I wished them harm. They also stated that what had made them say they were going hunting and to build a barricade, was not fear of their enemies, nor the wish to hunt, but their fear of all the other pataches which were with me, because, on the night they had sent for me, they had heard that they were all to be killed. They felt that I could not defend them against the others, who were much more numerous, and so they had used this craftiness, in order to get away quietly. Had there been only our two pataches, they would have stayed a few days longer. They begged of me, when I returned with my companions, not to bring any other people. I told them I had not brought these, but that they had followed me without my asking them, and that in future I should proceed in a different fashion from what I had done in the past, at which declaration they were highly pleased.

And again they began to recite what they had promised me touching the exploration of the country. And on my part I promised them with God's help to do what I had said. They requested me once more to give them a man, and I said that if there were any amongst us who would like to go, I should be very glad to send one.

They told me that there was a trader called Bouvier, captain of a patache, who had asked them to take a youth, but that they had been unwilling to do so, until they heard from me, whether I should agree; for they were uncertain whether we were friends, although he had come in my company to barter with them. They said that they were not under any obligation whatsoever to him, but that he was offering to make them large presents.

I replied that we were not enemies and that often they had seen us talking together; but so far as trade was concerned, each did what he could, and that Bouvier perhaps wished to send this youth, as I had sent mine, hoping for future advantage, much as I also might expect from them. Still it was their duty to decide to whom they owed most and from whom they should expect most.

They told me there was no comparison between what they owed to each of us; for I had given them much assistance in their wars with their enemies, and had offered them my personal help for the future. And since they had always found me truthful in such matters, everything now depended upon my good pleasure. They said that what had made them speak of the matter was the gifts that he had offered them, and that even if this lad should go with them, that fact could lay them under no obligation to Bouvier, comparable to their indebtedness to me, and moreover could make no difference in the future, seeing they only took him in order to have Bouvier's presents.

I replied that it was a matter of indifference to me whether they took this lad with them or not, and that if they took him indeed with small recompense, I should be sorry; but if Bouvier made them good presents, I should be glad, provided the lad stayed with Iroquet, as they promised me he would. When, for the last time, they had told me their desires and I had told them mine, there was an Indian who had been three times a prisoner of the Iroquois, but who had very luckily escaped, who resolved to go with nine others on the war-path, in order to avenge himself for the cruelties his enemies had inflicted upon him. All the chiefs begged of me to dissuade him if I could; for he was very brave and they feared lest he and his little band might become so deeply involved with the enemy, that he would never return. To satisfy the chiefs I spoke to him, setting forth all the reasons I could think of; but they were of little use; for showing me his hacked-off fingers, as well as the great cuts and burns on his body, where they had tortured him, he replied that it was impossible for him to live unless he killed some of his enemies, and took vengeance upon them. He said that his heart told him that he must set off as soon as possible, and he did go, firmly resolved to fight bravely.

Having finished with them, I asked them to bring me back to our patache. To do this, they made ready eight canoes, with which to run the rapids, and they stripped naked, but left me in my shirt; for it often happens that some are lost in running the rapids. Consequently they keep close to one another, in order to give prompt help, if a canoe should happen to capsize. They told me that if unfortunately my canoe should upset, since I did not know how to swim, I ought under no circumstances to let go, but to keep hold of the small pieces of wood in the centre of the canoe; for they would easily rescue me. I assure you that even the bravest people in the world who have not seen nor passed this place in small boats such as theirs, could not do so without great apprehension. But these tribes are so clever at shooting rapids, that this is easy for them. I ran this one with them, a thing I had never done before, nor had any other Christian, except my young man of whom I have already spoken. And we came to our pinnaces where I found quarters for a good many of them, and I had a discussion with Bouvier, who was afraid lest I might hinder his young lad from going off with the Indians. On the following day they set off for home with this youth, who cost his master dearly. I suppose he hoped to recover in this way the rather large losses which he, like many others, had suffered in this year's expedition.

There was a young man of our party who decided to go home with the Charioquois Indians, who live about a hundred and fifty leagues from the rapids. He went with Savignon's brother, one of the chiefs, who promised me to show him as much as he could. Bouvier's lad went home with the Algonquin, Iroquet, who lives some eighty leagues from the rapid. They went off quite happy and contented.

After the departure of these Indians, we still waited for the three hundred others, who, we were informed, were to come, on the strength of the promise which I had made to them. Seeing that they did not arrive, the pataches all decided to induce some Algonquins who had come from Tadoussac, to set off to meet them, promising to give them something when they should get back, which was to be at the latest within nine days; for we wished to be sure whether the Algonquins

were coming or not, in order to return to Tadoussac. This they agreed to do, and accordingly one canoe set off.

On the fifth of July arrived a canoe from the Algonquins who had promised to come to the number of three hundred. We learned from it that the canoe which had left us had reached their country, and that its occupants, being wearied with the distance they had travelled, were resting. These men informed us that their tribe would soon come and redeem the promise they had made; and would not be more than eight days late; but that there would only be twenty-four canoes, inasmuch as one of their chiefs and many of their tribe had died of a fever which had broken out amongst them. Moreover, they had sent many braves on the war-path; and this it was that had hindered them from coming. We decided to wait for them.

When this period had expired without their coming, Pont-Gravé left the rapid on the eleventh of the month to attend to some business at Tadoussac, and I remained to await the Indians.

On that same day there arrived a patache with provisions for the numerous pinnaces at the rapid; for our bread, wine, meat, and cider had given out some days before, and our only recourse was to catch fish, to the good water of the river, and to some native roots, which things did not fail us in any way. Had it not been for them we should have been obliged to return. That same day arrived an Algonquin canoe, which assured us that, on the following day, the twenty-four canoes would arrive, twelve of which were ready to go on the war-path.

On the twelfth day of the month the Algonquins arrived with some few furs. Before beginning to barter they offered a present to a Montagnais Indian, the son of Annadabigeau, recently deceased, in order to appease and comfort him upon his father's death. Shortly after this they decided to make gifts to all the captains of the pataches. To each they gave ten beaver-skins, and in giving these they said that they were sorry they had not more of them; but that the war to which the majority were on their way was the cause of the small number. Still they hoped that we should take what they offered in a kindly spirit; for they were all friendly to us, and to me, who was sitting beside them, above all the others, who were well-disposed to them only on account of their beaver-skins. For they found that the others were not like me, who had always assisted them, and had never been double-tongued like the others.

I replied that all those whom they saw assembled were their friends, and that perhaps should an opportunity occur, they would not fail to do their duty; that we were all friends and that they should continue to be well-disposed towards us; for we would make them presents in exchange for what they gave us, and I hoped they would trade in peaceable fashion. They did so, and each one carried away what he could.

The next day they brought me secretly forty beaver-skins, assuring me of their friendship, and saying they were very glad of the decision I had taken with the Indians who had left for home, that we should make a settlement at the rapids. I reassured them on this point, and made them a present in return.

After this was done, they decided to go and get the body of Outetoucos, who was drowned at the rapid, as we have already related. They proceeded to the spot where the body was, disinterred it and carried it to St. Helen's island, where they performed their usual ceremonies of singing and dancing over the grave, with feasts and banquets afterwards. I asked them why they disinterred the body. They answered that if their enemies found the grave, they would do so, and would cut the body into several pieces, which they would hang upon trees to insult them. For this reason they said that they carried the body to a spot away from the trail, and as secretly as they could.

On the fifteenth of the month arrived fourteen canoes whose leader was called Tecouehata. On their arrival all the other Indians took up their arms and went through drill movements. Having turned about and danced enough, the others who were in their canoes began also to dance, at the same time making various movements with their body. The singing over, they landed with a few furs and made presents like those the others had given. We in return made them similar presents of equal value. The next day they bartered the little they had, and made me especially a present of thirty beaver-skins, for which I recompensed them. They begged me to continue to be friendly to them, and this I promised to do. They discussed with me very particularly about some explorations in the north which might prove advantageous. And on this subject, they said to me that if

any of my companions would go with them, they would show him something which would please me; and that they would treat him like one of their own children. I promised to give them a young lad, whereat they were much pleased. When he said good-bye to me to set off with them, I gave him a very particular memorandum of the things he should observe. After they had bartered the small quantity of goods they had, they separated into three parties: one to go on the war-path, another to go by way of the Great Rapid, and another to go by way of a small river which empties into that of the Great Rapid. They set off on the eighteenth of the month, and we also on the same day.

That day we made thirty leagues, the distance from the rapid to Three Rivers, and on the nineteenth we reached Quebec, which is also thirty leagues from Three Rivers. I induced nearly everyone to remain at this settlement, then had some repairs made and some rose-bushes planted. I had some split oak put on board, to be tested in France both for wainscoting and for window-frames. On the following day, the twentieth of July, I set out thence and on the twenty-third arrived at Tadoussac, where, with the approval of Pont-Gravé, I made up my mind to return to France. Having given directions about the things at our settlement, according to the charge given to me by the Sieur de Monts, on the eleventh of August I embarked in the ship of Captain Tibaut, of La Rochelle. During the voyage we had plenty of fish, such as dorados, tunnies, and pilot-fish. The last resemble herrings, and gather about certain planks covered with barnacles, which is a sort of shell-fish, which attach themselves thereto, and increase with the lapse of time. Sometimes there is such a quantity of these small fish, that it is wonderful to see. We caught also porpoises and other varieties of fish. We had fairly good weather as far as Belle-Isle, where we were caught in a fog which lasted three or four days. Then the weather turning fine, we sighted Alvert and arrived at La Rochelle on the tenth of September, 1611.

709. 1611–1612. Champlain explains some of the problems of maintaining a French presence in New France.

S. de Champlain, Les voyages (1613), Bk. 4,

Chap. 4, translated in H. P. Biggar (and others),
The Works of Samuel de Champlain, *II (1922),*
215–221.

4

Upon my arrival at La Rochelle, I went to see the Sieur de Monts at Pont in Saintonge, to inform him of all that had happened during my expedition, and of the promise made to me by the Ochateguins and Algonquins upon the conditions which I accepted to assist them in their wars. The Sieur de Monts, after hearing the whole story, decided to go to Court, to get the matter settled. I started off ahead to go there as well, but on the way was held up by a wretched horse which fell upon me and nearly killed me. This fall delayed me a long time; but as soon as I was in a fit condition, I set out to complete my journey, and to meet the Sieur de Monts at Fontainebleau. The latter, on his return to Paris, had an interview with his partners; but these were unwilling to continue the partnership any longer, since they had no mandate to exclude anyone from our new discoveries and from bartering with the inhabitants of the region. When the Sieur de Monts saw this, he came to terms with his partners for what remained in the settlement of Quebec, paying them a sum of money for their share in the business. He sent out a few men to protect the settlement, hoping still to receive a monopoly from His Majesty. While he was occupied in this pursuit, unexpected and important business forced him to abandon it, and to me he left the task of finding ways and means.

Whilst I was in the midst of this business, the vessels arrived from New France, and in them some of those people from our settlement whom I had sent with the natives into the interior. They brought me rather good news, to the effect that more than two hundred Indians had come down in the expectation of finding me at the great rapid of St. Louis, where with the intention of giving them the assistance for which they had asked, I had agreed to meet them. When they saw that I had not kept my promise, they were much annoyed. However, apologies, which they accepted as real, were made by our men, who assured them that in the following year I should certainly come, and that they also must not fail to appear. They promised that they would not; but several others, who

had forsaken their former traffic at Tadoussac, came to the rapids with a number of small pinnaces, to see whether they could carry on barter with these tribes, to whom they affirmed that I was dead, whatever our men might say to the contrary. Thus does jealousy steal into bad natures in opposition to worthy objects. They only want people to run a thousand risks in discovering nations and countries in order that they may keep the profits and the others the hardships. It is unreasonable when one has caught the sheep for another to have the fleece. Had they been willing to share our explorations, use their resources, and risk their persons, they would have shown that they possessed honour and a love of renown; but, on the contrary, they clearly show that they are driven by pure malice to seek to enjoy equally with us the fruits of our labours.

This topic prompts me again to say something to show how some try to turn men aside from worthy enterprises, like the people of St. Malo and others, who say that the profit from these discoveries belongs to them, because Jacques Cartier, who first visited Canada and the islands of Newfoundland, came from their town; as if that town had contributed to the expenses of the said discoveries of Jacques Cartier, who went there by the command, and at the expense, of King Francis I, in the years 1534 and 1535, to explore these lands now called New France. If then Cartier made these discoveries at the expense of His Majesty, all his subjects are entitled to the same rights and liberties therein as the people of St. Malo, and these cannot prevent any who have made discoveries at their own expense, as has been shown to be the case in regard to the discoveries described above, from the peaceable enjoyment thereof; wherefore they should not claim a right to anything to which they themselves have not contributed; and their reasons in this respect are poor and weak.

And to show more fully to those who would maintain this plea, that they have no ground to stand on, let us take the case of a Spaniard or other foreigner having discovered lands and treasures at the expense of the king of France; would the Spaniards or other foreigners lay claim to these discoveries and treasures, because the discoverer was a Spaniard or other foreigner? No, there is no ground for this; the discoveries would certainly belong to France, so that the people of St. Malo cannot claim these, as we have shown, because Cartier came from their town; but all they can do, because he came from their city, is to esteem him, and to give him the praise which is his due.

Moreover, Cartier on his voyage never passed beyond the great rapid of St. Louis, and did not make explorations, either to the north or south of the river St. Lawrence. His narratives give no evidence of this, and in them he speaks only of the river Saguenay, of Three Rivers and of the Ste Croix, where he wintered in a fort near our settlement. For had he made other explorations, he would not have omitted to speak of them as he has done of what he did describe; which shows that he left out all the upper part of the river St. Lawrence, from Tadoussac to the Great Rapid, where it is difficult to explore territory, and where he was unwilling to run risks or to leave his pinnaces and adventure himself. Thus his work has re-

mained without results, until within the last four years, when we built our settlement at Quebec, and having completed the building, I ventured to pass the rapid, in order to assist the Indians in their wars, and to send men there to become acquainted with the tribes, their manner of life and to see what their territory is like. Having spent our time to this good purpose, is it not right that we should enjoy the fruits of our labours, since His Majesty [Louis XIII], up to the present, has not provided the funds for assisting those who undertake such projects?

I hope that some day, for the service of God, for his own glory, and for the good of his subjects, His Majesty may by God's grace succeed in bringing many poor tribes to the knowledge of our faith, in order that later on they may enjoy the heavenly kingdom.

NOTES ON THE MAPS

112. 1569. Eastern North America on the Mercator World Map.

Rotterdam, Maritiem Museum 'Prins Hendrick.' Reproduced in V. van 't Hoff, *Gerard Mercator's Map of the World 1569* (s'Gravenhage, 1961).

The very large printed world map which Gerard Mercator produced at Antwerp in 1569 represented the finest piece of world cartography yet attempted and was to remain influential for more than a generation. He incorporated much of the older French information on the St. Lawrence without elaborating it unduly. His Newfoundland ("Terra de Bacallaos") contained much detail, but is still a group of islands. The whale is prominent at sea southeast of Newfoundland. His profile of the eastern mainland is primarily a Spanish one, with its Cabo de Arenas (Monomoy Point) carried far to the south. A great river flows from an extensive Appalachian range (on which there existed little evidence at this date) into the sea north of the Florida peninsula and is reminiscent of that on Jacques le Moyne de Morgues's map of Florida of 1591. This river most likely represents the Savannah rather than the St. Johns. The proportions and relations of land and water are carefully regulated, and this is the first "true chart" for sailing east and west, though the precise means by which Mercator solved (empirically) the nautical triangle are not known.

113. Whaling off the North American Coasts.

    a. 1546. Whaling Shown off the Coast of Labrador.

    Manchester, John Rylands University Library.

    The Pierre Desceliers map is the earliest to show Frenchmen (probably French Basques) whaling off the coast of Labrador.

    b. 1631. Later View of Whaling Operations off Greenland.

    Samuel Purchas, *Pilgrimes* (London, 1625) was the first to give this detailed picture of the operation of the Greenland whale fishery. It was later reproduced, with a revealing text, in E. Pelham, *Gods power and providence* (London, 1631).

Though later and applicable to Greenland where there was probably no whale fishing before 1612, the pictures at the sides give some idea of how the whale fishery was carried on in the Strait of Belle Isle much earlier.

114. 1612. Newfoundland and the Gulf of St. Lawrence, Champlain's Engraved Map of New France.

Samuel de Champlain, *Les voyages* (1613). Reproduced in Samuel de Champlain, *Works*, ed., H. P. Biggar. 6 vols. and portfolio (Toronto: Champlain Society, 1922–1937), portfolio; and reprinted, 7 vols. (Toronto, 1971), Vol. VII.

115. 1537. A View of the Supposed Northwest Passage on the Frisius-Mercator Globe.

Vienna, Österreichische Nationalbibliothek.

Gemma Frisius and Gerard Mercator made a globe in 1537 which included the supposed discovery of a Northwest Passage by Sebastian Cabot. This depiction was taken up and elaborated by other cartographers.

116. 1538. The Gerard Mercator World Map of 1538, Giving Details of Supposed Polar Passages.

In A. E. Nordenskjold, *Facsimile-atlas to the Early History of Cartography* (Stockholm, 1889), Plate XLVIII.

117. 1558. Falsified Zeno Chart, Said to Belong to 1380, of the Northern Regions.

Nicolo Zeno, *Commentarii* (Venice, 1558), invented this chart as being one compiled by ancestors of his, Nicoló and Antonio Zeno, in 1380. Its invention of islands like Frisland, Icaria, and Estotiland, combined with the adoption of the fifteenth-century view of Greenland ("Engronelant") as a peninsular extension of Europe, bemused cartographers (e.g., Mercator) and explorers (e.g., Frobisher) for more than a generation.

118. 1576. Sir Humphrey Gilbert's Map of the Supposed Northwest Passage.

Sir Humphrey Gilbert, *A discourse of a discoverie for a newe passage to Cataia* (London, 1576).

By 1576 Gilbert had long advocated the existence of a Northwest Passage. The map in his published tract was influenced by Abraham Ortelius's world map of 1564. It showed a very simplified North America. See Quinn, *Gilbert* (1940), I.

119. 1578. George Best's World Map, Showing the Supposed Northern Passages.

George Best, *A true discourse of the late voyages of discoverie, for the finding of a passage to Cathaya* (London, 1578).

120. 1578. George Best's Schematic View of Martin Frobisher's Discoveries, 1576–1578.

George Best, *A true discourse of the late voyages of discoverie, for finding of a passage to Cathaya* (London, 1578).

Taken with Best's own general view of the Northwest Passage and the falsified Zeno map, this represents a crudely effective indication of what Frobisher believed his voyages to have accomplished.

121. 1582. Michael Lok's Map, Showing Passages Around and Through North America.

Published by Richard Hakluyt, *Divers voyages* (London, 1582).

Lok adopts all the theories that indicate that North America is divisible into islands, narrow in width, easily traversed by a Northwest Passage.

122. 1592. The Northern Hemisphere According to Christian Sgrooten.

Madrid, Biblioteca Nacional; manuscript atlas, prepared for Philip II.

This is mainly of interest for its picture of Labrador, with a great inlet, an open Northwest Passage, and with some information on Frobisher's voyages. It is otherwise a conventional representation. See Cumming, Skelton and Quinn, *Discovery of North America* (1971), p. 221.

123. 1593. A Polar View of North America by Cornelis de Jode.

Cornelis de Jode, *Speculum orbis terrae* (Antwerp, 1593) gave an elaborate view of North America in his polar-centered map of the northern hemisphere.

124. 1596. The Americas, as Engraved by Francis Pisard.

London, British Library, Map Library.

Published by Theodor de Bry, Frankfurt-am-Main, 1596.

125. 1608. Engraving of Champlain's Sketch of the Site at Québec.

Samuel de Champlain, *Les voyages* (Paris, 1613).

Champlain shows the turn in the St. Lawrence River which gives the northern promontory its strategic importance. He located his first *habitacion* on the level space below the heights, but from the first used the latter as an observation post.

126. 1611. Engraving of Marc Lescarbot's "Figure de la Terre Neuve."

Marc Lescarbot, *Histoire de la Nouvelle France*, 2nd edition (Paris, 1611).

Lescarbot's map does not compare in quality with Champlain's, but it was published first. It is valuable in giving names and locations for Indian tribes, though some depend on Cartier; he also gives impressions of corn and some fruits. Curiously, he names Cape Breton "Bacaillos."

127. 1612. Samuel de Champlain's Published Map of New France.

Samuel de Champlain, *Les voyages* (Paris, 1613).

Champlain was able in this map to clear up many ambiguities about the St. Lawrence Valley, as a result of his expeditions in 1603 and from 1608 to 1611. He linked his own results to the English discovery of Hudson Bay, while for Acadia he used his unpublished map of his 1604–1607 expeditions.

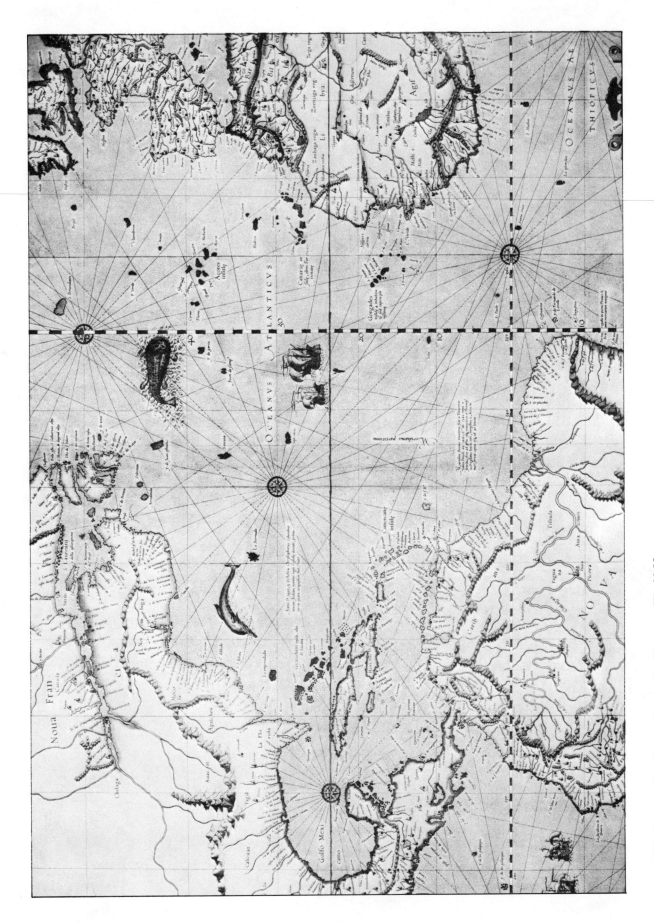

112. 1569. Eastern North America on the Mercator World Map.

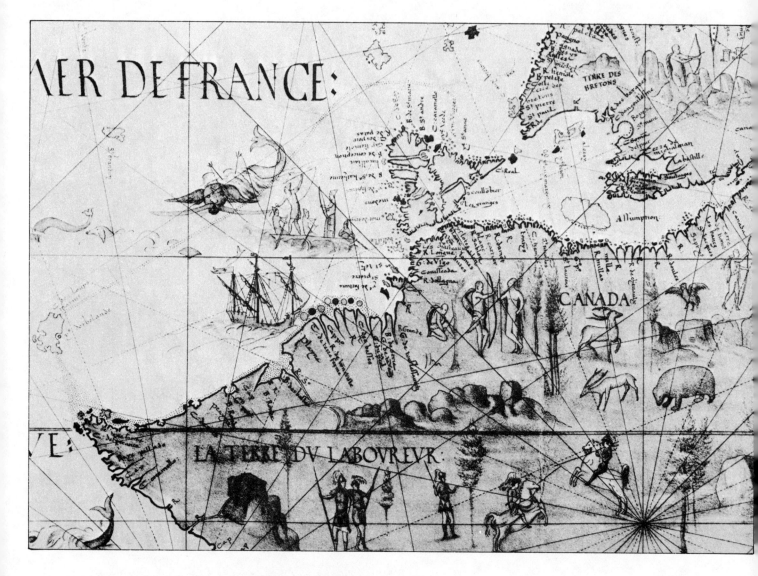

113. *Above and opposite.* Whaling off the North American Coasts.

A Whale is ordinarly about 60 foote longe

The Seamoree is in quantity as bigg as an oxe

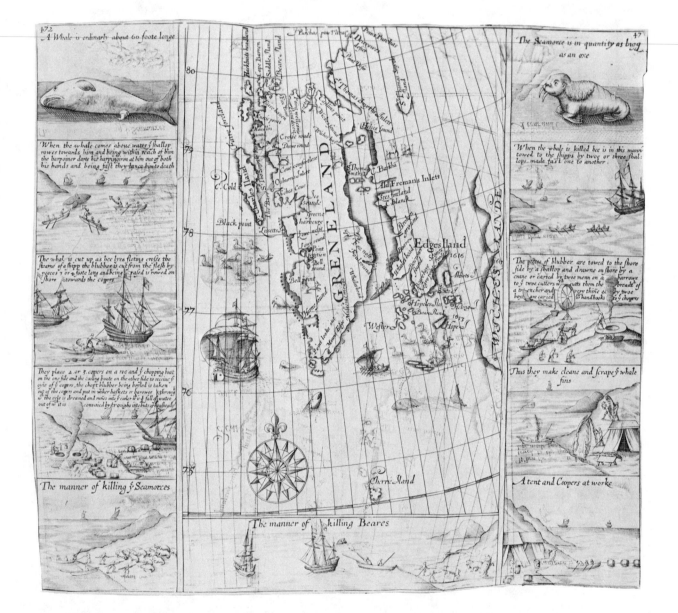

When the whale comes aboue water y° shallop rowes towards him and being within reach of him the harpiner darts his harpingiron at him out of both his hands and being fast they lance him to death

When the whale is killed hee is in this manner towed to the shipps by twoe or three shallops made fast one to another

The whale is cut up as hee lyes floting crose the sterne of a shipp the blubber is cut from the flesh by peeces 3 or 4 foote long and being y° rased is rowed on shore towards the coopers

The peeces of blubber are towed to the shore side by a shallop and drawne on shore by a crane or carted by twoe menn on a barrowe to y° twoe cutters w° cutts them the breadth of a trencher and euery thine cut by twoe boyes are caried w° handhooks y° choppers

They place 2 or 3 coopers on a rve and y° chopping boat on the one side and the cooling boate on the other side to receiue y° oyle of y° coopers, the chopt blubber being boyled is taken out of the coopers and put in wher baskets or harrowes y° thrown in the oyle is dreaned and roies into y° cooler w° is full of water out of w° it is conueid by troughs into huts of the sheap

Thus they make cleane and scrape y° whale fins

The manner of killing y° Seamorees

A tent and Coopers at worke

GRENELAND

Edges Iland

WICHES LANDE

The manner of killing Beares

Cherrie Iland

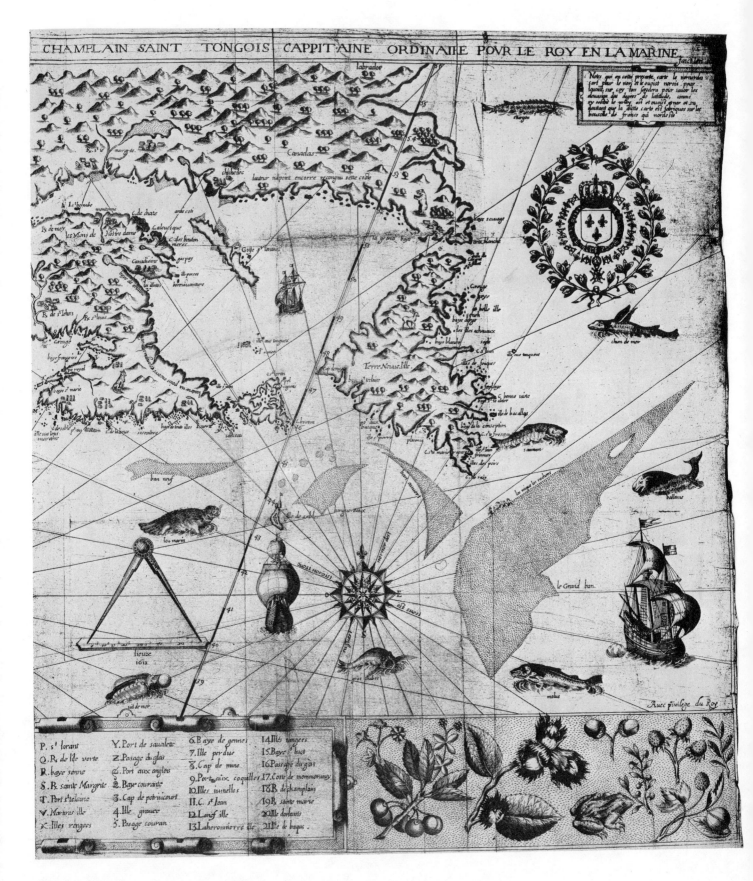

114. 1612. Newfoundland and the Gulf of St. Lawrence in the Engraved Champlain Map of New France from *Les voyages*.

115. 1537. A View of the Supposed Northwest Passage on the Frisius-Mercator Globe.

116. 1538. The Gerard Mercator World Map of 1538, Giving Details of Supposed Polar Passages.

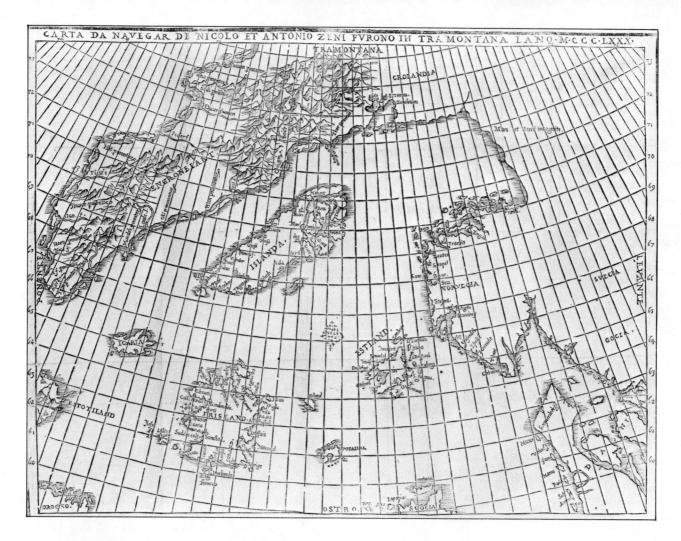

117. 1558. Falsified Zeno Chart, Said to Belong to 1380, of the Northern Regions.

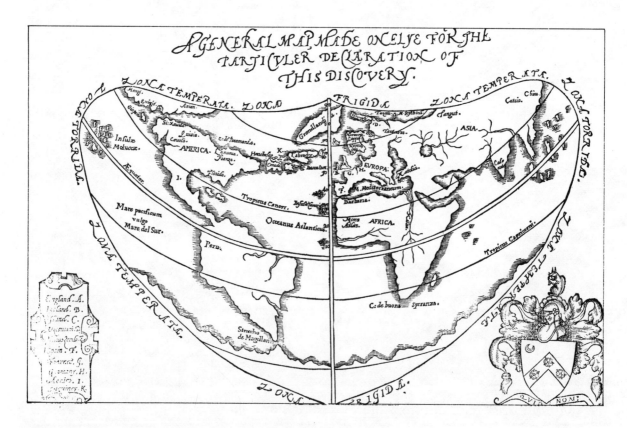

118. 1576. Sir Humphrey Gilbert's Map of the Supposed Northwest Passage.

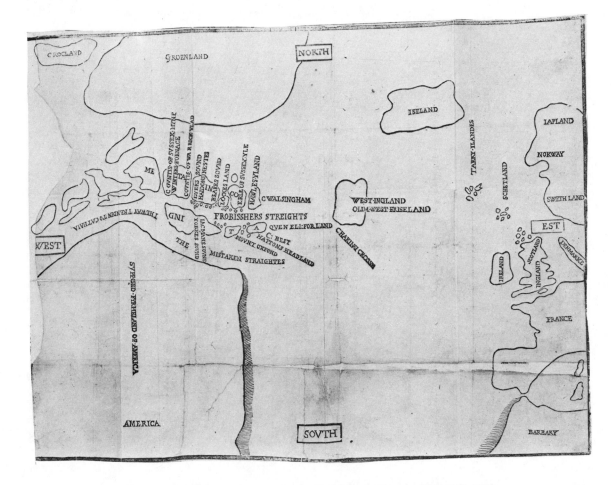

119. 1578. George Best's World Map, Showing the Supposed Northern Passages.

120. 1578. George Best's Schematic View of Martin Frobisher's Discoveries, 1576-1578.

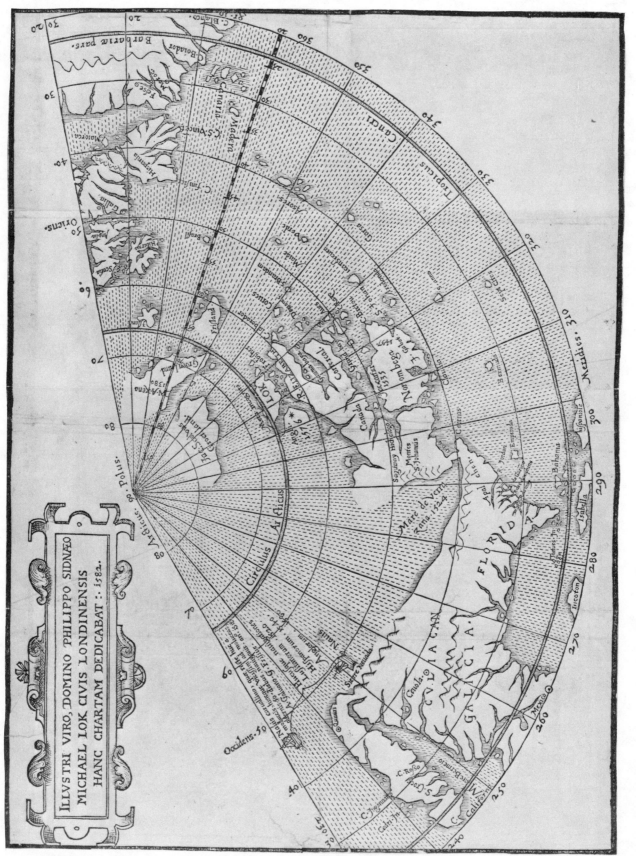

121. 1582. Michael Lok's Map, Showing Passages Around and Through North America.

122. 1592. The Northern Hemisphere According to Christian Sgrooten.

123. 1593. A Polar View of North America by Cornelis de Jode.

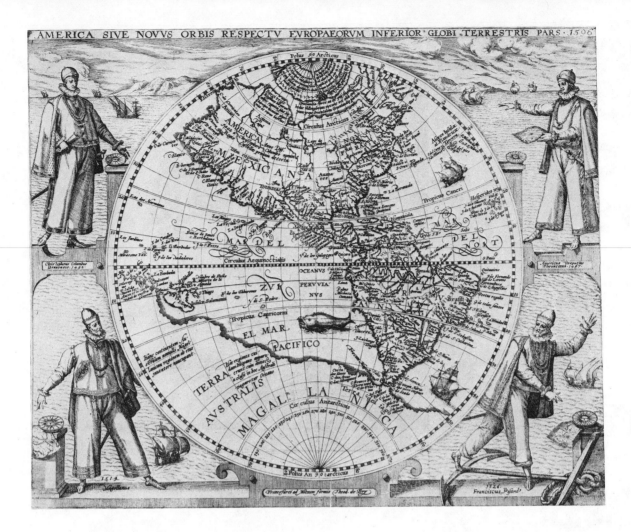

124. 1596. The Americas, as Engraved by Francis Piscard.

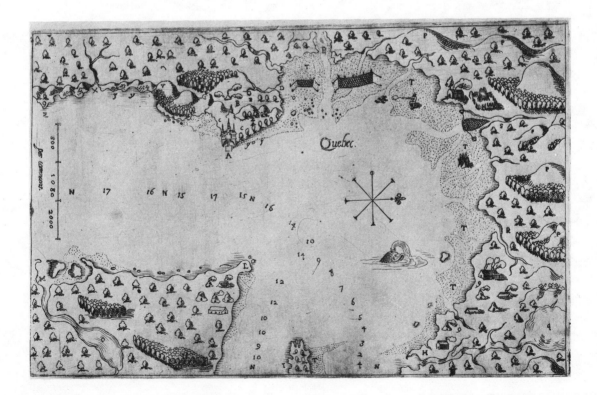

125. 1608. Engraving of Champlain's Sketch of the Site at Québec.

126. 1611. Engraving of Marc Lescarbot's "Figure de la Terre Neuve."

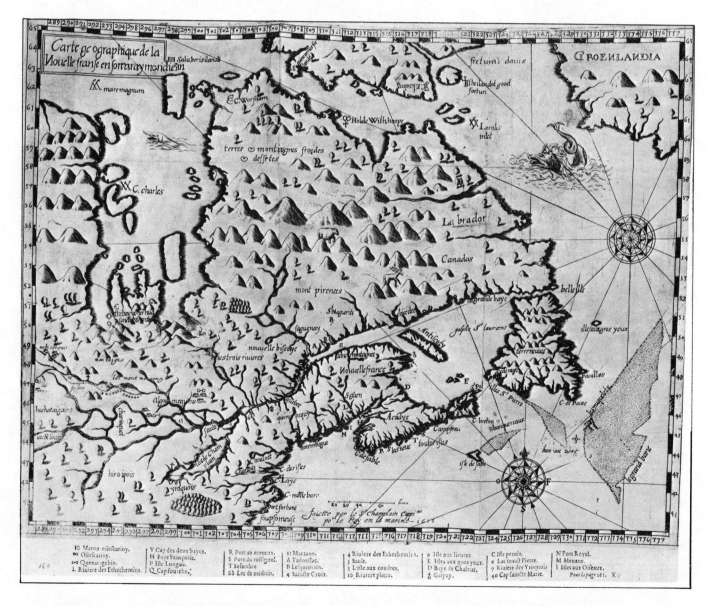

127. 1612. Samuel de Champlain's Published Map of New France.